CAMBRIDGE CLASSICAL TEXTS AND
COMMENTARIES

EDITORS

C. O. BRINK   D. W. LUCAS   F. H. SANDBACH

10

THE TRAGEDIES OF
ENNIUS

THE TRAGEDIES OF
ENNIUS

THE FRAGMENTS
EDITED WITH AN INTRODUCTION
AND COMMENTARY

BY

H.D.JOCELYN
Reader in Latin in the
University of Sydney

CAMBRIDGE
AT THE UNIVERSITY PRESS
1967

Published by the Syndics of the Cambridge University Press
Bentley House, 200 Euston Road, London, N.W. 1
American Branch: 32 East 57th Street, New York, N.Y. 10022

© Cambridge University Press 1967

Library of Congress Catalogue Card Number: 67-11525

Printed in Great Britain
at the University Printing House, Cambridge
(Brooke Crutchley, University Printer)

PA
6382
.A2
1967b

CONTENTS

v

PREFACE

This book contains material from a dissertation submitted in the year 1961 to the University of Cambridge for the degree of Doctor of Philosophy. No alterations of substance were made to the typescript after June 1966. I have tried, using printed editions of the authors who quote Ennius, to present the evidence which exists concerning each tragedy whose title is known and to discuss the questions to which this evidence is relevant. I have put together under the rubric INCERTA those pieces of verse which are quoted by ancient authors in company with Ennius' name and which have been attributed by one modern scholar or another to the tragedies.

My debts are many. The Faculty of Archaeology, History and Letters of the British School at Rome, the Faculty Board of Classics in the University of Cambridge, the Council of St John's College, Cambridge, and the Senate of the University of Sydney gave me financial help at various times. Dr W. Ehlers allowed me in the northern summers of 1957 and 1958 to use the archive and library of the Institute for the *Thesaurus Linguae Latinae*. Professor O. Skutsch read and criticised a section of my typescript, showed me unpublished work of his own and discussed several problems with me at great length. Mr D. W. Lucas and Dr D. R. Shackleton Bailey read sections of my typescript and made criticisms. Professor C. O. Brink read many drafts of the whole work, devoted much time to writing extensive criticisms of these drafts, tolerated occasional unwillingness to accept good advice and encouraged me in moments of weariness to persevere. The officers of the Cambridge University Press indulged my vagaries and lavished their skill on the somewhat forbidding material with which

vii

I supplied them. Professor S. Mariotti and Mr F. H. Sandbach corrected and improved the proof pages in many places. I thank these whom I have named and the many others whose friendship, knowledge and wisdom I exploited.

H. D. JOCELYN

New Haven, Connecticut
March 1967

INTRODUCTION

I. ATHENIAN DRAMA AND THE ROMAN FESTIVALS

The twenty-two dramatic treatments of Greek heroic legend whose remains are discussed in this volume were adapted from Athenian tragedies between the years 203 B.C. and 169 for performance at *ludi scaenici*. These *ludi scaenici* formed an important element both of the regular yearly festivals managed by the civil magistrates in honour of Iuppiter, Apollo, Ceres, Magna Mater and Flora and of those held for some special purpose, such as to thank a deity for a magistrate's military success or to honour the spirit of a deceased member of the ruling class.[1] They were believed to have been introduced to Rome from Etruria in 364 as a means of placating the divine senders of a plague.[2] The old agricultural festivals of the so-called Calendar of Numa, which continued to be managed by the priests, had no place for them.[3] The earliest adaptation of an Athenian play which scholars of the first century B.C. could find recorded was performed at *ludi scaenici* in 240, the year following the first capitulation of Carthage to Roman arms.[4]

---

[1] See Habel, *RE* Suppl. v (1931), s.v. *ludi publici*, 608 ff., L. R. Taylor, *TAPhA* LXVIII (1937), 284 ff. For the continuing religious associations of the *ludi scaenici* see J. A. Hanson, *Roman Theater-Temples* (Princeton, 1959), pp. 3 ff.

[2] Cf. Festus, p. 436.23 ff., Livy 7.2, Valerius Maximus 2.4.4.

[3] Naevius (*Com.* 113) identified the old *Liberalia* with the Attic Διονύσια. Plautus however (*Cist.* 89, 156, *Curc.* 644, *Pseud.* 59) seems to have thought the differences too great to justify the identification. Tertullian's statement (*De spect.* 10.19) that scenic games were properly called *Liberalia* is based on second-hand theorising rather than firm knowledge.

[4] H. Mattingly Jr., *CQ* N.S. VII (1957), 159–63, produces no good reason for doubting the veracity of the *antiqui commentarii* consulted by Varro (Gellius 17.21.42), Atticus and Cicero (*Brut.* 72, *Tusc.* 1.3, *Cato* 50). Accius, whose *Didascalica* set the first production of a play by Livius Andronicus in 197,

Scholars and literary amateurs of the first century B.C. regarded those plays of the previous two centuries whose scenes were set in Greece as being the work of the men who wrote the Latin acting scripts and yet were conscious that particular Greek tragedies and comedies underlay them all.[1] The Greek philosophical dialogues which Cicero adapted were full of quotations from Attic drama. Cicero sometimes replaced these with quotations from the scripts of Latin stage adaptations and sometimes with his own translations of the verses quoted. In the first case he either left the quotation anonymous or named the Latin adapter while in the second he always named the Greek

---

may have been quite well aware that Naevius and Plautus had produced plays before this date (see W. Hupperth, *Horaz über die scaenicae origines der Römer* [Diss. Köln, 1961], pp. 5 ff., 10 ff., H. Dahlmann, 'Studien zu Varro, "De poetis"', *Abh. Ak. d. Wiss. u. d. Lit. Mainz, Geistes- u. Sozialw. Kl.* 1962, Nr. 10, 29 ff., C. O. Brink, 'Horace and Varro', *Entretiens Hardt* IX [1963], 192). E. Fraenkel seems to have based his view that Livius produced only one play, and that a tragedy, in 240 (*RE* Suppl. v [1931], s.v. *Liuius*, 598 f.) on Cicero, *Brut.* 72, *Tusc.* 1.3, *Cato* 5. These passages should not be pressed nor, it must be admitted, should Gellius' words *Liuius poeta fabulas docere...coepit*. However according to Cassiodorus (*Chronica*) Livius produced both a tragedy and a comedy in 239. This date is a clear error for 240 but the rest of Cassiodorus' statement may be reliable. For Livius as the founder of both comedy and tragedy cf. Donatus, *De com.* 5.4, *Gloss. Lat.* 1 128, s.v. *comoedia*, 1 568, s.v. *tragoedia*.

[1] There is nothing in ancient discussions of republican tragedy and comedy to support the statement frequently made in modern times that the Latin poets occasionally wrote quite independently of particular Greek models (cf. J. J. Scaliger, *Coniectanea in M. Terentium Varronem de lingua Latina* [Paris, 1565], p. 6, H. Columna, *Q. Ennii Poetae Vetustissimi quae supersunt Fragmenta* [Naples, 1590], p. 408, F. Nieberding, *Ilias Homeri ab L. Attio Poeta in Dramata Conuersa* [Conitz, 1838], p. 3, T. Ladewig, *Analecta Scenica* [Neustrelitz, 1848], pp. 8, 29, 38, G. Boissier, *Le poète Attius* [Paris, Nîmes, 1857], p. 60, W. S. Teuffel, *Caecilius Statius, Pacuuius, Attius, Afranius* [Tübingen, 1858], pp. 23, 29, U. von W., in T. von Wilamowitz-Moellendorff, *Die dramatische Technik des Sophokles* [Berlin, 1917], p. 315 n. 1, J. Vahlen, *Ennianae Poesis Reliquiae²* [Leipzig, 1903], p. ccvii [very tentatively], E. M. Steuart, *AJPh* XLVII [1926], 276, J. Heurgon, *Ennius* II [Paris, 1958], p. 143). Cicero, *Fin.* 1.7 refers to the relations between Ennius' *Annales* and Homer's epics; *Gloss. Lat.* 1 568, s.v. *tragoedia* (*tragoedias autem Ennius* FERE *omnes ex Graecis transtulit*), to plays on Roman historical themes such as the *Sabinae* (cf. Horace, *Ars* 285–8).

dramatist.[1] Scholars normally at this time gave the name of the Latin poet and his Latin title when quoting from an acting script but very occasionally gave the title of the Greek original; on one occasion a play is quoted with the name of the author of the original as well as that of the adapter.[2] The writers of the third and second century acting scripts were by now thought of with varying degrees of admiration as the fathers of an indigenous Roman literature and it is clear that performances of these scripts were advertised with their names to the fore.

When the early adaptations were being made a different attitude to them probably prevailed among the managers of the *ludi scaenici* and the citizens who attended the theatre. The literary and artistic culture that had spread out from Athens over the whole Greek-speaking world was then making the same appeal to certain of the Roman governing class as it had to the rulers of Etruria and other barbarians in earlier centuries. The works that had been produced for performance at the festivals of Dionysus were among the brightest jewels of that culture. They could have been produced in the original Greek at the Roman *ludi*, as in later times they perhaps sometimes were,[3] but one of the purposes of the *ludi* was to impress the peers of the presiding magistrate and their clients. To many of these Greek culture in its less adulterated forms was an alien and suspect thing. The pride of the majority in Roman race, language and tradition was satisfied by the form in which the Greek works were presented; the enthusiasm of the minority

---

[1] Cf. G. Przychocki, *Eos* XXXII (1929), 215 ff., Fraenkel, *Gnomon* VI (1930), 663. Seneca followed Cicero's practice; contrast *Epist.* 115.14–15 with 95.53 and 102.16.

[2] See below, p. 59.

[3] The evidence collected by F. G. Welcker, *Die griechischen Tragödien mit Rücksicht auf den epischen Cyclus* (*RhM* Suppl. II, Bonn, 1839–41), pp. 1323 ff., is of an ambiguous kind. Polybius 30.22, Tacitus, *Ann.* 14.21, Plutarch, *Brut.* 21 do not necessarily refer to drama at all. Suetonius (*Iul.* 39, *Aug.* 43) talks of performances by 'omnium linguarum histriones'.

for classical Greek culture by their advertisement as the works of the classical Athenian tragedians and comedians. Slaves and foreign immigrants did the work of adaptation and it is unlikely that their names carried much weight while they lived. The uncertainty among Roman scholars about the authorship of certain comic scripts popularly ascribed to Plautus[1] may have been partly due to failure by the magistrates of earlier times always to record the Latin poet's name in their *commentarii*. A Sophocles might be made a magistrate at Athens but at Rome a magistrate could be pilloried for having an Ennius in his retinue.[2]

The opening speech of the *Rudens* describes a storm as follows (83–8): *pro di immortales, tempestatem quoiusmodi | Neptunus nobis nocte hac misit proxuma. | detexit uentus uillam — quid uerbis opust? | non uentus fuit uerum Alcumena Euripidi, | ita omnis de tecto deturbauit tegulas; | inlustriores fecit fenestrasque indidit.* It is unclear whether the speaker has in mind a stormy reaction by the heroine of Euripides' play to her husband's accusations[3] or a real storm within the action of that play;[4] likewise whether the identification stood in the Diphilian original[5] or was added by Plautus himself.[6] In any case one cannot imagine such a state-

[1] Cf. Terence, *Eun.* 25 (?), Varro, *Ling.* 6.89, Gellius 3.3.
[2] For the traditional Roman suspicion of the maker of verses cf. Cato, *Mor.* 2 *poeticae artis honos non erat; si quis in ea re studebat aut sese ad conuiuia adplicabat grassator uocabatur.* [3] Cf. Plautus, *Amph.* 812 ff.
[4] So R. Engelmann, *Ann. Ist. Corrisp. Arch.* XLIV (1872), 16, *Beiträge zu Euripides I: Alkmene* (Berlin, 1882), p. 11, *Archäologische Studien zu den Tragikern* (Berlin, 1900), pp. 59–60.
[5] So S. Vissering, *Quaestiones Plautinae* 1 (Amsterdam, 1842), p. 42, T. Bergk, *Ind. lectt. Marburg* 1844, XI (= *Kl. phil. Schr.* I 225), Ladewig, *Anal. scen.* p. 5.
[6] So Fraenkel, *Plautinisches im Plautus* (Berlin, 1922), p. 68 (= *Elementi Plautini in Plauto* [Florence, 1960], p. 64); cf. the Addenda to the Italian translation, p. 403. The addition of the Greek poet's name suggests Plautine authorship; for the late fourth century method of referring to famous tragedies cf. Menander, *Epitr.* 767 τραγικὴν ἐρῶ σοι ῥῆσιν ἐξ Αὔγης ὅλην (contrast Aristophanes, *Thesm.* 134 ff.).

ment being made on the Roman stage unless a play about Alcmena had already appeared there and been advertised as being in some sense Euripides' 'Αλκμήνη. Admittedly there is no undisputed evidence elsewhere for the existence of an adaptation of this play,[1] but considering the fragmentary record of third and second century dramatic production[2] we should not be surprised to find such a reference in the *Rudens*. The prologues of the *Poenulus* (*v.* 1) and the *Eunuchus* (*vv.* 9, 19–20) refer to Latin versions of Greek plays in this way although it was theatrically possible for the speakers to use the first century's customary mode of reference if it had then been in general use.

The only Greek plays which are said by knowledgeable ancient authorities to have been adapted for performance at Roman *ludi* in the late third and early second centuries were originally composed for the festivals of Dionysus at Athens in the fifth, fourth and early third centuries.[3] The only dramatists among the famous Greeks mentioned in Plautus' comedies are the Athenians, Euripides,[4] Diphilus and Philemon.[5] The forms of comedy written by Epicharmus and others at Syracuse in the fifth century and by Rhinthon at Tarentum in the third and the imitations of Athenian drama made by Machon and the

---

[1] O. Ribbeck (see *Corollarium* in *Tragicorum Romanorum Fragmenta*[2] [Leipzig, 1871], p. LXIII) took Marius Victorinus, *Gramm.* VI 8.6 ff. to refer to tragic personages rather than to titles; hence *Alcumena* does not appear in his 'index fabularum'. Plautus, *Amph.* 91 ff. can be plausibly interpreted as referring to the play postulated. See also below, p. 63.

[2] Of the 130 comic titles once attributed to Plautus we now know only 53. Several tragic titles occur only once or twice in our sources, sometimes even without the Latin adapter's name (*Laomedon* at Schol. Veron. Verg. *Aen.* 2.81; *Penthesilea* at Festus, p. 206.3).

[3] Bergk, *Commentationum de Reliquiis Comoediae Atticae Antiquae Libri II* (Leipzig, 1838), p. 148, explained the fragment of Varro's *De poetis* quoted by Priscian, *Gramm.* II 469.9—*deinde ad Siculos se adplicauit*—as referring to Plautus (cf. Horace, *Epist.* 2.1.58) but thought that Varro was speaking generally of the reputed πρῶτος εὑρετής of the comic genre.

[4] *Rud.* 86.

[5] *Most.* 1149. Philemon was not, of course, an Athenian by birth.

tragedians of the 'Pleiad' for the festival of Dionysus established at Alexandria by Ptolemy Philadelphus (285–247)[1] obtained for themselves a certain literary notoriety and it is not utterly impossible that plays from Alexandria[2] and Magna Graecia[3] were adapted for the Roman stage. Ennius adapted non-dramatic works by Epicharmus, Archestratus, Sotades and Euhemerus for the private delectation of his aristocratic patrons and perhaps imitated Callimachus' Αἴτια in the proem of his epic Annales[4] but the public presentation of dramatic works outside the classical Athenian repertoire would have been quite another matter. As late as 45, when a large number of poetical works from Alexandria and other Hellenistic centres had achieved a sort of second-grade classical status and were being enthusiastically studied and imitated by poets writing in Latin, Cicero chose adaptations of the non-dramatic poems of Euphorion to set against what he believed to be a version by Ennius of a Euripidean tragedy.[5] New plays continued to be presented at the Dionysiac competitions of Athens until well into the first century A.D.[6] but no playwright productive

---

[1] Cf. Wilamowitz, Hellenistische Dichtung I (Berlin, 1924), pp. 166 ff.

[2] So A. Rostagni, RFIC XLIV (1916), 379–97 (= Scritti Min. II ii 3–22); cf. M. Lenchantin De Gubernatis, MAT LXIII (1913), 389 ff., Ennio (Torino, 1915), pp. 62 ff. For detailed criticism of Rostagni's argument see N. Terzaghi, AAT LX (1925), 660 ff. (= Stud. Graec. et Lat. [Torino, 1963], 686 ff.).

[3] So T. B. L. Webster, 'Alexandrian Epigrams and the Theatre', in Miscellanea di studi Alessandrini in memoria di Augusto Rostagni (Torino, 1963), 531–43, Hellenistic Poetry and Art (London, 1964), pp. 269 ff., 282 ff., 290 f.

[4] So K. Dilthey, De Callimachi Cydippa (Leipzig, 1863), pp. 15 f., F. Skutsch, Aus Vergils Frühzeit (Leipzig, 1901), pp. 34 ff., S. Mariotti, Lezioni su Ennio (Pesaro, 1951), p. 60, O. Skutsch, The Annals of Quintus Ennius (London, 1953), p. 10; contra E. Reitzenstein, in Festschrift R. Reitzenstein (Leipzig, 1931), 63 ff., R. Pfeiffer, Callimachus I (Oxford, 1949), p. 11, G. Marconi, RCCM III (1961), 224 ff.

[5] Tusc. 3.45. For Cicero's belief (apparently false) that Ennius' Andromacha was an adaptation of a tragedy by Euripides see Opt. gen. 18.

[6] Cf. Dio Chrysostom, Or. 19. The competition for new plays was over by the late second century (Lucian, Enc. Dem. 27). Οἱ περὶ τὸν Διόνυσον τεχνῖται often included tragic and comic poets as well as actors (see below, p. 16).

between 240 B.C. and the fall of the Roman senatorial regime seems to have gained more than an ephemeral repute. Ziegler's view[1] that the Latin playwrights adapted contemporary Greek work thus lacks all probability.

Besides the six classical Athenian dramatic poets Roman audiences are reported to have seen in Latin linguistic dress Aristarchus, a contemporary of Euripides whose name figured in accounts of the development of tragedy and from whose hand seventy titles were known to ancient scholars,[2] Alexis, Posidippus, Apollodorus and Demophilus.[3] Only the last mentioned is absent from the Greek record but that may be an accident and there is no good reason to suppose that the original of the *Asinaria* was composed either outside Athens or by a contemporary of Plautus. Of the comedians Menander was plainly the one most often performed and of the tragedians Euripides.

The classical six had certainly acquired most of their later pre-eminence in Greece by 240 B.C. A competition for actors held at Athens in 254 employed three old satyr plays, three old tragedies and three old comedies, one each by Diphilus, Menander and Philemon.[4] Aristophanes' comedy Βάτραχοι shows Aeschylus, Sophocles and Euripides standing out in public esteem as early as the end of the fifth century. From

---

[1] *RE* 2 vi ii (1937), s.v. *Tragoedia*, 1984.

[2] *Souda* A 3893 Adler. A third century B.C. papyrus (*Flinders Petrie Papyri Part II*, ed. J. P. Mahaffy [Dublin, 1893], pp. 158–9 [= nr. 1594 Pack²]) contains scraps of what looks like a collection of epigrams addressed to famous poets; in them and their titles are legible the names Aristarchus, Astydamas and Cratinus. See R. Reitzenstein, *BPhW* xiv (1894), 155–9.

[3] At *Epist.* 2.1.163 ff. Horace is talking generally. He names Thespis because of his fame as the πρῶτος εὑρετής of tragedy; cf. above, p. 7 n. 3, on the reference to Epicharmus at *v.* 58.

[4] See B. D. Meritt, *Hesperia* vii (1938), 116 ff., A. Körte, *Hermes* lxxiii (1938), 123 ff., A. W. Pickard-Cambridge, *The Dramatic Festivals of Athens* (Oxford, 1953), pp. 123 f.

the record of theatrical revivals in Athens and elsewhere[1] and the character of allusions to tragedy in fourth and third century comedy[2] it is clear that Euripides' popularity far surpassed that of the other two quite early and continued to do so. Menander gained a similar position among comedians, although exactly when is hard to say.[3] Nevertheless for some time other tragedians and comedians continued to have their works revived. There are recorded performances of tragedies by the fourth-century poet Chaeremon and the otherwise unknown Archestratus[4] and performances of comedies by Anaxandrides, Posidippus and Philippides.[5] The scholars of the Alexandrian Museum thought Ion and Achaeus worthy to stand beside Aeschylus, Sophocles and Euripides,[6] doubtless in obedience to a common opinion. The Ptolemaic rubbish tips of Oxyrhynchus and other Greek settlements of the Egyptian countryside provide evidence of a taste in tragic poetry more extensive

---

[1] For the literary and inscriptional evidence see Welcker, Die griech. Trag. pp. 1275 ff., A. Müller, Lehrbuch der griechischen Bühnenalterthümer (Freiburg, 1886), pp. 390 f., NJbb xxIII (1909), 36 ff., Pickard-Cambridge, Dramatic Festivals, pp. 100 ff., M. Kokolakis, Πλάτων xII (1960), 67 ff. The evidence from figurative monuments collected by Webster (CQ xLII [1948], 15 f., Hermes LxxxII [1954], 295 ff., Monuments Illustrating Tragedy and Satyr Play [BICSL Suppl. xIV (1962)]) is ambiguous; it has to be interpreted with the aid of knowledge provided by literature and lapidary inscriptions; it does not provide new knowledge.

[2] See A. Pertusi, Dioniso xvI (1953), 27 ff., xIX (1956), 111 ff., 195 ff.

[3] On Menander's posthumous fame see A. Dain, Maia xv (1963), 278 ff. The material concerning comedy in late antiquity collected by Webster (AJA LxvI [1962], 333 ff.) refers almost exclusively to Menander.

[4] I.G. v 2.118 (saec. II a Chr. = S.I.G.³ 1080). Given the context, Webster's view (Hellenistic Poetry and Art, p. 16) that Archestratus was a contemporary poet seems most unlikely. L. Moretti's doubts (Athenaeum xxxvIII [1960], 272) as to whether I.G. xII 1.125 (saec. II a Chr.) refers to the classical Sophocles are likewise unjustified.

[5] I.G. II² 2323a (Anaxandrides 311), 2323 col. iii (Posidippus 181), col. v (Philippides 155).

[6] Anecd. Graec. Par. IV 196.20, Tzetzes, Proleg. Lyc. p. 3.8 Scheer.

and catholic than that possessed by the schoolmasters of the urban centres of later antiquity.[1] Where playwrights were concerned the tragic and comic repertory of the third and second century Roman theatre probably reflected that of contemporary Greek theatres. But in actual plays the Romans seem to have had their own taste. Many scholars have noted the extraordinary preponderance among surviving tragic titles of those connected with the Trojan cycle of heroic legends.[2] These legends had long been of particular interest to the ruling families of Greek states of recent origin; in these there was a keen desire to find the same links with the heroic past as Argos, Thebes and Athens possessed.[3] The wanderings of the Greek and Trojan heroes after the destruction of Troy were easily embroidered to suit any state in the Mediterranean area. The families of the cities of Etruria and Latium, as of other non-Greek speaking communities, early took an interest in the legends that fascinated their Greek neighbours. Long before the earliest adaptation of an Attic tragedy speakers of Latin imitated as best they could the sounds of the Greek heroes' names[4] and were accustomed to see representations of incidents from the legends on works of art.[5] There is

---

[1] On the comparatively large number of Euripidean plays absent from the selection of the later schools which are represented in Ptolemaic papyri see C. H. Roberts, *MusH* x (1953), 270. The proportion of tragic papyri which cannot be attributed to the classical trio seems to be much greater among the Ptolemaic than among the Roman; cf. nos. 169 ff. and 1707 ff. in the second edition of R. A. Pack's catalogue (Ann Arbor, 1965).

[2] E.g. Welcker, *Die griech. Trag.* pp. 1344, 1350, Ribbeck, *Die römische Tragödie im Zeitalter der Republik* (Leipzig, 1875), p. 632.

[3] Cf. T. J. Dunbabin, *PBSR* xvi (1948), 11 ff., for the claims of South Italian cities to be founded by Greek heroes after the fall of Troy.

[4] On the inscriptions on the Praeneste mirrors and caskets (*C.I.L.* I² 547–70) see R. S. Conway, *The Italic Dialects* (Cambridge, 1897), pp. 315 ff. On the forms of names used by the early poets see J. Wackernagel, *Philologus* lxxxvi (1931), 143 (= *Kl. Schr.* I 755).

[5] See I. S. Ryberg, *An Archaeological Record of Rome from the Seventh to the Second Century B.C.* (London, 1940 [Studies and Documents xiii]), *passim*.

good evidence that by the end of the third century many Roman aristocrats liked to think of themselves as the descendants of the Trojans led to Latium by Aeneas.[1] At least one family, the Mamilii of Tusculum, was advertising itself by the end of the second century as sprung from Ulysses.[2] During the first century the Iulii claimed descent from Aeneas himself and the Memmii from Mnestheus.[3] These genealogical obsessions must have been encouraged by the constant performance of the old adaptations of tragedy at the *ludi* but it would not be fanciful to see in them one of the forces directing the choice of the magistrates who first had the adaptations made in the third and second centuries.

II. THE HELLENISING OF THE ROMAN STAGE

The history of the *ludi scaenici* down to 240 is wrapped in obscurity. The accounts which serious scholars wrote have come down to us in somewhat garbled form and it is clear that they were based much more on Greek theories about the origins of Attic drama[4] than on documentary evidence about

---

[1] The time of this story's birth and the speed of its growth are disputed. For the extreme views on either side cf. J. Perret, *Les origines de la légende troyenne de Rome* (Paris, 1942), pp. 451 ff., A. Alföldi, *Early Rome and the Latins* (Ann Arbor, 1963), pp. 278 ff.

[2] See Festus, pp. 116.7 ff., Livy 1.49.9, Dionysius Hal. 4.45.1, F. Münzer, *Römische Adelsparteien und Adelsfamilien* (Stuttgart, 1920), p. 65 (on numismatic evidence).

[3] See Alföldi, 'The Main Aspects of Political Propaganda on the Coinage of the Roman Republic', in R. A. G. Carson and C. H. V. Sutherland (edd.), *Essays in Roman Coinage presented to H. Mattingly* (Oxford, 1956), pp. 79 f.

[4] See F. Leo, *Hermes* xxiv (1889), 67 ff. (= *Ausg. kl. Schr.* i 283 ff.), xxxix (1904), 63 ff., G. L. Hendrickson, *AJPh* xv (1894), 1 ff., xix (1898), 285 ff., F. Solmsen, *TAPhA* lxxviii (1947), 252 ff., J. H. Waszink, *Vigiliae Christianae* ii (1948), 224 ff., K. Meuli, *MusH* xii (1955), 206 ff., Brink, *Entretiens Hardt* ix (1963), 175 ff.

what went on in Rome before 240. Nevertheless some elements of these accounts seem to come from intelligent observation of post-240 stage practices and their general evolutionary approach is preferable to that of certain modern idealist accounts. The survival of words of probable Etruscan origin, like *histrio, persona*[1] and *scaena*,[2] in the vocabulary of first-century theatrical practice suggests that some of the early performers did come from Etruria and may have brought Etruscan theatrical ways with them. The word *satura* itself can be plausibly interpreted as Etruscan.[3] The word must have denoted at one time some sort of stage performance. It can hardly be a mere invention on the model of Aristotle's τὸ σατυρικόν.[4] All, however, that Livy's story at 7.2.4 ff. implies is that the *histriones* presented on a *scaena* at public festivals arrangements of words in a variety of metrical patterns accompanied by pipe music and called *saturae*. There is no suggestion that these *saturae* involved consistent acts of impersonation.[5] Indeed the use of the word as a book title by Ennius, Pacuvius[6] and Varro[7] and what we know of the form of their books[8] carries the very opposite suggestion.

---

[1] See W. Deecke, *Etruskische Forschungen und Studien* VI (Stuttgart, 1884), p. 47, F. Skutsch, *ALL* XV (1908), 145, P. Friedländer, *Glotta* II (1910), 164, v. Blumenthal, *RE* XIX i (1937), s.v. *Persona*: 1. *Die Theatermaske*, 1036 ff.

[2] See W. Schulze, *Kuhns Zeitschr.* LI (1923), 242 (= *Kl. Schr.* 638 f.); A. Ernout discusses objections raised to Schulze's view in *BSL* XXX (1929), 122 n. 2 (= *Philologica* I [Paris, 1946], p. 50 n. 2).

[3] See P. Meriggi, *Studi Etruschi* XI (1937), 157, 197, B. Snell, *SIFC* N.S. XVII (1940), 215 f. For criticism see F. Altheim, *Geschichte der lateinischen Sprache* (Frankfurt am M., 1951), pp. 363 ff.

[4] The title *Satura* attributed to the scenic poets Naevius (Festus, p. 306.29), Pomponius (*Gramm.* II 200.7, 282.16) and Atta (Isidore, *Orig.* 6.9) looks like a useful piece of evidence but does not materially help the argument.

[5] Talk of 'dramatic' *satura* is confused and misleading.

[6] Diomedes, *Gramm.* I 485.32 ff.   [7] Quintilian, *Inst.* 10.1.93.

[8] The *quattuor libri saturarum* mentioned by Porphyrio (Hor. *Sat.* 1.10.46) and quoted by Nonius, Macrobius and the Danieline Servius must be a late arrangement. There is no getting round the plain words of Diomedes (Suetonius): *olim carmen quod ex uariis poematibus constabat satira uocabatur quale scripserunt Pacuuius et Ennius.*

The aristocracies of Etruria imported from Greece and had made by local artists objects decorated with pictorial representations of the heroic legends as early as the sixth century.[1] Etruscan or Etruscanised names were given to the gods and heroes.[2] A writer of the late second or early first century, a certain Volnius, is said[3] to have composed tragedies in the Etruscan language. Modern scholars have often suggested that Volnius worked in a tradition that went back beyond 240. The idea is not an improbable one but unambiguous evidence is lacking. Excavation of tombs has produced frescos portraying many aspects of pre-240 scenic performances, but so far of nothing like an Attic tragedy. The nearest approach to drama is in pictures of entertainments involving a masked performer.[4] Vase-paintings and reliefs on cinerary urns which have heroic themes can all be easily interpreted as going back to Greek originals.[5] One can, however, leave open the possibility that forerunners and contemporaries of the 240 B.C. Latin-speaking *histriones* performed Etruscan adaptations of the Athenian classics.

Campanian farce was performed at *ludi scaenici* in Rome during the first century and later both in Latin and in Oscan.[6] Plautus makes an obvious reference to the stock character Bucco

---

[1] See J. D. Beazley, *Etruscan Vase-Painting* (Oxford, 1947), p. 8, L. Banti, *Die Welt der Etrusker* (Stuttgart, 1960), pp. 116 f., R. Hampe and E. Simon, *Griechische Sagen in der frühen etruskischen Kunst* (Mainz, 1964).

[2] See E. Fiesel, *Namen des griechischen Mythos im Etruskischen* (Göttingen, 1928). [3] Varro, *Ling.* 5.55.

[4] See S. De Marinis, *Enciclopedia dell'Arte Antica* VI (1965), s.v. *Phersu,* 119.

[5] A series of third-century cinerary urns (E. Brunn and G. Körte, *I rilievi delle urne etrusche* I–III [Rome and Berlin, 1870–1916]) are often taken to be based on a Greek artist's versions of scenes from Euripidean tragedies. A. Piganiol, *Recherches sur les jeux romains* (Strasbourg, 1923), pp. 32 ff., argued that they represent Etruscan adaptations of plays by Euripides made for performance at funeral games.

[6] See Varro, *Ling.* 7.29, Strabo 5.233, Cicero, *Fam.* 7.1.3, Diomedes, *Gramm.* I 489.32 ff.

at *Bacch.* 1088 and another to Manducus at *Rud.* 535. The name Maccus[1] suggests that Plautus may at one time have been himself an actor in this kind of drama. Livy leaves it unclear when precisely he thought Campanian farce was first performed at the *ludi scaenici* but it seems likely that the aediles would have presented this kind of drama before they tried the more sophisticated Athenian kind. There were plainly no links between the *histriones* and the performers of farce in Livy's own day and it is therefore hazardous to suppose either that they had more than accidental relations in the third century or that the form of Campanian drama had any considerable influence on the form which Athenian drama assumed on the Roman stage.

The years between 240 and the middle of the next century saw considerable reorganisation of the old magisterial festivals as well as the establishment of new ones. One of the principal innovations was the regular performance of Latin versions of the classics of Attic drama. Many Greek states had reformed their ancient festivals in similar fashion or introduced new ones on the model of the Athenian festivals of Dionysus.[2] As early as the fifth century Archelaus of Macedon established a festival in honour of Zeus and the Muses of which scenic performances were an important element.[3] Philip,[4] Alexander[5] and the successor kings[6] often had tragedies and comedies performed at the monster public festivals they delighted in arranging. Even the old musical festivals of Pythian Apollo were forced to admit the Athenian newcomers, tragedy and comedy.[7] To cater for the

---

[1] *Asin.* 11, *Merc.* 10, Gellius, 3.3; cf. Varro, *Ling.* 7.104 (?: Maccius *F*), Leo, *Plautinische Forschungen*[2] (Berlin, 1912), p. 85.

[2] See W. W. Tarn and G. T. Griffith, *Hellenistic Civilisation*[3] (London, 1952), pp. 113 ff. on Greek festivals between Alexander's death and 189 B.C.

[3] Diodorus 17.16.3.   [4] Demosthenes 19.192 ff.

[5] Plutarch, *Alex.* 4, 29, Athenaeus 12.538 F.

[6] Diodorus 20.108.1.

[7] Plutarch, *Mor.* 674D, Philostratus, *Soph.* pp. 238.20 ff., 269.1 ff., *Apoll.* 6.10 (pp. 109.35 ff.).

demand guilds of itinerant theatrical workers and performers, οἱ περὶ τὸν Διόνυσον τεχνῖται,[1] established themselves. Stray references in literature and a great number of lapidary inscriptions record their activities from early in the third century in most parts of the Greek-speaking world. On at least two occasions in the first half of the second century[2] they performed at Rome.

The Greek cities with which members of the Roman ruling class had their first direct contacts after the long period of cultural isolation following the expulsion of the second Tarquin[3] were those of southern Italy and Sicily. Three of the four known dramatists of the third century came to Rome from this area. Hiero II of Syracuse visited Rome in 237, according to Eutropius[4] *ad ludos spectandos*. Permanent theatres had been erected in the wealthier cities as early as the fifth century.[5] Athenian drama was well known. Aeschylus visited the court of Hiero I and produced the Πέρσαι and the Αἰτναῖαι in Syracuse.[6] Those Athenian prisoners taken in 413 who could recite Euripides were, according to legend,[7] released by their admiring captors. The tyrant Dionysius not only invited Athenian poets

---

[1] See Welcker, *Die griech. Trag.* pp. 1303 ff., O. Lüders, *Die Dionysischen Künstler* (Berlin, 1873), P. Foucart, *De collegiis scenicorum artificum apud Graecos* (Paris, 1873), Poland, *RE* 2 v ii (1934), s.v. *Technitai* (Nachträge), 2473 ff., Pickard-Cambridge, *Dramatic Festivals*, pp. 286 ff.

[2] At the *ludi* celebrated by M. Fulvius Nobilior in 186 (Livy 39.22.2) and those celebrated by L. Scipio in the same year (Livy 39.22.10). Cf. Polybius 30.22 for the *ludi* of L. Anicius in 167. There is no need to suppose that they performed in tragedy or comedy.

[3] See Altheim, *Epochen der römischen Geschichte* i (Frankfurt am M., 1934), pp. 128 ff., A. Blakeway, *JRS* xxv (1935), 136, Ryberg, *An Archaeological Record of Rome*, pp. 3, 79, 107, 204 f.

[4] 3.1–2.

[5] On the theatre of Syracuse, which seems to have been dedicated about 460 B.C., see G. E. Rizzo, *Il Teatro Greco di Siracusa* (Milan, Rome, 1923). On the other theatres of Magna Graecia see B. Pace, *Dioniso* x (1947), 266 ff., A. von Gerkan, in *Festschrift A. Rumpf* (Cologne, 1965), pp. 82 ff.

[6] *Vita*, 9, 18. [7] Plutarch, *Nic.* 29.

to his court but composed tragedies himself for performance at the Athenian festivals.[1] An early South Italian kalyx krater (400–390) depicting the punishment of a thief in a stage comedy has an inscription in what is possibly Attic dialect and iambic verse.[2] It is probably an accident that activity by οἱ περὶ τὸν Διόνυσον τεχνῖται is not recorded until the mid first century.[3] Nevertheless the Dorian cities had theatrical traditions of their own, independent at least in origin of the Athenian theatre,[4] and it is possible that the texts of Athenian plays were used by actors costumed differently from Athenian actors and on stages different in character from the Athenian.[5] In any case one may reasonably seek the inspiration of at least some of the changes made to the Roman *ludi scaenici* between 240 and the turn of the century in the stage practices of Magna Graecia.

However one imagines the amalgam of Etruscan, Italiote Greek and perhaps Oscan elements in the practice of the late third century Roman *histriones* it is plain that the adapters of Athenian tragic and comic scripts had to deal with a theatrical situation very different in the one case from that which faced

---

[1] See Niese, *RE* v (1905), s.v. *Dionysios* [1], 900 f., for references.

[2] See Beazley, *AJA* LVI (1952), 193, Webster, *CQ* XLII (1948), 25, in *Festschrift B. Schweitzer* (Stuttgart, 1954), pp. 260 f.

[3] Plutarch, *Brut.* 21 (Naples). *I.G.* XIV 12, 13 (Syracuse), 615 (Rhegium) are undated.

[4] On the so-called Φλύακες see Pollux 9.149, Athenaeus 14.621 F (= Sosibius).

[5] It is only a possibility. The evidence of painted pottery will not bear the weight of the interpretations often placed upon it. Late fifth and fourth century Apulian, Lucanian and Campanian wares have representations of stage performances of both comic (see A. D. Trendall, *Phlyax Vases* [*BICSL* Suppl. VIII (1959)], Webster, *Monuments Illustrating Old and Middle Comedy* [*BICSL* Suppl. IX (1960)]) and tragic (see Webster, *Monuments Illustrating Tragedy and Satyr Play*) type. The costume of the comic actors is clearly local. In the absence of fully comparable Athenian material it is difficult to pass judgment on the elaborate costume of the tragic actors. The low stage raised on columns with steps leading up to it seems quite different from what we know of the contemporary Athenian stage.

Euripides in the fifth century and in the other from that which faced Menander in the late fourth; different again from that of contemporary Athens and other Greek-speaking states.

Roman stages in stone at the time of Vitruvius differed considerably in dimensions from contemporary Greek.[1] The stages in wood of the third and second centuries no doubt differed similarly from contemporary Greek stone structures. Archaeological investigation and close study of the surviving dramatic texts have made it clear that the classical Athenian stage differed yet again in dimensions, and quite radically.[2]

The flat area directly in front of the stage where the Athenian choruses sang and danced was occupied by seats for part of the audience.[3] Adaptations of comedy clearly dispensed with the dancing chorus. Ancient students tell us so[4] and surviving comic scripts either do not have the actor's introduction of the first choral ode conventional in late fourth century Attic comedy[5] or replace it with something else. Plautus writes at *Bacch.* 107: *simul huic nescioqui turbare qui huc it decedamus,*[6] while Terence leaves an awkward break at *Haut.* 170.[7] The performance of the *tibicen* indicated at *Pseud.* 573 a and the lecture of the *choragus* at *Curc.* 462–86 probably replaced choral odes in Plautus' originals. The difficulty which ancient students, who must have possessed the Greek scripts, found in imposing a five-act division on the

---

[1] 5.6.2, 5.7.
[2] See Pickard-Cambridge, *The Theatre of Dionysus in Athens* (Oxford, 1946), pp. 5 ff., Webster, *Greek Theatre Production* (London, 1956), pp. 22, 170.
[3] Vitruvius should not be taken to imply at 5.6.2 that before 194 this area was left free of spectators; see Livy 34.44.5.
[4] Cf. Donatus, Ter. *Eun.* praef. 1.5, Euanthius, *De fab.* 3.1, Diomedes, *Gramm.* I 491.29 f. The statement at *Gloss. Lat.* I 128.6—*apud Romanos quoque Plautus comoediae choros exemplo Graecorum inseruit*—may refer to the fishermen of *Rud.* 290–324 and the *aduocati* of *Poen.* 504–816.
[5] Cf. Antiphanes, fr. 91, Alexis, fr. 107, Menander, *Epitr.* 33–5, *Perik.* 71–2, *Dysk.* 230–2.
[6] Cf. Leo, *Hermes* XLVI (1911), 292 ff.
[7] Cf. F. Skutsch, *Hermes* XLVII (1912), 141 ff.

Latin versions suggests that the Latin poets often covered up the breaks by rewriting the actors' dialogue. Classical tragedy differed from comedy in that the chorus sometimes had a role integral to the action and it was almost impossible for Latin adapters to remove it in these cases. Plautus appears to refer to a Roman tragic chorus at *Amph.* 91–2. Ancient students interpreted parts of Latin tragic scripts as utterances of a chorus[1] and the remains of Ennius' adaptation of Euripides' Μήδεια contain unmistakeable signs[2] that the original chorus of Corinthian women was retained. Horace's discussion of the chorus at *Ars* 193 ff. may be based on a Greek theoretical discussion and may at times adduce arguments quite inapplicable to Roman practice,[3] but it is hard to believe that the despised republican playwrights abandoned the chorus and that Horace passed over in silence such a divagation from the Attic practice he so much admired.[4] The Roman choruses could not have danced in the classical Greek manner.[5] The extent to which they were present

---

[1] Cf. Varro, *Ling.* 6.94, Gellius 19.10.12 (but see commentary on fr. xcix), Terentianus Maurus 1934.

[2] See *Commentary* on frs. cv and cx.

[3] Cf. Latte, *Hermes* lx (1925), 5 ff., Brink, *Horace on Poetry: Prolegomena* (Cambridge, 1963), pp. 114 f.

[4] H. Plank, *Q. Ennii Medea commentario perpetuo illustrata* (Diss. Göttingen, 1807), pp. 56 ff., and A. La Penna, *Maia* v (1952), 95, seem to banish the chorus from the early republican stage. Most students allow it in some form; cf. A. G. Lange, *Vindiciae Tragoediae Romanae* (Leipzig, 1822), p. 22 n. 31, Welcker, *Die griech. Trag.* p. 1368, Grysar, *SB Vienna* 1855, 365 ff., 384 ff., O. Jahn, *Hermes* II (1867), 227 ff., Ribbeck, *Die röm. Trag.* pp. 632 ff., L. Mueller, *Q. Ennius. Eine Einleitung in das Studium der römischen Poesie* (St Petersburg, 1884), p. 79, Leo, *De Tragoedia Romana Obseruationes Criticae* (Göttingen, 1910), pp. 14 ff. (= *Ausg. kl. Schr.* I 203 ff.), *Pl. Forsch.*[2], p. 96, *Geschichte der römischen Literatur* I (Berlin, 1913), pp. 193 ff., E. S. Duckett, *Studies in Ennius* (Diss. Bryn Mawr, 1915), pp. 53 ff., Fraenkel, *Pl. im Pl.* p. 336 (= *Elementi*, p. 320), Wł. Strzelecki, in *Tragica* I (Wrocław, 1952), pp. 54 ff.

[5] Post-fifth-century Attic tragedians reduced considerably the role of the chorus. There is considerable evidence that later productions of classical plays sometimes dispensed with a full chorus; cf. E. Capps, *AJA* x (1895), 287, Leo, *RhM* lii (1897), 509 ff., A. Körte, *NJbb* v (1900), 81 ff., P. Venini, *Dioniso* xvi

during the actions of tragedies and their mode of giving utterance must remain obscure.[1]

The left-hand end (from the point of view of the spectators) of the Roman stage pretty clearly was the conventional point of entry for travellers from abroad.[2] There is some evidence that this reversed the Attic convention.[3]

At Athens tragic acting and comic acting were considered quite different skills.[4] At Rome on the other hand it was not unusual for an actor to perform in both genres.[5] The scholars of late antiquity thought[6] that the adapters of comedy had more than the classical Athenian trio of actors to employ.[7] If masks were not in use before the end of the second century[8] there had to be as many actors as characters. The early adapters of comedy seem to have taken advantage of a greater number of available actors in order to alter whole scenes of their originals. The *Stichus* is the only one of Plautus' pieces that could be easily

---

(1953), 3, Webster, *Hermes* LXXXII (1954), 294 ff. A third century B.C. papyrus of Euripides' Ἱππόλυτος omitting the choral lyrics has now turned up (Pap. Sorb. 2252). W. S. Barrett, *Euripides: Hippolytos* (Oxford, 1964), p. 438 n. 2 compares Pap. Hib. I 4, long thought to be of Euripides' Οἰνεύς.

[1] Leo's theory that Ennius always made the coryphaeus utter trochaic tetrameters and kept the other choreutae mute goes far beyond the evidence. At least one Ennian choral utterance (fr. cx) is more plausibly scanned as in lyric verses and Leo himself admitted lyric scansion of choral utterances in the other tragedians.

[2] Cf. Plautus, *Amph.* 333, *Men.* 555, *Rud.* 156, Terence, *Andr.* 734, M. Johnston, *Exits and Entrances in Roman Comedy* (New York, 1933), pp. 64 ff.

[3] Pollux, 4.126. See W. Beare, *CQ* XXXII (1938), 205 ff. (= *Roman Stage*[3], pp. 248 ff.), Pickard-Cambridge, *Theatre of Dionysus*, pp. 234 ff.

[4] Cf. Plato, *Politeia* 3.395 A.

[5] Cf. Plautus, *Poen.* I ff., Cicero, *Orat.* 109.

[6] Cf. Diomedes, *Gramm.* I 490.27 ff.

[7] The existence of the convention of three actors at the time when classical tragedy and classical comedy were actually written has been denied; for the evidence and discussion see Pickard-Cambridge, *Dramatic Festivals*, pp. 137 ff., K. Schneider, *RE* Suppl. VIII (1956), s.v. Ὑποκριτής, 190 ff. Menander's Δύσκολος can be arranged for three actors; cf. G. P. Goold, *Phoenix* XIII (1959), 144 f., J. G. Griffith, *CQ* N.S. x (1960), 113 ff.

[8] See below, p. 22.

performed with three principals.[1] Terence's pieces, on the other hand, are perhaps all just actable with three. Nevertheless the didascaliae of the *Adelphi* and the *Hecyra* mention each two principals, something unparalleled in Greek didascaliae.[2] Terence was much more faithful than his predecessors to the texts of his originals but the producers of his plays may have still employed the traditional Roman number of actors.[3] Horace's polemic at *Ars* 192 suggests that contemporary producers of tragedy at Rome still employed more than three actors.

The amount of singing required in the actors' parts in Attic drama was very much less than in the Roman versions[4] but there is no evidence that the Athenian actors did not do their own singing. According to Livy 7.2.9–10 the Roman *histriones* merely mimed the *cantica* while a singer accompanied the *tibicen*. It is difficult to believe that tragedy and comedy were performed this way. The trochaic and anapaestic verses of Ennius' *Andromacha* quoted by Cicero at *Sest.* 120–2 were certainly uttered by the actor Aesopus. At *De orat.* 1.254 and *Leg.* 1.11 Cicero talks of the actor Roscius singing in old age. Livy may have been thinking of the contemporary pantomime.[5]

There is very little evidence as to how the *histriones* were costumed in the third century and early second. One piece[6] suggests that tragic actors wore the dress that normally distinguished the priestly order of *flamines*. The accounts of comic costume by the Greek Pollux (4.118–20) and the Roman Donatus (*De com.* 8.6) do not tally and may reflect real dif-

---

[1] Cf. Leo, *NGG, Phil.-hist. Kl.* 1902, 391.

[2] Cf. that of the Δύσκολος.

[3] K. Dziatzko, *RhM* xx (1865), 591, and F. Schoell, *NJbb* cxix (1879), 41 ff., discuss the Terentian didascaliae without reaching any satisfactory conclusion.

[4] See below, p. 29. Euripides, *Or.* 1369 ff. would have needed a highly skilled singer.

[5] Cf. Ribbeck, *Die röm. Trag.* p. 634.

[6] *Gloss. Lat.* 1 128, 568, Servius auct. *Aen.* 4.262; see I. Hilberg, *WSt* xiii (1891), 170 f.

ferences between Greek and Roman stage practice. Romans of the first century believed that the wearing of masks by the *histriones* in performances of tragedy and comedy was a recent innovation.[1]

At Athens the writers of tragedy and comedy were usually native Athenians, sometimes of aristocratic birth. During the fourth century a number of foreigners came to the city to practise the two arts. There was a tradition of poetry held in honour by all. The prime object of the poet was to win the prize in the competition to which he submitted his work. Performers likewise were usually citizens of respectable status and competed for prizes from the year 449 onwards.[2] At Rome writing verse became in the course of time a respectable activity for gentlemen, acting never. In the third and early second centuries both the making of acting scripts and the performance of them were lowly activities.[3] A magistrate would use either his own slaves, freedmen and clients for the spectacles he was providing at the *ludi* or hire professional poets and actors.[4] There is no clear evidence for poetic competitions during republican times.[5]

---

[1] See Cicero, *De orat.* 3.221, Festus, s.v. *personata*, p. 238.12 ff., Donatus, *De com.* 6.3, Diomedes, *Gramm.* I 489.11 ff., C. Saunders, *AJPh* XXXII (1911), 58 ff. The sceptical attack on the tradition by A. S. F. Gow, *JRS* II (1912), 65 ff., and Beare, *CQ* XXXIII (1939), 139 ff. (cf. *Roman Stage³*, pp. 192 ff., 303 ff.) is unconvincing. Donatus' belief (*Ad. praef.* 1.6, *Eun.* praef. 1.6) that Terence's actors wore masks was probably based on the illustrations of the text current in his day; see Leo, *RhM* XXXVIII (1883), 342 f. The prologue of Plautus' *Poenulus* was spoken by one of the actors who changed his costume in some way (123, 126) in order to play one of the ordinary roles. This shows nothing about the distribution of roles within the action.

[2] On Athenian actors see Pickard-Cambridge, *Dramatic Festivals*, pp. 127 ff.

[3] See B. Warnecke, *NJbb* XXXIII (1914), 95 ff., *RE* VIII ii (1913), s.v. *Histrio*, 2117, 2125 ff. T. Frank's challenge to the orthodox view (*CPh* XXVI [1931], 11 ff.) is unconvincing.

[4] For the giving of a *pretium* to poets cf. Terence, *Eun.* 20, Horace, *Epist.* 2.1.175, Gellius 3.3, Suetonius, *Vit. Ter.* 3.14.

[5] Plautus, *Cas.* 17 and Terence, *Phorm.* 16–17 are clearly metaphorical; cf. Volcacius Sedigitus *ap.* Gell. 15.24, Horace, *Epist.* 2.1.181.

Comic poets often had to plead for a quiet hearing. They ended their scripts with an appeal for applause, as in their originals,[1] but made no request for victory.[2] Tragic scripts seem to have ended similarly.[3] There were however acting competitions.[4] The language of Plautus, *Trin*. 706 suggests that they went back beyond the time of composition of this script.[5]

As time passed the differences between the external conditions of the Roman stage and those of the contemporary Athenian lessened but during the period when the first adaptations of classical Athenian drama were made they remained considerable and inevitably affected the poetic form of the adaptations.

III. ATHENIAN DRAMA AND THE ROMAN POETS

The only evidence for what the Latin poets themselves thought about the process of adapting the Athenian classics is found in five comic prologues from the years 166–161, those of Terence's *Andria, Hauton timoroumenus, Eunuchus, Phormio* and *Adelphi*. Terence can be seen struggling against two contradictory but related movements of taste, one favouring the work of the older poets against the new, the other demanding faithful versions of the Athenian classics. He appeals to the commonly

---

[1] Cf. Posidippus, Pap. Heid. 183; Menander, *Dysk.* 965 ff., *Epitr.* fr. 11 Körte, *Misoumenos* D → col. ii. 36–8 Turner, *Sikyonios* in Pap. Sorb. 2272 e col. B. 11 ff. (= 420 ff. Kassel).

[2] There was sometimes a prayer for the success of Roman arms in the prologue; cf. Plautus, *Asin.* 15.

[3] Cf. Horace, *Ars* 155, Quintilian, *Inst.* 6.1.52; contrast Euripides, *I.T.* 1497 ff., *Or.* 1691 ff., *Phoin.* 1764 ff.

[4] Cf. Cicero, *Att.* 4.15.6. It is noteworthy that the ivy of Dionysus (see Olck, *RE* v (1905), s.v. *Epheu,* 2838) was replaced by Apollo's palm (see Steier, *RE* xx i (1941), s.v. *Phoinix,* 401).

[5] Plautus, *Amph.* 69 and *Poen.* 37 may be actors' interpolations from a later time.

recognised authority of Naevius, Plautus and Ennius in defence of the liberties he has taken with his originals.[1] The argument proceeds within the context of comedy but we need not suppose that Naevius and Ennius regarded the adaptation of tragedy as fundamentally different. The Athenians always kept the tragedian's craft rigidly distinct from the comedian's[2] and required much less originality from the tragedian in the matter of plot construction.[3] At Rome on the other hand Livius and his immediate successors cultivated the two genres together and brought their respective forms much closer than they had been at Athens.[4]

Terence's thinking made the conventionally sharp ancient distinction between the subject-matter and plot of a play (*argumentum*) and the verbal manner in which the poet presented those things (*oratio, stilus*).[5] The distinction between one *argumentum* and another was at the same time much less sharp for him than it was for certain contemporary critics and is for the modern scholar. Speaking of Menander's Περινθία and 'Ανδρία he declared: *qui utramuis recte norit ambas nouerit*.[6] The scanty remains of the Περινθία make it appear to us to have had a very different *argumentum* from the 'Ανδρία but a poet busy providing scripts for set occasions would naturally have been more struck by their similarities. Terence's predecessors appear to have been much busier than he was and we can well believe that they regarded many plays as very like others and did not

---

[1] *Andr.* 18–19; cf. *Haut.* 20–1.

[2] Cf. Plato, *Politeia* 3.395 A. *Ion* 534 C and *Symp.* 223 D deal with an ideal situation.

[3] Cf. Antiphanes, fr. 191. On the views of Aristotle (*Poet.* 9.1451 b 21–6, 14.1453 b 25) see Brink, *Horace*, pp. 103 ff.

[4] See below, pp. 31 ff, 38 ff.

[5] *Andr.* 9–12, *Haut.* 6, 46. Cf. Aristotle, *Poet.* 6.1449 b 24 ff., Horace, *Ars* 40 ff., 119 ff., Plutarch, *Mor.* 347 E–F (anecdote about Menander's mode of composition).

[6] *Andr.* 10. Cf. also *Eun.* 41 *nullumst iam dictum quod non dictum sit prius.*

think close fidelity to the particular *argumentum* of a play much of a virtue.

In discussing the school exercise of παράφρασις[1] and his own adaptations of Greek philosophical dialogues[2] Cicero, who was well acquainted with the texts of many Greek and Latin plays and knew at first hand the workings of the Roman theatre, thought it proper and persuasive to use the analogy of the behaviour of the old republican poets towards the texts of their originals.

The schools of third and second century Greece employed two exercises akin to the translation of poetical works from one language into another. In the one poetic texts were interpreted word for word in the everyday language.[3] In the other a rhetorical equivalent of the substance of a poem or prose work was sought; the student had to present this substance in such a way as to please the sort of audiences he was being trained to persuade; it was important that he should use the vocabulary and mode of expression appropriate to public oratory.[4] Roman schools took over both exercises, at first using Greek texts and then, as the indigenous literature grew in bulk, Latin ones. The continued use of Greek texts naturally came under attack and defenders of the practice tossed up the notion that the paraphrast should attempt to improve on his original.[5] This notion ceases to be surprising when one remembers the sharp ancient distinction between a work of art's substance and its verbal or material form; the one was constant and to an extent beyond

---

[1] *Opt. gen.* 18.   [2] *Ac.* 1.10, *Fin.* 1.4–7.

[3] Cf. the paraphrases of the *Iliad* found on papyrus (nos. 1157 ff. in Pack's catalogue) and the literary references to the exercise collected by H.-I. Marrou, *Histoire de l'éducation dans l'antiquité*[3] (Paris, 1958), pp. 231 ff., G. Giangrande, *Eranos* LX (1962), 152 ff.

[4] Cf. Plutarch, *Dem.* 8.2, Dio Chrys. *Or.* 18.19, Theon, *Progymn.* 4, Hermogenes, *Meth.* 24.

[5] Cf. Quintilian, *Inst.* 10.5.5, Pliny, *Epist.* 7.9.3.

time and space, the other was very much fixed in its creator's particular time and could not be exactly reproduced in another's; adaptation alone was possible. The old dramatic adaptations of Sophocles, Euripides and Menander were much admired in some quarters in the mid first century and some were thought to excel their originals.[1] Accordingly Cicero argues in his treatise *De optimo genere oratorum* that the paraphrases he and others made of the Attic orators were of the same character as the dramatic adaptations and deserved the approbation accorded these.

At *Ac.* 1.1–10 Cicero is concerned to rebut the view that readers who knew Greek would not bother with philosophical dialogues written in Latin. Such men, he argues, read with pleasure the Latin adaptations of Aeschylus, Sophocles and Euripides made by the poets of the previous century, *qui non uerba sed uim Graecorum expresserunt poetarum*; they will get even more pleasure out of the philosophical dialogues of Roman writers *si, ut illi Aeschylum Sophoclem Euripidem, sic hi Platonem imitentur Aristotelem Theophrastum*. His distinction between *uis* and *uerba* is the one informing *Opt. gen.* 14–23.[2] The poets, in his view, did not offer a word for word representation of the substance of their originals but achieved in their own medium effects similar to those which the Athenian poets had achieved in theirs. Both sets of poets had their own excellences.

At *Fin.* 1.4–7 Cicero makes his case against those who scorned Latin philosophical dialogues more detailed and sophisticated. Such men, he argues, read *fabellas Latinas ad uerbum e Graecis expressas* and must therefore be foolish to ignore works of a more serious kind which do not merely reproduce the words of someone like Aristotle in the manner of a grammatical exercise

---

[1] Cf. Cicero, *Tusc.* 2.49, Varro *ap.* Suet. *Vit. Ter.* 3.
[2] Cf. also the hexameters of Caesar and Cicero on Terence (Suetonius, *Vit. Ter.* 7).

but treat Aristotelian themes afresh in the manner of a Theophrastus. Where his own dialogues depend closely on a classical Greek philosopher they depend, he suggests, in the way that Ennius' epic depends on Homer and Afranius' *fabulae togatae* on Menander,[1] not in the way Ennius' *Medea* depends on Euripides. The character of his argument forces him to attribute less independence to the dramatic poets and more to himself than he does at *Ac.* 1.1–10.[2] Nevertheless he does not assimilate the republican plays completely with the grammatical kind of translation. He writes of them as possessing a literary value of their own independent of their degree of fidelity to the original Greek. He dismisses Atilius as a bad writer, not as an inaccurate translator.

Ancient scholars regarded the tragedies and comedies of the republican period as different in kind from their originals. The *argumenta* belonged to Greece, only the words to the Latin poets.[3] It is easy to misunderstand their view. It was not one denigratory of the Latin poets. There would have been a strong temptation for Romans to consider the construction of a plot a smaller matter than the provision of adequate words. Such detailed comparisons of the texts of the Latin plays and their Greek originals as were made[4] resembled those made between Latin and Greek poems united only in genre, for example

---

[1] Cf. Afranius, *Com. tog.* 25–8, Macrobius, *Sat.* 6.1.1–7.

[2] It was not only in his public orations that Cicero tailored his statements of fact according to circumstance and audience; one might compare with *Ac.* 1.1–10 and *Fin.* 1.4–7 his description of the *libri academici* at *Att.* 12.52.3: *apographa sunt, minore labore fiunt* (on the context of this remark see D. R. Shackleton Bailey, *Towards a Text of Cicero 'Ad Atticum'* [Cambridge, 1960], pp. 61 f.).

[3] Cf. Donatus, Ter. *Andr.* 9 *scribit enim Terentius qui uerba adhibet tantum; facit Menander qui etiam argumentum componit.* Leo, *Pl. Forsch.*[2], p. 87 n. 1, compares Marcus Pomponius Bassulus, *C.L.E.* 97, *Menandri paucas uorti scitas fabulas...ipsus etiam sedulo finxi noua* and Pliny, *Epist.* 6.21.

[4] Cf. Gellius 2.23, 11.4, the scholia to Terence's comedies *passim*.

between the *Aeneid* and Homer's epics.[1] Argument about the
text of a Latin play and its correct interpretation based itself on
such comparisons[2] with a rarity that is significant. Most discussion, including that of the Latin poet's alleged misunderstandings of his original, was carried on in terms deriving from the
discussion of rhetorical παράφρασις.[3] Students were interested in
how effectively the Latin poet used his medium in dealing with
the Greek substance. We thus often find the same language used
to describe his degree of success as is used of Virgil's treatment
of a Homeric motif.

Modern views of the relationship between the comedies and
tragedies of the early republic and the Attic plays that lie behind
them have often been subconsciously coloured by the attitude
to the translation of the Hebrew and Greek scriptures imposed
until recently by the Christian sects upon their members; the
words of the original as well as its substance were in orthodox
theory sacred and should either be left alone or respected by the
translator; the idioms and rhetorical modes of the translator's
own culture ought not to replace those of the original.[4] The
practice of successful translators of these writings has of course
always diverged to a greater or lesser extent from the orthodox
theory but the word 'translation' has come to have associations
that can only be misleading in the discussion of pagan Latin
literature. Accordingly I make little use of it.

---

[1] Cf. Sidonius' comparison of the *Hecyra* of Terence with Menander's
᾽Επιτρέποντες (*Epist.* 4.12).

[2] Cf. Donatus, *Andr.* 204, 483, 592, 801, *Eun.* 46, *Hec.* 58.

[3] The σύγκρισις of two authors writing within the same genre was a regular
exercise of the Greek schools; see F. Fock, *Hermes* LVIII (1923), 327 ff.

[4] Cf. Hieronymus, *Epist.* 57.

IV. THE FORM OF ROMAN TRAGEDY

Thirty-two tragic scripts have been transmitted to us from the Athenian theatre more or less in their entirety. Of these we possess small sections of the Latin adaptations of possibly twelve. All twelve seem to have contained a much lower proportion of that type of verse which was uttered by the actor without any accompaniment from the piper[1] than did their originals.[2] The remains of third and second century Latin tragedy taken together show a tendency for poets to move

---

[1] My argument does not require an answer to the question how Greek and Roman actors actually delivered verses while the piper was playing. At Athens stichic tetrameters were recited in a mode (παρακαταλογή) different from that used for trimeters on the one hand and from that used for verses of lyric type on the other (for the sparse evidence see Pickard-Cambridge, *Dramatic Festivals*, pp. 153 ff.). Ancient editors of Latin comic scripts deployed a set of symbols—DV (*deuerbium*), C (*canticum*) and MMC (*mutatis modis canticum*: see Donatus, *Ad.* praef. 7) which suggests that Roman actors used a similar triple mode of delivery. I assume that both at Athens and at Rome iambic trimeters were normally spoken without accompaniment (this is implied in such comparisons with ordinary speech as at Aristotle, *Poet.* 4.1449a21–8, 22.1459a 10–14, *Rhet.* 3.8.1408b32–6, Cicero, *Orat.* 189–91, Horace, *Ars* 80–2) while all other types of verse received an accompaniment of some kind (cf. Aristophanes, *Orn.* 222, Menander, *Dysk.* 879, Xenophon, *Symp.* 6.3, Plautus, *Pseud.* 573a, *Stich.* 762, 769, Cicero, *De orat.* 1.254, *Orat.* 183–4, *Ac.* 2.20, *Diu.* 2.113, *Tusc.* 1.106). There is evidence for occasional Greek (Plutarch, *Mor.* 1140 f., Athenaeus, 14.636B, Lucian, *De Salt.* 27, Pap. Osl. 1413 [see *SO* XXXI (1955), 1 ff.]) and Roman (see *Commentary* on fr. CIV; the irregularities in the distribution of the symbols C and DV in the Palatine manuscripts of Plautus are relatively very few and should be treated as errors of transmission [so Ritschl, *RhM* XXVI (1871), 616 (= *Opusc.* III 22 ff.), Bergk, *Philologus* XXXI (1872), 229 ff. (= *Kl. phil. Schr.* I 192 ff.)] rather than as evidence for republican theatrical practice [so R. Klotz, *Grundzüge altrömischer Metrik* (Leipzig, 1890), pp. 379 ff., A. Klotz, *Würzb. Jbb.* II (1947), 305 f.]) departures from the norm but these are too few to affect my argument significantly. I have not found it useful always to distinguish between musically accompanied stichic verses and 'lyrics'.

[2] For the replacement of Greek trimeters by other types of verse in particular cases see *Commentary* on frs. LXXXIV, CV, CVII, CVIII, CIX.

closer to Attic practice as time passed.[1] Only one script of the kind of Attic comedy adapted at Rome survives in its entirety[2] but the lengthy pieces of Menander's Πλόκιον and Caecilius' adaptation quoted by Aulus Gellius (2.23) and the pieces of Terence's originals quoted in the scholia confirm the accuracy of Diomedes' statement at *Gramm.* I 490.22–3: *in Latinis... fabulis plura sunt cantica quae canuntur.*[3] The difference however grew less as the second century advanced.[4]

If, as seems likely,[5] the Latin poets not only dispensed with the choral songs of Attic comedy but modified the actors' parts at those points where, in their originals, the choral songs had been performed, the resultant continuous action would have been something very different from what Athenian audiences of the time of Menander were accustomed to see. The action of the average Attic tragedy at the time of Euripides could be said to have possessed a continuous character inasmuch as the interests of the members of the chorus were involved to a greater or

---

[1] Trimeters form about 40 per cent of Livius' measurable verses, 35 per cent of Naevius', 30 per cent of Ennius', 45 per cent of Pacuvius', 55 per cent of Accius'. Frequent uncertainty about the scansion of small fragments reduces the value of these figures. The difficulty of isolating choral fragments and the general uncertainty about the extent of the Roman tragic chorus' role make comparisons with Greek percentages thoroughly ambiguous. I note for what it is worth the fact that trimeters form about 65 per cent of the verses of the Ὀρέστης.

[2] On the relationship between the verse quoted by Festus, p. 174.18 as by *Plautus in Dyscolo* and Menander's Δύσκολος see Strzelecki, *GIF* XII (1959), 305 ff., C. Questa, *RCCM* I (1959), 307 ff., T. Mantero, in *Menandrea* (Univ. di Genova, Ist. di Fil. Class., 1960), 125 ff.

[3] Cf. Quintilian, *Inst.* 10.1.99 *licet Terenti scripta ad Scipionem Africanum referantur (quae tamen sunt in hoc genere elegantissima et plus adhuc habitura gratiae si intra uersus trimetros stetissent)*, Marius Victorinus, *Gramm.* VI 78.20 *scio plurimos affirmare Terentianas uel maxime fabulas metrum ac disciplinam Graecarum comoediarum non custodisse, id est quas Menander Philemon Diphilus et ceteri ediderunt.*

[4] In *c.* 18,400 Plautine verses there are *c.* 8,200 trimeters (38 per cent), in *c.* 6,000 Terentian 3,100 (52 per cent). Menander's Δύσκολος has 813 trimeters in 969 actors' verses (84 per cent).

[5] See above, pp. 18 f.

lesser extent in it. Nevertheless the songs of the chorus very often had little relevance to the action and were always performed away from the area used by the actors. The Latin poets did not abolish the tragic chorus but what they could do with it was limited by the fact that their choral performers had to use the same comparatively restricted area as their actors; the elaborate dancing of fifth-century Athens was impossible and without this the songs of the Attic poets would have had little theatrical value. It is possible, therefore, that they dispensed with some of the songs of their originals and pruned others severely. In any case the action of a Roman tragedy as it revealed itself in the theatre would have had much more continuity than that of any fifth-century Athenian play.

The dramatic material which the Latin poets put into musically accompanied verse differs not only in quantity but also in kind from what can be found in the scripts of classical Attic tragedy and comedy. The Attic comedians rarely went beyond the simpler stichically arranged types of verse[1] and did not allow the action to progress in scenes accompanied by music. The tragedians often gave their actors metrically complex utterances and made them take part in lyric dialogues both with the chorus and with one another. It would be difficult however to point to a long musically accompanied scene in which vital information was given and the action made serious progress.[2]

It is plain that the first Latin poets set the scripts of comedy and tragedy they chose to adapt in one dramatic mould and that during the time of the republic this mould was never broken

---

[1] F. Marx, Plautus Rudens: Text und Kommentar (Abh. Sächs. Ak., Phil.-hist. Kl. xxxviii [1928], v), pp. 254 ff., collects the little that can be found of lyric verse. There is somewhat more in the remains of the so-called 'Middle Comedy' (see Leo, RhM xl [1885], 164).

[2] Cf. Wilamowitz, Menander. Das Schiedsgericht (Berlin, 1925), p. 169 n. 1, G. Pasquali, Enciclopedia Italiana xxvii (1935), s.v. Plauto, 528.

despite an ever increasing desire on the part of critics for the main features of the two Attic genres to be faithfully reproduced. Two historically credible kinds of explanation have been offered of their behaviour. According to one[1] they adapted the Attic scripts to a contemporary type of musical stage performance. According to the other[2] they simply merged the theatrical forms of Attic tragedy and Attic comedy. The latter explanation does not cover all the facts, the former has to postulate an entity for whose existence there is little solid evidence. The issue is an important one and cannot be brushed aside with idle talk about Roman creativeness. The paucity of our knowledge of what went on during the third century in the theatres of Etruria and the Greek and Oscan speaking cities of the South makes it incapable of settlement.

The scholars who first edited and discussed the early Latin theatrical scripts found it possible to use the same general type of metrical description as had been applied at Alexandria and Pergamum to the scripts of Attic drama and other Greek poems.[3] Some areas of the Latin scripts gave more trouble than

---

[1] Cf. Wilamowitz, *NGG, Phil.-hist. Kl.* 1896, 228, *Griechische Verskunst* (Berlin, 1921), p. 125, O. Crusius, *Philologus* LV (1896), 384, Leo, *Die plautinischen Cantica und die hellenistische Lyrik (Abh. Gött. Gesellschaft* N.F. 17 [1897]), pp. 78 ff., *Gesch.* pp. 121 ff., R. Reitzenstein, *NGG, Phil.-hist. Kl.* 1918, 233 ff., O. Immisch, *SB Heidelberg, Phil.-hist. Kl.* XIV (1923), 7, 1 ff., H. Drexler, *Plautinische Akzentstudien* II (Breslau, 1932), pp. 358 ff. These discussions concentrate their attention on Plautine comedy and more or less ignore tragedy.

[2] Cf. Bergk, *Philologus* XXXI (1872), 246 n. 23 (= *Kl. Phil. Schr.* I 207 n. 23), Wilamowitz, *Hermes* XVIII (1883), 248 f., Fraenkel, *Pl. im Pl.* pp. 340 ff., 366 ff. (= *Elementi*, pp. 324 ff., 346 ff.; see also *Addenda*, p. 439), *RE* Suppl. VI (1935), s.v. *Naevius*, 632 ff.

[3] Two closely related systems of description can be observed in the remains of Latin metrical discussion and traced back to Greek theorists (see Leo, *Hermes* XXIV [1889], 280 ff.). From one system come the terms *senarius, septenarius* and *octonarius*, which first appear in Varro (cf. Diomedes, *Gramm.* I 515.3 ff., Rufinus, *Gramm.* VI 555.5 ff.) and Cicero (*Orat.* 184, 189, *Tusc.* I.106)

others. Stichic arrangements of iambic, trochaic, cretic, bacchiac, anapaestic and dactylic verses were readily discernible, although the number of departures from the classical patterns and the comparatively high degree of metrical and prosodical licence caused disquiet.[1] The two manuscript traditions of Plautine comedy and stray remarks in late grammatical writing provide evidence on how the more complex areas were divided into metrical cola.[2] Very little is known about how the resulting cola were analysed. Here the absence of exact Attic analogues was particularly bothersome to scholars.[3]

The scholars' mode of description may have encouraged the strange notion that the Latin poets got their metrical patterns from careless and incompetent examination of the scripts of Attic drama.[4] Modern students of republican drama have found this notion unpalatable and many put forward the equally implausible one that Livius Andronicus—an immigrant Greek—deliberately altered the patterns in the light of his intuitive perception of the nature of the Latin language.[5] Attempts have

---

and are still commonly used in modern discussion. Those who coined these terms do not seem to have thought that their objects of description differed in nature from Greek verses. Many ancient (e.g. Anon. *Gramm.* VI 286.14: *hic Latine senarius quod pedes sex simplices habeat, Graece trimeter quod tres* συζυγίας *habeat appellatur*) and modern students (e.g. those who allow word accent as an element in the structure of early Latin verse) have made the two sets of terms cover differences of metrical nature. I use the terms trimeter, tetrameter and catalexis in talking of both Greek and Latin verse simply for descriptive convenience and leave the theoretical issues open.

[1] Cf. Marius Victorinus, *Gramm.* VI 81.1 ff., Euanthius, *De fab.* 3.3.

[2] See below, p. 51.

[3] Cf. Charisius, p. 375.13 ff. (*De saturnio*), Rufinus, *Gramm.* VI 561.8 ff. (quoting a bewildered comment by Sisenna on a passage of apparent anapaests in Plautus).

[4] Cf. Horace, *Ars* 251 ff., *Epist.* 2.1.69 ff. Marius Victorinus (*Gramm.* VI 78.19 ff.) records a notion based on similar premises, to the effect that those who adapted the comedies of Menander took their metrical patterns from Aristophanes.

[5] Cf. R. Klotz, *Grundzüge*, pp. 29 ff., Leo, *Gesch.* pp. 62 ff.

been made to argue that the catalectic trochaic tetrameter (*septenarius*)[1] and the iambic trimeter (*senarius*)[2] used by Livius and other adapters of Attic drama owed something to verse forms already established in Rome in 240. These attempts can be criticised in detail[3] but their approach to the problem is basically sound. The Latin dramatic poets had Latin-speaking actors and a Latin-speaking audience to deal with as well as scripts in Attic Greek. It is likely that the earliest of them would have arranged the words of the new type of stage performance in patterns like those which actors were used to mouthing and audiences to hearing.

The most striking features of the Latin scripts are the presence of large blocks of verses which Attic scripts either do not show at all or do so only sporadically in lyric contexts,[4] the presence of certain types of short verse quite absent from Attic scripts,[5] the polymetry and absence of strophic corresponsion in extended

---

[1] Cf. Immisch, *SB Heidelberg, Phil.-hist. Kl.* xiv (1923), 7, 27 ff., Fraenkel, *Hermes* lxii (1927), 357 ff. (= *Kl. Beitr.* ii 11 ff.), Altheim, *Geschichte der lateinischen Sprache*, pp. 366 ff.

[2] Cf. Altheim, *Glotta* xix (1930), 24 ff., S. Mariotti, *Livio Andronico e la traduzione artistica* (Milan, 1952), p. 33 n. 3.

[3] Cf. G. Pasquali, *Preistoria della poesia Romana* (Florence, 1936), pp. 46 ff.

[4] I note in the meagre remains of Latin tragic scripts blocks of acatalectic trochaic (e.g. Ennius 185–6, 296–7) and iambic tetrameters (e.g. Ennius 322–31; cf. Sophocles' satyr play Ἰχνευταί, 238 ff.), of cretic (e.g. Ennius 81–3; cf. Aeschylus, *Choe.* 783, 794, *Hik.* 418–27, Euripides, *Or.* 1419–24; the 'cretics' of Eubulus [fr. 112] and Aristophanes are of a quite different kind [see Leo, *Die plaut. Cant.* p. 74]) and bacchiac tetrameters (e.g. Ennius 290, 293–5; cf. Aeschylus, *Ag.* 1103, 1110, *Choe.* 349–50, 367–8, *Prom.* 115, fr. 23, fr. 341, Sophocles, *Phil.* 396–7, 511–12, Euripides, *Ba.* 994, 1016, *Hel.* 642–3, *Herakles* 906, *Ion* 1446–7, *Or.* 1437–40, *Phoin.* 295, 1536, *Rhes.* 706–8, 724–6, Aristophanes, *Thesm.* 1143–4).

[5] E.g. Livius, *Trag.* 20–2 *da mihi hasce opes, quas peto, quas precor: porrige, opitula* (—∪— ∪— | —∪— —∪— | —∪∪∪ ∪ —; cf. Plautus, *Most.* 690–746, *Pseud.* 1285–334; but for a different metrical interpretation see Leo, *RhM* xl (1885), 166, *De Trag. Rom.* p. 13 [= *Ausg. kl. Schr.* i 202]). On Roman 'clausulae' see Marius Victorinus, *Gramm.* vi 79.1 ff.

lyric structures,[1] the high degree of metrical[2] and prosodical[3] variation in some types of verse, the extremely frequent co-incidence of metrical and rhetorical units,[4] the regularity of certain caesurae and diaereses,[5] the avoidance of certain shapes of words in particular metrical positions[6] and the blurring of the sharp Attic distinctions between comic and tragic verses. There is a little evidence suggesting that certain types of verse used only in comedy at Athens appeared in both the tragic and the comic scripts of the Latin poets. An ancient writer on metric[7] seems to have read a catalectic iambic tetrameter in a tragic script[8] and at least two others can now be read among the extant fragments.[9] The same writer also quotes[10] a catalectic anapaestic tetrameter whose language is thoroughly tragic and several extant fragments of indubitable tragic origin are open

---

[1] The fragmentary transmission makes definite statements about the tragic scripts difficult but I note Ennius 43–9 + 69–73, 80–94. Similar structures are rare in Attic scripts (but cf. Euripides, *Or.* 1369 ff., Aristophanes, *Batr.* 1309 ff.). The corresponsion which F. Crusius (*Die Responsion in den plautinischen Cantica* [*Philologus* Suppl. XXI 1, 1929]) and others have claimed to find in various Roman lyrics (for more recent discussion of the issue see G. Maurach, *Untersuchungen zum Aufbau plautinischer Lieder* [Göttingen, 1964]) is quite different from the Attic type.

[2] The use of long syllables in the 'pure' elements of iambic and trochaic metra was one of the main causes of the criticism mentioned above, p. 33. For metrical hiatus in tragedy see *Commentary* on *v.* 17, fr. XV, fr. XXVII *h*, *v.* 126, fr. LXVI, *v.* 154; for 'split anapaests', etc., on fr. XII.

[3] For iambic shortening in tragedy see *Commentary* on fr. IX; for *ille* (two morae), etc., on *v.* 33; for prosodical hiatus, on *v.* 173, fr. XCVI.

[4] See *Commentary* on fr. CX.

[5] See *Commentary* on fr. IV.

[6] See *Commentary* on *v.* 126, fr. CIV, fr. CLX.

[7] *Gramm.* VI 613.12 (for the writer's identity see G. Schultz, *Hermes* XXII [1887], 265, Leo, *Hermes* XXIV [1889], 282 n., R. Heinze, *SB Leipzig, Phil.-hist. Kl.* 1918, 4, p. 21 n. 1 [= *Vom Geist des Römertums*³, p. 241 n. 32]).

[8] J. Kraus (*RhM* VIII [1853], 531 ff.), L. Mueller (*NJbb* XCVII [1868], 432 f.) and others have dismissed the verse quoted—*haec bellicosus* (Carrio: *bellicosis* cod.) *cui pater mater* (Carrio: *mater pater* cod.) *cluet Minerua*—as a grammatical concoction. It could also, of course, be a paratragic verse from comedy.

[9] Pacuvius 131–2, Accius 64–5. See Strzelecki, in *Tragica* I, pp. 43 ff.

[10] *Gramm.* VI 614.3.

to this metrical interpretation.[1] The so-called 'uersus Reizianus'[2] has been detected by modern scholars in Naevius, *Trag.* 13[3] and Ennius 246.[4]

The number of perceptible differences in the metrical structure of Latin comic and tragic scripts is small.

The comic scripts contain short groups of words which could be interpreted as dactylic[5] but nothing like Ennius, *Trag.* 43–6 (four dactylic tetrameters) or 250 (dactylic hexameter).[6] Early Latin tragic trimeters and tetrameters show, when examined in large groups, somewhat less resolution of long elements and replacement of short elements by longs and double shorts than do contemporary comic verses, less synaloephe and synizesis of adjacent vowels, less tolerance of hiatus[7] and 'split anapaests' and less treatment of normally iambic sequences of syllables as pyrrhic. No shape of trimeter or tetrameter, however, seems to occur in comic scripts and not in tragic.[8] Whereas comic ana-

---

[1] E.g. Ennius 5, 365–6. See Strzelecki, in *Tragica* II (Wrocław, 1954), pp. 93 ff.

[2] This verse does occur in Attic tragedy (e.g. Sophocles, *Ai.* 408–9) but is extremely rare.

[3] W. M. Lindsay, *Early Latin Verse* (Oxford, 1922), p. 279 n. 2.

[4] See *Commentary* on fr. CXIX.

[5] See W. Meyer, *Über die Beobachtung des Wortaccentes in der altlateinischen Poesie* (*Abh. Bayer. Ak.* XVII, 1886), pp. 93 ff. Leo (*Die plaut. Cant.* pp. 50, 52) however argued that Plautus' –∪∪–∪∪ –∪∪– is a form of the glyconic.

[6] More tragic hexameters may lurk among the verses quoted in our sources with only Ennius' name and assigned by Vahlen to the *Annales*.

[7] See B. Maurenbrecher, *Hiatus und Verschleifung im alten Latein* (Leipzig, 1899), pp. 225 f.

[8] Strzelecki (*De Senecae Trimetro Iambico Quaestiones Selectae* [Kraków, 1938], pp. 94 ff.) follows F. A. Lange (*Quaestiones Metricae* [Diss. Bonn, 1851]) in arguing that tragic trimeters and tetrameters of the republican period as well as of the imperial period never have a short syllable occupying the element preceding a final cretic-shaped word or word-group. Quite savage emendation is required to make some transmitted verses conform to 'Lange's law'. However, even if such a law did bind republican tragic verses, the strong tendency of comic verses to have a long syllable at the point in question would have made its rhythmical effect scarcely perceptible to a listening audience. The operation

paests contain with great frequency[1] sequences of syllables normally iambic scanned as pyrrhic, there is little prosodic variation of any kind in tragic anapaests. The latter have diaeresis between metra and divide disyllabic elements between words[2] rather more often than do comic anapaests. The cretic and bacchiac verses of comedy stand apart from other types of comic verse in the small amount of metrical and prosodical variation they contain[3] but not, apparently, from their tragic counterparts.

This blurring of the Attic metrical distinctions springs not only from the fact that there was one and not two dramatic traditions at Rome but also from the different way in which the Latin-speaking poets and their audience viewed the personages and the subject-matter of the two Attic genres. For the average Athenian the themes of tragedy were ancient history, the heroes remote and extraordinary beings. It was fitting that they should speak in tight rhythmical patterns. Comedy on the other hand usually dealt with the contemporary life of Athens, by the late fourth century almost exclusively so. Its chief personages were city-dwelling property holders and the rhythms of their speech needed to be only sufficiently distinct from those of every day to mark their slightly elevated position in Athenian society. For Romans of the third century B.C. the personages of both genres were almost equally remote in space and time. They differed in little more than social class and poets would have

---

of 'Porson's law', on the other hand, helped to make a group of Attic trimeters or tetrameters rhythmically very different from a group of their comic counterparts.

[1] With much greater frequency, in fact, than iambic and trochaic verses; see A. Spengel, *Reformvorschläge zur Metrik der lyrischen Versarten bei Plautus* (Berlin, 1882), pp. 309 ff.

[2] See J. Perret, *REL* XXXIII (1955), 352 ff.

[3] See O. Seyffert, *De Bacchiacorum Versuum Vsu Plautino* (Diss. Berlin, 1864), A. Spengel, *Reformvorschl.* pp. 113 ff., 193 ff., G. Jachmann, *Glotta* VII (1916), 39 ff., *RhM* LXXI (1916), 527 ff.

found the sharpness of the metrical differences between the plays they were adapting meaningless from a theatrical point of view. They did not, however, totally obliterate the differences. Scholastic tradition must have had a strong hold even then.[1]

The general linguistic form of the two Roman genres no more reproduced the Attic situation than did the metrical. At Athens even in the sixth century it was understood and expected that poets should use for serious themes a vocabulary remote from that of everyday life. The tragedians had audiences acquainted with several different types of poetry whose forms had been shaped in communities speaking distinct dialects of the Greek language and which enjoyed universal cultural prestige. They found a ready acceptance of the convention according to which one set of non-Attic words informed the utterances of the actors and another those of the chorus. The comedians first gained public recognition some time after the conventions of tragedy had been firmly established and always thought of their genre as the polar opposite of tragedy. By the time of Menander their normal vocabulary scarcely differed from that used in contemporary polite society.[2] In third-century Latium there seem to have been no commonly recognised traditions of public poetry—extempore compositions are another matter—and speakers of the Roman dialect probably already looked down on others. The Latin poets could not have reproduced the Attic situation even if they had so desired. In place of the three very distinct vocabularies of the Attic stage they offered one, based largely on that regularly used in the

---

[1] The formulations of some scholars (e.g. R. Klotz, *Grundzüge*, p. 22) on this issue are misleading. See Lindsay, *E.L.V.* p. 274.

[2] For the language of tragedy see Aristotle, *Poet.* 22.1458a18 ff., *Rhet.* 3.7.1408a10 ff. The observations concerning the two genres at Cicero, *Opt. gen.* 1, Quintilian, *Inst.* 1.8.8, 10.2.22 probably derive to some extent from Greek sources.

houses of the great Roman families[1] but drawing also on the special languages of religion,[2] law,[3] and public administration[4] and apt to resurrect obsolete morphology,[5] to produce new words[6] and to vary the usage of common words and phrases[7] for the purpose of amplifying the tone of discourse. At the same time they indulged freely in hyperbole[8] and metaphor[9] and created artificial patterns of words and phrases to a much greater extent than any of the classical Attic poets.[10] Some Roman critics[11] deplored the absence of the sharp Attic distinctions of language between republican comedy and tragedy. Nevertheless the mode of speech normal to the personages of tragedy had from the beginning a certain character of its own, being much more artificial and remote from that of every day, and was frequently aped for comic effect by the slaves of early comedy.[12] The modern student cannot often isolate in the remains of the Latin tragic scripts words and turns of phrase and

---

[1] For the aristocratic connections of most of the Latin poets there is good evidence. The silence of our sources in regard to the rest should not be treated as evidence of popular connections. The management of the *ludi* was firmly in the hands of the aristocracy.

[2] See *Commentary* on fr. IV, *v.* 41, *v.* 42, fr. XVIII, fr. XXVII *h*, fr. XXXIV, *v.* 103, fr. LXXXVI, fr. CX, *v.* 247, fr. CXXI, *v.* 280, *v.* 287.

[3] See *Commentary* on fr. XIV, *vv.* 48–9, fr. XXVII *h*, fr. XLV, fr. LXIV, fr. LXXXVII, *v.* 272.

[4] See *Commentary* on fr. I, *vv.* 5, 6, 74–5, 123, 137, fr. LXXV, *vv.* 173, 200, 212, 214, fr. CV.

[5] See *Commentary* on *vv.* 37, 59, 79, 112, 151, 183, 248.

[6] See *Commentary* on *vv.* 5, 17, 20, 25, 26, 45, 68, 91, 93, fr. XXXVIII, *vv.* 110, 111, 113, 115, 136, 138, 150, 169, 246, 279.

[7] See *Commentary* on *vv.* 2, 33, 35, 39, 43, 44, 46, 61, 71, 72, 74–5, 76–7, 88, 95, 105, 127, 134, 156, 166, 168, 232, 267, 299.

[8] See *Commentary* on *vv.* 24, 41, 73, 272, 281.

[9] See *Commentary* on *v.* 3, fr. XII, *vv.* 35, 43–4, 53, 57, 96, fr. XLII, *vv.* 143, 144, 165, 171, 180, 187, 188–9, 216, 229–30, 243, 245, 304.

[10] See *Commentary* on fr. I, *vv.* 4, 6–7, 8, 9, frs. IX, XIV, *vv.* 17, 19, 21, 24, 34, 39, 54, 57, 62, 63, 74–5, 76–7, 83, 87, 90, 94, 100, 105, 192.

[11] E.g. Horace, *Ars* 86 ff., Gellius 2.23.21. Cf. Schol. Soph. *Ai.* 1127, Schol. Eur. *Andr.* 32, Plutarch, *Mor.* 853 C–D.

[12] Cf. Plautus, *Pseud.* 702–7 . . . *ut paratragoedat carnufex.*

label them with certainty as peculiarly tragic. Nevertheless some words and phrases can be shown from their comparative frequencies in the tragic and comic scripts and the contexts in which they occur to have possessed a more elevated tone than others.[1] The Latin distinctions were ones of degree, not of kind.

As the second century advanced and the two Roman genres came more and more to be cultivated by specialist poets, the language of comedy moved away from that of tragedy and approached the common language.[2] That of tragedy on the other hand seems to have become more elaborate and artificial.[3]

Both the Attic and the Latin poets varied their metrical patterns according to the substance and tone of the actor's speech. At Aeschylus, *Pers.* 176, for example, the Queen interrupts a highly emotional dialogue with the chorus in trochaic tetrameters to recount a dream in trimeters.[4] The dialogue in various musically accompanied metres at Plautus, *Persa* 482–548 is interrupted twice while a letter is read out in trimeters.[5] At Plautus, *Rud.* 1338 iambic tetrameters cease as one of the actors begins to recite an oath. Such changes of metre within a scene are on the whole uncommon. A scene is usually set either in trimeters or in musically accompanied verses. In Attic scripts an increase in uncommon vocabulary and rhetorical embellishment of the phrase becomes noticeable when trimeters are

---

[1] See *Commentary* on *vv.* 3, 7, 9, 13, 17, 18, 21, 22, 29, 66, 89, 100, 116, 162, 178, 213, 215, 218, 219, 222, 225, 237, 238, 242 et al.

[2] Cf. Euanthius, *De fab.* 3.5 *tam illud est admirandum* (scil. *in Terentio*) *quod et morem retinuit ut comoediam scriberet et temperauit affectum ne in tragoediam transiliret, quod cum aliis rebus minime obtentum et a Plauto et ab Afranio et Appio et multis fere magnis comicis inuenimus.*

[3] Cf. Cicero, *Orat.* 36 on the styles of Ennius and the other writers of tragedy.

[4] Cf. the two speeches from Accius' *Brutus* quoted by Cicero, *Diu.* 1.44; the king describes a dream in trimeters, the *coniectores* give their interpretation in trochaic tetrameters.

[5] Cf. Plautus, *Bacch.* 997 ff., *Pseud.* 998 ff.

abandoned even if only stichic tetrameters replace them.[1] In the comic scripts of Plautus the difference in stylistic level between the trimeters of the action and the musically accompanied verses is very pronounced. In those of Terence this difference is much smaller but still perceptible. In the remains of the late second century tragic scripts of Accius, trimeters seem not to differ from the musically accompanied verses. The small amount of material available from early tragedy and the uncertain scansion of many small fragments make it hard for one to be positive, but the proposition that early writers of tragedy did not make a distinction between the two types of verse parallel with that made in contemporary comedy is on general grounds unlikely. There are some signs that Ennius kept the trimeters of the tragic action much less elaborate than other verses.[2] Prologue trimeters, as in comedy, would have occupied a special position.[3]

---

[1] Cf. Wilamowitz, *SB Berlin* 1916, 73 f. (= *Kl. Schr.* 1 423 f.).

[2] See *Commentary* on *v.* 9, fr. IX, *v.* 17, *v.* 19.

[3] The fact that the early Latin poets imitated in their own way the genre distinctions of Greek poetry was pointed out by Ritschl (*Parerga zu Plautus und Terenz* I [Leipzig, 1845], p. 112) and Bergk (*NJbb* LXXXIII [1861], 631 [= *Kl. phil. Schr.* I 302]). The latter also remarked on the way in which the sung verses of drama (both tragedy and comedy) differed stylistically from the spoken. Important illustrations of the way epic style differed from tragic have been given by Fraenkel, *RE* Suppl. V (1931), s.v. *Livius*, 603 ff. and of the distinctions between the two types of verse within comedy by Leo (*NGG, Phil.-hist. Kl.* 1895, 415 ff. [= *Ausg. kl. Schr.* I 49 ff.]), Fraenkel (*Pl. im Pl.* pp. 209 ff. [= *Elementi*, pp. 199 ff.], *Iktus und Akzent im lateinischen Sprechvers* [Berlin, 1928], p. 93 n. 1), E. Lindholm (*Stilistische Studien zur Erweiterung der Satzglieder im Lateinischen* [Lund, 1931], pp. 94 ff.) and H. Haffter (*Untersuchungen zur altlateinischen Dichtersprache* [Berlin, 1934], *passim*). Haffter asserts (p. 124) that 'die tragischen Senare im Gebrauche aller hier besprochenen Stilmittel in keiner Weise von den Langversen der gleichen Gattung sich unterscheiden'. The general approach of these scholars has been attacked by M. Lenchantin De Gubernatis (*Athenaeum* XIII [1935], 278 ff.) from the point of view of idealist aesthetics and by M. Leumann (*MusH* IV [1947], 116 ff. [= *Kl. Schr.* pp. 131 ff.]) on empirical grounds. Lenchantin contributes nothing of substance to the argument. Leumann merely reiterates that the Latin distinctions are not exactly parallel with the Greek distinctions.

Three sources have been suggested for the origin of the types of phrasal elaboration characteristic of certain parts of early Roman drama: the modes of public speaking taught in Greek schools and practised by Roman politicians,[1] the Attic τραγική λέξις and the formulae of Roman law and religion.[2] A parallel for every type of Latin elaboration can be found in the scripts of Attic tragedy but some, like alliteration, are relatively uncommon and the rate of occurrence of the others rarely approaches even that of the spoken verses of Terentian comedy. The paucity of what survives of Roman legal and religious formulae makes discussion difficult. Many were taken over as they stood by the dramatists or used as models for new creations but they never seem to have provided more than a light antique colouring to the style of an actor's speech. Our actual knowledge of third and second century Roman oratory is slight but we can guess that men prepared to tolerate the hellenisation of their community's religion and public art would not have neglected the powerful aids to political success offered by the techniques of speaking taught in contemporary Greek schools. Those Latin poets who had received their education in Greek-speaking communities could not have escaped the influence of the ῥήτορες. Those who had close personal relations with their Roman patrons could not fail to be interested in the debates of the senate, the law courts and the assemblies.[3] Here, in turns of phrase and sentence with which orators raised their discourse above the commonplace and worked on the emotions of their hearers, lay ready material for dramatists trying to construct a poetic style for a people poor in distinctively poetic traditions. It seems unlikely that Cato would have delivered himself

---

[1] Cf. E. Norden, *Die antike Kunstprosa* II[1] (Leipzig, 1898), pp. 839, 889, Leo, *Analecta Plautina* II (Göttingen, 1898) (= *Ausg. kl. Schr.* I 123 ff.), *Gesch.* pp. 34 ff., F. Eckstein, *Philologus* LXXVII (1921), 173.

[2] Cf. Fraenkel, *Pl. im Pl.* pp. 356 ff. (= *Elementi*, pp. 338 ff.).

[3] For Ennius' interest in public speaking see *Ann.* 303 ff.

publicly in language more elaborate than that of his philhellene peers and elders, and yet those long passages of his orations which are preserved usually show much more adornment than is observable even in the scripts of Attic tragedy.[1] The trimeters of comic prologues have a high degree of elaboration, Terence's at times even more than his musically accompanied verses, and it is perhaps significant that the prologists of the *Amphitruo*[2] and the *Hauton timorumenus*[3] cast themselves explicitly as *oratores*. It would be foolish to assert that the Attic τραγικὴ λέξις had no influence on poets constantly adapting Attic plays but the forms of elevated speech already familiar to third and second century Roman audiences should be considered the dominating influences.

V. ENNIUS

Like all the early poets of whom we know anything Ennius came from outside Latium and must have acquired his Latin as a second or third language. He was a Messapian of high birth[4] who in adolescence had received a Greek literary education[5] and in manhood had served as a soldier of fortune in one of the South Italian units of the Roman army,[6] high enough in the

---

[1] R. Till (*Die Sprache Catos* [*Philologus* Suppl. XXVIII 2, 1935]) perceived this but drew the unlikely conclusion that Cato's oratorical style was influenced by that of Ennius' poetry.   [2] 20, 33 f., 50.   [3] 11 f.

[4] See Silius 12.393, Servius, *Aen.* 7.691, *Souda* E 1348 (Aelian). It is possible, of course, that Ennius had claimed only to come from the land of King Messapus.

[5] This is all that Festus, p. 374.8 f. and Suetonius, *De gramm.* 1 mean by the terms *Graecus* and *semigraecus*. Whether he had received a philosophical or rhetorical training as well we cannot say for sure but the general features of his poetry and certain particular fragments (cf. among those of tragedy IV, CX, CLXXXVIII) suggest he had both. See H. Fränkel, *Hermes* LXVII (1932), 308 ff., LXX (1935), 62 ff.

[6] See Cornelius Nepos, *Cat.* 1.4, Cicero, *Cato* 10, Ps. Aurel. Victor, *De uir. illustr.* 47.1. On Iapygian and Messapian units fighting in 225 see Polybius 2.24.11.

ranks[1] to be able to make the acquaintance of the quaestor M. Porcius Cato. He lived with one servant in his own house in the artisans' quarter on the Aventine and for some time pursued the profession of *grammaticus*.[2] He is known to have been on intimate terms with various politically active members of the aristocracy, at first with Cato, who brought him to Rome in his entourage in 203, and later with men of factions hostile to Cato's. The political debates of 203–169 sometimes seem[3] to make themselves heard in the scripts of the tragedies he adapted for the festivals managed by his aristocratic patrons. Like Livius and Naevius he adapted comedies as well as tragedies and like Naevius he composed plays of the tragic type on themes from Roman history.

In a medieval glossary there appears in a discussion of the history of tragedy the interesting note: *tragoedias autem fere omnes ex Graecis transtulit, plurimas Euripidis* (Lindsay: *Euripides* codd.), *nonnullas Aristarchi* (Lindsay: *Aristarchus* codd.).[4] The source of the note is obscure[5] but there is no reason to think it an invention. It may come from one of Varro's treatises by way of Suetonius. One of Ennius' titles, *Achilles*, is attributed elsewhere[6] to Aristarchus and four, *Alexander, Andromacha, Hecuba* and *Medea*,[7] to Euripides. Of the seventy tragic scripts of

---

[1] Silius 12.394–5 *Latiaeque superbum | uitis adornabat dextram decus* suggests that he was a centurion, but such statements need to be treated with caution.

[2] I do not share Fraenkel's doubts about Suetonius, *De gramm.* 1 (*RE* Suppl. v [1931], 601).

[3] See *Commentary* on frs. LXXXIV, CV.

[4] *Gloss. Lat.* I 568. Cf. Donatus' addition to Suetonius' *Life* of Terence, 10, *duae ab Apollodoro translatae esse dicuntur comico, Phormio et Hecyra; quattuor reliquae a Menandro*.

[5] Cf. H. Usener, *RhM* XXVIII (1873), 417 ff. (= *Kl. Schr.* III 36 ff.). On the 'Glossary of Ansileubus' or 'Liber Glossarum' in general see G. Goetz, *Abh. sächs. Ges., Phil.-hist. Kl.* XIII (1893), 256 ff., Lindsay, *CQ* XI (1917), 119 ff. *Glossaria Latina* I (Paris, 1926), p. 8, S. Timpanaro, *StudUrb*, Serie B, XXXI (1957), 178. [6] Plautus, *Poen.* 1, Festus, p. 282.10.

[7] Varro, *Ling.* 7.82, Cicero, *Opt. gen.* 18, Gellius 11.4, Cicero, *Fin.* 1.4.

Aristarchus possessed by the Alexandrian library we know from Greek sources the title of only one, Τάνταλος,[1] but of the seventy catalogued under the name of Euripides we seem to know all the titles and can guess with a fair amount of certainty at their general themes.[2] If the story of Ptolemy and the Lycurgean text of the classical tragedians[3] has any basis in fact these could have been the only ones surviving in Athens in c. 330 B.C. and it is most unlikely that scripts of the other plays would have survived for long anywhere else. *Andromacha*, despite the statements of Varro, *Ling.* 7.82 and Cicero, *Opt. gen.* 18, cannot be regarded as an adaptation of any of the Euripidean seventy.[4] Neither can *Aiax*, *Eumenides*, *Hectoris lytra*, *Nemea* or *Telamo*. There is nothing on the other hand in the remains of *Alexander*, *Andromeda*, *Erectheus*, *Hecuba*, *Iphigenia*, *Melanippa*, *Phoenix*, *Telephus* or *Thyestes* to make one wish to deny Euripidean provenance. About *Athamas*, *Alcmeo* and *Cresphontes* there is doubt. The title *Medea* covers two plays, one quite certainly a version of Euripides' Μήδεια, the other possibly a version of his Αἰγεύς. Vahlen is wrong to dismiss[5] the plain statement of the glossary article that Ennius adapted more than one play by Aristarchus. There are several possibilities among the extant titles and in any case we cannot be sure that these titles exhaust Ennius' tragic production.[6]

The texts which Ennius worked from very likely resembled

---

[1] F. Blass, *Literarisches Centralbl.* 1893, 1434, restored ἐπὶ τοῦ Ἀχιλλ]έως τοῦ Ἀριστάρχου in the Flinders Petrie papyrus mentioned above, p. 9 n. 2.

[2] Cf. Wilamowitz, *Analecta Euripidea* (Berlin, 1875), pp. 144 ff., W. Schmid, *Geschichte der griechischen Literatur* I iii (Munich, 1940), pp. 329 f. There are a number of titles too many; see E. G. Turner, in *Acta of the 9th International Congress of Papyrology, Oslo 1958* (Oslo, 1962), 1 ff., for further evidence that two scripts bore the title Φρίξος.

[3] Plutarch, *Mor.* 841 F, Galen, *Hipp. Epid.* 2.4.

[4] See *Commentary*, pp. 236 ff.   [5] *E.P.R.*[2], p. CCI.

[6] See Varro, *Ling.* 5.14 (= fr. CLXXXVI) and below, p. 62, 7.13 (= fr. CXC) and below, p. 62.

those found in certain third century B.C. papyri from which the Alexandrian colometry of the lyrical passages is absent.[1] Philological examination of the tragic texts had already progressed a long way by 203[2] and Ennius doubtless possessed and used commentaries upon them. The suggestion, however, that what they contained sometimes radically affected Ennius' own version[3] seems an unlikely one. We must distinguish between versions of poems made for dramatic presentation to audiences largely ignorant of literary Greek and versions of such poems as Aratus' Φαινόμενα made for circulation in books. Only the latter were aimed at people who knew the Greek originals (and perhaps, in some cases, the scholarly apparatus as well) and who would set the versions against the originals.[4] Ennius had no motive that we can see for worrying about the exact interpretation of the Greek tragic texts.

Unlike the classical Greek dramatists Ennius probably did not compose his own musical scores.[5] Some of the classical scores still existed in his day[6] but even then Greek musicians

---

[1] For an account of these papyri see G. Zuntz, *An Inquiry into the Transmission of the Plays of Euripides* (Cambridge, 1965), pp. 250 f.

[2] Cf. Wilamowitz, *Einleitung in die attische Tragödie* (Berlin, 1889), pp. 134 ff.

[3] Cf. Leo, *Pl. Forsch.*[2] p. 98, *Gesch.* p. 192.

[4] On Cicero's version of Aratus' Φαινόμενα and the scholia see Leo, *Hermes* XLIX (1914), 192 f. (= *Ausg. kl. Schr.* I 279 f.); on Varro Atacinus and the scholia to Apollonius' epic see E. Hofmann, *WSt* XLVI (1928), 161. Acceptance of H. Fränkel's view (*Hermes* LXVII [1932], 306; cf. Mariotti, *Livio Andronico*, p. 28) of the relationship between the scholia and Livius' version of the Odyssey would entail regarding this poem as quite a sophisticated piece of work.

[5] Cf. the didascaliae to Terence's comedies and Donatus, *De com.* 8.9 *deuerbia histriones pronuntiabant, cantica uero temperabantur modis non a poeta sed a perito artis musicae factis.* Cicero however talks at *Leg.* 2.39, perhaps loosely, of 'modi Liuiani et Naeuiani'.

[6] The discussion of Dionysius Hal. at *De comp. uerb.* 11.63–4 implies that students of his day had access to at least some of the score to Euripides' Ὀρέστης. A iii–ii B.C. papyrus of the score to *vv.* 338–43 of the tragedy (no. 411 in Pack's catalogue) survives; see Turner, *JHS* LXXVI (1956), 95 ff.

were composing new scores for parts of the old scripts[1] and it seems likely that the music composed for the Roman *tibiae*[2] and that for the αὐλός of classical Athens differed as widely as did the metrical patterns imposed on the Latin and Greek words.

VI. THE HISTORY OF THE TEXT OF ENNIUS' TRAGEDIES

Ennius' plays were well known to theatre goers in 166 B.C.[3] and no doubt had been for some time.[4] These and other plays of the early period[5] were constantly produced at first century B.C. festivals. The last public performance of a play by Ennius which is clearly recorded took place at the *ludi Apollinares* of 54 B.C.[6] Accius' *Tereus* was performed in its entirety in 44[7] and extracts from Pacuvius' *Armorum iudicium* and Atilius' *Electra*

---

[1] Cf. Latte, *Eranos* LII (1954), 125 ff., LIII (1955), 75 f., S. Eitrem and L. Amundsen, *SO* XXXI (1955), 26 ff.

[2] An instrument that probably came to Rome from Etruria (cf. Livy 9.30.5–10); it is usually assumed to have been of the same character as the fifth-century Athenian αὐλός.

[3] See Terence, *Andr.* 18.

[4] Plautus, *Bacch.* 214 is the earliest evidence for the performance of old plays at the Roman festivals. Many imitations of Ennian passages, of which the most convincing is *Bacch.* 933 *o Troia o patria o Pergamum o Priame periisti senex* ∼ *Trag.* 87 *o pater o patria o Priami domus*, have been found in the comic scripts attributed to Plautus. There is a clear reference to Ennius' *Achilles* at *Poen.* 1 (see *Commentary* on fr. 1) but no certainty that Plautus (d. *c.* 184) made it.

[5] Varro expected the readers of his treatise *De lingua Latina* to be acquainted with the plot of a play by Livius about Teucer (7.3) but Cicero's disdainful remarks at *Brut.* 71 suggest that only the learned knew Livius' plays at first hand. The *Equos Troianus* produced by Pompey in 55 (see Cicero, *Fam.* 7.1.2) was probably Naevius' tragedy.

[6] See Cicero, *Att.* 4.15.6. It is uncertain what kind of performance Ovid is referring to at *Rem.* 383, or even whether the script of Ennius' *Andromacha* was used.

[7] See Cicero, *Att.* 16.2.3, 16.5.1, *Phil.* 1.36. Cf. Ribbeck, *Quaestionum scenicarum Mantissa*, in *Tragicorum Latinorum Reliquiae* (Leipzig, 1852), p. 326.

47

were sung at Julius Caesar's funeral games.[1] At the time when Horace was composing *Epist.* 2.1.23 ff. the old poets still enjoyed great popularity in the theatre and the emperor Augustus notoriously favoured their work.[2] Nero (A.D. 54–68) had the *Incendium* of Afranius staged with a realism that gained notoriety.[3] Quintilian's discussion at *Inst.* 11.3.178–82 suggests that at least some of the comedies of Terence were regularly performed in his time. It is difficult to tell when fresh information based on knowledge of the contemporary theatre ceased to be inserted in commentaries upon these plays but the reference to use of female actors at Donatus, *Ter. Andr.* 716 looks quite late.

Only three names of post-republican comic poets are certainly known, those of Fundanius,[4] Marcus Pomponius Bassulus,[5] and Vergilius Romanus.[6] Quintilian could find none of sufficient commonly recognised standing to set beside the classical Greeks.[7] Many on the other hand tried their hand at tragedy. The *Thyestes* of Varius was performed at the festival held to celebrate Octavian's victory at Actium[8] and reliable witnesses attest the performance of tragedies by Pomponius in the theatre.[9] Some wrote tragedies explicitly for private recitation.[10] That other tragedians whose names are recorded intended their work for performance in the public theatres is not stated in the ancient sources and has often been denied by modern students. Ovid's *Medea* was much admired as late as Quintilian's time.[11] The plays of Varius, Gracchus, Pomponius and

---

[1] See Suetonius, *Iul.* 84.
[2] See Suetonius, *Aug.* 89.1.
[3] Suetonius, *Ner.* 11.
[4] Horace, *Sat.* 1.10.42.
[5] *C.L.E.* 97.
[6] Pliny, *Epist.* 6.21.1–4.
[7] *Inst.* 10.1.99.
[8] Cod. Paris. 7530, cod. Casin. 1086.
[9] Pliny, *Epist.* 7.17.11, Tacitus, *Ann.* 11.13. For relations between Pomponius and Seneca see Quintilian, *Inst.* 8.3.31.
[10] See Tacitus, *Dial.* 2 ff.
[11] See Quintilian, *Inst.* 10.1.98, Tacitus, *Dial.* 12.

Seneca were drawn upon by the elder Pliny in his treatise on Latin morphology and by Caesius Bassius in his treatise on Latin metric. These treatises are probably the ultimate sources of the quotations scattered through the handbooks of late antiquity. Seneca's alone of the mythological plays written in Latin survived in their entirety until the age of printing.[1]

The almost total silence of our literary sources concerning the production of complete tragedies at the festivals of Latin-speaking communities after the first century A.D.[2] may have no significance at all. Most extant late writers, both pagan and Christian, were hostile to the theatre[3] and, if plays enjoying the educational prestige attaching to the names tragedy and comedy had been performed there, these writers would have been unwilling to advertise the fact. The notion that the mass of the population of Rome became too degenerate, both morally and culturally, to tolerate high comedy and tragedy has nothing to commend it. Gladiatorial contests and knock-about farce were without a doubt extremely popular long before the advent of the Attic type of drama and the performers of the latter always had to contend with audience behaviour which would have been unthinkable in Athens.[4] There is no reason to think that mass tastes ever altered in one direction or the other, but some that, except during the period of economic collapse in the third century A.D., a superficial knowledge of and respect for the high poetic genres increased among the upper classes.

---

[1] Varius' *Thyestes* may have reached the age of Charlemagne (see A. E. Housman, *CQ* XI [1917], 42, and, *contra*, Lindsay, *CQ* XVI [1922], 180).

[2] The evidence is collected by Welcker, *Die griech. Trag.* pp. 1319, 1477 ff., A. Müller, 'Das Bühnenwesen in der Zeit von Constantin dem Grossen bis Justinian', *NJbb* XXIII (1909), 36 ff. (esp. 40 f.), L. Friedländer, *Darstellungen aus der Sittengeschichte Roms*[9] (Leipzig, 1921), vol. II, pp. I ff., 112 ff., 118 ff.

[3] This hostility was no new thing among pagan aristocrats (cf. Cicero, *Sest.* 119, *S. Rosc.* 46, Livy 7.2) no mere reflection of Plato's ancient prejudices.

[4] See Plautus, *Amph.* 51 ff., Terence, *Hec.* I ff., 25 ff. Cf. Polybius' description (30.22) of the *ludi* celebrated by Anicius.

Terence's work formed part of the regular syllabus of Latin literature[1] while that of the Attic dramatists was necessary reading for every student of Greek.[2] Roman houses of the wealthier sort were frequently adorned with figurative representations of various aspects of comic and tragic theatrical performances.[3] It seems to me likely that those who managed the *ludi* would have at least occasionally paid obeisance to cultural tradition and allowed the performance of plays commonly read in the schools. One might have expected a comedy of Terence, possibly a comedy of Plautus[4] or an Attic play according to the original script,[5] but hardly any work of the other Roman dramatic poets.[6]

Somewhat more is known and can be conjectured about the fate of those Ennian scripts which were recorded in books and circulated among the Roman reading public.

In the early part of the second century B.C. the scripts of plays performed at *ludi scaenici* may have been seen by few people outside the actor's companies. As late as 161 Terence could claim, apparently in good faith, that he did not know that Menander's Κόλαξ had already been adapted for performance on

---

[1] With Cicero, Sallust and Virgil Terence formed the 'quadriga' of Arusianus Messius (see Cassiodorus, *Inst. diu.* 15.7).

[2] On knowledge of Greek in the West see P. Courcelle, *Les lettres grecques en occident, de Macrobe à Cassiodore*[2] (Paris, 1948), H.-I. Marrou, *Saint Augustin et la fin de la culture antique*[4] (Paris, 1958), pp. 27 ff., 631 ff.

[3] For the archaeological evidence see M. Bieber, *The History of the Greek and Roman Theater* (Princeton, 1961), pp. 227 ff., Webster, *AJA* LXVI (1962), 333 ff. Bieber and Webster grossly overestimate the value of this evidence. Changes in the form of artistic representations need not reflect the fashions of the contemporary theatre.

[4] Arnobius 7.33, however, is no evidence for a performance of the *Amphitruo*.

[5] See above, p. 5 n. 3. It is perhaps significant that Juvenal speaks of the performance of tragedy at Roman festivals (6.67 ff., 396 f.) but names Sophocles alone of actual tragedians (6.634 ff.). Even Persius refers to Menander's Εὐνοῦχος (5.161 ff.) rather than to Terence's adaptation (contrast Horace, *Sat.* 2.3.259 ff.).

[6] For their neglect in the schools see below, pp. 55 ff.

the Roman stage.[1] The sources of Suetonius' treatise *De grammaticis et rhetoribus* knew of no serious philological activity in Rome until the year after Ennius' death and the state of the text of the extant comedies of Plautus makes it plain that the first scientific editors had to deal with scripts which had passed through the hands of professional actors and were rarely, if ever, able to obtain a Plautine autograph.[2] Ennius' tragic scripts were frequently reused at the early festivals and they may have suffered the same sort of damage that can be observed in the extant text of Plautine comedy.

Editions of the *Annales* employing the conventions established at Alexandria for the editing of classical Greek poetry are recorded with the names of C. Octauius Lampadio and Q. Vargunteius[3] but no ancient author mentions an edition of Ennius' tragedies. Nevertheless we may guess on the analogy of what the extant texts suggest for the comedies of Plautus and Terence[4] that they were also edited in the Alexandrian manner, each one prefixed with διδασκαλίαι containing, amid other information, the title and author of the Greek original and with Ennius' name and the title commonly given to his adaptation suffixed. The discussions of the metricians[5] and such quotations as that of *v.* 44 by Ciccro at *Orat.* 155 provide solid evidence that the ancient editions presented the lyric passages divided into cola.

---

[1] *Eun.* 30 ff.

[2] For the theatrical transmission of the texts of comedy see F. Osann, *Analecta critica* (Berlin, 1816), pp. 147 ff., Ritschl, *Parerga*, pp. 88 ff.

[3] Cf. Gellius 18.5.11, Suetonius, *De gramm.* 2, Fronto, p. 15.13 ff. van den Hout, Frag. Paris. *Gramm.* VII 534.4, Timpanaro, *SIFC* N.S. XXI (1946), 49 ff.

[4] Cf. W. Studemund, in *Festgruss der philologischen Gesellschaft zu Würzburg an die XXVI. Versammlung deutscher Philologen* (Würzburg, 1868), p. 48, Leo, *RhM* XL (1885), 161 ff., *Die plaut. Cant.* pp. 5 ff., *Pl. Forsch.*[2], pp. 29 ff., *Gesch.* pp. 356 ff., Pasquali, *Storia della tradizione e critica del testo*[2] (Florence, 1952), pp. 350 ff.

[5] One is echoed by Cicero at *De orat.* 3.183. Cf. Varro *ap.* Rufin. *Gramm.* VI 556.7 (on Accius).

Between 169 and the period from which the first extant prose works containing literal quotations come considerable changes in Latin orthographical convention took place. There are comparatively few traces in these quotations of the orthographical peculiarities which mark early second century public inscriptions and the text of Plautus' comedies offered by the Ambrosian codex. To what extent modernisations come from the first philological edition of the tragedies rather than from the heedlessness of quoters or the scribes who copied the works of the quoters cannot now be fully ascertained.[1] One would suppose that titles were peculiarly liable to modernisation, especially those of tragedies still performed in the late republican theatre. I have tried to avoid medieval and renaissance forms in printing titles and quotations but not to impose any further rationality on the chaos of the παράδοσις.

During the late second and most, if not all, of the first century B.C. the tragedies of Ennius and other Latin poets were read and studied intensively in schools.[2] They were used as a quarry by rhetoricians seeking examples of certain types of argument and figurated speech as well as by grammarians seeking unusual words and anomalous forms of accidence and syntax. Orators quoted famous passages in the Senate and the law courts.[3] Literary men bandied brief, allusive quotations with each other in private letters[4] and introduced quite lengthy

---

[1] Cf. the way quotations of Herodotus in Greek rhetorical works (e.g. the treatise Περὶ ὕψους) tend to lose their ionicisms.

[2] Cf. Rhetor inc. Her. 4.7 on the copying out of Ennian sententiae and Pacuvian messenger-speeches; Cicero, De orat. 1.246 on the learning of Pacuvius' Teucer by heart.

[3] C. Titius, 'uir aetatis Lucilianae', quite certainly alluded in a speech to Ennius 72-3 (Macrobius, Sat. 3.13.13). L. Sempronius Atratinus may, like Crassus and Cicero (Cael. 18), have alluded to the Medea at the trial of M. Caelius Rufus in 56 B.C. (Chirius Fortunatianus 3.7).

[4] Cf., apart from Cicero, Varro, Epist. Iuli Caesaris ap. Non. p. 263.3 (~ Cicero, Att. 13.47.1). Fam. 9.16.4 shows that Paetus quoted from Accius' Oenomaus in a letter to Cicero.

quotations into philosophical dialogues.[1] Poets made elaborate imitations not only in the genre of tragedy[2] but also in others, particularly that of epic.[3]

A very considerable amount of what we possess of Ennius' tragic writing is embedded in works of this period preserved either more or less whole, or in epitomes such as that by Pompeius Festus of the lexicon of Verrius Flaccus, or in quotations by the authors of late antiquity.[4] Not all this comes directly from whole texts of the tragedies or even from the memory of the quoters. The practice of borrowing examples from previous writers rather than collecting them afresh had already begun in the sphere of technical writing.[5]

---

[1] Cf., apart from Cicero, Varro, Γεροντοδιδάσκαλος *ap.* Non. p. 261.7.

[2] On Asinius Pollio see Tacitus, *Dial.* 21.

[3] For Virgil's *Aeneid* and tragedy see Macrobius, *Sat.* 6.1–3, Norden, *P. Vergilius Maro: Aeneis Buch VI*[2] (Leipzig, 1916), pp. 241, 263 f., 304, 370 f.

[4] Cf. the quotation of the *Alcmeo* in the piece of Cicero's *Hortensius* quoted by Priscian (*Gramm.* II 250.12); of the *Medea* in the piece of Varro's Γεροντοδιδάσκαλος quoted by Nonius (p. 261.7).

[5] On the quotations of poetry in the anonymous rhetorical treatise addressed to Herennius and Cicero's *De inuentione* see D. Matthes, *Lustrum* III (1958), 81 ff.; in the extant books of Varro's *De lingua Latina* R. Reitzenstein, *M. Terentius Varro und Johannes Mauropus* (Leipzig, 1901), H. Dahlmann, *Varro und die hellenistische Sprachtheorie* (Berlin, 1932), R. Schröter, 'Studien zur varronischen Etymologie', *Abh. Ak. d. Wiss. u. d. Lit. Mainz, Geistes- u. Sozialw. Kl.* 1959, Nr. 12; in the lexicon of Verrius Flaccus, R. Reitzenstein, *Verrianische Forschungen* (Breslau, 1887), Strzelecki, *Quaestiones Verrianae* (Warsaw, 1932). W. Zillinger, a scholar who made a very detailed study of Cicero's poetic quotations (*Cicero und die altrömischen Dichter* [Diss. Erlangen, 1911]), writes as if Cicero always quoted either directly from a whole text or from memory of a whole text. He notes (p. 84) without offering any explanation that the mode of quotation employed in the *Orator* varies strikingly. At 164 a famous speech (Trag. inc. 80–2: probably from Pacuvius' *Iliona*) is quoted as if it were well known to the reader: *nisi forte sic loqui paenitet: 'qua tempestate Helenam Paris' et quae sequuntur*; Cicero's writings are full of similar quotations (e.g. *Diu.* 2.112, *Tusc.* 3.53, 3.58, etc.). At 155, on the other hand, in a discussion of anomalous accidence, two verses of tragedy (Ennius 44 and Pacuvius 82) metrically complete and yet defective in sense are quoted without apology; this is a mode of quotation frequently employed by the lexicographer Verrius Flaccus (cf. Vahlen, *E.P.R.*[2], p. LXVII, L. Rychlewska, *Eos* XLIII (1948/9), fasc. 1, 186 ff.). It

Ennius' *Telephus* seems to have been read in the school attended by the fable writer Phaedrus (born in 17 B.C.).[1] However it is doubtful whether, at least in the schools of the capital, this and other tragedies long survived the attack of such partisans of modern poetry as Q. Caecilius Epirota and Remmius Palaemon.[2] Early imperial prose and poetry show no sign of the sort of acquaintance with the scripts of republican tragedy that grammar-school study might have provided. The fact that Seneca's quotations are few and mostly, if not all, at second hand is much more significant than the frequency of his denunciations.[3] The links that can be found between his tragic scripts and those of the republican poets[4] are nowhere near as extensive as those, for example, between Virgil's *Aeneid* and Ennius' *Annales* and may be due to imitation of Ovid and Varius, who, whatever formal critical views they acquired, would have remained deeply affected by what they read at school.[5] The argument of Tacitus' *Dialogus* shows what conven-

is more likely that Cicero took the two verses from a grammarian's treatise than that he himself employed deliberately in a literary dialogue a technical mode of quotation. The quotation of two tragic verses (Trag. inc. 194–5) as if they came from a scene of Terence's *Phormio* at *Orat.* 157 indicates even more plainly Cicero's dependence on a grammatical source; this is a type of error found repeatedly in authors who take blocks of quotations from their predecessors (cf. Strzelecki, *Quaest. Verr.* pp. 3 ff., on Paulus' epitome of Festus' epitome of Verrius Flaccus).

[1] Cf. 3, epil. 33–4. It is possible that Phaedrus read the trimeter he quotes in a collection of *sententiae*. On the use of such collections in schools see K. Horna, *RE* Suppl. VI (1935), s.vv. *Gnome, Gnomendichtung, Gnomologien*, 74 ff., J. Barns, *CQ* XLIV (1950), 126 ff.

[2] Cf. Suetonius, *De gramm.* 16, 23. These *grammatici* followed rather than created a fashion; cf. Cicero, *Tusc.* 3.45, Horace, *Epist.* 1.19.7–8, 2.1.50–3, *Ars* 259–62, Ovid, *Am.* 1.15.19, *Trist.* 2.259–60.

[3] Cf. *De ira* 3.37.5, *Epist.* 58.5, *ap.* Gell. 12.2.2.

[4] Cf. G. Carlsson, 'Die Überlieferung der Seneca-Tragödien', *Lunds Univ. Årsskrift*, N.F. Avd. I, Bd. 21, No. 5 (1926), 58 ff. F. Strauss had denied that there were any (*De ratione inter Senecam et antiquas fabulas Romanas intercedente* [Diss. Rostock, 1887]).

[5] Asinius Pollio wrote tragedies in conscious imitation of the republican poets (see Tacitus, *Dial.* 21).

tional attitudes were like during the reign of the Flavian emperors. For Curiatus Maternus, defending poetry against the sneers of the practical orator, Ovid's *Medea* and Varius' *Thyestes* are the classics of tragedy; Marcus Aper, defending modern oratory and attacking that of the ancients (i.e. of those after Cassius), can bring against the latter as an apparently irrefutable charge the fact that they frequently imitated the style of the republican tragedians. It would be wrong however to accept Leo's theory[1] that no one in Rome read the older republican poetry during the Julio-Claudian and early Flavian periods and that texts disappeared from libraries both public and private. The violence with which the fashionable view was expressed and remarks like that of Seneca at *Epist.* 114.13—*multi ex alieno saeculo petunt uerba*—suggest that some did not follow fashion.[2]

The fashion of admiring the old republican poets which M. Valerius Probus was supposed to have introduced[3] and which made the emperor Hadrian express a preference for Ennius' epic poetry over Virgil's[4] caused the scripts of at least some of Ennius' tragedies to be sought out and consulted. Fronto's pupil, Marcus Aurelius, the future emperor, Aulus Gellius (b. 123, educated in Rome)[5] and Apuleius (b. about 123, educated in Carthage) seem occasionally to quote from them at first hand. But while the books of the *Annales* were often read in second-century schools[6] the tragedies probably were not. In

---

[1] See *Pl. Forsch.*[2] pp. 26 ff.

[2] Tacitus (*Ann.* 13.15) describes Britannicus uttering a poem that could have been the famous canticum from Ennius' *Andromacha* (fr. xxvii).

[3] Suetonius, *De gramm.* 23. Signs of change can be seen in the tone of Martial at 11.90.6 and Quintilian at *Inst.* 1.8.8 (contrast 10.1.97). On Probus see N. Scivoletto, *GIF* xii (1959), 97 ff., K. Büchner, in H. Hunger et al., *Geschichte der Textüberlieferung der antiken und mittelalterlichen Literatur* i (Zürich, 1961), pp. 335 ff.   [4] Spartianus, *Hadr.* 16.6.

[5] On Gellius' sources see L. Mercklin, *NJbb* Suppl. iii (1857–60), 633 ff., C. Hosius, *A. Gellii Noctium Atticarum Libri XX*, vol. i (Leipzig, 1903), pp. xvi ff.

[6] Cf. Gellius 16.10, 18.5, 20.10.2.

general discussions of archaic poetry preserved from this century Ennius always figures as a writer of epic, never of tragedy; Pacuvius and Accius are usually named as the great tragedians of the Republic.[1]

The only person after Apuleius who can be shown with probability to have handled a roll or codex containing an Ennian tragedy is the early fourth century grammarian Nonius Marcellus. The *Telephus* and the *Hectoris lytra* appear to have been among those republican poems which he excerpted himself.[2] At some time in the fifth or the sixth century a reader of Orosius' *Historiae* consulted a copy of the seventh book of the *Annales* in order to gloss the historian's text.[3] However, to judge by Macrobius' remarks about the literary tastes of his contemporaries,[4] not even this work could have found a great many readers. The quotations of the tragedies which appear in works composed after Nonius' lexicon are probably all second or third hand. This cannot be indubitably demonstrated in every case but the frequency with which the authors of late antiquity admit to using older material[5] and the number of coincidences both between blocks of quotations in early and late technical

---

[1] See Fronto, p. 131.13, Gellius 13.2.1, Diomedes, *Gramm.* I 490.12 ff. (Suetonius?). This had long been the orthodox view (cf. Ovid, *Am.* 1.15.19, *Trist.* 2.359, Velleius 1.17.1, 2.9.3, Columella I praef. 30, Persius 1.76–8, Martial 11.90.6, Tacitus, *Dial.* 20, Quintilian, *Inst.* 10.1.97) and was perhaps as old as Horace, *Epist.* 2.1.55–6. Horace nevertheless thought Ennius' dramatic verse worthy of assault. Cicero joined Ennius with Pacuvius and Accius to form a classical tragic trio (*De orat.* 3.27, *Orat.* 36, *Opt. gen.* 18, *Ac.* 1.10, *Fin.* 1.4).

[2] Cf. Lindsay, *Nonius Marcellus' Dictionary of Republican Latin* (Oxford, 1901); for further analysis of the structure of Nonius' work along the same lines see Lindsay, *Philologus* LXIV (1905), 438 ff., Strzelecki, *Eos* XXXIV (1932–3), 113 ff., *De Flauio Capro Nonii Auctore* (Kraków, 1936), Rychlewska, in *Tragica* II, pp. 117 ff.

[3] See Norden, *Ennius und Vergilius: Kriegsbilder aus Roms grosser Zeit* (Leipzig, 1915), pp. 78 ff.   [4] See *Sat.* 1.4.17, 6.1.2, 6.1.5, 6.3.9, 6.9.9.

[5] Cf., in particular, Priscian, *Gramm.* III 418.10 (at the beginning of a work which contains some of the longest quotations of republican tragedy extant).

writing and between arguments illustrated by particular quotations of republican poetry in early and late literary prose[1] should compel scholars to be at least hesitant in postulating a direct connection between any tragic fragment preserved in a work of late antiquity and a whole tragic text.

From this point the history of the text of Ennius' tragedies is coincident with those of the many works which carry quotations from them. Our evidence for some quotations is comparatively old (e.g. the fourth-century palimpsest of Cicero's *De republica*), for others recent (e.g. the book printed at Basle in 1521 containing Rufinian's *De figuris sententiarum et elocutionis*), for some copious and good, for others (particularly lexicographical quotations) bad. I have found it necessary to express doubt concerning, or disbelief in, the παράδοσις at many points. Sometimes the ancient quoter had a faulty text[2] or misread[3] or misunderstood an accurate text,[4] but most errors must come from the inattention or incompetence of medieval scribes. Lack of knowledge of the original context often prevented them from reading obscure groups of letters correctly and continues to prevent modern scholars from correcting their errors in a manner likely to convince others.

---

[1] On Rufinian see Marx, *BPhW* x (1890), 1008, A. Gantz, *De Aquilae Romani et Iulii Rufiniani Exemplis* (Diss. Königsberg, 1909), W. Schaefer, *Quaestiones Rhetoricae* (Diss. Bonn, 1913); on Charisius and Diomedes, K. Barwick, *Remmius Palaemon und die römische Ars Grammatica* (*Philologus* Suppl. xv 2, 1922); on St Jerome, C. Kunst, *De S. Hieronymi Studiis Ciceronianis* (Diss. Vienna, 1918), p. 142; on the Ciceronian scholiasts, P. Hildebrandt, *De Scholiis Ciceronis Bobiensibus* (Diss. Göttingen, 1894), pp. 34 ff.; on Macrobius and the Virgilian scholiasts, H. D. Jocelyn, *CQ* N.S. xiv (1964), 280 ff., xv (1965), 126 ff.; on Priscian, L. Jeep, *Philologus* lxvii (1908), 12 ff., lxviii (1909), 1 ff.

[2] Cf. the reading of *v.* 209 *caesae accidissent abiegnae...trabes* (see Commentary).

[3] Cf. Nonius' placing of fr. lxxiii under the lemma VAGAS.

[4] Cf. Verrius' placing of fr. xcviii under the lemma PEDVM, *baculum*. Similar errors may have been made by Cicero or his source concerning the *exitium* of *v.* 44 (*Orat.* 155) and by Nonius' source, Lindsay's list 27 'Alph. Verb', concerning the *regredere* of *v.* 7 (p. 166.21).

VII. THE TITLES OF ENNIUS' TRAGEDIES

Most of the titles which head the quotations made by the ancient grammarians consist of proper names—*Achilles, Aiax, Alcmeo, Alexander, Andromacha, Andromeda, Athamas, Cresphontes, Erectheus, Hecuba, Iphigenia, Medea, Melanippa, Nemea, Phoenix, Telamo, Telephus, Thyestes*. One title contains a Latin adjective—*Medea exul*; one the name of the author of the Attic original—*Achilles Aristarchi*; three contain Greek words not domiciled in second-century Latin—*Andromache aechmalotis, Eumenides, Hectoris lytra (Lytra)*. Some of the spellings used by the grammarians could not possibly come from Ennius himself and there is reason to suppose that some of the very titles are equally late. Certain modern scholars have inferred from the titles *Achilles Aristarchi, Andromache aechmalotis* and *Medea exul*[1] that the grammarians quote from two Ennian plays about Achilles, from two about Andromache and from two about Medea. The substance of the grammarians' quotations supports strongly the idea of two Medea plays but leaves the issue open in the case of *Achilles* and *Andromacha*.[2]

Andromache aechmalotis should be considered along with the title *Aiax mastigophorus* which Nonius appears to attribute to Livius Andronicus at p. 207.32, the title *Philoctetes Lemnius* which Varro attributes to Accius at *Ling.* 7.11 and the titles *Phasma* and *Synaristosae* under which pieces of the comedies of Plautus otherwise known as *Mostellaria* and *Cistellaria* respectively are quoted in Verrius Flaccus' lexicon.[3] What has hap-

---

[1] Stephanus' notion that *Hectoris lytra* and *Lytra* denote distinct plays has never found favour (*Fragmenta Poetarum Veterum Latinorum* [Geneva, 1564]).

[2] See *Commentary*, pp. 161 ff., 234 ff.

[3] Cf. Festus, pp. 158.33, 394.18 for *Phasma* (contrast p. 166.19); pp. 390.8, 480.23 (for new evidence on the text see Fraenkel, *Philologus* LXXXVII [1932], 117 ff. [= *Kl. Beitr.* II 33 ff.]) for *Synaristosae* (contrast p. 512.10).

pened in each case is that some grammarian, not necessarily Nonius or Verrius, headed his quotation with the title of the Latin poet's Attic original taken from the διδασκαλίαι of the edition he consulted. Sheer caprice would have been his motive, not a desire to distinguish one play from another or to indicate titles actually used in the theatre for revival productions.[1]

The mode of quotation used at Festus p. 282.9—*Ennius in Achille Aristarchi*—has no exact parallel in the remains of Latin lexicography. Nevertheless its similarity with the mode of reference used in the prologue of Plautus' *Poenulus*[2] should be treated as accidental. P. Scriverius[3] thought that the quoter was trying to distinguish the play he was quoting from a second play about Achilles by Ennius; Bergk[4] from a play about Achilles by another Latin poet. I suggest a more humdrum explanation: the quoter, not necessarily Verrius Flaccus in the first instance,[5] was simply looking at or recalling the διδασκαλίαι at the beginning of the roll instead of the Latin title written at the end and on the σίλλυβος.

The titles *Eumenides* and *Hectoris lytra* would have been incomprehensible to those members of Ennius' first audiences who were ignorant of literary Greek. They do not appear outside the works of the grammarians Verrius, Nonius and

---

[1] Plautus, *Cas.* 32 may simply give a translation of Diphilus' title Κληρού-μενοι; there is no need to suppose that the revival performance for which some learned person composed the extant prologue was not advertised with the title *Casina*. Osann, *Anal. crit.* p. 164, lumped *Sortientes* and *Phasma* together as revival titles. Ritschl, *Parerga*, pp. 159, 165, 206, wrote more carefully; he treated *Sortientes* as a revival title and *Phasma* as a title used either for learned purposes or for stage revivals. Many later scholars (e.g. A. O. F. Lorenz, *Plautus: Mostellaria* [Berlin, 1866], pp. 2 f., Lindsay, *The Ancient Editions of Plautus* [Oxford, 1904], p. 1 n.) have adopted Osann's view of the Festus quotations alleging it to be Ritschl's.

[2] See above, p. 7.

[3] *Collectanea Veterum Tragicorum Fragmenta* (Leiden, 1620), p. 8.

[4] *Ind. lectt. Marburg* 1844, XI (= *Kl. phil. Schr.* I 225).

[5] See *Commentary*, p. 161 n. 1.

Diomedes. It is possible that in the early second century the plays were advertised with other titles and that these titles were either unknown to[1] or ignored by the grammarians who used the plays as a quarry for unusual Latinity. The twenty-one comedies which ancient scholars agreed to be genuinely Plautine all had titles attaching to them which could be understood by speakers of Latin, some proper names (*Amphitruo*, etc.), some straight translations of the Attic title (*Mercator* ~ Ἔμπορος, etc.), some of a native Latin type (*Cistellaria* ~ Συναριστῶσαι, etc.).[2] Terence retitled his version of Apollodorus' Ἐπιδικαζόμενος as *Phormio* but allowed his other five comedies to be advertised with transliterations of their Attic titles although these must have been incomprehensible to many spectators. It is reasonable to suppose that Terence was following a new fashion in tune with the growing Hellenisation of the Roman stage and to suspect that all titles attaching to comedies and tragedies of earlier times which require a knowledge of Greek for their comprehension may have been bestowed by students of the Latin scripts rather than their authors.[3]

---

[1] Nonius seems to have possessed a roll containing the *Hectoris lytra*; see *Commentary*, p. 290.

[2] The *fabula -aria* type of title continued to be used in the next century for freshly composed Atellane farces.

[3] The small number of purely Greek titles from the third and early second century and of purely Latin titles from the late second was discussed by Osann, *Anal. crit.* pp. 161 ff., and Ritschl, *Parerga*, pp. 139 ff. Ritschl argued that theatrical practice fluctuated until Plautus established the fashion of using Latin titles. This is historically implausible and the evidence can be interpreted more economically in the way I have suggested. The trimeter *Acontizomenus fabula est prime proba* quoted by Charisius, p. 273.11 ff. may come from a prologue written for a revival performance of Naevius' version of an Ἀκοντιζόμενος (cf. Plautus, *Cas.* 31). On the other hand the practice of Caecilius and Pacuvius, like that of Terence, may well have fluctuated. The title *Hypobolimaeus Rastraria* which Nonius attributes to Caecilius on a number of occasions (pp. 16.17, 40.3, 89.14, 147.6, 176.6, 505.29) looks like a conflation of an old-style title, which must have been Caecilius' own, and a transliteration of the title of the Attic original. Since Cicero quotes the titles *Niptra* (*Tusc.* 2.48) and *Synephebi* (*Fin.* 1.4, *Opt. gen.* 18, *Nat. deor.* 3.72, *Cato* 24, *Tusc.* 1.31) and since their use gave

The title *Medea exul*, like the title *Hector proficiscens* attributed
to Naevius by Priscian at *Gramm.* II 400.1, could in principle
be interpreted as a mere translation of a Greek title (e.g.
Μήδεια φεύγουσα) made either by Ennius himself or by a grammarian.[1] Greek grammarians commonly invented such titles
when they wished to distinguish two scripts by the one poet
about the one hero or heroine.[2] However the tragic verses
quoted along with *Medea exul* clearly belong to the version of
the extant Euripidean Μήδεια which is elsewhere quoted with
the title *Medea*.[3] Among the seventy tragedies of Euripides
known to the scholars of Alexandria[4] there was one apart from
the extant Μήδεια which had the Colchian woman as a personage. But this is regularly quoted in our sources as the
Αἰγεύς. We should therefore suppose that *Medea exul* is a title
of the type of *Parasitus piger* and *Parasitus medicus* (Plautus),
Hercules furens and *Hercules Oetaeus* (Seneca), and was applied
by some grammarian to Ennius' adaptation of Euripides'
Μήδεια in order to distinguish it from another tragedy by
Ennius about Medea.

A large number of fragments of tragic verse are quoted by
Cicero and Varro without any mention of the title of the par-

him stylistic pain (cf. *Tusc.* 3.65 *ille Terentianus ipse se poeniens, id est* ἑαυτὸν
τιμωρούμενος) we may suppose that no others were known for Pacuvius'
version of Sophocles' Νίπτρα and Caecilius' version of Menander's Συνέφηβοι
in the middle of the first century. Whether these plays ever possessed Latin
titles is now anybody's guess.

[1] The titles *Faenerator* and *Subditiuus* which Nonius (pp. 150.2, 543.23,
204.33, 514.31) attributes to Caecilius could be grammarians' translations of
Greek titles. Nonius quotes a *Hypobolimaeus* at p. 178.16 (for *Hypobolimaeus
Rastraria* see above, p. 60 n. 3) and an *Obolostates* at pp. 98.6, 154.10, 277.33,
279.40, 508.12.

[2] The *Souda* gives an Αἴας μαινόμενος to Astydamas, an Ἀχιλλεὺς Θερσιτο-
κτόνος to Chaeremon and a Ἡρακλῆς περικαιόμενος to Spintharos. The
absence of companions for these three plays in our sources is due to the rarity
with which the three tragedians are quoted.

[3] See *Commentary*, p. 342.   [4] See above, p. 45.

ticular tragedy from which they come or their author. Sometimes, however, the hero or heroine who spoke them is named. The first editor of the Ennian fragments, Stephanus, printed under the extant titles only those fragments whose quoters made a specific assignation. Columna and subsequent editors have with varying degrees of confidence attempted to assign for themselves the fragments which are quoted without assignation. They have assumed that Cicero and Varro knew at first hand all the plays which are named by Verrius, Nonius, Priscian and other grammarians and that they knew no play outside those named in our grammatical sources. These assumptions are not necessarily valid. Where Ennius is concerned there is no sign at all that Cicero knew the *Andromeda*, *Nemea* or *Phoenix*, few that he knew the *Athamas*, *Erectheus*, or *Hecuba*. On the other hand he quotes no tragic verse as by Ennius which cannot be easily assigned to one of the known titles. Varro quotes two fragments as by Ennius which require textual emendation of a very unconvincing kind to make them fit any of the twenty-two plots to which we can attach titles.

At *Ling.* 5.14 (fr. CLXXXVI) Varro quotes a fragment—*o terra Thraeca* (Fleckeisen: *treca* F) *ubi Liberi fanum inclutum* | *Maro locaui*—which would appear to the unprejudiced observer to come from the prologue of a play set in Thrace which was spoken by Maro the son of Dionysus (Liber). Leo[1] compared the opening verses of Euripides' 'Ηλέκτρα: ὦ γῆς παλαιὸν "Αργος, 'Ινάχου ῥοαί, ὅθεν...ἔπλευσε, and "Αλκηστις: ὦ δώματ' 'Αδμήτει' ἐν οἷς ἔτλην ἐγώ.... Ribbeck[2] altered *locaui* to *locauit* and interpreted the words as part of an apostrophe to the birthplace of Eumolpus in the *Erectheus*. Vahlen[3] gave them to the Polymestor of the *Hecuba*.

---

[1] *Gesch.* p. 187 n. 2. Cf. Bergk, *Philologus* XXXIII (1874), 291 (= *Kl. phil. Schr.* I 358).

[2] *Quaest. scen.* p. 262.   [3] *E.P.R.*[2] p. 194.

The fragment quoted by Varro at *Ling.* 7.13 (fr. cxc)—*extemplo acceptum me necato* (Scaliger: *negato* F) *et filium*—can be got into the *Andromacha* with Vossius' change of *acceptum* to *acceptam*[1] or into the *Hecuba* with F. H. Bothe's further change of *filium* to *filiam*.[2]

In assigning the fragments I have followed the method of Columna rather than that of Stephanus; more for the convenience of discussion than out of any confidence in my own ability to determine with certainty the plays which Cicero and Varro quoted on particular occasions. Nevertheless some assignations are more probable than others and I have tried to render explicit the reasoning behind those which I make.

Titles are sometimes omitted from the quotations of Festus, Nonius and Diomedes. In these cases it is unmethodical to assign the quotations to plays which are never formally quoted by these grammarians. The extant commentaries on Terence, Virgil, Horace and Cicero rarely give a title when they refer to Ennius. Where they do it is always a title we know from other sources. I am accordingly sceptical about O. Skutsch's suggestion[3] that Terence quotes the first verse of an *Alcumena* by Ennius at *Eun.* 590—*qui templa caeli summa sonitu concutit*[4]—and that Donatus (see Ennius, *Trag.* fr. cLxi*b*) recognised the connection. In any case, while it seems reasonably certain that Plautus refers to a Latin version of Euripides' 'Αλκμήνη at *Rud.* 86,[5] there are no good grounds for thinking Ennius the only person to have written tragedy at Rome in the early decades of the second century and thus necessarily the author of the version.

---

[1] *Castigationes et Notae*, p. 17 (in Scriverius, *Collectanea*).
[2] F. H. Bothe, *Poetae Scenici Latinorum*, vol. v (Leipzig, 1834), p. 48, compared Euripides, *Hek.* 391 ὑμεῖς δέ μ' ἀλλὰ θυγατρὶ συμφονεύσατε. Columna's discussion at *Q. Ennii Frag.* pp. 362–3 foreshadowed both suggestions.
[3] *HSCPh* LXXI (1967), 128.
[4] Cf. Plautus, *Rud.* 1 *qui gentes omnes mariaque et terras mouet*.
[5] See above, p. 6.

THE FRAGMENTS

Testes cuiusque tragoediae ratione fere temporum
ordinaui. testium codices siglis notaui usitatis.

ACHILLES

I

Plautus, *Poen.* 1:

> Achillem Aristarchi mihi commentari lubet;
> inde mihi principium capiam, ex ea tragoedia.
> sileteque et tacete atque animum aduortite.
> audire iubet uos imperator histricus (histrycus *codd.*),
> 5 bonoque ut animo sedeate in subselliis
> et qui esurientes (D^4: csuplentes BCD^1) et qui saturi
>   uenerint.
> qui edistis multo fecistis sapientius;
> qui non edistis saturi fite fabulis.
> nam cui paratumst quod edit, nostra gratia
> 10 nimia est stultitia sessum inpransum incedere.
> exsurge praeco, fac populo audientiam.
> iam dudum exspecto si tuom officium scias;
> exerce uocem quam per uiuisque et colis.
> nam nisi clamabis tacitum (*Turnebus*: ta titum *B*: statim
>   *CD*) te obrepet fames.
> 15 age nunc reside duplicem ut mercedem feras.
> bonum factum, †esse† edicta ut seruetis mea.
> scortum exoletum ne quis in proscaenio
> sedeat, neu (*Camerarius*: niue *codd.*) lictor uerbum aut
>   uirgae muttiant,
> neu dissignator praeter os obambulet,
> 20 neu sessum ducat dum histrio in scaena (scena *codd.*) siet.
> diu qui domi otiosi dormierunt, decet
> animo aequo nunc stent uel dormire temperent.
> serui ne obsideant, liberis ut sit locus,
> uel aes pro capite dent; si id facere non queunt

25   domum abeant, uitent ancipiti infortunio,
      ne et hic uarientur uirgis et loris domi
      si minus curassint (cura sint *codd.*) †quom eri ueniant
          domum†.
      nutrices pueros infantis minutulos
      domi ut procurent, neu quae spectatum adferat
30   ne et ipsae sitiant et pueri pereant (*CD*: pertant *B*:
          peritent *T*) fame
      neue esurientes hic quasi haedi obuagiant.
      matronae tacitae spectent, tacitae rideant (redeant *C*:
          rediant *B*: reddeant *D*),
      canora hic uoce sua tinnire temperent,
      domum sermones fabulandi conferant
35   ne et hic uiris sint et domi molestiae.
      quodque ad ludorum curatores attinet,
      ne palma detur quoiquam artifici iniuria,
      neue ambitionis caussa extrudantur foras
      quo deteriores anteponantur bonis.
40   et hoc quoque etiam quod paene oblitus fui:
      dum ludi fiunt in popinam pedisequi
      inruptionem facite; nunc dum occasio est,
      nunc dum scribilitae aestuant occurrite.
      haec quae imperata sunt pro imperio histrico,
45   bonum hercle factum, pro se quisque ut meminerit.
      ad argumentum nunc uicissatim uolo
      remigrare ut aeque mecum sitis gnarures (*T*: siti signa
          rures *BCD*);
      eius nunc regiones limites confinia
      determinabo; ei (*codd. Plauti*: eius *codd. Non.* p. 11.25)
          rei ego sum factus finitor.

II

(*a*) Cicero, *Verr.* 2.1.46: Delum uenit. ibi ex fano Apollinis religiosissimo noctu clam sustulit signa pulcherrima atque antiquissima, eaque in onerariam nauem suam conicienda curauit. postridie cum fanum spoliatum uiderent ii qui Delum incolebant, grauiter ferebant; est enim tanta apud eos eius fani religio atque antiquitas ut in eo loco ipsum Apollinem natum esse arbitrentur. uerbum tamen facere non audebant, ne forte ea res ad Dolabellam ipsum pertineret. tum subito tempestates coortae sunt maximae, iudices, ut non modo proficisci cum cuperet Dolabella non posset sed uix in oppido consisteret.

> *ita magni fluctus eiciebantur.*   1

hic nauis illa praedonis istius, onusta signis religiosis, expulsa atque eiecta fluctu frangitur; in litore signa illa Apollinis reperiuntur; iussu Dolabellae reponuntur. tempestas sedatur, Dolabella Delo proficiscitur.

(*b*) Schol. Gronouianus: ITA MAGNI FLVCTVS EICIEBANTVR. Enniano hemistichio usus est ex ea tragoedia quae Achilles inscribitur.

III

Festus, p. 282.9:

> *prolato aere astitit,*   2

Ennius in Achille Aristarchi cum ait, significat clipeo ante se protento.

IV

(*a*) Festus, p. 394.33: SVBICES Ennius in Achille pro subiectis posuit cum dixit nubes:

> *per ego deum sublimas subices*   3
> *umidas unde oritur imber sonitu saeuo et spiritu.*

III in Achille *Scaliger*: achillae in *F*
IV (*a*) 3 deum subices *F*   4 inde oritur imber sonitus aeuo spiritu *F*

(*b*) Gellius 4.17.13: congruens igitur est ut subices etiam, quod proinde ut obices compositum est, u littera breui dici oporteat.

14: Ennius in tragoedia quae Achilles inscribitur subices pro aere alto ponit, qui caelo subiectus est, in his uersibus: 'per ego deum sublimas subices humidas unde oritur imber sonitu saeuo et strepitu'. plerosque omnes tamen legere audias u littera producta.

(*c*) Nonius, p. 169.1: SVBICES noue positum; non a subiciendo sed altitudine. Ennius Achille (acille *codd.*): 'per ego deum sublimas subicis umidas unde oritur imber'.

V

Nonius, p. 147.18: OBVARARE, peruertere, deprauare; dictum a uaris. Ennius Achille:

†nam consilius† *obuarant quibus tam concedit hic ordo.* 5

VI

Nonius, p. 166.20: REGREDERE, reuocare. Ennius Achille:

quo nunc incerta re atque inorata gradum 6
regredere conare?

VII

Nonius, p. 277.23: DEFENDERE, †tueri† depellere (debellare ueri *A⁴*). Ennius Achille:

serua ciues, defende hostes cum potes defendere. 8

VIII

Nonius, p. 472.26: PROELIANT. Ennius Achille:

†inta† *mortales inter sese pugnant proeliant.* 9

V acille *codd.*: 5 nam consiliis ius *Timpanaro*
VII in achille *Gen.*: in chille (achilleo *B²*) que te *B*
VIII 9 inta mortales *LB⁴C⁴*: ita mortales *A⁴*: mortales interea *Klussmann*: interea mortales *Lachmann*

IX

Isidorus, *Diff.* 1.218: inter famam et gloriam: gloria quippe uirtutum est, fama uero uitiorum. Ennius in Achille:

> *summam tu tibi pro mala uita famam extolles*   10
> *et pro bona paratam gloriam.*
> *male uolentes* [enim] *famam tollunt, bene uolentes gloriam.*

AIAX

X

Cicero, *Off.* 1.114: suum quisque igitur noscat ingenium acremque se et bonorum et uitiorum suorum iudicem praebeat, ne scaenici plus quam nos uideantur habere prudentiae. illi enim non optumas sed sibi accommodatissimas fabulas eligunt: qui uoce freti sunt Epigonos Medumque (Medeamque *X*), qui gestu Melanippam (melenippam *B*: menalippam *bX*), Clytemestram (clitemestram *Lp*: clitimestram *c*), semper Rupilius quem ego memini Antiopam (Anthiopam *Z*), non saepe Aesopus Aiacem.

XI

(*a*) Varro, *Ling.* 6.6: cum stella prima exorta...id tempus dictum a Graecis ἑσπέρα, Latine uesper; ut ante solem ortum quod eadem stella uocatur iubar, quod iubata. Pacui dicit pastor...Enni Aiax:

> *lumen iubarne in caelo cerno?*   13

(*b*) Varro, *Ling.* 6.81: cerno idem ualet. itaque pro uideo ait Ennius: 'lumen iubarne in caelo cerno?'

IX 12 enim *del. Ribbeck*
XI (*a*) Ennii *Laetus*: ennius *F*

(c) Varro, *Ling.* 7.75: possunt triones dicti, VII quod ita sitae stellae ut ternae trigona faciant. †aliquod†

76: 'lumen iubarne in caelo cerno?' iubar dicitur stella lucifer †quae† in summo quod habet lumen diffusum ut leo in capite iubam. huius ortus significat circiter esse extremam noctem. itaque ait Pacuius...

XII

Festus, p. 482.3: TVLLIOS al⟩ii dixerunt esse silanos, alii (ali *F*) riuos, alii (ali *F*) uehementes proiectiones sanguinis arcuatim fluentis quales sunt Tiburi in Aniene. Ennius in Aiace:

†a iax† *misso sanguine tepido tullii efflantes uolant.*   14

XIII

Nonius, p. 393.7: STATIM producta prima syllaba, a stando, perseueranter et aequaliter significat...Ennius Aiace:

qui rem cum Achiuis gesserunt statim.   15

ALCMEO

XIV

(a) Cicero, *De orat.* 3.154: nouantur autem uerba quae ab eo qui dicit ipso gignuntur ac fiunt uel coniungendis uerbis ut haec: 'tum pauor sapientiam omnem (mihi *add. M*: sapientiam mihi omnem '*pars integrorum*' [*Vahlen*]; *cod.* G *Non.* p. 16.7: omnem sapientiam mihi *cod.* L *Non.*) exanimato (exanimo *B*) expectorat (expectarat *A*) (*v.* 17)'; 'num non uis huius me uersutiloquas malitias'. uidetis enim et 'uersutiloquas' et 'expectorat' ex coniunctione facta esse uerba, non nata. sed saepe uel sine coniunctione...

XII ennius inaiacea. iax *F*   14 tulii *F*: tullii *codd. Pauli*
XIII 15 achibidis *A⁴*

(*b*) Cicero, *De orat.* 3.217: aliud enim uocis genus iracundia sibi sumat, acutum...aliud miseratio ac maeror, flexibile...
   218: aliud metus, demissum et haesitans et abiectum:

> *multis sum modis circumuentus, morbo exilio atque inopia.*   16
> *tum pauor sapientiam omnem exanimato expectorat.*
> †alter† *terribilem minatur uitae cruciatum et necem;*
> *quae nemo est tam firmo ingenio et tanta confidentia*
> *quin refugiat timido sanguen atque exalbescat metu.*   20

   219: aliud uis, contentum...

(*c*) Cicero, *Tusc.* 4.19: quae autem subiecta sunt sub metum, ea sic definiunt: pigritiam...terrorem...timorem...pauorem metum mentem loco mouentem, ex quo illud Enni ($V^{rec}M$: Ennius X) 'tum pauor sapientiam omnem exanimato (omnem mihi ex anima *codd.*) expectorat (K^2: expectaret X: expectoret B: expelleret V^{rec}) (*v.* 17)'; exanimationem...conturbationem ...formidinem...

(*d*) Cicero, *Fin.* 4.62: hoc uero te ferre non potuisse, quod antiqui illi quasi barbati, ut nos de nostris solemus dicere, crediderint (crediderunt *RNV*), eius, qui honeste uiueret, si idem etiam bene ualeret, bene audiret, copiosus esset, optabiliorem fore uitam melioremque et magis expetendam quam illius, qui aeque uir bonus multis modis esset, ut Enni Alcmeo, 'circumuentus morbo exilio atque inopia (*v.* 16)'.

(*e*) Cicero, *Fin.* 5.31: quis est enim aut quotus quisque (est *add. codd. Non. p. 224.18*), cui, mors cum adpropinquet, non 'refugiat timido sanguen (refugiat timidos anguis *BERN*[1]: refugiat timido sanguis N^2V: fugiat timido sanguen *codd. Non.*) atque exalbescat metu (*v.* 20)'.

(*f*) Cicero, *Hortens.* frag. *ap.* Prisc. *Gramm.* II 250.12: ut ait Ennius, 'refugiat timido sanguen atque exalbescat metu (*v.* 20)'.

XIV (*b*) 16 modis sum *L*   17 omnem mi *P*: omnem mihi *VO*   18 alter *L*: *om. M*   minitatur *L*   20 sanguine *L*

XV

(a) Cicero, *Ac.* 2.52: illud enim dicimus non eandem esse uim neque integritatem dormientium et uigilantium nec mente nec sensu...quod idem contingit insanis, ut et incipientes furere sentiant et dicant aliquid quod non sit id uideri sibi et cum relaxentur sentiant atque illa dicant Alcmeonis:

> *sed mihi neutiquam cor consentit cum oculorum aspectu.*   21

(b) Cicero, *Ac.* 2.88: dormientium et uinulentorum et furiosorum uisa inbecilliora esse dicebas quam uigilantium siccorum sanorum. quo modo? quia cum experrectus esset Ennius non diceret se uidisse Homerum sed uisum esse, Alcmeo autem: 'sed mihi neutiquam cor consentit — (*v.* 21)'. similia de uinulentis...

89: quid loquar de insanis?... quid ipse Alcmeo tuus, qui negat cor sibi cum oculis consentire, nonne ibidem incitato furore:

> *unde haec flamma oritur?*   22

et illa deinceps:

> †incede incede† *adsunt; me expetunt.*

quid cum uirginis fidem implorat:

> *fer mi auxilium, pestem abige a me,*
> *flammiferam hanc uim quae me excruciat.*   25
> *caeruleae incinctae igni incedunt,*
> *circumstant cum ardentibus taedis.*

num dubitas quin sibi haec uidere uideatur? itemque cetera:

> *intendit crinitus Apollo*
> *arcum auratum luna innixus;*
> *Diana facem iacit a laeua.*   30

qui magis haec crederet si essent quam credebat quia uidebantur? apparet enim iam cor cum oculis consentire.

XV (b) 23 incaede incaede *V*   26 ceruleae (cerulaeae *B*) incincte igni *codd.*: caeruleo incinctae angui *Columna*

(c) Festus, p. 162.14:
NEVTIQVAM pro
cum ait 'sed
lorum aspect (v. 21)
neutiquam

XVI

Nonius, p. 127.13: IAMDIV pro olim...Ennius Alcmeone:

factum est iam diu. 31

ALEXANDER

XVII

(a) Cicero, *Att.* 8.11.3: uoluisti enim me quid de his malis sentirem ostendere. προθεσπίζω igitur, noster Attice, non hariolans ut illa (*Pius*: utilia *codd.*) cui nemo credidit sed coniectura prospiciens: 'iamque mari (maria *codd.*) magno—(v. 43)'. non multo, inquam, secus possum uaticinari. tanta malorum impendet Ἰλιάς.

(b) Cicero, *Orat.* 155: atque etiam a quibusdam sero iam emendatur antiquitas, qui haec reprehendunt. nam pro deum atque hominum fidem deorum aiunt. ita credo hoc illi nesciebant. an dabat hanc licentiam consuetudo? itaque idem poeta qui inusitatius contraxerat 'patris mei meum factum pudet (v. 37)' pro meorum factorum, et 'texitur exitium examen rapit (v. 44)' pro exitiorum, non dicit liberum ut plerique loquimur ...at ille alter in Chryse...

156: ...atqui (*uulgo*: et quid *Heerdegen*: quid *A*: et qui *L*) dixit Accius...

(c) Cicero, *Diu.* 1.66: inest igitur in animis praesagitio (*uulgo*: praesagatio *codd.*) extrinsecus iniecta atque inclusa diuinitus. ea

---

XV (c) NEVTIQVAM pro nullo modo — *Paulus*

75

si exarsit acrius furor appellatur cum a corpore animus abstrac-
tus diuino instinctu concitatur.

> sed quid oculis rapere uisa est derepente ardentibus? 32
> ubi illa paulo ante sapiens †uirginali† modestia?

> mater, optumatum multo mulier melior mulierum,
> missa sum superstitiosis hariolationibus; 35
> †neque† me Apollo fatis fandis dementem inuitam ciet.
> uirgines uereor aequalis, patris mei meum factum pudet,
> optumi uiri. mea mater, tui me miseret, mei piget.
> optumam progeniem Priamo peperisti extra me. hoc dolet:
> men obesse, illos prodesse, me obstare, illos obsequi. 40

o poema tenerum et moratum atque molle. sed hoc minus ad
rem.

67: illud quod uolumus expressum est ut uaticinari furor uera
soleat.

> adest adest fax obuoluta sanguine atque incendio. 41
> multos annos latuit. ciues ferte opem et restinguite.

deus (restinguit deus AV) inclusus corpore humano iam, non
Cassandra loquitur.

> iamque mari magno classis cita 43
> texitur. exitium examen rapit.
> adueniet. fera ueliuolantibus
> nauibus compleuit manus litora.

tragoedias loqui uideor et fabulas.

XVII (c) 32 rabere *Lambinus 1573*   33 ⟨aut⟩ ubi *Lachmann*   uirginale *B¹*
34 optumatum *uulgo*: optumarum *Porson*: optuma tum *AVB*   36 meque
Grotius: namque me *Hottinger*: namque *Ribbeck*   37 uereor *Ribbeck*: uero⁕⁕
(o *ex e corr.*) *B*: uero *AV*   39 peperisti *Marsus*: repperisti *AVB*   40 me⁕
B   42 referte *AV*   45 aduenit et fera *V²*   46 complebit *P*

(*d*) Cicero, *Diu*. 1.114: multos nemora siluaeque, multos amnes aut maria commouent, quorum furibunda mens uidet ante multo quae sint futura. quo de genere illa sunt:

> *eheu uidete:*   47
> *iudicauit inclitum iudicium inter deas tris aliquis,*
> *quo iudicio Lacedaemonia mulier Furiarum una adueniet.*

eodem enim modo multa a uaticinantibus saepe praedicta sunt.

(*e*) Cicero, *Diu*. 2.112: at multi saepe uera uaticinati, ut Cassandra: 'iamque mari magno—(*v.* 43)' eademque paulo (populo *V*) post: 'eheu uidete (*v.* 47)'.

113: num igitur me cogis etiam fabulis credere? quae delectationis (*ed. Veneta 1471*: delectationes *AVB*) habeant quantum uoles, uerbis sententiis numeris cantibus adiuuentur; auctoritatem quidem nullam debemus nec fidem commenticiis rebus adiungere.

XVIII

Cicero, *Diu*, 1.42: haec etiamsi ficta sunt a poeta non absunt tamen a consuetudine somniorum. sit sane etiam illud commenticium quo Priamus est conturbatus quia

> *mater grauida parere se ardentem facem*   50
> *uisa est in somnis Hecuba. quo facto pater*
> *rex ipse Priamus somnio mentis metu*
> *perculsus curis sumptus suspirantibus*

XVII *Trag. inc. *ap.* Quintil. *Inst.* 9.3.77 Hecuba hoc dolet pudet piget, Varro, *Men.* frag. *ap.* Non. pp. 112.21, 328.28 adest fax inuoluta incendio (incendii *codd.* Non. *p. 328.29*), Vergilius, *Aen.* 2.569–74 Tyndarida aspicio...illa...Troiae et patriae communis Erinys | abdiderat sese; ex Vergilio Lucanus 10.59
XVIII *Ouidius, *Epist.* 17.237–8 fax quoque me terret quam se peperisse cruentam | ante diem partus est tua uisa parens.
XVII (*d*) 48 inter *add.* *B^c*: intus *V^b*
XVIII 50 se *om.* H

exsacrificabat hostiis balantibus.
tum coniecturam postulat pacem petens,   55
ut se edoceret obsecrans Apollinem
quo sese uertant tantae sortes somnium.
ibi ex oraclo uoce diuina edidit
Apollo puerum primus Priamo qui foret
postilla natus temperaret tollere;   60
eum esse exitium Troiae, pestem Pergamo.

sint haec ut dixi somnia fabularum...

XIX

Varro, *Ling.* 6.83: ab auribus uerba uidentur dicta audio et
ausculto; aures (*A. Spengel*: auris *O. Mueller*: audio *F*) ab aueo
(*Laetus*: abaucto *F*), quod his auemus discere (*uulgo*: dicere *F*)
semper, quod Ennius uidetur ἔτυμον ostendere uelle in Alexandro cum ait:

iam dudum ab ludis animus atque aures auent   62
auide exspectantes nuntium.

propter hanc aurium auiditatem theatra replentur.

XX

Varro, *Ling.* 7.82: apud Ennium: 'Andromachae nomen qui
indidit recte ei indidit (*v.* 99)'. item:

quapropter Parim pastores nunc Alexandrum uocant.   64

imitari dum uoluit (*Aldus*: uolunt *F*) Euripidem (euripeden *F*)
et ponere ἔτυμον, est lapsus; nam Euripides quod Graeca posuit,
ἔτυμα sunt aperta. ille ait ideo nomen additum Andromachae,
quod ἀνδρὶ μάχεται (*Aldus*: andromache · quod andromachete
F); hoc Enni (ennii *F*) quis potest intellegere in uersu (*Turnebus*:

54 et sacrificabat *H*   56 doceret *V*   58 ubi *B*   60 temptaret tollere
H: tempora extollere *V^c*

inuersum *F*) significare 'Andromachae nomen qui indidit recte
indidit' aut Alexandrum ab eo appellatum in Graecia qui Paris
fuisset, a quo Herculem quoque cognominatum Alexicacon, ab
eo quod defensor esset hominum?

XXI

(*a*) Festus, p. 240.10:
antiquos u
dicisum est i
nifici ait neque
in Alexandro
†amidio† *purus put⟨us⟩*   65
sycophanta est
quo certior sc
putatum dici sol
ta id est pura fact

(*b*) Gellius, 7.5.10: scriptum est autem 'purum putum' non in
Carthaginiensi solum foedere sed cum in multis aliis ueterum
libris tum in Q. quoque Ennii tragoedia, quae inscribitur
Alexander, et in satira M. Varronis, quae inscripta est δὶς
παῖδες οἱ γέροντες.

XXII

Festus, p. 416.35: STOLIDVS, stultus. Ennius lib. 1...et in
Alexandro:

  hominem appellat. 'quid †lasciui† stolide?' non intellegit.   66

et Caecilius...

XXI (*a*) PVTVS antiqui dicebant pro puro, unde putatae uites et arbores, quod
decisis inpedimentis remanerent purae. aurum quoque putatum dici solet, id
est expurgatum, et ratio putata, id est pura facta — *Paulus*
XXII 66 lasciuis *Scaliger*

XXIII

Festus, p. 494.33: TAENIAS Graecam uocem sic interpretatur
Verrius, ut dicat ornamentum esse laneum capitis honorati, ut
sit apud Caecilium...Ennius in Alexandro:

> *uolans de caelo cum corona et taeniis.*   67

Accius...

XXIV

Macrobius, *Sat.* 6.1.61 (7: dicam itaque primum quos ab aliis
traxit uel ex dimidio sui uersus uel paene solidos): 'multi
praeterea quos fama obscura recondit (Verg. *Aen.* 5.302)'.
Ennius in Alexandro:

> *multi alii aduentant, paupertas quorum obscurat nomina.*   68

XXV

Macrobius, *Sat.* 6.2.18 (1: locos locis componere sedet animo
ut unde formati sint quasi de speculo cognoscas): 'o lux
Dardaniae spes o fidissima Teucrum (Verg. *Aen.* 2.281)' et
reliqua. Ennius in Alexandro:

> *o lux Troiae, germane Hector,*   69
> *quid ita cum tuo lacerato corpore miser?*
> *aut qui te sic respectantibus tractauere nobis?*

XXIV *ex Vergilio Statius, *Theb.* 6.560.
XXV *Vergilius, *Aen.* 2.281–6 o lux Dardaniae, spes o fidissima
Teucrum, | quae tantae tenuere morae? quibus Hector ab oris |
exspectate uenis? ut te post multa tuorum | funera, post uarios
hominumque urbisque labores | defessi aspicimus. quae causa
indigna serenos | foedauit uoltus? aut cur haec uolnera cerno?,
6.500–2 Deiphobe armipotens, genus alto a sanguine Teucri, | quis
tam crudelis optauit sumere poenas? | quoi tantum de te licuit?

XXV 70 ita cumque tuo *T* miser ⟨ades⟩ *Mariotti*: miser ⟨es⟩ *Vahlen*

XXVI

Macrobius, *Sat.* 6.2.25: 'cum fatalis equus saltu super ardua uenit | Pergama et armatum peditem grauis attulit aluo (Verg. *Aen.* 6.515–16)'. Ennius in Alexandro:

> *nam maximo saltu superauit grauidus armatis equus*   72
> *qui suo partu ardua perdat Pergama.*

ANDROMACHA

XXVII

(*a*) Cicero, *Sest.* 120: quid fuit illud quod, recenti nuntio de illo senatus consulto quod factum est in templo Virtutis ad ludos scaenamque perlato, consessu maximo summus artifex et mehercule semper partium in re publica (*Naugerius*: in TR.PL. *codd.*) tam quam in scaena optimarum, flens et recenti laetitia et mixto dolore ac desiderio mei, egit apud populum Romanum multo grauioribus uerbis meam causam quam egomet de me agere potuissem? summi enim poetae ingenium non solum

---

XXVI *Lucretius 1.476–7 nec clam durateus Troianis Pergama partu | inflammasset equos nocturno Graiugenarum; Vergilius, *Georg.* 3.139–41 exactis grauidae cum mensibus errant, | non illas grauibus quisquam iuga ducere plaustris, | non saltu superare uiam sit passus, *Aen.* 2.237–8 scandit fatalis machina muros | feta armis, 328–9 arduus armatos mediis in moenibus adstans | fundit equos, 6.515–16 cum fatalis ecus saltu super ardua uenit | Pergama et armatum peditem grauis attulit aluo; Ouidius, *Ars* 1.364 militibus grauidum laeta recepit equum; Macrobius, *Sat.* 3.13.13 nam Titius in suasione legis Fanniae obicit saeculo suo quod porcum Troianum mensis inferant, quem illi ideo sic uocabant, quasi aliis inclusis animalibus grauidum, ut ille Troianus equus grauidus armatis fuit.

XXVI 72 nunc maxima P

arte sua sed etiam dolore exprimebat. †qua enim† (qua enim
ui *Koechly*)

> qui rem publicam certo animo adiuuerit 74
> statuerit, steterit cum Achiuis—

uobiscum me stetisse dicebat, uestros ordines demonstrabat.
reuocabatur ab uniuersis.

> re dubia 76
> haut dubitarit uitam offerre nec capiti pepercerit.

121: haec quantis ab illo clamoribus agebantur. cum iam
omisso gestu uerbis poetae et studio actoris (*Heruagius*: auctoris
codd.) et exspectationi nostrae plauderetur:

SVMMVM AMICVM SVMMO IN BELLO

— nam illud ipse actor adiungebat amico animo et fortasse
homines propter aliquod desiderium adprobabant —

SVMMO INGENIO PRAEDITVM.

tum (*G*: tam *P*: iam *ed. Ascens. 1531*) illa quanto cum gemitu
populi Romani ab eodem paulo post in eadem fabula sunt acta.

'o pater—   (*v.* 87).'

me, me ille absentem ut patrem deplorandum putabat (*ed.
Ascens. 1531*: putarat *codd.*), quem Q. Catulus, quem multi alii
saepe in senatu patrem patriae nominarant. quanto cum fletu de
illis nostris incendiis ac ruinis, cum patrem pulsum, patriam
adflictam deploraret, domum incensam euersamque. sic egit ut,
demonstrata pristina fortuna, cum se conuertisset,

'haec omnia uidi inflammari (*v.* 92)'

fletum etiam inimicis atque inuidis excitaret.

122: pro di immortales. quid? illa quem ad modum dixit
idem. quae mihi quidem ita acta et scripta uidentur esse ut uel a
Q. Catulo, si reuixisset, praeclare posse dici uiderentur; is enim

---

XXVII (*a*) 77 haut *Madvig*: *ut (*fuit* aut) *P*: ut *G* dubitari *G* uitam
Naugerius: uiam *codd.* pepercerit *uulgo*: peper *P*¹: pepercit *P*ᶜ*G*

libere reprehendere et accusare populi non numquam temeri-
tatem solebat aut errorem senatus.

'o (P: uero G) ingratifici Argiui (argui P[1]), immunes (schol.
Bob.: inanes codd.) Grai, inmemores benefici (benefitii
codd.)'.

non erat illud quidem uerum; non enim ingrati, sed miseri,
quibus reddere salutem a quo (P: quod G) acceperant non
liceret, nec unus in quemquam umquam gratior quam in me
uniuersi; sed tamen illud scripsit disertissimus poeta pro †me†
(Telamone Lambinus), egit fortissimus actor, non solum optimus, de me, cum omnis ordines demonstraret, senatum equites
Romanos uniuersum populum Romanum accusaret.

'exulare sinitis (ed. Ascens. 1531: sinite codd.), sistis (si istis codd.)
pelli (P: belli G), pulsum patimini'.

quae tum significatio fuerit omnium, quae declaratio uoluntatis
ab uniuerso populo Romano in causa hominis non popularis,
equidem audiebam (ed. Ascens. 1531: audiebamus codd.);
existimare facilius possunt qui adfuerunt.

123: et quoniam huc me prouexit oratio, histrio casum meum
totiens conlacrimauit, cum ita dolenter ageret causam meam, ut
uox eius illa praeclara lacrimis impediretur; neque poetae,
quorum ego semper ingenia dilexi, tempori meo defuerunt;
eaque populus Romanus non solum plausu sed etiam gemitu
suo comprobauit. utrum igitur haec Aesopum potius pro me
aut Accium dicere oportuit, si populus Romanus liber esset, an
principes ciuitatis? nominatim sum appellatus in Bruto.

'Tullius qui libertatem ciuibus stabiliuerat'.

miliens reuocatum est. parumne uidebatur populus Romanus
iudicare id a me et a senatu esse constitutum quod perditi ciues
sublatum per nos criminabantur?

(b) Cicero, De orat. 3.102: numquam agit hunc uersum Roscius eo gestu quo potest...quid ille alter? 'quid petam praesidi

(praesidii *codd.*)? (*v.* 81)' quam leniter, quam remisse, quam non actuose. instat enim: 'o pater o patria o Priami domus (*v.* 87)'. in quo tanta commoueri actio non posset, si esset consumpta superiore motu et exhausta.

(*c*) Cicero, *De orat.* 3.183: est autem paean hic posterior non syllabarum numero sed aurium mensura, quod est acrius iudicium et certius, par fere cretico, qui est ex longa et breui et longa, ut 'quid petam praesidi (praesidii *codd.*) aut exsequar? quoue nunc (*v.* 81)'.

(*d*) Cicero, *De orat.* 3.217: aliud enim uocis genus iracundia sibi sumat, acutum, incitatum, crebro incidens... aliud miseratio ac maeror, flexibile plenum interruptum flebili uoce: ...et illa: 'o pater o patria o Priami domus (*v.* 87)'; et quae sequuntur 'haec omnia uidi (uidet *M*) inflammari, Priamo ui uitam euitari (ui uitam uitari *L*: uitam euitaret *M*) (*vv.* 92–3)'. aliud metus, demissum et haesitans et abiectum...

(*e*) Cicero, *Orat.* 92: translata dico, ut saepe iam, quae per similitudinem ab alia re aut suauitatis aut inopiae causa transferuntur; immutata (*Schütz*: mutata *AL*), in quibus pro uerbo proprio subicitur aliud quod idem significat sumptum ex re aliqua consequenti.

93: quod quamquam transferendo fit, tamen alio modo transtulit cum (*L*: quod *A*) dixit Ennius †arcem et urbem orbas (*L*: arcent urbem orbam *A*) (*v.* 83?) alio modo si pro patria arcem dixisset et horridam Africam terribili tremere tumultu cum dicit pro Afris immutate Africam†

(*f*) Cicero, *Tusc.* 1.85: sit igitur aliquis qui nihil mali habeat, nullum a fortuna uolnus acceperit. Metellus ille honoratis (*V²*: honoratus *X*) quattuor filiis aut (*K*: at *GRV*) quinquaginta Priamus, e (*V²*: *om. X*) quibus septemdecim iusta uxore natis. in utroque eandem habuit fortuna potestatem, sed usa in altero

ANDROMACHA

est. Metellum enim multi filii filiae nepotes neptes in rogum inposuerunt, Priamum tanta progenie orbatum, cum in aram confugisset, hostilis manus interemit. hic si uiuis filiis incolumi regno occidisset 'astante ope barbarica, tectis caelatis laqueatis (*vv.* 89–90)' utrum tandem a bonis an a malis discessisset? tum profecto uideretur a bonis. at certe ei melius euenisset, nec tam flebiliter illa canerentur: 'haec omnia uidi inflammari, Priamo ui uitam euitari, Iouis aram sanguine turpari (*vv.* 92–4)'. quasi uero ista ui (*Petrus Crassus*: uel *codd.*) quicquam tum potuerit ei melius accidere. quodsi ante occidisset, talem (*Dauisius*: tamen *codd.*) euentum omnino amisisset; hoc autem tempore sensum amisit malorum.

(*g*) Cicero, *Tusc.* 1.105: sed plena errorum sunt omnia. trahit Hectorem ad currum religatum Achilles; lacerari eum et sentire, credo, putat. ergo hic ulciscitur, ut quidem sibi uidetur; at illa sicut acerbissimam rem maeret:

uidi, uidere quod me passa aegerrume,   78
Hectorem curru quadriiugo raptarier.

quem Hectorem, aut quam diu ille erit Hector? melius Accius et aliquando sapiens Achilles: 'immo enimuero corpus Priamo reddidi, Hectora (*Nieberding*: Hectorem *codd.*) abstuli'. non igitur Hectora traxisti, sed corpus, quod fuerat Hectoris.

(*h*) Cicero, *Tusc.* 3.44: quaerendum igitur quem ad modum aegritudine priuemus eum qui ita dicat:

'pol mihi fortuna magis nunc defit quam genus.
namque regnum suppetebat mi, ut scias quanto e loco,
quantis opibus, quibus de rebus lapsa fortuna accidat
(*vv.* 338–40)'.

XXVII (*g*) 79 curro GK¹R *et fort.* V¹ (-u *in ras.*)

quid? huic calix mulsi impingendus est, ut plorare desinat, aut aliquid eius modi? ecce tibi ex altera parte ab eodem poeta:

> *ex opibus summis opis egens Hector tuae.* 80

huic subuenire debemus; quaerit enim auxilium.

> *quid petam praesidi aut exequar? quoue nunc* 81
> *auxilio exili aut fugae freta sim?*
> *arce et urbe orba sum. quo accedam? quo applicem?*
> *cui nec arae patriae domi stant, fractae et disiectae iacent,*
> *fana flamma deflagrata, tosti †alii† stant parietes,* 85
> *deformati atque abiete crispa.*

scitis quae sequantur et illa in primis (*Tregder*: illum primis *X*: illud in primis *V*^{c}ς):

> *o pater, o patria, o Priami domus,* 87
> *saeptum altisono cardine templum.*
> *uidi ego te adstante ope barbarica,*
> *tectis caelatis laqueatis,* 90
> *auro ebore instructam regifice.*

45: o poetam egregium. quamquam ab his cantoribus Euphorionis contemnitur. sentit omnia repentina et necopinata esse grauiora. exaggeratis igitur regiis (ς: regis *X*) opibus, quae uidebantur sempiternae fore, quid adiungit?

> *haec omnia uidi inflammari,* 92
> *Priamo ui uitam euitari,*
> *Iouis aram sanguine turpari.*

praeclarum carmen. est enim et rebus et uerbis et modis lugubre. eripiamus huic aegritudinem. quo modo? conlocemus in culcita plumea...

XXVII (*h*) 81 praesidii *X*   82 exilii *X*   fugae ς *Bentley*: fuga *X*   85 alti *M*^{2}ς   89 adstantem (m *eras. in V*) *X*   90 laqueatis *codd.*: lacuatis *Seruius auct. Aen. 1.726*   91 regificem (m *exp. K*^{1}*B*) *X*   94 sanguine *KR*^{c} *codd. Non. p. 181.1*: sanguinem *GR*^{1}*V*

(*i*) Cicero, *Tusc.* 3.53: Karthaginienses multi Romae seruie-
runt, Macedones rege Perse capto; uidi etiam in Peloponneso,
cum essem adulescens, quosdam Corinthios. hi poterant omnes
eadem illa de Andromacha (ς: antromacha *X*) deplorare:
'haec omnia uidi (*v.* 92)'. sed iam (etiam *KR*) decantauerant
fortasse. eo enim erant uoltu, oratione, omni reliquo motu et
statu, ut eos Argiuos aut Sicyonios (sicionios *K*¹*R*) diceres
(dicere *X*: *corr.* *V*ᶜ), magisque me mouerant Corinthi subito
aspectae (aspecta *X*: *corr.* *V*²) parietinae quam ipsos Corinthios,
quorum animis diuturna cogitatio callum uetustatis obduxerat.

XXVIII

(*a*) Cicero, *De orat.* 2.155: '...miror cur philosophiae sicut
Zethus ille Pacuuianus prope bellum indixeris'.

156: 'minime', inquit Antonius; 'ac sic decreui philosophari

XXVII *Plautus, *Bacch.* 933–4 o Troia o patria o Pergamum o
Priame periisti senex | qui misere male mulcabere quadringentis
Philippis aureis; Sallustius, *Iug.* 14.17 nunc uero exul patria domo,
solus atque omnium honestarum rerum egens, quo accedam aut quos
appellem?; Vergilius, *Aen.* 1.483 ter circum Iliacos raptauerat
Hectora muros, 2.241–2 o patria (O PATRIA. uersus Ennianus—
Seruius) o diuom domus Ilium et incluta bello | moenia Dardanidum,
272–5 raptatus bigis ut quondam aterque cruento | puluere perque
pedes traiectus lora tumentis. | ei mihi (EI MIHI. Ennii uersus—
Seruius) qualis erat, quantum mutatus ab illo | Hectore, 499–505 uidi
ipse furentem | caede Neoptolemum geminosque in limine Atridas, |
uidi Hecubam centumque nurus Priamumque per aras | sanguine
foedantem quos ipse sacrauerat ignis. | quinquaginta illi thalami, spes
tanta nepotum, | barbarico postes auro spoliisque superbi | pro-
cubuere; Porcius Latro *ap.* Sen. *Contr.* 2.1.1 uidi ego magni exercitus ducem sine comite fugientem, uidi...limina deserta...nam
quid ex summis opibus ad egestatem deuolutos loquar?; Tacitus,
Ann. 13.15 ille constanter exorsus est carmen quo euolutum eum
sede patria rebusque summis significabatur.

potius, ut Neoptolemus apud Ennium, "paucis; nam omnino (quam omnino *HE²*) haud placet'".

(*b*) Cicero, *Rep.* 1.30: Aelius Sextus...Zethum illum Pacuui nimis inimicum doctrinae esse dicebat; magis eum delectabat Neoptolemus Enni qui se ait philosophari (filosofari *cod.*) uelle set paucis; nam omnino haud placere.

(*c*) Cicero, *Tusc.* 2.1: Neoptolemus quidem apud Ennium philosophari sibi ait necesse esse (est *H*) sed paucis; nam omnino haud placere. ego autem, Brute, necesse mihi quidem esse arbitror philosophari — nam quid possum praesertim nihil agens agere melius? — sed non paucis ut ille...

2: sed tamen in uita occupata atque, ut Neoptolemi tum erat, militari pauca ipsa multum saepe prosunt et ferunt fructus...

(*d*) Gellius 5.15.9: hos alios talis argutae delectabilisque desidiae aculeos cum audiremus uel lectitaremus neque in his scrupulis aut emolumentum aliquod solidum ad rationem uitae pertinens aut finem ullum quaerendi uideremus, Ennianum (ennianum autem *RV*) Neoptolemum probabamus, qui profecto ita ait:

> philosophandum est paucis; nam omnino haud placet. 95

(*e*) Gellius 5.16.5: sed hic aeque (*Petschenig*: eaque *codd.*) non diutius muginandum eiusdemque illius Enniani Neoptolemi, de quo supra scripsimus, consilio utendum est, qui degustandum ex philosophia censet, non in eam ingurgitandum.

(*f*) Apuleius, *Apol.* 13: da igitur ueniam Platoni philosopho uersuum eius de amore ne ego necesse habeam contra sententiam Neoptolemi Enniani pluribus philosophari.

XXIX

Cicero, *Att.* 4.15.6: redii Romam Fontei causa a.d. VII.Id. Quint. veni spectatum (*Graeuius*: spectaculum *codd.*) primum magno et aequabili plausu (sed hoc ne curaris; ego ineptus qui

scripserim); deinde Antiphonti operam. is erat (*Victorius*:
miserat *codd.*) ante manu missus quam productus. ne diutius
pendeas, palmam tulit; sed nihil tam pusillum nihil tam sine
uoce nihil tam — uerum haec tu tecum habeto. in Andromacha tamen maior fuit quam Astyanax (*Victorius*: Astyanax
nam *Cratander*: astya [*uel* astia] nam Δ: astra nam ΠΦ), in
ceteris parem habuit neminem.

XXX

Cicero, *Opt. gen.* 18: huic labori nostro duo genera reprehen-
sionum opponuntur. unum hoc: 'uerum (*uulgo*: uerbum G)
melius Graeci'. a quo quaeratur ecquid (*uulgo*: et quid G)
possint ipsi (*uulgo*: illi G) melius Latine? alterum: 'quid istas
potius legam quam Graecas?' idem (*uulgo*: id est G) Andriam et
Synephebos nec minus Terentium et Caecilium quam Menandrum legunt, nec Andromacham aut Antiopam aut Epigonos
Latinos †recipiunt†, sed tamen Ennium et Pacuuium et
Accium potius quam Euripidem et Sophoclem legunt. quod
igitur est eorum in orationibus e Graeco (*Lambinus*: a greco G)
conuersis fastidium, nullum cum sit in uersibus?

XXXI

Cicero, *Ac.* 2.20: quam multa quae nos fugiunt in cantu exau-
diunt in eo genere exercitati qui primo inflatu tibicinis Antiopam esse aiunt aut Andromacham, cum id nos ne suspicemur
quidem.

XXXII

Cicero, *Diu.* 1.23: sus rostro si humi A litteram inpresserit,
num propterea suspicari poteris Andromacham Enni (Ennii
$A^c V^c$) ab ea posse describi?

XXXIII

Varro, *Ling.* 5.19: omnino †eo magis puto a chao chouũ† et hinc caelum, quoniam, ut dixi, 'hoc circum supraque quod complexu continet terram', cauum caelum. itaque dicit Andromaca Nocti:

> *quae caua caeli* 96
> *signitenentibus conficis bigis.*

et Agamemno: 'in altisono caeli clipeo (vv. 188–9)'; cauum enim clipeum. et Ennius item ad cauationem: 'caeli ingentes fornices'.

XXXIV

Varro, *Ling.* 7.6: templum tribus modis dicitur: ab natura, ab auspicando, a similitudine; natura in caelo, ab auspiciis in terra, a similitudine sub terra. in caelo templum dicitur, ut in Hecuba... in terra, ut in Periboea...sub terra, ut in Andromacha:

> *Acherusia templa alta Orci saluete infera.* 98

XXXV

Varro, *Ling.* 7.82: apud Ennium:

> *Andromachae nomen qui indidit recte indidit.* 99

item...imitari dum uoluit (*Aldus*: uolunt *F*) Euripidem (euripiden *F*) et ponere ἔτυμον, est lapsus. nam Euripides (euripedes *F*) quod Graeca posuit, ἔτυμα sunt aperta. ille ait ideo

---

XXXIV *Trag. inc. *ap.* Cic. *Tusc.* 1.48 quae est anus tam delira quae timeat ista quae uos uidelicet si physica non didicissetis timeretis 'Acherunsia templa alta Orci pallida leti nubila (letio nubila *GK*[1] [b *post* o *add.* *K*[c]]*R*: let//o nubila *V* [leto nubila *B*]) tenebris loca'?
XXXV *Cicero, *Att.* 2.1.5 ego illam odi male consularem. ea est enim seditiosa, ea cum uiro bellum gerit.

XXXIII Andromacha Nocti 'quae *Laetus*: Andromeda Nocti 'quae *Scaliger*: androma noctique *F*
XXXV 99 recte ei indidit *F*

nomen additum Andromachae quod ἀνδρὶ μάχεται (*Aldus*: andromache· quod andromachete *F*). hoc Enni (Ennii *F*) quis potest intellegere in uersu (*Turnebus*: inuersum *F*) significare 'Andromachae nomen qui indidit recte indidit' aut...

XXXVI

Varro, *Ling.* 10.70: †de genere† multi utuntur non modo poetae sed etiam plerique †haec primo† omnes qui soluta oratione loquuntur ⟨* * *⟩ dicebant ut quaestorem praetorem sic Hectorem Nestorem. itaque Ennius ait:

> Hectoris natum de Troiano muro iactari.   100

Accius haec in tragoediis largius a prisca consuetudine mouere coepit et ad formas Graecas uerborum magis reuocare.

XXXVII

Festus, p. 384.16:   ʏssɪ dicebantur
Naeuius: 'odi' inquit
inde aperte dice
times? Ennius in sexto
ntus in occulto mussa
s in Andromacha: *di* 101
on est: nam mussare si
s in Agnorizomene:
'quod potes sile cela oc tege
tace mussa manc'. sᴠᴍ pro eum

XXXVIII

Nonius, p. 76.1: ᴀᴠɢɪꜰɪᴄᴀᴛ, auget. Ennius Andromaca:

> †quid fit seditio tabesne an numerus† *augificat* †suos†.   102

XXXVI 100 iactari *uulgo*: lactari *F*
XXXVII sᴠᴍᴍᴠssɪ, murmuratores. Naevius: 'odi' inquit 'summussos, proinde aperte dice quid sit'. Terentius (*sic*) mussare pro tacere posuit cum ait: 'sile cela occulta tege tace mussa' — *Paulus*
XXXVIII andromaga *L*[1]   102 tabetne *Lipsius*   numeros *ed. princ.*

XXXIX

Nonius, p. 292.7: EXANCLARE etiam significat perpeti. Ennius Andromache aechmaloto:

> quantis cum aerumnis illum exanclaui diem.　　　　　103

XL

(a) Nonius, p. 401.37: SVMMVM, gloriosum, laudabile... Ennius Andromache aechmaloto (andromaca haec malo codd.): 'annos multos longinque (longique codd.) ab domo bellum gerentes summum summa (summam A^4) industria'.

(b) Nonius, p. 515.12: LONGINQVE et LONGITER pro longe. Ennius Andromache aechmaloto:

> annos multos longinque a domo　　　　　104
> bellum gerentes summum summa industria.

XLI

Nonius, p. 504.18: LAVERENT (uulgo: lauere codd.) etiam inde manauit. Ennius Andromaca:

> nam ubi introducta est puerumque ut lauerent locant　　　　　106
> in clipeo.

XLII

Nonius, p. 505.12 SONVNT etiam inde manauit. Ennius Andromache aechmalotide:

> nam neque irati neque blandi quicquam sincere sonunt.　　　　　108

XXXIX Andromache aechmaloto 'quantis Gerlach: Andromache aechmalo-
tidi 'quantis Roth: andromache malo torquantis (torquentis LB^4) codd.　　103
exanclaui eum diem A^4L^2
XL (b) accius andromache ei malo (mala C^4) codd.
XLI 106 puerorumque G　　107 clypeo Aldus: cypeo LBamb.: cipeo HG
XLII andromace ethemapotide codd.　　108 quiquam codd.: corr. L^2

XLIII

Nonius, p. 515.24: RARENTER... Ennius Andromacha:

> sed quasi aut ferrum aut lapis 109
> durat rarenter gemitum †conatur trabem†

XLIV

(a) Servius, Aen. 1.224: ueliuolum duas res significat, et quod uelis uolatur, ut hoc loco, et quod uelis uolat, ut Ennius: 'naues (nauius C) ueliuolas'. qui et proprie dixit.

(b) Macrobius, Sat. 6.5.10: (1: multa quoque epitheta apud Vergilium sunt quae ab ipso ficta creduntur sed et haec a ueteribus tracta monstrabo) despiciens mare ueliuolum (Aen. 1.224) ...Ennius in quarto decimo...idem in Andromache:

> rapit ex alto naues ueliuolas. 111

ANDROMEDA

XLV

Festus, p. 312.7: QVAESO, ut significat idem quod rogo, ita quaesere ponitur ab antiquis pro quaerere, ut est apud Ennium lib. II...et in Cresphonte...et in Andromeda:

> liberum quaesendum causa familiae matrem tuae. 112

XLIII 109 quasi ferrum B^4C^4 110 conatu trahens *Lipsius*
XLIV (b) andromache rapit A: dromachera alpit N: dromachera capit P: dromacera apice T: dromache rapit RF uelicolas F
XLV andromedoa liberum quae sčdm (i.e. secundum) F

XLVI

(*a*) Festus, p. 448.19:
saxa et difficili
ri insuetae, aut
lere. Ennius i̇n An
tita saxo atque host
unde scrupulosam
in se asperi. Corne̩l
IIII: his tum iniectus
et quaedam dubitatio

(*b*) Nonius, p. 169.25: SCABRES pro scabra es (*Quicherat*: scapres pro scabres *codd.*). Ennius Andromeda:

> *scrupeo inuestita saxo atque ostreis* †quam excrabrent†.   113

XLVII

Festus, p. 514.22: VRVAT. Ennius in Andromeda significat circumdat, ab eo sulco, qui fit in urbe condenda uruo aratri, quae fit forma simillima uncini curuatione buris et dentis, cui praefigitur uomer. ait autem:

> *circum sese uruat ad pedes a terra quadringentos* †caput†.   114

XLVIII

Nonius, p. 20.18: CORPORARE est interficere et quasi corpus solum sine anima relinquere. Ennius Andromeda:

> *corpus contemplatur unde corporaret uulnere.*   115

XLVI (*a*) SCRVPI dicuntur aspera saxa et difficilia attrectatu; unde scrupulosam rem dicimus, quae aliquid in se habet asperi — *Paulus*
XLVI (*b*) 113 screpeo *L*   squamae scabrent *Mercerus*

XLIX

(*a*) Nonius, p. 165.8: †reciproca animum in quam odiose†
Ennius Andromeda: 'rursus (riscus *B^A*) prorsus reciprocat
fluctus (fructus *codd.*) feram'.

(*b*) Nonius, p. 384.32: RVRSVS, retro...Ennius Andromeda:

rursus prorsus reciprocat fluctus †feram†.   116

L

Nonius, p. 183.18: VISCERATIM, per uiscera (per uiscera *C^A D^A*:
om. L). Ennius Andromeda:

alia fluctus differt dissupat   117
uisceratim membra; maria salsa spumant sanguine.

LI

Priscianus, *Gramm.* II 293.5: inueniuntur tamen quaedam
pauca feminini generis, quae ex masculinis transfigurantur non
habentibus neutra, quae et animalium sunt demonstratiua,
naturaliter diuisum genus habentia, quae differentiae causa
ablatiuo singulari 'bus' assumentia faciunt datiuum et ablati-
uum pluralem, quod nulla alia habet declinatio in 'bus' termi-
nans supra dictos casus, ut 'a' longam in eis paenultimam habeat,
ut 'his natabus', 'filiabus', 'deabus', 'equabus', 'mulabus',
'libertabus', 'asinabus'... et 'filiis' tamen in eodem genere
dictum est. Ennius in Andromeda:

filiis propter te obiecta sum innocens Nerei.   119

[id est natis pro natabus] id est Nerei filiabus.

LI andromeada *Rr*: andromedia *GK*

ATHAMAS

LII

Charisius, p. 314.9 EVHOE...Ennius in Athamante:

> *his erat in ore Bromius, his Bacchus pater,* 120
> *illis Lyaeus uitis inuentor sacrae.*
> *tum pariter* †euhan euhium†
> *ignotus iuuenum coetus alterna uice*
> *inibat alacris Bacchico insultans modo.*

CRESPHONTES

LIII

Rhetor incertus, *Her.* 2.38: utuntur igitur studiosi (studiose *M*) in confirmanda ratione duplici conclusione hoc modo:

> *iniuria abs te adficior indigna pater.* 125
> *nam si inprobum esse Cresphontem existimas,*
> *cur me huic locabas nuptiis? sin est probus,*
> *cur talem inuitam inuitum cogis linquere?*

quae hoc modo concludentur, aut ex contrario conuertentur aut ex simplici parte reprehendentur (reprehendetur *M*). ex contrario (contraria *M*) hoc modo:

> *nulla te indigna nata adficio iniuria.* 129
> *si probus est, collocaui. sin est inprobus,*
> *diuortio te liberabo incommodis.*

LII 120 his erat *Fabricius*: is erat *N*   121 illis Lyaeus uitis *n*[1]: illis ✳ uitis *n*: illis lisaeus uitis *N*   122 tum pariter euhan ⟨euhoe euhoe⟩ euhium *Fabricius*: tum pariter euchoe neucheum *Cauchii exc.*   123 iuuenem *Cauchii exc.*   124 insultans *ed. princ.*: insultas *N*

LIII 126 chresponthe *H*: chrespontem *BC*: chresponthem *PΠ*: threspontem *E* existimabas *bd*   127 sin est *EC*: sine si *M*   128 linquere *ΠBC*: liquere *M*: relinquere *E*   129 nuta *M*   130 est locaui sin (sin autem *bl*) *E*: es collocabisin *M*: est te locaui *Oudendorp*   131 te liberabo *Omnibonus*: libero te *M*: liberabo te *E*

ex simplici parte reprehendetur si (sed *M*) ex duplici conclusione alterutra pars diluitur, hoc modo:

'nam si inprobum esse Cresphontem (esse chrespontem *M*:
  threspontem esse *E*) existimas (existimabas *bd*),
cur me huic (huius *Cd*: his *bl*) locabas nuptiis? ::duxi
  probum.
erraui. post cognoui et fugio (fugio nunc *E*) cognitum'.

ergo reprehensio huiusmodi conclusionis duplex est; auctior
(acutior *CBE*) illa superior, facilior haec posterior ad cogi-
tandum.

LIV

Festus, p. 312.7: QVAESO, ut significat idem quod rogo, ita
quaesere ponitur ab antiquis pro quaerere, ut est apud Ennium
lib. II...et in Cresphonte:

ducit me uxorem liberorum sibi quaesendum gratia.   132

LV

Festus, p. 334.8: REDHOSTIRE, referre gratiam...nam et hostire (hostiae *F*) pro aequare posuerunt. Ennius in Cresphonte:

audi atque auditis hostimentum adiungito.   133

LVI

Gellius 7.16.8: sed neque solus Catullus ita isto uerbo (*i.e.*
'*deprecor*'; *92.3*) usus est. pleni sunt adeo libri similis in hoc
uerbo significationis, ex quibus unum ct alterum quae sub-
petierant apposui.

9: Q. Ennius in Erectheo non longe secus dixit quam
Catullus...signat abigo et amolior uel prece adhibita uel quo
alio modo.

10: item Ennius in Cresphonte:

ego meae cum uitae parcam, letum inimico deprecer.   134

LIV chresponte *F*
LV chresponte *F*   133 audi *Scaliger*: audis *F*
LVI 134 cum meae *codd.*: *transp. Bothe*

LVII

Nonius, p. 144.12: NITIDANT, abluunt (*F³mg.*: albunt *F³*:
aluunt *L¹C⁴D⁴*.); dictum a nitore. Ennius Cresphonte:

†opie†   135

eam secum aduocant, eunt ad fontem, nitidant corpora.

LVIII

Nonius, p. 471.2: SORTIRENT pro sortirentur...MODERANT pro
moderantur...SORTIVNT. Ennius Cresphonte:

an inter se sortiunt urbem atque agros.   137

LIX

Macrobius, *Sat.* 6.2.21 (cf. fr. xxv): 'nec te tua funera mater |
produxi pressiue oculos aut uulnera laui (Vergilius, *Aen.* 9.486–
7)'. Ennius in Cresphonte:

neque terram inicere neque cruenta conuestire corpora   138
mihi licuit neque miserae lauere lacrimae salsum sanguinem.

ERECTHEVS

LX

Festus, p. 158.10:

       aerumnas. NEMINIS
       et quis diceret cum sit
       uitio creatis neminisque
       us Erectheo: *lapideo sunt* 140
       corde multi quos non miseret neminis. NEMO

LVII cresponte *codd.*   136 ad fortem *codd.*: *corr.* F²
LVIII cresfonte *codd.*   137 inter sese *Vossius*
LIX cresiphonte *P*: cressiphonte *NRFA*   138 conuertire *T*: conuertere *A*
139 mihi corpora *codd.*: *transp. Bothe*
LX NEMINIS genitiuo casu Cato (*sic*) usus est, cum dixit: 'sunt multi corde quos
non miseret neminis' — *Paulus*

LXI

Gellius 7.16.9: Q. Ennius in Erectheo non longe secus dixit quam Catullus (cf. fr. LVI):

†qui† *nunc*

inquit

> *aerumna mea libertatem paro,*   141
> *quibus seruitutem mea miseria deprecor.*

LXII

Macrobius, *Sat.* 6.4.6 (1: ego conabor ostendere hunc studio-sissimum uatem et de singulis uerbis ueterum aptissime iudicasse et inseruisse electa operi suo uerba quae nobis noua uideri facit incuria uetustatis): 'tum ferreus hastis | horret ager (Vergilius, *Aen.* 11.601–2)'. HORRET mire se habet. sed et Ennius in quarto decimo...et in Erectheo:

> *arma* †arrigunt† *horrescunt tela.*   143

EVMENIDES

LXIII

Nonius, p. 292.18: EXANCLARE, effundere. Ennius Eumeni-dibus:

> *nisi patrem materno sanguine exanclando ulciscerem.*   144

LXI erictheo *V*: eripiteo (eripite o *B⁴*) *codd. Non. p. 290.18*   141 cui *codd. Non.* erumnam ea (erumnam et a *L*) *codd. Non.*: erumpna ea *V* libertate para *codd. Non.*   142 meam miseriam (meam miseria *A⁴*: mea miseriar *E*) *codd. Non.*
LXII erectheo *RFA*: erecteo *NP*: erictheo *T*   143 horrigunt *N*: argunt *A*

LXIV

Nonius, p. 306.32: FACESSERE significat recedere. Ennius Eumenidibus:

> *dico uicisse Orestem. uos ab hoc facessite.*   145

LXV

Nonius, p. 474.35: OPINO pro opinor...Ennius Eumenidibus:

> *tacere opino esse optumum et pro uiribus*   146
> *sapere, atque fabulari tute noueris.*

LXVI

Nonius, p. 505.16: EXPEDIBO pro expediam...Ennius Eumenidibus:

> *id ego aecum ac iustum fecisse expedibo atque eloquar.*   148

HECTORIS LYTRA

LXVII

Festus, p. 334.8: REDHOSTIRE, referre gratiam...nam et hostire pro aequare posuerunt. Ennius in Cresphonte...et in Hectoris lytris:

> *quae mea comminus machaera atque hasta* †hospius manu†.   149

LXIV 145 edico *L. Mueller*: dico ego *Scaliger* Orestem *ed. princ.*: oresten *codd.* nuossab (nuosab *B*) A^A facessit (facessi L^1) *codd.*: *corr. Vrbin. 307*
LXV 147 atquea A^A tate C^A
LXVI 148 ac iustum fecisse *Jocelyn*: ac ius fuisse *Gulielmius*: accius fecisse *codd.*
LXVII innectoris lyrisque mea *F*: *corr. Vrsinus* 149 hostibis eminus *Timpanaro*: hostiuit e manu *Scaliger*

LXVIII

Nonius, p. 111.7: FVAM, sim uel fiam...Ennius Hectoris lytris:

at ego omnipotens 150
ted exposco ut hoc consilium Achiuis auxilio fuat.

LXIX

Nonius, p. 222.25: SPECVS genere masculino...Ennius Lytris:

inferum uastos specus. 152

LXX

Nonius, p. 355.3: OCCVPARE est proprie praeuenire...Ennius Hectoris lytris:

Hector †ei summa† *armatos educit foras* 153
castrisque castra ultro iam ferre occupat.

LXXI

Nonius, p. 399.8: SPERNERE rursum segregare. Ennius Hectoris lytris:

melius est uirtute ius: nam saepe uirtutem mali 155
nanciscuntur; ius atque aecum se a malis spernit procul.

LXXII

Nonius, p. 407.24: TENACIA est perscuerantia et duritia. Ennius Hectoris lytris:

†ducet quadrupedum iugo inuitam† 157
doma infrena et iunge ualida quorum tenacia infrenari minis.

LXVIII haectoris lytris (listris B^4) *codd.* 150 a ego *L* 151 ted *Bothe*: te *codd.* auxilio *Vossius*: auxilii *codd.*
LXX haectoris listris *codd.* 153 ui summa *Mercerus* foras *Iunius*: in foras *codd.* 154 conferre *Vossius*
LXXI haectoris lystris (listris *G*: lytris L^1) *codd.* 155 ius *Bentinus*: eius *codd.* 156 nanciscu tur *L*: nascuntur *G* atque cum *L*
LXXII haectoris listris (lystris *Bamb.*) *codd.* 158 iunge *Lipsius*: iuge *codd.*

LXXIII

Nonius, p. 467.23: VAGAS pro uagaris...Ennius Hectoris lytris:

constitit credo Scamander, arbores uento uacant.   159

LXXIV

Nonius, p. 469.25: CVNCTANT pro cunctantur...Ennius... idem Hectoris lytris:

qui cupiant dare arma Achilli †ut ipse† *cunctent.*   160

LXXV

Nonius, p. 472.21: CONMISERESCIMVS...Ennius Hectoris lytris:

                 †ser uos et uostrum†   161
imperium et fidem Myrmidonum, uigiles, conmiserescite.

LXXVI

Nonius, p. 489.29: TVMVLTI. Ennius Hectoris lytris:

quid hoc hic clamoris, quid tumulti est? nomen qui usurpat meum? 163

LXXVII

Nonius, p. 490.6: STREPITI pro strepitus. Ennius Hectoris lytris:

quid in castris strepiti est?   164

LXXIII hectoris (haectoris *HBamb.*) lystris (litris *Bamb.*) *codd.*   159 arboris *codd.* uacant *Columna*: uagant *codd.*
LXXIV hectoris (haectoris *HBamb.*) lytris (lystris *H*²) *codd.*   160 ut ipsi *Iunius* cunctet *A*⁴
LXXV ectoris lystris (haectori listris *Bamb.*) *codd.*   161 ser uos et uostrum (useruos ũrorũ *Bamb.*) *codd.*: per uos et nostrum *Palmerius*
LXXVI haectoris lystris (litris *H*¹: listris *H*²) *codd.*   163 qui tumulti *C*⁴
LXXVII haectoris lystris (lytris *Bamb.*) *codd.* 164 strepitus *G*

LXXVIII

Nonius, p. 504.30 SONIT pro sonat... Ennius Hectoris lytris:

aes sonit, franguntur hastae, terra sudat sanguine.   165

LXXIX

Nonius, p. 510.32: SAEVITER pro saeue... Ennius Hectoris lytris:

saeuiter fortuna ferro cernunt de uictoria.   166

LXXX

Nonius, p. 518.3: DEREPENTE... Ennius Hectoris lytris:

ecce autem caligo oborta est, omnem prospectum abstulit.   167
derepente contulit sese in pedes.

LXXXI

Diomedes, *Gramm.* I 345.3: similiter halare et halitare (alare et alitare *A*: alere et alitare *B*: halere et halitare *M*). Ennius in Lytris:

sublime iter ut quadrupedantes flammam halitantes.   169

LXXXII

Diomedes, *Gramm.* I 387.21: est tertium his (*i.e. odi et memini*) simile, ut quidam putant — nec enim defuerunt qui hoc uerbum praesentis temporis esse dicerent —, noui nouisti nouit; et id simile est instanti et perfecto, ut memini... apud ueteres

---

LXXVIII haectoris lystris *codd.*   165 aes sonit *Nic. Faber*: et sonit *codd.*
LXXIX haectoris lystris *codd.*
LXXX hectoris (haectoris *HBamb.*) lystris *codd.*   167 aborta *LA⁴B⁴*   168 se sese *G*   in pede *C⁴*
LXXXI lustris *codd.*   169 sublime iter ut *B*: lublime iter *A*: lublime item *M* quadrupedantis *B*   alitantes *B*

pluraliter huius uerbi instans colligitur, cum nomus dicunt pro
eo quod est nouimus, ita ut Ennius in Lytris:

> *nos quiescere aequum est; nomus ambo Vlixem.* 170

HECVBA

LXXXIII

Varro, *Ling.* 7.6: templum tribus modis dicitur: ab natura, ab
auspicando, a similitudine; natura in caelo, ab auspiciis in terra, a
similitudine sub terra. in caelo templum dicitur, ut in Hecuba:

> *o magna templa caelitum commixta stellis splendidis.* 171

in terra, ut in Periboea...sub terra, ut in Andromacha...

LXXXIV

Gellius 11.4.1: Euripidis uersus sunt in Hecuba uerbis,
sententia, breuitate insignes inlustresque; Hecuba est ad Vlixen
dicens (293–5):

2:
> τὸ δ' ἀξίωμα, κἂν κακῶς (κακὸς *codd. Gell.*) λέγῃ, τὸ σὸν
> νικᾷ (πείσει, πείθει *codd. Eur.*)· λόγος γὰρ ἔκ τ' ἀδοξούντων
> ἰὼν
> κἀκ τῶν δοκούντων αὑτὸς (*Porson*: αὐτὸς *codd.*) οὐ ταὐτὸν
> σθένει.

3: hos uersus Q. Ennius, cum eam tragoediam uerteret, non
sane incommode aemulatus est. uersus totidem Enniani hi sunt:

> *haec tu etsi peruerse dices, facile Achiuos flexeris:* 172
> *nam cum opulenti locuntur pariter atque ignobiles,*
> *eadem dicta eademque oratio aequa non aeque ualet.*

LXXXII lustris *codd.*
LXXXIII inecuba F   171 caelitum *Scioppius*: caeli tum F
LXXXIV 172 haec tametsi X   173 namque opulenti cum *Scaliger*: nam
opulenti quum *Porson*   pariter et Π   174 dicta atque eadem Π

4: bene, sicuti dixi, Ennius; sed ignobiles tamen et opulenti ἀντὶ ἀδοξούντων καὶ δοκούντων satisfacere sententiae non uidentur; nam neque omnes ignobiles ἀδοξοῦσι, neque omnes opulenti εὐδοξοῦσιν.

LXXXV

Nonius, p. 115.28: GVTTATIM...Ennius Hecuba:

†uide hinc meae inquam† *lacrumae guttatim cadunt.*　　175

LXXXVI

Nonius, p. 116.31: GRATVLARI, gratias agere. Ennius Hecuba:

Iuppiter tibi summe tandem male re gesta gratulor.　　176

LXXXVII

Nonius, p. 153.22: PERBITERE, perire...Ennius Hecuba:

set numquam scripstis quis parentem aut hospitem　　177
necasset †quos quis† *cruciatu perbiteret.*

LXXXVIII

Nonius, p. 223.24: SALVM neutri generis est uulgari consuetudine. masculini. Ennius Hecuba:

undantem salum.　　179

LXXXIX

(a) Nonius, p. 224.6: SANGVIS masculino genere in consuetudine habetur...neutro. Ennius Hecuba:

heu me miseram. interii. pergunt lauere sanguen sanguine.　　180

LXXXV haecuba *codd.*　175 uide hunc meae in quem *Mercerus*: uide hanc meae in quam *Vossius*　lacrumae *B⁴*: lacrimae *F³*: meae *L*
LXXXVI 176 iupiter *codd.*: corr. *L²*
LXXXVII 177 scripstis *Vossius*: scripsistis *codd.*　qui *Iunius*　178 necasset quo quis cruciatu *Iunius*: necassat quos quis cruciatur *codd.*
LXXXIX (a) hecuba heu *B⁴*: hecubae heu *L¹*: hecuba eheu *F³*　180 labere *codd.*

(*b*) Nonius, p. 466.18: LAVARE, cum sit eluere et emaculare et aquis sordida quaeque purgare, uetustatis auctoritas posuit etiam polluere... Ennius Hecuba (heucuba *LBamb.*: ecuba *G*): 'heu me miseram (miserum *C⁴*). interii. pergunt lauere sanguen sanguine (sanguen *om. L¹*)'.

(*c*) Nonius, p. 503.38: LAVIT pro lauat...LAVERE inde tractum est...Ennius...idem Hecuba: 'heu me miserum. interii. pergunt lauere (labere *codd.*) sanguinem (*LA⁴*: sanguen sanguinem *B⁴C⁴*)'.

XC

Nonius, p. 342.23: MODICVM in consuetudine pausillum uolumus significare; modicum ueteres moderatum et cum modo (commodo *A⁴*: commodum *LD⁴*) dici uolunt...Ennius Hecuba:

> quae tibi in concubio uerecunde et modice morem gerit. 181

XCI

Nonius, p. 474.32: MISERETE. Ennius Hecuba:

> miserete †manus† date ferrum qui me anima priuem. 182

XCII

(*a*) Nonius, p. 494.3: PAVPERIES pro paupertate. Ennius Hecuba: 'senex sum: utinam moriar mortem oppetam priusquam eueniat quod in pauperie mea (pauperie *D⁴*: pauperiem *C⁴*) senex grauiter gemam'.

(*b*) Nonius, p. 507.19: EVENAT pro eueniat. Ennius Hecuba:

> senex sum: utinam mortem obpetam priusquam euenat 183
> quod in pauperie mea senex grauiter gemam.

XC haecuba *L*: heccuba *Gen.H*   181 in cubio *A⁴D⁴*
XCI ecuba *codd.*

IPHIGENIA

XCIII

Rhetor incertus, *Her.* 3.34: cum uerborum similitudines imaginibus exprimere uolemus, plus negoti suscipiemus et magis ingenium nostrum exercebimus. id nos hoc modo facere oportebit. 'iam domum ultionem (domu ultionem *l*: domui ultionem *C*: domi ultionem *HPΠBC²l²bdp*: domum itionem *p m. 2, librarius cod. Bernensis 469 in marg., Victorius*) reges Atridae parant'. in loco †constituere† (*PΠB*: construere *H*: oportet constituere *bl*: constituere oportet *Cd*) manus ad caelum tollentem Domitium cum a Regibus Marciis loris caedatur: hoc erit 'iam domum ultionem (domū ultionem *l*: domū ultiones *M*: domi ultionem *bd*) reges'. in altero loco Aesopum et Cimbrum subornari, ut agant (*W. Kroll*: ut ad *M*: ut uel uagantem *E*) Iphigeniam (ephigeniam *codd.*), in Agamemnonem et (*PΠB*: in agamen non emit *H*: in agamen nomen et *C*: *om. E*) Menelaum (*om. E*): hoc erit 'Atridae parant'. hoc modo omnia uerba erunt (*CE*: erant *M*) expressa.

XCIV

Cicero, *Tusc.* 1.116: clarae uero mortes pro patria oppetitae non solum gloriosae rhetoribus sed etiam beatae uideri solent... Menoeceus non praetermittitur qui item oraculo edito largitus est patriae suum sanguinem. Iphigenia (⟨nam⟩ Iphigenia *Vahlen*) Aulide duci se immolandam iubet ut hostium (sanguis *superscriptum habet V*) eliciatur suo.

XCV

(*a*) Cicero, *Rep.* 1.30: in ipsius paterno genere fuit noster ille amicus dignus huic ad imitandum, 'egregie cordatus homo, catus Aelius Sextus', qui egregie cordatus et catus fuit et ab

Ennio dictus est, non quod ea quaerebat quae numquam inueniret, sed quod ea respondebat quae eos qui quaesissent et cura et negotio soluerent, cuique contra Galli studia disputanti in ore semper erat ille (*utrum* ᴀ *in* ε *an* ε *in* ᴀ *correcta sit, diiudicare non potuit Ziegler*) de Iphigenia (ifigenia *cod.*) Achilles:

> *astrologorum signa in caelo quid sit obseruationis?*   185
> *cum Capra aut Nepa aut exoritur nomen aliquod beluarum,*
> *quod est ante pedes nemo spectat, caeli scrutantur plagas.*

(*b*) Cicero, *Diu.* 2.30: Democritus tamen non inscite nugatur, ut physicus, quo genere nihil est adrogantius. 'quod est ante pedes nemo spectat, caeli scrutantur plagas'. uerum is tamen habitu extorum et colore declarari censet haec dumtaxat: pabuli genus et earum rerum quas terra procreet uel ubertatem uel tenuitatem; salubritatem etiam aut pestilentiam extis significari putat.

(*c*) Seneca, *Apocol.* 8.2: si mehercules a Saturno petisset hoc beneficium, cuius mensem toto anno celebrauit, Saturnalicius (*Bücheler*: saturnaliaeius *codd.*) princeps, non tulisset illud, nedum ab Ioue, quem (*Gronouius*: illum deum abiouem [abioue *VL*] qui *codd.*), quantum quidem in illo fuit, damnauit incesti...

     3: ...hic nobis curua corriget (*Sonntag*: corrigit *codd.*)? quid in cubiculo suo faciat nescit (*Bücheler*: nescio *codd.*), et iam caeli scrutatur plagas.

(*d*) Nonius, p. 145.12: NEPAM quidam cancrum putant ad illud Plauti (*Cas.* 443) 'retrouorsum cedam: imitabor nepam (nepa *C*ᴬ*D*ᴬ)' et illud aliud 'aut cum nepa †esset†'. dubium in utroque. nam uere nepa scorpius dicitur.

(*e*) Donatus, Ter. *Ad.* 386 (386–8 istuc est sapere, non quod ante pedes modost | uidere sed etiam illa quae futura sunt | prospicere): NON QVOD ANTE PEDES MODO EST VIDERE. hoc

sumpsit poeta de illo in (in *V*: *om. C*) †syrum† (Syrium
Schoell: physicum *Lindenbrog*) peruulgato ancillae dicto: 'quod
ante pedes est non uident, caeli scrutantur (uidet caeli scrutatur
V) plagas'.

XCVI

(*a*) Varro, *Ling.* 5.19: omnino †eo magis puto a chao chouū†
et hinc caelum, quoniam, ut dixi, 'hoc circum supraque quod
complexa continet terram', cauum caelum. itaque dicit
Andromacha nocti (*uide fr. XXXIII*)...et Agamemno: 'in
altisono caeli clipeo'. cauum enim clipeum. et Ennius item ad
cauationem: 'caeli ingentes fornices (*v.* 319)'.

(*b*) Varro, *Ling.* 7.73:

> *quid noctis uidetur? in altisono*   188
> *caeli clipeo temo superat*
> ⟨*plaustri*⟩ *stellas sublimum agens*
> *etiam atque etiam noctis iter.*

hic multam noctem ostendere uolt a temonis motu; sed temo
unde et cur dicatur latet. arbitror antiquos rusticos primum
notasse quaedam in caelo signa, quae praeter alia erant insignia
atque ad aliquem usum †culturae† tempus designandum
conuenire animaduertebantur.

XCV *Cicero, *Tusc.* 5.114 et cum alii saepe quod ante pedes esset
non uiderent, ille (*FBV^{rec et b}*: illa *X*) in (5: *om. XF*) infinitatem
omnem peregrinabatur, ut nulla in extremitate consisteret, *Nat.
deor.* 3.40 singulas enim stellas numeras deos eosque (easque *P*) aut
beluarum nomine appellas ut Capram, ut Nepam (*cod. Vrsini*: lupam
AVB), ut Taurum, ut Leonem, aut rerum inanimarum, ut Argo, ut
Aram, ut Coronam; Poeta incertus, *Aetna* 254–6 nam quae mortali
spes est, quae amentia maior, | in Iouis errantem regno perquirere
diuos, | tantum opus ante pedes transire ac perdere segnem (*Schrader*:
segne est *G*: segnes *x*); ex Cicerone Minucius Felix 12.7, Augustinus,
Conf. 10.16.25, Ambrosius, *Noë* 7.17, Paulinus Nolanus, *Epist.* 12.5.
XCVI (*b*) 190 ⟨plaustri⟩ stellas *Jocelyn* sublimum agens *Jocelyn*: sublimis
agens *Turnebus*: sublime agens *F*

74: eius signa sunt quod has septem stellas Graeci ut Homerus uocant ἅμαξαν et propinquum eius signum βοώτην (bootem signum F), nostri eas septem stellas †boues et temonem et prope eas axem† triones enim et boues appellantur a bubulcis etiam nunc cum arant terram...

75: temo dictus a tenendo: is enim continet iugum. et plaustrum appellatum a parte totum, ut multa. possunt triones dicti, vii quod ita sitae stellae, ut ternae trigona faciant †aliquod†

(c) Festus, p. 454.37:
septem stellae appell
bus iunctis quos trio
appellent quod iunç
quasi terrionem
quod id astrum Graec
partem quandam
Ennius: 'superat
et physici eum summ
conten...temp
aiunt, quod ita sunt
ut ternae proximae
trigona

(d) Apuleius, Socr. 2: suspicientes in hoc perfectissimo mundi, ut ait Ennius, clipeo miris fulgoribus uariata caelamina.

XCVII

Festus, p. 218.21: OB praepositione antiquos usos esse pro ad testis est Ennius, cum ait lib. xiv...et in Iphigenia:

> Acherontem obibo ubi Mortis thesauri obiacent. 192

eiusdem autem generis esse ait obferre, obtulit, obcurrit, oblatus, obiectus. mihi non satis persuadet.

XCVII ephigenia W: hiphigenia X   192 obibo ed. princ.: adibo W: adhibo
X   obiacent X: adiacent W

XCVIII

(*a*) Festus, p. 292.7: PEDVM est quidem baculum incuruum quo pastores utuntur ad conprehendendas oues aut capras; a pedibus. cuius meminit etiam Vergilius in Bucolicis, cum ait (5.88): 'at tu sume pedum'. sed in eo uersu, qui est in Iphigenia Enni:

> *procede: gradum proferre pedum,*
> *nitere, cessas o fide?*

193

id ipsum baculum (*Vrsinus*: iaculum *F*) significari cum ait Verrius, mirari satis non possum, cum sit ordo talis, et per eum significatio aperta: gradum proferre pedum cessas nitere.

(*b*) Schol. Veronensis, Verg. *Ecl.* 5.88: pedum autem est baculum recuruum quo pastores utuntur * | aut adminiculum pedum sit, ut ait Ennius in Iphigenia (ifigenia): 'gradum proferre pedum nitere cessas o fide' * * | pastores pedes ouium (*Keil*: bouium) retrahere soleant.

XCIX

Gellius 19.10.4: ...cumque architectus dixisset necessaria uideri esse sestertia ferme trecenta, unus ex amicis Frontonis: 'et praeter propter' inquit 'alia quinquaginta'...

6: 'non meum' inquit 'hoc uerbum est, sed multorum hominum, quos loquentis id audias;

7: quid autem id uerbum significet, non ex me, sed ex grammatico quaerundum est'...

11: atque ibi Iulius Celsinus admonuit in tragoedia quoque Enni, quae Iphigenia inscripta est, id ipsum, de quo quaerebatur, scriptum esse et a grammaticis contaminari magis solitum quam enarrari.

XCVIII (*a*) iphigeniae *F*   194 o fide *om. F et fortasse Festus*

12: quocirca statim proferri Iphigeniam Q. Enni iubet. in eius tragoediae choro inscriptos esse hos uersus legimus:

> *otio qui nescit uti* 195
> *plus negoti habet quam cum est negotium in negotio.*
> *nam cui quod agat institutum est* †*in illis*† *negotium,*
> *id agit, ⟨id⟩ studet, ibi mentem atque animum delectat suum;*
> †*otioso initio*† *animus nescit quid uelit.*
> *hoc idem est: em neque domi nunc nos nec militiae sumus.* 200
> *imus huc, hinc illuc; cum illuc uentum est, ire illinc lubet.*
> *incerte errat animus, praeter propter uitam uiuitur.*

13: ... 'audistine', inquit, 'magister optime, Ennium tuum dixisse praeter propter et cum sententia quidem tali quali seuerissimae philosophorum esse obiurgationes solent? petimus igitur, dicas, quoniam de Enniano iam uerbo quaeritur, qui (*uulgo*: quid *codd.*) sit remotus (*Hosius*: motus *codd.*) huiusce uersus sensus: "incerte errat animus praeter propter uitam uiuitur"'.

C

Iulius Rufinianus, *Rhet.* 11, p. 41.28: ἀγανάκτησις, indignatio, quae fit maxime pronuntiatione. Ennius in Iphigenia:

> *Menelaus me obiurgat; id meis rebus regimen restitat.* 203

CI

Iulius Rufinianus, *Rhet.* 37, p. 47.16: σύγκρισις siue ἀντίθεσις, comparatio rerum atque personarum inter se contrariarum, ut

> *ego proiector quod tu peccas. tu* †*delinquas*† *ego arguor.* 204
> *pro malefactis Helena redeat, uirgo pereat innocens?*
> *tua reconcilietur uxor, mea necetur filia?*

XCIX 196 negotii *codd.*   197 in illis δ: in illo γ   negotio ΠΧ   198 ⟨id⟩ studet *Ribbeck*   199 otioso in otio *Lipsius*   200 nec *uulgo*: de *codd.*   201 hunc δ   hinc illinc Z: illuc hinc Q   ire illuc Q   lubet *Beroaldus*: iubet *codd.*   202 uita *Salmasius*
C 203 restitat *Bentley*: restat *ed. Basil.*
CI 204 delinquis R. *Stephanus*   206 necetur filia *Columna*: negetur filia mea *ed. Basil.*

CII

Servius auctus, *Aen.* 1.52: sane uasto pro desolato ueteres ponebant. Ennius Iphigenia:

> quae nunc abs te uiduae et uastae uirgines sunt.   207

ponebant et pro magno. Clodius Commentariorum: 'uasta inania magna'.

MEDEA EXVL; MEDEA

CIII

(*a*) Rhetor incertus, *Her.* 2.34: item uitiosa expositio quae nimium longe repetitur...hic id, quod extremum dictum est, satis fuit exponere, ne Ennium et ceteros poetas imitemur, quibus hoc modo loqui concessum est:

> utinam ne in nemore Pelio securibus   208
> caesa accidisset abiegna ad terram trabes,
> neue inde nauis inchoandi exordium   210
> cepisset, quae nunc nominatur nomine
> Argo, quia Argiui in ea delecti uiri
> uecti petebant pellem inauratam arietis
> Colchis, imperio regis Peliae, per dolum.
> nam numquam era errans mea domo efferret pedem   215
> Medea animo aegro amore saeuo saucia.

CIII (*a*) 208 utinam *CE*: uti iam *M*   209 caesa accidisset abiegna *scripsit Ennius: fortasse errauit rhetor*: caesae *codd.*   accidissent *B*Π: ///// cidissent *P*[1]: accedissent *H*: cecidissent *P²CE*   abiegnae *EB*Π*CP²*: ad ignē *H*: abignę *P*[1] 210 nauis *E*: naues *M*   inchoandi *b*: inchoandas *H*: inchoansas *P*[1]: inchoans Π: inchoanda *B*: inchoandae *CP²d*: inchoandum *l*   211 cepisset *M*: coepisset *bdH²*Π*C*: caepisset *Bl*   212 argu *M*   qui (qua *PB*) argiui in eadem lecti uiri *M*: qua argiui delecti uiri *E*   214 pelire *M*   215 nam (utinam *C*) numquam era (hera *C*) errans mea domo efferret pedem *BC*: nam numquam era mea errans medea domo efferret pedem *d*: nam numquam hera errans mea medea efferret pedem (pellem *b*) domo *bl*: nam numquam errans mea efferret pedem *M*   216 *non habent codices rhetoris*: medea egro amore saucia *in cod. P margine m. 2 additum*

nam hic satis erat dicere, si id modo quod satis esset curarent
(curassent *E*) poetae: 'utinam ne era errans (hera errans *CBE*:
erra ueras *H*: erra erra errans *P*: trans Π) mea domo efferret
pedem (*M*: mea efferret pedem domo *E*) Medea (Medeas
*HP*¹) animo (*b*: animū *d*: homo *H*: homodo *P*: *om*. Π*BCl*)
aegro (egro *b*) amore saeuo (amores reuo *M*: amore *BE*: *om*. Π)
saucia'.

(*b*) Cicero, *Inu.* 1.91: remotum est quod ultra quam satis est
petitur...huiusmodi est illa quoque conquestio: 'utinam ne in
nemore Pelio securibus caesae accidissent (*H*³: accedissent *M*:
concidissent *S*²*i*: cecidissent *J*) abiegnae (*P*³ *in marg.*: *om. C*) ad
terram trabes (*vv.* 208–9)'. longius enim repetita est quam res
postulabat.

(*c*) Cicero, *Cael.* 18: ...conduxit in Palatio non magno domum. quo loco possum dicere id quod uir clarissimus, M.
Crassus, cum de aduentu regis Ptolemaei quereretur, paulo
ante dixit: 'utinam ne in nemore Pelio (peleo *P*) (*v.* 208) —'
ac longius mihi quidem (*V*: quidem mihi Ππ) contexere hoc
carmen liceret: 'nam numquam era (eram *GE*) errans (*v.* 215)'
hanc molestiam nobis exhiberet 'Medea (mede *P*) animo aegro
(aegra *H*) amore saeuo saucia (*v.* 216)'. sic enim, iudices,
reperietis quod, cum ad id loci uenero, ostendam, hanc
Palatinam Medeam eamque migrationem huic (*Kayser*:
migrationemque huic *codd*.) adulescenti causam siue malorum
omnium siue potius sermonum fuisse.

(*d*) Cicero, *Fin.* 1.4: in quibus hoc primum est in quo admirer,
cur in grauissimis rebus non delectet eos sermo patrius, cum
idem fabellas Latinas ad uerbum e Graecis expressas non inuiti
legant. quis enim tam inimicus paene nomini (nomini pene *BE*)
Romano est, qui Enni (ennii *codd*.) Medeam aut Antiopam
Pacuui (pacuuii *codd*.) spernat aut reiciat, quod se isdem
Euripidis fabulis delectari dicat, Latinas litteras oderit?...

5: ...an 'utinam (*Muretus*: at utinam *ABERN*: aut umnam *V*) ne in nemore (*v.* 208)' nihilo minus legimus quam hoc idem Graecum, quae autem de bene beateque uiuendo a Platone disputata sunt, haec explicari non placebit Latine?

(*e*) Cicero, *Tusc.* 1.45: ...qui ostium Ponti uiderunt et eas angustias per quas penetrauit ea quae est nominata 'Argo, quia Argiui in ea (in ea *add.* K^c) delecti (KV^2B: dilecti GRV^1) uiri uecti petebant pellem inauratam arietis (*vv.* 212–13)'.

(*f*) Cicero, *Nat. deor.* 3.75: utinam igitur ut illa anus optat 'ne in nemore Pelio securibus caesae accidissent (cecidissent B^2) abiegnae (abiegne B^2: abigne $APVB^1$) ad terram trabes (*vv.* 208–9)', sic istam calliditatem hominibus di ne dedissent...

(*g*) Cicero, *Fat.* 34: itaque non sic causa intellegi debet ut quod cuique antecedat id ei causa sit sed quod cuique (antecedat id ei [*corr. ex* id et]...cuique *in mg. antiquissimus corrector add. A:* /// antecedat id, *litura del.* efficientes *B*: id et causa *V*) efficienter (efficientur V^1B^1) antecedat (antecedant A^pV^p), nec quod in campum descenderim (descenderint V^p) id fuisse causae (causa *B*) cur pila luderem (lauderem A^p)...ex hoc genere illud est Enni (ennii V^cB^c) 'utinam ne in nemore Pelio securibus accidissent (B^1: accedissent *V*: cecidissent A^2B^2) abiegnae (abi*egnac *A*: abiaegne *V*) ad terram trabes (trabas V^1) (*vv.* 208–9)'. licuit uel altius: utinam ne in Pelio nata ulla umquam esset (esse B^p) arbor. etiam supra: utinam ne esset (esse V^p) mons Pelius. similiterque superiora repetentem regredi infinite licet. 'neue inde nauis inchoandi exordium cepisset (B^p: coepisset *AV*) (*vv.* 210–11)'. quorsum haec praeterita? quia sequitur illud: 'nam numquam era errans mea domo ecferret (haec ferret A^pV^p: ha *paene erasae B*) pedem Medea animo aegro amore saeuo (amores aeuo B^p: amores V^p: more A^p) saucia (*vv.* 215–16)'. †non ut eae res (ut heres V^2) causam adferrent amoris†

(*h*) Cicero, *Top.* 61: hoc igitur sine quo non fit ab eo in quo certe fit diligenter est separandum. illud enim est tamquam 'utinam ne in nemore Pelio (*v.* 208)'. nisi enim accidissent (*AaV*: cecidissent *OjbcdL*β) abiegnae ad terram trabes, Argo illa facta non esset, nec tamen fuit in his trabibus efficiendi uis necessaria. at cum in Aiacis nauim crispisulcans igneum fulmen iniectum est, inflammatur nauis necessario.

(*i*) Varro, *Ling.* 7.33: sic dictum a quibusdam ut una canes, una trabes 'remis rostrata per altum'. Ennius: 'utinam ne in nemore Pelio (polio *F*) securibus caesa accidisset (cesa saccidissent *F*) abiegna ad terram trabes (*vv.* 208–9)'. cuius uerbi singularis casus rectus (*Scioppius*: recte *F*) correptus (*Laetus*: correctus *F*) ac facta trabs.

(*k*) Quintilianus, *Inst.* 5.10.84: recte autem monemur causas non utique ab ultimo esse repetendas, ut Medea: 'utinam ne in nemore Pelio (*v.* 208)'. quasi uero id eam fecerit miseram aut nocentem, quod illic ceciderint abiegnae (*AB*: ceciderit abiegna *P*) ad terram trabes (*v.* 209).

(*l*) Iulius Victor, *Rhet.* 12, p. 415.24: uitiosum genus argumentationis...ut remotum, quod ulterius quam satis est petitur, ut: si in nemore Pelio non cecidissent trabes, hoc scelus factum non esset.

(*m*) Donatus, Ter. *Phorm.* 157: VTINAM NE PHORMIO. uetus elocutio utinam ⟨ne⟩ (*add. Stephanus*), ut Ennius in Medea: 'utinam ne in nemore Pelio umquam sectae cecidissent (cecidissent caesae *V*) ad terram trabes (*vv.* 208–9)'.

(*n*) Hieronymus, *Epist.* 127.5.2: hanc multos post annos imitata est Sophronia et aliae, quibus rectissime illud Ennianum aptari potest 'utinam ne in nemore Pelio (*v.* 208)'.

(*o*) Priscianus, *Gramm.* II 320.15: uetustissimi tamen etiam trabes pro trabs proferebant. Ennius in Medea: 'utinam ne in nemore Pelio securibus caesa (cessa *GL*) accedisset (*K*: accidisset *r*: cecidisset *h Coloniensis*) abiegna in terram (in terram abiegna *codd*.) trabes (*vv.* 208–9)'.

(*p*) Priscianus, *Gramm.* III 423.35: nec solum comici huiusce-modi sunt usi iambis sed etiam tragici uetustissimi, ut Ennius in Medea: 'utinam ne in nemore Pelio securibus caesae cecidissent abiegnae ad terram trabes, neue inde (*RVBa*: neuenide *A*) nauis inchoanda exordium cepisset (*V*: coepisset *A*) quae nunc

---

CIII *Pomponius, *Atell. ap.* Non. p. 516.12 occidit taurum toruiter, me amore sauciauit (*Lipsius*: me amores amauit *codd*.); Catullus 64.1–7 Peliaco quondam prognatae uertice pinus | dicuntur liquidas Neptuni nasse per undas | Phasidos (fascidicos *X*: *al*. phasidos *add. rmg*: fasidicos *O*) ad fluctus et fines Aeetaeos (*uulgo*: ceticos *O*: oeticos *X*), | cum lecti iuuenes, Argiuae robora pubis (*uulgo*: pupis *O*: puppis *X*), | auratam optantes Colchis auertere pellem | ausi sunt uada salsa cita decurrere puppi, | caerula uerrentes abiegnis aequora palmis, 171–2 utinam ne tempore primo | Gnosia Cecropiae tetigissent litora puppes, 250 multiplices animo uoluebat saucia curas; Lucretius 4.1048 idque petit corpus mens unde est saucia amore; Horatius, *Epod.* 16.57–8 non huc Argoo contendit remige pinus, | neque impudica Colchis intulit pedem; Vergilius, *Ecl.* 4.34–5 et altera quae uehat Argo | delectos heroas, 8.47–8 saeuus amor docuit natorum sanguine matrem | commaculare manus; Phaedrus 4.7.4–9 parua (*Rigault*: par *P*) libellum sustine patientia, | seueritatem frontis dum placo tuae | et in cothurnis prodit Aesopus nouis (*Pithoeus*: nobis *P*). | utinam nec (*Bongars*: ne *PR*) umquam Pelii (*Salmasius*: pelei *P*) nemoris iugo | pinus bipenni concidisset Thessala | nec ad professae mortis audacem uiam | fabricasset Argus opere Palladio ratem; Poeta incertus *ap.* Gell. 19.11.4 anima aegra (*codd*.: aegra amore *Camerarius*) et saucia | cucurrit ad labeas mihi; Apuleius, *Met.* 4.32 sed Psyche uirgo uidua domi residens deflet desertam suam solitudinem aegra corporis, animi saucia (*uulgo*: animis audacia *codd*.); Orosius 1.12.10 nolo meminisse Medeae amore saeuo sauciae et pignorum paruulorum caede gaudentis.

nominatur nomine Argo, qua uecti Argiui dilecti uiri petebant illam pellem inauratam arietis Colchis imperio regis Peliae per dolum. nam numquam era errans mea domo efferret pedem (*vv.* 208–15)'.

CIV

Cicero, *De orat.* 3.217: aliud enim uocis genus iracundia sibi sumat, acutum, incitatum, crebro incidens...aliud miseratio ac maeror, flexibile, plenum, interruptum, flebili uoce:

> *quo nunc me uortam? quod iter incipiam ingredi?* 217
> *domum paternamne? anne ad Peliae filias?*

CV

(*a*) Cicero, *Fam.* 7.6.1: tu modo ineptias istas et desideria urbis et urbanitatis depone et, quo consilio profectus es, id adsiduitate et uirtute consequere. hoc tibi tam ignoscemus nos amici quam ignouerunt Medeae quae Corinthum arcem altam habebant matronae opulentae optumates, quibus illa manibus gypsatissimis persuasit ne sibi uitio illae uerterent quod abesset a patria. nam

> *multi suam rem bene gessere et publicam patria procul;* 219
> *multi qui domi aetatem agerent propterea sunt improbati.*

CIV *C. Gracchus *ap.* Cic. *De orat.* 3.214 et Quintil. *Inst.* 11.3.115 quo me miser conferam? quo uortam? in Capitoliumne? at fratris sanguine redundat (*L*: madet *M*). an domum? matremne ut miseram lamentantem uideam et abiectam?; Catullus 64.177–81 nam quo me referam? quali spe perdita nitor? | Idomneosne (*E. Fraenkel*: idoneos [idmoneos *X*] ne *V*) petam montes? at (*Muretus*: a *V*) gurgite lato | discernens ponti (*O*: pontum *X*) truculentum ubi diuidit aequor? | an patris (*R*: impatris *O*: in patris *G*) auxilium sperem? quemne ipsa reliqui, | respersum iuuenem fraterna caede secuta?

CIV 218 paternam *L*   ad Peliae *uulgo*: ad Paeliae *P*: appellare *M*

2: quo in numero tu certe fuisses, nisi te extrusissemus. sed plura scribemus alias. tu, qui ceteris cauere didicisti, in Britannia ne ab essedariis decipiaris caueto et (quoniam Medeam coepi agere) illud semper memento:

> *qui ipse sibi sapiens prodesse non quit nequiquam sapit.*   221

(b) Cicero, *Off.* 3.62: nemo est qui hoc uiri boni fuisse neget; sapientis negant, ut si minoris quam potuisset uendidisset. haec igitur est illa pernicies, quod alios bonos, alios sapientes existimant. ex quo Ennius nequiquam sapere sapientem qui ipse sibi prodesse non quiret. uere id quidem, si quid esset prodesse mihi cum Ennio conueniret.

CVI

Cicero, *Tusc.* 3.63: sunt autem alii quos in luctu cum ipsa solitudine loqui saepe delectat, ut illa apud Ennium nutrix:

> *cupido cepit miseram nunc me proloqui*   222
> *caelo atque terrae Medeai miserias.*

CVII

Cicero, *Tusc.* 4.69: quid ait ex tragoedia princeps ille Argonautarum?

> *tu me amoris magis quam honoris seruauisti gratia.*   224

quid ergo? hic amor Medeae quanta miseriarum excitauit incendia. atque ea tamen apud alium poetam patri dicere audet se (ς'V³: sed X) coniugem habuisse illum 'Amor quem dederat qui plus pollet potiorque est patre'.

CV (a) 221 nequicquam *R*
CVI 223 Medeai *Turnebus*: medeae *codd.*
CVII 224 tum amoris *K*: tum ea moris *R*   seruauisti *ed. Cratandrina*: seruasti *codd.*

CVIII

Cicero, *Nat. deor.* 3.65:

nequaquam istuc istac ibit; magna inest certatio.   225
nam ut ego illi supplicarem tanta blandiloquentia
ni ob rem—

66: parumne ratiocinari uidetur et sibi ipsa nefariam pestem machinari? illud uero quam callida ratione:

qui uolt quod uolt ita dat ⟨semper⟩ se res ut operam dabit.   228

qui est uersus omnium seminator malorum.

ille trauersa mente mi hodie tradidit repagula   229
quibus ego iram omnem recludam atque illi perniciem dabo
mihi maerores, illi luctum, exitium illi, exilium mihi.

hanc uidelicet rationem, quam uos diuino beneficio homini solum tributam dicitis, bestiae non habent.

67: uidesne igitur quanto munere deorum simus adfecti? atque eadem Medea (Media *A¹VB¹*) patrem patriamque fugiens

'postquam (posquam *A*) pater
adpropinquat iamque paene ut conprehendatur parat,
puerum interea obtruncat membraque articulatim diuidit
perque agros passim dispergit corpus; id ea gratia
ut, dum nati dissipatos artus captaret parens,
ipsa interea effugeret, illum ut maeror tardaret sequi,
sibi salutem ut familiari pareret parricidio.'

huic ut scelus sic ne ratio quidem defuit.

CVIII 225 istac ibit *B¹*: isthaec ibit *V²*: ista ibit *AV¹B²*   226 illi *Ribbeck*: illis *codd.* subplicarem *A* blandiloquenti *codd.*   227 ni ob rem *Vahlen*: aniobe *B*: niobem *AV*   228 qui uult *A²V²B*: qui uult esse *pauci deteriores, Dauisius* quod uult *A²V²B* ut adat *V¹* ⟨semper⟩ se *Jocelyn*   229 transuersa *V²* 230 perniciem *V²*: pernitiem *A²B²*: permiiem *A¹V¹B¹*   231 exitium *V²B²*: exitum *AV¹B¹*

CIX

(*a*) Varro, *Men.* fr. *ap.* Non. p. 261.7: non uides apud
⟨Ennium⟩ (*add. Aldus*) esse scriptum 'ter sub armis malim
uitam cernere quam semel modo parere'?

(*b*) Varro, *Ling.* 6.81: cerno idem ualet. itaque pro uideo ait
Ennius...ab eodem est quod ait Medea:

> nam ter sub armis malim uitam cernere 232
> quam semel modo parere.

quod, ut decernunt de uita eo tempore, multorum uidetur uitae
finis.

(*c*) Nonius, p. 261.18: CERNERE rursum dimicare uel conten-
dere...Ennius in Medea exule: 'nam ter (te *codd.*) sub armis
malim (maculim L^1) uitam (E^1: uita *codd.*) cernere'.

CX

Probus, Verg. *Ecl.* 6.31-3 (namque canebat uti magnum per
inane coacta | semina terrarumque animaeque marisque fuissent
| et liquidi simul ignis): ...Aemilius Asper cum hunc locum
(*Aen.* 6.724-6) adnotaret sic ait: 'haec membra naturae sic solet
iungere ut in tria diuidat. nam et alibi: "maria ac terras caelum-
que profundum (*Aen.* 1.58)" et Homerus similiter: ἐν μὲν
γαῖαν ἔτευξ', ἐν δ' οὐρανόν, ἐν δὲ θάλασσαν (*Il.* 18.483)'. sed et
Homerum ipso hoc loco possumus probare quattuor elemen-
torum mentionem fecisse. nam ἐν μὲν γαῖαν ἔτευξεν Achilles
significatur, ut homo terrenus, cui arma fiebant, ἐν δ' οὐρανὸν
aerem scilicet in quo ista fiebant: ignem extrinsecus adhibebi-
mus in ipso Volcano. similiter et Ennius in Medea exule in his
uersibus:

CIX (*b*) 232 nam *non habet* F: *fortasse non attulit Varro* multa cernere F

Iuppiter tuque adeo summe Sol qui res omnis inspicis   234
quique tuo lumine mare terram caelum contines
inspice hoc facinus prius quam fit. prohibessis scelus.

nam (*Keil*: iam *codd.*) et hic Iuppiter et Sol pro igni, qui mare et terram et caelum continet, ⟨ut⟩ (*add. Keil*) non dubie (dubium *MP*) caelum pro aere dixerit.

CXI

(*a*) Nonius, p. 38.29: ELIMINARE, extra limen eicere... Ennius Medea exule:

    antiqua erilis fida custos corporis,   237
    quid sic te extra aedis exanimatam eliminat?

(*b*) Nonius, p. 292.20: ELIMINARE est exire. Ennius Medea exule: 'antiqua erilis (edilis *codd.*) fida custos corporis quid †sit† extra aedis exanimata (examinata [examinate *L¹*] *codd.*) eliminat'. Accius Phoenissis...

CXII

(*a*) Varro, *Ling.* 7.9: in hoc templo faciundo arbores constitui fines apparet et intra eas regiones qua oculi conspiciant, id est tueamur, a quo templum dictum, ut contemplare, ut apud Ennium in Medea: 'contempla et templum Cereris ad laeuam aspice'.

(*b*) Nonius, p. 469.34: CONTEMPLA... Ennius Medea:

    asta atque Athenas anticum opulentum oppidum   239
    contempla et templum Cereris ad laeuam aspice.

CX 236 facimus *V* fit *VE*: sit *MP* prohibessis *Bothe*: prohibesse *V*: prohibe ẽẽ P: prohibe prohibe esse *M*: prohibe *E*
CXI (*a*) ennium et ea exule *L¹*: ennius metea exule *L²*: ennius mede exule *G* 238 sic te *Mercerus*: sit *codd.* exanimatam eliminat *Jocelyn*: exanimata eliminas *Mercerus*: examinata elimina *codd.*
CXII (*b*) 239 anticum *Roth*: antiquum *uulgo*: anti eum *codd.* opulenteum *LC⁴* 240 et templum Cereris ad laeuam aspice *non habent codices: fortasse omisit Nonius*

CXIII

Nonius, p. 84.31: CETTE significat dicite uel date; ab eo quod cedo...Ennius in Medea:

saluete optima corpora. 241
cette manus uestras measque accipite.

CXIV

Nonius, p. 170.8: SVBLIMARE, extollere. Ennius Medea:

sol qui candentem in caelo sublimat facem. 243

CXV

Nonius, p. 297.16: EFFERRE significat proferre...Ennius Medea:

utinam ne umquam †mede† cordis cupido corde pedem extulisses 244

CXVI

Nonius, p. 467.7: AVCVPAVI, actiuum positum pro passiuo... Ennius Medea:

fructus uerborum aures aucupant. 245

MELANIPPA

CXVII

Cicero, *Off.* 1.114: *uide fr.* X.

CXVIII

Gellius 5.11.11–14: '...inter enim pulcherrimam feminam et deformissimam media forma quaedam est, quae et a nimiae pulcritudinis periculo et a summae deformitatis odio uacat;

CXV 244 Medea Colchis *Lipsius*

qualis a Quinto Ennio in Melanippa perquam eleganti uocabulo stata (*PR*: tecta *V*) dicitur, quae neque κοινή futura sit neque ποινή'. quam formam (*P²*: quam in formam *codd.*) modicam et modestam Fauorinus non mi hercule inscite appellabat 'uxoriam'. Ennius autem in ista quam dixit (dixi *R*) tragoedia eas fere feminas ait incolumi pudicitia esse quae stata forma forent.

CXIX

(*a*) Nonius, p. 170.10: SVPERSTITENT (superstent *D⁴*), saluent. Ennius Melanippa:

> regnumque nostrum ut sospitent superstitentque.   246

(*b*) Nonius, p. 176.2: SOSPITENT, saluent. Ennius Melanippa (menalippa *G*): 'regnumque nostrum sospitent superstitentque'.

CXX

Nonius, p. 246.9: AVSCVLTARE est obsequi... Ennius Melanippa:

> mi ausculta nate: pueros cremari iube.   247

CXXI

Nonius, p. 469.3: AVGVRO... Ennius Melanippa:

> †certo hic est nulla† quin monstrum siet.   248
> hoc ego tibi dico et coniectura auguro.

CXXII

Macrobius, *Sat.* 6.4.7 (*cf. fr. LXII*): 'splendet tremulo sub lumine pontus (Vergilius, *Aen.* 7.9)'. TREMVLVM LVMEN de imagine rei ipsius expressum est. sed prior Ennius in Melanippe:

> lumine sic tremulo terra et caua caerula candent.   250

CXIX (*a*) 246 superstitent *Acidalius*
CXX menalippa *codd.*   247 mi *Vossius*: mihi *codd.*   cremitari *Bothe*
CXXI menalippo (melanippo *L¹*) *codd.*   248 certo hic est nullum *B⁴*: certatio hic est nulla *Passeratius*

PHOENIX

CXXIII

(a) Gellius 6.9.15: praeterea inueni a uerbo scindo simili ratione non sciderat, sed sciciderat dictum esse...

17: Ennius quoque ⟨* * *⟩

(b) Priscianus, *Gramm.* II 516.14: scindo scidi. uetustissimi tamen etiam scicidi (sciscidi *R*) proferebant...Ennius in Melanippa:

cum saxum sciciderit   251

NEMEA

CXXIV

Nonius, p. 183.14: VENOR, circumuenior. Ennius Nemea:

teneor consaepta, undique uenor.   252

CXXV

Priscianus, *Gramm.* II 171.4: hic et haec et hoc pecus. Ennius in Nemea:

pecudi dare uiuam marito.   253

potest tamen figurate hoc esse prolatum, ut si dicam 'aquila maritus' uel 'rex auium'.

PHOENIX

CXXVI

Gellius 6.17.1: percontabar Romae quempiam grammaticum ...discendi magis studio et cupidine, quid significaret obnoxius quaeque eius uocabuli origo ac ratio essct...

CXXIII (b) menalippa *BD*   251 scisciderit *R*
CXXIV 252 consepta (concepta *G*) *codd.*
CXXV nemia *L*: neinea *G*   253 pecudi *ex* peculi *corr. K*: pecodi *G*   uiua *Dresd. 1.2 Erl. 1.2 Lips. 2 Krehlii*: uerba *Palmer*

125

10: iam uero illud etiam Q. Enni quo pacto congruere tecum (congrueret equum *codd.*) potest, quod scribit in Phoenice in his uersibus?

> *sed uirum uera uirtute uiuere* †animatum adiecit†   254
> *fortiterque* †innoxium uocare† *aduersum aduersarios.*
> *ea libertas est qui pectus purum et firmum gestitat;*
> †aliae† *res obnoxiosae nocte in obscura latent.*

CXXVII

(*a*) Helenius Acro, Ter. *Ad.* 45–6 (semper parce ac duriter | se habere) *ap.* Charisium, p. 257.6: secundum antiquorum consuetudinem. nam et Ennius in Phoenice:

> *quam tibi ex ore orationem duriter dictis dedit.*   258

(*b*) Nonius, p. 512.1: DVRITER pro dure...Ennius Phoenice (foenice *G*: fenice *LH*): 'quam tibi ex ore orationem duriter dictis dedit'.

CXXVIII

Nonius, p. 91.4: CVPIENTER, cupidissime...Ennius Phoenice:

> †stultus est qui cupida† *cupiens cupienter cupit.*   259

CXXIX

Nonius, p. 245.30: ARGVTARI dicitur loquacius (*H*³: loquacium *codd.*) proloqui. Ennius Phoenice:

> †tum tu isti credere† *atque exerce linguam ut argutarier*
> *possis.*   260

CXXVI phonice *codd.*   254 animatum addecet *Carrio*   255 innoxium
uacare *P*: innoxium stare *Bentley*   257 obnoxiosae *Acidalius*: obnoxiose *V*:
obnoxio se *P*: obnoxie se *R*
CXXVII (*a*) poinice *N*
CXXVIII foenice *codd.*
CXXIX Ennius Phoenice 'tum *Mercerus*: ennius quo enicetum *codd.*   260
tum tu isti crede te *Haupt*: tum tu isti crede *L*¹ *Turnebus*   lingua *LA*⁴*B*⁴

CXXX

Nonius, p. 507.22: FAXIM, fecerim. Ennius Phoenice:

    plus miser sim si scelestum faxim quod dicam fore.   261

CXXXI

Nonius, p. 510.32: SAEVITER pro saeue...Ennius Phoenice:

    saeuiter suspicionem ferre falsam futtilum est.   262

CXXXII

Nonius, p. 514.12: FVTTILE, futtiliter. Ennius Phoenice:

    ut quod factum est futtile amici uos feratis fortiter.   263

CXXXIII

Nonius, p. 518.3: DEREPENTE...Ennius Phoenice:

    ibi tum derepente ex alto in altum despexit mare.   264

TELAMO

CXXXIV

(*a*) Cicero, *Nat. deor.* 3.79: Telamo autem uno uersu locum totum conficit cur di homines neglegant:

    nam si curent, bene bonis sit, male malis; quod nunc abest.   265

(*b*) Cicero, *Diu.* 1.132: nunc illa testabor non me sortilegos neque eos qui quaestus causa hariolentur, ne (ς: nec *AVB*)

CXXX fenice (foinice *Bamb.*) *codd.*   261 sim *Delrius*: sum *codd.* scelestum *ed. princ.*: scelestim (scclestem *A^A*) *codd.*
CXXXI fonice *LG*: foenice *HBamb.*   262 futtulum *D^A*
CXXXII foenice *codd.*   263 amici *codd.*: a me id *O. Skutsch*: a me *Buecheler* feratis *ed. princ.*: fueratis *codd.*
CXXXIII foenicae *LGH*: phenice *Bamb.*

psychomantia quidem quibus Appius, amicus tuus, uti solebat, agnoscere; non habeo denique nauci (*Marsus*: non ab eodem sanci *AV*: non ab eodem sancti *Bᵖ*: non ab eodem sanxi *Bᶜ*) Marsum augurem, non uicanos haruspices, non de circo astrologos, non Isiacos (isiagos *Bᵖ*) coniectores, non interpretes somniorum; non enim sunt hi aut scientia aut arte diuini sed superstitiosi uates inpudentesque harioli,

> *aut inertes aut insani aut quibus egestas imperat,*　　　　266
> *qui sibi semitam non sapiunt alteri monstrant uiam;*
> *quibus diuitias pollicentur, ab iis drachumam ipsi petunt.*
> *de his diuitiis sibi deducant drachumam, reddant cetera.*

atque haec quidem Ennius, qui paucis ante uersibus esse deos censet, sed eos non curare opinatur 'quid agat humanum genus.' ego autem, qui et curare arbitror et monere etiam ac multa praedicere, leuitate, uanitate, malitia exclusa (ς: exclusam *AVB*) diuinationem probo.

(c) Cicero, *Diu.* 2.104: primum enim hoc sumitis: 'si sunt di, benefici in homines sunt'. quis hoc uobis dabit? Epicurusne, qui negat quicquam (**quicquam *AB*: atquicquam *Vᵖ*) deos nec alieni curare nec sui? an noster Ennius (nostert *AVᵖ*: nosterrenius *Bᵖ*), qui magno plausu loquitur adsentiente populo:

> *ego deum genus esse semper dixi et dicam caelitum,*　　　　270
> *sed eos non curare opinor quid agat humanum genus.*

et quidem cur sic opinetur rationem subicit, sed nihil est necesse dicere quae secuntur; tantum sat est intellegi, id sumere istos pro certo quod dubium controuersumque sit.

CXXXIV (b) 268 ab iis *Lambinus*: ab his *AVB*　dracmam *A*: dragmam *VBᶜ*: drachman *Bᵖ*　269 drachumam *AVᵖBᵖ*: dracmam *Vᶜ*: dragmam *Bᶜ*
CXXXIV (c) 271 curarare *B*

CXXXV

Festus, p. 218.2: OBSIDIONEM potius dicendum esse quam obsidium adiuuat nos testimonio suo Ennius (pacuuius X) in
Telamone quom (cum X) ait:

> scibas natum ingenuum Aiacem cui tu obsidionem paras.   272

CXXXVI

Nonius, p. 85.20: CLARET, clara est uel clareat (uel clare $C^A D^A$).
...Ennius Telamone:

> nam ita mihi Telamonis patris atque Aeaci et proaui Iouis   273
> †gratia ea est† atque hoc lumen candidum claret mihi.

CXXXVII

Nonius, p. 159.38: PORCET significat prohibet...Ennius
Telamone:

> deum me sentit facere pietas, ciuium porcet pudor.   275

CXXXVIII

(a) Nonius, p. 172.19: SQVALAM pro squalidam. Ennius
Telamone:

> strata terrae lauere lacrimis uestem squalam et sordidam.   276

(b) Nonius, p. 503.38: LAVIT pro lauat...LAVERE inde tractum est...Ennius Telamone: 'strata terra (terrae EP) lauere
(labere codd.) lacrimis uestem squalidam (squalem P^1) et
sordidam'.

CXXXV 272 ingenuum *ed. princ.*: ingenium *codd.*
CXXXVI 273 atque *codd.*: aui *Bergk*   Aeaci et *Bergk*: faciet *codd.*   touis *L*
CXXXVIII talamone *codd.*

CXXXIX

Nonius, p. 475.20: PARTIRET pro partiretur... Ennius Telamone:

eandem me in suspicionem sceleris partiuit pater. 277

CXL

Nonius, p. 505.35: AVDIBO pro audiam. Ennius Telamone:

more antiquo audibo atque auris tibi contra utendas dabo. 278

CXLI

Diomedes, *Gramm.* I 382.10: cui enim in dubium cadit quin abnuo abnuis dicamus? uerum apud ueteres et (*Putschius*: est *codd.*) abnueo dictum annotamus, ut Ennius...idem (*BM*: item *A*) in Telamone (*M*: telamonem *AB*) ex eo futurum:

abnuebunt 279

TELEPHVS

CXLII

(*a*) Festus, p. 128.24: MVTTIRE (mutire *codd.*), loqui. Ennius in Telepho:

palam muttire plebeio piaculum est. 280

(*b*) Phaedrus 3, epil. 33:

ego quondam legi quam puer (*Pithoeus*: pueri *PR*)
            sententiam
'palam muttire plebeio periculum est'
dum sanitas constabit pulchre meminero (*Rittershausen*:
         memini *P*: memin. *R*).

CXXXIX 277 eamdem *codd.* in om. *A⁴*: in me *Delrius*
CXL telemone *codd.* 278 atque *Cᴬ Montepess. Oxon.*: neque *LAᴬBᴬ Paris. 7665* utendos *CᴬDᴬ*
CXLI 279 abnuebant *B*: abnueḃ *M*
CXLII (*a*) 280 muttire (mutire *IR*) *codd. Pauli*: mutire *codd. Festi*

CXLIII

(*a*) Festus, p. 440.35:

cultum et sord
tum quod proximae
scium accedit; in
diti paludum squ
in Telepho: 'quam ue
stola'. SQVARROSOS

(*b*) Nonius, p. 537.23: STOLAM ueteres non honestam uestem solum, sed etiam omnem quae corpus tegeret. Ennius Telepho:

†cedo et caueo cum uestitus† *squalida saeptus stola.*　　　281

idem in eadem:

regnum reliqui saeptus mendici stola.　　　282

CXLIV

Nonius, p. 15.3: ENODA significat explana; et (ex $C^A D^A$) quae sit proprietas, manifestum est, hoc est, nodis exsolue... Ennius Telepho:

uerum quorum liberi leto dati　　　283
sunt in bello non lubenter haec enodari audiunt.

CXLV

Nonius, p. 232.17: ADVORSVM rursum apud significat... Ennius Telepho:

te ipsum hoc oportet profiteri et proloqui　　　285
aduorsum †illam mihi†

CXLIII (*a*) SQVALIDVM, incultum et sordidum; quod proxime similitudinem habeat squama piscium, sic appellatum — *Paulus.*
CXLIII (*b*) telefo *codd.*　281 cedo et caueo conuestitus *Columna*　282 septus *codd.*　mendici *Iunius*: medici *codd.*
CXLIV telefo *codd.*　283 laeto *L*
CXLV telefo *codd.*

CXLVI

Nonius, p. 342.6: MACTARE malo adficere significat...Ennius
Telepho:

> qui illum di deaeque magno mactassint malo. 287

CXLVII

Nonius, p. 429.1: inter urbem et ciuitatem hoc interest.
urbs est aedificia (aedificatio H^1), ciuitas incolae...Ennius
Telepho:

> sed ciuitatem uideo Argiuum incendere. 288

CXLVIII

Nonius, p. 490.10: ITINER pro iter. Ennius Telepho:

> deumque de consilio hoc itiner credo conatum modo. 289

THYESTES

CXLIX

(a) Cicero, De orat. 3.164: nolo esse uerbum angustius id quod
translatum sit quam fuisset (quam fuisset om. M) illud (illum M)
proprium ac suum:

> quidnam est obsecro quod te adiri abnutas? 290

melius esset uetas, prohibes, absterres; quoniam ille dixerat
'ilico istic. ne contagio mea bonis umbraue obsit (vv. 293–4)'.

(b) Cicero, Tusc. 3.25: nunc aegritudinem si possumus depel-
lamus...taetra enim res est, misera, detestabilis...

CXLVI tennius telefo codd.   287 dii codd.
CXLVII telefus et LA^4: telefo et B^4 288 incendier Aldus
CXLVIII telefo (telepo L^1) codd.
CXLIX (a) 290 quod M: quid L   adiri L: abire M: adirier Vahlen 1854

26: qualis enim tibi ille uidetur?

> *Tantalo prognatus Pelope natus qui quondam a socru*   291
> *Oenomao rege Hippodameam raptis nanctus nuptiis.*

Iouis iste quidem pronepos. tamne ergo abiectus tamque fractus?

> *nolite*

inquit
>   *hospites ad me adire. ilico istic.*   293
> *ne contagio mea bonis umbraue obsit.*
> *tanta uis sceleris in corpore haeret.*

tu te (tune R^2) Thyesta damnabis orbabisque luce propter uim sceleris alieni?

CL

(*a*) Cicero, *Pis.* 43: neque uero ego, si umquam uobis mala precarer, quod saepe feci, in quo di immortales meas preces audierunt, morbum aut mortem aut cruciatum precarer. Thyestea est ista exsecratio, poetae uolgi animos, non sapientium, mouentis, ut tu naufragio expulsus uspiam 'saxis fixus asperis, euisceratus' latere penderes, ut ait ille, 'saxa spargens tabo sanie et (et *om.* ω) sanguine atro'.

(*b*) Cicero, *Tusc.* 1.106: exsecratur luculentis sane uersibus apud Ennium Thyestes, primum ut naufragio pereat Atreus; durum hoc sane; talis enim interitus non est sine graui sensu; illa inania

> *ipse summis saxis fixus asperis, euisceratus,*   296
> *latere pendens, saxa spargens tabo sanie et sanguine atro.*

CXLIX *Cicero, *Verr.* 2.1.81 nisi tanta acerbitas iniuriae, tanta uis sceleris fuisset.

CL *Lucilius *ap.* Non. p. 405.3 latere pendens, saxa spargens tabo sanie et sanguine atro.

CXLIX (*b*) 291 socru *Bentley*: socero *codd.*   292 hippodamiam R^2 nactus KR^c: nactu'st *Bentley*   293 illic o G^1KV^1 (l *exp.* G^2V^2)   295 ⟨meo⟩ tanta *Bentley*

non ipsa saxa magis sensu omni (omnia X: a *exp.* V^1) uacabunt quam ille latere pendens cui se hic cruciatum censet optare. quae (V^2: quam X) essent dura si sentiret (ς: sentirent X), nulla ⟨sunt⟩ (*add.* ς) sine sensu. illud uero perquam inane

> *neque sepulcrum quo recipiat habeat, portum corporis,*   298
> *ubi remissa humana uita corpus requiescat malis.*

uides quanto haec in errore uersentur. portum esse corporis et requiescere in sepulcro putat mortuum. magna culpa Pelopis qui non erudierit filium nec docuerit quatenus esset quidque curandum.

CLI

Cicero, *Orat.* 183: in uersibus res est apertior, quamquam etiam a modis quibusdam cantu remoto soluta esse uidetur (*uulgo*: uideatur *AL*) oratio, maximeque id in optimo quoque eorum poetarum qui λυρικοί a Graecis nominantur, quos (*L*: eos *A*) cum cantu spoliaueris nuda paene remanet oratio.

184: quorum similia sunt quaedam etiam apud nostros (*L*: illos *A*), uelut illa (*A*: ille *L*) in Thyeste:

> *quemnam te esse dicam qui tarda in senectute—*   300

et quae sequuntur; quae, nisi cum tibicen accessit, orationis sunt solutae simillima.

CLII

Cicero, *Brut.* 78: C. Sulpicius Gallus...hoc praetore ludos Apollini faciente, cum Thyesten fabulam docuisset Q. Marcio Cn. Seruilio consulibus, mortem obiit Ennius.

CLIII

(a) Cicero, *Nat. deor.* 2.4: quid enim potest esse tam apertum tamque perspicuum, cum caelum suspeximus caelestiaque contemplati sumus, quam esse aliquod numen (nomen B^1) prae-

---

CLI 300 quin *L*   senecta *Bothe*

stantissimae mentis quo haec regantur? quod ni ita (quot nuta B^1) esset, qui potuisset adsensu omnium dicere Ennius 'aspice hoc sublime candens quem inuocant (inuocat B^1) omnes Iouem' — illum uero et Iouem et dominatorem rerum et omnia motu regentem et, ut idem (em* A) Ennius, 'patrem diuumque hominumque' et praesentem ac praepotentem deum?

(*b*) Cicero, *Nat. deor.* 2.64: sed ipse Iuppiter, id est iuuans pater, quem (V: partem quae B^1: partemque A) conuersis casibus appellamus a iuuando (adiuuando B^1) Iouem, a poetis 'pater diuomque hominumque' dicitur...

65: hunc igitur Ennius, ut supra dixi, nuncupat ita dicens 'aspice hoc sublime (suplimim B^1) candens, quem inuocant omnes Iouem' planius (planus A^1) quam (*PB*: quem AHV^1: que V^2) alio loco idem '†cuit† quod in me est exsecrabor hoc quod lucet (licet V) quicquid est (*v.* 342)'.

(*c*) Cicero, *Nat. deor.* 3.10: primum fuit, cum caelum suspexissemus, statim nos intellegere esse aliquod numen quo haec regantur. ex hoc illud etiam 'aspice hoc sublime candens (cadens A^1V) quem inuocant omnes Iouem'.

(*d*) Cicero, *Nat. deor.* 3.40: sit sane deus ipse mundus (mundus deus ipse P). hoc credo illud esse 'sublime (sublime esse P) candens quem inuocant (inuocans A^1) omnes Iouem'.

(*e*) Festus, p. 400.17: SVBLIMEM est in altitudinem elatum, ut ⟨* * *⟩ Ennius in Thyeste:

aspice hoc sublime candens quem uocant omnes Iouem.   301

(*f*) Apuleius, *Mund.* 33: namque habitus orantium sic est, ut manibus extensis ⟨in⟩ (*uulgo*: extensis *codd.*) caelum precemur. Romanus etiam poeta sic sensit: 'aspice hoc sublime (*BF*: sub

---

CLIII (*e*) SVBLIMEM (*MPEGR*: sublime *TI*: sublimen *L*) est in altitudinem elatum, id autem dicitur a limine superiore quia supra nos est — *Paulus*

lumine *PL*) candens (*B*: cadens δ) quem inuocant (inuocans *B*) omnes Iouem'. unde illa quae uidentur suntque omnibus praestantiora, easdem sublimitates regionum tenent...

(*g*) Probus, Verg. *Ecl.* 6.31–3: principem habuerunt Empedoclem Agrigentinum qui de his ita scribit: τέσσαρα δὴ πάντων ῥιζώματα πρῶτον ἔασιν Ζεὺς ἀργής... ut accipiamus Ζεὺς ἀργὴς ignem, qui sit ʒέων et candens, quod ignis est proprium, de quo Euripides...et Ennius: 'aspice hoc sublime candens quem uocant omnes Iouem'.

CLIV

Nonius, p. 90.13: CONGLOMERARE, inuoluere, superaddere. Ennius Thyeste:

> eheu mea fortuna ut omnia in me conglomeras mala.   302

CLV

Nonius, p. 97.29: DELECTARE, inlicere, adtrahere. Ennius Thyeste:

> set me Apollo ipse delectat ductat Delphicus.   303

CLVI

Nonius, p. 110.11: FLACCET, languet, deficit...Ennius Thyeste:

> sin flaccebunt condiciones repudiato et reddito.   304

CLVII

Nonius, p. 255.25: CREPARE, ferire. Ennius in Thyeste:

> sed sonitus auris meas pedum pulsu increpat.   305

CLIV Ennius in Thieste *ed. a. 1476*: ennius tithe *codd.*   302 eheu mea *Lachmann*: eumea *codd.*
CLV Thyeste set *Mercerus*: theestes et *codd.*   303 delficus *codd.*
CLVI 304 sin flaccebunt *Gulielmius*: inflaccebunt *codd.*

CLVIII

Nonius, p. 261.13: CERNERE, iudicare...Ennius Thyeste:

impetrem facile ab animo ut cernat †uitalem babium† 306

CLIX

Nonius, p. 268.9: CONTINGERE, euenire...Ennius Thyeste:

quam mihi maxime hic hodie contigerit malum. 307

CLX

Nonius, p. 369.29: PVTARE, animo disputare...Ennius Thyeste:

ibi quid agat secum cogitat parat putat. 308

INCERTA

CLXI

(*a*) Terentius, *Eun.* 586–91:

egomet quoque id spectare coepi et, quia consimilem luserat
iam olim ille ludum, inpendio magis animus gaudebat mihi.
deum sese in hominem conuortisse atque in alienas tegulas
uenisse clanculum! per inpluuium fucum factum mulieri!
at quem deum! qui templa caeli summa sonitu concutit.
ego homuncio hoc non facerem?

(*b*) Donatus: QVI TEMPLA CAELI SVMMA (summo *T*) SONITV
CONCVTIT. ab auctoritate personae (persona *TC*) ut fit (sit *C*) in
exemplis. SONITV CONCVTIT. parodia de Ennio. TEMPLA CAELI
SVMMA. tragice (sūma tragice *V*: sumairagica *C*: sūma ragica *T*),
sed de industria, non errore.

CLVIII thyste *codd.*   306 cernet *A*[A]
CLIX tyeste *codd.*
CLX thieste *codd.*   308 cogitet *LB*[A]   paritat *Buecheler*

CLXII

(*a*) Rhetor incertus, *Her.* 2.39: item uitiosum est cum id pro
certo (*E*: quō id proco *P*¹: quid [u *in ras.*] praeco *H*: quae id
pro quo *BC*¹) sumitur quod inter omnes †constat†, quod etiam
nunc in controuersia (controuersia est *blC*: controuersia sit *d*),
hoc modo:

> *eho tu: di quibus est potestas motus superum atque inferum*   309
> *pacem inter sese conciliant, conferunt concordiam.*

nam ita pro suo iure hoc exemplo utentem (*Kayser*: usum *E*:
utuntur *M*) Thesprotum (*M*: threspontem *E*) Ennius induxit
quasi iam (*E*: quaesitam *M*) satis certis rationibus ita (id ita *Hl*)
esse demonstrasset.

(*b*) Cicero, *Inu.* 1.91: controuersum est in quo ad dubium
demonstrandum dubia causa adfertur hoc modo: 'eho tu: di
(*P*¹: dii *C*) quibus est potestas motus superum atque inferum
pacem inter sese conciliant, conferunt concordiam'.

CLXIII

Rhetor incertus, *Her.* 4.18: conpositio est uerborum constructio
...ea conseruabitur si...et si uitabimus eiusdem litterae
nimiam adsiduitatem; cui uitio uersus hic erit exemplo — nam
hic nihil prohibet in uitiis alienis exemplis uti —: 'o Tite tute
Tati tibi tanta tyranne tulisti (*cf. Prisc. Gramm.* II 591.12 *et al.*)'
et hic eiusdem poetae:

> *quicquam quisquam* †quemquam† *quemque quisque conueniat*
> *neget.*   311

CLXII (*a*) 309 eho tu dii quibus *E*: studiis *M*   est potestas *E*: est potest at *H*:
est potest aut *PB*: esse potest aut Π: est potestas ut *C*   motus *E*: motum *M*
310 pace enim *M*: pacem *E*   sese *M*: se *E*
CLXIII 311 quicquam quisquam quemq; *E*: qui oquam quicquam quemq
(quemquam *P*) quemq; *P*¹*B*: quicquam quisquam quemquam quemque *P*²*C*:
quicquam quicq quemq *H*: quicquam quicquam quemq; Π

CLXIV

(*a*) Cicero, *S. Rosc.* 89: uerum ego forsitan propter multi-
tudinem patronorum (ς: paternorum Σς) in grege (ς: gregem
Σς) adnumerer, te pugna Cannensis accusatorem sat bonum
fecit. multos caesos non ad Trasumennum (trahasymennum Σ:
trasimennum ς) lacum sed ad Seruilium uidimus.

90:

   quis ibi non est uulneratus ferro Phrygio?   312

non necesse est omnis commemorare Curtios Marios denique
Memmios (*Vrsinus*: mammeos *codd.*) quos iam aetas a proeliis
auocabat, postremo Priamum ipsum senem, Antistium quem
non modo aetas sed etiam leges pugnare prohibebant.

(*b*) Schol. Gronouianus: FERRO FRVGIO. in Ennio haec fabula
inducitur, Achilles (*Eberhard*: achillis *C*) quo tempore propter
Briseidem cum Graecis pugnare noluit; quo etiam tempore
Hector classem eorum incendit. in hac pugna Vlixes uulneratus
inducitur et fugiens ⟨ad⟩ (*add. Graeuius*) Achillen uenit. cum
interrogaretur ab Aiace cur fugisset, ille ut celaret dedecus
†uitium†: 'quis enim uulneratus ferro Frugio?'

CLXV

(*a*) Cicero, *Balb.* 36: in quo erat accusatoris interpretatio
indigna (*uulgo*: digna in *codd.*) responsione, qui ita dicebat
'comiter' esse 'communiter' quasi uero priscum aliquod aut
insolitum uerbum interpretaretur. comes (comites *E*) benigni
faciles suaues homines esse dicuntur; 'qui erranti (eranti *P¹*)
comiter (*P*: com [*erasa lineola supra* -m] *G*: comiti *E*) monstrat
(monstrant *GE*) uiam' benigne, non grauate; 'communiter'
quidem certe non conuenit.

CLXIV (*a*) 312 Brugio *Osann*

(b) Cicero, *Off.* 1.51: omnium (*Zumpt*: omnia *codd.*) autem communia hominum (*ZLp*: omnium *c*) uidentur ea quae sunt generis eius quod ab Ennio positum in una re transferri in permultas (*ZL*: multas *pʃ*) potest:

> *homo qui erranti comiter monstrat uiam*   313
> *quasi lumen de suo lumine accendat facit.*
> *nihilo minus ipsi lucet cum illi accenderit.*

52: ...sed (et *p*) quoniam copiae paruae singulorum sunt, eorum autem qui his egeant infinita est multitudo, uulgaris liberalitas referenda est ad illum Enni (ennii *codd.*) finem 'nihilominus ipsi lucet' ut facultas (ni[c]hilominus scilicet ut facultas *L¹[c]*: nihilominus ipsi luceat ut facultas *L²pʃ*) sit qua in nostros simus liberales.

CLXVI

Cicero, *De orat.* 1.199: quid est enim praeclarius quam honoribus et rei publicae muneribus perfunctum senem posse suo iure dicere idem quod apud Ennium dicat ille Pythius Apollo, se esse eum unde sibi, si non populi et reges, at omnes sui ciues consilium expetant suarum (suarum summarum *codd. integri plerique*: summarum *codd. Lagomarsiniani*) rerum incerti;

>   *quos ego mea ope ex*   316
> *incertis certos compotesque consili*
> *dimitto ut ne res temere tractent turbidas.*

200: est enim sine dubio domus iuris consulti totius oraculum ciuitatis.

CLXVII

Cicero, *De orat.* 2.221: quod est hominibus facetis et dicacibus difficillimum, habere hominum rationem et temporum et ea quae occurrunt (*A¹*: occurrant *codd.*), cum salsissime dici pos-

---

CLXV (b) 313 comiter *ZL*: comiti *p*: communiter *c*   315 q nichilo *c* ipsi luceat *ZX*: ipsi ut luceat *ʃ*
CLXVI 316 ope mea *Reisig*   317 compotes *integri paene omnes* (*Vahlen*)

sunt, tenere. itaque non nulli ridiculi homines hoc ipsum non insulse interpretantur. dicere enim aiunt Ennium (*L*: enim aiunt *H*: enim aut *AE*) flammam a sapiente (flammam a sapiente *L*: pienti *H* [*post xxxvi litt. sp.*] *AE*) facilius ore in ardente opprimi quam bona dicta teneat; haec scilicet bona dicta quae salsa sint; nam ea dicta appellantur proprio iam nomine.

CLXVIII

(*a*) Cicero, *De orat.* 3.162: primum est fugienda dissimilitudo:

> *caeli ingentes fornices.*   319

quamuis sphaeram in scaenam, ut dicitur, attulerit Ennius, tamen in sphaera fornicis similitudo inesse non potest.

(*b*) Varro, *Ling.* 5.19: a chao cauum (*Laetus*: chouũ *F*) et hinc caelum...et Ennius item ad cauationem: 'caeli ingentes fornices'.

CLXIX

(*a*) Cicero, *Rep.* 1.49: concordi populo et omnia referente ad incolumitatem et ad libertatem suam nihil esse inmutabilius, nihil firmius...itaque cum patres rerum potirentur numquam constitisse ciuitatis statum; multo iam id in regnis minus quorum, ut ait Ennius, 'nulla (*Mai*: nulla regni *cod.*) sancta societas nec fides est'.

(*b*) Cicero, *Off.* 1.26: maxime autem adducuntur (ad hoc adducuntur *p*) plerique ut eos (uti eos *p*) iustitiae capiat obliuio cum in (in *om. pς*) imperiorum honorum gloriae cupiditatem inciderunt (*Zp*: inciderint *cς*). quod enim est apud Ennium,

> *nulla sancta societas nec fides regni est,*   320

id latius patet. nam quicquid eiusmodi est in quo non possint (*Z*: possunt *XKς*) plures excellere, in eo fit plerumque (plerumque fit *p*) tanta contentio ut difficillimum sit seruare sanctam societatem.

CLXX

Cicero, *Orat.* 155: idem poeta qui inusitatius contraxerat
'patris mei meum factum pudet' pro meorum factorum (*cf. fr.*
XVIIb)...non dicit liberum ut plerique loquimur cum cupidos
liberum aut in liberum loco dicimus sed ut isti uolunt:

> *neque tuum umquam in gremium extollas liberorum ex te genus.* 321

CLXXI

(*a*) Cicero, *Orat.* 155: non dicit liberum ut plerique loquimur
...sed ut isti uolunt (*cf. fr.* CLXX)...et idem: 'namque
Aesculapi (*L*: excola*** *A*) liberorum (*v.* 326)'.

(*b*) Cicero, *Tusc.* 2.38: quin etiam uidemus ex acie efferri saepe
saucios, et quidem rudem illum et inexercitatum quamuis leui
ictu ploratus turpissimos edere. at uero ille exercitatus (exercitus
K^1) et uetus ob eamque rem fortior medicum modo requirens a
quo obligetur

> *o Patricoles*

inquit   *ad uos adueniens auxilium et uestras manus*   322
> *peto priusquam oppeto malam pestem mandatam hostili manu —*
> *neque sanguis ullo potis est pacto profluens consistere —*
> *si qui sapientia magis uestra mors deuitari potest;*   325
> *namque Aesculapi liberorum saucii opplent porticus.*
> *non potest accedi.*

certe Eurypylus hic quidem est! hominem exercitum! ubi
tantum luctus continuatur (ς: luctum continuatus *GKR*) uide
quam non flebiliter respondeat, rationem etiam adferat cur
aequo animo sibi ferendum sit: *qui alteri exitium parat,*
> *eum scire oportet sibi paratam pestem ut participet parem.*   328

abducet (abducit V^2) Patricoles credo ut conlocet in cubili

CLXX 321 neque tuum *A*: neque tu *L*
CLXXI (*b*) 326 esculapi *K*: aesculapii *GRV*   328 exitium G^2V^2: exitum
G^1V^1 329 paratum *Bentley*

$(V^2\varsigma$: cubiculi X), ut uulnus obliget (non obliget K). si quidem homo esset — sed nihil uidi minus (uidiminus V^c: uidimus X). quaerit enim quid actum sit: 330

eloquere eloquere res Argiuum proelio ut se sustinet.

non potest ecfari tantum dictis quantum factis suppetit laboris.

quiesce igitur et uolnus alliga. etiam si Eurypylus posset non posset Aesopus. 333

ubi fortuna Hectoris nostram acrem aciem inclinatam—

et cetera explicat in dolore; sic est enim intemperans militaris in forti uiro gloria. ergo haec ueteranus miles facere poterit, doctus uir sapiensque non poterit?

CLXXII

Cicero, *Orat.* 160: Burrum semper Ennius, numquam Pyrrhum; 334

ui patefecerunt Bruges,

non Phryges. ipsius antiqui declarant libri.

CLXXIII

Cicero, *Fin.* 2.41: nec uero audiendus Hieronymus, cui summum bonum est idem quod uos interdum uel potius nimium saepe (minimum sepe V: sepe minimum BE) dicitis, nihil dolere. non enim si malum est dolor carere eo malo satis est ad bene uiuendum. hoc dixerit potius Ennius:

nimium boni est cui nihil est mali. 335

nos beatam uitam non depulsione mali sed adeptione boni iudicemus.

CLXXIII *Publilius Syrus, *Sent.* 430 nimium boni est in morte cui nil sit mali.

331 ecfari V: hecfari K: haecfari GR 333 haectoris X inclinatam 〈dedit〉 *Ribbeck*
CLXXII 334 Bruges *Victorius*: fruges *FPM*: phruges O: phryges A

CLXXIV

Cicero, *Tusc.* 3.5: at et morbi perniciosiores pluresque sunt animi quam corporis. hi enim ipsi odiosi sunt quod ad animum pertinent eumque sollicitant,

> *animus*que *aeger*

ut ait Ennius

> *semper errat;*   336
> *neque pati neque perpeti potest, cupere numquam desinit.*

CLXXV

Cicero, *Tusc.* 3.39: quid ergo? huiusne uitae propositio et cogitatio aut Thyestem leuare poterit aut Aeetam (aetam *X*: oetam *K²R^c*), de quo paulo ante dixi, aut Telamonem pulsum patria exulantem atque egentem...

43: ad hancine igitur uitam Telamonem illum reuocabis ut leues aegritudinem?...

44: ...quaerendum igitur quem ad modum aegritudine priuemus (*K²R²V³*: priuemur *X*) eum qui ita dicat:

> *pol mihi fortuna magis nunc defit quam genus.*   338
> *namque regnum suppetebat mi, ut scias quanto e loco,*
> *quantis opibus, quibus de rebus lapsa fortuna accidat.*

quid? huic calix mulsi impingendus est, ut plorare desinat... ecce tibi ex altera parte ab eodem poeta: 'ex opibus summis opis egens Hector tuae (*cf. fr.* xxvii h)'. huic subuenire debemus...

46: ...eripiamus huic aegritudinem...

CLXXVI

Cicero, *Tusc.* 4.70: quis est enim iste amor amicitiae? cur neque deformem adulescentem quisquam amat neque formosum senem? mihi quidem haec in Graecorum gymnasiis

---

CLXXV 339 neque *K*   mi *Grotius*: mihi *X*

nata consuetudo uidetur, in quibus isti liberi et concessi sunt amores. bene ergo Ennius:

flagiti principium est nudare inter ciuis corpora.   341

qui ut sint, quod fieri posse uideo, pudici, solliciti tamen et anxii sunt, eoque magis quod se ipsi continent et coercent.

CLXXVII

Cicero, *Nat. deor.* 2.64: sed ipse Iuppiter, id est iuuans pater...
   65: hunc igitur Ennius, ut supra dixi, nuncupat ita dicens 'aspice hoc sublime candens quem inuocant omnes Iouem' planius quam (*PB*: quem *AHV*^{1}: que *GV*^{2}) alio loco idem

†cui† *quod in me est exsecrabor hoc quod lucet quicquid est.*   342

CLXXVIII

Cicero, *Diu.* 1.88: Amphilochus et Mopsus Argiuorum reges fuerunt sed iidem augures, iique urbis in ora ma0rituma Ciliciae Graecas condiderunt. atque etiam ante hos Amphiaraus et Tiresias, non humiles et obscuri neque eorum similes, ut apud Ennium est,

qui sui quaestus causa fictas suscitant sententias,   343

sed clari et praestantes uiri qui auibus et signis admoniti futura dicebant.

CLXXIX

Cicero, *Diu.* 2.57: Democritus quidem optumis uerbis causam explicat cur ante lucem galli canant (*B*: cantant *AV*); depulso enim de pectore et in omne corpus diuiso et mitificato (modificato *V*^{2}) cibo cantus edere quiete satiatos; qui quidem silentio noctis (noctis *ex corr. B*), ut ait Ennius,

fauent faucibus russis   344
cantu plausuque premunt alas.

CLXXVI 341 flagitii *X*   ciues *G*(?)*R*^{rec}
CLXXVII 342 qui *Gulielmius*   licet *V*
CLXXVIII 343 ficta *B*^{b}: factas *V*
CLXXIX 345 cantu *V*^{c}*B*^{b}: cantus *AV*^{b}*B*^{c} lausuque *AV*^{b}

CLXXX

Cicero, *Diu*, 2.127: iam uero quis dicere audeat uera omnia (A^cB: ueras omnia A^p: uera somnia V) esse somnia?

> *aliquot somnia uera*

inquit Ennius
> *sed omnia non necesse est.* 346

CLXXXI

(*a*) Cicero, *Off.* 1.61: itaque in probris (inprobis *Lpb*) maxime in promptu est si quid tale dici potest: 'uos enim (etenim *ps̄*) iuuenes animum geritis muliebrem, illa uirgo uiri'; et si quid eiusmodi:

> *Salmacida spolia sine sudore et sanguine.* 347

(*b*) Festus, p. 439.10: SALMACIS nomine nympha, Caeli et Terrae filia, fertur causa fontis Halicarnasi aquae appellandae fuisse Salmacidis (*uulgo*: salamcidis *F*); quam qui bibisset uitio inpudicitiae mollesceret. ob eam rem †que id† eius aditus, angustatus parietibus, occasionem largitur iuuenibus petulantibus antecedentium puerorum puellarumque uiolandarum (*Augustinus*: uitolandarum *F*) quia non patet effugium (*Timpanaro*: patefugium *F*). Ennius: 'Salmacida spolia (salmacidas polla *F*) sine sanguine et sudore'.

CLXXXII

Cicero, *Off.* 2.23: omnium autem rerum nec aptius est quicquam ad opes tuendas ac tenendas (tuendas *Lp*: tuendas tenentes *P*: tenendas ac tuendas *Hs̄*) quam diligi nec alienius quam timeri. praeclare enim Ennius:

> *quem metuunt oderunt; quem quisque odit periisse expetit.* 348

CLXXXII *Hieronymus, *Epist.* 82.3.2 quem metuit quis odit, quem odit perisse cupit.

CLXXX 346 non necesse est *F*: nonnunc haec esset *AV*: non nunc necesse est, sed nunc *linea transuersa del. B*
CLXXXII 348 perisse *codd.* expetit *ZLp*: cupit *c*

CLXXXIII

Cicero, *Off.* 2.62: propensior benignitas esse debebit in calami-
tosos nisi forte erunt digni calamitate. in iis tamen qui se
adiuuari uolent (uolunt *b*), non ne adfligantur sed ut altiorem
gradum ascendant, restricti omnino esse nullo modo debemus
sed in deligendis (diligendis *Lp*) idoneis iudicium et diligentiam
adhibere. nam praeclare Ennius:

> *benefacta male locata malefacta arbitror.* 349

CLXXXIV

(*a*) Cicero, *Off.* 3.104: sed in iure iurando non qui metus sed
quae uis sit debet intellegi (intellegi debet *Xʒ*). est enim ius
iurandum affirmatio religiosa; quod autem affirmate et (*Zpʒ*:
affirmat et *c*) quasi deo teste promiseris, id tenendum est. iam
enim non ad iram deorum, quae nulla est, sed ad iustitiam et ad
fidem (ad iustitiam et fidem *Lc*: ad fidem et iustitiam *p*)
pertinet. nam praeclare Ennius:

> *o Fides alma apta pinnis et ius iurandum Iouis.* 350

qui ius igitur (igitur ius *Xʒ*) iurandum uiolat, is fidem uiolat
quam in Capitolio uicinam Iouis optimi maximi (ioui *c*), ut in
Catonis oratione est, maiores nostri esse uoluerunt.

(*b*) Apuleius, *Socr.* 5: neue per ista iuretur, cum sit summi
deorum hic honor proprius. nam et ius iurandum Iouis (*Brant*:
iurandum iouis iurandum *codd.*) dicitur, ut ait Ennius.

CLXXXV

Cicero, *Lael.* 64: quid? haec ut (ut *om. P*) omittam, quam graues,
quam difficiles plerisque uidentur calamitatum societates! ad

---

CLXXXIII 349 benefacta *Z*: bene facta *ʒ*: beneficia *X*   male facta *codd.*

quas non est facile inuentu qui descendant (discendant *P*:
distendant *M*: discedant *K*). quamquam Ennius recte:

> amicus certus in re incerta cernitur. 351

tamen haec duo leuitatis et infirmitatis plerosque conuincunt,
aut si in bonis rebus contemnunt aut in malis deserunt.

CLXXXVI

Varro, *Ling.* 5.14: locus est ubi locatum quid esse potest, ut
nunc dicunt collocatum. ueteres id dicere solitos apparet...
apud Ennium:

> o terra Thraeca ubi Liberi fanum inclutum 352
> Maro locaui.

CLXXXVII

Varro, *Ling.* 5.23: terra, ut putant, eadem et humus; ideo
Ennium in terram cadentis dicere:

> cubitis pinsibant humum. 354

CLXXXVIII

Varro, *Ling.* 5.64: terra Ops, quod hic omne opus et hac opus
ad uiuendum, et ideo dicitur Ops mater quod terra mater. haec
enim

> terris gentis omnis peperit et resumit denuo. 355

quae dat cibaria, ut ait Ennius, quae quod gerit fruges Ceres.
antiquis enim quod nunc G C (*Lachmann*: & *F*).

65: idem hi dei Caelum et Terra, Iuppiter (Iupiter *F*) et Iuno
quod, ut ait Ennius,

> istic est is Iuppiter quem dico, quem Graeci uocant 356
> aerem, qui uentus est et nubes, imber postea,
> atque ex imbre frigus, uentus post fit, aer denuo.

CLXXXVI 352 Thraeca *Fleckeisen*: treca *F*   inclutum *Gulielmius*: inciuiũ *F*
353 miro *ut uid. ras. ex* maro *F*   locauit *Ribbeck*
CLXXXVIII 356 iupiter *F*   358 uentus *Laetus*: uentis *F*

†haec propter† *Iuppiter sunt ista quae dico tibi.*
†qua† *mortalis atque urbes beluasque omnis iuuat.*

quod hinc (*L. Spengel*: hic *F*) omnes et sub hoc, eundem appellans dicit 'diuumque hominumque pater rex'.

CLXXXIX

Varro, *Ling.* 7.12: tueri duo significat, unum ab aspectu, ut dixi, unde est Enni (*C. O. Mueller*: enī *F*) illud:

> *tueor te senex? pro Iuppiter!* 361

...alterum a curando ac tutela...

CXC

Varro, *Ling.* 7.12: quare a tuendo et templa et tesca dicta cum discrimine eo quod dixi.
13: etiam indidem illud Enni (*Scaliger*: enī *F*):

> *extemplo acceptum me necato et filium.* 362

extemplo enim est continuo quod omne templum esse debet continuo saeptum (septum *F*) nec plus unum introitum habere.

CXCI

Varro, *Ling.* 7.16: Ennius:

> *ut tibi Titanis Triuia dederit stirpem liberum.* 363

Titanis Triuia Diana est, ab eo dicta Triuia quod in triuio ponitur fere in oppidis Graecis uel quod luna dicitur esse, quae in caelo tribus uiis mouetur, in altitudinem et latitudinem et longitudinem. Titanis dicta quod eam genuit, ut (*L. Spengel*: ut ni *F*) Plautus (*cf. Bacch. 893*), Lato.

---

359 iupiter *F*
CLXXXIX 361 iupiter *F*
CXC 362 acceptū, cc *ex* u *corr. F*: acceptam *Vossius*   necato *Scaliger*: negato *F*

CXCII

Varro, *Ling.* 7.19: Enni (ennii *F*):

> *Areopagitae quid dedere* †quam pudam†   364

Areopagitae ab Areopago; is locus (*Laetus*: his locis *F*) Athenis.

CXCIII

Varro, *Ling.* 7.48: apud Ennium:

> *quaeque in corpore caua caeruleo*   365
> *caeli cortina receptat.*

caua cortina dicta quod est inter terram et caelum ad similitudinem cortinae Apollinis; ea a corde quod inde sortes primae
existimatae.

CXCIV

Varro, *Ling.* 7.49: apud Ennium:

> *quin inde inuitis sumpserint perduellibus.*   367

perduelles dicuntur hostes.

CXCV

Varro, *Ling.* 7.87: lymphata dicta a lympha; ⟨lympha⟩ (*add. L.
Spengel*) a Nympha, ut quod apud Graecos Θέτις, apud Ennium:

> *Thelis illi mater.*   368

CXCVI

Varro, *Ling.* 7.89: apud Ennium:

> *si uoles aduortere animum comiter monstrabitur*   369

comiter hilare ac lubenter cuius origo graeca κῶμος (*Aldus*:
comos *F*).

CXCIII 365 quaeque in corpore caua caeruleo *Bergk*: caua quaeque in corpore
caeruleo *Turnebus, Aduers. XXIII.17*: quaeque in corpore causa ceruleo *F*
366 caeli cortina receptat *Turnebus*: cẹlo orta nare ceptat *F*
CXCIV 367 uindictam uictis *Scaliger*
CXCV 368 Thelis *Turnebus*: thetis *F*

CXCVII

(*a*) Varro, *Ling.* 7.93: euax uerbum nihil significat sed effutitum naturaliter est— ut apud Ennium:

> *hehae! ipse clipeus cecidit.* 370

(*b*) Grammaticus incertus, *Gramm.* v 574.24: clipeus (*L*: clypeus *M*) generis masculini, ut Ennius: 'cecidit clipeus (*L*: clypeus *M*)'.

CXCVIII

Varro, *Ling.* 7.93: euax uerbum nihil significat sed effutitum naturaliter est— ut...apud Ennium:

> *heu mea puella* †spe† *quidem id succenset tibi.* 371

CXCIX

Varro, *Ling.* 7.101: apud Ennium:

> *uocibus concide* †facimus et† *obrutus.* 372

mussare dictum quod muti non amplius quam MV dicunt.

CC

Rutilius Lupus 1.12: Διαφορά. hoc schema ⟨est⟩ (*add. Ruhnken*) cum uerbum iteratum aliam sententiam significat ac significauit primo dictum (*Stephanus*: dictum est *codd.*)...item in Enni uersu (*Halm*: Enni uersus *Meineke*: uniuersum *codd.*):

> *mulierem: quid potius dicam aut uerius quam mulierem?* 373

CCI

Paulus, p. 110.16: METVS feminine (femine *R*) dicebant. Ennius:

> *uiuam an moriar nulla in me est metus.* 374

CXCVIII 371 ipse quidem *Lachmann*
CXCIX 372 facito musset *L. Mueller*
CCI 374 meto *R*

CCII

Festus, p. 166.11: NAVCVM ait Ateius Philologus poni pro nugis. Cincius quod oleae nucisque intus sit. Aelius Stilo omnium rerum putamen. glosematorum autem scriptores fabae grani quod haereat in fabulo. quidam ex Graeco, quod sit ναὶ καὶ οὐχί, leuem hominem significari. quidam nucis iugulandis, quam Verrius iugulandam uocat, medium uelut dissepimentum. Plautus...et Naeuius...sed ⟨et⟩ (*uulgo*: sed *F*) Ennius:

> *illic est nugator nihili non nauci homo.*   375

CCIII

Festus, p. 218.2: OBSIDIONEM potius dicendum esse quam obsidium adiuuat nos testimonio suo Ennius (pacuuius *X*) in Telamone quom (cum *X*) ait...item alio loco:

> *Hector qui haud cessat obsidionem obducere.*   376

CCIV

Festus, p. 388.25:

traxit. SOSP
omnes ferre auc
Afranius in Ep
seruent tuis
'maxime Teu⟨crorum ductor quo sospite⟩
numquam'. Enṇ
parentem et pa
sospitem. Acc   377
rite ad patri
set. Ennius uid

CCII 375 illic *Vrsinus*: illuc *F*   nihili *Vrsinus*: nihil *F*
CCIV SOSPES, saluus. Ennius tamen sospitem pro seruatore posuit. SOSPITARE est bona spe adficere aut bonam spem non fallere — *Paulus*

CCXV

Hieronymus, *Epist.* 60.14.4: Naeuius poeta 'pati' inquit 'necesse est multa mortalem mala'. unde... prudenterque Ennius

> *plebes*

ait

> *in hoc regi antestat: loco licet*   388
> *lacrimare plebi, regi honeste non licet.*

ut regi, sic episcopo. immo minus (plenius *G*) regi quam episcopo (quam episcopo regi *G*: episcopo quam regi Ψ). ille enim nolentibus praeest, hic uolentibus.

CCXVI

Diomedes, *Gramm.* I 345.1: item adeo adis: hoc iteramus adito aditas dictitantes, ut Ennius:

> *ad eum aditauere.*   390

CCXVII

Diomedes, *Gramm.* I 400.15: plura enim uerba quae uulgo passiuo more declinamus apud ueteres diuersa reperiuntur enuntiata declinatione.... moro... Ennius (Ennius *om. B*):

> †an aliquid quod dono illi morare sed accipite†   391

CCXVIII

(*a*) Diomedes, *Gramm.* I 447.5: homoeoteleuton est oratio similibus clausulis terminata, id est pari uerborum exitu finita, ut apud Ennium:

> *eos reduci quam relinqui, deuehi quam deseri*   392
> *malui.*

CCXV 388 plebis Φ: plebs *mDB p.c.m*² regio *GAKΦΨB* antistat *GKB*: antistet *m a.c.m*² (antesto *in mg. m*²): antistant Ψ   389 lacrimari Φ*B*
CCXVI ut Ennius 'ad eum aditauere' *huc transposuit Scioppius*
CCXVII 391 morares sed ς
CCXVIII (*a*) 392 eoste duci *M*: eos deduci *AB*   quam relinqui *om. ABM* deuihi *M*: deuei *A*   deserit *M*   393 maluit *B*

(*b*) Donatus, *Gramm.* IV 398.24: homoeoteleuton est cum simili modo (est cum similiter *P*: est oracio cum simili modo *S*) dictiones plurimae finiuntur ut 'eos reduci (eos reuei *S*) quam relinqui deuehi (relinquere deuei *S*) quam deseri malui'.

(*c*) Charisius, p. 370.27: homoeoteleuton est oratio pari uerborum exitu finita ut 'hos reduci (seduci *N*) quam relinqui, deuehi (deui *N*) quam deseri malui (maḷlu *N*)'.

CCXIX

Seruius auct., Verg. *Georg.* 1.12–13 (cui prima frementem | fudit equom): nonnulli uero ob hoc 'cui prima frementem fudit aquam' legunt quod ueteres murmura aquae fremitum dicebant. Ennius:

    ager oppletus imbrium fremitu.   394

CCXX

(*a*) Seruius auct., Verg. *Georg.* 4.170–1 (fulmina massis | cum properant): fulmina properant uetuste ait, ut...et Ennius: 'festinat diem'.

(*b*) Servius auct., Verg. *Aen.* 9.401 (properet per uolnera mortem): aut deest adire (*Commelinus*: audire *F*) aut deest ad... aut certe antique properet mortem, ut...Ennius:

    festiuum festinant diem.   395

CCXXI

Seruius, Verg. *Aen.* 1.4 (saeuae memorem Iunonis ob iram): cum a iuuando dicta sit Iuno quaerunt multi cur eam dixerit saeuam et putant temporale epitheton quasi saeua circa

---

CCXX (*b*) 395 festiuum *Danielis*: festinum *F*   dies *F*

Troianos, nescientes quod saeuam dicebant ueteres magnam,
ut Ennius:

> *induta fuit saeua stola.* 396

id est magna.

CCXXII

Seruius auct., Verg. *Aen.* 2.62 (certae occumbere morti):
OCCVMBERE MORTI. nouae locutionis figura et penitus remota.
Ennius:

> *ut uos nostri liberi* 397
> *defendant, pro uostra uita morti occumbant obuiam.*

CCXXIII

Seruius auct., Verg. *Aen.* 3.241 (ferro foedare uolucres):
FOEDARE, cruentare. Ennius:

> *ferro foedati iacent.* 399

CCXXIV

Seruius, Verg. *Aen.* 6.686 (effusaeque genis lacrimae): GENIS,
palpebris. Ennius de dormiente:

> *inprimitque genae genam.* 400

CCXXV

Seruius, Verg. *Aen.* 7.319–20 (nec face tantum | Cisseis
praegnas ignis enixa iugalis): CISSEIS, regina Hecuba, filia
secundum Euripidem Cissei (cisei *ASL*), quem Ennius Pacuuius
et Vergilius sequuntur; nam Homerus Dymantis (dimantis
codd.) dicit. haec se facem parere uidit et Parin creauit qui causa
fuit incendii.

CCXXI 396 inducta (*corr.*) N
CCXXII 397 nñ *C*: uñ *C*⁵: uestri *f*   398 uestra *C*⁵*f* obuiam *om. f*
CCXXIV 400 inprimit *M* rene *H*: genaeque *M*

CCXXVI

Seruius, Verg. *Aen.* 9.255–6 (integer aeui | Ascanius): INTEGER
AEVI, adulescens cui aetas integra superest, unde Ennius

> *deos aeui integros* 401

dicit quibus multum aeui superest.

CCXXVII

Seruius auct., Verg. *Aen.* 9.747 (hoc telum mea quod ui dextera
uersat): VERSAT, librat, iactat. et est Ennianum

> *uersat mucronem.* 402

COMMENTARY

ACHILLES

The title *Achilles* is given to Ennius by Verrius Flaccus,[1] Gellius,[2] Nonius,[3] Isidore[4] and a late commentator on Cicero's orations.[5] Nonius gives the same title to Livius[6] and to Accius.[7] One of Verrius' quotations[8] allows us to see that the author of Ennius' original was the mid fifth century poet Aristarchus of Tegea. The reference to an *Achilles Aristarchi* in the prologue of Plautus' *Poenulus* must be to Ennius' adaptation.[9]

The themes of the three tragedies are not readily discernible from the fragments quoted. Livius may have dealt with incidents of Achilles' life on

---

[1] Festus, p. 282.9 depends on Strzelecki's '5 lists from archaic poetry' (cf. *Quaest. Verr.* pp. 81 ff.); p. 394.33 on the '17 lists from archaic authors'.

[2] 4.17.14 depends on a grammatical source, probably one of the writings of Probus or Sulpicius Apollinaris.

[3] Pp. 147.19 and 166.20 depend on list 27 of Lindsay's 41, 'Alph. Verb'; p. 169.2 perhaps on Gellius 4.17.14 (cf. Strzelecki, in *Aus der altertumswissenschaftlichen Arbeit Volkspolen* [*Schr. der Sekt. für Altertumswiss. der Dt. Akad. der Wiss. zu Berlin* XIII, Berlin, 1959], pp. 81 ff.); p. 277.26 perhaps on list 1 'Gloss. i'; p. 472.26 on list 26 'Gloss. iii' or list 27.

[4] Nothing precise can be said about the source of *Diff.* 1.218. Isidore's polymathy depends notoriously on the work of writers who were not even themselves given to original research (on Isidore in general see J. Fontaine, *Isidore de Séville et la culture classique dans l'Espagne wisigothique* [Paris, 1959]). The effort to distinguish carefully between words of related meaning had long been encouraged by rhetoricians and lexicographers (see M. L. Uhlfelder, *De Proprietate Sermonum uel Rerum: A Study and Critical Edition* [American Academy in Rome, 1954], pp. 1 ff.).

[5] The source of Schol. Gron., Cic. *Verr.* 2.1.46 is obscure. The identification of unacknowledged quotations in the text of Cicero's speeches was undertaken by commentators as early as the first century A.D. and probably earlier (cf. Asconius, *Pis.* 82).

[6] The source of pp. 365.37 and 473.18 is obscure.

[7] The source of pp. 98.4, 110.13, 277.37 and 503.34 is obscure. It is certainly a different one from that which provided the *Myrmidones* quotations at pp. 109.31, 120.31, 137.33, 234.8, 261.24, 262.15, 396.31, 433.1 and 502.1, namely Lindsay's list 17 'Accius iii' (cf. also P. Schmidt, *De Nonii Marcelli auctoribus grammaticis* [Leipzig, 1868], pp. 52 ff., in particular p. 59 n. 26). H. Düntzer's theory (*L. Liuii Andronici Fragmenta* [Diss. Berlin, 1835], p. 20) that the titles *Achilles* and *Myrmidones* refer to the one script thus remains a possible one.

[8] Festus, p. 282.9. See *Introduction*, p. 59.

[9] See *Introduction*, p. 7.

Scyros,[1] Accius with the siege of Troy.[2] Ennius' tragedy was certainly set near a field of battle and Welcker interpreted most of the fragments with great plausibility as coming from a scene in which Agamemnon's ambassadors attempt to persuade the sulking Achilles to rejoin the fight with the Trojans.[3] Later students have made only slight modifications to Welcker's reconstruction.

Achilles appeared in three other tragedies by Ennius, *Hectoris lytra*, *Iphigenia* and *Telephus*. The *Hectoris lytra* was set in the Greek camp before Troy; so too the *Aiax*, Pacuvius' *Armorum iudicium*, Accius' *Armorum iudicium*, *Myrmidones*, *Epinausimache* and *Nyctegresia*. Several of these plays are quoted outside grammatical literature in loose and allusive ways,[4] and it is rarely possible for the modern student to assign them accurately. Even when Ennius' name is mentioned we are hindered by our ignorance of how far forward from the embassy the action of the *Achilles* went and how far back from Priam's visit to Achilles' tent that of the *Hectoris lytra* went.

At *S. Rosc.* 89 Cicero is speaking about the great number of professional prosecutors slain during the Sullan proscriptions. There spring to his mind famous slaughters in Roman history and in heroic legend, in particular that of the Achaeans by their ships at the hands of Hector. One of his sentences— *quis ibi non est uulneratus ferro Phrygio?*—consists of three trochaic metra and is said by a scholiast to come from an address by Ulysses to Ajax outside the tent of Achilles in a tragedy by Ennius (fr. CLXIV). Osann,[5] Welcker and Bergk[6]

---

[1] Cf. E. Bickel, *RhM* LXXXVI (1937), 1 ff.

[2] This would be certain if the title *Myrmidones* referred to the same script. On the fragments of the *Myrmidones* see Welcker, *Die Aeschylische Trilogie* (Darmstadt, 1824), pp. 420 ff., G. Hermann, *De Aeschyli Myrmidonibus Nereidibus Phrygibus Dissertatio* (Leipzig, 1833), pp. 6 ff. (= *Opusc.* V 140 ff.), W. Schadewaldt, *Hermes* LXXI (1936), 49 ff. (= *Hellas und Hesperien* [Zürich, 1960], 191 ff.), C. B. Earp, *A Study of the Fragments of Three Related Plays of Accius* (Diss. Columbia, 1939), pp. 24 ff., G. Barabino, in 'Αντίδωρον *H. E. Paoli oblatum* (University of Genoa, 1956), pp. 57 ff.

[3] *Die griech. Trag.* p. 933. Cf. Düntzer, *L. Liuii Andron. Frag.* p. 20. A. Schöll's reconstruction (*Beiträge zur Kenntnis der tragischen Poesie der Griechen*, I [Berlin, 1839], pp. 485 ff.) is not worth discussing.

[4] Horace doubtlessly has a Latin tragic Achilles in mind at *Ars* 120–2— *honoratum si forte reponis Achillem | inpiger, iracundus, inexorabilis, acer | iura neget sibi nata, nihil non adroget armis*—but it would be foolish to guess which one. Cicero distinguishes 'Achilles Homericus' (*De orat.* 3.57, *Tusc.* 3.18, 4.52, *Diu.* 1.65, *Att.* 9.5.3), 'Accius et aliquando sapiens Achilles' (*Tusc.* 1.105) and 'ille de Iphigenia Achilles' (*Rep.* 1.30) but frequently alludes to tragic versions of incidents of the Trojan siege without naming the author.   [5] *Anal. crit.* p. 13 n. 6.

[6] *Ind. lectt. Marburg* 1844, X ff. (= *Kl. phil. Schr.* I 222 ff.), altering *Vlixes uulneratus...cum interrogaretur ab Aiace* to *Eurypylus...Achille*.

assigned it to the *Achilles*. Ribbeck[1] accepted Schöll's reconstruction of the *Hectoris lytra*,[2] according to which the action began even before Patroclus' departure to do battle with the Trojans, pointed out the large number of extant fragments referring to battle and assigned *quis ibi non est uulneratus ferro Phrygio?* to that play. Schöll's reconstruction is by no means certain and while there is positive evidence that Cicero knew the script of the *Achilles* there are very few signs that he knew the *Hectoris lytra*. At an earlier point in his speech for Roscius, where he describes the embassy of the decurions of Ameria to Sulla (26), there is a verbal parallelism with fr. VI of the *Achilles*. On the other hand, when later in the speech he describes the murder of the elder Roscius, he asks his hearers (98): *non uersatur ante oculos uobis in caede Glaucia? non adest iste T. Roscius? non suis manibus in curru conlocat Automedontem illum, sui sceleris acerbissimi nefariaeque uictoriae nuntium?* and the scholiast comments (p. 312.17): *Automedon Achillis auriga fuit. posteaquam Achilles Hectorem uicit, posuit aurigam suum in curru ut iret et nuntiaret occisum Hectorem.* This departs from Homer's version of the story and it is possible that Cicero had a tragedy in mind. However the tragedy could hardly have been Ennius' *Achilles*. The whole question of fr. CLXIV must accordingly be left open.

At *Tusc.* 2.38 Cicero quotes a dialogue in iambic tetrameters between Eurypylus, who had been wounded in battle, and Patroclus (fr. CLXXI). It is clear that we have here a dramatisation of the incident described by Homer at *Il.* 11.806 ff. G. Hermann[3] assigned it to Accius' *Myrmidones* but a phrase is also quoted at *Orat.* 155 and Bergk[4] showed from an analysis of Cicero's method of quotation here that Ennius must be the author. Bergk assigned the dialogue to the *Achilles*; Ribbeck and Vahlen on the other hand assigned it to the *Hectoris lytra*. The problem is similar to that of fr. CLXIV. Two points are worth making, although they do not help much to resolve the problem. First, fr. CLXIV and fr. CLXXI appear to come from similar kinds of scene and it is a little difficult to imagine them both in the one play. Secondly, the Eurypylus of fr. CLXXI appears to have given after his dialogue with Patroclus a lengthy description of the battle. The iambic tetrameters may replace trimeters of the original but the argumentative structure of the scene must belong to the Greek poet.[5] Such accounts of events offstage were usually given by unnamed messengers even in late fifth century Attic tragedy.[6] One

---

[1] *Quaest. scen.* pp. 276 f.; cf. *Die röm. Trag.* pp. 118 ff.
[2] *Beitr.* pp. 472 ff. See below, p. 290.
[3] *De Aeschyli Myrmidonibus*, p. 8 (= *Opusc.* V 142).
[4] *Ind. lectt. Marburg* 1844, VIII ff. (= *Kl. phil. Schr.* I 220 ff.). Cf. below, p. 205.   [5] *Andria* 28 ff., however, could be Terence's invention.
[6] Fraenkel, however (*De Media et Noua Comoedia Quaestiones Selectae* [Diss. Göttingen, 1912], pp. 43 ff.), compares Pap. Hib. 1.4 (p. 22: Euripides?).

should hesitate to attribute such an advanced dramatic technique to Aristarchus.

The words quoted by Cicero at *Orat.* 160 (fr. CLXXII)—*ui patefecerunt Bruges*—and by Verrius at Festus, p. 218. 2 (fr. CCIII)—*Hector qui haud cessat obsidionem obducere*—as by Ennius clearly belong to an account of Hector's attack on the Greek encampment. The tragedy must be either the *Achilles* or the *Hectoris lytra.*

The words quoted by Varro at *Ling.* 7.93 (fr. CXCVII): *hehae! ipse clipeus cecidit*, by Nonius at p. 205.30 (fr. CCXIV): *crassa puluis oritur, omnem peruolat caeli fretum*, and by the commentators on Virgil's *Aeneid* at 3.241 (fr. CCXXIII): *ferro foedati iacent*, and 9.747 (fr. CCXXVII): *uersat mucronem*, as by Ennius belong to one or more battle descriptions. The *Erectheus*[1] is as likely in each case to be the source as either the *Achilles* or the *Hectoris lytra.*

The Ennian reference to Achilles' mother quoted by Varro at *Ling.* 7.87 (fr. CXCV) could as easily come from the *Achilles* or the *Hectoris lytra* as from the *Iphigenia.*[2]

Ribbeck compared the words quoted by Gellius at 19.8.6, *eo ego ingenio natus sum: amicitiam atque inimicitiam in frontem promptam gero*, with Homer, *Il.* 9.312–13 ἐχθρὸς γάρ μοι κεῖνος ὁμῶς Ἀΐδαο πύλησιν, | ὅς χ' ἕτερον μὲν κεύθῃ ἐνὶ φρεσίν, ἄλλο δὲ εἴπῃ and assigned them to the *Achilles.* They could have been spoken by the Achilles of the *Hectoris lytra* or the *Telephus* equally well,[3] or indeed by several other Ennian heroes. Gellius' mode of quotation, *Q. Ennius in illo memoratissimo libro*, implies, however, that he is not quoting a dramatic poem.[4] Ladewig[5] suggested that at *Mur.* 60, *non multa peccas, inquit ille fortissimo uiro senior magister, sed ⟨si⟩ (si* add. ed. Ascens. 1511) *peccas te regere possum*, Cicero quotes from a scene of Accius' *Myrmidones* in which Achilles is admonished by his one-time tutor Phoenix about his refusal to help the hard-pressed Greeks. Ennius' *Achilles* is just as likely to be the source.

I

The prologue of the *Poenulus* poses two questions of importance to students of the *Achilles.* The first one is whether we have a parody of a scene set at a place of public assembly; the second is whether we have extensive verbal quotations of Ennius' script.

---

[1] Cf. fr. LXII.

[2] Welcker, *Die griech. Trag.* p. 934 n. 1, suggested the *Achilles.* Vahlen, *E.P.R.*[2], p. 159, the *Iphigenia.*

[3] Welcker, *Die griech. Trag.* p. 489 n. 11, assigned them to the *Telephus.* They have no parallel in Euripides' *I.A.* and it is difficult to imagine a context in which Ennius could have introduced them himself in his version of that play.

[4] Cf. L. Havet, *RPh* XIV (1890), 45, Timpanaro, *SIFC* N.S. XXIII (1948), 6 ff.   [5] *Anal. scen.* p. 3 n. 1.

Schöll, who seems to have believed that the comic prologue was a mere translation of that of the Καρχηδόνιος without any necessary reference to Ennius' version of Aristarchus' 'Αχιλλεύς, argued that the tragic scene showed the assembly described in *Iliad* I, which was summoned to consider what to do about the plague sent by Apollo upon the Greek army. O. Jahn[1] imagined an assembly in which Achilles slew Thersites. Vahlen[2] drew attention to the one described in *Iliad* IX at which Agamemnon announced his decision to placate Achilles. This kind of view is beset with serious difficulties. The staging of a scene set at a place of assembly is hard to visualise: hard in the theatre of Dionysus at Athens, even harder in a Roman theatre where the flat space in front of the stage was occupied by part of the audience.[3] In extant Attic tragedies the proceedings of assemblies are regularly reported by messengers;[4] the scene of Aeschylus' Εὐμενίδες is a special case. Furthermore, if Scriverius' hypothesis of two plays by Ennius about Achilles has to be abandoned, we are faced with a shift of scene within the one play: from the assembly ground to Achilles' tent. The scene shifts in Aristophanes' Βάτραχοι (180) but nowhere in comedy of the classical period or its Roman adaptations;[5] in Aeschylus' Αἰτναῖαι (fr. 26 Mette) and Εὐμενίδες (234, 488) and in Sophocles' early tragedy Αἴας (815) but nowhere in the tragedies of Euripides or other late tragedies so far as we can determine. It is likely that even if a Roman poet chose an early Attic tragedy to adapt he would have obliterated any shifts of scene. Two opinions are admittedly possible on this point but Roman tragedies with shifts of scene should not be postulated unnecessarily. One could avoid the difficulties I have sketched by interpreting verses 3–49 of the prologue as a parody of commands given by Ennius' Achilles to the soldiers guarding his tent.[6]

E. Klussmann[7] argued that *v.* 3 of the prologue, *sileteque et tacete atque animum aduortite* and *v.* 11, *exsurge praeco fac populo audientiam* were verbatim quotations of the script of the *Achilles*. In his first edition of the fragments of tragedy Ribbeck printed these verses and part of *v.* 4, *audire iubet uos imperator*, as coming from the hand of Ennius. All subsequent editors of the fragments of Ennius' tragedies have accepted this idea. Of editors of the *Poenulus* Leo accepted *vv.* 3–4, *sileteque et tacete atque animum aduortite.* | *audire*

---

[1] *Hermes* III (1869), 191.   [2] *E.P.R.*², p. 118.

[3] See *Introduction*, p. 18.

[4] Cf. Euripides, *Hek.* 521 ff., *I.A.* 1543 ff., *Or.* 884 ff.

[5] H. W. Prescott, *CPh* VIII (1913), 14 ff., tried to explain the muddle at *Amphitruo* 629–32 by postulating a shift of scene from the harbour to the palace.

[6] For doubts about the usual view taken of the *Poenulus* prologue cf. F. Stoessl, *RE* XXIII ii (1959), *Nachträge*, s.v. *Prologos*, 2370.

[7] *NJbb* Suppl. XI (1845), 325.

iubet uos imperator, as a quotation and rejected *v*. 11. Lindsay on the other hand added *v*. 16, *bonum factum* †esse† *edicta ut seruetis mea*, to the quotations alleged by Klussmann and Ribbeck.

The verses *exsurge praeco, fac populo audientiam*[1] and *bonum factum* †esse† *edicta ut seruetis mea* obviously spring straight from the discourse the comic poet gives his actor. There is no reason at all to treat them as quotations of another play. *Sileteque et tacete atque animum aduortite.* | *audire iubet uos imperator* may be of similar character.

The word *commentari* is wrongly interpreted at *T.L.L.* III 1864.19 as 'afferre'. There is no good parallel for this meaning. What we have is probably a piece of actors' jargon: 'apply the mind to, study, con (with a view to acting a role)'; cf. Plautus, *Cist.* 509, *Truc.* 735 ff., Cicero, *S. Rosc.* 82, *Brut.* 87, 301. The sentence *inde mihi principium capiam ex ea tragoedia* need mean no more than 'I, who have often played the title role in the *Achilles*, will open this comedy like the *Achilles*, i.e. with a general's speech'.

The verb *silete*[2] and the copula *-que et*[3] had a pompous tragic ring but the commonplace *tacete* must have come παρὰ προσδοκίαν with similar effect to *histricus* in *v*. 4 and *fabulis* in *v*. 8. Where one word of a tautological pair is rarer and more elevated than the other it normally comes second.[4]

Audire iubet uos imperator looks superficially like part of a quotation of a tragic herald's address but one wonders why the prologising actor, who elsewhere speaks with the voice of a magistrate, should begin his edict so ineffectively.

I should take the phrase as a pompous variant of *uos audire iubeo* and compare the Euripidean Orestes' address to his dead father at *Or.* 1225–30 and the words of the Plautine Jupiter to Alcmena reported at *Amph.* 1064–5: *Alcumena adest auxilium: ne time.* | *et tibi et tuis propitius caeli cultor aduenit.*[5] Roman magistrates used a phrase like *uos audire iubeo* at *contiones*[6] and Caesar was not the only one to talk of himself in the third person; Cicero addressed Catiline with *exire ex urbe iubet consul hostem* (*Catil.* 1.13).

---

[1] Cf. Plautus, *Asin.* 4 *face nunciam* (Linge: *iam nunc* codd.) *tu praeco omnem auritum poplum*.

[2] Only four times in comedy.

[3] Rare in comedy and then only in phrases of some dignity concluding a metrical unit; see *T.L.L.* v ii 887.36 ff.

[4] For such tautologies in Roman tragedy see below on Ennius, *v*. 9.

[5] Cf. the way those personages of comedy who are given to paratragic pomposity sometimes issue greetings in the third person: Plautus, *Amph.* 676, *Bacch.* 243, *Epid.* 126–7, *Merc.* 713, *Poen.* 685–6, *Trin.* 435–6, 1151–2, Terence, *Eun.* 270–1.

[6] Cf. Livy 2.7.8 *ibi audire iussis consul laudare fortunam collegae*, Horace, *Sat.* 2.3.77 *audire atque togam iubeo componere* (parody).

Words and phrases from Ennius' *Achilles* doubtlessly do occur in the *Poenulus* prologue, perhaps here and there right down to *v.* 49, but the modern scholar is in no position to isolate them. The similarity between *sileteque et tacete atque animum aduortite* and Aristophanes, *Thesm.* 381 σῖγα σιώπα πρόσεχε τὸν νοῦν pointed out by Fraenkel[1] is not so very great if I am right about the tone of *tacete* and in any case could be explained by the fact that both Athenian and Roman public assemblies were rather noisy. There is no need to invoke Aristarchus as the link between the two verses.

II

The words which the scholiast alleges to come from Ennius' *Achilles* stand out stylistically from Cicero's discourse. The use of *ita* as a causative particle, frequent in drama, seems not to occur elsewhere in Cicero's orations. Words of the length of *eiciebantur*, much affected by tragedy, rarely end a Ciceronian sentence. From the preceding sentence O. Plasberg[2] extracted the tetrameter *ibi tum subito sunt coortae tempestates maximae*, remarking the absence elsewhere in Cicero's orations of the verb *cooriri*. The absence of this verb and the commonness of its simple form has no significance, for Cicero nowhere has *tempestas orta est* or anything like it; the purist Caesar obviously found nothing poetical in *tempestas coorta est* (cf. *Gall.* 4.28.2, 5.10.2, 7.61.1, *Ciu.* 1.48.1). However the plural *tempestates* would have raised the tone of the sentence above the ordinary (see below on *v.* 46).

The alleged Ennian words can be scanned as either *ita magni fluctus eiciebantur* ∪ — or — ∪ — *ita magni fluctus eiciebantur* ∪ —. In neither case is the scholiast's term 'hemistichium' an accurate description. Similar phrases in the scholia on Virgil's poems frequently cover what are not verbal quotations of earlier hexametric poems but mere loose imitations.[3]

It is accordingly possible that Cicero was using antique phraseology to embroider his near-miraculous story and had no thought of Ennius' *Achilles*. I think it certain enough that a storm caused by an angry Apollo formed part of either the background or the action of this play. It was Apollo who caused Agamemnon to insult Achilles[4] and ultimately brought about his death. A commentator saw a similarity, either real or imaginary, between Cicero's storm and Ennius' and pointed it out.[5] The Leiden scholia look like the end of a long process of epitomising. What we now read on *Verr.* 2.1.46 may be the work of someone rewriting an earlier and perhaps more accurate note.

---

[1] *Beobachtungen zu Aristophanes* (Rome, 1962), pp. 119 ff.
[2] In Vahlen, *E.P.R.*², *addenda*, p. 304.
[3] See *CQ* N.S. xv (1965), 139 ff. [4] *Il.* 1.8 f.
[5] For detailed knowledge of republican drama in the extant commentaries see the Bobbio scholia to *Sest.* 102, 117, 118, 120, 122, 123, 126.

COMMENTARY

Ita magni fluctus eiciebantur need be no more a verbatim quotation of tragedy than is *nisi tanta acerbitas iniuriae, tanta uis sceleris fuisset* at 2.1.81 (~ Ennius, *Trag.* 295) or *semper nobis uigilandum, semper laborandum uidemus* at 2.5.181 (~ Accius, *Trag.* 214).

1 fluctus eiciebantur: cf. Ovid, *Fast.* 3.521 *eiecta si forte tenebitur unda,* *T.L.L.* v ii 309.17 ff.

III

The three words come from a description of battle and probably refer to the stance normally adopted by Ajax (cf. Homer, *Il.* 7.219 ff., Anon. *Culex* 315 f.).

2 prolato aere: Festus' explanation could be misleading. *Scuto proiecto* was probably the set phrase in the contemporary military language; cf. Quadrigarius *ap.* Gell. 9.13.16 *constiterunt: Gallus sua disciplina scuto proiecto cantabundus; Manlius...,* Sisenna *ap.* Macr. *Sat.* 6.4.15 *scutis proiectis tecti... coniciunt,* Livy 7.10.9 *proiecto laeua scuto...deiecit,* 32.25.10 *cum proiecto prae se clipeo staret.* Ennius would have used *proferre* to fit the fabled hugeness of Ajax's shield. Here as elsewhere he gave his hero archaic weaponry; contemporary Roman soldiers carried the oblong *scutum* made of wood, linen, leather and metal insets (Polybius 6.23).

In Roman poetry relating to the heroic age *aes* is common for protective armour in general,[1] but outside the phrase under discussion there is no clear example of its standing metonymically for a particular shield. *Ferrum* however frequently denotes a particular offensive weapon.

IV

This is the beginning of either an oath or a supplication, the normal forms of which on the republican stage were *per Iouem iuro* et sim. and *per deos immortales obsecro* et sim. Ennius' personage invokes the divinised atmosphere. This was a notion familiar to Greeks of the Hellenistic period but perhaps as strange to early second century Romans as it was to fifth-century Athenians. Such oaths as those at Euripides, *Ion* 870, ἀλλ' οὐ τὸ Διὸς πολύαστρον ἕδος, and fr. 487, ὄμνυμι δ' ἱερὸν αἰθέρ' οἴκησιν Διός,[2] Aristophanes ridiculed as both irreligious and nonsensical (*Batr.* 100, *Thesm.* 272; cf. *Neph.* 627, 814 ff.). Philemon however could make the new god speak a comic prologue (fr. 91). Whether Ennius took this invocation from Aristarchus' play or from his own general acquaintance with Euripidean tragedy and Greek

---

[1] See *T.L.L.* 1 1073.73 ff. Cf. the same use of χαλκός in Greek poetry.
[2] Contrast Sophocles, *Ant.* 758 οὐ τόνδ' Ὄλυμπον, *O.T.* 1087.

philosophical speculation must remain uncertain. Certainly the divinised atmosphere appears frequently in his remains: e.g. *Trag.* 233–4, 342, 355–60. Here it is invoked in the style usual with the traditional deities.

The philosophical tone suggests that Ennius' speaker might be Phoenix, Achilles' one-time tutor.

The old editors scanned the words transmitted as two iambic trimeters. This involves treating the first syllable of *subices* as short, contrary to the testimony of Gellius and the normal behaviour of such words in republican drama.[1] Recent editors follow Lachmann[2] in taking *per ego deum sublimas subices* as the end of a trochaic tetrameter lacking the normal diaeresis.[3] Cf., however, Vahlen, *E.P.R.*[2], pp. LXX f.

3–4 per ego deum sublimas subices | umidas: the disjunction of *per* from its object probably had an antique ring even in supplications during the second century. It does not occur in extant comic oaths (but cf. Ovid, *Met.* 3.658, *Fast.* 2.841) and is rare, comparatively speaking, in comic supplications (cf. Plautus, *Bach.* 905, *Men.* 990, *Poen.* 1387, *Rud.* 627, Terence, *Andr.* 538, 834). *Ego* is usually accompanied by an oblique case of the second person pronoun in these disjunctions but cf. Plautus *Rud.* 627.

For the two adjectives in asyndeton split by their noun cf. Ennius, *Ann.* 395 *indigno bello confecit acerbo*, *Trag.* 296 *summis saxis fixus asperis*, Plautus, *Persa* 707–8 *longa nomina | contorplicata habemus*, *Rud.* 907 *qui salsis locis incolit pisculentis*, *Trin.* 297–8 *nil ego istos moror faeceos mores turbidos quibus boni dedecorant se*, Porcius Licinus, fr. 1.2 *bellicosam in Romuli gentem feram*.

Sublimis (*-us*) was a word of some dignity; it occurs nine times in republican tragedy, not at all in comedy except in the set phrases *sublimem rapere* (*arripere*) and *sublimem ferre* (*auferre*).

Subex, 'something laid underneath' or 'something raised up from underneath',[4] seems not to occur elsewhere in Latin. The adjective *umidas* and the relative clause *unde oritur imber sonitu saeuo et spiritu* indicate that the lower atmosphere is referred to.[5] The rareness of similar formations in tragedy makes it unlikely to be a poetic coinage. Ennius may be using a word of the architectural vocabulary metaphorically: *subices* would be the

---

[1] M. W. Mather, *HSCPh* VI (1895), 83 ff., 99, 130 ff., and C. Exon, *Hermathena* XIII (1905), 129 ff., find five certain cases in which the first syllable of a *iacio* compound is treated as short.

[2] On Lucretius 3.227 (Leipzig, 1850).   [3] Cf. Ennius, *Trag.* 74, 151, 196, 231.

[4] For *subicere*, 'raise up', cf. Virgil, *Ecl.* 10.73–4, *Georg.* 2.19, 4.385, *Aen.* 12.287–8. *Sub-* in origin indicated a movement from below; see P. Lejay, *RPh* XL (1916), 181 ff.

[5] Cf. Euripides, fr. 941.1–2 ὁρᾷς τὸν ὑψοῦ τόνδ' ἄπειρον αἰθέρα | καὶ γῆν πέριξ ἔχονθ' ὑγραῖς ἐν ἀγκάλαις;

COMMENTARY

blocks out of which the vault of heaven was constructed; for similar meta-
phors cf. Euripides, *Hek.* 1100–1 οὐράνιον | ὑψιπετὲς ἐς μέλαθρον, Ennius,
Trag. 319 *caeli ingentes fornices* (cf. Septuag. *Is.* 40.22 ὁ στήσας ὡς καμάραν
τὸν οὐρανόν), *Ann.* 49 *caeli caerula templa*, 60 *caenacula...caeli*, 615 *porta...
caeli*, *Sat.* 4 *pilatas...aetheris oras*, Accius, *Trag.* 531 *alto ab limine caeli*. The
absence of close parallels for some of the Latin metaphors in extant Attic
tragedy no doubt reflects the fact that arches and vaults were unknown in
the public buildings of fifth-century Athens.[1]

4 unde oritur imber: where a traditional deity is invoked, in both Greek
and Roman literature, a relative clause frequently indicates his permanent
habitat or function:[2] cf., in Roman drama, probably reflecting the language
of Roman cult as much as that of the Attic originals, Ennius, *Trag.* 234 *sol
qui res omnis inspicis*, Accius, *Trag.* 581–2 *sol qui...flammam...explicas*, *Trag.*
inc. 19–20 *o sancte Apollo qui umbilicum certum terrarum obtines* | *unde super-
stitiosa primum saeua euasit uox foras*, 216 *Liber qui augusta haec loca Cithaeronis
colis*, Plautus, *Bacch.* 172–3 *Apollo qui aedibus* | *propinquos nostris accolis*, *Poen.*
1187–8 *Iuppiter qui genus colis alisque hominum, per quem uiuimus uitalem aeuom*,
| *quem penes spes uitae sunt hominum omnium.*

sonitu saeuo et spiritu: cf. Accius, *Trag.* 392 *ingenti sonitu et spiritu*, Virgil,
Aen. 6.557 *saeua sonare.*
The play with the sounds *U* and *S* may be intended to represent the stormy
weather being referred to; cf. Plautus, *Amph.* 1062 *strepitus crepitus sonitus
tonitrus*, Pacuvius, *Trag.* 336 *strepitus fremitus clamor tonitruum*, Horace,
Epod. 10.19 *Ionius udo cum remugiens sinus*, Virgil, *Georg.* 4.260 ff. *tum sonus
auditur grauior tractimque susurrant*, etc., *Aen.* 1.85 ff. *una Eurusque Notusque
ruont*, etc. Yet alliteration and assonance are so common in the remains of
tragedy, in every kind of context[3] and particularly at the ends of metrical

---

[1] See H. Plommer, *Ancient and Classical Architecture* (London, 1956),
pp. 244 ff.
[2] See Norden, *Agnostos Theos* (Leipzig, 1913), pp. 168 ff.
[3] For alliteration of noun and determinant cf. Livius 33 *mare magnum*, 37
struices saxeas, Naevius 8 *praesens pretium*, 21 *corporis custodias*, Ennius 3 *sublimas
subices*, 4 *sonitu saeuo*, 29 *arcum auratum*, 34 *mulier melior*, 43 *mari magno*, 44
exitium examen, 57 *sortes somnium*, 96 *caua caeli*, 139 *salsum sanguinem*, 171 *stellis
splendidis*, 189 *caeli clipeo*, 207 *uiduae et uastae uirgines*, 215 *era errans*, 216 *animo
aegro*, 223 *Medeai miserias*, 237 *custos corporis*, 239 *opulentum oppidum*, 244
cupido corde, 250 *caua caerula*, 254 *uera uirtute*, 256 *pectus purum*, 296 *summis saxis*,
305 *pedum pulsu*, 333 *acrem aciem*, Pacuvius 70 *propinquitate parti*, 80 *antiqui
amici*, 82 *portentum pauos*, 177 *regina rerum*, 232 *caelitum camilla*, 246 *manuum
mollitudine*, 251 *sparteis serilibus*, 252 *scruposam specum*, 309 *dictio Delphis*, 386

units[1] that it is always hazardous to link the sound of a phrase with its sense. In the present case it is worth pointing out that the triple alliteration of s is not as common as that of c and p, sounds which begin just as many words in the tragic lexicon, and that u (long) assonances are quite uncommon. Ennius took this element of his tragic style from his Latin predecessors rather than from Attic tragedy, which, although not averse to phonetic effects, sought them very sparingly.[2] Their presence in contemporary hymns and prayers[3] enabled them to lend weight to the utterances of the tragic heroes.

v

Timpanaro's restoration *nam consiliis ius obuarant...*[4] is the most economical and convincing so far offered. The resulting anapaests would come from a denunciation by Achilles of his Greek enemies.

5 obuarant: not elsewhere in Latin; the simple verb *uarare* seems to occur only in the technical vocabulary of the land surveyors (cf. Grom. pp. 285–6, 288–91). In the case of verbs of the common language tragedy often forms compounds with *ob-* where comedy uses the simple form or another compound: e.g. Ennius 41 *obuoluere*, 192 *obire* and *obiacere*, 326 *opplere*, 376 *obducere*, Pacuvius 213 *obnuntiare*, Accius 285 *obtui* (319), 344 *oblectare*, Trag. inc. 254 *obrigescere*.

quibus tam concedit hic ordo: the more influential among the Greek βασιλῆες.

---

incicorem iracundiam, 387 *consilium cicur*, 418 *saeuitiam Salaciae*, Accius 71 *animo aegroto*, 150 *salutis spes supremas*, 176 *satias sanguinis*, 297 *abundantem antiquam amnem*, 331 *lucifera lampade*, 421 *liberorum leto*, 453 *mansues misericordia*, 467 *uis ueritatis*, 468 *animum atrocitatem*, 501 *horrida honestitudo*, 517 *serpentis squamae*, 565 *uis uolneris*, 566 *stellas septem*, 573 *crepitu clangente*, 581 *candido curru*, 583 *aduerso augurio*, 647 *more multarum*, 659 *satias supplici*.

[1] For alliteration of the three concluding words cf. Naevius 13, 28, 35, 45, Ennius 4, 34, 55, 62, 118, 138, 203, 211, 217, 219, 250, 258, 259, 262, 281, 287, 303, 310, 317, 318, 329, 347, 350, 365, Pacuvius 93, 118, 246, 292, Accius 16, 22, 158, 198, 200, 201, 223, 229, 288, 434, 445, 449, 453, 509, 520, 573, 630.

[2] For a passage roughly parallel with Ennius, *Trag.* 3–4 cf. Aeschylus, *Hik.* 33–6 ἔνθα δὲ λαίλαπι | χειμωνοτύπῳ βροντῇ στεροπῇ τ' | ὀμβροφόροισίν τ' ἀνέμοις ἀγρίας | ἁλὸς ἀντήσαντες ὄλοιντο. For alliteration of noun and determinant cf. Sophocles, *Ai.* 55, 445; of the last three words in a metrical unit cf. Aeschylus, *Ag.* 1430, Sophocles, *Ai.* 445, 687, *El.* 210, Euripides, *Ba.* 1298, *Rhes.* 383.

[3] Cf. those recorded by Cato, *Agr.* 132 ff.

[4] *SIFC* N.S. XXII (1947), 69 ff. Cf. Havet, *RPh* XXXI (1907), 133.

For *tam* with verb cf. Plautus, *Bacch.* 778 (= *adeo*), Ennius, *Trag.* 380 (= *tamen*).

Hic ordo was a phrase regularly used by Roman senators referring to their assembled peers (e.g. Cicero, *Pis.* 6, 8, 40, 45 et al.). Cf. Plautus' parody at *Cist.* 22–4 *decet pol, mea Selenium, | hunc esse ordinem beniuolentis inter se | beneque amicitia utier.*

VI

For a parallel situation cf. Seneca, *Thy.* 429–30 *quae causa cogit, genitor, a patria gradum | referre uisa?* Ennius' speaker may be one of the ambassadors sent to placate Achilles.

Cicero perhaps has this passage in mind when at *S. Rosc.* 26 he says of the ambassadors sent to Sulla: *Ameriam re inorata reuerterunt.* The phrase *re inorata* occurs nowhere else in Latin. Cicero has *rem agere* and *rem dicere* quite commonly in his orations, *rem orare* not at all; he has *causam agere* and *causam dicere* also commonly, *causam orare* only once (in the early *Pro Quinctio* 43; cf. *Brut.* 47).

6 incerta re atque inorata: for the word-order cf. Plautus, *Amph.* 33 *iustam rem et facilem*, Terence, *Andr.* 132 *bene dissimulatum amorem et celatum*; see Haffter, *Untersuchungen*, p. 73.

Orare, 'speak, say' (cf. Varro, *Ling.* 7.41), seems to have been obsolete even in Ennius' time in the vernacular except for the legalistic phrases *aequom orare* and *ius orare.*

In Ennius' time the absolute phrase, especially where it had a preponderantly temporal significance, characterised the official language rather than the ordinary vernacular. It is a noticeable feature of the style of speeches in comedy parodying the reports which generals made of their achievements;[1] wherever else it appears the context has a markedly formal tone. It is not very common even in tragedy; Ennius has 51 *quo facto*, 71 *respectantibus...nobis*, 176 *male re gesta*, 299 *remissa humana uita*, Pacuvius 411 *occidente sole.*

6–7 gradum | regredere conare: Nonius' source may have made the sort of error that Caesellius made over the gender of *cor* in *Ann.* 382 (Gellius 6.2.3 ff.). *Regredere* is not elsewhere recorded in Latin and *regredi* is common only in the historians. The grammarian could have mistaken *regredere*, a second person singular present indicative,[2] for an infinitive and *conare*, an imperative, for an indicative.

---

[1] E.g. Plautus, *Amph.* 188 f., 654 ff., *Bacch.* 1070 f., *Persa* 753 ff. See Fraenkel, *Pl. im Pl.* pp. 236 f., *Addenda* to Italian trans. p. 429, Haffter, *Untersuchungen*, p. 49.

[2] The form normally ended in -*re* in republican drama; for statistics on Plautus' usage see C. M. S. Müller, *Glotta* XVII (1928), 137 ff.

Gradus, 'act of taking a step', occurs only once in comedy outside Plautus (Terence, *Phorm.* 867), is avoided by Caesar, and is rarely used by Cicero. Sallust and Livy, on the other hand, have it often in accounts of military activities. Republican (12 instances) and Senecan tragedy (65) have it in all kinds of contexts. Plautus' 22 instances can all be interpreted as parody of either military or tragic language; he has neither *gradum regredere* nor *gradum referre* nor *gradum repedare* (so Pacuvius, *Trag.* 400); *redire* (142 instances; Terence 89), *reuerti* (27; Terence 10), *reuenire* (17; Terence 0), *recedere* (10; Terence 0) express the idea for him.

For the etymological figure cf. Euripides, *Alk.* 869 πόδα πεζεύων, Plautus, *Poen.* 514 *istoc grassari gradu.* Such figures frequently occur in the plays of Plautus in all kinds of contexts from the ludicrous to the highly pathetic. They are much less common in the rest of comedy.[1] Ennius has them often in both tragedy (36 *fatis fandis*, 48 *iudicauit...iudicium*, 93 *uitam euitari*, 115 *corpus...corporaret*, 211 *nominatur nomine*, 236 *facinus...fit*) and epic (*Ann.* 50 *uoce uocabam*, 77 *curantes...cum cura*, 244 *faceret facinus*, 314 *factumque facit*, 452 *longiscere longe*, 458 *riserunt...risu*); in the rest of tragedy I find only Naevius 39 *inflexu flectitur*, Pacuvius 239 *nuncupasti nomine*, Trag. inc. 82 *partu...parit*, 185 *dominare domino*. They occur fairly frequently in Attic tragedy but it was their use by Roman public men in solemn contexts[2] that made them attractive to a poet seeking a theatrical equivalent of the Attic τραγικὴ λέξις.

If *conare* is to be understood in Nonius' sense, it means 'are you about to?, are you preparing to?'; cf. Pacuvius, *Trag.* 227, Terence, *Phorm.* 52, *Haut.* 240, Cicero, *Fam.* 5.12.1, Propertius 1.6.19.

VII

These words would have been addressed to the sulking Achilles. For their sentiment cf. Homer, *Il.* 9.251 φράζευ ὅπως Δαναοῖσιν ἀλεξήσεις κακὸν ἦμαρ, Aeschylus, *Myrm.* fr. 132 τί ποτ' ἀνδροδάικτον ἀκούων ἰὴ κόπον οὐ πελάθεις ἐπ' ἀρωγάν;

The Latin wording suggests the conditions under which contemporary Romans fought rather than those of the Greek heroic age. Homer's Achilles was in no sense a fellow citizen of Agamemnon, Ulysses, Ajax and the rest. Nevertheless the Attic tragedians represented the expedition against Troy as promoting a panhellenic interest and employed arguments proper to city-state patriotism (e.g. Euripides, *I.A.* 1368–401). To be compared with Ennius' tetrameter are two passages of Plautus, the slave Toxilus' parody of

---

[1] See Haffter, *Untersuchungen*, pp. 10 ff.
[2] Cf. Lex XII tab. 12.2 *si seruos furtum faxit noxiamue no⟨x⟩it.*

the Roman general's prayer of thanksgiving at *Persa* 753–62 (753 *hostibus uictis ciuibus saluis*) and Pleusicles' monologue on the dishonourable actions caused by love at *Mil.* 1284–9 (1289 *mitto iam ut occidi Achilles ciuis passus est*).

8 serua ciues, defende hostes: such asyndetic antithesis is extremely common in tragedy: cf. Ennius 24 *fer mi auxilium, pestem abige a me*, 38 *tui me miseret, mei piget* et al.

For the rhyming metra cf. Ennius, *Trag.* 205 *Helena redeat uirgo pereat*, 224 *tu me amoris magis quam honoris*, Naevius, *Com.* 76 *alii adnutat alii adnictat*, Plautus, *Amph.* 683 *sic salutas atque appellas*, 1013 *in medicinis in tonstrinis, Bacch.* 64, *Curc.* 179, 285, 286, 297, *Epid.* 198, 230, 231, *Men.* 403, 1015, *Merc.* 493, 833, *Mil.* 331, *Pseud.* 695, *Truc.* 824. The laws governing the structure of trochaic tetrameters all but prevent such rhymes in Attic tragedy.[1] Comedy, despite its looser metrical structure, has very few. To the Aristophanic examples collected by Fraenkel, *Hermes* LXII (1927), 365 ff. (= *Kl. Beitr.* II 19 ff.), may be added Menander, *Dysk.* 717.

Ennius' use of *defendere* probably had an archaic tone even at the time of writing. The only parallel in comedy is Plautus, *Rud.* 774 *ut illas serues uim defendas* (contrast *Bacch.* 846 et al.).

cum potes defendere: verbs are frequently repeated in adjacent clauses in both tragedy and early comedy.[2]

VIII

Welcker took this fragment to refer to a particular battle and to come from a speech made by one of the ambassadors to the sulking Achilles. Klussmann's palaeographically attractive restoration of the corrupt beginning, *int⟨ere⟩a*, would make such an interpretation almost inevitable. *Mortales*, however, unaccompanied by any determinant, is taken most naturally as 'men in general'. The fragment could come from a moralising speech comparing the bellicosity of men with the peaceful ways of the gods.[3]

9 mortales: substantive *mortalis* was probably little used in the vernacular. But tragedy has it 5 times as against *uir* 20 and *homo* 10. The Plautine ratio is

---

[1] The nearest I can find is Euripides, *I.A.* 869 χὤτι μ' ἐν ταῖς σαῖσι φερναῖς.

[2] Outside the prologues (*Andr.* 10, 17, 18–19, *Haut.* 13–14, 20–1, *Eun.* 4–5, 27–8, 41, *Phorm.* 9–10, 11, 22–3, 31, *Hec.* 10–11, *Ad.* 18–19) Terence tends to avoid such repetition.

[3] The gods depicted in early Greek epic and extant Attic tragedy are very far from peaceful but certain philosophers substituted a more edifying picture (cf. Cicero, *Nat. deor.* 2.78), and Ennius seems to have made one of his tragic heroes give voice to their doctrine at fr. CLXII.

45:246:780, the Terentian 0:65:177, that of the rest of comedy 2:5:23. Caesar avoids the word and Cicero uses it sparingly (in the set phrases: *multi mortales, omnes m., cuncti m.*). The historians have it often.

pugnant proeliant: for the near tautology cf. Homer, *Il.* 2.121 πολεμί-ζειν ἠδὲ μάχεσθαι, Plautus, *Curc.* 179 *sibi pugnas sibi proelia*, Lucretius 2.118 *proelia pugnas edere*, 4.967 *pugnare ac proelia obire*, Virgil, *Aen.* 11.912 *ineant pugnas et proelia temptent.* Such tautologies are much more common in Roman tragedy (cf. Ennius 65, 117, 148, 148, 156, 181, 198, 207, 246, 276, 285, 303, Pacuvius 32, 36, 44, 98, 175, 223, 303, 340, 369, 384, Accius 66, 90, 114, 136, 554, 587, Trag. inc. 73, 145) than in Attic. The Latin poets were probably using the associations they had in the minds of their hearers with the abundant style of the official language.[1] Only one of the Ennian examples occurs in a trimeter. In comedy Plautus restricted them by and large to the trimeters of the prologue and the musically accompanied verses of the action.[2] Later drama employed them much more sparingly, tragedy blurring the old distinction between trimeters and musically accompanied verses.

The 'asyndeton bimembre' has many parallels in the remains of Ennius' tragedies (36, 65, 74–5, 90, 91, 116, 117, 166, 303), fewer in those of Pacuvius (175, 263, 310, 384) and Accius (66, 114, 394), still fewer, comparatively speaking, in Attic tragedy.[3] The official language again probably provided the impetus.[4] Comic asyndeta either consist of old-fashioned proverbs or formulae of the official language or occur in the company of other stylistic devices aping the style of tragedy.

The deponent form *proeliantur* may have been regular in the common language in Ennius' time (there is, of course, no significance in its absence from comedy) as it was later and replaced with *proeliant* in this verse for the sake of homoeoteleuton.

IX

The text which the codices of Isidore present is full of difficulties.

The verbal repetition *extolles...tollunt* is of a type common in republican drama[5] but the two *sententiae* do not seem quite appropriate to the one con-

---

[1] Cf. *C.I.L.* I² 614 (189 B.C.) *L. Aimilius L. f. inpeirator decreiuit...agrum oppidumqu. quod ea tempestate posedisent, item possidere habereque iousit.*

[2] Cf. Haffter, *Untersuchungen*, pp. 63 ff.

[3] Of cases accompanied by alliteration and homoeoteleuton I note Aeschylus, *Ag.* 1410 ἀπέδικες ἀπέταμες, 1553, *Pers.* 426, Euripides, *Alk.* 173, *Or.* 1302.

[4] Cf. Lex XII tab. 6.3 *usus auctoritas fundi biennium est*, 8.10 *uinctus uerberatus igni necari iubetur.*

[5] Cf. Pacuvius, *Trag.* 38–9 *non tam illum adpetit...quam illum eumpse* (Vossius: *eum ipsum* codd.) *lapidem...petit*, 410 *intuentur nec tuendi satietas capier*

175

text. Whereas the first deals with evil livers and good livers, the second deals with the evilly disposed and the well disposed. Editors of Isidore have treated the second as written by the bishop[1] but Ribbeck's removal of *enim* produced a perfectly good trochaic tetrameter. L. Mueller inserted an *idem alibi* in front of the tetrameter.

The Latinity of *summam tu tibi pro mala uita famam extolles et pro bona paratam gloriam* is dubious at only one point. Comedy, Caesar, Cicero, the historians and the classical poets have the phrase *gloriam (laudem) parere* regularly. But *gloriam parare* is possible in republican tragedy. The metre of Ennius, *Trag.* 141 protects the hemistich *libertatem paro* against any suspicions that might be raised against it by the regularity of *libertatem parere* elsewhere in Latin. Ribbeck produced, with two alterations, quite regular trochaic verse: *summam tu tibi | pro mala uita famam extolles, pro bona partam gloriam.* The treatment of *mala* and *bona*, words normally iambic in shape, as pyrrhic has good parallels in the iambic and trochaic verses of tragedy: e.g. Livius, *Trag.* 11, Ennius, *Trag.* 16, 41, 84, 163, 164, 181, 187, 258, 323, 327, 331, Pacuvius, *Trag.* 58–9, 236, Accius, *Trag.* 133, 147. Vahlen produced trochaic rhythm without alteration to the tradition by dividing the epithet *mala* and its noun *uita* between verses. I can find no good parallel for this in early dramatic verse.[2]

The distant disjunction of the anteposed epithet *summam* counts somewhat against trochaic or iambic measurement. There are no parallels in any kind of tragic verse before Accius (*Trag.* 234[1]–5, 658–9).[3]

I have no solution to these problems.

For the sentiments cf. Cato, *Or.* 17 *si quid uos per laborem recte feceritis labor ille a nobis cito recedet, bene factum a uobis, dum uiuitis, non abscedet; sed si qua per uoluptatem nequiter feceritis, uoluptas cito abibit, nequiter factum illud apud uos semper manebit*, Cicero, *Tusc.* 3.3 *est enim gloria solida quaedam res et expressa, non adumbrata: ea est consentiens laus bonorum, incorrupta uox bene iudicantium de excellenti uirtute, ea uirtuti resonat tamquam imago. quae quia recte factorum*

---

potest, Plautus, *Aul.* 202–3, *Bacch.* 980, *Capt.* 65–6, *Men.* 122–3, *Pseud.* 549–50, Terence, *Hec.* 8, *Phorm.* 265, Fraenkel, in *Studien zur Textgeschichte und Text-kritik* (Cologne, 1959), pp. 21 f. If one excludes phrases like κατίδετ' ἴδετε (Euripides, *Med.* 1252; see Elmsley *ad loc.*) the type is very uncommon in Attic drama.

[1] So too Scriverius; see *Collectanea*, p. 182.

[2] But cf. Ennius, *Trag.* 283–4 *dati | sunt*, 316–17 *ex | incertis.*

[3] Ennius and Pacuvius disjoin epithet and noun with scarcely any greater boldness or frequency than do the comedians; like the latter they disjoin much more often in musically accompanied verses than in spoken trimeters. Accius appears to have made no distinction between sung and spoken verse and to have been about three times as free as his predecessors in placing epithets.

plerumque comes est, non est bonis uiris repudianda. illa autem, quae se eius imitatricem esse uolt, temeraria atque inconsiderata et plerumque peccatorum uitiorumque laudatrix, fama popularis, simulatione honestatis formam eius pulchritudinemque corrumpit.
For the distinguishing of words related in meaning cf. Euripides, *Andr.*
319–22 ὦ δόξα δόξα μυρίοισι δὴ βροτῶν | οὐδὲν γεγῶσι βίοτον ὤγκωσας μέγαν, | εὔκλεια δ᾽ οἷς μὲν ἔστ᾽ ἀληθείας ὕπο | εὐδαιμονίζω, *Med.*
1229–30 ὄλβου δ᾽ ἐπιρρυέντος εὐτυχέστερος | ἄλλου γένοιτ᾽ ἂν ἄλλος, εὐδαίμων δ᾽ ἂν οὔ, Accius, *Trag.* 4–9, 296, *Trag. inc.* 30. Grammatical and rhetorical theorising provided the impetus as much in second-century Rome as in fifth-century Athens.

   10 tu tibi: cf. Plautus, *Asin.* 524, *Curc.* 9, *Pseud.* 936, et al.

   famam extolles: cf. Naevius, *Trag.* 7 *desubito famam tollunt si quam solam uidere in uia,* Plautus, *Persa* 351 *inimici famam non ita ut natast ferunt, Trin.* 186 *hascine propter res maledicas famas ferunt,* 689 *ne mi hanc famam differant.* There is a tendency in tragedy to replace simple verbs regular in the common language by compounds with *ex-*; see below on *v.* 20.

AIAX

The title *Aiax* is given to Ennius by Verrius[1] and Nonius.[2] Nonius gives the same title to Livius.[3] Livius' one fragment, *mirum uidetur quod sit factum iam diu,* is of indeterminate subject-matter.[4] The fragment of Ennius' play quoted by Verrius suggests that the death of Ajax was the main theme. Vahlen interpreted the fragment quoted by Nonius in such a way as to carry the action back to the debate over whether Achilles' armour should be given to Ajax or to Ulysses.

   Greek sources record the title Αἴας against the names of Sophocles, Carcinus, Theodectes and the younger Astydamas. Scaliger's view[5] that Ennius adapted Sophocles' extant Αἴας would be upset if Vahlen were right about fr. xiii or if it could be shown that Livius had already adapted this play.

---

[1] Festus, p. 482.5.   [2] P. 393.15.
[3] P. 127.20. The source is obscure at all three places.
[4] Ribbeck (*Die röm. Trag.* p. 26) and Leo (*De Trag. Rom.* p. 6 [= *Ausg. kl. Schr.* I 195]) refer it to Greek ingratitude towards Ajax, Ribbeck supplying *mirum uidetur quod sit factum iam diu* ⟨*oblitos esse*⟩?, Leo ⟨*mortalibus*⟩ *mirum uidetur quod sit factum iam diu;* cf. Sophocles, *Ai.* 646 ff., 1266 ff.
[5] *Coniect. Varr. Ling.,* on 6.6.

At least two other republican tragedies, Pacuvius' *Armorum iudicium* and Accius' tragedy of the same name, had Ajax the son of Telamon as a central figure. The action of Accius' tragedy almost certainly included the death of Ajax.[1] Ajax appeared as a minor figure in a second Ennian tragedy, either the *Achilles* or the *Hectoris lytra*.[2]

Cicero distinguishes between 'Homericus Aiax' (*Diu.* 2.82, *Tusc.* 4.49) and 'Aiax fabulaeque' (*Scaur.* 3). He refers to tragic presentations of the debate between Ajax and Ulysses before the judges (*Off.* 3.98), Ajax's demented attack on Ulysses (*De orat.* 3.162, *Ac.* 2.89) and Ajax's death (*Tusc.* 4.52, *Off.* 1.113, *Scaur.* 3). Since he nowhere quotes Livius verbally and on one occasion refers to his plays with some disdain,[3] we may suppose that the *Aiax* to which he refers at *Off.* 1.114 is Ennius' tragedy.

Ribbeck[4] attributed the trimeter quoted by Cicero at *Off.* 1.61 without name of author and by Festus at p. 439.17 with that of Ennius (fr. CLXXXI) —*Salmacida spolia sine sudore et sanguine*—to a scene of the *Aiax* in which Ajax molested a herd of cattle, imagining the cattle to be the Greek princes who had deprived him of Achilles' armour.[5] The attribution is plausible. It would not conflict with the view that Ennius adapted Sophocles' Αἴας. In this play Ajax's treatment of the cattle was described by Athena but a Latin adaptation might well have substituted an actual scene. In adapting the Ἀδελφοί of Menander, where, it seems,[6] the young man's seizure of the girl from the procurer was merely reported, Terence added after the introductory dialogue between the two old men a scene showing the actual seizure. This must be the scene which, in the prologue,[7] Terence claims to be a careful version of a scene of Diphilus' Συναποθνῄσκοντες omitted from Plautus' adaptation of that play. Ennius of course was one of the playwrights to whose authority Terence appealed in justification of his free treatment of Menander's text. However I leave the fragment among the *incerta*.

The Laurentian codex of Varro's treatise *De lingua Latina* has at 6.6 a piece of verse introduced by the words 'ennius aiax'. At three points in books 5 and 6 Varro heads quotations of tragedy with the name of the speaker (5.18–20, 6.2–7, 6.81–2), twice clearly distinguishing this name with that of the author of the tragedy: 6.6 *Pacui dicit pastor*, 6.7 *in Bruto Cassii* (sic) *quod dicit Lucretia* (cf. 7.3 *etiam Teucer Liuii post* XV *annos ab suis qui sit ignoretur*).

---

[1] Welcker, *RhM* III (1829), 54 n. 39, and G. Hermann, *De Aeschyli Tragoediis Fata Aiacis et Teucri Complexis Dissertatio* (Leipzig, 1838), pp. 5 ff. (= *Opusc.* VII 365 ff.), thought that Pacuvius' tragedy also extended as far; but cf. Leo, *De Trag. Rom.* p. 12 (= *Ausg. kl. Schr.* I 201).

[2] Ennius, *Trag. fr.* CLXIV b. See above, p. 162.   [3] *Brut.* 71.

[4] *Quaest. scen.* p. 272; cf. *Die röm. Trag.* pp. 131f.

[5] Cf. *Trag. inc.* 47–8.

[6] Cf. *Ad.* 88–92.   [7] *Ad.* 6–11.

Cicero frequently employs the same method of citing drama.[1] His purpose is sometimes to mark off a Latin poet's handling of the personage from a famous Greek handling but usually to separate two well-known Latin handlings. We may therefore accept as very probable Laetus' reading *Enni*(*i*) *Aiax* at Varro, *Ling*. 6.6.[2]

Scaliger excluded the words which Varro quotes—*lumen iubarne in caelo cerno*—from Ennius' *Aiax* on the grounds that there is nothing corresponding in the text of Sophocles' Αἴας. So much the worse, one might reply, for the view that Ennius adapted Sophocles' play. In fact the words clearly come from a scene set just before dawn[3] and one need postulate very little change to the opening of the Αἴας in order to accommodate them in a typical second century B.C. Latin version. It is impossible to imagine them in either the *Achilles* or the *Hectoris lytra*. I therefore follow Columna in printing them as a fragment of the *Aiax*.

Some words quoted by Nonius at p. 207.32—*praestatur uirtuti laus gelu set multo ocius* †*uenio LB*⁴/*uento F*³† *tabescit*—in order to illustrate *gelu* neuter appear to contain a *sententia* relating to the transitoriness of a man's repute among his fellows. Ribbeck[4] saw the similarity with Sophocles, *Ai*. 1266–71 φεῦ τοῦ θανόντος ὡς ταχεῖά τις βροτοῖς | χάρις διαρρεῖ καὶ προδοῦσ' ἁλίσκεται, | εἰ σοῦ γ' ὅδ' ἀνὴρ οὐδ' ἐπὶ σμικρῶν λόγων, | Αἴας, ἔτ' ἴσχει μνῆστιν, οὗ σὺ πολλάκις | τὴν σὴν προτείνων προύκαμες ψυχὴν δορί· | ἀλλ' οἴχεται δὴ πάντα ταῦτ' ἐρριμμένα and, with the help of cod. Vrbinas 308, corrected the introductory *titus liuius pisi adtacematico foro* to *Liuius in Aiace mastigophoro*. Sophocles' extant Αἴας was often called by ancient scholars Αἴας μαστιγοφόρος[5] so as to distinguish it from his tragedy concerning the Locrian Ajax. There can be little doubt therefore that *praestatur...tabescit* comes from a Latin version of Sophocles' Αἴας μαστιγο-

---

[1] E.g. *Tusc*. 1.105 *Accius et aliquando sapiens Achilles*, 1.106 *apud Ennium Thyestes*, 2.1 *Neoptolemus...apud Ennium*, 2.48 *in Niptris ille sapientissimus Graeciae...Pacuuius*, 3.62 *ille Agamemno Homericus et idem Accianus*, 3.63 *illa apud Ennium nutrix*, 3.65 *ille Terentianus 'ipse se poeniens'*, 4.67 *ille apud Trabeam*, 4.67 *Naeuianus ille...Hector*, *Fin*. 1.3 *Terentianus Chremes*, 4.62 *Enni Alcmeo*, *Rep*. 1.30 *Zethum illum Pacuui*, *Nat. deor*. 2.89 *ille apud Accium pastor*, *Diu*. 1.44 *Superbi Tarquini somnium de quo in Bruto Acci loquitur ipse*, 1.131 *ille Pacuuianus qui in Chryse physicus inducitur*, 2.133 *Pacuuianus Amphio*, *De orat*. 1.199 *apud Ennium...ille Pythius Apollo*, *Fam*. 7.33 *Philoctetes apud Accium*.

[2] Vahlen, *E.P.R.*¹, p. 95, *RhM* XVI (1861), 578 (= *Ges. phil. Schr*. I 417), suggested independently *Enni*(*i*) *Aiax* and *Ennianus Aiax*.

[3] Cf. A. La Penna, *Maia* V (1952), 94.

[4] *Monatsb. Preuss. Ak. d. Wiss. z. Berlin* I (1854), 45–6.

[5] Cf. the hypothesis of this play and Athenaeus 7.277C.

φόρος.[1] It is, however, by no means certain that Livius was the author of the version. I should like to dagger *pisi* and mark after it a lacuna; this lacuna would have contained *gelu* in the nominative or accusative case and another name, perhaps that of Ennius rather than that of Livius, as the author of *Aiax mastigophorus*. I should regard the *Aiax mastigophorus* piece as an intruder in Nonius' *gelu/gelus* article.

The type of ablative of comparison presented by the transmitted text is unparalleled in archaic Latin[2] but *gelu* can hardly be taken otherwise and such ablatives as that in Plautus, *Poen.* 812 *leuior pluma est gratia* are not very different.[3] It is thus plain that the quotation does not illustrate Nonius' lemma, *gelu* neuter (or, for that matter, *gelus* masculine).

The third book of Nonius' dictionary ('de indiscretis generibus') appears to have used a work of Flavius Caper as its base and to have supplemented the quotations it drew from Caper with quotations from the 41 lists drawn on in the other books.[4] A quotation of an *Aiax mastigophorus* of Livius could not come at this point from any of the 41 lists. There is no evidence that Caper quoted any Livian tragedy by name, very little that he quoted any at all.[5] The historian Titus Livius, on the other hand, who is quite absent from the 41 lists,[6] seems to have been quoted often by Caper.[7] Two quite certain quotations of the historian appear in Nonius' third book[8] and one rather dubious one.[9] I should therefore postulate that Nonius took from Caper a piece of the historian illustrating *gelu* neuter and added from memory the

---

[1] The arguments which K. Ziegler, *RE* 2 vi ii (1937), s.v. *Tragoedia*, 1985, brings against identifying the substance of *praestatur...tabescit* with that of Sophocles, *Ai.* 1266 ff. are quite inconclusive. For the introduction of imagery foreign to the original cf. Livius, *Carm.* fr. 16 *igitur demum Vlixi cor frixit prae pauore* ~ Homer, *Od.* 5.297; Ennius, *Trag.* 229–30 *ille trauersa mente mi hodie tradidit repagula* | *quibus ego iram omnem recludam* ~ Euripides, *Med.* 365 ff.

[2] See E. Löfstedt, *Syntactica* I² (Lund, 1942), pp. 304 ff.

[3] See Drexler, *Gymnasium* LXIII (1956), 165.

[4] See Strzelecki, *Eos* XXXIV (1932/3), 113 ff., *De Flauio Capro*, pp. 1 ff.

[5] Ribbeck includes in his collection the pieces attributed simply to 'Livius' at Nonius, p. 197.31 and Priscian, *Gramm.* II 231 . 11.

[6] *Titus Liuius* at p. 368.29 is an obvious error. The words *uestis pulla purpurea ampla* could be a version of Homer, *Od.* 19.225. Nonius quotes *Liuius in Odyssia* at p. 475.16 and 493.16 and introduces apparent versions of *Od.* 1.169 and 1.136 with *Liuius* at pp. 509.28 and 544.20. Livian tragic titles come into the dictionary in plenty from the alphabetical lists of adverbs and verbs and from glossaries dependent on Verrius Flaccus.

[7] Cf. Priscian, *Gramm.* II 141.1 – 171.15, 194.1 – 282.18.

[8] P. 196.16 *Titus Liuius* (= 6.40.18), p. 197.20 *Liuius lib. XII* (= 22.14.8).

[9] P. 194.20 *Liuius lib. IX: auratae uaginae aurata baltea illis erant*; cf. Homer, *Od.* 11.610.

AIAX

Aiax mastigophorus piece, failing to see that it did not illustrate his lemma. He might have seen it in his alphabetical list of verbs illustrating the uncommon *tabescere*.[1] I should further postulate that the archetype of our manuscripts of Nonius' dictionary had lost all but the first word of the Titus Liuius quotation as well as the name of the author of the *Aiax mastigophorus*.[2] In any case *praestatur...tabescit* should be excluded from the tragic fragments of Livius. There is at least some possibility that it belongs to Ennius.

X

See above, p. 178.

XI

Columna's inclusion of the *aliquod* of *Ling.* 7.75, which makes no sense at all in the context of Varro's preceding discussion, in the Ennian fragment[3] is unconvincing. The fragment occurs at 6.6 and 6.81 with no trace of an *aliquod* and one can offer no explanation as to why the word should have been omitted at these two places and included at 7.75. The *in altisono caeli clipeo* of 5.19 is deprived of its introductory *Agamemno* at 7.73 because that is not the style of introduction normal in book 7[4] but extended to *quid noctis uidetur in altisono caeli clipeo temo superat stellas sublime agens etiam atque etiam noctis iter* because a different point is at issue.

13 **lumen iubarne**: *iubar* is sometimes taken as a neuter adjective with *lumen*. The word appears as a masculine noun in the highly artificial language of Ennius' epic[5] but is normally a neuter. The terms of the discussion at *Ling.* 6.6 and 7.76 suggest that Varro took it as a noun here. Vahlen punctuated his text: *aliquod lumen, iubarne? in caelo cerno*, interpreting it as 'aliquod lumen (φῶς τι) in caelo cerno: iubarne est?'[6]

For *iubar* as the morning star cf. Ennius, *Ann.* 557, Lucretius 5.697, Anon. *Aetna* 333; contrast Plautus' *diurna stella* (*Men.* 175) and Pomponius' *lucifer* (*Atell.* 74).

---

[1] Strzelecki, *De Flauio Capro*, p. 30 n. 1, sees the difficulty of tracing it to either Caper or the 41 lists and assumes it to be from a marginal scholium.
[2] Similar lacunae have to be postulated at pp. 75.8, 90.10, 116.8, 170.12 (*liuius antiopa!*), 176.12, 209.25, 223.2, 479.13, 515.12, et al.
[3] Cf. Vahlen, *Ind. lectt.* Berlin 1880, 14 (= *Op. ac.* I 115).
[4] At 7.72–6 Varro quotes many of the same passages as he does at 5.18–20, 6.2–7, and 6.81–2, in all probability from the same source; he alters the mode of introduction of each passage to one of those usual in book 7.
[5] 557 *interea fugit albus iubar Hyperionis cursum* (~ ὁ φωσφόρος). Cf. Anon. *Aetna* 333.
[6] *E.P.R.*², p. 122. Cf. *Op. ac.* I 115.

181

COMMENTARY

Lumen was a word of poetic tone: it occurs 12 times in republican tragedy, its synonym *lux* only twice; in comedy on the other hand *lux* occurs 29, *lumen* 4 times (at Plautus, *Cist.* 643, *Truc.* 518 as a poeticism for *uita*; at *Curc.* 95, 117 in paratragic dialogue). Most formations in *-men* had a similar tone; H. Ploen[1] counted 18 in 1,940 verses of republican tragedy, 8 of which do not occur at all in comedy, and only 24 in 30,000 verses of comedy.

cerno: in the meaning 'perceive' this verb occurs 8 times in republican tragedy (∼ *uidere* 45, *audire* 11, *intellegere* 9) and only 7 in comedy (∼ *uidere* 1,270, *audire* 540, *intellegere* 125).

XII

The corpse of Ajax is being described: cf. Sophocles, *Ai.* 917–19 οὐδεὶς ἄν, ὅστις καὶ φίλος, τλαίη βλέπειν | φυσῶντ' ἄνω πρὸς ῥῖνας ἔκ τε φοινίας | πληγῆς μελανθὲν αἷμ' ἀπ' οἰκείας σφαγῆς, 1411–13 ἔτι γὰρ θερμαὶ | σύριγγες ἄνω φυσῶσι μέλαν | μένος.

For the imagery of *tullii efflantes uolant* cf. Homer, *Od.* 22.18–19 αὐτίκα δ' αὐλὸς ἀνὰ ῥῖνας παχὺς ἦλθεν | αἵματος ἀνδρομέοιο, Sophocles, *Ant.* 1238–9 καὶ φυσιῶν ὀξεῖαν ἐκβάλλει ῥοὴν | λευκῇ παρειᾷ φοινίου στα-λάγματος, Euripides, *Hek.* 567–8 τέμνει σιδήρῳ πνεύματος διαρροάς · | κρουνοὶ δ' ἐχώρουν, *Rhes.* 790–1 θερμὸς δὲ κρουνὸς δεσπότου πάρα σφαγαῖς | βάλλει με δυσθνῄσκοντος αἵματος νέου, Lucretius 2.354 *san-guinis exspirans calidum de pectore flumen,* Virgil, *Aen.* 9.414–15 *uoluitur ille uomens calidum de pectore flumen | frigidus,* 700–1 *reddit specus atri uulneris undam | spumantem, et fixo ferrum in pulmone tepescit,* 11.668 *sanguinis ille uomens riuos.*

Vahlen understood the transmitted text as ⟨*ferro percussus iacet*⟩ | *Aiax: misso sanguine tepido tullii efflantes uolant.* The resulting enjambement *iacet* | *Aiax,* the asyndeton *Aiax: misso* and the dactylic word *sanguine* occupying the third foot of the trochaic tetrameter are all highly unusual. Compara-tively speaking, even fewer so-called 'split anapaests' and the like are trans-mitted in the iambic and trochaic verses of early tragedy than in those of comedy[2] and most that are transmitted occur in the company of other kinds of anomaly.[3] The only credible restoration is Hermann's *animam misso sangui*

---

[1] *De Copiae Verborum Differentiis inter Varia Poesis Romanae Antiquioris Genera Intercedentibus* (Diss. Strasbourg, 1882), p. 36.

[2] The situation in comedy was observed and described by Hermann, *Ele-menta Doctrinae Metricae* (Leipzig, 1816), p. 78, Ritschl, *Prolegomena* to Plautus' *Trinummus* (Bonn, 1848), pp. CCLXX ff., Lachmann on Lucretius 2.719 and C. F. W. Mueller, *Nachträge zur plautinischen Prosodie* (Berlin, 1871), pp. 12 ff. Opinions have differed widely about the cases which defy the rigid rules laid down by these early critics.

[3] Cf. Ennius, *Trag.* 33, 86, 204, 263. For a permissive discussion of the Ennian examples see Vahlen, *Hermes* XVII (1882), 604 ff.

tepido tullii efflantes uolant.[1] However the ablative *sangui* seems to be un-exampled in extant Latin and present participles rarely govern objects in the remains of republican drama.[2]

14 misso sanguine tepido: the participle seems to have a present force; cf. Naevius, *Trag.* 15 *laetus sum laudari me abs te pater a laudato uiro,* Livy 1.37.1, 2.36.1, Servius, Verg. *Georg.* 1.206–7.

For *mittere* 'emittere' cf. Lucretius 2.194 *quod genus e nostro cum missus corpore sanguis | emicat exsultans alte spargitque cruorem.* It is possible that *sanguinem mittere* was the regular phrase in Ennius' day but more likely that we have an archaising removal of the customary prefix; cf. in Attic tragedy αἰνεῖν, ἦσθαι, θνῄσκειν, κτείνειν, ὀλλύναι, in Ennius' adaptations *missa sum* (35 = *emissa sum*), *uereor* (37 = *reuereor*), *sumptus* (53 = *consumptus*), *statuerit* (75 = *constituerit*), *locant* (106 = *collocant*), *linquere* (128 = *relinquere*), *cernunt* (166 = *decernunt*), *ibit* (225 = *abibit*), *parat* (308 = *comparat*), *putat* (308 = *reputat*).

tullii: not elsewhere, it seems, in recorded Latin; perhaps a word of rustic tone even in Ennius' day. Tragedy admitted few words which obviously originated outside the dialect of Latin spoken by the Roman upper classes. The classical grammarians branded the *ungulus* of Pacuvius, *Trag.* 64 and 215 and the *famulus* of Trag. inc. 138 as Oscan. For words of Greek origin see below on *v.* 67.

efflantes: for the intransitive use cf. Lucretius 6.682, 699. Intransitive *flare* is very common.

XIII

Ribbeck set these words in a speech like that which Ulysses delivers at the end of Sophocles' Αἴας (cf. 1338–41 ἀλλ' αὐτὸν ἔμπας ὄντ' ἐγὼ τοιόνδ' ἐμοὶ | οὐκ ἀντατιμάσαιμ' ἂν ὥστε μὴ λέγειν | ἕν' ἄνδρ' ἰδεῖν ἄριστον Ἀργείων, ὅσοι | Τροίαν ἀφικόμεσθα, πλὴν Ἀχιλλέως). Vahlen on the other hand[3] suggested that they come from a speech by Nestor in which he advises that the Trojans should be consulted as judges in the dispute between Ulysses and Ajax. Neither view is entirely satisfactory.

The words refer to σταδίη ὑσμίνη (cf. Homer, *Il.* 13.313 f., 713, Strabo 10.449), a form of fighting in which Telamonian Ajax was pre-eminent.

---

[1] On Sophocles, *Ai.* 918, ed. 3 (according to Ribbeck). Cf. Euripides, *Ba.* 620 θυμὸν ἐκπνέων, *Or.* 1163 πάντως ἐκπνέων ψυχὴν ἐμήν, Plautus, *Persa* 638 *animam ecflauit,* Virgil, *Aen.* 2.532 *concidit ac multo uitam cum sanguine fudit.*

[2] Cf., however, Ennius, *Trag.* 55, 63, 105, 190–1, Terence, *Andr.* 75, *Eun.* 584, *Hec.* 163, 365–6.   [3] *E.P.R.*², pp. CCI, 121.

I should interpret them as part of a sentence to the effect that Ajax was one of those *qui rem cum Achiuis gesserunt statim*, i.e. as belonging to a free version of Sophocles, *Ai*. 1266 ff. (esp. 1269–70 οὗ [Agamemnon] σὺ [Ajax] πολλάκις | τὴν σὴν προτείνων προὔκαμες ψυχὴν δορί).

The phrase *rem gerere* belonged properly to the official language (cf. Varro, *Ling*. 6.77 *imperator quod dicitur res gerere in eo neque facit neque agit, sed gerit, id est sustinet*). Where warlike operations were concerned *cum* could be used not only of hostility to an enemy (Cicero, *Prou*. 15, *Off*. 3.108, Livy 7.26.13, 9.16.2, 28.12.1) but also of co-operation with a colleague (Anon. *Bell. Afr*. 10.1, Livy 10.21.14, 21.40.3).

15 Achiuis: 6 times in tragedy and once in comedy (Plautus, *Bacch*. 936) of the heroes who besieged Troy. *Graeci*, the name by which second-century Romans knew the Greeks, does not occur in tragedy. There are three instances however of *Graecia*. *Achiui* would have been the old Latin name for the Greeks settled in Campania ('Αχαιϝοί); how it was preserved until the time of the tragic poets is hard to say.

statim: not in republican drama outside the five passages quoted by Nonius to illustrate the meaning 'perseueranter et aequaliter'. Terence, *Phorm*. 790, Plautus, *Amph*. 239 and 276 neither confirm nor disprove Nonius' strange doctrine about the quantity of the *a*. The text of the Afranius piece is unsound while the Ennius piece under discussion could be scanned either × – *qui rem cum Achiuis gesserunt statim* or, no less plausibly, *qui rem cum Achiuis gesserunt statim* ∪ –; in the latter case the law of Bentley and Luchs (see below on *v*. 308) would require a long *a*.

ALCMEO

Nonius gives the title *Alcmeo* to Ennius once[1] and to Accius nine times.[2] The stories about the hero Alcmeo related by the mythographers are many

---

[1] The source of p. 127.15 is Lindsay's list 28 'Alph. Adverb'.

[2] Most of the quotations come from Lindsay's list 5 'Accius i'. About pp. 181.16 and 184.1, where the codices give *Alcmena/-e* as the title, there is some doubt. Ribbeck argued (*NJbb* LXXVII [1858], 192 ff. [in Ritschl, *Opusc*. II 512 ff.]; cf. Ritschl, *RhM* VIII [1853], 477, XII [1857], 102 f. [= *Opusc*. II 475 f., 485 f.]) from the discussion of Marius Victorinus at *Gramm*. VI 8.6 ff. and Priscian at *Gramm*. II 29.7 ff. and from the readings of the codices of Nonius' lexicon at pp. 16.19 (*alcimeone*), 116.14 (*alcimachone*) and 393.28 (*alcemeone*) that Ennius spelled the hero's name 'Alcumeo' and Accius 'Alcimeo'. Two distinct questions have been muddled here: first, what form did the dramatists use

and difficult to sort out.[1] He killed his mother Eriphyle because of her betrayal of his father Amphiaraus. Like Orestes, an Argive of later times, he was pursued by the Furies from one foreign city to another and protected against these demons by Apollo. He produced children by at least three women, Manto, the daughter of the Theban seer Teiresias, Alphesiboea (Arsinoe, according to Apollodorus), the daughter of Phegeus, king of Psophis, and Callirrhoe, the daughter of the river god Achelous. The necklace with which Eriphyle had been bribed to betray Amphiaraus was also the instrument of Alcmeo's destruction. When Callirrhoe learned that it had been given to her predecessor Alphesiboea she demanded it for herself. Alcmeo went to Psophis to recover it and was slain by the brothers of Alphesiboea.

The one fragment of Ennius' tragedy quoted by Nonius—*factum est iam diu*—appears to refer to the killing of Eriphyle and to set the scene away from Argos at a time long afterwards.[2] Of the eight fragments of Accius' tragedy two are potentially informative. That quoted at p. 487.29, *qui ducat cum te uiderit socerum generibus tantam esse inpietatem?*, was very plausibly interpreted by Welcker[3] as coming from an address to Phegeus by one of his sons after the discovery of Alcmeo's plot to recover the necklace. No satisfactory interpretation of the quotation at p. 393.26, *suos deseruit liberos. superstites sunt*, has been found. G. Krókowski[4] referred it to the children Alcmeo had of Manto and set Accius' tragedy in Corinth around the theme of Alcmeo's reunion with the children. According to Apollodorus (3.7.7.2) Alcmeo had entrusted them to the care of the king of Corinth. It is thus difficult to explain the word *deseruit* in the Accian fragment. Psophis remains a more likely scene for the tragedy than Corinth.

Alcmeo was quite certainly a personage of Accius' *Epigoni* and possibly of

---

in the text of their plays?; second, what form appeared at the colophon and upon the σίλλυβος of the rolls consulted by Nonius and the lexicographers upon whom Nonius drew? The texts of republican drama present the name only twice: Plautus at *Capt.* 562 almost certainly wrote *Alcumeus*; at Accius, *Trag.* 78 one could restore the genitive of this form or the classical *Alcmeonis* (so L. Mueller, *De Accii Fabulis Disputatio* [Berlin, 1890], pp. 8 f., referring to Varro, *Ling.* 10.70 and Accius' introduction of Greek forms of proper names) equally as well as *Alcimeonis* (Ribbeck: *almeonis* codd.).

[1] See C. Robert, *Die griechische Heldensage* III i (Berlin, 1921), pp. 956 ff. The principal sources are Apollodorus 3.7.5 ff. and Pausanias 8.24.7 ff.

[2] Cf. Cicero's reference to the *exsultatio...senium matricidarum* at *Har. resp.* 39.

[3] *Die griech. Trag.* p. 283.

[4] In *Tragica* II, 57 ff. (68).

the *Eriphyla*[1] and the *Alphesiboea*.[2] The *Epigoni* was set in Argos and dealt with the killing of Eriphyle and the second Argive expedition against Thebes. The one fragment of the *Eriphyla*—*Pallas bicorpor anguium spiras trahit*—is enigmatic. Those of the *Alphesiboea* have been interpreted to refer to Alcmeo's second visit to Psophis and his death at the hands of the brothers of Alphesiboea[3] but if this was the theme of Accius' *Alcmeo* one ought not to postulate without very good reason a second handling of it. L. Mueller[4] referred the fragments quite plausibly to a play about the revenge Alphesiboea took on her brothers,[5] H.J. Mette[6] to a play about Alcmeo's first coming to Psophis and marriage with Alphesiboea.

Cicero frequently mentions Alcmeo (*Tusc.* 3.11, *Fin.* 4.62, *Ac.* 2.52, 88, 89); he describes him as a *uir bonus* (*Fin.* 4.62)[7] and quotes two tragic speeches from his mouth, one in trochaic tetrameters (*De orat.* 3.154, 218, *Tusc.* 4.19, *Fin.* 4.62, 5.31, *Hortensius ap.* Prisc. *Gramm.* II 250.12—fr. XIV), the other in a mixture of anapaests and no longer discernible metra (*Ac.* 2.52, 88–9—fr. XV). Ennius' name is three times connected with the former but not at all with the latter. Columna gave it to Ennius[8] and subsequent editors have all followed him.

The speech in lyrics is addressed to a *uirgo* and describes an attack by the Furies upon Alcmeo and the arrival of Apollo and Diana to rescue him. The context of Cicero's discussion and Alcmeo's words *sed mihi neutiquam cor consentit cum oculorum aspectu* make it clear that the demons are figments of the hero's imagination and could hardly have been represented on the stage by actors.[9]

---

[1] Quoted only by Priscian at *Gramm.* II 236.6.

[2] Quoted by Nonius at pp. 15.6, 73.25, 136.16, 279.35, 280.4, 469.25, 485.25, 497.2, 512.14 from Lindsay's list 5 'Accius i', the same source as provided most of the *Alcmeo* quotations. P. Schmidt (*De Nonii Marcelli auctoribus grammaticis*, pp. 52–65) demonstrated this fact and thus destroyed Bothe's theory that *Alcmeo* and *Alphesiboea* were alternative titles of the one play.

[3] Cf. Schöll, *Beitr.* pp. 132 ff., Welcker, *Die griech. Trag.* pp. 278 ff., Hartung, *Euripides restitutus* I (Hamburg, 1843), pp. 187 ff., H. Grotemeyer, *De L. Accii tragoediis* (Diss. Münster, 1851), p. 55, Ribbeck, *Die röm. Trag.* pp. 501 f., Schadewaldt, *Hermes* LXXX (1952), 46 ff. (= *Hellas und Hesperien*, 316 ff.).

[4] *De Accii fabulis*, pp. 10 f.; cf. Robert, *Die griech. Heldensage* III i, p. 963.

[5] Cf. Propertius 1.15.15–16.   [6] *Lustrum* IX (1964), 142 f.

[7] Cf. Ovid, *Met.* 9.408 *facto pius et sceleratus eodem*.

[8] Stephanus (p. 109) had expressly excluded it.

[9] This was first seen by Wilamowitz, *Ind. schol. Göttingen* 1893, 12–17 (= *Kl. Schr.* I 185–91), cf. G. Perrotta, *SIFC* N.S. VI (1928), 127–32. Cicero thrice (*S. Rosc.* 67, *Pis.* 46, *Leg.* 1.40; cf. Suetonius, *Ner.* 34) refers to stage Furies using a poetic phrase—*taedis ardentibus*—which occurs in the tragic anapaests. Ennius' *Eumenides* contained real stage Furies and it is possible that the phrase occurred

The audience would have seen only Alcmeo's reactions, as in the parallel situation of Euripides' 'Ορέστης.[1]

Cicero's phraseology at *Ac. 2.89, quid? cum uirginis fidem implorat...*, contains nothing foreign to his usage[2] but it looks as if he is echoing the tragic Alcmeo's actual address to a person unknown. Otherwise he would have given the person's name or status (i.e. *ancillae* or *filiae*). In any case, whether the phraseology belongs to Cicero or to Ennius, it suggests strongly that the person addressed appeared to be Alcmeo's social superior (i.e. some citizen of the town to which he had come). In such passages of republican comedy as Plautus, *Amph.* 376 *pro fidem Thebani ciues*, *Amph.* 1130 *di obsecro uostram fidem, Men.* 999–1000 *perii, opsecro uestram fidem | Epidamnienses subuenite ciues, Rud.* 615–24 *pro Cyrenenses populares uostram ego imploro fidem ...ferte opem inopiae...uostram iterum imploro fidem | qui prope hic adestis... ferte suppetias* the word *fides* had its old sense of 'protective power' and called to mind the client–patron relationship.[3] If in comedy a character entrusted himself to the *fides* of a social inferior as at Terence, *Eun.* 885–7, *nunc ego te in hac re mi oro ut adiutrix sies; | ego me tuae commendo et committo fide; | te mihi patronam capio Thais, te obsecro*, a mildly humorous effect was being sought from the incongruity of the language. The word *uirgo* normally denoted in tragedy and comedy a young woman of free status not yet married or a woman in the hands of a slave dealer who had not yet been sold on the retail market. Hartung's view[4] that the *uirgo* was Tisiphone, the daughter whom Alcmeo had had by Manto and bought by mistake in a slave market, and that the scene was parallel with that of Euripides, *Ion* 725 ff. is therefore hardly a credible one.[5] Welcker's view[6] that the *uirgo* was the daughter of

---

there. On the other hand Cicero's language tends to take on a poetic colouring whenever he speaks of the heroic world, whether or not he has a particular Roman tragedy in mind; the only other occurrence of *taeda* in his works is at *Verr.* 2.4.106, where he recounts the wanderings of Ceres. Zillinger, *Cicero und die altrömischen Dichter*, p. 29, is wrong in any case to treat the three passages as *testimonia* to the *Alcmeo*.

[1] *Or.* 253 ff. Cf. Aeschylus, *Choe.* 1048 ff., Euripides, *El.* 1342, *I.T.* 281 ff. Servius appears to say in a note on *Aen.* 4.473 that in a play of Pacuvius real Furies attacked Orestes as he came out of Apollo's temple but Virgil's comparison of the figures of Dido's dream with the demons that beset Pentheus and Orestes only has point if these were imaginary demons.

[2] See *T.L.L.* VI i 665.73 ff. on *fidem alicuius inplorare*.

[3] See Fraenkel, *RhM* LXXI (1916), 193 ff. (= *Kl. Beitr.* I 21 ff.).

[4] *Euripides restitutus* II (Hamburg, 1844), p. 536; cf. Ladewig, *Anal. scen.* p. 29.

[5] Hartung himself was troubled by the word *uirgo* and suggested that it was used to prevent anybody thinking that Alcmeo was guilty of incest as well as matricide.   [6] *Die griech. Trag.* pp. 575 ff.

COMMENTARY

Phegeus is tenable but one finds it a little odd that the king's unmarried daughter should be standing in the street in such a way as to be accosted by a derelict madman.[1] I therefore suggest that the *uirgo* was a priestess of Apollo,[2] the god of purification and healing who played the same role in the story of Alcmeo as in that of Orestes. If so the scene of action would be in front of a temple and Psophis could perhaps be ruled out as the city to which Alcmeo had come; any action there would have taken place outside Phegeus' palace.[3]

The trochaic tetrameters which Cicero quotes at *De Orat.* 3.218 are corrupt at a vital point but I think it can be argued[4] that they were spoken by an Alcmeo aware that the Furies belonged to his own imagination rather than the external world and afraid of the outcome of a legal trial that he was to face.

Many Greek tragedians are credited with an Ἀλκμέων: Sophocles, Euripides, Timotheus (*I.G.* II² 3091.5 f.), Agathon, Astydamas, Theodectes, Euaretus (*I.G.* II² 2320.26 f.) and Nicomachus of Alexandreia Troas (*Souda* N 396). Euripides wrote two plays which the more careful of ancient scholars distinguished with the phrases διὰ Κορίνθου and διὰ Ψωφῖδος. Without knowing about the διὰ Κορίνθου quotations Bentley[5] postulated the existence of two plays, one set in Psophis and dealing with Alcmeo's first visit, his purification by Phegeus and his marriage with Phegeus' daughter. Welcker[6] and Wilamowitz[7] reconstructed the Ἀλκμέων διὰ Ψωφῖδος according to Bentley's view, Wilamowitz pointing out that the distinguishing phrase in the title seemed to exclude as the theme Alcmeo's second visit to Psophis and murder there at the hands of Phegeus' sons. Schöll[8] and Hartung[9] however reconstructed the play around this theme and fairly recently there

---

[1] In Attic drama, as in fifth and fourth century Attic society, neither unmarried girls nor matrons normally went outside unaccompanied or conversed with strangers; cf. Sophocles, *Ant.* 578 f., *El.* 516 ff., Euripides, *Andr.* 876 ff., *El.* 343 f., 1072 ff., *Hek.* 974 f., *Herakleidai* 474 ff., *I.A.* 735, 1028 ff., *Phoin.* 88 ff., Aristophanes, *Lys.* 16, Menander, *Dysk.* 205 ff., 218 ff., Headlam and Knox on Herodas 1.37 (Cambridge, 1922).

[2] Cf. Euripides, *Tr.* 252–3 ἤ τὰν τοῦ Φοίβου παρθένον, ᾇ γέρας ὁ | χρυσοκόμας ἔδωκ' ἄλεκτρον ζόαν.

[3] A fourth-century tragedy might have had a palace and a temple. No more than one stage building need be postulated for any extant fifth-century piece except the Ἀνδρομάχη, which was not written for performance in Athens; see Pickard-Cambridge, *Theatre of Dionysus*, pp. 30, 52 ff.

[4] See below on fr. XIV.

[5] *Epistola ad Jo. Millium* (Oxford, 1691), pp. 17 ff.

[6] *Die griech. Trag.* pp. 575 ff.

[7] *Ind. schol. Göttingen* 1893, 12 ff. (= *Kl. Schr.* 1185 ff.). Cf. *Euripides: Herakles²* (Leipzig, 1895), p. 123 n. 22.

[8] *Beitr.* pp. 132 ff.

[9] *Euripides restitutus* I, pp. 187 ff.

has come to light a scrap of papyrus which seems to many to settle the issue in their favour. G. Vitelli saw that Pap. S.I. 13.1302 and the quotation of Euripides' 'Αλκμέων at Stobaeus 4.19.25 coincided and W. Schadewaldt[1] interpreted the enlarged fragment as coming from the 'Αλκμέων διὰ Ψωφῖδος: from a scene in which Phegeus, having learnt of Alcmeo's return to Psophis, tells a slave and the chorus not to reveal the news to his daughter. Schadewaldt's arguments however are far from conclusive and he makes no attempt to explain the title phrase διὰ Ψωφῖδος.[2]

As Ennius' original three Greek plays have been proposed: the 'Αλκμέων διὰ Ψωφῖδος,[3] the 'Αλκμέων διὰ Κορίνθου[4] and Theodectes' 'Αλκμέων.[5]

Since we know Ennius to have adapted many tragedies by Euripides there is a good chance that Euripides provided the original of the *Alcmeo*. The three fragments usually assigned to this play do not exclude the 'Αλκμέων διὰ Κορίνθου or an 'Αλκμέων διὰ Ψωφῖδος dealing with the first visit. It would be difficult however to make them deal with the second visit. I interpret fr. XIV as spoken by an Alcmeo afraid of the outcome of a legal trial. Some verses quoted by Stobaeus, apparently as from Euripides' 'Αλκμέων (Ακμ' 8.12; fr. 67), refer very plainly to such an episode and were argued by T. Zieliński[6] to have a metrical technique typical of the later Euripides. The 'Αλκμέων διὰ Κορίνθου was produced after Euripides' death while the 'Αλκμέων διὰ Ψωφῖδος appeared in 438 B.C. Both Zieliński's argument and mine are shaky ones, mine much more than Zieliński's, but if they have arrived at the truth they give grounds for thinking that Hartung was right about Ennius' original. The identification of words[7] and common motifs[8] as Euripidean does not help the argument. Such things could come from any play about Alcmeo or any play about a matricide. One might as well argue

---

[1] *Hermes* LXXX (1952), 46 ff. (= *Hellas und Hesperien*, 316 ff.).

[2] See the criticism of H. van Looy, *Zes Verloren Tragedies van Euripides* (Brussels, 1964), pp. 78–103 and 310–12 (summary in French).

[3] So A. Matthiae, *Euripides* IX (Leipzig, 1829), p. 20, Welcker, *Die griech Trag.* pp. 575 ff., Wilamowitz, *Ind. schol. Göttingen* 1893, 14 ff. (= *Kl. Schr.* I 187 ff.), Vahlen, *E.P.R.*², p. CCII, Leo, *Hermes* XLII (1907), 153 (= *Ausg. kl. Schr.* II 409), *Gesch.* p. 190 n. 1.

[4] So Hartung, *Euripides restitutus* II, p. 534; cf. Ladewig, *Anal. scen.* p. 29 (arguing that Cicero's phrase *uir bonus* excludes the two visits to Psophis).

[5] So Ribbeck (tentatively), *Quaest. scen.* 268 f., *Die röm. Trag.* pp. 197 ff., G. Perrotta, *SIFC* N.S. VI (1928), 127 ff.

[6] *Mnemosyne* L (1922), 319 ff.

[7] Welcker compared *exalbescat* of *v.* 20 with Hesychius I, p. 237 Latte, s.v. ἀργαίνειν.

[8] Wilamowitz compared the fit of madness with Tatian 24; Leo Alcmeo's *inopia* (*v.* 16) with Photius Berol. 39.8.

from the similarity which Columna observed between *incede incede adsunt adsunt me me expetunt* (his text of *v.* 23) and Euripides, *Or.* 257 αὖται γὰρ αὖται πλησίον θρῴσκουσί μου that Ennius adapted the Ὀρέστης.

XIV

Corruption at the head of *v.* 18 stands in the way of an uncontroversial interpretation of this fragment. I shall argue that the speaker allegorised the Furies as what he suffered in consequence of mental and physical illness, exile and lack of friends and the spirit of Eriphyle as his fear of the result of a trial he was soon to face.

The *alter* of *v.* 18 has always given trouble. Columna stopped the quotation of Ennius' *Alcmeo* at *expectorat*,[1] apparently thinking that Cicero began the quotation of another play at *alter*. Plank[2] and Bothe correctly extended the quotation to *metu* but offered no explanation of *alter*. After fifty years of honourable struggle with the problem Vahlen despaired with the words '*Alter* qui explicem non habeo, nisi forte interceptum est, errore aut consulto de more Ciceronis, quod excipiebat *Alter*'.[3] This does not, of course, solve anything.

Ribbeck proposed in his first edition and stuck in his third to the emendation *mater*, imagining that Alcmeo, like his fellow matricide Orestes, was pursued by the spirit of his mother as well as by the Furies. He could have adduced in support Aeschylus, *Eum.* 94–139 and Euripides, *Or.* 255–6.[4] The emendation is much superior to Vahlen's similarly inspired *ultor*.[5] Such emendations assume that Ennius' tetrameters describe a vision of demons, if not actual demons. But this is what the anapaests quoted by Cicero at *Ac.* 2.89 do (fr. xv) and it is not likely that Ennius' play had two scenes of this kind. Furthermore the verse form and the wording of the fragment under discussion suggest that Alcmeo is speaking at a moment of comparative rationality[6] and trying to explain why 'neutiquam cor consentit cum oculorum aspectu'.

In the phrase *multis sum modis circumuentus* there is the same military metaphor as in *v.* 23 *me expetunt*, 24 *fer mi auxilium*, 26 *incinctae igni incedunt*,

---

[1] Stephanus gave *circumuentus morbo exilio atque inopia* to the *Alcmeo* but seems to have lost Cicero's quotation at *De orat.* 3.218.

[2] *Q. Ennii Medea*, p. 105.

[3] *E.P.R.*[2], p. 123.

[4] Cf. also Virgil, *Aen.* 4.471–3, Ovid, *Met.* 9.409–10 *attonitusque malis, exul mentisque domusque | uultibus Eumenidum matrisque agitabitur umbris* (of Alcmeo himself).

[5] *Ind. lectt. Berlin* 1888–9, 3 (= *Op. ac.* I 401).

[6] Cf. *vv.* 34–42 and 43–9 (Cassandra's speech of apology in trochaic tetrameters followed by her prophecy in dactyls and other lyric verses).

ALCMEO

27 *circumstant*. But instead of the three Furies[1] three less demonic entities surround Alcmeo: *morbus*, *exilium* and *inopia*. *Morbus* is his sick state of body and mind,[2] *exilium* his homelessness,[3] *inopia* his lack of funds[4] and powerful friends.[5] The three allegorical Furies are accompanied not by the spirit of Eriphyle but by *pauor*, a state of neurotic fear. The mode of attack employed by *pauor* is described in *vv*. 17–18. Some scholars have tried to make *pauor* the subject of the verb *minatur* as well as of *expectorat*, emending *alter* accordingly.[6] But the shrewdest suggestion has come from Bergk who proposed[7] that *alter terribilem* be altered to *atra bilis mihi*. This emendation is false but it did not deserve the scorn that Ribbeck poured upon it.[8] Greek philosophers devoted much speculation to the phenomena of clairvoyance and prophecy[9] and many explained them as mental aberrations arising out of an excess of black bile. It is unlikely that Ennius, prone as he was to indulge in tragic philosophising,[10] and ready to represent the emotion of fear in physical terms in *v*. 20, would have introduced black bile stark naked without a word of explanation. But Bergk's feeling that prophecy is involved in Ennius' discourse was just. Ennius' discourse makes sense if for *alter* is substituted something like *animus* or *mens enim*.

---

[1] The late fifth century Attic tragedians make the Furies three in number; cf. Euripides, *Or*. 408, 434, 1650, *Tr*. 457, E. Wüst, *RE* Suppl. VIII (1956), s.v. *Erinys*, 122.

[2] Cf. Euripides, *Or*. 34–5 ἐντεῦθεν ἀγρίᾳ συντακεὶς νόσῳ νοσεῖ | τλήμων Ὀρέστης ὅδε, 227 ff., 395, 407, 480, 792, 800, 881 ff., 1016, Timocles *ap*. Athen. 6.223 B ὁ νοσῶν δὲ μανικῶς Ἀλκμέων ἐσκέψατο.

[3] The normal lot of the parricide in the heroic world of tragedy (cf. Aeschylus, *Choe*. 1034 ff., Euripides, *Herakles* 1322, *Hik*. 148, *I.T*. 80, 929, *Or*. 898–900) and historical Athens (cf. Demosthenes 23.42). The sentence of death passed on Orestes in Euripides' Ὀρέστης (902–56) is represented as a barbarous one.

[4] For the exile's poverty cf. Euripides, *Herakles* 1325 ff., *Med*. 551 ff., Seneca, *Thy*. 303 f., 923 ff.

[5] Cf. Plautus, *Rud*. 617 *ferte opem inopiae* and see below on *vv*. 89 (*ups*) and 173 (*opulentus*). The parricide of the heroic world of tragedy was spurned as one dangerously polluted (cf. Euripides, *I.T*. 947 ff.; contrast Homer, *Il*. 2.661 ff., *Od*. 15.280–1); drought struck the cities where Alcmeo was allowed to live (Apollodorus 3.7.5.3).

[6] *Adeo* was suggested by Vahlen (*Ind. lectt. Berlin* 1887–8, 6 n. [= *Op. ac*. I 382 n.]), *tetrum* by L. Mueller (*Q. Enni Carminum Reliquiae* [St Petersburg, 1884], p. 113).

[7] *Philologus* XXXIII (1874), 283 (= *Kl. phil. Schr*. I 362).

[8] *Ad Tragicos Addenda* in *Comicorum Romanorum Fragmenta*[2] (Leipzig, 1873), pp. CXIII–CXIV, *RhM* XXIX (1874), 218.

[9] Cf. Plato, *Phaidr*. 244D, *Tim*. 71E, Cicero, *Diu*. 1.63, 81, Lucretius 1.132 ff., 4.757 ff.   [10] See above on fr. IV, below on fr. XCIX.

The prophetic powers of the mind are frequently mentioned in Attic[1] and Roman drama.[2] It is evil that normally appears to the mind when it is in a prophetic state.

For *minari* 'prophesy evil at the hands of a third party' cf. Cicero, *Carm.* fr. 10.28–9 *oracla...tristis minitantia casus*, Manilius 1.892–4 *talia significant lucentes saepe cometae:* | *funera cum facibus ueniunt, terrisque minantur* | *ardentes sine fine rogos*, Seneca, *Nat.* 2.39.2 *ubi rebus quietis nec agentibus nec cogitantibus quicquam fulmen quidem interuenit et aut minatur aut promittit aut monet*, *Oed.* 20–1 *thalamos parentis Phoebus et diros toros* | *gnato minatur inpia incestos face*, *Octauia* 236–7 *gentibus clades nouas* | *minantur astra*, Statius, *Theb.* 2.348 *exta minantia diuos*, Ps. Quintil. *Decl.* 4.12 *minatus est mihi manus meas meus animus*.

T.L.L. IV 1219.67 seems to take *uitae* as a genitive depending on *cruciatum* and compares Porphyrio, Hor. *Sat.* 1.1.78 *pulcher et grauis sensus recusantis diuitias, quae cruciatum uitae domino adferant*. But Alcmeo is already suffering mental torture; it is not merely threatened or prophesied. I should take *uitae* as *uitae* (meae) (for the omission cf. *v.* 295 *tanta uis sceleris in corpore* [meo] *haeret*, *vv.* 340–1 *ut scias quanto e loco*, | *quantis opibus, quibus de rebus lapsa fortuna* [mea] *accidat*), i.e. as (mihi) *uiuenti*. For this personal use of the abstract *uita* cf. Plautus, *Asin.* 16–17 *sicut tuom uis unicum gnatum tuae* | *superesse uitae sospitem et superstitem*, *Trin.* 57 *deosque oro ut uitae tuae superstes suppetat*, Cicero, *Mil.* 86 *neque ullo in loco potius mortem lacerari quam in quo uita esset damnata*, *Sest.* 83 *eius igitur uitam quisquam spoliandam ornamentis esse dicet, cuius mortem ornandam monumento sempiterno putaretis?*, Propertius 2.1.73–4 *Maecenas...et uitae et morti gloria iusta meae*, 4.7.69 *sic mortis lacrimis uitae sanamus amores*, Valerius Maximus 3.4.5 *cuius uita triumphauit, mors Papia lege damnata est*, 9.2 ext. 10 *Etrusci...amari uitae pariter ac mortis tortores*.

The object of fear is *cruciatus et nex*. The real demons of Aeschylus' *Eumenides* and the imaginary ones of Euripides' plays[3] threaten Orestes with these very things. But if my interpretation of the fragment is correct Ennius'

---

[1] E.g. Aeschylus, *Pers.* 10–11 κακόμαντις...θυμός, Euripides, *Andr.* 1072 πρόμαντις θυμὸς ὥς τι προσδοκᾷ, Trag. inc. 176 πηδῶν δ' ὁ θυμὸς ἔνδοθεν μαντεύεται, Menander, *Misoumenos* c↓ 16–17 Turner μαντεύεθ' ἡ ψυχή τι μου Γέτα κακόν· | δέδοικα.

[2] E.g. Plautus, *Aul.* 178 *praesagibat mi animus frustra me ire quom exibam domo*, *Bacch.* 679 *animus iam istoc dicto plus praesagitur mali*, Terence, *Haut.* 236 *nescioquid profecto mi animus praesagit mali*, Pacuvius, *Trag.* 78 *propemodum animus coniectura de errore eius augurat*, Seneca, *Thy.* 957–8 *mittit luctus signa futuri* | *mens, ante sui praesaga mali*; cf. in dactylic verse, Calvus, fr. 10 *mens mea dira sibi praedicens omnia uaecors*, Virgil, *Aen.* 10.843 *adgnouit longe gemitum praesaga mali mens*.

[3] Aeschylus, *Eum.* 267, 305 f., 422 f., Euripides, *Or.* 260 f. (cf. 438 ff.), *I.T.* 285 f.

Alcmeo must fear them from somewhere else, most likely the civil authorities. Euripides allegorised Orestes' imaginary assailants as the naggings of a guilty conscience.[1] The fourth-century orator Aeschines allegorised the Furies of the contemporary stage as the insatiable lusts of a bad man's heart driving him on to further crime.[2] An allegory very similar to the one I am attributing to Ennius appears in Lucretius' versification of Epicurean teachings at 3.978–1023: *atque ea nimirum quaecumque Acherunte profundo | prodita sunt esse in uita sunt omnia nobis. . . Cerberus et Furiae iam uero et lucis egestas. . . | qui neque sunt usquam nec possunt esse profecto: | sed metus in uita poenarum pro male factis | est insignibus insignis, scelerisque luella, | carcer et horribilis de saxo iactus deorsum, | uerbera carnifices robur pix lammina taedae; | quae tamen etsi absunt at mens sibi conscia factis | praemetuens adhibet stimulos torretque flagellis, | nec uidet interea qui terminus esse malorum | possit nec quae sit poenarum denique finis | atque eadem metuit magis haec ne in morte grauescant. | hic Acherusia fit stultorum denique uita.* The demons with which the poets populate the underworld are here reinterpreted as the punishments which await the guilty man in this world.

A difficulty remains: the Alcmeo of an Attic play might have had to fear death from the civil authorities if he faced a trial in Argos but any trial in a foreign city, if we can go by the analogy of that of Orestes in Athens as depicted by Aeschylus, could have resulted, at the worst for him, only in expulsion. I therefore suggest that, whereas the text of the play Ennius was adapting made Alcmeo express fear about the outcome of a trial to decide whether he should be admitted to the community he had approached, Ennius gave the hero the fears that a contemporary Roman parricide might have. There are signs that he rewrote the trial scene of Aeschylus' *Eumenides* with Roman conditions likewise in mind.[3]

L. Hostius was executed just after the Hannibalic war for murdering his father,[4] in a manner that greatly impressed the theatre audience for whom Ennius was writing. In adaptations of Attic comedy Plautus alludes at least twice quite unmistakeably to the *culleus* in which Roman parricides were put.[5] The phrase *cruciatum et necem* perhaps came straight from the language of the lawyers[6] and in any case could not help drawing the attention of the

---

[1] *Or.* 395 ff.: cf. Cicero, *S. Rosc.* 67, *Pis.* 46, *Har. resp.* 39, *Leg.* 1.40, *Parad.* 18, Juvenal 13.193–5, Quintilian, *Decl.* 314, p. 236.9.

[2] *Tim.* 190.   [3] See below on fr. LXIV.   [4] Plutarch, *Rom.* 22.5.

[5] *Epid.* 349 ff., *Pseud.* 212 ff. For the origin of this practice, apparently unknown to Greek communities, see Latte, *TAPhA* LXVII (1936), 24 ff., *RE* Suppl. VII (1940), s.v. *Todesstrafe*, 1614, *ZSavSt* LXVII (1950), 51 ff.

[6] Cicero uses the nominal phrase *cruciatus et mors* regularly in referring to judicial executions (*Verr.* 2.5.72, 134, 138, 153 et al.; cf. Ulpian, *Dig.* 4.6.3 et al.). The word *nex* was probably already uncommon in ordinary parlance in Ennius' own day; it occurs only 8 times in republican drama (~ *mors* 69).

audience to contemporary Roman judicial practice. The Romans regularly tortured criminals before executing them.[1] The Athenians on the other hand were notoriously gentle. Torture does not appear in the executions their tragic poets described[2] and the only case recorded from historical Athens is of a slave condemned for poisoning.[3] A proposal to torture the condemned Phocion was greeted with horror.[4]

16 multis sum modis: the archaic dramatists normally joined *multis* and *modis* so closely as to measure the phrase $-\cup\cup-$ or even to write it as *multimodis*. But there is no need to entertain Bothe's *multis modis sum c.* For the disjunction cf. Plautus, *Bacch.* 507 *a: ego istanc multis ulciscar modis.* Five of the six verbs in the passage are hoisted towards the head of their respective clauses. This type of word order is a marked feature of the archaic tragic style. And in all archaic writing, and some classical, whenever a part of *esse* for some reason precedes its complement, it tends to go to the second position of the clause; see M. Seyffert, *Cicero: Laelius*, ed. 2 (Leipzig, 1876), pp. 441–2, J. Wackernagel, *IF* 1 (1892), 428–9 (= *Kl. Schr.* 1 96–8).

circumuentus: cf. Horace, *Ars* 169 *multa senem circumueniunt incommoda.*

morbo exilio atque inopia: for the syntactical arrangement of the triad (*a, b* atque *c*) cf. Plautus, *Bacch.* 1113, 1181, *Men.* 174, Terence, *Ad.* 846, *Haut.* 777–8, 893, Ennius, *Ann.* 108.

17 tum pauor sapientiam omnem exanimato expectorat: I follow the reading of the 'codices mutili' at *De orat.* 3.218; for the omission of the anaphoric pronoun cf. Plautus, *Cas.* 621–2 *occidi,* | *cor metu mortuumst, membra* (mihi) *miserae tremunt,* Terence, *Eun.* 665–6 *audieram . . . uerum* (mihi) *miserae non in mentem uenerat.* Tragedy was prone to omit such pronouns when the context was unambiguous; cf. Ennius 19–20, 38, 304, Pacuvius 257, 259, 263, 264, 266, 328, 350, 351, Accius 13 et al. All the personal pronouns and pronominal adjectives are, perhaps because of their undignified lack of size, much less common in tragedy than in comedy.[5] Hiatus at the

---

[1] Cf. Cicero, *Verr.* 2.5.14, 118. Livy's statement, *in aliis gloriari licet, nulli gentium mitiores placuisse poenas* (1.28.11), is pious nonsense.

[2] Cf. the discussion of Orestes' punishment at Euripides, *Or.* 857 ff.

[3] Antiphon 1.20. See Latte, *RE* Suppl. VII (1940), 1609–10.

[4] Plutarch, *Phoc.* 35.

[5] Ennius has *ego* etc. about once in 49 words, Pacuvius 1 in 53, Accius 1 in 57, Terence 1 in 27. *Tu* etc. occurs about once in 75 words of Ennius, 1 in 62 of Pacuvius, 1 in 77 of Accius, 1 in 37 of Terence. *Is* etc. occurs about once in 188 words of Ennius, 1 in 145 of Pacuvius, 1 in 182 of Accius, 1 in 60 of Terence. Significantly *is* etc. is extremely rare in the elevated language of Ennius' epic, extremely common in the remains of his prose treatise *Euhemerus* (1 in 700 ∼ 1 in 25).

diaeresis of the trochaic tetrameter is not elsewhere transmitted in the remains of Ennius' tragedies[1] but is so frequently in the comedies of Plautus. Terence seems to have avoided it[2] but Accius allowed it a few times[3] and it would be hypercritical to deny it to Ennius.

Fear is one of the incorporalia most commonly personified in republican drama: cf. Naevius, *Trag.* 40 *nos duplicat aduenientis timos*, Pacuvius, *Trag.* 292 *ecfare quae cor tuum timiditas territet*, Accius, *Trag.* 122 *uos hic non mertet metus*, Plautus, *Amph.* 1079, *Cas.* 653, 704, *Cist.* 688 a, *Mil.* 1233, *Rud.* 686, 703. Incorporalia and abstracts govern transitive verbs much more often in Latin tragedy than in Attic. In the latter the construction scarcely occurs outside gnomic utterances and passages where the line between personification and demonology is hard to draw (cf. Aeschylus, *Ag.* 1306, *Choe.* 288, *Eum.* 88, *Hik.* 736, *Pers.* 703, *Prom.* 181 ~ Homer, *Il.* 11.37, 13.299, Aeschylus, *Theb.* 45). In Latin tragedy I note it at Livius 13, Naevius 40, Ennius 17, 25, 68, 102, 156, 199, 222, 271, 275 (*bis*), 305, 333, Pacuvius 6, 58, 60, 67, 109, 119, 137, 150, 161, 170, 179, 211, 222, 224, 241, 257, 276 (*bis*), 277, 292, 299, 303, 306 (*bis*), 309, 368, 374, 388, 396, 412; Accius 13, 16, 88, 98, 99, 102, 118, 122, 138, 152, 155, 176, 188, 272, 286, 303 (*bis*), 316, 344, 352, 387, 419, 453, 456, 479, 492, 503, 516, 555, 564, 566, 568, 580, 587, 621; Trag. inc. 58, 93, 148, 247. Only two of the Ennian examples occur in spoken trimeters but Pacuvius and Accius appear to have constructed their trimeters in this way more often than they did their musically accompanied verses. Occasionally, as in the verse under discussion, the verb governs an abstract as well: e.g. Pacuvius 60, 276, 292, 306; Accius 99, 176, 188, 352, 456, 621; Trag. inc. 58, 148 (cf. Aeschylus, *Hik.* 498; Sophocles, *Ant.* 389, 1028; Euripides, *Phoin.* 944: about the only clear examples in these three plays). The construction is comparatively rare in comedy and where it does occur it tends to be accompanied by other devices designed to elevate the style; sung verses show it very much more often than do spoken; see Haffter, *Untersuchungen*, pp. 86 ff.

For *tum* 'praeterea' cf. Ennius, *Ann.* 77 *curantes magna cum cura tum cupientes regni*, Plautus, *Men.* 258 ff., Terence, *Phorm.* 327 f.

Pauor was a word of some elevation, occurring 5 times in tragedy and not at all in comedy. It is absent from Caesar and from Cicero, except for three passages in the Tusculans (4.16, 4.19, 5.52) where he is making fine psychological distinctions. Abstract formations in -*or* tended generally to have a lofty tone; Ploen counted 26 in 1,940 verses of tragedy and only 35 in 30,000 of comedy.

---

[1] But cf. *vv.* 148, 149.

[2] For a defence of the few cases transmitted see A. Klotz, *Hermes* LX (1925), 325 ff.

[3] *Trag.* 13, 149, 231, 301, 451, 476.

COMMENTARY

Sapientia occurs twice elsewhere in tragedy. It is more common (21 instances) in comedy than other abstracts in -entia and -antia but rare compared with its synonym consilium.

For sapientiam...expectorat cf. Plautus, Truc. 77–8 Phronesium | suom nomen omne ex pectore exmouit meo, Bacch. 653, Pseud. 144, Truc. 603, Catullus 76.22, Lucretius 3.908, 4.908. The verb expectorare occurs elsewhere in archaic and classical literature only in Accius (Trag. 301, 595). The type of formation was probably as bizarre to archaic ears as to classical.[1] The only parallels I can find are, in comedy, egurgitare (Plautus, Epid. 582) and, in tragedy, eliminare (Ennius 238, Pacuvius 134, Accius 448, 592).

For the redundancy of pauor...exanimato continued by terribilem... timido...metu cf. Plautus, Amph. 1079–81 eadem nos formido timidas terrore inpulit...ita mihi animus etiam nunc abest, Cist. 688–8a intus paueo et foris formido, ita nunc utrubique metus me agitat.

18 terribilem: elsewhere in republican drama only at Trag. inc. 96. Formations with -bilis (-biliter) are numerous in tragedy, comparatively rare in comedy.

minatur: scarcely preferable to minitatur, the reading of the 'codices integri'; both forms occur frequently in drama and in Cicero's writings, the latter having the simple predominating (39:22 in the orations, 10:4 in the philosophical dialogues, 8:5 in the letters, neither in the rhetorical writings at all), the former the intensive (23:8 in comedy, 1:1 [?] in tragedy).

uitae cruciatum et necem: see above, p. 193.

19–20 quae nemo est...quin refugiat timido sanguen atque exalbescat metu: Vahlen's supplement ⟨cum aduentare uideat⟩ removes the anacoluthon at the price of even greater syntactical complication. It would be better to understand refugiat timido sanguen atque exalbescat as a pictorial substitute for a verb like timeat and quae (i.e. cruciatum et necem) as its object; cf. Aeschylus, Theb. 289–90 μέριμναι 3ωπυροῦσι τάρβος | τὸν ἀμφιτειχῆ λεών, Hik. 566–7 δείματι θυμὸν | πάλλοντ' ὄψιν ἀήθη, Euripides, Or. 860, Ba. 1288.

For the physical effect of fear cf. Aeschylus, Ag. 1121–2 ἐπὶ δὲ καρδίαν ἔδραμε κροκοβαφὴς | σταγών, Aristotle, fr. 243 Rose, Lucretius 3.152 ff.

19 tam firmo ingenio et tanta confidentia: the second phrase repeats the substance of the first at slightly greater length (5:8 syllables) and with choicer vocabulary. Plautus has (Rud. 645) quis homost tanta confidentia but

[1] Cf. Quintilian, Inst. 8.3.31.

comedy on the whole has the phrase-type 'est+ablative of abstract noun' much less often than the type 'est ingenio+adjective'. The anaphora tam... tanta elevates the tone further.

The long verses of Ennian tragedy and Plautine comedy share a marked tendency to make the second phrase of a pair longer than the first. Where the substance of the second repeats that of the first in comedy, the speaker is usually a personage of low degree taking off the ways of speaking usual in tragedy. Such tautologies are rare in Attic tragedy and restricted to highly emotional passages;[1] they are common in the Latin adaptations: Livius 21, Ennius 19, 40, 61, 83, 163, 174, 193–4, 204, 205–6, 217, 252, 278, 310, Pacuvius 50, 155, 164, 256, Accius 15, 60, 87, 154, 207, 364, 365, 510, 583, 608. Only two of the Ennian examples are in trimeters, one of the Pacuvian and three of the Accian. This may, however, be partly an accidental effect of the length of the verse.[2]

20 refugiat: once elsewhere in republican tragedy (Trag. inc. 189), and once in comedy (Caecilius 236) with little perceptible difference in meaning from the extremely common simple form of the verb. Ennius' *respectare* (71), Pacuvius' *retinere* (263) and Accius' *remanere* (447), *reticere* (95) and *reuisere* (336) similarly replace the simple forms used by the common language.

sanguen: not elsewhere in republican drama; for *sanguis* cf. Ennius, *Trag.* 324, Trag. inc. 209, Plautus, *Merc.* 550; for *sanguinem* Plautus, *Bacch.* 372 et al. *Sanguen* appears in epic at Ennius, *Ann.* 113, in oratory at Cato, fr. 211.

exalbescat: only here, Cicero, *De orat.* 1.121, *Ac.* 2.48 and Gellius 12.1.12. The prefix picks up *exanimato* and *expectorat* in *v.* 17 and amplifies the tone rather than alters or extends the sense of what is being said. Other compounds with *ex-* likewise replacing the simple form in tragedy are *edocere* (Ennius 56, Pacuvius 374), *eloqui* (Ennius 330, Accius 301), *enitere* (Accius 235[1]), *exaudire* (Accius 281), *exposcere* (Ennius 151), *exsacrificare* (Ennius 54), *exsuperare* (Trag. inc. ap. Cic. Tusc. 4.77, Pacuvius 404), *exsuscitare* (Accius 199). Plautus' *exaugere*, *exdissertare*, *exobsecrare*, *exputare* *erogitare*, *extumere* appear to be of a paratragic character. The prefix ἐκ- performed a similar function in Attic tragedy.[3]

---

[1] Cf. Euripides, *Hel.* 483 τί φῶ; τί λέξω;, *Alk.* 21 θανεῖν...καὶ μεταστῆναι βίου, 108 ἔθιγες ψυχᾶς, ἔθιγες δὲ φρενῶν.

[2] On the whole subject see Lindholm, *Stilistische Studien*, pp. 94 ff., Haffter, *Untersuchungen*, pp. 53 ff.

[3] See Wilamowitz, *Herakles*[2], on *v.* 155, A. Meillet, *Aperçu d'une histoire de la langue grecque*[3] (Paris, 1930), p. 209, Fraenkel, *Aeschylus: Agamemnon* (Oxford, 1950), on *v.* 1033.

The inchoative form of the verb probably had a poetic tone. Such forms are comparatively rare in the fragments of Ennius' tragedies but pullulate in those of his *Annales* and the rest of republican tragedy. This situation may be partly due to the nature of the sources of Nonius' lexicon, which included only two actual scripts of Ennius' tragedies. Ploen[1] counted 85 inchoative formations in comedy but it would be wrong to think that many came from ordinary Roman speech. 64 of them occur only in Plautus' plays and many of these nowhere else in Latin. Very often a paratragic tone is plainly detectable in the context of occurrence.

XV

For the context see above, p. 187. I should add only that Apollo and Diana were of a similar nature to the three Furies: figments of Alcmeo's imagination rather than real personages appearing on stage. They perhaps symbolised Alcmeo's hope of release from his sufferings.

The words of *v.* 21, *sed mihi neutiquam cor consentit cum oculorum aspectu*, suggest that Alcmeo is speaking at a moment of relative sanity.[2] It would therefore be preferable to scan them as part of a trochaic tetrameter (lacking the final two elements ∪ —) than as anapaests. However a convincing supplement is hard to find. Ribbeck's *aspectu ⟨truci⟩* is quite unsatisfactory; Pacuvius, *Trag.* 2–3 *quadrupes...aspectu truci* belongs to a quite different kind of context.

Cicero quotes neither *v.* 22 nor *v.* 23 in its entirety and scribes have corrupted what he does quote of the latter.[3] Ribbeck printed *v.* 23 as a very unconvincing catalectic trochaic tetrameter—*incedunt incedunt adsunt adsunt me med expetunt*—and *vv.* 24–7 as two acatalectic tetrameters, thus making the dactyl-shaped end of *ardentibus* coincide with the end of a foot.[4] The old editors took *vv.* 24–30 as a series of anapaestic dimeters with hiatus between *v.* 28 and *v.* 29. In his Epistle to Mill (p. 26) Bentley pointed out that the anapaestic systems of classical Greek and Roman poetry avoided this kind of hiatus. Bücheler argued that *v.* 28 was defective at the beginning; Ribbeck[5]

---

[1] *De Cop. Verb. Diff.* p. 79.

[2] Cf. Euripides, *Hel.* 575 οὔ που φρονῶ μὲν εὖ, τὸ δ' ὄμμα μου νοσεῖ;

[3] Vahlen (cf. *Ind. lectt. Berlin* 1887–8, 7 [= *Op. ac.* I 383]) takes *incede incede* as addressed by Alcmeo to himself. Of his parallels only Euripides, *El.* 112–13 could be persuasive and there the interpretation of the Greek is disputed. In any case it is hard to see what point such a self-address on Alcmeo's part would have.

[4] Cf. above on fr. XII. A. Spengel, *Reformvorschl.* p. 192, drew attention to this and the lack of pure theses in Ribbeck's alleged trochaics.

[5] *Coroll.* pp. XVII f.

supplied ⟨*eccum*⟩ *intendit*, Vahlen[1] *hac*, Plasberg[2] *dextra*. None of these suggestions is convincing and the words transmitted make reasonable sense as they stand. The only parallel hiatus in tragic anapaests, that between Ennius, *Trag.* 91 and 92, coincides with a strong rhetorical pause but the small number of archaic anapaests surviving and the large number of anomalies transmitted in other kinds of archaic verse make regularisation a dubious procedure.

21 cum oculorum aspectu: the phrases *oculis aspicere* et sim. are common in comedy (Plautus, *Cas.* 939–40, *Men.* 1001, *Mil.* 1217 et al.) but the abstract noun *aspectus* occurs only twice (Plautus, *Epid.* 572; Turpilius 75). Tragedy, on the other hand, has *aspectus* five times. The formation of abstract substantives in -*tus* (-*sus*) was much affected by the more elevated genres of archaic poetry; Ploen counted 63 such formations in 1,940 verses of tragedy and only 125 in 30,000 of comedy.

Cum oculorum aspectu stands for little more than *cum oculis*; cf. Euripides, *I.A.* 233–4 τὰν γυναικεῖον ὄψιν ὀμμάτων | ὡς πλήσαιμι, *I.T.* 1167 ὄψιν δ' ὀμμάτων ξυνήρμοσεν. This type of periphrasis, in which the adjective or defining genitive carries the main idea, is common in both Attic and Roman tragedy: where nouns in -*tus* (-*sus*) are concerned I note Ennius 123 *iuuenum coetus*, 245 *fructus uerborum*, 305 *pedum pulsu*, 309 *motus superum atque inferum*, 394 *imbrium fremitu*, Pacuvius 68 *triplicem...partum*, 303 *beluarum ac ferarum aduentus*, 328 *paternum aspectum*, Accius 515 *ex tuo...satu*, 608 *belli fluctus*, 618 *mediocri satu*.

22 unde haec flamma oritur: for fire as a sign of the onset of madness cf. Aeschylus, *Ag.* 1256 (Cassandra) παπαῖ οἶον τὸ πῦρ · ἐπέρχεται δέ μοι, Sophocles, *El.* 887–8 εἰς τί μοι | βλέψασα θάλπει τῷδ' ἀνηκέστῳ πυρί;, Virgil, *Aen.* 7.354–6 *ac dum prima lues udo sublapsa ueneno | pertemptat sensus atque ossibus implicat ignem | necdum animus toto percepit pectore flammam.*

Flamma appears to have been a word of elevated tone. It occurs 10 times in tragedy, only 4 in comedy (∼ *ignis* 1:26).

23 †incede incedet† adsunt: Alcmeo does not name the fiends whom he imagines to be attacking him; probably *ominis causa* (cf. Sophocles, *O.K.* 128, Euripides, *Or.* 409).

Adesse is commonly used in prayers invoking the aid of a deity (cf. the augural prayer quoted by Servius at *Aen.* 8.72 *adesto Tiberine cum tuis undis*, Catullus 62.25 et al.). For use of normally auspicious vocabulary from the sacral language in inauspicious contexts see below on *v.* 144.

---

[1] *Ind. lectt. Berlin* 1887–8, 4 n. (= *Op. ac.* 1 380 n.).
[2] Using an idea put forward by Zillinger, *Cicero und die altrömischen Dichter*, p. 109 n. 3.

me expetunt: the compound verb picks up *exilio...exanimato expectorat ...exalbescat* in fragment XIV and is itself picked up by *excruciat*. For *expetere* 'petere, attack' I can instance only Plautus, *Bacch.* 51 *duae unum expetitis palumbem.*

24 fer mi auxilium, pestum abige a me: chiasmus is a common adornment of the more emotional speeches of both Attic tragedy (e.g. Euripides, *Alk.* 215-17, *Ba.* 74-5, 902-3) and the Latin adaptations (e.g. Ennius 143, 159, 165, 310, Pacuvius 77, 92, 113-14, 155, 253-4, 276, 335, 336, Accius, 15, 156, 303, 365).

24-5 pestem abige a me, | flammiferam hanc uim quae me excruciat: vision and reality here begin to fuse, so that it is not clear whether Alcmeo is referring to the flames of the Furies' torches or to the fever (πυρετός) from which he is suffering. *Pestis* may be a tragic hyperbole for *febris* or *morbus*; it is normally used of a plague which attacks a whole population (cf. Ennius, *Ann.* 559). The phrases *morbum abigere* and *febrem abigere* are common in Latin medical writing (cf. *T.L.L.* I 97.41 ff.).

Flammiferam hanc uim is a periphrasis for *has tantas flammas*; cf. Trag. Graec. inc. 90 πυρὸς...μένος, Lucretius 2.215 *uis flammea*, Anon. *Aetna* 567 *incendi uis.*

The compound adjective *flammifer* does not occur again before Ovid. Such adjectives are rare in comedy (Plautus has *dulcifer, furcifer, trifurcifer, lucrifera, flabellifera*), comparatively common in tragedy (*frondifer* at Naevius 22, *frugifer* at Trag. inc. 164, *horrifer* at Pacuvius 82 and Accius 566, *lucifer* at Accius 331, *mortifer* at Trag. inc. 87). Classical dactylic poetry employs them sparingly, Seneca's mythological tragedy freely.[1]

26 caeruleae incinctae igni incedunt: Columna rewrote this as *caeruleo incinctae angui incedunt*, thinking, no doubt, that there was enough talk of fire elsewhere in the canticum and explicitly quoting in support of his alterations Virgil, *Georg.* 4.482-3 *caeruleosque implexae crinibus anguis | Eumenides* and Ovid, *Met.* 4.482-3 *cruore rubentem | induitur pallam, tortoque incingitur angue.* To these might be added Hesiod, *Asp.* 233-4 ἐπὶ δὲ ζώνῃσι δράκοντε | δοιὼ ἀπηωρεῦντ' ἐπικυρτώοντι κάρηνα (the Gorgons), Aeschylus, *Choe.* 1049-50 φαιοχίτωνες καὶ πεπλεκτανημέναι | πυκνοῖς δράκουσιν, Euripides, *Ba.* 697-8 καταστίκτους δορὰς | ὄφεσι κατεζώσαντο (Maenads), Catullus 64.258 *sese tortis serpentibus incingebant.*

Against himself in favour of *caeruleae* (sc. *Furiae*) Columna quoted *Orph. H.* 70.6-7 κυανόχρωτοι ἄνασσαι, ἀπαστράπτουσαι ἀπ' ὄσσων |

---

[1] Cf. K. Münscher, *Bursians Jahresb.* CXCII (1922), 200 ff.

ALCMEO

δεινὴν ἀνταυγῆ φάεος σαρκοφθόρον αἴγλην. To this should be added Hesiod, *Asp.* 249 Κῆρες κυάνεαι, Virgil, *Aen.* 7.346 *huic dea caeruleis unum de crinibus anguem*, Statius, *Theb.* 1.110 *et caerulei redeunt in pectora nodi*.

Incinctae igni can stand, interpreted either as 'wearing belts of fire' (no more bizarre than Euripides, *I.T.* 288 ἢ δ' ἐκ χιτώνων πῦρ πνέουσα) or as 'armed with fiery weapons' (cf. Virgil, *Aen.* 9.74 *facibus pubes accingitur atris*, 12.811 *flammis cincta* [Iuno], Seneca, *Tro.* 560–1). Ennius' love of redundant expression needs no further illustration.

The form *caeruleus* occurs once elsewhere in republican drama, likewise in anapaests (Plautus, *Trin.* 834).

Incinctae is picked up by *incedunt...intendit...innixus.* The compound verb *incingere* is absent from comedy and classical prose. Other *in-* compounds replacing simple verbs of the common language in tragedy are *inaudire* (Pacuvius 35), *inaurare* (Ennius 213), *inesse* (Ennius 225), *infrenare* (Ennius 158), *inhorrescere* (Pacuvius 411), *inniti* (Ennius 29), *insultare* (Ennius 124), *inuestire* (Ennius 113), *inuisere* (Accius 237).

27 circumstant cum ardentibus taedis: for the torches of the Erinyes cf. Aristophanes, *Plout.* 423–5 ἴσως Ἐρινύς ἐστιν ἐκ τραγῳδίας· | βλέπει γέ τοι μανικόν τι καὶ τραγῳδικόν. | — ἀλλ' οὐκ ἔχει γὰρ δᾷδας, Aeschines, *Tim.* 190 καθάπερ ἐν ταῖς τραγῳδίαις Ποινὰς ἐλαύνειν καὶ κολάζειν δᾳσὶν ἡμμέναις. There is no clear evidence in the text of Εὐμενίδες that Aeschylus' Erinyes carried torches.

Taeda occurs twice in tragedy, not at all in comedy (~ *fax* 1:5); it was probably a word of the sacral language.

28 crinitus Apollo: Φοῖβος ἀκερσοκόμης (Homer, *Il.* 20.39); cf. Virgil, *Aen.* 9.638. *Crines* usually denoted the hair of the Roman *matrona* in its characteristic arrangement; cf. Plautus, *Mil.* 792, *Most.* 226 (in both passages the Attic original is handled freely).

29 arcum auratum: for Apollo's golden bow cf. Aeschylus, *Eum.* 181–2 πτηνὸν ἀργηστὴν ὄφιν, | χρυσηλάτου θώμιγγος ἐξορμώμενον. Ennius' use of the adjective *auratus*, properly 'gilded', rather than *aureus* may be a piece of rationalism.

luna: 'the curve of the bow'; cf. the use of the denominative *lunare* at Propertius 4.6.25 *aciem geminos...lunarat in arcus*, Ovid, *Am.* 1.1.23 *lunauitque genu sinuosum fortiter arcum*.

innixus: not elsewhere in republican drama; *niti* occurs 6 times in comedy, 4 in tragedy.

Diana facem iacit: Apollo's sister normally carries a bow (Euripides, *Hipp.* 167, 1422, 1451, Naevius *ap.* Macr. *Sat.* 6.5.8, Accius, *Trag.* 52, 167) but for the torch cf. Sophocles, *O.T.* 204 ff., *Tr.* 205 ff., Euripides, *I.T.* 21.

XVI

See above, p. 185.

ALEXANDER

The title *Alexander* is given to Ennius by Varro, Verrius, Gellius and Macrobius. Varro, Verrius and Gellius quote what they do to illustrate points of lexicography. Macrobius' quotations come from an account of those verses and passages of Virgil's poems which were thought to have been based on work by the older Latin poets.

Alexander was another name of the Trojan hero Paris. One story, as old as the Κύπρια and Homer, *Il.* 24.28 ff., told of how the three goddesses, Hera, Athena and Aphrodite, came to him when he was minding cattle on Mount Ida and got him to settle a dispute as to who among them was the most beautiful. Another story, as old as Pindar, *Paian* 8 *e*.5 ff., told of how he was exposed at birth on the advice of seers, rescued and raised by herdsmen of Mount Ida; at athletic games celebrated in his memory by his father Priam he competed with and defeated his brothers, Hector and Deiphobus; angry at being defeated by an apparent slave, Deiphobus plotted to kill Alexander but at the critical moment the facts of Alexander's birth came out and he was received back into the royal house.[1]

Tragedies by Euripides and Sophocles dealt with Alexander's recognition.[2] The pieces attributed to Ennius' *Alexander* can all be interpreted with some plausibility as coming from a play with the same theme.

---

[1] For the second story see Apollodorus 3.12.5.2 ff. and Hyginus, *Fab.* 91. Its relations with the first story are obscure; cf. C. Robert, *Bild und Lied* (Berlin, 1881), pp. 233 ff., *Hermes* IL (1914), 315 f., *Die griech. Heldensage* III ii (Berlin, 1923), pp. 977 ff., 1071 ff.

[2] Sophocles, fr. 90 N.² (Steph. Byz. p. 139.20) is quite unambiguous. Direct quotations of Euripides' 'Αλέξανδρος in Greek authors are uninformative and early students were led badly astray by their belief that its title was 'Αλεξάνδρα. J. Barnes (*Euripides: quae extant omnia* [Cambridge, 1694]) seems to have been the first to make the recognition of Alexander Euripides' theme. Osann, in F. A. Wolf's *Analecta Litteraria* II (Berlin, 1818), pp. 529 ff., got rid of the title 'Αλεξάνδρα and argued that Hyginus, *Fab.* 91 summarised the plot. The matter was put beyond all doubt by the papyrus fragments published in 1922 (by W. Crönert, *NGG, Phil.-hist. Kl.,* 1–17).

C. O. Mueller referred Varro's quotation at *Ling.* 6.83 (fr. XIX), *iam dudum ab ludis animus atque aures auent | auide exspectantes nuntium*, to the games at which Alexander defeated his brothers.

Welcker[1] interpreted Macrobius' quotation at *Sat.* 6.1.61 (fr. XXIV), *multi alii aduentant paupertas quorum obscurat nomina*, as coming from the messenger's speech which recounted the games and as describing Alexander's companions. This interpretation is confirmed to some extent by the fact that Virgil's imitation occurs in his list of those who came to compete in the foot-race at the funeral games for Anchises (*Aen.* 5.293 ff.). In Homer's foot-race, which was Virgil's main object of imitation at this point, there competed only three prominent heroes, Ajax, Odysseus and Antilochus (*Il.* 23.740 ff.). Virgil's imitations frequently reflect the context as well as the wording of the older Latin poet's verses.[2]

Macrobius' quotations at *Sat.* 6.2.18 and 25 (frs. XXV and XXVI) refer to events which occurred in time after the death of Alexander. They were for a long time partly responsible for the notion that Ennius wrote two plays, an *Alexander* and an *Alexandra*, the latter dealing with the prophetess Cassandra and set after the fall of Troy. Taking up a hint of Columna's, Vossius interpreted the quotations as from a speech by Cassandra describing a vision of the future. This interpretation is supported by the fact that Virgil imitates the first in the speech made by the ghost of Hector to the sleeping Aeneas on the night of Troy's fall (*Aen.* 2.281 ff.) and both in the conversation between Aeneas and the shade of Deiphobus in the underworld (*Aen.* 6.500 ff.).

At *Ling.* 7.82 (fr. XX) Varro quotes a verse of Ennius—*quapropter Parim pastores nunc Alexandrum uocant*—which can only come from a play about Alexander's early life. Varro asserts that Ennius took his etymology straight from Euripides and it would seem fair to suppose that he believed the Latin *Alexander* to be an adaptation of Euripides' Ἀλέξανδρος.[3] This play was the only one of the Alexandrian seventy[4] in which such an etymology could have been found.

Commenting on Virgil, *Aen.* 7, 319–20 *nec face tantum | Cisseis praegnas ignis enixa iugalis*, where Juno is prophesying the same troubles for Aeneas and his bride Lavinia as struck Paris and Helen, Servius comments: CISSEIS *regina Hecuba filia secundum Euripidem Cissei quem Ennius Pacuuius et Vergilius sequuntur; nam Homerus Dymantis dicit. haec se facem parere uidit et Parin creauit qui causa fuit incendii* (fr. CCXXV).[5] Columna and succeeding editors of Ennius

---

[1] *Die griech. Trag.* p. 467.

[2] Cf. Norden, *Ennius und Vergilius, passim, Aeneis VI*[2], pp. 365 f.

[3] F. Vater, *Untersuchungen über die dramatische Poesie der Griechen* I (Berlin, 1843), p. 23 (cf. Leo, *Gesch.* p. 189 n. 2), tried to deny that this was implied by Varro's discourse.   [4] See *Introduction*, p. 45.

[5] Cf. *Aen.* 10.705 ff. and Servius' note.

thought that Servius refers to Ennius' version of Euripides' Ἑκάβη. B. Snell argued[1] that Servius' comment shows him to have believed that Ennius adapted the Ἀλέξανδρος. It shows nothing of the sort. The bulk of what Servius says probably comes from the same mythological source as lies beneath Hyginus, *Fab.* 91.1...*Hecubae, Cissei siue Dymantis filiae. uxor eius praegnas in quiete uidit se facem ardentem parere* and Apollodorus 3.12.5.2 Ἑκάβην τὴν Δύμαντος ἢ ὥς τινές φασι Κισσέως...ἔδοξεν Ἑκάβη καθ' ὕπνους δαλὸν τεκεῖν διάπυρον, τοῦτον δὲ πᾶσαν ἐπινέμεσθαι τὴν πόλιν καὶ καίειν. The similarity between Hyginus and Ennius, *Trag.* 50–1 *mater grauida parere se ardentem facem | uisa est in somnis Hecuba* is an accidental one.[2] The information about Euripides' view of Hecuba's parentage might refer to the Ἑκάβη (*v.* 3) or to several of his other plays including the Ἀλέξανδρος. The information about Ennius' view would have been added by Servius or some preceding scholiast and might just as readily refer to Ennius' version of the Ἑκάβη as to his *Alexander*. Nothing is implied about the relationship between Greek and Latin plays.

The pieces attributed by ancient authors to the Latin *Alexander* are not such as could prove wrong Varro's belief that it had a Euripidean original.

A number of pieces of tragic verse quoted by Cicero without either the name of the author or the title of the play are commonly given by modern scholars to the *Alexander*.

At several points of his dialogue on divination Cicero illustrates the phenomenon of ecstatic prophecy with the utterances of the Cassandra of a Latin tragedy as she beholds a series of visions of the events which culminated in the destruction of Troy. *Diu.* 2.112 (fr. xviie) gives the proof, if proof be required, that 1.67 (fr. xviic) and 1.114 (fr. xviid) quote the same speech.[3] There is, however, one difficulty. The quotation at 1.67 strongly suggests that the tragedy is set within the walls of Troy (*ciues ferte opem*), while the context of the quotation at 1.114 suggests that Cicero believed it to be set on Mount Ida or perhaps by the sea shore (*multos nemora siluaeque multos amnes aut maria commouent*). Cicero's dialogue shows many signs of hasty composition and it could be that he decorated his adaptation of some Greek account of the causes of ecstatic prophecy with more from the same speech which he had quoted at 1.67 and did not stop to think whether it was completely appropriate.[4]

---

[1] *Euripides' Alexandros* (*Hermes* Einzelschr. v [1937]), p. 59.

[2] There is no common linguistic peculiarity such as the *se...uisa est* which links Ovid, *Epist.* 17.237–8 with Ennius.

[3] T. C. W. Stinton, *Euripides and the Judgement of Paris* (London, 1965), pp. 68 f., toys with the idea that separate speeches are quoted.

[4] Cf. Philippson, *BPhW* xlii (1922), 102. At *Tusc.* 3.44 f. Cicero quotes a speech by the Ennian Andromache (fr. xxviih) although only a speech by a male personage would fully suit the context.

It has been argued[1] that while the verses quoted in 1.66 and 1.67 come from the same play the first group comes from near the end and the second from near the beginning. Now it is true, as Cicero himself admits, that the first group does not illustrate the phenomenon of ecstasy (*o poema tenerum et moratum atque molle. sed hoc minus ad rem*). Furthermore some scholars[2] have been tempted to reverse Cicero's order, thinking that the second group were accompanied in utterance by the unmaidenly behaviour remarked on and apologised for in the first group.[3] But the rationale of Cicero's mode of quotation, his failure to make clear in his discourse that the first two verses quoted were not uttered by Cassandra and the enormous extent of his quotation, suggest that he consulted a text of the tragedy rather than his memory and copied out the verses which struck his sensibilities, both those relevant to his argument and those not. A papyrus roll would have carried the text in Cicero's day and rolls were far more easily consulted in one place than in two and more likely to be read frontwards than backwards. As to the second point it is an error to think that a seer's description of his or her vision was necessarily accompanied by signs of violent physical disturbance;[4] at Euripides, *Tr.* 308–461 physical disturbance seems to have come first, then rational discourse, then prophecy.

Cicero's discussion of the correct form of the second declension genitive plural at *Orat.* 155–6 takes examples from the work of three writers of tragedy. The third is mentioned by name, Accius; the second, 'ille alter in Chryse', must be Pacuvius; the first can only be Ennius. These were in Cicero's day the three classic Latin tragedians.[5] Two of the four examples of Ennius' usage come from the speech of Cassandra quoted at *Diu.* 1.66–7. Study of Cicero's mode of quotation throughout the whole discussion of the σύνθεσις of individual words at *Orat.* 149–64 confirms our impression that *Diu.* 1.66–7 quotes from the one speech. The quotation of *texitur exitium examen rapit*, a metrical unit making no sense, at 155 and the attribution of two tragic verses to Terence's *Phormio* at 157 suggests that here Cicero's examples are drawn from a grammarian's treatise rather than from his own direct reading. Errors of attribution are common in the blocks of illustrative passages which went from one grammarian to another. Verrius Flaccus is known to have been prone to quoting units of metre rather than units of

---

[1] Tentatively by G. Murray, *Greek Studies* (Oxford, 1946), p. 130, and strongly by F. Scheidweiler, *Philologus* XCVII (1948), 324 n. 1.

[2] E.g. Düntzer, *Zeitschr. f. d. Alt.* 1838, 61–2, Hartung, *Euripides restitutus* II, p. 244.

[3] Cf. Euripides, *Or.* 281 ff.

[4] For this cf. Plautus, *Truc.* 600 ff., Virgil, *Aen.* 6.46 ff., Seneca, *Ag.* 710 ff., Lucan 5.161 ff.

[5] Cf. Cicero, *Opt. gen.* 18, *Ac.* 1.10, *De orat.* 3.27.

sense;[1] he must have been following a practice already well established at the time of composition of the *Orator*. Grammarians also tended to quote from successive parts of the one speech or scene; the lexicon of Nonius Marcellus provides many examples. At *Orat*. 157 a quotation of Ter. *Phorm*. 390 follows one of 384, while the three quotations of Pacuvius' *Chryses* at 155 appear to be successive verses. One would expect the two Ennian pieces, *patris mei meum factum pudet* and *texitur exitium examen rapit*, to be of similar character.

Columna suggested in his commentary that the verses in question belonged to the same scene as provided those attributed by Macrobius to the *Alexander* at *Sat*. 6.2.18 and 25. Ribbeck was the first editor to include them in a collection of the *Alexander* fragments. There is no place for them in any other known tragedy of Ennius or, indeed, of his republican fellows.[2]

At *Diu*. 1.42, in an account of prophetic dreams, Cicero quotes twelve trimeters from the prologue of a Latin tragedy describing the dream which led to the exposure of Alexander on Ida (fr. xvIII). B. Heath[3] seems to have been the first to assign them to the *Alexander*. It is possible that they come from one of the other known republican tragedies which dealt with the fate of members of the Trojan royal house, *Equos Troianus*, *Hector proficiscens*, *Andromacha*, *Hectoris lytra*, *Hecuba*,[4] *Iliona*, *Astyanax* or *Troades*. The prologue of Euripides' Φοίνισσαι, a tragedy set at the time of the Argive siege of Thebes, went back to events before the birth of Oedipus. I have nevertheless thought it hypercritical to separate a description of Alexander's birth from the only Latin tragedy known to deal with him.

A number of brief pieces quoted by Cicero, Verrius, Quintilian and Charisius have been attributed at various times to the *Alexander*. In no case is the substance sufficiently specific to justify the attribution.

Barnes[5] set in Cassandra's canticum the iambics and trochaics quoted by Cicero at *Diu*. 2.115, *o sancte Apollo qui umbilicum certum terrarum obsides,* | *unde superstitiosa primum saeua euasit uox fera.*

Snell[6] set the trimeter quoted without author's name in Festus' epitome of Verrius at p. 306.10, *omnis aequalis uincebat quinquertio*, in the messenger's speech describing the games. Ribbeck[7] had compared Sophocles, Ἠλέκτρα 690–3 and assigned the verse to Atilius' version of this play. There is no evidence however that Verrius ever quoted Atilius.

---

[1] See *Introduction*, p. 53.

[2] Bothe made the strange suggestion (*P.S.L.* vol. v, p. 275) that they be placed in Accius' *Hecuba* or *Troades*.

[3] *Notae* (Oxford, 1762), p. 163.

[4] Aldus Manutius and Welcker (*Die griech. Trag.* p. 463 n. 3) proposed Ennius' *Hecuba*: Bothe Accius' *Hecuba*.

[5] *Euripides*, p. 517.

[6] *Euripides' Alexandros*, p. 38.

[7] *Die röm. Trag.* p. 609.

ALEXANDER

Hartung[1] set the trimeter given to Ennius in Paulus' epitome of Festus at p. 507.12 (fr. CCVIII), *is habet coronam uitulans uictoria*, in a speech by Deiphobus. C. Lefke[2] compared part of the Strasbourg papyrus of Euripides' Ἀλέξανδρος: ποῦ νῦ⟨ν ἂ⟩ν εἴη καλλίνικα ἔχων στέφη ; | — πᾶν ἄστυ πληροῖ Τρωικὸν γαυρούμενος (= fr. 43.41–2 Snell); this appears to come from a conversation between Hecuba and Deiphobus after Priam's decision to let Alexander's victory stand.

Lange[3] set the example of ὁμοιοτέλευτον quoted by Quintilian at *Inst.* 9.3.77, *Hecuba hoc dolet pudet piget*, in Cassandra's *canticum*, after the words *superstitiosis hariolationibus*. Vahlen[4] suggested that the phrase might come after *illos obsequi*. Its substance would be quite otiose anywhere in the *canticum*. N. Terzaghi[5] interpreted it as either a misquotation by Quintilian or an imitation of Ennius by another tragedian.

Ribbeck[6] set the example of emotional speech quoted by Charisius at p. 315.19, *heus heus pater heus Hector*, in the same canticum. The phrase seems as otiose here as does *Hecuba hoc dolet pudet piget*.

XVII

(c) Cicero quotes remnants of a scene in which Cassandra behaves at first with virginal propriety, then goes into an ecstatic trance, returns momentarily to mental normality, realises the cause of her ecstasy, and is finally confronted by a series of visions of the fate of Troy and its ruling family.

Verses 32–3 are spoken by the chorus leader[7] and *vv.* 41–2 provide indirectly the answer to his question. It was the presence of Alexander either inside the palace or on stage and a dim perception of his identity that caused Cassandra's eyes to burn and her general demeanour to alter. Her plea to the citizens of Troy (other bystanders as well as members of the chorus) in *v.* 42 only makes dramatic sense if the spectators have seen or can see on stage the physical Alexander.[8] Verse 39, *optumam progeniem Priamo peperisti extra me*, on

---

[1] *Euripides Restitutus* II, p. 238.
[2] *De Euripidis Alexandro* (Diss. Münster, 1936), p. 63.
[3] *Vindiciae Tragoediae Romanae*, p. 48.
[4] *E.P.R.²*, p. 128.   [5] *BFC* XXXIV (1927/28), 43.
[6] *Quaest. scen.* p. 260.
[7] Editors of Cicero and Ennius seem to me quite wrong in making Hecuba the speaker without at the same time changing *uisa est* to *uisa es* and *illa* to *ista*.
[8] The appeal to the body of citizens at a moment of danger (see W. Schulze, 'Beitr. z. Wort- und Sittengeschichte 11', *SB Berlin* 1918, 481 ff. [= *Kl. Schr.* 160 ff.]) is a common motif of tragedy (cf. Sophocles, *O.K.* 884, Euripides, *Herakleidai* 69–70, *I.T.* 1422–30, *Or.* 1621–4) and comedy (cf. Aristophanes, *Neph.* 1322–3, Plautus, *Aul.* 406, *Men.* 1000, *Most.* 1031, *Rud.* 615–26, Terence, *Ad.* 155–6).

207

the other hand sounds very oddly if Alexander has already been recognised by his family. There is tragic irony here. Only the spectators are as yet fully aware that the bearer of fire and destruction has arrived. We cannot now decide whether Alexander is visible to the spectators as Cassandra speaks or whether he is off stage, i.e. inside the palace. There are good parallels for both possibilities. In Euripides' Βάκχαι Pentheus sees the handsome stranger standing on stage as a bull (920 ff.) and Agave describes the head of Pentheus which she carries in her hands as that of a mountain lion (1168 ff.). In Aeschylus' 'Αγαμέμνων Cassandra cries out at the culminating point of her series of visions of past and future events in the Atreid palace ἄπεχε τῆς βοὸς | τὸν ταῦρον (1125–6), meaning Clytaemnestra and Agamemnon whom the spectators have just seen enter the palace.

Welcker[1] made Cassandra utter her prophecies as Deiphobus was attempting to kill Alexander (Hyginus, *Fab.* 91.6); Hartung[2] after Alexander had been recognised as Priam's son. Vater,[3] on the other hand, argued that the scene comes from very early in the play, long before Alexander had arrived from the arena where the games were held. Such a view would demand a very forced interpretation of Ennius' words but some sort of parallel is offered by Ovid's account at *Epist.* 5.115–20 of a vision which Cassandra saw before Helen's arrival in Troy.

Ps. Longinus refers at 15.4 to a graphic utterance by Cassandra in a play by Euripides, quoting the beginning of a trimeter: ἀλλ' ὦ φίλιπποι Τρῶες (fr. 935). Wilamowitz[4] pointed out that of the Alexandrian seventy the only one to which Ps. Longinus could be referring is the 'Αλέξανδρος. Hartung's guess[5] that Ps. Longinus quotes the original of Ennius' *ciues ferte opem* is thus very likely correct.

Lefke[6] argued that *vv.* 32–3 (reading *rabere* rather than *rapere*) were a version of those Euripidean trimeters preserved in Strasbourg as

$$x - \cup - x - \cup]\eta\varsigma \; \text{ἤκουσ' ἔπος}$$
$$x - \cup - x - \cup \; \beta]\alpha\kappa\chi\epsilon\acute{\upsilon}\epsilon\iota \; \varphi\rho\acute{\epsilon}\nu\alpha.$$

Snell[7] accepted this argument and argued further from the appearance of the papyrus that the verses belonged in the first scene near verses restored by Wilamowitz as

καὶ μὴν δέ]δορκα παῖδα Κ[ασάνδραν σέθεν
ἤκουσα]ν ἀδύτων ὧ[δε Φοιβείων πάρος.

---

[1] *Die griech. Trag.* pp. 472 ff.   [2] *Euripides Restitutus* II, pp. 244 f.
[3] *Untersuchungen*, p. 23; cf. Snell, *Euripides' Alexandros*, pp. 24 ff.
[4] *Anal. Eurip.* p. 148.   [5] *Euripides Restitutus* II, p. 244.
[6] *De Eur. Alex.* p. 97.   [7] *Euripides' Alexandros*, p. 25.

To Snell the words preserved implied that Cassandra prophesied the destruction of Troy in this first scene. One of two embarrassing conclusions would have to follow from this: either that Vater's interpretation of the Ennian scene was correct, for two prophecies could hardly be expected in the one play, or that Ennius did not adapt the Euripidean play at all. It is likely enough that Cassandra did appear in the first scene of the Ἀλέξανδρος and that someone did say of her: βακχεύει φρένα. But no one could argue that this phrase comes necessarily from a description of her behaviour at the moment of speaking. Several possibilities are open.

Iamque at *v.* 43 indicates that Cicero omitted[1] the beginning of the Ἰλιὰς *malorum*, perhaps an account of the Greek chieftains assembling their forces at Aulis. Ennius' Cassandra actually sees the Greek ships sweeping across the water (*texitur...rapit*), the soldiers disembarked on the shore (*compleuit*), the three goddesses judged on Mount Ida (*iudicauit*). She perceives the evil to come intellectually rather than visually; hence the future tenses *adueniet...* *adueniet.*[2]

While conversing with her mother the Ennian Cassandra speaks in stichic trochaic tetrameters and continues with these verses even after she has realised who the stranger is. From Ps. Longinus' quotation it is clear that iambic trimeters stood at this point in Euripides' play. The first scenes of the Latin prophecy are described in dactylic verses; the more sophisticated spectators would perhaps have associated the rhythm with that of the Greek oracles recorded in the Sibylline books. Whether any Latin oracles were composed in hexameters before the publication of Ennius' *Annales* we do not know.[3] Other scenes of the prophecy are described in metres now difficult to discern. The change of metre at *v.* 43 is paralleled at Euripides, *Tr.* 444, where Cassandra passes from trimeters to trochaic tetrameters for the climax of her prophecy, and Seneca, *Oed.* 233, where the contents of an oracle are given in dactylic hexameters after a description of the medium's behaviour in trochaic tetrameters. It was rash of Strzelecki[4] to argue from an alleged imitation by Seneca at *Ag.* 693–774 that Euripides cast Cassandra's prophecy in iambic trimeters from beginning to end.

---

[1] For Cicero's habit of making omissions from the middle of a quotation without warning cf. *De orat.* 2.327 and Terence, *Andr.* 117–29, *Att.* 7.3.10 and Terence, *Eun.* 114–15.

[2] For prophecies (future tenses) alternating with visions (present and perfect tenses) cf. Aeschylus, *Ag.* 1090–172, Pindar, *Pyth.* 4.49, 8.45 ff., Horace, *Carm.* 1.15, Virgil, *Aen.* 6.86 ff., Tibullus 2.5.39 ff.

[3] O. Skutsch, *CR* N.S. VIII (1958), 47, denies the possibility with unnecessary firmness.

[4] *De Senecae Agamemnone Euripidisque Alexandro* (Wrocław, 1949), p. 21.

32 sed quid oculis rapere uisa est: for the use of *sed* when something new is seen or heard to happen on stage cf. Plautus, *Amph.* 270, 1130 et al. Lambinus' *rabere*[1] is quite unnecessary. In any case *rabere* would be used metaphorically, 'rage like a mad dog', and hardly need to be accompanied by *uisa est*.

For *oculis rapere*, 'use the eyes as if they were hands to grab with' cf. Trag. inc. 48 *oculis postremum lumen radiatum rape*, Plautus, *Poen.* 277 *haec tanta oculis bona concipio*, Virgil, *Georg.* 2.230 *locum capies oculis*. The normal phrase in comedy is *oculis aspicere* (*uidere, intueri, cernere*). Attic tragedy has ὀφθαλμοῖς (ὄμμασι, ὄσσοις) ὁρᾶν (δέρκεσθαι) but nothing like *oculis rapere*. Plautus frequently transfers the qualities and functions of one part of the body to another for comic effect[2] with no analogues in the Νέα and few in the 'Αρχαία.

oculis...derepente ardentibus: cf. Plautus, *Capt.* 594 *ardent oculi* (of an apparent madman), Virgil, *Aen.* 2.404-5 *Cassandra...ad caelum tendens ardentia lumina frustra*.

Derepente occurs 4 times in tragedy, 6 in comedy (Plautus, *Men.* 874, *Most.* 488, Terence, *Hec.* 518, 554, Turpilius 3, Com. inc. 22). The simple form *repente* occurs only once in tragedy but 13 times in comedy. The contexts of occurrence of *derepente* in comedy confirm the statistical indication that it had a high-falutin tone.

33 ubi illa paulo ante sapiens †uirginali† modestia: Lachmann (on Lucretius 1.186) removed the hiatus *paulo | ante* by supplying ⟨*aut*⟩ *ubi...* and accepted the old interpretation of *uirginali* as *uirginali(s)*,[3] despite the unusual division of the fifth foot of the tetrameter[4] and the necessity of scanning *illa* as two morae.[5] This nevertheless remains the most economical restoration so far suggested. O. Skutsch argues tentatively for *sapiens illa uirginalis paulo ante ubi modestia* or *ubi illa paulo ante* ⟨*apta*⟩ *sapiens uirgin[al]i modestia*.[6]

For *illa paulo ante...modestia* cf. Plautus, *Persa* 385 *non tu nunc hominum mores uides..?*, *Poen.* 725 *rem aduorsus populi saepe leges*.

Sapere, sapiens usually have a personal reference in both tragedy and comedy but cf. Pacuvius, *Trag.* 6 *quod coniectura* (Roth: *consectura* codd.) *sapiens aegre contuit* (Vossius: *contulit* codd.). Tragedy is prone to apply to the

---

[1] This was suggested in the margin and the notes of his 1573 edition. The notion that it occurs in manuscripts seems to come from a misreading of Muretus, *Variarum Lectionum libri XV* (Antwerp, 1580), IX 19.

[2] See Fraenkel, *Pl. im Pl.* p. 107 n. 1 (= *Elementi*, p. 101 n. 1).

[3] Cf. Leo, *Pl. Forsch.²*, p. 290 n. 1.   [4] Cf. above on fr. XII.

[5] See F. Skutsch, *Plautinisches und Romanisches* (Leipzig, 1892), pp. 116 f.

[6] *HSCPh* LXXI (1967), 133.

inanimate and the abstract adjectives and participles used properly of living things: e.g. Ennius 35 *superstitiosis hariolationibus*, 53 *curis...suspirantibus*, Pacuvius 36, 47, 109, 147, 386, Accius 33, 38, 46, 133, 315, 398, 412, 453, 501, Trag. inc. 20, 58, 59, 114.

34 mater, optumatum multo mulier melior mulierum: there is no need to tamper with *optumatum* (*optuma tum* codd.) or any of the other words transmitted. Asconius and Nonius cite passages of Cicero containing the genitive plural *optumatum*[1] while considerable contamination of the vowel and consonantal stems of the third declension is recorded elsewhere in early Latin texts. *Optumarum* would be more normal (cf. *C.I.L.* I² 9.1 f. *honc oino ploirume cosentiont Romane duonoro optumo fuise uiro*, Plautus, *Amph.* 676–7 *Amphitruo uxorem salutat laetus speratam suam | quam omnium Thebis uir unam esse optumam diiudicat, Capt.* 836 *quantum est hominum optumorum optume*) but Ennius appears to have made his Medea call the women of Corinth *matronae opulentae optumates* (see below on fr. cv) and Plautus has the similar formation *summas* three times of members of the Athenian land-owning class (*Cist.* 25, *Pseud.* 227, *Stich.* 492; cf. the humorous *infumas* at *Stich.* 493). In the political pamphlets of the first century the senatorial supporters of the *status quo* referred to themselves regularly as *optumates*.[2] The word suggested social and moral excellence as well as wealth and power (*ops*).

For the pleonasm *optumatum...melior* cf. Aeschylus, *Hik.* 524–6 μακάρων | μακάρτατε καὶ τελέων | τελειότατον, Sophocles, *O.T.* 334, κακῶν κάκιστε, Naevius, *Com.* 118 *pessimorum pessime*, Plautus, *Capt.* 836 *optumorum optume, Men.* 817 *miserorum miserrumus*, Horace, *Sat.* 1.3.136 *magnorum maxime.*

For *mulier melior mulierum* cf. Aeschylus, *Hik.* 524–5 ἄναξ ἀνάκτων μακάρων | μακάρτατε, Sophocles, *O.T.* 660 τὸν πάντων θεῶν θεὸν πρόμον, Plautus, *Capt.* 333 *optumusque hominum es homo,* 540, 825, *Trin.* 1115, Terence, *Phorm.* 853, *Hec.* 861, *Ad.* 218.

For the comparative *melior* representing the superlative cf. Plautus, *Capt.* 825 *regum rex regalior,* Varro, *Rust.* 2.5.10 *Epirotici meliores totius Graeciae.* Ennius aims at a certain kind of parechesis comparatively rare in Attic tragedy (cf. however Sophocles, *Tr.* 947 ΠΟΤΕΡα ΠρΟΤΕΡον ἐπιστένω, Euripides, *I.T.* 1339 ΗΜΕΝ ΗΜΕΝοι, *Phoin.* 1174 ΕΧῶν ΕΧῶρει et al.) but very common in the Latin adaptations (e.g. Naevius 35 *ACReM ACRiMoniam,* 39 *inFLExV FLECtitVr,* Pacuvius 37 *praeGRAnDi GRADu,* 53 *STVdIo obSTVpIda,* 203 *uMoREM riMaREM,* 246 *MiNVaM MaNVuM* et al.).

---

[1] Nonius, p. 409.32, Asconius, p. 71.14 Stangl.
[2] Cf. Rhet. inc. *Her.* 4.45 et al.

COMMENTARY

It is unlikely that Euripides made his Cassandra address her mother in such a bloated style (cf. *Tr.* 353 μῆτερ πύκαζε...). The early Latin adapters of Greek poetry tended to add descriptive matter to vocatives (e.g. Livius, *Carm.* fr. 14 *sancta puer Saturni filia regina* ~ *Od.* 4.513 Πότνια "Ηρη, Ennius, *Trag.* 237 *antiqua erilis fida custos corporis* ~ Euripides, *Med.* 49 παλαιὸν οἴκων κτῆμα δεσποίνης ἐμῆς, *Trag.* 234 *summe Sol qui res omnis inspicis* ~ Euripides, *Med.* 1251 παμφαὴς ἀκτὶς 'Αελίου) and to other cases in solemn narrative (e.g. Livius, *Carm.* fr. 15 *apud nympham Atlantis filiam Calypsonem* ~ *Od.* 4.557 νύμφης ἐν μεγάροισι Καλυψοῦς, Ennius, *Trag.* 214 *imperio regis Peliae* ~ Euripides, *Med.* 6 Πελία). We may have here a reflection of the modes of speech employed in upper-class Roman society on formal occasions.

35 missa sum superstitiosis hariolationibus: the expression is as bizarre and resistant to rational analysis as that of the Aeschylean Cassandra at *Ag.* 1209 τέχναισιν ἐνθέοις ἠρημένη.

I should guess that Ennius thought of his Cassandra as a horse ridden by the power of clairvoyance; cf. Virgil, *Aen.* 6.77–101...*Phoebi nondum patiens...si...possit excussisse deum...fatigat | os rabidum, fera corda domans, fingitque premendo...ea frena furenti | concutit et stimulos sub pectore uertit Apollo.* This field of imagery is commonly used in connexion with non-prophetic madness (e.g. Aeschylus, *Prom.* 597, 883, Euripides, *Hipp.* 237, *I.T.* 81, *Or.* 36, *El.* 1253). Here there are obvious sexual associations.[1]

For *missa sum*, 'emissa sum, immissa sum', cf. Cicero, *Fin.* 1.2 *difficilem quandam temperantiam postulant in eo quod semel iam missum coerceri reprimique non potest,* Tibullus 1.4.32 *qui prior Eleo est carcere missus equus,* Propertius 3.11.62, Seneca, *Med.* 874. For the replacement of compound verbs with their simple forms in tragedy see above on *v.* 14.

Superstitiosus, 'παραστατικός, prophetic', is normally used of persons in republican drama[2] but cf. Trag. inc. 18 *superstitiosa...uox.*

The noun *hariolatio* occurs elsewhere in Latin only at Gellius 15.18.3. The great majority of forms in -*tio* in republican drama (Ploen counts 18 in tragedy, 123 in comedy) retain a strong verbal force.

The plurals of abstract nouns and incorporalia occur frequently in tragedy: e.g. Ennius 36 *fatis,* 44 *exitium,* 53 *curis,* 103 *aerumnis,* 223 *miserias,* 231

---

[1] Female ecstatic seers were sometimes regarded as Apollo's concubines; see Herodotus 1.182, Ps. Longinus 13.2, Pausanias 10.12.2, Apollodorus, *Epit.* 6.3, Norden, *Aen. VI*[2], pp. 145 f., Latte, *HThR* xxxiii (1940), 9, P. Amandry, *La Mantique apollinienne à Delphes* (Paris, 1950), pp. 117 f.

[2] Plautus, *Amph.* 323, *Curc.* 397, *Rud.* 1139, Pacuvius, *Trag.* 216. See E. Linkomies, *Arctos* ii (1931), 73 ff., E. Benveniste, *REL* xvi (1938), 35, Latte, *Römische Religionsgeschichte* (Munich, 1960), p. 268 n. 1.

maerores, Pacuvius 81, 155, 175, 319, 356, Accius 15, 36, 42, 73, 94, 109, 154, 156, 160, 171, 175, 195, 219, 224, 293, 352, 468, 481, 550, 553, 577, 587, 621, 694. They are not excluded from comedy, even by Terence, and do not seem to have been felt as such outright poeticisms as their equivalents were on the Attic stage.

36 †neque† me Apollo fatis fandis dementem inuitam ciet: it would be natural to understand transmitted *neque* as negativing the whole sentence[1] if it were not for the context. Vahlen takes the word closely with *inuitam* and compares Aeschylus, *Ag.* 1202 ff. and Euripides, *Tr.* 451 ff. Neither of these passages implies that Cassandra welcomed or enjoyed the physical presence of Apollo. In any case Ennius' Cassandra goes on to express shame at her periodic fits. The relevant parallels are Aeschylus, *Ag.* 1174 ff., 1215 f., Euripides, *I.A.* 760, *Tr.* 408 ff., where Cassandra is assumed to behave under an external, unwanted compulsion.[2] Hottinger's *namque me Apollo* is palaeographically attractive but the division of the first foot dactyl is odd (see above on fr. XII); likewise the use of *namque* before a consonant (absent from comedy; but cf. Livius, *Carm.* fr. 20, Naevius, *Trag.* 41 [?], Ennius, *Trag.* 339). Ribbeck's *namque Apollo* is a little more convincing than Grotius' *meque Apollo* (for the omission of the anaphoric pronoun see above on *v.* 17).

Fari occurs five times in tragedy, of the utterances of ordinary men as well as of seers. Comedy has it only in the idiomatic phrases *fando accipere* (Plautus, *Amph.* 588) and *fando audire* (*Epid.* 496) and the comic creation *ingenium fans atque infans* (*Persa* 174). The substantive *fatum*, 'statement about the future', sometimes 'event (usually evil) prophesied', perhaps never 'fate',[3] is fairly common in both genres. For the etymological figure cf. Euripides, *Phoin.* 409 ἔχρησ' Ἀδράστῳ Λοξίας χρησμόν τινα.

Ciet probably comes from the same field of imagery as *missa sum*.

37 uirgines uereor aequalis: for *uereor*, 'αἰσχύνομαι', I can find no exact parallel. It seems to be a poetical replacement of the compound *reuereor* (cf. Plautus, *Epid.* 173 *filium reuereor*).

Cassandra has ceased to be herself properly a *uirgo*; she is now the *paelex* of Apollo. Aeschylus had represented his Cassandra as a social outcast: *Ag.* 1273–4 καλουμένη δὲ φοιτὰς ὡς ἀγύρτρια | πτωχὸς τάλαινα λιμοθνὴς ἠνεσχόμην. Women of the ruling class did not go in for ecstatic prophecy either in fifth-century Athens or in second-century Rome.

---

[1] But cf. Terence, *Phorm.* 114.
[2] Cf. Timpanaro, *SIFC* XXI (1946), 58 f.
[3] See below, p. 305.

patris mei meum factum pudet: 'I am ashamed at what my father thinks of the things I do.' *Pudet* does not seem to be accompanied elsewhere by two genitives in this way.

Genitive plural *meum* is transmitted three times elsewhere in republican tragedy (Pacuvius 80, 401, Accius 424), not at all in comedy except in the company of *maiorum* and *parentum*.

39 progeniem...peperisti: the stock phrase in republican drama was *puerum* etc. *parere*. Here we have a poetic substitute preserving the alliteration. *Progenies* occurs three times elsewhere in republican drama (Terence, *Phorm.* 395, Pacuvius, *Praet.* 1, Accius, *Trag.* 50; cf. Lucilius 800) in the meaning 'ancestry'; for the meaning 'offspring' cf. *C.I.L.* I² 15 *progeniem genui*, Cicero, *Tusc.* 1.85 *Priamum tanta progenie orbatum*.

hoc dolet: for the rhyme *ciet...pudet...piget...dolet* extending over four trochaic tetrameters I can find no parallel in Greek or Latin drama. Over two it is quite common: e.g. Aeschylus, *Pers.* 171 f., 247 f., Euripides, *Ba.* 618 f., 622 f., 628 f., *I.A.* 338 f., 361 f., 392 f., Plautus, *Amph.* 308 f., 358 f., 366 f., 368 f., 413 f., 415 f., 435 f., 547 f., 806 f., 1127 f.

40 men obesse, illos prodesse, me obstare, illos obsequi: for the exclamatory accusative and infinitive involving a pronoun or pronominal adjective and the particle *-ne* cf. Plautus, *Pseud.* 202 *a*: *huncine hic hominem pati colere iuuentutem Atticam,* 371, Terence, *Andr.* 689, *Eun.* 644, Cicero, *S. Rosc.* 95, Horace, *Sat.* 1.9.72–3, 2.4.83, 2.8.67, Virgil, *Aen.* 1.37. A similar type of expression is common in Attic drama and oratory; cf. Aeschylus, *Ag.* 1662 ff. ἀλλὰ τούσδ᾽ ἐμοὶ ματαίαν γλῶσσαν ὧδ᾽ ἀπανθίσαι..., *Eum.* 837–9, Sophocles, *Ai.* 410–11, Demosthenes 21.209, 25.91. Elaborate gesturing would have probably accompanied an excited tone of voice.

For the tautology of the two phrases see above on *v.* 19.

Similar anaphora of the personal pronoun occurs in highly emotional passages of comedy; cf. Plautus, *Asin.* 148 *te ego ut ulciscar, te ego ut digna es perdam, Men.* 1015, *Mil.* 331, 1386, *Truc.* 441, Terence, *Eun.* 193 ff.

41 adest adest fax obuoluta sanguine atque incendio: this vision looks like a doublet of the dream which Hecuba had of giving birth to a fiery torch when pregnant with Alexander. Among the many accounts of this dream only Ovid's (*Epist.* 17.237 ff.) mentions fire as well as blood. For the combination cf. Euripides, *I.T.* 288 πῦρ πνέουσα καὶ φόνον, Virgil, *Aen.* 2.210 *oculos suffecti sanguine et igni*. Blood was a common ingredient of Roman portents (e.g. Cicero, *Diu.* 1.46, 1.98, 1.99, 2.58, Livy 22.1.10, 21.63.13, 23.31.15 et al.).

For the gemination of the present indicative cf. Euripides, *Alk.* 259 ἄγει μ' ἄγει μέ τις (vision of death), Virgil, *Aen.* 6.46 *deus ecce deus*, Ovid, *Met.* 15.677 *en deus est deus est*. Comedy doubles vocatives and imperatives fairly frequently.

Obuoluere was certainly archaic in tone in Cicero's day. Of the three examples in his writings two are in legal contexts and one in a reference to heroic legend (*Verr.* 5.72, *Inu.* 2.149, *Orat.* 74); he has *inuoluere* often. We cannot be certain about Ennius' day: the only other occurrence of *obuoluere* in republican drama is at Plautus, *Most.* 424 in a speech in high-falutin style by a slave; *inuoluere* does not occur at all.

Incendium is used elsewhere in republican drama only metaphorically (Plautus, *Asin.* 919, *Merc.* 590); in classical Latin it is used of fires rather larger than those one would associate with a torch.

42 ferte opem: a high-falutin variant of *ferte auxilium*; perhaps from the sacral language (cf. Trag. inc. 241, Terence, *Andr.* 473, *Ad.* 487, Turpilius, *Com.* 118); the tone is elevated at Plautus, *Bacch.* 637, *Mil.* 1387, *Rud.* 617.

43–4 iamque mari magno classis cita | texitur: cf. Virgil, *Aen.* 6.4–5 *et litora curuae | praetexunt puppes*. Cicero uses a related field of imagery when he turns Homer, *Il.* 2.303–4 χθιζά τε καὶ πρωΐζ' ὅτ' ἐς Αὐλίδα νῆες Ἀχαιῶν | ἠγερέθοντο κακὰ Πριάμῳ καὶ Τρωσὶ φέρουσαι into *Argolicis primum ut uestita est classibus Aulis, | quae Priamo cladem et Troiae pestemque ferebant* (*Diu.* 2.63).

For the alliterative phrase *mare magnum*, 'open sea', cf. Livius, *Trag.* 33, Ennius, *Ann.* 445, Lucretius 2.1, Cicero, *Fam.* 16.9.4, *Rep.* 6.2т.

For the omission of *in* cf. Lucretius 2.1 *mari magno turbantibus aequora uentis*, Virgil, *Aen.* 3.204 *erramus pelago*, 6.697 *stant sale Tyrrheno classes*, Cicero, *Fin.* 5.9 *natura sic ab iis inuestigata est, ut nulla pars caelo mari terra, ut poetice loquar, praetermissa sit*. There is a closely parallel phrase at Sophocles, *Tr.* 114–15 κύματ' ἂν εὐρέϊ πόντῳ βάντ' ἐπιόντα τ' ἴδοι. Ennius frequently dispenses with prepositions in the manner of Attic tragedy: e.g. at *Trag.* 45, 76, 214, 218, 299, 330.

Citus accompanies a verb in four obviously paratragic passages of comedy (Plautus, *Amph.* 244, 1111, 1115, *Stich.* 391); cf. Sophocles, *O.K.* 307 δεῦρ' ἀφίξεται ταχύς et al. The adverbial use of adjectives is common in Ennius' epic poetry (e.g. *Ann.* 21, 35, 40, 42, 80, 85, 203, 519) but rare in early tragedy; cf. however Accius 396, 403, 570, 576, Trag. inc. 63, 75.

For the present tense in a vision of the future cf. Homer, *Od.* 20, 351 ff., Aeschylus, *Ag.* 1072–177, Euripides, *Alk.* 252–5, Virgil, *Aen.* 7.98 (Servius' reading of the text), Ovid, *Epist.* 5.115–20. The so-called 'prophetic future' is somewhat different; see below on *v.* 61. Cassandra actually sees the events as they happen.

44 exitium examen rapit: cf. Virgil, *Aen.* 12.450 *ille uolat campoque atrum rapit agmen aperto*, Livy 3.23.3 *citatum agmen Tusculum rapit*, 23.36.3 *citatum agmen praeter Capuam rapit*, 25.35.1 *ad Hasdrubalem Hamilcaris citatum agmen rapiunt*.

Examen is used instead of *agmen* for the sake of alliteration with *exitium*; but cf. Plautus, *Truc.* 314 *neque istuc insegesti tergo coget examen mali*, Propertius 2.32.41 *in tanto stuprorum examine*.

Rapere, 'make to move quickly', is a usage foreign to comedy but common in tragedy: e.g. Ennius 111 *rapit ex alto naues ueliuolas*, Accius 396, Trag. inc. 196, 237.

45–6 … fera ueliuolantibus | nauibus compleuit manus litora: cf. Virgil, *Aen.* 6.5–6 *iuuenum manus emicat ardens | litus in Hesperium*. Many take *nauibus* as instrumental. It is perhaps a pregnant ablative of separation (i.e. *nauibus egressa compleuit*).

The tense of *compleuit* is confirmed by the textually quite secure *tractauere* of *v.* 71.

The disjunction puts a heavy emphasis on *fera*; cf. the way in which Virgil's Aeneas speaks of the Greeks and their gods at *Aen.* 2.29, *hic saeuus tendebat Achilles*, and 2.326–7 *ferus omnia Iuppiter Argos | transtulit*.

Ships frequently fly in ancient poetry (Aeschylus, *Hik.* 734, *Pers.* 559, Euripides, *Hel.* 147, *Med.* 1, *Tr.* 1086, Virgil, *Aen.* 3.124), sometimes by means of their oars (Homer, *Od.* 11.125, Euripides, *I.T.* 1346, Propertius 4.6.47), sometimes, as here, by means of their sails (Hesiod, *Erg.* 628, Aeschylus, *Prom.* 468, Euripides, *Hipp.* 752, Ennius, *Trag.* 111, Lucretius 4.390, 5.1442, Virgil, *Aen.* 3.520, Ovid, *Pont.* 4.5.42).

The *ueliuolans* type compound is common in archaic Latin epic (Naevius, *Carm.* fr. 30 *arquitenens*, Ennius, *Ann.* 81 *altiuolans*, 181 *bellipotens*, 181 *sapientipotens*, 195 *belligerans*, 303 *suauiloquens*, 458 *omnipotens*, 541 *altitonans*, ap. schol. Iuuenalis 7.134 [see Wessner, *BPhW* xliii (1923), 572 ff.] *multisonans*) and in tragedy (Ennius 97 *signitenens*, 150 *omnipotens*, Accius 52, 167 *arquitenens*, 127 *armipotens*, Trag. inc. 36 *crispisulcans*, 150 *praepotens*). Plautus has a number of *-potens* compounds in prayers and paratragic speeches (*omnipotens* at *Poen.* 275; *multi-* at *Bacch.* 652, *Cas.* 841, *Trin.* 820; *prae-* at *Poen.* 1182; *ante-* at *Trin.* 1116; *salsi-* at *Trin.* 820; *uiri-* at *Persa* 252; *caeli-* at *Persa* 755). They have no counterpart in Greek and very few appear in classical Latin poetry. It is tempting to say that the republican poets got them by adoption or extension from the contemporary sacral language but extant prayers have nothing like them.

The plural *litora* stands for the singular in republican drama only here and at Accius, *Trag.* 526 (anapaests); cf. ἀκταί in Attic tragedy. Other plural concretes standing for singulars in Latin tragedy are *aequora* (Accius

224), *caua* (Ennius 96), *delubra* (Accius 527), *freta* (Trag. inc. 183), *lumina* (Naevius 28), *pectora* (Trag. inc. 96), *Pergama* (Livius 2, Ennius 74), *sceptra* (Accius 3, Trag. inc. 104), *stagna* (Accius 335), *tecta* (Trag. inc. 242), *templa* (Ennius 98, 171, Pacuvius 311, Accius 529), *terga* (Livius, *Ino* 3), *thesauri* (Ennius 192).

(*d*) Haupt observed trochaic rhythm in the words of this quotation.[1] *Eheu uidete* might just as readily be regarded as a colon reizianum as the end of an acatalectic tetrameter.[2]

The tense of *iudicauit* should be preserved along with that of *compleuit* in *v*. 46, *tractauere* in *v*. 71 and *superauit* in *v*. 72. The future would be absurd after the imperative *uidete*. Cassandra's mode of speech is the same as that of the Aeschylean Cassandra at *Ag.* 1214–22, Euripides' Alcestis at *Alk.* 259–63 and Virgil's Venus at *Aen.* 2.604–18 (*aspice...Neptunus...fundamenta quatit...Iuno Scaeas saeuissima portas | prima tenet...iam summas arces Tritonia — respice — Pallas | insedit...ipse pater...*); all are pointing out things invisible to ordinary mortals.

Cassandra could scarcely be referring to common knowledge about the historical past;[3] *uidete* makes it plain that she is describing a vision. The vision on the other hand could be of a past event. Ancient diviners were capable of seeing the past as well as the future.[4] Cicero, however, obviously understood *iudicauit* as referring to the future and although he was capable of mishandling pieces of dramatic poetry for the sake of his argument we should not abandon his interpretations of them without good reason.

Whether the vision is of the past or the future it occurs out of chronological order.[5] This is odd. Aeschylus' Cassandra (*Ag.* 1072 ff.) has her visions in strict chronological order; so too Seneca's (*Ag.* 726 ff.).

If the vision is of the past the Latin Alexander would have been aware from the beginning of the action that he was something other than an ordinary slave. Yet in Euripides' tragedy the recognition was as much a surprise to him as it was to his parents. The debate with Deiphobus assumes that he was precisely what he seemed to be. If, on the other hand, the vision is of the future, it is odd that after being recognised as a prince of the royal house he

---

[1] *Philologus* III (1848), 547 (= *Opusc.* I 209).

[2] See Mariotti, *Lezioni su Ennio*, p. 134. But for the rarity of this colon in the company of trochaic verses see Maurach, *Philologus* CVII (1963), 252.

[3] So Bücheler, *RhM* XXVII (1872), 477.

[4] Cf. Homer, *Il.* 1.70, Hesiod, *Th.* 38, Aeschylus, *Ag.* 1072–330, Euripides, *I.T.* 1259–68, Virgil, *Georg.* 4.392–3, Ovid, *Met.* 1.517–18.

[5] Cicero's words at *Diu.* 2.112—Cassandra '*iamque mari magno*' eademque paulo post '*eheu uidete*'—establishes the order of the fragments. Plank, *Q. Ennii Medea*, p. 118, was wrong to reverse them.

should go back to herding cattle on Ida. Certainly in epic poetry the Trojan princes are often described as herdsmen[1] and in tragic allusions to the story of the judgment Alexander is usually described as a herdsman.[2] However the 'Αλέξανδρος, like many of Euripides' plays, brought the heroes into a world similar to the contemporary one, where a member of a wealthy and powerful family was the last person likely to spend time tending cattle.

The phrase *inclitum iudicium* is odd in the dramatic context. One could take the epithet as belonging in substance with *inter deas tris*.[3] But this is a bold enallage for republican tragedy. The tragedian may be writing with the fame of the judgment in his own day in mind. At *Trag.* 211–12, with no prompting from his original, Ennius makes his actor speak like a contemporary scholiast rather than a person of the heroic age.

The words *Lacedaemonia mulier Furiarum una adueniet* are usually taken as a close translation of a Greek sentence containing the word 'Ερινύς.[4] The Roman adapters of tragedy certainly called the 'Ερινύες who pursued matricides *Furiae*.[5] Cicero[6] translated Sophocles, *Tr.* 1051–2 καθῆψεν ὤμοις τοῖς ἐμοῖς 'Ερινύων | ὑφαντὸν ἀμφίβληστρον as *haec me inretiuit ueste furiali*. At Euripides, *Tr.* 456–7 there is a sentence parallel in structure with Ennius': οὐκέτ' ἂν φθάνοις ἂν αὔραν ἱστίοις καραδοκῶν, | ὡς μίαν τριῶν 'Ερινὺν τῆσδέ μ' ἐξάξων χθονός. In substance, however, it is not. Euripides' emphasis is on the wickedness of Agamemnon; Cassandra will be the immediate cause of his just destruction and is fittingly compared with an 'Ερινύς. Ennius' emphasis is on the wickedness of Helen herself; she is compared with a *Furia* because Cassandra thinks of her as a bringer of fire and destruction to Troy; the cause of her coming, Alexander's decision in favour of Aphrodite, could hardly be thought a punishable act of wickedness.

The semantic area of 'Ερινύς in Attic tragedy and that of *Furia* in recorded Latin are not exactly co-extensive. The 'Ερινύς was a spirit of ven-

---

[1] Cf. Homer, *Il.* 5.313, 6.25, 421 ff., 11.101 ff., 14.445, 15.547 f., 20.89 ff., 188 ff.; for stories recorded outside Homer see Robert, *Bild und Lied*, p. 234, *Die Griech. Heldensage* III ii, p. 978 n. 3.

[2] Cf. Sophocles, fr. 469, Euripides, *Andr.* 274 ff., *Hec.* 629 ff., *Hel.* 23 ff., 357 ff., 678, 708, *I.A.* 76, 180 ff., 573 ff., 1283 ff., Trag. Graec. inc. 286, Accius, *Trag.* 610, Seneca, *Ag.* 730 ff. (contrast the vagueness of Euripides, *Tr.* 919 ff.).

[3] I am grateful for the suggestion to E. W. Handley. For enallage in tragedy see below on *v.* 57.

[4] So they were understood by Virgil at *Aen.* 2.569–73: *Tyndarida aspicio... Troiae et patriae communis Erinys*; by Fraenkel, on Aesch. *Ag.* 749, p. 347 ('Euripides has adopted this conception in his *Alexandros* if, as is probable, the words of Ennius go back to the original'); and by Wüst, *RE* Suppl. VIII (1956), 118.

[5] Cicero, *S. Rosc.* 67, *Pis.* fr. 3, 46, *Leg.* 1.40, *Parad.* 18.   [6] *Tusc.* 2.20.

geance and justice, never one of random destruction.[1] *Furia* on the other hand was frequently used, like the abstracts *pestis, pernicies, labes, exitium*, to indicate mad, wicked and/or destructive persons whose presence made other persons equally mad, wicked and/or destructive: e.g. Cicero, *Dom*. 99, 102, *Har. resp.* 4, 11, *Sest.* 33, 39, 109, 112, *Vat.* 31, 33, 40, *Pis.* 8, 26, 91, *Fam.* 1.9.15, *Quint. fr.* 3.1.11, Horace, *Sat.* 1.8.45, Livy 21.10.11, 30.13.12. Not one of the persons so indicated had any kind of justice on his or her side, at least not in the view of the indicator. What *Furia* denoted before the Latin poets took it up it is hard to say. Certainly it was the horrific external aspect of the Attic 'Ερινύς, their fiery torches and serpentine adornment, rather than their role as the keepers of a primitive system of justice that impressed the imagination of all poets after the fifth century, both Greek and Latin.

What Cicero quotes at *Diu*. 1.114 may therefore be not a close adaptation of verses of Euripides' 'Αλέξανδρος but a careless injection by Ennius into the speech he wrote for his Cassandra of matter quite foreign to the 'Αλέξανδρος. The words *eheu uidete... adueniet* could have led into a description, based on one in the 'Αλέξανδρος, of a vision of the night of Troy's fall with Helen waving, like a *Furia* from a tragedy, a torch to signal the Greek attackers.[2]

Snell[3] argued from the shape of the debate between Hecuba and Helen in Euripides' Τρῳάδες that there had been no reference to the contest of the goddesses in the 'Αλέξανδρος, the first member of the 415 B.C. trilogy: whereas Helen merely alludes to the dream of Hecuba (919 ff.), something which was described at length in the prologue of the 'Αλέξανδρος, she gives a most detailed account of how the three goddesses came to Alexander on Ida; the words with which she introduces her account, ἐνθένδε τἀπίλοιπ' ἄκουσον ὡς ἔχει, imply that Euripides is setting something new before his audience; again the scorn which Hecuba in her reply pours upon Helen's story[4] and the rationalism with which she explains Alexander's departure for Sparta, treating Aphrodite as a symbol of the foolishness engendered by sexual lust, would have appeared rather strange to the audience of 415, if, in the earlier play, the divinely inspired Cassandra had described a vision of the beauty contest. Scheidweiler[5] and Strzelecki[6] have argued that Ennius'

---

[1] Wüst, *RE* Suppl. VIII (1956), 118, takes too narrowly modern a view of justice. The exact point at Aeschylus, *Ag*. 749 and Euripides, *Or*. 1389 is obscure and disputed but in neither case could Helen be regarded as a criminal; in the one the crime was Alexander's insult to Menelaus' hospitality, in the other Laomedon's perjury.

[2] Cf. Virgil, *Aen*. 6.517 ff., Tryphiodorus 512 ff.

[3] *Euripides' Alexandros*, pp. 53 f.

[4] Stinton, *Euripides and the Judgement*, pp. 38 n. 1, 64 ff., argues that Hecuba does not express disbelief at 969 ff.

[5] *Philologus* XCVII (1948), 334.   [6] *De Senecae Agamemnone*, p. 11 n. 19.

words *eheu uidete. iudicauit inclitum iudicium* etc. destroy Snell's position. Things are the other way around. Properly interpreted the Latin words confirm it.[1]

48–9 iudicauit inclitum iudicium...quo iudicio: the spelling *inclutus* seems to be the earliest recorded in inscriptions and there are traces of it in the manuscript tradition of several republican authors. The word was probably not in common use in Ennius' day. It occurs only three times in comedy, all three in paratragic contexts (Plautus, *Mil.* 1227, *Persa* 251, *Pseud.* 174), three times in tragedy. Classical Latin confines it to poetry and history.

The phrase *iudicium iudicare* does not occur elsewhere in republican drama or in Cicero. *Rem iudicare* and *iudicium dare* are Cicero's regular phrases. Ennius however may have employed a contemporary legalism;[2] for etymological figure in the language of law and poetry see above on *v.* 6.

Relative clauses repeat the antecedent noun fairly frequently in the elevated parts of comedy (e.g. Plautus, *Aul.* 561, *Cas.* 309–11, *Epid.* 41, 1015–16, *Rud.* 997, Terence, *Haut.* 20, *Hec.* 10–11). The phenomenon does not seem to occur in Attic drama but is common in Latin legal texts.[3] Many of the Latin dramatic examples have as here a juridical flavour.

48–9 ...inter deas tris aliquis...Lacedaemonia mulier Furiarum una adueniet: there is probably a deliberate antithesis here between the three Olympian goddesses and the three underworld *Furiae*.

For the appellation of Helen cf. Euripides, *Andr.* 486 ἡ Λάκαινα, Horace, *Carm.* 3.3.25, Virgil, *Aen.* 6.511.

For *Furiarum una adueniet*, 'she will arrive like one of the three Furies', cf. the construction of Horace, *Epist.* 2.2.99–100 *discedo Alcaeus puncto illius; ille meo quis?* | *quis nisi Callimachus?*, Propertius 2.2.6–7 *incedit uel Ioue digna soror,* | *aut...Pallas,* Martial 1.62.6 *Penelope uenit, abit Helene.*

XVIII

There is some dispute as to where the quotation begins. *Quia* is given by some editors to Cicero's discourse, by others to the tragedian's trimeters.

The words *sit sane illud commenticium quo Priamus est conturbatus* form a logical unity which the addition of *quia mater grauida parere se ardentem facem*

---

[1] Snell himself saw the difficulty upon which Scheidweiler and Strzelecki pounce; see *Euripides' Alexandros*, p. 54.
[2] Cf. *C.I.L.* I² 583 (122 B.C.).4 *ioudicium ioudicatio leitisque aestumatio, quei quomque ioudicium ex h.l. erunt, eorum h.l. esto.*
[3] See W. Kroll, *Glotta* III (1910–12), 8 f.

uisa est in somnis Hecuba embarrasses if it does not destroy. It is therefore tempting to make *quia* begin a syntactically independent quotation. But such quotations usually have a logical unity; they do not begin with adverbial clauses hanging in the air. In any case it is difficult to imagine what could have formed the substance of the principal clause omitted from the quotation of the tragic narrative.

I do not think it has been noticed that Cicero's discourse paraphrases to some extent what he actually quotes: *quo Priamus est conturbatus* ~ *quo facto...Priamus...mentis metu perculsus*. It is more usual for Cicero to introduce a direct quotation with a paraphrase of what comes before (e.g. *Tusc.* 1.45, 1.69). The dialogue on divination was composed in obvious haste and we must regard the *quia* in question as Cicero's own inelegant link between his allusion to the dream of Hecuba and his quotation of Ennius' poetic account. Vahlen's suggestion that Cicero omitted a word like *mea* from the head of what he quotes is attractive.

There have been many guesses at the identity of the prologue speaker: Düntzer suggested Cassandra, Hartung Venus, Crönert Hecuba, W. Schmid[1] some subordinate person. An interpretation by O. Skutsch of fr. XXIII would seem to me to give some support to Hartung's view.

In adapting Euripides' story of Hecuba's dream Ennius was forced by the exigencies of his medium to treat the dream as a Roman *prodigium* in need of *procuratio*. The phrases *exsacrificabat hostiis...pacem petens...edidit...temperaret tollere* seem to have been borrowed from the contemporary sacral language. There are signs that the substance of the Euripidean narrative has been altered out of respect for Roman religious feeling.

Most other extant accounts of Hecuba's dream[2] make Hecuba take religious action.[3] Certainly no Roman *paterfamilias* would have allowed a woman to interfere in so important a matter[4] and it is possible that Ennius departed from the Euripidean account at this point.[5]

The fear which the Latin narrative attributes to Priam may also be an Ennian addition. The Romans regarded all *prodigia* as signs of divine dis-

---

[1] *Geschichte der griechischen Literatur* I iii, p. 475 n. 11.

[2] Hyginus, *Fab.* 91, Dictys 3.26, Schol. Eur. *Andr.* 293, Schol. A, Hom. *Il.* 3.325, Tzetzes, *Anteh.* 43; *aliter* Lycophron 224, Apollodorus 3.12.5.2, Ovid, *Epist.* 16.47 ff.

[3] Cf. Aeschylus, *Pers.* 176, Euripides, *Hek.* 87, *I.T.* 42.

[4] See Snell, *Euripides' Alexandros*, p. 59 n. 3.

[5] Cf. Terence's alteration to Apollodorus's narrative at *Phorm.* 91; according to Donatus: *Apollodorus tonsorem ipsum nuntium facit, qui dicat se nuper puellae comam ob luctum abstulisse, quod scilicet mutasse Terentium, ne externis moribus spectatorem Romanum offenderet.*

pleasure and fear was their automatic response.[1] For the persons of Ionian epic and Attic tragedy a τέρας could presage good as readily as evil. The words of Clytemnestra at Sophocles, *El.* 644 ff. (esp. 646–7 εἰ μὲν πέφηνεν ἐσθλά... εἰ δ' ἐχθρά) are typical. Cicero adapted *Il.* 2.320–1 ἡμεῖς δ' ἑσταότες θαυμάζομεν οἷον ἐτύχθη. | ὡς οὖν δεινὰ πέλωρα θεῶν εἰσῆλθ' ἑκατόμβας as *nos autem TIMIDI stantes mirabile monstrum | uidimus in mediis diuom uersarier aris* (*Diu.* 2.64), thus importing a quite un-Homeric but thoroughly Roman attitude to the prodigy.

To judge by *Andr.* 293 ff. and *Tr.* 919 ff., Euripides very likely made Apollo's order one to kill the child.[2] Ennius may have used the legal circumlocution *tollere temperare* rather than a word like *necare* (cf. Plautus, *Truc.* 399) out of euphemism or with contemporary Roman practice in regard to unwanted children in mind.[3]

Hyginus, *Fab.* 91, Dictys 3.26, Schol. Eur. *Andr.* 293, Schol. A, Hom. *Il.* 3.325 and Tzetzes, *Anteh.* 43 make Hecuba herself consult μάντεις/*coniectores* about the dream, Apollodorus 3.12.5.2 makes Priam consult Aesacus, while Mythogr. Vatic. 2.197 makes Priam interpret the dream himself; according to the Latin trimeters, on the other hand, Priam goes direct to Apollo. Robert[4] and Snell[5] argue that the mythographers, for all their divergences among themselves, reflect Euripides' account of events more truly. In the view of Robert and Snell the Greeks always consulted μάντεις in such circumstances; they never approached the gods directly.

I think it can be demonstrated with some probability that Ennius here followed Euripides quite faithfully. Apollo was himself a μάντις, the μάντις of Zeus (cf. Aeschylus, *Eum.* 17–19 τέχνης δέ νιν Ζεὺς ἔνθεον κτίσας φρένα | ἵζει τέταρτον τόνδε μάντιν ἐν θρόνοις· | Διὸς προφήτης δ' ἐστὶ Λοξίας πατρός) and at the moment of prophecy no clear distinction was made between the God and his human medium (cf. Cicero, *Diu.* 1.67 *deus inclusus corpore humano iam, non Cassandra loquitur*). Where the Delphic oracle was concerned the Greek poets spoke regularly of the god as the giver of answers (e.g. Homer, *Od.* 8.79–81, Pindar, *Ol.* 7.32–4, Aeschylus, *Prom.* 655–69, *Cho.* 269–90, Sophocles, *O.T.* 69–150, 787–93, *O.K.* 84–105, Euripides, *Hel.* 148–50, *I.T.* 82–94, 972–8, *Ion* 66–75, *Med.* 667–81, *Phoin.* 13–20). Prose writers

---

[1] See R. Bloch, *Les prodiges dans l'antiquité classique* (Paris, 1963), pp. 13 ff., 84 ff.

[2] However parallel stories in Attic drama sometimes vary for no apparent reason; contrast Sophocles, *O.T.* 1174 and Euripides, *Phoin.* 25 on the baby Oedipus.

[3] Cf. Terence's departure from Menander's text at *Ad.* 275; according to Donatus: *Menander mori illum uoluisse fingit, Terentius profugere.*

[4] *Die griech. Heldensage* III ii, p. 980.

[5] *Euripides' Alexandros*, p. 59 n. 3.

on the other hand represented the answer as coming from the Pythian priestess (e.g. Herodotus *passim*; cf. Cicero, *Diu.* 1.81). The only references to the medium in Attic tragedy are at Aeschylus, *Eum.* 1 ff., Sophocles, *O.T.* 711 ff. and Euripides, *Ion* 91–2. We may believe that Euripides made Priam (or, rather, Hecuba; see above, p. 221) consult an Asiatic oracle of Apollo and that Ennius followed him in speaking of the god as the μάντις; the mythographers made various guesses as to who the human medium was.[1]

50–1 parere se ardentem facem | uisa est in somnis: Buecheler's *parere* ⟨*ex*⟩ *se* assimilates Ennius' construction to the form normal in archaic and classical Latin.[2] However Ovid's imitation at *Epist.* 17.237–8, *fax quoque me terret quam se peperisse cruentam | ante diem partus est tua uisa parens,* justifies the transmitted text; cf. also Plautus, *Curc.* 260–1 *hac nocte in somnis uisus sum uiderier | procul sedere longe a me Aesculapium,* Gellius 15.22.8 *uisum sibi esse ait in quiete ceruam...ad se reuerti.* Ennius conflated the two logical constructions *parere se...facem uidit* and *parere...facem uisa est.*[3]

51 quo facto: picked up at *v.* 55 by *tum,* at *v.* 58 by *ibi.* Despite the absence of this phrase in particular from the rest of republican drama and the rareness in general of the ablative absolute and the conjunctive relative pronoun one should not tinker with the transmitted text.

52–3 ... somnio mentis metu | perculsus: Lambinus regularised *mentis* to *mentem* but such genitives are common in republican drama (cf. Plautus, *Epid.* 138 *desipiebam mentis,* *Trin.* 454 *satin tu's sanus mentis aut animi tui,* *Aul.* 105 *discrucior animi,* Terence, *Hec.* 121 *animi ut incertus foret*).

53 curis sumptus suspirantibus: *cura* usually occurs in the singular in both tragedy (5 times) and comedy (52). There is no other certain example of the plural in tragedy, but in elevated parts of comedy there are five (Plautus, *Rud.* 221, Terence, *Andr.* 260, *Hec.* 230, 817, Turpilius 52).

For *curis sumptus* cf. Terence, *Phorm.* 340 *ille et cura et sumptu absumitur.* But *sumptus* here probably stands for *consumptus.* For the metaphor cf. Homer, *Il.* 6.202 ὃν θυμὸν κατέδων (Cicero, *Tusc.* 3.63 *ipse suum cor edens*), [Theocritus] 30.21 ὁ πόθος καὶ τὸν ἔσω μύελον ἐσθίει, Ennius, *Ann.* 335–6 *curumue...quae nunc te coquit,* Plautus, *Epid.* 320 *exspectando exedor miser atque*

---

[1] For gods speaking directly to inquirers in Latin poetry cf. Plautus, *Men.* 840–1, Virgil, *Aen.* 3.84–99, 7.81–101, Seneca, *Thy.* 679 ff. For the human medium cf. Seneca, *Oed.* 223 ff.

[2] E.g. Plautus, *Mil.* 389, Cicero, *Diu.* 1.49.56, 57 et al.

[3] Cf. *Trag.* 329 (*eum scire oportet sibi paratam pestem ut participet parem* = *paratam pestem + paratum pestem ut participet*).

exenteror, Truc. 593 *qui ipsus se comest,* Lucretius 3.993–4 *exest anxius angor | aut...scindunt... curae,* Catullus 66.23 *exedit cura medullas,* Livy 40.54.1 *maerore consumptus...decessit.*

Suspirantibus is perhaps better taken as a bold heightening of the personification (cf. Sophocles, *Ai.* 957 μαινομένοις ἄχεσιν) rather than as an instance of the 'tropus quo id quod efficit ex eo quod efficitur ostendimus'.[1] The effect is much more bizarre than that of any of the adjectives and participles defining abstracts listed above on *v.* 33. Closely parallel is the humanist reading of Lucretius 5.747 *crepitans dentibus algor.*

54 exsacrificabat hostiis balantibus: for the offering of sacrifice after dreams, visions, omens, portents, etc. cf. Aeschylus, *Pers.* 201 ff., *Choe.* 523 ff., Sophocles, *El.* 405 ff., Menander, *Dysk.* 417 ff., Plautus, *Amph.* 1126–7 *iube uasa pura actutum adornari mihi, | ut Iouis supremi multis hostiis pacem expetam, Curc.* 270–3 *pacem ab Aesculapio | petas, ne forte tibi eueniat magnum malum, | quod in quiete tibi portentumst...quae res male uortat tibi,* Virgil, *Aen.* 3.176 ff., 4.56 ff., 5.743 ff., 8.544 ff., Tibullus 1.5.13.

The compound *exsacrificare* occurs nowhere else in recorded Latin. Vahlen interprets: 'ἐκθύεσθαι *uelut* ἄγος Herodotus (6.91) *aliique*'. But there is no question of pollution here. We may regard the form as simply a poetic coinage; *exsacrificabat* forms a trio with the unusual, if not unique, compounds *edoceret* and *edidit*; cf. above on *v.* 20.

The simple *sacrificare* occurs 21 times in comedy. It is absent from Caesar and Cicero (except for *Nat. deor.* 2.67) but common in Livy. The word probably belonged to the sacral language in the first century, and was avoided by the purists because of its similarity to certain poetical formations with *-ficus, -ficare* and *-ficabilis.*

For the narrative imperfect standing within a succession of aorist and historic present tenses cf. Naevius, *Carm.* fr. 3 *postquam auem aspexit in templo Anchisa, | sacra in mensa Penatium ordine ponuntur; | immolabat auream uictimam pulchram,* fr. 24 *isque susum ad caelum sustulit suas †res ammullus† gratulabatur diuis,* Virgil, *Aen.* 3.32 ff. *insequor...et...sequitur...Nymphas uenerabar agrestis | Gradiuumque patrem, Geticis qui praesidet aruis, | rite secundarent uisus omenque leuarent. | ...auditur....* The contexts are all liturgical but what significance this has, if any, I cannot say. See Mariotti, *Bellum Poenicum,* pp. 75 f.

Hostia was a word of the sacral language, 'victim offered to appease the wrath of the gods'.

Balans was probably a poeticism (cf. Ennius, *Ann.* 186, Lucretius 2.369, 6.1132, Virgil, *Georg.* 1.272, *Aen.* 7.538) modelled partly on such sacral

---

[1] Quintilian 8.6.27; cf. Rhet. inc. *Her.* 4.32. For a discussion of this phenomenon in classical poetry see Norden, *Aen. VI*², pp. 138 f.

terms as (*hostia*) *bidens, lactens,* etc., and partly on the Greek μηκάς (of sheep Euripides, *Kykl.* 189; of goats Homer, *Il.* 11.383, Sophocles, fr. 468).

For the three-syllable rhyme *suspirANTIBVS . . . balANTIBVS* in iambic trimeters cf. Trag. inc. 133–5 *caelum nitescere, arbores frondESCERE,* | *uites laetificae pampinis pubESCERE,* | *rami bacarum ubertate incuruESCERE,* Plautus, *Pseud.* 67–8, 805–6. It occurs sporadically in the trimeters of Attic tragedy: e.g. Sophocles, *Ai.* 807–8, 1085–6, *O.T.* 110–11, Euripides, *Hipp.* 727–8, *Herakleidai* 541–2, *Med.* 408–9, Agathon, fr. 11.

55 tum coniecturam postulat: for *coniectura* of the interpretation of dreams cf. Plautus, *Curc.* 246, *Rud.* 612, 771; for *somnium conicere* Plautus, *Curc.* 253 (~ Euripides, *I.T.* 55 τοὔναρ δ᾽ ὧδε συμβάλλω τόδε). The usage seems to have arisen from the use of lots in dream interpretation (*sortes conicere*).[1]

Abstract formations with -*ura* are not common in republican drama. Ploen counts only 4 in tragedy, 20 in comedy.

pacem petens: for *pax,* 'grace, favour', cf. Ennius, *Trag.* 380, Plautus, *Amph.* 32, 1127, *Curc.* 270, *Merc.* 678; this meaning was probably still alive only in liturgical phrases like *pacem peto* et al. No exact equivalent need have stood in the prologue of the Ἀλέξανδρος; such dreams were not an automatic sign of divine displeasure for the Greek mind. Cf. Cicero's version of Homer, *Il.* 2.305–6 ἡμεῖς δ᾽ ἀμφὶ περὶ κρήνην ἱερούς κατὰ βωμούς | ἔρδομεν ἀθανάτοισι τεληέσσας ἑκατόμβας: *nos circum latices gelidos fumantibus aris* | *aurigeris* diuom placantes numina *tauris* (*Diu.* 2.63).

56 ut se edoceret obsecrans: the compound *edocere* occurs twice in tragedy, the simple *docere* once; in comedy the ratio is 6:26.

57 quo sese uertant tantae sortes somnium: for the sequence of tenses —*postulat* (historic present). . .*edoceret*. . .*uertant*—cf. Plautus, *Pseud.* 795–6 *quin ob eam rem Orcus recipere ad se hunc noluit* | *ut esset hic qui mortuis cenam coquat.*

With *quo sese uertant sortes* Ennius is revivifying the faded metaphor of *coniectura.* The lots are shaken in the turning urn. Cf. Horace, *Carm.* 2.3.26–8 *omnium* | *uersatur urna serius ocius* | *sors exitura,* Virgil, *Aen.* 3.375–6 *sic fata deum rex* | *sortitur uoluitque uices,* Seneca, *Tro.* 974 *uersata dominos urna captiuis dedit.*

For the enallage in *tantae sortes somnium,* cf. Ennius, *Trag.* 123 *ignotus iuuenum coetus,* 401 *deos aeui integros,* Pacuvius, *Trag.* 20 *mea propages sanguinis,*

---

[1] Cf. G. P. Shipp, *CR* LI (1937), 209 ff.

Accius, *Trag.* 566–7 *horrifer Aquilonis stridor*, Trag. inc. *ap.* Cic. *Tusc.* 1.48 *pallida leti...loca*. Republican tragedy normally keeps epithets with the nouns to which they belong in sense.

For *tantus*, 'so extraordinary', cf. Plautus, *Amph.* 1036 *neque ego umquam tanta mira me uidisse censeo*, 1057 *ita tanta mira in aedibus sunt facta*, Accius, *Praet.* 31 *di rem tantam haut temere inprouiso offerunt*.

58–9 ibi ex oraclo uoce diuina edidit | Apollo: cf. Pindar, *Ol.* 7.32–4 τῷ μὲν ὁ χρυσοκόμας εὐ|ώδεος ἐξ ἀδύτου ναῶν πλόον | εἶπε, Euripides, *I.T.* 976–7 ἐντεῦθεν αὐδὴν τρίποδος ἐκ χρυσοῦ λακών, | Φοῖβός μ' ἔπεμψε δεῦρο..., Plautus, *Men.* 840 *ecce Apollo mihi ex oraclo imperat*.

For the phrase *ex oraclo edere* cf. Cicero, *Fin.* 5.79, *Ad Brut.* 1.2a.3.

Edere, 'announce publicly', belonged properly to the official language. For *edere* of the pronouncements of the keepers of the Sibylline oracles cf. Livy 21.62.8, 22.10.10 et al.

For the pleonasm of *uoce diuina edidit Apollo* cf. Homer, *Od.* 8.79 χρείων μυθήσατο Φοῖβος Ἀπόλλων, Pindar, *Isth.* 8.45 ὡς φάτο Κρονίδαις | ἐνέποισα θεά, Aeschylus, *Ag.* 205 εἶπε φωνῶν, *Choe.* 279 πιφαύσκων εἶπε, Sophocles, *Ai.* 757 ὡς ἔφη λέγων, *Ant.* 227 ψυχὴ γὰρ ηὔδα πολλά μοι μυθουμένη, Catullus, 64.321 *talia diuino fuderunt carmine fata*, Cicero, *Carm.* fr. 22.22 *tum Calchas haec est fidenti uoce locutus* (*Diu.* 2.63 = Homer, *Il.* 2.322).

59–60 primus Priamo qui foret | postilla natus: *forem* as the perfect participle's auxiliary occurs on only nine other occasions in republican drama (Pacuvius, *Trag.* 300, Plautus, *Amph.* 21, *Curc.* 449, *Mil.* 1083, *Most.* 494, 800, *Poen.* 262, *Rud.* 218, Caecilius, *Com.* 45); thrice the participle is *natus* (contrast Plautus, *Cas.* 46, *Persa* 634, Terence, *Hec.* 279). The contexts of occurrence in comedy have a tone either of legal formality or of paratragedy.

puerum...temperaret tollere: for *temperare* and infinitive the only parallels in drama are Plautus, *Poen.* 22, 33, 1036; in all three passages the speaker appears to be aping the language of the magistrates.

For the phrase *puerum...tollere* cf. Trag. inc. 85 *ego cum genui tum morituros sciui et huic rei sustuli*, Plautus, *Amph.* 501 *quod erit natum tollito*, *Truc.* 399, Terence, *Andr.* 219, 401, 464, *Haut.* 626–7, Cicero, *Att.* 11.9.3, Horace, *Sat.* 2.5.46 et al. The phrase reflects a Roman family ritual wherein the *paterfamilias* picked up from the hearth the child he intended to rear as his own.[1] It is often said[2] that Attic drama used the verb ἀναιρεῖσθαι of a similar ritual.

---

[1] Cf. Augustine, *Ciu.* 4.11.

[2] Cf. E. Samter, *Familienfeste der Griechen und Römer* (Berlin, 1901), pp. 59 ff., O. Schrader, *Sprachvergleichung und Urgeschichte*[3] (Jena, 1907), p. 345.

This appears to be untrue. In contexts parallel with the Roman ones the verb τρέφειν is used (e.g. Menander, *Perik.* 370, 382); ἀναιρεῖσθαι refers regularly to the taking up to rear of another person's child (e.g. Aristophanes, *Neph.* 531, Menander, *Sam.* 140, 159, 196, *Epit.* 74, 87, 154, *Perik.* 14).[1] Plutarch uses ἀναιρεῖσθαι to turn the *tollere* of his Latin source when speaking of the children Antony had by Cleopatra (*Ant.* 36) but this tells us nothing about fifth and fourth century B.C. Attic usage. There is no direct evidence that Athenian families employed a ritual like the Roman. On the fifth day after birth the Athenian child whom the father had decided to have reared was carried ceremonially around the hearth.[2] One can only guess at the significance attached to the two rituals in Athenian and Roman society respectively but it must have been roughly similar. Athenian society is no more likely than Roman to have possessed both.

61 eum esse exitium Troiae, pestem Pergamo: while Attic drama has regularly τὰ πέργαμα (except in two lyric passages, Euripides, *I.A.* 773, *Tr.* 1065, where the city as a whole is clearly meant), Roman has *Pergamum* (except at Livius, *Trag.* 2, Ennius, *Trag.* 73, Seneca, *Ag.* 206, *Troad.* 472, 889). *Pergamum* indicated the *arx*, *Pergama* perhaps the walls surrounding the arx, *Troia* the *urbs agrique*. For *Troia* (Τροία) and *Pergamum* (Πέργαμα) in conjunction cf. Sophocles, *Ph.* 353, Euripides, *Andr.* 292–3, Plautus, *Bacch.* 1053, Virgil, *Aen.* 2.554–6, 3.349–51.

Esse stands for *fore*. The present tense is frequently used in Attic drama in prophecies (e.g. Aeschylus, *Ag.* 126, *Prom.* 848, Euripides, *Hipp.* 47, Aristophanes, *Hipp.* 127) as well as in descriptions of visions. For the indirect reporting of such prophecies cf. Aeschylus, *Choe.* 1030–2 τὸν πυθόμαντιν Λοξίαν, χρήσαντ᾽ ἐμοὶ | πράξαντα μὲν ταῦτ᾽ ἐκτὸς αἰτίας κακῆς | εἶναι, Apollodorus 3.12.5.3 οὗτος (sc. Αἴσακος) εἰπὼν τῆς πατρίδος γενέσθαι τὸν παῖδα ἀπώλειαν ἐκθεῖναι τὸ βρέφος ἐκέλευε.[3]

For *eum esse exitium Troiae* cf. Plautus, *Bacch.* 1054 *sciui ego iam dudum fore me exitium Pergamo*, Virgil, *Ecl.* 3.101, *Aen.* 2.190–1, Horace, *Carm.* 1.15.21. The predicative dative is normal (e.g. Plautus, *Bacch.* 947, 953, Cicero, *Mur.* 56 et al.). Ennius was probably seeking concinnity with the following phrase. *Exitium* is not elsewhere used of single individuals in drama or in Cicero; *pestis*, on the other hand, is commonly so used (e.g. Plautus, *Pseud.* 204, Terence, *Ad.* 189).

---

[1] *Tollere* was used in this sense also by the Roman poets: e.g. Plautus, *Cist.* 124, 167, 184 et al.

[2] Cf. Plato, *Theait.* 160E. Plautus appears to have generalised a detailed reference to this ritual at *Truc.* 424.

[3] For the phenomenon in classical Latin see E. Wistrand, *Horace's Ninth Epode* (Göteborg, 1958), pp. 29 ff., 49 ff.

COMMENTARY

XIX

For the context of this fragment see above, p. 203.
Welcker thought that Priam was the speaker. The Strasbourg papyrus
revealed that the Euripidean Priam was present at the games. Crönert
accordingly made Hecuba the speaker.

62–3 ab ludis...nuntium: cf. Plautus, *Bacch.* 197 *quod ab illoc attigisset
nuntius*, 528, Cicero, *Att.* 13.47.1 (alluding to a passage of tragedy).

62 animus atque aures auent: a periphrasis for *audire aueo*. Cf. Sophocles, *Ai.* 686 τοὐμὸν ὧν ἐρᾷ κέαρ, Euripides, *Hipp.* 173 τί ποτ' ἔστι μαθεῖν
ἔραται ψυχή, 912 ἡ γὰρ ποθοῦσα πάντα καρδία κλύειν, *Hyps.* 1.3.15
τάδε μοι τάδε θυμὸς ἰδεῖν ἵεται, Plautus, *Cist.* 554 *animus audire expetit*,
Catullus 46.7 *iam mens praetrepidans auet uagari*, Cicero, *Phil.* 5.13 *auet
animus apud consilium illud pro reo dicere* (a passage of excited rhetoric).
Auere does not occur elsewhere in republican drama. Cicero alone of
classical writers uses it frequently.

63 auide expectantes: the adverb is probably to be construed with
expectantes rather than *auent*. Rhetorical pause usually coincides with metrical
pause. Where a verb is accompanied by an etymologically related adverb the
adverb usually precedes: e.g. Ennius, *Trag.* 259 *cupienter cupit*, Plautus, *Capt.*
250 *memoriter meminisse*, *Cas.* 267 *cupide cupis*, *Curc.* 535 *propere properas*, 688
propere propera, *Most.* 985 *me eius...misere miseret*, *Persa* 427 *ualide ualet*, *Poen.*
606 *sapienter sapit*, 921 *iterum iterem*, *Pseud.* 358 *cursim curram*, *Rud.* 1265 *iterum
...itera*, *Truc.* 61 *tempestiuo temperent*, 354 *nitide nitet*, Pomponius, *Atell.* 109
memore meministi. However the adverb does occasionally follow: e.g. Plautus,
Amph. 417 *memorat memoriter*, *Men.* 146 *ecquid adsimulo similiter*, 151 *caueo
cautius*, *Poen.* 562 *meministis memoriter*, Afranius, *Com. tog.* 294 *curre cursim*,
365 *memini memoriter*.

XX

For the Greek etymology see Apollodorus 3.12.5.4 ἔτρεφεν ὀνομάσας
Πάριν· γενόμενος δὲ νεανίσκος καὶ πολλῶν διαφέρων κάλλει τε καὶ
ῥώμῃ αὖθις Ἀλέξανδρος προσωνομάσθη, λῃστὰς ἀμυνόμενος καὶ τοῖς
ποιμνίοις ἀλεξήσας.

For the giving of a name according to the character or circumstances of
the person to bear it cf. Aeschylus, *Prom.* 848 ff., Euripides, *Hel.* 8 ff., *Ion*
661 ff., *I.T.* 32 f., Plautus, *Capt.* 285 ff., *Pseud.* 653 ff., *Stich.* 174 ff. Plautus
was obviously not troubled by the sort of objection which Varro has to
Ennius' method of adaptation; the three passages I have quoted could all be
his own additions to the substance of his originals. The Attic tragedians were

228

ALEXANDER

in the same theoretical difficulty with the portrayal of barbarians; they ignored it except when it was dramatically convenient to draw attention to linguistic differences.[1]

XXI

65 purus putus: cf. Plautus, *Pseud.* 988–9 *oh ! Polymachaeroplagides | purus putus est ipsus,* 1200 *purus putus hic sucophantast,* Varro, *Men.* 432 (Nonius, p. 27.23) *Chrysosandalos locat sibi amiculam de lacte et cera Tarentina quam apes Milesiae coegerint ex omnibus floribus libantes, sine osse et neruis, sine pelle, sine pilis puram putam proceram candidam teneram formosam.*

XXII

Welcker referred this fragment to an account of Deiphobus addressing the victorious Alexander; Ribbeck to one of how Alexander's favourite steer was taken away from him.

66 hominem appellat: 'eum appellat'; the usage is common in republican drama; cf. Terence, *Andr.* 744 and Donatus *ad loc.*; J. Köhm, *Altlateinische Forschungen* (Leipzig, 1905), p. 89 n. 1, counts 120 instances in Plautus, 34 in Terence.

stolide: 14 times in republican drama as against *stultus* 102, absent from Caesar and Cicero (except *Top.* 59), fairly common in the historians; the word probably had a high-falutin tone even in Ennius' day. Ploen counts 40 formations with *-idus* in comedy and 27 in tragedy, 10 of which do not appear at all in comedy.

XXIII

Welcker, Hartung and Ribbeck referred this fragment to Ἔρως/*Amor*, C. O. Mueller to Νίκη/*Victoria*. The latter was commonly represented in ancient art and literature as winged and bearing a crown and fillets, cf. Euripides, *I.T.* 1497–9 ὦ μέγα σεμνὴ Νίκη τὸν ἐμὸν | βίοτον κατέχοις | καὶ μὴ λήγοις στεφανοῦσα, Sallust *ap.* Macrob. *Sat.* 3.13.8 *praeterea tum sedenti in transenna demissum Victoriae simulacrum cum machinato strepitu tonitruum coronam ei imponebat, tum uenienti ture quasi deo supplicabatur,* Livy 7.12.13 *unicum ducem qui nihil agenti sibi de caelo deuolaturam in sinum uictoriam censeat.*

Welcker suggested two possible contexts:[2] a description of the games by a messenger and Cassandra's account of her vision of the contest of the goddesses. Welcker's first idea seems to me to have been the better one. We

[1] E.g. Aeschylus, *Ag.* 1061, *Hik.* 118. Cf. Pacuvius, *Trag.* 364.
[2] *Die griech. Trag.* pp. 467, 1582.

now know (see fr. 18 Snell) that in Euripides' play a messenger described Paris being crowned by human hands as victor in the contest. It is unlikely that any ancient tragedian would have had a personage describe a visible intervention by a supernatural being in such events. I would suggest that the Latin trimeter comes from the messenger's report of a prayer uttered by Alexander to his patroness Venus[1] asking for victory in the contest; cf. Odysseus' prayer to Athena during Homer's foot-race at *Il.* 23.768 ff., Cloanthus' prayer to the 'di quibus imperium est pelagi' during Virgil's boat-race at *Aen.* 5.235 ff.

In the view of O. Skutsch[2] the verse is best interpreted as the opening of a prologue spoken by *Victoria*.[3] This seems to me possible on the further supposition that Ennius replaced a prologue by Aphrodite in his original with one by the abstract *Victoria*. It is difficult to imagine Νίκη, who was associated in the Athenian mind with Athena, opening a Euripidean play about the period of Troy's prosperity. At Rome on the other hand *Victoria* was associated with Venus rather than with Minerva.

67 cum corona et taeniis: cf. Thucydides 4.121 ... δημοσίᾳ μὲν χρυσῷ στεφάνῳ ... ἰδίᾳ δὲ ἐταινίουν τε καὶ προσήρχοντο ὥσπερ ἀθλητῇ, Aristophanes, *Batr.* 392–5 καὶ | τῆς σῆς ἑορτῆς ἀξίως | παίσαντα καὶ σκώψαντα νι|κήσαντα ταινιοῦσθαι, schol. *ad loc.* ταινιοῦσθαι · ἀντὶ τοῦ στεφανοῦσθαι · ταινία γὰρ τὸ ῥάμμα τοῦ στεφάνου, Plato, *Sympos.* 212 ε ἐστεφανωμένον αὐτὸν κιττοῦ τέ τινι στεφάνῳ δασεῖ καὶ ἴων, καὶ ταινίας ἔχοντα ἐπὶ τῆς κεφαλῆς πάνυ πολλάς, Virgil, *Aen.* 5.269 (describing the victors in the boat race) *puniceis ibant euincti tempora taenis*, Servius *ad loc.* PVNICEIS TAENIS *uittis roseis; et significat lemniscatas coronas quae sunt de frondibus et discoloribus fasciis, et sicut Varro dicit, magni honoris sunt.* 'taenis' *autem modo uittis; alias uittarum extremitates dicit ut* (7.352) 'fit longae taenia uittae'.

Corona, 'στέφανος', is common in republican drama; *taenia,* 'ταινία' rare. *Corona* must have been a borrowing by the sacral language from South Italian Greek; κορώνη does not appear in extant Attic literature in the meaning 'corona, στέφανος'. *Taenia* also probably came from this source rather than the Attic plays adapted by the poets. The common language contained a large number of obvious borrowings from Greek. The poets restricted these in comedy largely to the speech of slaves and persons of low degree and used them even less in tragedy. Ennius has only *barbaricus, corona, drachuma, exanclare, machaera, ostreum, philosophari, salus, stola, taenia, thesaurus.*

---

[1] Pompey's temple to *Venus uictrix* was called by Tiro *aedes Victoriae* (Gellius 10.1.7).

[2] Expressed in private conversation, 11 October 1965. See now *HSCPh* LXXI (1967), 126 f.

[3] Plautus refers to such a tragic prologue at *Amph.* 41–2.

XXIV

For the context of this fragment see above, p. 203.

68 aduentant: only here in tragedy and five times in comedy; *aduenire* on the other hand is extremely common in both genres. Tragedy frequently uses an intensive form with no perceptible difference of meaning from the simple form normally used in comedy: e.g. *abnutare* (Ennius 290), *aditare* (Ennius 390), *concursare* (Accius 398), *increpitare* (Trag. inc. 234), *initare* (Pacuvius 1), *perrogitare* (Pacuvius 315), *proiectare* (Ennius 204), *raptare* (Ennius 79), *subiectare* (Pacuvius 334), *succussare* (Accius 568), *uolitare* (Trag. inc. 183). Comedy has large numbers of similar verbs banned from the Latin of the classical purists; it is erroneous to label them all vulgarisms; many must have been poetic formations.

paupertas quorum obscurat nomina: a periphrasis for *pauperes atque ignobiles*; cf. *v.* 309 *di quibus est potestas motus superum atque inferum* ∼ *di superi atque inferi*.

For the sentiment cf. Euripides, *El.* 37–8, *Phoin.* 442–3, fr. 326.3–4, fr. 362.11 ff.

XXV

For the context of this fragment see above, p. 203. For the idea of a mutilated spirit cf. Homer, *Od.* 11.40–1, Seneca, *Oed.* 617 ff. For the incident described cf. Homer, *Il.* 22.463–4, Sophocles, *Ai.* 1030–1, Euripides, *Andr.* 107–8, Ennius, *Trag.* 78–9, Virgil, *Aen.* 1.483, 2.272–3.

It is difficult to fit the words transmitted in Macrobius' codices into any or the metrical patterns found in republican drama and yet they are not indubitably corrupt. The question *quid ita cum tuo lacerato corpore miser* has seemed to many to lack a verb but an actor could well have interpreted *ita* with a gesture of the hand; cf. Plautus, *Rud.* 809 *adsistite ambo. sic. audite nunciam*, Ennius, *Trag.* 293 *nolite hospites ad me adire. ilico istic*.

Trochaic and bacchiac scansion have been tried. Vahlen[1] produced a trochaic system: *o lux Troiae, germane Hector,* | *quid ita cum tuo lacerato corpore* | *miser ⟨es⟩ aut qui te sic respectantibus* | *tractauere nobis?*; Leo[2] a slightly more convincing system: *o lux Troiae, germane Hector,* | *quid ita cum tuo lacerato* | *corpore ⟨abiectus's⟩ miser aut qui* | *te sic respectantibus* | *tractauere nobis?* Mariotti[3] took *o lux Troiae, germane Hector* as an anapaestic dimeter and the rest as bacchiac verse: *quid ita cum tuo lacerato corpore* | *miser ⟨ades⟩ aut qui te sic*

---

[1] *Hermes* XII (1877), 400, XV (1880), 262.
[2] *De Trag. Rom.* p. 20 (= *Ausg. kl. Schr.* I 210). Cf. *Die plaut. Cant.* pp. 29 ff.
[3] *Lezioni su Ennio*, p. 133.

respectantibus | *tractauere nobis?*[1] However of the ten alleged bacchiac metra only one is purely so and wherever a run of indisputable bacchiacs occurs in contemporary comedy pure metra predominate.[2] I leave the question open.

69 o lux Troiae: 'o help of Troy'; cf. Homer, *Od.* 16.23 Τηλέμαχε γλυκερὸν φάος, Sophocles, *El.* 1354–5 ὦ φίλτατον φῶς, ὦ μόνος σωτὴρ δόμων | ᾿Αγαμέμνονος, Euripides, *Hek.* 841 ὦ δέσποτ᾿, ὦ μέγιστον ῞Ελλησιν φάος, *Herakles* 531 ὦ φίλτατ᾿ ἀνδρῶν, ὦ φάος μολὼν πατρί, Trag. inc. *ap.* Page, *G.L.P.* 162 ff. ῞Εκτορ... πάτρᾳ καὶ ἐμοὶ μέγα φῶς, Accius, *Trag.* 163 a: ⟨He⟩*ctor lux Dardaniae*, Plautus, *Mil.* 1344 *quae res? quid uideo? lux salue*, *Stich.* 618 *o lux oppidi.*

70 quid ita cum tuo lacerato corpore miser: for the adnominal use of *cum* cf. Ennius, *Trag.* 235 *quique tuo cum lumine mare terram caelum contines*, *Ann.* 54 *Tiberine tuo cum flumine sancto*, Plautus, *Curc.* 191 *tun etiam cum noctuinis oculis 'odium' me uocas?*, *Pseud.* 967 *heus tu qui cum hirquina barba astas.*

71 aut qui te sic respectantibus tractauere nobis: for *aut* introducing a question which is not an alternative to the previous one cf. Plautus, *Amph.* 409 *quid igitur ego dubito aut qur non intro eo in nostram domum?*, *Poen.* 994 *quoiates estis aut quo ex oppido?*

With the phrase *respectantibus...nobis* is to be contrasted Plautus, *Amph.* 998 *hic deludetur...uobis inspectantibus* and Cicero, *Manil.* 33 *cum prope inspectantibus nobis classis ea...a praedonibus capta atque depressa est.* The absolute phrase with *inspectante* or *inspectantibus* is normal in Caesar and Cicero.

For *tractare*, 'drag up and down, round and about', cf. Ennius, *Ann.* 137 *tractatus per aequora campi*, Lucretius 3.888–9 *malis morsuque ferarum* | *tractari.*

The stylistic level of the termination in *-ere* is obscure. D. W. Pye[3] counted 12 instances in tragedy against 4 of *-ērunt*, 52 in Plautine comedy against 100, 28 in Terentian comedy against 25. Ennius' *tractauere* differs from the great majority of comic forms in *-ere* in occurring before a word beginning with a consonant. Havet[4] thought that on the few occasions where this happens in comedy the poet had some special rhythmical or stylistic motive.

---

[1] Strzelecki, in *Tragica* I, 61 f., approves Mariotti's colometry but supplies *ess* instead of *ades.*

[2] Cf. A. Spengel, *Reformvorschl.* pp. 260 ff.

[3] *Trans. Phil. Soc.* 1963, 1 ff.   [4] *RPh* XXXI (1907), 230 ff.

ALEXANDER

XXVI

Cassandra describes a vision with *nam maximo saltu superauit grauidus armatis equus* and expresses a foreboding about the future with *qui suo partu ardua perdat Pergama.* Modern editors follow Vossius in writing *superabit.* There is no good syntactical reason for abandoning the transmitted text. *Perdat* is a prospective subjunctive.[1] For the sequence cf. Plautus, *Epid.* 285 *repperi haec te qui abscedat suspicio,* Cicero, *S. Rosc.* 32 *etiamne ad subsellia cum ferro atque telis uenistis ut hic aut iuguletis aut condemnetis?*

The image of the pregnant mare leaping appears first in extant Greek literature at Aeschylus, *Ag.* 824–6: πόλιν διημάθυνεν 'Αργεῖον δάκος, | ἵππου νεοσσός, ἀσπιδηφόρος λεώς, | πήδημ' ὀρούσας ἀμφὶ Πλειάδων δύσιν; cf. Euripides, *Tr.* 9–12 ὁ γὰρ Παρνάσιος | Φωκεὺς 'Επειός, μηχαναῖσι Παλλάδος | ἐγκύμον' ἵππον τευχέων ξυναρμόσας, | πύργων ἔπεμψεν ἐντὸς ὀλέθριον βρέτας, Lycophron 342, Antiphilus, *A.P.* 9.156, Tryphiodorus 389. Something of its clarity is allowed to fade by Ennius' masculine adjective *grauidus.*

The words which Macrobius quotes show no sign of corruption and yet they are difficult to reduce to metrical order. *Nam maxumo saltu superauit grauidus armatis equus* can be treated as an iambic tetrameter acatalectic without diaeresis. Such verses are common in comedy both in company with other types of verse (breaking into anapaests at Plautus, *Amph.* 1061, into trochees at *Amph.* 1071) and in stichic runs. They are also common in tragedy (cf. *vv.* 138–9, 163–4, 171, 322–32). Vahlen treats *qui suo partu ardua perdat Pergama* as trochaic despite the resulting dactylic word *ardua* in the third foot (see above on fr. XII).

72–3 nam maxumo saltu superauit...Pergama: *Pergama* has to be taken ἀπὸ κοινοῦ with *superauit;* cf. Plautus, *Persa* 524 *ac suo periclo is emat qui eam mercabitur.*

Saltus, 'leap', occurs only here in republican drama; it is absent from Caesar and Cicero (except for *Cato* 19) but frequent in dactylic verse, both archaic (Ennius, *Ann.* 129, Lucretius 5.559, 1318) and classical (Virgil, *Georg.* 3.141, *Aen.* 2.565 et al.).

Superare is used of physical movement only here, *v.* 189 and Plautus, *Stich.* 365 (cf. 279) in republican drama; it is absent from Caesar and Cicero but common in Virgil (*Georg.* 3.141, 3.270 et al.) and Livy (6.2.11 et al.).

73 qui suo partu ardua perdat Pergama: the plural *Pergama* occurs elsewhere in republican drama only at Livius, *Trag.* 2. Here Ennius may have in mind the walls of the citadel; hence the plural (after *moenia*).

---

[1] Cf. Plautus, *Asin.* 29 *dic...quod te rogem,* Catullus 64.330, Virgil, *Aen.* 1.287.

233

Arduus is normally used of mountains, mountain paths, etc.; rarely of walls, ramparts, etc. in either classical prose (but cf. Varro, *Rust.* 1.14.3, Cicero, *Rep.* 2.11, Tacitus, *Hist.* 3.30) or classical verse (but cf. Virgil, *Aen.* 12.745, Ovid, *Met.* 3.61).

ANDROMACHA

The title *Andromacha* is given to Ennius by Cicero, Nonius,[1] Macrobius and Servius.[2] The Danieline Servius gives the same title to Novius, a writer of *abulae Atellanae* who sometimes parodied tragic themes (*Georg.* 1.266).

Behind three of Nonius' citations (p. 76.1 *andromaca*, p. 504.18 *andromaca*, p. 515.28 *andromacha*) appears to lie the archaic form *Andromaca*; behind four (p. 292.7 *andromache malo tor*, p. 402.3 *andromaca haec malo*, p. 505.12 *andromace ethemapotide*, p. 515.13 *andromache eimalo*) a classical transliteration of Ἀνδρομάχη αἰχμαλωτίς.[3] In the one case Ennius' own title would have been given, in the other the title of his Greek original.[4] Nothing in the pieces quoted alongside these titles suggests that two distinct scripts were in the possession of the grammarians who first quoted them.

The title *Andromacha* appears without an author's name at Cicero, *Tusc.* 3.53, *Ac.* 2.20, *Att.* 4.15.6, Varro, *Ling.* 7.6, and Festus, p. 384.21. Combination with *Tusc.* 3.44 and *Orat.* 93 makes it certain that at *Tusc.* 3.53 Cicero means a play by Ennius. Since no Latin tragedy *Andromacha* apart from that by Ennius is known editors have interpreted the other passages likewise.[5] Ovid may refer to the play at *Rem.* 383.

---

[1] All seven of Nonius' citations appear to come from the sources defined by Lindsay as list 27 'Alph. Verb' and list 28 'Alph. Adverb'. At the end of the article on *summus* (pp. 401.23 – 402.5) comes the same passage which at p. 515.13 illustrates the adverb *longinque* and quite certainly comes from list 28. It must have been added to the *summus* article when the book *De uaria significatione sermonum* was being organised alphabetically. The presence of Accius' name at p. 515.12 must be an error of the transmission.

[2] Servius, *Aen.* 1.224 and Macrobius, *Sat.* 6.5.10 appear to draw ultimately on the same source; see *CQ* N.S. xv (1965), 135 ff.

[3] The first to glimpse the truth was C. L. Roth, who, in the edition of Nonius which he published with F. D. Gerlach at Basle in 1842, suggested in the apparatus at p. 292.8 *Andromacha aechmalotide*. Cf. Propertius 2.20.1–2 *quid fles | anxia captiua tristius Andromacha?* Ribbeck's *Andromaca aecimalotide* (ed. 2, p. 23) and Wölfflin's *Andromaca aecmaloto* (*ALL* viii [1893], 234) confuse things.   [4] See *Introduction*, pp. 58 f.

[5] Very little is preserved of the quotation at Festus, p. 384.21. It is odd that ⟨*Enniu*⟩*s in Andromacha* should have been written rather than *idem in Andromacha*. Perhaps one should restore ⟨*Nouiu*⟩*s in Andromacha*.

ANDROMACHA

The personage who gave her name to the tragedy was the wife of Hector and the action took place after the fall of Troy. Opinions have differed about the scene. Columna set it in the camp of the Greek chieftains preparing to return to their homes and made the killing of Andromache's son Astyanax the central theme. Mercerus[1] interpreted Nonius as quoting from two scripts, one an adaptation of Euripides' extant Ἀνδρομάχη with the title *Andromache-Molottus*, the other an adaptation of the Τρῳάδες. Düntzer[2] rejected the idea of two scripts and by adducing some dubious parallels between the Ennian fragments and Seneca's *Troades* made the killing of Polyxena as well as that of Astyanax a theme of the play. Welcker[3] imagined one play with a title like *Andromache in Molottis* and set its scene at the court of Helenus, the brother of Hector, in Epirus.[4] Roth's elucidation of the text of Nonius, p. 292.7 as *Ennius Andromache aechmalotidi* confirmed Columna's view. One might compare Euripides, *Tr.* 677–8 ναυσθλοῦμαι δ' ἐγὼ | πρὸς Ἑλλάδ' αἰχμάλωτος ἐς δοῦλον ζυγόν. The heroine of Euripides' Ἀνδρομάχη is frequently referred to as αἰχμαλωτίς or αἰχμάλωτος (583, 871, 908, 932, 962, 1059, 1243) but this is to distinguish her from Neoptolemus' regular spouse Hermione; one could hardly imagine the word in a title of the play. Ladewig[5] suggested that Cicero's argument at *Tusc.* 3.53 only has point if Andromache's lament referred to recent events. Ribbeck[6] settled the issue by directing attention to Cicero, *Att.* 4.15.6. The central event of Ennius' play must have been the killing of Astyanax.[7] Proper interpretation of Cicero, *Orat.* 93, *Tusc.* 3.44 and *Sest.* 121[8] confirms Düntzer's view[9] that the killing of Polyxena also took place during the action of the play.

Speeches by and about Andromache (Varro, *Ling* 5.19,[10] 7.82), Astyanax (Varro, *Ling.* 10.70) and Neoptolemus (Cicero, *De orat.* 2.156, *Rep.* 1.30,

---

[1] In his second edition of Nonius (Paris, 1614). He granted the possibility of a title Ἀνδρομάχη ἡ ἐν Μολοττοῖς.

[2] *Zeitschr. f. d. Alt.* 1838, 47 ff.   [3] *Die griech. Trag.* p. 1200.

[4] Cf. Euripides, *Andr.* 1243 ff., Virgil, *Aen.* 3.294 ff.

[5] *Anal. scen.* p. 36.

[6] *Quaest. scen.* pp. 257 ff.

[7] Terzaghi, *BFC* XXXII (1925), 16 f., nevertheless wanted to put the verses about the women of Sparta quoted by Cicero at *Tusc.* 2.36 (= Trag. inc. 205–8) into Ennius' *Andromacha* because of their similarity with Euripides, *Andr.* 595 ff.

[8] See below on fr. XXVIIa.

[9] Accepted by Ribbeck and tacitly controverted by Vahlen in *E.P.R.*²; cf. Vahlen's interpretation of Varro, *Ling.* 7.6.

[10] I supply *Androma⟨ca⟩ Nocti* with Pomponius Laetus rather than *Androm⟨ed⟩a Nocti* with Scaliger.

Tusc. 2.1, Gellius 5.15.9, 5.16.5, Apuleius, *Apol.* 13) quoted along with Ennius' name have no place in any other play of his which is quoted in our sources and should be placed in the *Andromacha*.[1]

One other republican tragedy about the killing of Astyanax is known, Accius' *Astyanax*.[2] The monument set up for P. Numitorius Hilarus on the via Salaria late in the first century B.C. represents against a Roman stage background Ulysses leading away Astyanax and Andromache standing by.[3] Speculation about the author of this play is vain.

I have followed Columna in giving the two trimeters quoted by Cicero at *Tusc.* 1.105 to the *Andromacha* (fr. XXVII *g*) for four, perhaps not sufficient, reasons. First, the form of *Hectorem* excludes Accius as the author;[4] secondly, Cicero's *illa* suggests that he has already before referred to the speech from which he quotes and the quite certain reference to the *Andromacha* at 1.85 is the only reference one could connect. Thirdly, the long quotation from the *Andromacha* at 3.44–6 (fr. XXVII *h*) shows that Ennius' heroine did indeed speak of Hector in trimeters; fourthly the *uidi* of *v.* 78 seems to be picked up at *vv.* 89 and 92.

Cicero and Varro seem to have believed that Euripides was the author of Ennius' original. On the implications of *Ling.* 7.82 see above, p. 203. At *Opt. gen.* 18 Jahn made large-scale deletions in order to cure an obviously ailing text: *idem Andriam et Synephebos nec minus* [Terentium et Caecilium quam Menandrum legunt nec] *Andromacham aut Antiopam aut Epigonos Latinos recipiunt.* [sed tamen Ennium et Pacuuium et Accium potius quam Euripidem et Sophoclem legunt]. This seems rather drastic surgery but even if we permit it we must still take seriously the statements that are made. The alleged interpolator could have got his information about *Andria*, *Synephebi* and *Antiopa* from *Fin.* 1.4 but that about *Andromacha* and *Epigoni* appears only here and it is difficult to see how it could have been invented. An interpolator with no genuine knowledge would surely have inserted the name of Aeschylus.[5]

The extant Ἀνδρομάχη cannot be a candidate. The play known to ourselves and to the ancients as Τρῳάδες has Andromache as a personage and deals with the killing of Astyanax. Many of the fragments of Ennius' *Andromacha* have verbal analogues in this play as well as in Euripides'

---

[1] On Neoptolemus see Ribbeck, *Quaest. scen.* p. 258. Welcker, *Die griech. Trag.* pp. 1374 f., assumed the existence of a *Philoctetes* of Ennius in order to accommodate him.

[2] On this play see Zieliński, *Eos* XXXI (1928), 2 ff.

[3] See Pickard-Cambridge, *Dramatic Festivals*, p. 186 and fig. 57.

[4] Cf. Varro, *Ling.* 10.70.

[5] Cf. Cicero, *Ac.* 1.10.

Ἀνδρομάχη and Ἑκάβη.[1] Düntzer and Hartung[2] suggested that Ennius used the Τρῳάδες as the basis of his play and added speeches and scenes from Ἀνδρομάχη, Ἑκάβη and other plays. This theory implies a degree of freedom in adaptation far beyond that attributed by Terence to the early Latin poets.[3] In any case whatever play Varro had in mind it was not the Τρῳάδες. The etymology of Andromache's name in question does not occur in our text of this tragedy and could not be imagined in any other.[4] Furthermore there is no evidence that the Τρῳάδες was ever called Ἀνδρομάχη αἰχμαλωτίς. The only purpose of the epithet αἰχμαλωτίς would be to distinguish a script with the title Ἀνδρομάχη from that of the extant Ἀνδρομάχη and yet an epithet more unsuited to such a purpose it is hard to imagine.

Columna suggested that there existed another Euripidean Ἀνδρομάχη adapted by Ennius and known to Varro and Cicero but now quite lost.[5] This looks like a theory which could not be proved false but there is much to say against it. The title Ἀνδρομάχη αἰχμαλωτίς would have been a bad means of distinguishing the hypothetical play from the extant Ἀνδρομάχη. In any case the scholium on Euripides, Andr. 445 implies that the scholars of Alexandria could find no play by Euripides with the title Ἀνδρομάχη in the record of plays produced at Athenian festivals. We know the names and can guess at the themes of the seventy Euripidean tragedies possessed by these scholars[6] and there is no place among them for a second play about the killing of Astyanax or even for one containing the etymology of Andromache's name referred to by Varro. It is possible that such a play, written by Euripides for performance outside Athens, survived in the possession of actors and was adapted by Ennius. Possible, but unlikely. It is even more unlikely that Varro and Cicero alone of our witnesses should have known about it.

The conclusion seems inescapable that Cicero and Varro were in error, perhaps having been misled by a corrupt didascalic notice like that now pre-

---

[1] These were noticed long ago by Scaliger (*Coniect. Varr. Ling.*, on 10.70), who wrongly attributed the Latin fragments in question to the *Hecuba*, and by Columna. O. Schönberger (*Hermes* LXXXIV [1956], 255 f.) ought not to have produced as a novelty Columna's identification of 88 ff. and Euripides, *Tr.* 479 ff.

[2] *Euripides Restitutus* II, p. 284. Cf. Wilamowitz, *Hermes* LX (1925), 286 n. 2 (= *Kl. Schr.* IV 374 n. 2).

[3] See *Introduction*, p. 23.   [4] See below on fr. xxxv.

[5] Cf. Welcker, *Die Griech. Trag.* p. 1203, Vahlen, *E.P.R.*[2], p. CCIII. The pieces attributed to an Ἀνδρομάχη by Schol. Arist. *Batr.* 105 (fr. 144) and Stobaeus 1.3.23 (fr. 151) probably belong to the Ἀνδρομέδα. Artemidorus, p. 284.13 Pack, whatever the truth about the verse quoted (*Syleus*, fr. 687.1), refers to a scene of the extant Ἀνδρομάχη.   [6] See *Introduction*, p. 45.

fixed to Terence's *Hecyra*, where the name of the famous Menander has replaced that of the obscure Apollodorus, or else having applied their general knowledge of Ennius' predilection for Euripides falsely to the particular case. Such similarities as have been pointed out between the Latin *Andromacha* and the three Euripidean plays are either accidental (the plays have a similar background of events) or may be due to the fact that Ennius translated a Greek imitator of Euripides. In the fourth century[1] and even in the fifth[2] Attic tragedians were not averse to copying a predecessor's phrases and themes when handling a similar subject. Fourth-century tragedies seem to have been filled, like contemporary comedies, with echoes of the universally popular Euripides. A play about Andromache and Astyanax is recorded against the name of Antiphon.[3] There is insufficient evidence to discuss purposefully Morel's theory[4] that the papyrus published by E. Lobel in *Greek Poetry and Life* (Oxford, 1936), 295 ff., comes from a text of Antiphon's play and that this play was Ennius' original.

XXVII

(a) From section 118 to section 123 Cicero describes scenic performances at *ludi* of some extraordinary character held on the day when the Senate decreed his recall from exile. He alleges that the actors and the audience understood various speeches in the old second-century plays performed as referring to himself and his enemy Clodius.[5] He names the *fabula togata* he quotes at section 118 as the *Simulans* and the *fabula praetexta* at 123 as the *Brutus*. In the intermediate sections he quotes three pieces of musically accompanied tragic verse, the middle one of which (section 121) plainly comes from the canticum quoted at length at *Tusc.* 3.44–5 and attributed explicitly to Ennius at *Orat.* 93 and to the *Andromacha* at *Tusc.* 3.53. He introduces this middle quotation with the words *ab eodem paulo post in eadem fabula sunt acta.* It would seem therefore that the first of the anonymous quotations—*qui rem publicam certo animo adiuuerit statuerit steterit cum Achiuis...re dubia haud dubitarit uitam offerre nec capiti pepercerit*—belongs to the *Andromacha* and that the third could

---

[1] Athenaeus 10.454 B–E alleges that Theodectes borrowed from Agathon and Agathon from Euripides the device of describing the letters of the name ΘΗΣΕΥΣ.

[2] The hypothesis of Aeschylus' Πέρσαι reports an opinion of Glaucus that Aeschylus copied the Φοίνισσαι of Phrynichus. Servius (*Aen.* 4.694) alleges that the Thanatos of Euripides' Ἄλκηστις was borrowed from Phrynichus.

[3] See Aristotle, *Eth. Eud.* 7.4.1239a37.

[4] *BPhW* LVII (1937), 558 ff.

[5] Cf. Cicero's account of the behaviour of the actor Diphilus at the *ludi Apollinares* of 59 at *Att.* 2.19.3 and Suetonius' accounts of certain actors of imperial times at *Aug.* 53, 68, *Tib.* 45, *Galb.* 13.

(but need not necessarily) belong there too. In section 123 Cicero names the poet of the *Brutus* as Accius and the actor Aesopus. There is no necessary implication that Accius and Aesopus were responsible for the play or plays quoted in sections 120–2. On the other hand the words at the beginning of section 123, *et quoniam huc me prouexit oratio, histrio casum meum totiens con-lacrimauit, cum ita dolenter ageret causam meam, ut uox eius illa praeclara lacrimis impediretur; neque poetae, quorum ego semper ingenia dilexi, tempori meo defuerunt*, strongly suggest that the quotations of the previous sections came from more than one play but that only one actor was involved.[1]

A grave problem immediately presents itself. The canticum from the *Andromacha* was spoken by the heroine herself complaining of the destruction wreaked by the Greeks both upon her father's city and upon her husband's. The words quoted before the canticum—*qui rem publicam certo animo adiuuerit statuerit steterit cum Achiuis . . . re dubia haud dubitarit uitam offerre nec capiti pepercerit*—on the other hand laud someone who has co-operated with the Greeks. The words quoted after, *o ingratifici Argiui inmoenes Grai inmemores benefici,* | *exulare sinitis, sistis pelli, pulsum patimini*, upbraid certain races of Greeks for ingratitude to someone who has helped them.

In 1565 Lambinus substituted *Telamo* for *Simulans* in 118 and *pro Telamone* for *pro me* in 122. In 1573 he let *Simulans* be. His notes show that he was bothered by the presence of verses from Andromache's canticum. Paulus Manutius[2] argued that everything in 120–2 came from Accius' (*sic*) *Andromacha*[3] and that both the exiled Telamo and the bereft Andromache appeared in this play.

In 1828 there turned up certain scholia[4] which, though deriving in their present form from a fourth-century commentary on Cicero's orations, go back ultimately to quite early and genuinely learned work. They appear to assert that everything in 120–2 was uttered at a performance of the *Eurysaces* of Accius by the actor Aesopus:

SVMMVS ARTIFEX *actor illis temporibus notissimus tragicarum fabularum Aesopus egisse Accii fabulam, quae scribitur Eurysaces* (Gaumitz: *eurysace* C), *ita ut per omnem actionis cursum tempora rei publicae significarentur et quodammodo* (Orelli: *quodam* C) *Ciceronis fortuna deploraretur. ex quo illud probare contendit, omnes prorsus homines etiam infimae plebis restitutioni suae promptissime suffragatos.*

O IMMVNES GRAI *et haec uerba sunt de tragoedia: in qua uerbum istud immunes ingratos significat, quemadmodum* ✳✳✳✳✳✳✳✳✳✳✳✳✳✳✳✳✳ *munificos dicebant eos qui*

---

[1] For one actor appearing in several plays cf. Cicero, *Att.* 4.15.6. This seems to have been regular practice for a long period at the Athenian festivals; see Pickard-Cambridge, *Dramatic Festivals*, pp. 94 ff.

[2] *Commentarius* v iii (Venice, 1579), p. 62.

[3] Stephanus included the piece quoted by Nonius at p. 515.12 in such a play.

[4] Ed. A. Mai (Rome, 1828).

grati et liberales exstitissent. ergo uersus omnes tragici ad ipsum Ciceronem πλαγίως (Leo: *ab Aesopo* Luterbacher: ＊＊＊＊＊＊ C) *conuertuntur, ut aliud quidem in opere poetico fuerit, aliud uero in ipsius actoris significationibus.*

Madvig[1] declared that the scholiast was in error and that only the verses *o ingratifici Argiui, immunes Grai, immemores benefici, exulare sinitis, sistis pelli, pulsum patimini* belong to the *Eurysaces.* He made no suggestion as to how the two pieces *qui rem publicam certo animo adiuuerit statuerit, steterit cum Achiuis* and *re dubia haud dubitauit uitam offerre nec capiti pepercerit* might be placed in the *Andromacha.* Bergk[2] made Andromache appeal to the Greeks on her own behalf, reminding them of Priam's former services to them. Ladewig[3] made her ask the Greeks for mercy for Ajax, whom they were about to stone for the rape of Cassandra. J. Bake[4] deleted *in eadem fabula* and suggested that three tragedies are quoted in 120–2, one anonymous, a second the *Andromacha* and the third *Eurysaces.*

The way out now universally accepted was suggested first by F. Nieberding[5] and taken up by Ribbeck.[6] Nieberding set the *Eurysaces* in Salamis around the events narrated by Justinus at 44.3 and interpreted *qui rem publicam* etc. as spoken by someone about Teucer after he had been refused admittance to Salamis by Eurysaces, Telamo's heir.[7] Ribbeck combined the views of Lambinus with the new information offered by the scholia and set the *Eurysaces* in Aegina whither he imagined Telamo had fled after a revolution on Salamis. He interpreted *qui rem publicam* etc. as spoken about Telamo by Eurysaces who had come to Aegina with Teucer looking for his grandfather. Both Nieberding and Ribbeck treated the anapaests as inserted into Accius' canticum from Ennius' *Andromacha* by the actor Aesopus.

There is good evidence that ancient actors played fast and loose with authors' scripts. The scholia to the tragedies of Euripides are full of allegations of scenic interpolation.[8] In the very passage under discussion Cicero says that the actor added the tetrameter *summum amicum summo in bello*

---

[1] 'De emendandis Ciceronis orationibus pro P. Sestio et in P. Vatinium disputatio', in *Opuscula academica* (Copenhagen, 1834), 495 f.

[2] *Ind. lectt. Marburg* 1844, VIII. Bergk later withdrew; the text is altered at *Kl. phil. Schr.* I 219 f.

[3] *Anal. scen.* p. 36.

[4] *Scholica hypomnemata* I (Leiden, 1837), p. 119. Cf. Bergk, *Philologus* XXXI (1872), 238 n. 9 (= *Kl. phil. Schr.* I 200 n. 9).

[5] *Ilias Homeri ab L. Attio Poeta in Dramata Conuersa* (Conitz, 1838), p. 25.

[6] *In Tragicos Romanorum Poetas Coniectanea: Specimen I* (Diss. Berlin, 1849), p. 34, *Quaest. scen.* pp. 328 f., *Die röm. Trag.* pp. 419 ff.

[7] Cf. Welcker, *Die griech. Trag.* pp. 197 ff., Robert, *Die griech. Heldensage* III ii 2, p. 1483.

[8] Cf., for example, *Med.* 84, 148, 169, 228, 356, 380, 910.

summo ingenio praeditum to the Latin tragedian's script. Nevertheless it is hard enough to believe with Ladewig that the one personage uttered the verses quoted in 120–2 in different scenes. To have even the most patriotic of actors put them into the mouth of the one personage in the one scene is ludicrous.

If, however, we assume that Aesopus played two roles in *Andromacha* Cicero's quotations can be satisfactorily interpreted. With *qui rem publicam certo animo adiuuerit statuerit, steterit cum Achiuis* and *re dubia haud dubitarit uitam offerre nec capiti pepercerit* he was speaking the part of a Greek. Later in the play he assumed or reassumed the role of Andromache; hence Cicero's carefully chosen words *ab eodem paulo post in eadem fabula*. Masks were certainly employed by Roman actors in the mid first century,[1] whatever happened in Ennius' own day.[2] The Greek practice of performing tragedies with no more than three speaking actors probably came in along with the masks that made it possible.

Qui rem publicam certo animo adiuuerit statuerit, steterit cum Achiuis and *re dubia haud dubitarit uitam offere nec capiti pepercerit* could come from a speech by Ulysses in a debate over the demand of Achilles' ghost for the blood of Polyxene, pointing out the debt owed to the dead hero (cf. Euripides, *Hek.* 136 ff., 309 ff.).

My argument in brief is that Cicero described performances by Aesopus in Ennius' *Andromacha*, Accius' *Eurysaces* and *Brutus* and that in the *Andromacha* Aesopus played two roles, that of Ulysses and that of Andromache herself; a scholar recognised the tetrameters *o ingratifici Argiui inmoenes Grai inmemores benefici,* | *exulare ⟨sinitis sistis pelli, pulsum patimini* as coming from the *Eurysaces*; someone epitomising this scholar's commentary extended the *Eurysaces* quotations to include those which in reality came from the *Andromacha*.

Ennius' verses conjure up the city-state patriotism of second-century Rome rather than the panhellenism which the Attic tragedians attributed to the heroes who besieged Troy. The Euripidean Ulysses (*Hek.* 309–10) says of Achilles ἡμῖν δ' Ἀχιλλεὺς ἄξιος τιμῆς, γύναι, | θανὼν ὑπὲρ γῆς Ἑλλάδος κάλλιστ' ἀνήρ. The Latin tragedian makes his hero use one of the most hackneyed metaphors of Roman public life.

The tetrameter which Aesopus is reported to have added in the 57 B.C. performance of *Andromacha* looks as if it borrowed its play with the adjective *summus* from *v.* 105. *Praeditus* is very rare in republican drama (Plautus, *Amph.* 218, Terence, *Andr.* 98).

74–5 ...rem publicam certo animo adiuuerit | statuerit: for *certo animo* cf. Cicero, *Quinct.* 77, Anon. *Bell. Afr.* 41.
For *rem publicam adiuuare* cf. Cicero, *Phil.* 8.30, 10.26, *Off.* 1.123.

---

[1] Cf. Cicero, *De orat.* 2.193, 3.221.   [2] See *Introduction*, p. 22.

I can find no other instance of *rem publicam statuere*. It must be a tragic variant of *rem publicam constituere* (Cicero, *De orat.* 1.37, *Phil.* 2.92, 10.22 et al.). For the metaphor, difficult to parallel closely in Attic tragedy[1] or the language of Athenian politics, cf. Ennius, *Ann.* 500 *moribus antiquis res stat Romana uirisque*, Cicero, *Verr.* 3.223 *qui rem publicam sistere negat posse nisi...*, Virgil, *Aen.* 6.857–8 *hic rem Romanam magno turbante tumultu | sistet eques*.

steterit cum Achiuis: cf. Caesar, *Ciu.* 1.61 *quae superiore bello cum Sertorio steterant ciuitates.*
For the triple homoeoteleuton cf. Ennius, *Trag.* 90 *tectis caelatis laqueatis*, 308 *cogitat parat putat*, Accius, *Trag.* 437 *constitit cognouit sensit*, 550 *eiulatu questu gemitu*, Trag. inc. 21 *dolet pudet piget*. The phenomenon unobscured by synaloephe is hard to find in Attic tragedy; but cf. Aeschylus, *Prom.* 691 πήματα λύματα δείματα, Sophocles, *El.* 1235 ἐφηύρετ' ἦλθετ' εἴδεθ'.

76–7 re dubia | haud dubitarit uitam offere: for the phrase *re dubia* cf. Accius, *Trag.* 38–9 *ut quae tum absentem rebus dubiis coniugem | tetinerit nunc prodat ultorem* and contrast Plautus, *Epid.* 113 *is est amicus qui in re dubia re iuuat*, *Capt.* 406, *Most.* 1041, Sallust, *Iug.* 14.5, Livy 7.30.3, 29.25.3. In re (*rebus*) + epithet is the normal type of phrase in republican drama; the only other exceptions are at Trag. inc. 151 and two paratragic passages of Plautus, *Persa* 753 and *Truc.* 75.
For the play with verb and etymologically related adjective cf. Naevius, *Trag.* 15 *laetus sum laudari me abs te pater a laudato uiro*, Ennius, *Trag.* 351 *amicus certus in re incerta cernitur*, Accius, *Trag.* 314 *probis probatum potius quam multis fore*.
Caput offerre seems to have been the more common high-falutin variant of *se offerre* (Plautus, *Capt.* 230–1, Lucretius 3.1041, Cicero, *Sull.* 84 et al.). For *uitam offerre* cf. Cicero, *Sest.* 61.

nec capiti pepercerit: cf. Sophocles, *El.* 979–80 ὦ τοῖσιν ἐχθροῖς εὖ βεβηκόσιν ποτὲ | ψυχῆς ἀφειδήσαντε προὐστήτην φόνου, Euripides, *Herakles* 1146 τί δῆτα φείδομαι ψυχῆς ἐμῆς;, Ennius, *Trag.* 134 *ego cum meae uitae parcam letum inimico deprecer*, Plautus, *Rud.* 222 *uitae hau parco*, Cicero, *Nat. deor.* 3.15 *patriae consulerent, uitae non parcerent. Vitae alicuius parcere* seems to have been the common variant of *alicui parcere* but cf. Accius, *Trag.* 294.
This type of pleonasm whereby a negative phrase repeats the substance of the preceding positive phrase is fairly common in Attic tragedy: cf. Sophocles, *Tr.* 474 φράσω τἀληθὲς οὐδὲ κρύψομαι, Euripides, *Hek.* 668 ὄλωλας .οὐκέτ' εἶ et al. It is rare in republican drama.

---

[1] But cf. Euripides, *Tr.* 1160–1 μὴ Τροίαν ποτὲ | πεσοῦσαν ὀρθώσειεν, *Hik.* 1229–30 σύ με | ἐς ὀρθὸν ἴστη.

ANDROMACHA

(g) For the context of this fragment see above, p. 236.

78 uidi, uidere quod me passa aegerrume: contrast Plautus, *Bacch.* 1016
persuasumst facere quoius me nunc facti pudet, Cist. 504 *feci saepe quod factum
queror, Men.* 955 *ut parentur quibus paratis opus est* et al.
For the omission of *sum* cf. Plautus, *Men.* 119, *Most.* 84 et al.

79 curru quadriiugo: cf. Virgil, *Georg.* 3.18, *Aen.* 12.162, Ovid, *Am.*
3.2.66; *quadrigae* is the normal term in comedy (Plautus, *Amph.* 422 et al.) as
in classical prose and verse.

raptarier: twice elsewhere in republican drama (Plautus, *Aul.* 632, *Cist.*
216) as against *rapere* 55 times. The infinitive form in -*ier* seems to be no more
frequent in tragedy than in comedy; the common language used the form in
-*i*.

(h) Andromache seems to have described Hector's death in trimeters and
then broken into cretic tetrameters to lament her helplessness. For the use of
cretics in similar contexts cf. Plautus, *Cas.* 621 ff., *Rud.* 664 ff. For the contrast between the trimeters carrying the narrative and the musically accompanied verses carrying the expression of personal feelings cf. Euripides, *Andr.*
1–116, Terence, *Andr.* 206–27, *Haut.* 213–380, *Eun.* 292–390. Andromache
goes on to mourn the ruined state of the palace of her father Eetion in
trochaic tetrameters and the unseemly end of the once prosperous Priam in
anapaestic dimeters.

A number of the details of Ennius' metrical patterns are odd. Only one
other cretic tetrameter with an initial choriamb is transmitted in the remains
of republican verse with a fair degree of certainty (Plautus, *Truc.* 624) and
not so very many with any kind of choriamb.[1] The choriamb can be removed from *v.* 82 by treating the second *i* of *auxilio* as consonantal[2] but this
would be to replace one anomaly with another. Hiatus and *syllaba anceps* are
common enough after the second metron in cretic verse but not after
others.[3] The two cases of hiatus in *v.* 82 make it a very odd verse. The third
foot of *v.* 86 is constructed in an unusual way;[4] the *i* of *abiete* could be treated

---

[1] A. Spengel, *Reformvorschl.* pp. 21 ff., banned all choriambs from cretic
verse.
[2] For this phenomenon in dramatic verse see Marx, *Rudens*, pp. 194 f., O.
Skutsch, *Prosodische und metrische Gesetze der Iambenkürzung* (Göttingen,
1934), pp. 43 f. In epic hexameters Ennius has *auium* (*Ann.* 94), *Seruilius* (*Ann.*
251: *conpellat Seruilius sic*) and *insidiantes* (*Ann.* 436).
[3] Cf. Ritschl, *Prol. Trin.* p. cxcvi, C. F. W. Mueller, *Plaut. Pros.* p. 627.
[4] See above on fr. XII.

as prosodically null[1] but this again would be to replace one anomaly with another. Lindsay scanned the words *deformati atque abiete crispa* as an anapaestic dimeter[2] but offered no explanation of why Ennius should have changed the rhythm in the middle of the account of the burning of Eetion's palace. The dactyl in the final foot of *v.* 87 has few relatively certain analogues among the anapaestic verses of republican drama (but cf. Terence, *Andr.* 625, Accius, *Trag.* 571, Trag. inc. 96).

Despite these metrical anomalies the sense and rhetoric of all the words transmitted except *fuga* in *v.* 82 and *alii* in *v.* 85 appear to be excellent. The emendations offered by analogising metricians are singularly unpersuasive.[3]

Ennius makes his Andromache speak of herself as a stateless person in terms of Roman law and social practice (*opis egens...quid...praesidi?... quoue nunc auxilio exili aut fugae?...arce et urbe orba...quo applicem?*). One might compare the way in which Euripides' Medea draws upon the special language of Athenian law (*Med.* 386–8 τίς με δέξεται πόλις; | τίς γῆν ἄσυλον καὶ δόμους ἐχεγγύους | ξένος παρασχὼν ῥύσεται τοὐμὸν δέμας;) and contrast the quite general language of his Hecuba (*Hek.* 158–64 ὤμοι μοι | τίς ἀμύνει μοι· ποία γέννα; | ποία δὲ πόλις; | φροῦδος πρέσβυς, φροῦδοι παῖδες. | ποίαν ἢ ταύταν ἢ κείναν | στείχω; ποῖ δ᾽ ἥσω; ποῦ τις θεῶν | ἢ δαίμων νῶν ἐπαρωγός;). It looks as if Andromache has been offered her freedom by her Greek captors[4] and is bewailing her inability to profit from such freedom.

Ennius lays much emphasis on the religious aspects of the destruction of the palaces of Eetion and Priam, using, to some extent unavoidably, the Roman sacral language (*arae patriae domi...fana...domus, saeptum altisono cardine templum...Iouis aram*), and perhaps importing with Andromache's horror at the pollution by blood of Jupiter's altar feelings foreign to the world portrayed by Attic tragedy. Andromache speaks as if the destruction and pollution of the altars affects quite significantly her own wellbeing. One is reminded of the tone of Cicero's speech *De domo sua*[5] and the strange concern of Virgil's Aeneas for the images of the *Troiae penates*. The Homeric Andromache says nothing about altars in her account of the destruction of her father's kingdom (*Il.* 6.414–28). Euripides' Trojan women are similarly

---

[1] Cf. in epic verse Ennius, *Ann.* 104 *Ner(i)enem*, Lucretius 2.991 *or(i)undi*. Marx, *Rudens*, p. 195, allowed the phenomenon in dramatic verse.

[2] *ALL* vii (1892), 596.

[3] Cf. A. Spengel's transposition of *Priami* and *domus* (*Reformvorschl.* p. 326).

[4] Cf. Agamemnon's qualified offer to Hecuba at Euripides, *Hek.* 754 f.

[5] Cf. 109 *quid est sanctius...quam domus unius cuiusque ciuium? hic arae sunt, hic foci, hic di Penates.*

unconcerned for the altars of Troy.¹ It is the gods of Attic tragedy who worry about altars.² The human dispossessed have other worries.³

80 ex opibus summis opis egens Hector tuae: Vahlen compared Plautus, *Merc.* 111 *ex summis opibus uiribusque usque experire nitere*⁴ and supplied *uoco te*, assimilating the substance of the Latin words to that of Euripides, *Andr.* 523–5 ὦ πόσις πόσις εἴθε σὰν | χεῖρα καὶ δόρυ σύμμαχον | κτησαί-μαν Πριάμου παῖ and *Tr.* 587–90 μόλοις ὦ πόσις μοι...σᾶς δάμαρτος ἄλκαρ. It is better to take the phrase *ex opibus summis* as of the same type as those in Euripides, *Hek.* 55–6 ὦ μῆτερ ἥτις ἐκ τυραννικῶν δόμων | δούλειον ἦμαρ εἶδες, Ennius, *Ann.* 312–13 *mortalem summum Fortuna repente* | *reddidit e summo regno ut famul infimus esset*, Livy 2.6.2 *ne se ortum, eiusdem sanguinis, extorrem, egentem ex tanto modo regno cum liberis adulescentibus ante oculos suos perire sinerent*. For *opes* 'social position, power, influence' cf. Plautus, *Cist.* 494 *neque opes nostrae tam sunt ualidae quam tuae*, Ennius, *Trag.* 339–40 *ut scias quanto e loco,* | *quantis opibus, quibus de rebus lapsa fortuna accidit.* For *ops* 'protection afforded by such power to social equals' cf. Plautus, *Persa* 256 *ei egenti opem adferam*, Sallust, *Hist.* 2.47.4 *cum egens alienae opis plura mala exspectarem*, Cicero, *De orat.* 1.184 *praesidium clientibus, opem amicis...porri-gentem atque tendentem.*

For the polyptoton cf. Accius, *Trag.* 124 *ut mea ope opes Troiae integrem.*

81 quid petam praesidi aut exequar?: *exequar* is usually interpreted as 'quaeram'; P. Schmid, *T.L.L.* v ii.1850.26, refers to Cicero's remark *quaerit enim auxilium* and compares Plautus, *Epid.* 572 *quae exanimata ex-sequitur aspectum tuom.* The resulting pleonasm is possible for Ennius but can be removed by interpreting the second verb as 'consequar'; cf. Plautus, *Rud.* 261–2 *bonam atque obsequentem deam atque haud grauatam* | *patronam exsequontur benignamque multum.*

Praesidium denoted in the legal language the protection which a *patronus* gave his *clientes*; cf. Cicero, *De orat.* 1.184.

81–2 quoque nunc | auxilio exili aut fugae freta sim?: Bentley's *fugae* is an absolutely necessary correction. *Fuga* makes no sense. For the coupling of *exilium* and *fuga* cf. Plautus, *Merc.* 652 *quis modus tibi exilio tandem eueniet? qui*

---

¹ Cf. *Andr.* 103 ff., 394 ff., *Hek.* 475 ff., 905 ff., *Tr.* 98 ff., 474 ff., 577 ff., 1277 ff. At *Tr.* 1317 the θεῶν μέλαθρα simply take their place in the catalogue of destruction (cf. *Andr.* 1024 ff.).

² Cf. Aeschylus, *Ag.* 525 ff., Euripides, *Tr.* 15 ff., 69 ff.

³ It is not impossible that Ennius follows a Greek text closely; cf. Sophocles, *O.T.* 1378–9, Euripides, *Herakleidai* 876 ff.

⁴ Cf. Plautus, *Mil.* 620 *ea te expetere ex opibus summis.*

finis fugae?, Cicero, *Catil.* 1.22 et al. The lawyers made a fine distinction: cf. Marcianus, *Dig.* 48.22.5 *exilium triplex est: aut certorum locorum interdictio aut lata fuga...aut...relegatio in insulam.* If Ennius was adapting his Attic original closely at this point he would probably have had the one-word phrase φυγή in front of him.

For *-ue* connecting questions cf. Plautus, *Asin.* 636, *Rud.* 503. The comparative rarity of the usage suggests that it had a formal, perhaps legalistic, tone.

For *aut* linking near-synonyms cf. Plautus, *Amph.* 904 *si sis sanus aut sapias satis* et al.

Auxilium denoted the active assistance given to both *clientes* and *amici* in times of trouble.

83 arce et urbe orba sum: ἄπολίς εἰμι. A formula of the official language is employed. However there could have been a very similar phrase in Ennius' original; cf. Euripides, *Med.* 771 μολόντες ἄστυ καὶ πόλισμα Παλλάδος. For the Roman formula cf. the Fetial oath quoted at Festus, p. 102.11 *si sciens fallo tum me Diespiter salua urbe arceque bonis eiciat ut ego hunc lapidem* (N.B. Polybius' translation, 3.25.8 πάντων τῶν ἄλλων σῳζομένων ἐν ταῖς ἰδίαις πατρίσιν, ἐν τοῖς ἰδίοις νόμοις, ἐπὶ τῶν ἰδίων βίων ἱερῶν τάφων), Caecilius, *Com.* 146 *qui quasi ad hostis captus liber seruio salua urbe atque arce* (an addition to the Menandrian original), Cicero, *Diu.* 2.69 *ad arcem urbemque retinendam* (concerning the effect of an oracle), Livy 4.61.9, 24.37.6, 31.45.6, 37.37.2.

quo accedam? quo applicem?: cf. Sallust, *Iug.* 14.17 *quo accedam aut quos appellem?* The cretic rhythm suggests that we have *accĕdam* (*accidam*) rather than *accēdam*. The phrase *ad genua* is to be understood. For the use of *quo* in reference to persons cf. Plautus, *Merc.* 803, *Mil.* 119, *Stich.* 142. This and similar usages (e.g. of *unde*) are not common in republican drama; they may have had a legalistic tone. *Applicare* certainly recalls very forcibly the client–patron relationship; cf. Terence, *Andr.* 924–5 *ille...adplicat...ad Chrysidis patrem se, Haut.* 393 *hi se ad uos adplicant,* Cicero, *De orat.* 1.177 *qui Romam in exilium uenisset, cui Romae exulare ius esset, si se ad aliquem quasi patronum applicauisset intestatoque esset mortuus — nonne in ea causa ius applicationis... patefactum in iudicio atque inlustratum est a patrono?* For the intransitive use of *applicare* cf. that of *efflare* at *v.* 14 and of *recipere* at 298. *Supplicare* was regularly intransitive.

For the anaphora of the same form of the interrogative and the isocolon cf. Euripides, *Alk.* τί σὺ πρὸς μελάθροις, τί σὺ τῇδε πολεῖς;, 863 ποῖ βῶ, ποῖ στῶ; τί λέγω, τί δὲ μή;, Plautus, *Men.* 114–16 *rogitas...quid petam, quid feram.* Such phrases, where there are only two members, are normally linked by δέ in Attic drama and *aut* in Roman. The asyndeton increased the emotional intensity of the utterance.

84 cui nec arae patriae domi stant: the legal flavour of the preceding verses suggests that *nec* is an archaism (cf. Lex XII tab. 5.4 *cui suus heres nec escit*, 8.16 *quod nec manifestum erit*) rather than a Graecism ('ne...quidem', οὐδέ).

85 fana flamma deflagrata: *fanum* appears to be here used in its original sense of 'consecrated place'; cf. Livy 10.37.15 *fanum tantum, id est locus templo effatus, fuerat.*

Neither *deflagrare* nor *flagrare* occurs elsewhere in republican drama. In classical prose and verse the simple verb is much commoner than the compound.

85–6 tosti †alii† stant parietes, | deformati atque abiete crispa: all editors seem to have accepted the old correction *alti* and take *deformati atque abiete crispa* to refer to *parietes*. But the latter, though roasted, still stand upright (*tosti...stant*). Other things must have lost their original shape. *Alii* could be answered by another *alii* in the part of the quotation omitted by Cicero. If *alti* is read something like *postes* must be assumed to have stood in the second member of the antithesis. Cicero all but says that the phrase *deformati atque abiete crispa* is incomplete (*scitis quae sequantur*). For similar incomplete quotations cf. *Tusc.* 1.34, 1.106, 2.39, 3.53, 3.58.

Deformare does not occur elsewhere in republican drama. In classical Latin the word is confined to poetry and history.

87 o pater o patria o Priami domus: cf. Sophocles, *O.T.* 1394–5 ὦ Πόλυβε καὶ Κόρινθε καὶ τὰ πάτρια | λόγῳ παλαιὰ δώμαθ', Euripides, *Med.* 166 ὦ πάτερ ὦ πόλις.

For the parechesis *pater ~ patria* cf. Plautus, *Capt.* 43, *Men.* 1083, 1090, *Merc.* 660.

For the anaphora and ascending tricolon cf. Sophocles, *Ant.* 891–2 ὦ τύμβος, ὦ νυμφεῖον, ὦ κατασκαφὴς | οἴκησις ἀείφρουρος, Terence, *Ad.* 790 *o caelum o terra o maria Neptuni.* This type of phrasal arrangement, in which the third of three elements balances or outweighs the previous two, is much more common in Roman drama than in Attic and seems, relatively speaking, both more common in tragedy than comedy and more common in the musically accompanied parts of comedy than in the trimeters; see Lindholm, *Stilistische Studien*, pp. 26 ff.

For the vocative use of the nominative form cf. Trag. inc. 184–5 *o domus antiqua, heu quam dispari | dominare domino*, Novius, *Atell.* 40 *o domus parata*

COMMENTARY

pulchrae familiae festiuiter, Euripides, *Phoin.* 1500 ὦ δόμος ὦ δόμος. This use is quite distinct from Plautus' appositional nominatives (*Asin.* 691 *mi Libane ocellus aureus* et al.) and may justly be termed a Graecism.[1]

88 saeptum altisono cardine templum: a bizarre phrase. However, that the seat of Troy's government should be a *templum* reflects the ideas of contemporary Rome; cf. Varro, εἰσαγωγικῷ *ad Pomp.*, *ap.* Gell. 14.7.7 *docuitque . . . nisi in loco per augurem constituto, quod templum appellaretur, senatus consultum factum esset, iustum id non fuisse; propterea et in curia Hostilia et in Pompeia . . . cum profana ea loca fuissent, templa esse per augures constituta*, Servius auct. *Aen.* 1.446 *. . . erant tamen templa in quibus auspicato et publice res administrarentur et senatus haberi posset*, Cicero, *Leg.* 2.26 *quorum hic mundus omnis templum esset et domus*, Virgil, *Aen.* 7.174 (the palace of the king of Lanuvium), Seneca, *Thy.* 901–2 (the palace of Atreus). For *saepire* in connection with the enclosure of the *templum* cf. Varro, *Ling.* 7.13 *omne templum esse debet continuo septum nec plus unum introitum habere*, Festus, p. 146.12 MINORA TEMPLA *fiunt ab auguribus cum loca aliqua tabulis aut linteis sepiuntur, ne uno amplius ostio pateant, certis uerbis definita. itaque templum est locus ita effatus aut ita septus ut ex una parte pateat angulosque adfixos habeat ad terram.*

Door pivots are not mentioned in the remains of Attic tragedy although the appearance of persons from inside the stage house is frequently heralded by a noise from the opening door.[2] Gracchus mentions them twice.[3] Neither Attic nor Roman comedy refers much to them.[4]

Altisonus, 'ὑψηχής', occurs elsewhere only at Ennius, *Trag.* 188, *Ann.* 575, Cicero, *Carm.* fr. 19.1, Seneca, *Ag.* 582, *Herc. O.* 530, *Phaedr.* 1134, Juvenal 11.181. The only other possible formation with -*sonus* in republican tragedy is *suauisonus* (Naevius 20, Accius 572). There are none in comedy.

89 uidi ego te adstante ope barbarica: it is more likely that a scribe smoothed *adstante* to *adstantem* at *Tusc.* 3.45 than that Cicero twisted Ennius' phrase to suit himself at 1.85. Ennius is referring to the military support given to Troy by her Asian allies. Cf. Virgil, *Aen.* 8.685–8 *hinc ope barbarica*

---

[1] See J. Svennung, *Anredeformen* (Uppsala, 1958), p. 267.
[2] Euripides, *Hel.* 859–60, *Ion* 515–16, *Or.* 1366.
[3] *Trag.* 1 *o grata cardo regium egressum indicans*, 2 *sonat inpulsa regia cardo*; cf. Seneca, *Med.* 177 *sed cuius ictu regius cardo strepit?* Contrast Pacuvius, *Trag.* 214 *ualuae sonunt*, Accius, *Trag.* 30 *sed ualuae resonunt regiae*, 470 *atque adeo ualuas sonere sensi regias.*
[4] The στροφεύς, 'socket', appears at Aristophanes, *Thesm.* 487, fr. 255, Hermippus, fr. 47.9. The context at Plautus, *Curc.* 94 and 158 is paratragic. The normal advertisement for the newcomer from the stage house in Attic comedy is ἐψόφηκε τὴν θύραν et sim., in Roman *foris concrepuit* et sim.

uariisque Antonius armis | uictor ab Aurorae populis et litore rubro, | Aegyptum uiresque Orientis et ultima secum | Bactra uehit.

Βαρβαρικός does not occur in Attic tragedy and so is unlikely to be the immediate source of Ennius' *barbaricus*. The latter occurs elsewhere in republican drama only at Pacuvius, *Trag.* 270 and three high-falutin passages of Plautus, *Capt.* 492, 884, *Cas.* 748. In classical Latin its use is restricted, except for Livy 25.33.2, to poetry. *Barbarus* is frequent in comedy and classical prose. Similar forms in tragedy are *Delphicus* (Ennius 303), *modicus* (Ennius 181), *musicus* (Pacuvius 114), *tenebricus* (Pacuvius 158), *trabicus* (Pacuvius 406). Plautus has a large number at the ends of iambic trimeters and trochaic tetrameters. Their frequency in the Roman official language (*poplicus, ciuicus, hosticus, colonicus* et al.) gave them a formal tone.

For βάρβαρος/*barbarus* in the mouth of a non-Greek without any pejorative connotation cf. Aeschylus, *Pers.* 254–5 ὅμως δ' ἀνάγκη πᾶν ἀναπτύξαι πάθος, | Πέρσαι· στρατὸς γὰρ πᾶς ὄλωλε βαρβάρων (a Persian messenger speaking to his queen), Plautus, *Asin.* 11 *Demophilus scripsit, Maccus uortit barbare* (i.e. *Latine*), *Trin.* 19 *Philemo scripsit, Plautus uortit barbare*, Cicero, *Orat.* 160 *absurdum erat. . .in barbaris casibus Graecam litteram adhibere.*

90 tectis caelatis laqueatis: *tectis* is a poetic plural; cf. *Trag. inc.* 213, 242 and contrast Plautus, *Amph.* 1008 et al.

Coffered ceilings in private dwellings always indicated great luxury; cf. Lucretius 2.28, Cicero, *Tusc.* 5.62, Horace, *Carm.* 2.18.1, Anon. *Culex* 63–4, Seneca, *Nat.* 1 prol. 8, *Ep.* 90.42 (*non impendebant caelata laquearia*), 115.9, Plutarch, *Lycurgus* 13 (story of Leotychides the elder). That they are not mentioned in the remains of either Greek or Roman comedy is perhaps an accident. Aristophanes, *Sph.* 1215 and Diphilus, fr. 61 seem to refer to them. The lack of mention of them in extant Attic tragedy could be due to a deliberate avoidance by the poets of anachronism. If so Ennius has here added an architectural detail foreign to his original. Nothing corresponding with the *impluuium* mentioned at *Amph.* 1108, *Mil.* 159 et al., *Eun.* 589 could have stood in the comedies adapted by Plautus and Terence.

91 auro ebore instructam regifice: for *instruere* 'furnish richly' cf. Plautus, *Bacch.* 373, Cicero, *Nat. deor.* 2.95, Virgil, *Aen.* 1.637–8.

For ivory in domestic furniture cf. Homer, *Od.* 4.72–3 χαλκοῦ τε στεροπὴν κὰδ δώματα ἠχήεντα, | χρυσοῦ τ' ἠλέκτρου τε καὶ ἀργύρου ἠδ' ἐλέφαντος, 23.199–200 λέχος. . .δαιδάλλων χρυσῷ τε καὶ ἀργύρῳ ἠδ' ἐλέφαντι, Euripides, *I.A.* 582–3 ἐλεφαντοδέτων πάροι|θεν δόμων δὲ στάς (of Paris). There are surprisingly few mentions of ivory in extant Attic tragedy (Sophocles, fr. 1025.7, Euripides, *I.A.* 582, Achaeus, fr. 25.2). The notorious wealth of Troy is usually symbolised by gold (cf. Euripides, *Andr.* 168–9, *Hek.* 492, *Hel.* 928, *Tr.* 18, 994–5).

Regificus (*-e*) occurs only here in republican drama; it is rare in classical Latin (the lexica quote Virgil, *Aen.* 6.605, Val. Flacc. 2.652, Silius 11.271). Drama has the synonymous *regius* (*-e*) eight times. Other formations with *-ficus* in tragedy are *ingratificus* (Accius 364), *hostificus* (Accius 80, 83), *laetificus* (Trag. inc. 134), *largificus* (Pacuvius 414); comedy has *beneficus, damnificus, delenificus, falsificus, fumificus, furtificus, lucrificus* (?), *magnificus, maleficus, mirificus, munificus, spurcificus, ueneficus*. The common occurrence of *magnificus, maleficus* and *ueneficus* suggests that these belonged to the common language but the rest may be poetic creations. With the exception of the tragedies of Seneca[1] classical poetry has very few such formations.

92 inflammari: elsewhere in republican drama only at Accius, *Trag.* 14 (for the rarity of *flamma* see above on *v.* 22). *Incendere* occurs 13 times in comedy, once in tragedy.

93 ui uitam euitari: for the sound play cf. Turpilius, *Com.* 202 *quibus rebus uita amantum inuitari solet*, Trag. inc. 131 *uirginem me quondam inuitam per uim uiolat Iuppiter.*

Euitare (*uita*) occurs elsewhere in Latin only at Accius, *Trag.* 348 and Apuleius, *Met.* 3.8. For the formation cf. Plautus' *exanimare* (probably from the common language), *exossare, elinguare, exdorsuare, exoculare, euiscerare.* A different type of formation is represented by *expectorare* at *v.* 17.

Besides *perire, mori, necare* Ennius' tragic fragments contain a wide variety of periphrases for killing and dying: *uitam euitari,* 144 *materno sanguine exanclando,* 180 *pergunt lauere sanguen sanguine,* 182 *me anima priuem,* 183 *mortem obpetam,* 192 *Acherontem obibo,* 230 *perniciem dabo,* 283 *leto dati sunt,* 299 *remissa humana uita,* 323 *oppeto malam pestem,* 328 *exitium parat,* 329 *pestem ut participet.* Those of his successors have much less: Pacuvius 148 *leto dabit,* 286 *mortem... offeras,* 289 *macto inferis,* Accius 117 *leto offeres,* 433 *morte inbuturum manus,* 491 *mittis leto.* Plautus is probably parodying contemporary tragedy at *Asin.* 606–11 *...a uita abiudicabo...morti dedere...uitam largiar... uitam esse amissurum, Bacch.* 849 *exheredem fecero uitae suae,* 869 *animam amborum exsorbebo.* Few of the Ennian expressions have exact parallels in Attic tragedy.

94 Iouis aram sanguine turpari: no altar of *Iuppiter* stood in a Roman private house or even in the *Regia* or any of the *curiae*. Ennius is representing the Ζεὺς ἑρκεῖος (κτήσιος) of his original as best he can. With the exception

---

[1] See F. Skutsch, *Glotta* II (1909/10), 160 f. (= *Kl. Schr.* 386).

of the paratragic *Amphitruo* (cf. 1127) Roman comedies make the *Lares* the object of domestic cult (cf. Plautus, *Aul.* 2, 386, *Merc.* 830 ff. [contrast Euripides, *Phoin.* 631 ff.], *Mil.* 1339, *Rud.* 1207, *Trin.* 39).

For *aram sanguine turpari* cf. Lucretius 1.84–6 *Aulide quo pacto Triuiai uirginis aram | Iphianassai turparunt sanguine foede | ductores Danaum delecti, prima uirorum*, Sallust, *Hist.* 1.47, Virgil, *Aen.* 2.499–502. The Euripidean accounts of Priam's death (*Hek.* 21–4 ἐπεὶ δὲ Τροία θ' Ἕκτορός τ' ἀπόλλυται | ψυχή, πατρῷα θ' ἑστία κατεσκάφη, | αὐτὸς δὲ βωμῷ πρὸς θεοδμήτῳ πίτνει | σφαγεὶς Ἀχιλλέως παιδὸς ἐκ μιαιφόνου, *Tr.* 16–17 πρὸς δὲ κρηπίδων βάθροις | πέπτωκε Πρίαμος Ζηνὸς ἑρκείου θανών, 481–3 καὶ τὸν φυτουργὸν Πρίαμον... κατασφαγέντ' ἐφ' ἑρκείῳ πυρᾷ)[1] are unconcerned with the dirtying of the altar and it is possible that Ennius is here adding a horrific detail from the sphere of Roman tabu.

The Olympian deities of Attic tragedy certainly objected to suppliants at their altars being slain and only Artemis, to the horror of the poets who relate the stories, ever demanded to be propitiated with human blood.[2] But a regular and often mentioned part of the act of sacrifice was to pour the blood of the sacrificed animal over the altar.[3] This was done either indirectly by means of a σφαγεῖον or directly by cutting the animal's throat over the altar itself.[4] The mode of sacrifice practised at Rome differed in various details from the heroic and historical Athenian modes, for example in the boiling of the entrails of the slain animal in vessels separately. There is a strange reticence in our sources about what happened to the animal's blood in sacrifices *ritu Romano* to *Iuppiter* and the other *di superi*.[5] Livy's horrified description of Samnite ritual (10.41) and Virgil's account of Dido's terror as the wine she is

---

[1] Cf. Pindar, *Paian* 6.113 ff.

[2] Cf. the story of the substitution of the deer for Iphigenia and the language of Euripides' messenger, *I.A.* 1595 ὡς μὴ μιάνῃ βωμὸν εὐγενεῖ φόνῳ.

[3] Cf. Aeschylus, *Theb.* 275 μήλοισιν αἱμάσσοντας ἑστίας θεῶν, Euripides, *Ion* 1126–7 ὡς σφαγαῖσι Διονύσου πέτρας | δεύσειε δισσὰς παιδὸς ἀντ' ὀπτηρίων.

[4] Cf. Aeschylus, *Ag.* 232, Euripides, *El.* 813 ff., *Hel.* 1561 ff., *I.A.* 1578 ff., *I.T.* 26 ff.

[5] This was noticed by W. Warde Fowler, *The Religious Experience of the Roman People* (London, 1911), pp. 180, 196. Later writers (e.g. G. Wissowa, *Religion und Kultus der Römer*, ed. 2 [Munich, 1912], pp. 416 ff., Latte, *RE* ix i [1914], s.v. *immolatio*, 1129, *Röm. Rel.* p. 388) have seen no significance in it. Nothing about the *ritus Romanus* is to be learnt from *Ciris* 525 *sanguine taurorum supplex resperserat aras*, *Catalepton* 14.8 *uictima sacratos sparget honore focos*, Seneca, *Phaedr.* 498–9 *non cruor largus pias | inundat aras*. The silence of the *Aeneid*, stuffed as it is with Roman antiquarian lore, is eloquent. Lucretius 4.1236–7 *sanguine...conspergunt aras*, 5.1201–2 *aras sanguine...spargere*, and Arnobius 3.24 *nisi pecorum sanguine delibutas suas conspexerint arulas, suos deserunt...praesidiatus* are concerned with religious ritual in general.

COMMENTARY

pouring upon the altar turns to blood (*Aen.* 4.453–5) suggest that the
Romans feared to let blood of any sort stain certain altars. If this is so we have
part of an explanation why the Roman antiquarians believed that animal
sacrifice was unknown in early Rome.[1] Ennius' phrase *Iouis aram sanguine
turpari* may therefore be not a literal translation of some Attic poet's phrase
but an original creation aimed at superstitions peculiar to second-century
Romans.

Turpare does not occur elsewhere in republican drama and is very rare in
classical prose.

The two-syllable rhyme running over three anapaestic dimeters...
inflammari...euitari...turpari appears not to be paralleled in ancient drama.
Euripides has one-syllable rhyme over two dimeters often enough (e.g. *Hek.*
70–1, 111–12, 116–17, 127–8, 130–1, 142–3), Plautus two-syllable rhyme
over two (e.g. *Bacch.* 1094, *Rud.* 955–6a).

XXVIII

Aulus Gellius quotes *philosophandum est paucis* as the very words of Ennius.
Efforts to extract something different from Cicero's various paraphrases—
decreui philosophari...paucis; *se ait philosophari uelle sed paucis*; *philosophari sibi
ait necesse esse sed paucis*—should be abandoned.

In his first edition of the tragic fragments Ribbeck got from Gellius' discourse at 5.16.5 the trochaic tetrameter *degustandum ex philosophia non in eam
ingurgitandum*. L. Mercklin's arguments[2] against the particular form of
Ribbeck's verse have some weight but the mode of expression seems a little
drastic even for Gellius and we may in fact have a paraphrase diverging only
slightly from Ennius' own words. For the phrase *degustare ex philosophia* cf.
Laberius, *Mim.* 36 *sequere me in latrinum ut aliquid gustes ex Cynica haeresi*,
Tacitus, *Dial.* 31.7 *sed eum qui quasdam artes haurire, omnes libare debet*,
Quintilian, *Inst.* 12.2.4 *qui litteras uel primis ut aiunt labris degustarit*, Schol.
Pers. 3.52 *certe degustasti philosophiam*. For *in philosophiam ingurgitare* cf.
Cicero, *Fin.* 3.7 *quasi helluari libris*.

The words φιλόσοφος and φιλοσοφεῖν do not occur in extant Attic tragedy.[3] The activity of φιλοσοφία however is frequently represented under
the traditional heroic masks by the innovating Euripides: τοιοῦτός ἐστιν
ἀεί, τὰ ἡρωικὰ πρόσωπα εἰσάγων φιλοσοφοῦντα.[4] Neoptolemus'

---

[1] Cf. Dionysius Hal. *Ant. Rom.* 2.74.4, Ovid, *Fast.* 1.337 ff., Pliny, *Nat.*
18.7, Plutarch, *Rom.* 12, *Num.* 8, 16. Mere pythagoreanising will not suffice as
an explanation.
[2] *NJbb* Suppl. III (1860), 668.
[3] Trag. Graec. inc. 522 looks like comedy.
[4] Schol. *Hipp.* 953; cf. Athenaeus 13.561 A.

252

modified anti-intellectual sentiments were probably common among men of affairs both at Athens[1] and at Rome.[2] Ennius may have found them in his original or inserted them himself.[3] In any case he would have taken the word *philosophari* from the common language.

95 philosophandum est paucis: one must understand *uerbis*; cf. Plautus, *Aul.* 1 *nequis miretur qui sim paucis eloquar*, Terence, *Haut.* 10 *nunc quam ob rem has partis didicerim paucis dabo*.

haud placet: this and similar phrases occur at Plautus, *Merc.* 349, *Stich.* 297, *Pseud.* 653; *non placet* et sim. are much more common.

XXIX

Andromache was notoriously tall (cf. Ovid, *Ars* 2.645, 3.777, Juvenal 6.503, Dares 12); hence Antiphon's unsuitability for the role.

XXX

See above, p. 236.

XXXI

To explain this remark of Cicero's scholars often adduce Donatus, *De com.* 8.11: *huiusmodi carmina ad tibias fiebant, ut his auditis multi ex populo ante dicerent, quam fabulam acturi scaenici essent, quam omnino spectatoribus ipsius antecedens titulus pronuntiaretur.* But Cicero is patently referring to the personage from whom the aria comes, not the play as a whole. It is worth quoting his further remark at 2.86: *simul inflauit tibicen a perito carmen agnoscitur.* Donatus' statement may come from scholastic misinterpretation of *Ac.* 2.20 itself rather than observation of stage practice.

Cicero could have in mind the opening aria of a play.[4] If so it is hard to believe that connoisseurs came to the theatre not knowing what plays were to be performed. On the other hand, if he is referring to an aria within a play it is hard to believe that the connoisseurs recognised what personage was about to give utterance from knowledge of the music rather than from knowledge of the action of the play.

---

[1] Cf. Plato, *Gorg.* 484 c.

[2] Cf. Cicero, *Off.* 1.19, *Fin.* 1.1, Tacitus, *Agric.* 4.

[3] For Ennius' freedom in the matter of *sententiae* see below on fr. LXXXIV, fr. CV, fr. CVIII.

[4] Cf. Euripides' Ἰφιγένεια ἡ ἐν Αὐλίδι, ʿΡῆσος, Plautus' *Cistellaria*, *Epidicus*, *Persa* and *Stichus*, which all departed from the normal in having, according to the surviving scripts, musically accompanied openings.

These difficulties can be avoided by the assumption that Cicero had in mind a theatrical show like that given at the funeral games of the murdered Julius Caesar, where certain arias from Pacuvius' *Armorum iudicium* and Atilius' adaptation of Sophocles' Ἠλέκτρα particularly befitting the occasion were performed (Suetonius, *Iul.* 84, Appian, *B.C.* 2.146). On such an occasion it might well be that those with trained ears would first recognise the source of each aria.

XXXIII

Pomponius Laetus' *Androma⟨ca⟩ Nocti* is palaeographically at least as likely as Scaliger's *Androm⟨ed⟩a Nocti* and evidence exists that Varro and/or his sources knew the *Andromacha*, none that they knew the *Andromeda* of either Ennius or Accius.

The alleged similarity between the Latin anapaests and Aristophanes, *Thesm.* 1065–8 ὦ νὺξ ἱερὰ | ὡς μακρὸν ἵππευμα διώκεις | ἀστεροειδέα νῶτα διφρεύουσ' | αἰθέρος ἱερᾶς | τοῦ σεμνοτάτου δι' Ὀλύμπου, said by a scholiast to be τοῦ προλόγου τῆς Ἀνδρομέδας εἰσβολή, is not so very close. That Ennius gives the stars to Night's chariot rather than to the heaven matters little. More importantly Ennius' *conficis* suggests that darkness is disappearing; the Greek verses present the scene as still quite dark. In any case the similarities that do exist may be accidental. The personages of Attic tragedy frequently address the night: e.g. Sophocles, *El.* 201 ff., Euripides, *El.* 54, *Hek.* 68, *Or.* 174. Comedy sometimes parodies the device, sometimes uses it seriously: e.g. Aristophanes, *Batr.* 1331, Pap. Ant. 15 recto 9, Menander, fr. 789, Plautus, *Merc.* 3–5. Night's chariot might turn up anywhere; cf. Aeschylus, *Choe.* 660–1 τάχυνε δ', ὡς καὶ νυκτὸς ἅρμ' ἐπείγεται | σκοτεινόν, fr. 69.5–6 μελανίππου προφυγὼν | ἱερᾶς νυκτὸς ἀμολγόν, Euripides, *Ion* 1150–1 μελάμπεπλος δὲ νὺξ ἀσείρωτον ζυγοῖς | ὄχημ' ἔπαλλεν, Theocritus 2.166 ἀστέρες εὐκάλοιο κατ' ἄντυγα νυκτὸς ὀπαδοί, Cicero, *Arat.* 189–90 *hic tamen aeterno inuisens loca curriculo nox* | *signa dedit nautis* (∼ Aratus 408 ἀρχαίη νύξ), Virgil, *Aen.* 5.721 *et nox atra polum bigis subuecta tenebat*, Tibullus 2.1.87–8 *iam nox iungit equos, currumque sequuntur* | *matris lasciuo sidera* ⸢*ulua choro*, Anon. *Culex* 202 *iam quatit et biiuges oriens Erebeis equos nox*.

96 caua caeli: cf. Ennius, *Trag.* 250 *caua caerula*, Varro, *Men.* 270 *caeli cauernas*, Cicero, *Arat.* 252 *et late caeli lustrare cauernas* (translating nothing in Aratus), *Carm.* fr. 3.5, Lucretius 4.171, 391, 6.252, Cicero, *Arat.* 313–14 *et quantos radios iacimus de lumine nostro* | *quis hunc conuexum caeli contingimus orbem* (∼ Aratus 541 ὅσσον δ' ὀφθαλμοῖο βολῆς ἀποτείνεται αὐγή), Virgil, *Aen.* 4.451 *taedet caeli conuexa tueri*, 6.241 *supera ad conuexa ferebat*. The visible sky is frequently represented in republican tragedy as a hemispherical envelope or vault: cf. Ennius, *Trag.* 188–9 *in altisono caeli clipeo*, 319 *caeli ingentes fornices*, 365–6 *caua...caeli cortina*, Naevius *ap.* Varr. *Ling.* 7.7 *hemi-*

sphaerium ubi concha caerula septum stat. Such metaphors appear in late Greek poetry: e.g. Synesius, *Hymn.* 9.87 κύτος οὐρανῶν, Oppian, *Cyn.* 1.281 αἰθερίοισι γυάλοισι. Euripides' heroes refer often enough in oblique fashion to the scientific theory according to which the sky was, whatever its appearance, curved in the horizontal plane and the paths of the celestial bodies circular (e.g. fr. 593, fr. 919, fr. 941) but there seems to be no clear case in which they identify appearance and reality. W. S. Barrett should not have coupled[1] Euripides, *El.* 731 and fr. 114 with Plato, *Phaidr.* 247c and taken νῶτα as 'the top of what, viewed from the outside, is the sky's convexity'; this makes it impossible to explain why νῶτα is also used metaphorically of the sea (Euripides, *Hel.* 129, 774 et al.).

XXXIV

The first four words of Varro's quotation, *Acherusia templa alta Orci* (metrically a paroemiac), head an unattributed quotation of republican tragedy by Cicero at *Tusc.* 1.48: *quae est anus tam delira, quae timeat ista, quae uos uidelicet, si physica non didicissetis, timeretis,* '*Acherunsia templa alta Orci, pallida leti, nubila tenebris loca*'? *non pudet philosophum in eo gloriari, quod haec non timeat et quod falsa esse cognouerit?*

The words of Cicero's quotation form two anapaestic dimeters (for the fourth-foot dactyl cf. *v.* 87 *o pater o patria o Priami domus*; the enjambement could be avoided by placing *loca* before *pallida*). They make good, if incomplete, sense apart from the context of Cicero's discourse. Whereas the ordinary appellation of the underworld in republican drama is *Acheruns*, the words which Cicero quotes form a grandiose periphrasis based on Roman officialese: *loca* are the places where men go about their ordinary business, *templa* those where the senate and magistrates have dealings with the gods or with men under the protection of the gods:[2] Orcus, ruler of the dead,[3] keeps to his *templa* while the dead themselves inhabit the *pallida...nubila tenebris loca.* For *letum*, 'mortui' (manes, umbrae, simulacra, etc.), cf. the set funeral

---

[1] *Euripides: Hippolytos*, p. 186.

[2] Cf. the *carmen deuotionis* quoted by Macrobius, *Sat.* 3.9.7 *loca templa sacra urbemque eorum relinquatis...nostraque uobis loca templa sacra urbs acceptior probatiorque sit.* For the same phraseology used less precisely cf. Accius, *Trag.* 529–31 *Volcania templa sub ipsis* | *collibus, in quos delatus locos* | *dicitur alto ab limine caeli*, Cicero, *Manil.* 70 *testorque omnis deos et eos maxime qui huic loco temploque praesident.* Plautus parodies it on two occasions: *Mil.* 413–14 *quom me in locis Neptuniis templisque turbulentis* | *seruauit*; *Rud.* 906–9 *Neptuno has ego gratias meo patrono* | *qui salsis locis incolit pisculentis,* | *quom me ex suis locis pulcre ornatum expediuit* | *templis reducem, plurima praeda onustum.*

[3] Cf. G. P. Shipp, *Glotta* XXXIX (1961), 154 ff.

formula *ollus leto datus est* (Varro, *Ling.* 7.42, Festus, p. 304.1 ff.), Lucretius 3.42 *Tartara leti*, Virgil, *Georg.* 4.481–2. The word occurs frequently in republican epic and tragedy as a synonym of *mors*; it has a high-falutin tone wherever it occurs in comedy.[1]

The words which Varro attributes directly to the *Andromacha* form a slightly irregular iambic trimeter (see above on fr. xii). They can also be taken as a paroemiac followed by an anapaestic monometer. They make quite good sense, being a grim variant of the returning traveller's conventional address to his homeland.[2] The speaker would be someone on the point of death, possibly Astyanax, beholding in a vision the realm of Hades; cf. Euripides, *Hipp.* 1447 καὶ δὴ νερτέρων ὁρῶ πύλας.[3]

Most scholars since Stephanus' time seem to have assumed that Cicero quotes the very same speech as Varro does, some considering that Varro omitted *pallida leti nubila tenebris loca* after *Orci*, others that Cicero omitted *saluete infera* after this word. It is difficult to see how Varro could have omitted *pallida leti nubila tenebris loca*. If they formed one of the metrical units recognised by ancient editors of dramatic texts we would have a case parallel with the omission of *tibi utilisque habere* (an iambic dimeter catalectic) from the quotation of Plautus, *Cist.* 8–11 at *Ling.* 7.99.[4] But they do not form such a unit. It is possible that Cicero omitted *saluete infera* in order to merge the tragic piece into his own discourse. However the conglomeration of words that results from this hypothesis—*Acherusia templa alta Orci saluete infera pallida leti nubila tenebris loca*—ought not to be foisted on Ennius; *infera* goes tidily neither with *templa* nor with *loca*.

In difficulties like this one it is profitable to question basic assumptions. And indeed the assumption that Varro and Cicero are necessarily quoting the same passage is an arbitrary one. Lucretius repeats the two-word phrase *Acherusia templa* three times in the six books of his didactic poem (1.120, 3.25, 3.86). In the extant scripts of both Greek and Latin drama there recur phrases much longer than four-word ones. Cicero does not even say he is quoting Ennius. What he quotes should be assigned to the 'incertae incertorum fabulae'.

---

[1] Plautus, *Aul.* 661, *Merc.* 483, *Mil.* 1241.

[2] Cf. Aeschylus, *Ag.* 508, Sophocles, *El.* 67 ff., fr. 825.1, Euripides, *Herakles* 523 ff., frs. 558.1–2, 696.1–2, 817, Menander, frs. 1, 287, Plautus, *Bacch.* 170, *Stich.* 649.

[3] Vahlen compares Euripides, *Andr.* 413–14 ὡς σὺ μὴ θάνῃς | στείχω πρὸς Ἅιδην and 501–3 χέρας αἵματη|ρὰς βρόχοισι κεκλημένα | πέμπομαι κατὰ γαίας. These passages are not strictly parallel. The Euripidean Andromache is only threatened with death.

[4] See Leo, *Die plaut. Cant.* p. 6.

ANDROMACHA

XXXV

Vahlen's notion that this fragment refers to resistance by Andromache to Neoptolemus' sexual demands[1] is highly implausible. Indeed *bellum gerere* and *proelium facere* often suggest something very different in erotic contexts. The person with whom Andromache has been quarrelling could only be Neoptolemus. The issue would most likely be the proposal to sacrifice Polyxene to the shade of Achilles, Neoptolemus' father. Neoptolemus is nowhere represented as concerned in the killing of Astyanax.

Zillinger suggested[2] that Cicero had the Ennian Andromache in mind when, writing to Atticus in 60 (2.1.5), he said of Clodia, the wife of the consul Metellus, *sed ego illam odi male consularem. ea est enim seditiosa, ea cum uiro bellum gerit; neque solum cum Metello sed etiam cum Fabio.... Orelli and Buecheler[3] are likely to be right in proposing one of the perpetually quarrelsome *uxores dotatae* of comedy.[4]

For the declaration that a man's name suits his character, his deeds, or his fate cf. Aeschylus, *Ag.* 681–7 τίς ποτ' ὠνόμαξεν ὧδ' | ἐς τὸ πᾶν ἐτητύμως ...τὰν | δορίγαμβρον ἀμφινεικῆ | θ' Ἑλέναν;, *Hik.* 315, Sophocles, *Ai.* 430–1, fr. 880, Euripides, *Ba.* 508, *Rhes.* 158–9, *Phoin.* 636–7, fr. 517, *Telephos* Pap. Mediol. 1.11–13. For the rhetorical value of thus referring to the significance of a name cf. Aristotle, *Rhet.* 2.23.29, Cicero, *Inu.* 2.28, Quintilian, *Inst.* 5.10.30–1.

XXXVI

Scaliger struck out *Troiano* as a gloss, substituted *iactarier* for what he imagined to be *iactari* of the paradosis and joined the resulting trimeter with the two quoted by Cicero, *Tusc.* 1.105 (*vv.* 78–9). He seems to have thought the verses belonged to Ennius' *Hecuba*. Columna compared Euripides, *Andr.* 8–10 ἥτις πόσιν μὲν Ἕκτορ' ἐξ Ἀχιλλέως | θανόντ' ἐσεῖδον, παῖδα δ' ὃν τίκτω πόσει | ῥιφθέντα πύργων Ἀστυάνακτ' ἀπ' ὀρθίων and assigned the verses to the Latin *Andromacha*. But this makes sense only on the assumption that Ennius' play was set at some time well after the killing of Astyanax. Düntzer[5] proposed that *iubent* or *flagitant* be supplied with *iactari* and compared Euripides, *Tr.* 725 ῥῖψαι δὲ πύργων δεῖν σφε Τρωικῶν ἄπο.

---

[1] Vahlen compared Euripides, *Tr.* 658 ff., 673 ff., *Andr.* 38 ff., 111 ff.
[2] *Cicero und die altrömischen Dichter*, p. 88.
[3] *Ind. schol. Greifswald* 1868, 18 f. (= *Kl. Schr.* 1 646 f.).
[4] Ribbeck, *C.R.F.*[2], on Com. inc. 26, compared Axionicus, fr. 6.9 οἷον φίλερίς τίς ἐστι καὶ μάχεταί τί μοι, and Menander, fr. 251.6 Körte γυνὴ κρατεῖ πάντων ἐπιτάττει μάχετ' ἀεί. Cf. also Plautus, *Men.* 765 ff., Ovid, *Ars* 2.155.
[5] *Zeitschr. f. d. Alt.* 1838, p. 49.

100 Hectoris natum: substantival *gnatus* and *gnata* are normal in the manuscripts of Plautine and Terentian comedy;[1] even in the indirect and much modernised tradition of the fragments of tragedy these forms are as common as *natus* and *nata*. It is therefore unlikely that Ennius wrote *natum* here.

Outside the vocative the substantive *gnatus* had a markedly lofty tone; in comedy it occurs 131 times as against *filius* 318; in tragedy on the other hand it occurs 16 times as against *filius* only once.

de Troiano muro: there is no need to suppose that Servius auct. *Aen.* 3.489 (*Calchas cecinit deiiciendum ex muris Astyanacta...praecipitauit e muro*) is dependent on Ennius; Vahlen[2] ought not to have approved of Lachmann's alteration of *de* to *e*.

The use of the adjective *Troiano* instead of the genitive *Troiae* elevates the style; cf. Ennius, *Trag.* 124 *Bacchico...modo,* 144 *materno sanguine,* 208 *nemore Pelio,* 218 *domum paternam,* 237 *erilis...corporis,* 271 *humanum genus,* 323 *hostili manu,* Plautus, *Mil.* 13–15 *quemne ego seruaui in campis Curculionieis | ubi Bumbomachides Clutomestoridysarchides | erat imperator summus, Neptuni nepos.*

XXXVII

For doubts about the attribution to Ennius' tragedy see above, p. 234 n. 5.

Mussare, 'murmur, express displeasure quietly'[3] probably stood in some form among the words quoted.

XXXVIII

Augificare occurs only here in extant Latin. Lucretius 2.571 has the adjective *auctificus*. The verb is probably a coinage on the model of *magnificare*. The great frequency of the latter verb, *aedificare, ludificare* and *sacrificare* in comedy shows that such formations were not in themselves poetic; but the republican tragedians, in their search for diction distinct from that of every day, concocted several new ones. Pacuvius has *amplificare*, Accius *orbificare*.

XXXIX

This fragment looks like part of a lament either by Andromache or by a chorus of Trojan fellow captives. Mercerus compared Euripides, *Andr.* 111–12 πολλὰ δὲ δάκρυά μοι κατέβα χροός, ἁνίκ᾽ ἔλειπον | ἄστυ τε καὶ θαλάμους καὶ πόσιν ἐν κονίαις.

---

[1] See Köhm, *Altlat. Forsch.* p. 132. [2] *E.P.R.*[2], p. cciii n.
[3] Possibly the Greek μύζειν; cf. Leumann, in *Mélanges J. Marouzeau* (Paris, 1948), 381 f. (= *Kl. Schr.* 164 f.).

ANDROMACHA

103 quantis cum aerumnis: contrast Terence, *Hec.* 876 *ex quanta aerumna extraxeris.* The preposition *cum* rarely disjoins a noun from its preceding determinant in republican drama; I can find only Plautus, *Amph.* 245, *Asin.* 374, *Men.* 895, *Most.* 658, 977, *Persa* 54, Caecilius, *Com.* 59, Turpilius, *Com.* 168, Accius, *Trag.* 216. In the relatively few fragments of Ennius' epic on the other hand there are eight examples (51, 54, 77, 201, 338, 381, 444, 540). *Quantis* must therefore have received an unusually heavy emphasis.

illum exanclaui diem: the ironic flavour of Ennius' phrase is obscured by such parallels as Euripides, *Tr.* 433 δέκα γὰρ ἀντλήσας ἔτη, Cicero, *Carm.* fr. 22.27 *tot nos ad Troiam belli exanclabimus annos* (∼ Homer, *Il.* 2.328 ὣς ἡμεῖς τοσσαῦτ' ἔτεα πτολεμίξομεν αὖθι), Apuleius, *Met.* 6.11 *tetra nox exanclata.* In the minds of Attic theatre-goers ἀντλεῖν et sim. were associated with suffering when used metaphorically; the source of the metaphor was perhaps a nautical usage, 'draw off bilge-water'.[1] To judge by Livius, *Trag.* 30 *florem anclabant Liberi ex carchesiis, Carm.* fr. 36 *carnis uinumque quod libabant anclabatur* (∼ *Od.* 23.304–5 βόας καὶ ἴφια μῆλα | ἔσφαζον, πολλὸς δὲ πίθων ἠφύσσετο οἶνος), Plautus, *Stich.* 272–3 *ne iste edepol uinum poculo pauxillulo | saepe exanclauit submerum scitissume*[2] a non-metaphorical use of *anclare* et sim., associated with feasting and pleasure, was the one most familiar to Ennius' audience. *Anclare* may have been a word of the sacral language borrowed from some South Italian dialect of Greek.[3] If this is the case, there was a marked oxymoron perceptible to the first hearers of the words *quantis cum aerumnis illum exanclaui diem.*

XL

104–5 longinque a domo | bellum gerentes: contrast Cicero, *Manil.* 32 *fuit proprium populi Romani longe a domo bellare.* The adverb *longe* is common in republican drama and classical prose; *longinque* does not appear again after the present passage until Fronto, p. 132.2.

105 bellum . . . summum summa industria: *summa industria* and similar phrases are common; cf. Plautus, *Most.* 348 *summis opibus atque industriis,* Caesar, *Ciu.* 2.4.1, Cicero, *Brut.* 165, *Att.* 2.22.3, *Fam.* 13.10.3. *Summum bellum* must be a momentary creation for the sake of word play; Caesar and Cicero use repeatedly the phrase *magnum bellum.*

The use of the one adjective twice within the one phrase is common in

---

[1] See F. Solmsen, *Beiträge zur griechischen Wortforschung* I (Strasbourg, 1909), pp. 184 f.

[2] See also below on *v.* 144.

[3] Cf. *anclabris* in the Roman sacral language (Paulus, p. 10.18) and ἀντλητρία in the Athenian (Schol. Luc. *Dial. deor.* 2.1, p. 276.4 Rabe).

Attic tragedy (cf. Euripides, *El.* 337 and the examples collected by Denniston *ad loc.*), in Roman tragedy (cf. Ennius 128, 264, Accius 134, 206 [*quod re in summa summum esse arbitror*], 655) and the more elevated parts of Roman comedy (cf. Plautus, *Cist.* 288, 308, *Poen.* 1270, Terence, *Haut.* 4–5, *Phorm.* 587 et al.). Very frequently one of the adjectives is used either redundantly or in a fashion removed from common usage.

XLI

This fragment appears to come from a messenger's account of the funeral of Astyanax. Dead warriors were commonly carried on their shields (cf. Virgil, *Aen.* 10.506, 841) and the Andromache of Euripides' Τρῳάδες (1133 ff.) asked for Astyanax to be entombed in his father's shield; his corpse, however, was washed in the waters of the Scamander (1150 ff.).

106 locant: for the normal *collocant*. Plautus has the simple verb four times in military or para-military contexts (*Amph.* 351, *Curc.* 25, *Poen.* 612, *Rud.* 474) but elsewhere in republican Latin it is restricted to legal and financial contexts.

107 clipeo: *clypeo* would be an impossible spelling for Ennius' day. The manuscripts of Plautus have *clipeus* for the most part with an occasional *clupeus*. D at *Trin.* 719 has *clypeus*.

The *clupeus* was a circular bronze shield which covered everything from neck to calf, used according to Livy (1.43.2) by the first class of the old Servian army but long replaced by the oblong *scutum*. The adapters of both tragedy (Ennius 189, 370, Trag. inc. 62; cf. Pacuvius 186 *clupeat*) and comedy used the word to denote the Greek ἀσπίς. *Scutum* is absent from tragedy and comedy has it only in special contexts: Plautus, *Bacch.* 72 (pun); Plautus, *Trin.* 1034 and Turpilius, *Com.* 40 (moralising with reference to the interests of the spectators).

XLII

The speaker may be referring to the insincerity of public orators (cf. Euripides, *Hek.* 130 ff., 254 ff.). His metaphor is from the testing of pots for hidden cracks: cf. Plato, *Theait.* 179D διακρούοντα εἴτε ὑγιὲς εἴτε σαθρὸν φθέγγεται, Lucretius 3.870–3 *proinde ubi se uideas hominem indignarier ipsum,* | *post mortem fore ut aut putescat corpore posto* | *aut flammis interfiat malisue ferarum,* | *scire licet non sincerum sonere.*

Sonere was already restricted to tragedy and epic in the early second century. Plautus has *sonare* seven times.

ANDROMACHA

XLIII

Lipsius' alteration of the corrupt *trabem* to *trahens* seems to be generally accepted (cf. Ovid, *Met.* 11.709 *attonito gemitus a corde trahuntur* et al.). Vahlen scanned the fragment in his second edition as a trochaic pentameter. Hephaestion, 6.2, cites an example of this verse from Callimachus. There is no evidence of its existence in the extant scripts of Attic tragedy. Bentley thought he could find three examples in the comedies of Terence (*Eun.* 293, *Phorm.* 194, 485). Bergk[1] and Vahlen[2] thought they could add several examples from republican tragedy. None are convincing nor, in the state of the evidence, could they be.[3]

109 sed quasi aut ferrum aut lapis: cf. Aeschylus, *Prom.* 242 σιδηρό-φρων τε κἀκ πέτρας εἰργασμένος, Euripides, *Med.* 1279–81 τάλαιν' ὡς ἄρ' ἦσθα πέτρος ἢ σίδα|ρος, ἄτις...κτενεῖς.

110 rarenter: once elsewhere in tragedy, twice in comedy (Caecilius 135, 183); a poetic coinage, perhaps modelled on the antonym *frequenter*. *Raro* was the adverb normally used (4 times in Plautus, twice in Terence). A number of adjectives in *-us* have adverbs in *-ter* recorded fairly often in both tragedy and comedy but most such formations occur only in tragedy or at the ends of iambic and trochaic verses in Plautine (not Terentian) comedy.

XLIV

The other two pieces in Macrobius' *ueliuolus* article do not form metrical units but a strong tendency to quote such units is observable elsewhere in the discussion of Virgil's allegedly borrowed words. *Rapit ex alto naues ueliuolas* can be scanned as an anapaestic dimeter if *naues* is treated as a monosyllable (cf. Plautus, *Bacch.* 797, *Men.* 344).

111 ueliuolas: this compound occurs elsewhere at Ennius, *Ann.* 388, Laevius, fr. 11, Lucretius 5.1442, Virgil, *Aen.* 1.224, Ovid, *Pont.* 4.5.42, 4.16.21. No other compound in *-uolus* (*uolare*) seems to occur in republican or classical verse. Pliny has *altiuolus* twice (*Nat.* 10.42, 10.130). *-uolus* (*uelle*), apart from *maleuolus* and *beneuolus*, is almost as unproductive (Catullus has *multiuolus* [68.128] and *omniuolus* [68.140]). There seem to be no adjectives in -πετής (πέτομαι) in Ionic epic or Attic tragedy except ὑψιπετής.

---

[1] *Zeitschr. f. d. Alt.* 1855, 294, *Philologus* xxxiii (1874), 308 (= *Kl. phil. Schr.* I 114, 373 f.).
[2] *Ind. lectt. Berlin* 1888/9, 18 f. (= *Op. ac.* I 419 f.), *SB Berlin* 1901, 348 ff. (= *Ges. phil. Schr.* II 610 ff.), *Ind. lectt. Berlin* 1902/3, 4 ff. (= *Op. ac.* II 449 ff.).
[3] Cf. Timpanaro, *SIFC* N.S. xxi (1946), 77 ff.

261

ANDROMEDA

The title *Andromeda* is given to Livius by Nonius; to Ennius by Verrius, Nonius and Priscian; to Accius by Nonius, Macrobius (*Gramm.* v 606.38) and Priscian. Most of Nonius' quotations of the Accian *Andromeda* come from Lindsay's list 8 'Accius ii', a few from lexicographical sources. Two of his quotations of the Ennian tragedy appear to come from list 27 'Alph. verb' and two from 28 'Alph. adverb'; that at p. 20.19 heads a lemma following one illustrated by an 'Accius ii' citation and preceding lemmata illustrated from the same source; it appears to have displaced the present extra-citation, which comes from 'Accius ii' and illustrates the lemma somewhat better; one can only guess at its source.

The three sets of fragments can be interpreted so as to deal with the rescue by Perseus of Andromeda, the daughter of Cepheus and Cassiepeia, from a sea-monster. Scaliger's treatment of the text of Varro, *Ling.* 5.19 (see above on fr. xxxiii) has enforced among all students the belief that Ennius adapted the famous tragedy produced by Euripides in 412 B.C.[1] The title Ἀνδρομέδα is also recorded against the names of Lycophron, Phrynichus and Sophocles.

There is no clear evidence that any of the three Latin tragedies were known outside the ranks of the lexicographers after the second century B.C. At *Fin.* 2.105 Cicero translates himself a gnomic verse of Euripides' Ἀνδρομέδα which frequently turns up in extant Greek literature (fr. 133) and probably was quoted in his philosophical source.

Ribbeck[2] suggested that the words quoted by Festus at p. 488.23 probably as from Ennius (fr. ccvi)—*aspera saxa tesca tuor*—were spoken by Perseus when he arrived on stage and saw Andromeda chained to the rock; that the words quoted by Nonius at p. 197.3 as from Ennius (fr. ccxiii)—*et quis illaec est quae lugubri succincta est stola*—were spoken by Perseus when Andromeda's mother arrived on stage, that the words quoted by the Danieline Servius in his note on *Georg.* 1.12–13 (fr. ccxix)—*ager oppletus imbrium fremitu*—were spoken by Andromeda to Perseus, describing the floods which Poseidon had sent upon her land (Apollodorus 2.4.3.2).

Vahlen[3] set the tetrameter attributed to Ennius by Varro at *Ling.* 7.16 (fr. cxci)—*ut tibi Titanis Triuia dederit stirpem liberum*—in a plea by Andromeda to Perseus to take her away with him as his consort despite the wishes of her father.

---

[1] For Alexander's fondness for quoting this play see Athenaeus 12.537D.
[2] *Quaest. scen.* p. 261, *Die röm. Trag.* p. 165.
[3] *E.P.R.*[2], p. 138.

The content of none of the four fragments in question is specific enough to allow either acceptance or outright rejection of the modern attributions.[1]

XLV

Welcker[2] interpreted this fragment as from a speech by Andromeda when Cepheus went back on his promise (Apollodorus 2.4.3.4, Ovid, *Met.* 4.701 ff.) to give her in marriage to Perseus. The legal formulae employed by Ennius seem to me quite inappropriate in the mouth of a woman wishing to cohabit with a man against her father's will. They applied properly only to *matrimonium iustum*, not to *concubinatus*. I therefore accept Hartung's view[3] that the fragment is from the speech in which Cepheus made his original promise.

112 **liberum quaesendum causa**: Ennius' vocabulary was perhaps exactly that employed in contemporary Roman betrothals; cf. Plautus, *Capt.* 889 *liberorum quaerendorum causa ei credo uxor datast*, Varro *ap.* Macr. *Sat.* 1.16.18 *uxorem liberum quaerendorum causa ducere religiosum est*, Suetonius, *Iul.* 52, Gellius 4.3.2, 17.21.44. Parallel phraseology might have existed in Ennius' original; cf. Euripides, *Andr.* 4 δάμαρ δοθεῖσα παιδοποιὸς Ἕκτορι, *Herakleidai* 523–4, *Or.* 1080, Demosthenes 59.122 τὰς μὲν γὰρ ἑταίρας ἡδονῆς ἕνεκ᾽ ἔχομεν, τὰς δὲ παλλακὰς τῆς καθ᾽ ἡμέραν θεραπείας τοῦ σώματος, τὰς δὲ γυναῖκας τοῦ παιδοποιεῖσθαι γνησίως καὶ τῶν ἔνδον φύλακα πιστὴν ἔχειν, Menander, *Dysk.* 842–3 ἀλλ᾽ ἐγγυῶ παίδων ἐπ᾽ ἀρότῳ γνησίων | τὴν θυγατέρ᾽ ἤδη μειράκιόν σοι, *Perik.* 435–6, fr. 682.

Ennius' morphology must have had an archaic tone even in the second century. Plautus has the genitive *liberum* only once (*Most.* 120 [bacchiacs]) as against *liberorum* five times (*Capt.* 889, *Cist.* 777, *Men.* 59, *Most.* 121, *Poen.* 74). Apart from the first person singular present indicative Plautus has *quaesere* only at *Bacch.* 179 (parody of legal language; cf. 181 *uadatum amore uinctumque*).

familiae matrem tuae: cf. Gellius 18.6.8 *matronam dictum esse proprie quae in matrimonium cum uiro conuenisset, quoad in eo matrimonio maneret, etiamsi liberi nondum nati forent; dictamque ita esse a matris nomine non adepto iam sed cum spe et omine mox adipiscendi: unde ipsum quoque matrimonium dicitur; matrem autem familias appellatam esse eam solam quae in mariti manu mancipioque*

---

[1] With fr. cxci C. O. Mueller compared Euripides, *Med.* 714–15; with fr. ccxiii La Penna, *Maia* v (1952), 95, compared Aeschylus, *Choe.* 10–12 (without, however, asserting that Ennius adapted Aeschylus' play).

[2] *Die griech. Trag.* p. 661; cf. Vahlen, *E.P.R.*², p. 137.

[3] *Euripides Restitutus* II, p. 353.

esset, quoniam non in matrimonium tantum sed in familiam quoque mariti et in sui heredis locum uenisset. Comedy has the phrase *mater familias* five times in very formal contexts (Plautus, *Amph.* 831, *Merc.* 405, 415, *Stich.* 98, Terence, *Ad.* 747). It is odd that Ennius used the form *familiae* in such a context as this but *familias . . . tuae* may have sounded inelegant to second-century ears.

XLVI

This fragment describes the sea-monster; cf. Plato's description of Glaucus at *Politeia* 10.611D οἱ τὸν θαλάττιον Γλαῦκον ὁρῶντες οὐκ ἂν ἔτι ῥᾳδίως αὐτοῦ ἴδοιεν τὴν ἀρχαίαν φύσιν ὑπὸ τοῦ τά τε παλαιὰ τοῦ σώματος μέρη . . . λελωβῆσθαι ὑπὸ τῶν κυμάτων, ἄλλα δὲ προσπεφυκέναι, ὄστρεά τε καὶ φυκία καὶ πέτρας. For the second element of the description cf. Ovid, *Met.* 1.331–3 *supraque profundum | extantem atque umeros innato murice tectum | caeruleum Tritona uocat,* 4.725–7 *nunc terga cauis super obsita conchis | nunc laterum costas, nunc, qua tenuissima cauda | desinit in piscem, falcato uerberat ense.* It must come either from Andromeda's account of events leading to her enchainment or from a messenger's report of Perseus' encounter with the monster.

113 scrupeo inuestita saxo atque ostreis †quam excrabrent†: for the sound play cf. *Trag. inc.* 74 *per speluncas saxis structas asperis pendentibus,* Virgil, *Aen.* 6.471 *si dura silex aut stet Marpesia cautes*; see above on *v.* 4.

Scrupeus occurs elsewhere at Pacuvius, *Trag.* 310 and perhaps at Accius, *Trag.* 431. Plautus, *Capt.* 185, Pacuvius, *Trag.* 252, Lucretius 4.523 have *scruposus.* Neither word seems to occur in classical prose. It is an odd epithet for *saxum.* Adjectives in *-eus* indicating the material of which a thing is composed occur fairly often in both comedy and tragedy. Plautus uses the formation for comic effects (e.g. *oculeus, pugneus, stimuleus, uerbereus*) but the remains of tragedy have only one other neologism of the loose type affected by the classical dactylic poets:[1] *caeruleus* at Ennius 26.

The compound *inuestire* occurs elsewhere in Latin only at Maecenas, fr. *ap.* Sen. *Epist.* 114.5 and Seneca, *Herc. O.* 381. Comedy has *uestire* 9 times.

Scabrere seems to occur only here and at Pacuvius, *Trag.* 314. A number of similar formations occur in tragedy and are absent from comedy: e.g. *clarere, flaccere, frondere, languere, nigrere, pigrere, putrere, senere, stupere, tabere.*

XLVII

I have found no plausible explanation of this fragment.

---

[1] Cf. in contemporary epic Ennius, *Ann.* 577 *populea fruns.*

XLVIII

Ennius' trochaic tetrameter comes from a messenger's report of Perseus' encounter with the monster. For the structure and content of the sentence cf. Euripides, *I.A.* 1578–9 ἱερεὺς δὲ φάσγανον λαβὼν ἐπεύξατο, | λαιμόν τ' ἐπεσκοπεῖθ', ἵνα πλήξειεν ἄν. The Euripidean messenger used trimeters (cf. fr. 145).

115 corpus: here, properly, 'living body'; sometimes in high poetry 'cadauer' (e.g. Ennius, *Trag.* 138, Accius, *Trag.* 323, 655, 667; cf. σῶμα).

contemplatur: the active form of this verb was normally used in both tragedy and comedy. The deponent form is guaranteed by the metre here, Plautus, *Poen.* 1129, Terence, *Haut.* 617, *Phorm.* 210. It is difficult to see any semantic, stylistic or chronological pattern in the phenomena.

corporaret: 'that he might turn the beast's *corpus* into a *cadauer*'. Accius, *Trag.* 604 uses Ennius' neologism as a simple synonym for *interficere*. Words like *iugulare* (*iugulum*) and *obtruncare* (*truncus*) would have provided models. Plautus invented words in similar fashion for comic effect: cf. *Capt.* 84 *dum ruri rurant homines, Men.* 105 *domi domitus sum, Mil.* 34 *ne dentes dentiant.*

XLIX

Cf. Euripides, *Hek.* 28–9 κεῖμαι δ' ἐπ' ἀκταῖς, ἄλλοτ' ἐν πόντου σάλῳ, | πολλοῖς διαύλοις κυμάτων φορούμενος, Virgil, *Aen.* 6.362 *nunc me fluctus habet uersantque in litore uenti,* Lucan 8.698–9 *litora Pompeium feriunt truncusque uadosis* | *huc illuc iactatur aquis.* The fragment may come from the messenger's report of the encounter. If so *feram* can hardly be correct; only part of the beast would be carried back and forth by the tidal current. Bergk's *fera*[1] is ludicrous.

116 rursus prorsus: cf. Terence, *Hec.* 315 *trepidari sentio et cursari rursum prorsum.*

reciprocat: for *reciprocus* of tidal movement cf. Pliny, *Nat.* 2.213, 9.176, 16.170; for *reciprocare* cf. Cicero, *Nat. deor.* 3.24, Livy 28.6.10, Pliny, *Nat.* 2.212, 2.219 et al.

†feram†: comedy has *belua* and *bestia* often but not *fera.* Tragedy on the other hand has *fera* 7 times, *belua* twice and *bestia* not at all.

---

[1] *RhM* III (1835), 70; cf. Ribbeck, *Die röm. Trag.* p. 169 n. 191, Vahlen, *E.P.R.*[2], p. 136.

L

This fragment clearly comes from the messenger's report.

117 alia: 'reliqua'; cf. Plautus, *Amph.* 12 et al. It is difficult to see the point of the disjunction from *membra*.

differt dissupat: cf. Lucretius 1.651 *disiectis disque sipatis*, Cicero, *Leg. agr.* 1.2 *disperdat ac dissipet*, *De orat.* 1.187 *dispersa et dissipata*, *Leg.* 2.42 *distracti ac dissipati iacent*, *Nat. deor.* 2.41 *disturbat ac dissipat*, Caesar, *Gall.* 2.24.4 *diuersos dissipatosque*, 5.58.3 *dispersi ac dissipati*, Livy 2.28.3 *dispersam et dissipatam*. Contrast Accius, *Trag.* 587 *dissipent et disturbent* (text dubious). Tragedy has *dissupare* 3 times, comedy only once (Plautus, fr. 171).

118 uisceratim: 'with bits of flesh hanging'. The adverb does not occur elsewhere in Latin but is not necessarily a poetic coinage. *Guttatim* and *articulatim* are the only exactly parallel formations in tragedy. It may have belonged to the vocabulary of butchers; cf. Plautus' *assulatim* (*Capt.* 832, *Men.* 859), *frustillatim* (*Curc.* 576), *offatim* (*Truc.* 613), Caecilius' *ossiculatim* (*Com.* 50), Pomponius' *frustatim* (*Atell.* 177).

maria: a poetic plural. At Plautus, *Rud.* 1, *Trin.* 1087, Terence, *Ad.* 790 *maria* is a genuine plural. Nevertheless the context has in each case a heightened tone.

spumant sanguine: cf. Virgil, *Aen.* 6.87 *Thybrim multo spumantem sanguine cerno*, 9.456 *spumantis sanguine riuos*.

LI

These words were obviously spoken by Andromeda but it is difficult to imagine a context. Welcker put them in a speech by Andromeda trying to persuade her father to reverse his decision about Perseus, Hartung in a speech announcing her own decision to go with Perseus despite her parents' wishes. Webster[1] suggests that they are part of an apostrophe to Cassiepeia in Andromeda's prologue speech (...*crudelis mater*).

119 filiis...obiecta sum...Nerei: cf. Virgil, *Aen.* 10.88–90 *nosne tibi fluxas Phrygiae res uertere fundo* | *conamur? nos, an miseros qui Troas Achiuis* | *obiecit?* No clear distinction is made between the Nereids, their wrath, and the

---

[1] *BICSL* XII (1965), 29. Cf. Columna, *Q. Ennii Frag.* p. 410.

monster sent to avenge them. Vahlen interpreted *filiis Nerei* as *in gratiam Nereidum*, 'den Nereiden zu liebe' and compared Seneca, *Tro.* 248 *tuam natam parens Helenae immolasti.*

Plautus has *filiis* feminine at *Poen.* 1128 and *Stich.* 567. *Filiabus* occurs nowhere in republican drama.

ATHAMAS

The title *Athamas* is given eight times by Nonius to Accius[1] and once by Charisius to Ennius.[2] The five trimeters which Charisius quotes were once regarded with suspicion because of the similarity of their structure to that of imperial trimeters.[3] It is worth pointing out that Charisius quotes a large amount of indisputably republican verse in their company.

Cicero refers three times to the madness of Athamas,[4] at least once, it seems, with the theatre in mind.

It is impossible to make out with certainty the relationship of either tragedy to the saga of Athamas, his three wives and three sets of twin children.[5] Ennius' play concerned in some way the orgiastic worship of Dionysus. One of Athamas' wives, Ino, is reported to have looked after Dionysus as an infant and on another occasion to have been discovered by Athamas, after a long absence from home, consorting with bacchant women on Mount Parnassus.[6]

The title ᾿Αθάμας is recorded against the names of Aeschylus, Sophocles and Astydamas.

LII

The five trimeters must come from a messenger's speech describing a Bacchic orgy. It is interesting that males are alleged to have taken part in the orgy. The historical Boeotian orgiastic cult of Dionysus was exclusively

[1] Pp. 56.13, 315.19, 323.34, 416.13, 470.27, 488.36, 500.3, 524.21. All these quotations seem to come from Lindsay's list 8 'Accius ii'.

[2] The immediate source of pp. 312.3 ff. seems to have been the ᾿Αφορμαί of Julius Romanus.

[3] See Bothe, *P.S.L.* vol. v, p. 38, Welcker, *Die griech. Trag.* p. 1374, F. A. Lange, *Quaest. metr.* pp. 16, 30, B. Schmidt, *RhM* xvi (1861), 599. The objections of these scholars are answered by L. Mueller, *Q. Enni Reliquiae*, p. 238, and F. Skutsch, *RE* v (1905), 2619.58 ff.

[4] *Har. resp.* 39, *Pis.* 47, *Tusc.* 3.11. Cf. Apollodorus 3.4.3, Ovid, *Met.* 4.471, *Fast.* 6.484.

[5] See Robert, *Die griech. Heldensage* II i, pp. 41 ff.

[6] Cf. Hyginus, *Fab.* 4 (an account of the hypothesis of Euripides' ᾿Ινώ).

female except for the priestly leader until very late in antiquity.[1] Plautus
regarded the contemporary Italian form of the cult as a peculiarly feminine
business.[2] Such allegations of male participation as are found elsewhere in
literature (e.g. Euripides, *Ba.* 222 ff.; cf. Livy 39.8.5) are of a hearsay
character. The messenger of Euripides' Βάκχαι expressly refutes the sus-
picions of Pentheus (680 ff.).

120–1 his erat in ore Bromius, his Bacchus pater, | illis Lyaeus: for the
many names of Διόνυσος cf. Ovid, *Met.* 4.11–17 *turaque dant Bacchumque
uocant Bromiumque Lyaeumque | ignigenamque satumque iterum solumque
bimatrem; | additur his Nyseus indetonsusque Thyoneus | et cum Lenaeo genialis
consitor uuae | Nycteliusque Eleleusque parens et Iacchus et Euhan, | et quae
praeterea per Graias plurima gentes | nomina, Liber, habes,* Arrian, *Anab.* 5.2.5–7.
Attic tragedy has the names Βρόμιος (Aeschylus, *Eum.* 24 et al.) and
Βάκχος (Sophocles, *O.T.* 211 et al.); Λυαῖος however seems not to occur
before Leonidas of Tarentum (*A.P.* 6.154.1). Republican drama elsewhere
has *Bromius* (Plautus, *Men.* 835) and *Bacchus* (Plautus, *Men.* 835 [?], Pacuvius,
Trag. 310, 422) but not *Lyaeus.*

For *Bacchus pater* cf. Horace, *Carm.* 1.18.5. *Pater* was part of the cult
title of many very old Roman gods.[3] Ennius had the Roman *Liber pater*
in mind. Ζεῦ πάτερ occurs often enough in Attic drama but Βάκχε
πάτερ never.

For *erat in ore Bromius* cf. Terence, *Ad.* 93 *in orest omni populo* (sc. *Aeschinus*),
Cicero, *Rep.* 1.30 *in ore semper erat ille de Iphigenia Achilles,* *Leg.* 1.6 *ad eum,
qui tibi semper in ore est, Catonem...uenias, Tusc.* 1.116 *Harmodius in ore est et
Aristogiton,* Livy 9.10.3 *Postumius in ore erat, eum laudibus ad caelum ferebant.*

121 uitis inuentor sacrae: cf. Euripides, *Ba.* 279 βότρυος ὑγρὸν πῶμ'
ηὗρε, 378–86, 421–3, 534–5, Accius, *Trag.* 240 *Dionyse...uitisator,* Ovid,
Am. 1.3.11 *uitisque repertor.*

The noun *inuentor* occurs elsewhere in republican drama only at Terence,
Eun. 1034–5 *o Parmeno mi, o mearum uoluptatum omnium | inuentor inceptor
perfector,* a highly coloured passage. Tragedy and comedy employ such
formations freely, Plautine comedy much more freely than Terentian. Their
presence in the official language (*praetor, imperator* et al.) lent them a certain
dignity of tone.

---

[1] See M. P. Nilsson, *The Dionysiac Mysteries of the Hellenistic and Roman Age*
(Lund, 1957), pp. 14 f.
[2] Cf. *Amph.* 703, *Aul.* 408, *Bacch.* 53, *Cas.* 979–80, *Mil.* 851–6, 1016; most of
the contexts are Romanising ones.
[3] Cf. Gellius 5.12.5, Lactantius, *Diu. inst.* 4.3.11.

For *uitis...sacrae* cf. Euripides, fr. 765 οἰνάνθα τρέφει τὸν ἱερὸν βότρυν, Horace, *Carm.* 1.18.1 *nullam Vare sacra uite prius seueris arborem* (~ Alcaeus, fr. 342 Lobel and Page μηδ' ἐν ἄλλο φυτεύσῃς πρότερον δένδριον ἀμπέλω). Ennius' adjective seems to have something of the sense of ἱερός, 'supernaturally powerful' (cf. Hesiod, *Theog.* 93, Euripides, *Hipp.* 1206); it normally referred to things which already belonged to a god.

122 tum pariter †euhan euhium†: the context of Charisius' quotation demands the insertion of the cry *euhoe* (εὐοῖ; cf. Sophocles, *Tr.* 219 ἀνατα-ράσσει εὐοῖ μ' ὁ κισσός, Aristophanes, *Lys.* 1294) in some form. *Euhan* could be taken as a cry (εὐάν; cf. schol. Eur. *Phoin.* 656 γυναιξὶν εὐίοις...τὸ εὐοῖ εὐὰν ἐπιφθεγγομέναις) though elsewhere in Latin it occurs only as an epithet of the god (Lucretius 5.743, Ovid, *Met.* 4.15). *Euhium* likewise could be a cry (cf. Ovid, *Ars* 1.563 *pars clamant 'euhion euhoe'*, Persius 1.101–2 *et lyncem maenas flexura corymbis* | *'euhion' ingeminat*) as well as an epithet of the god (cf. Euripides, *Ba.* 157 εὖια τὸν εὖιον ἀγαλλόμεναι θεόν, Lucretius 5.743, Cicero, *Flacc.* 60, Horace, *Carm.* 1.18.9, 2.11.17). Vahlen understood *Euhan* ⟨'*euhoe euhoe*'⟩ *Euhium...inibat* (Fabricius' supplement) as the same type of phrase as Aristophanes' τὸν 'Αρμόδιον ᾄσεται (*Ach.* 980).[1] This leaves *pariter* an extraordinarily long way from its verb. For this reason Buecheler's supplement *euhoe cantans* is worth considering. One could keep Fabricius' supplement *euhoe euhoe* and alter *euhan* to *euhans* (εὐάζων; cf. Catullus 64.391, Virgil, *Aen.* 6.517); the cries *euhoe euhoe euhium* would then stand outside the construction of the sentence (cf. Sophocles, *Tr.* 219).

123 ignotus iuuenum coetus: there is no need to emend here. *Ignotus* is to be taken in sense with *iuuenum*. For enallage in republican tragedy see above on *v.* 57.

Ignotus can be taken as 'unknown to the speaker' (cf. Plautus, *Asin.* 494, *Capt.* 344, 542, *Rud.* 1043, 1044) or 'unknown to society at large, of low social degree' (cf. Terence, *Phorm.* 751). Dionysus was a notoriously democratic deity; cf. Euripides, *Ba.* 421–3, Aristophanes, *Batr.* 405 ff., Livy 39.8.3 *Graecus ignobilis in Etruriam primum uenit...sacrificulus et uates*, 39.17.6 *capita autem coniurationis constabat esse M. et C. Atinios de plebe Romana*; E. R. Dodds, *Euripides: Bacchae*[2] (Oxford, 1960), pp. 127 f.

Iuuenis occurs only once elsewhere in republican drama (Trag. inc. 210). Comedy has *adulescens* and *adulescentulus* commonly; neither of these words appears in tragedy. Cicero and Caesar are similarly shy of *iuuenis*.[2]

---

[1] Cf. also Demosthenes 18.260, Catullus 64.255, Juvenal 6.636, where the bacchic cry is treated as the internal object of the verb.

[2] See B. Axelson, in *Mélanges J. Marouzeau*, 7 ff.

The word perhaps belonged properly to the technical language of the military levy.

Coetus occurs only once elsewhere in republican drama: Plautus, *Amph.* 657, of a military encounter; it is common in classical Latin of an assembly of persons (often an illegal one, as opposed to a *contio* summoned by a magistrate).

123–4 alterna uice | inibat: 'the members of the male group were joining the female group one replacing another'. Cf. Manilius 1.258–9 *quae media obliquo praecingunt ordine mundum | solemque alternis uicibus per tempora portant.*

The accusative *uicem* is regular in comedy except at Plautus, *Amph.* 334, where editors follow Scaliger in altering the transmitted *uocis...uice.*

Inire is used metaphorically everywhere else in republican drama except at Trag. inc. 130.

124 alacris...insultans: cf. Cicero, *Att.* 1.16.7 *alacris exsultat improbitas in uictoria*, Livy 21.42.3 *alacer...exultans.* The adverb *alacriter* does not occur before Frontinus.

Insultare of physical movement occurs elsewhere in republican drama only at Terence, *Eun.* 285. It seems to be quite absent from classical prose. The simple verb *saltare* occurs 13 times in comedy, not at all in tragedy.

Bacchico...modo: 'Baccharum modo'. For the dance of the female bacchants cf. Sophocles, *Ant.* 1150–4, Euripides, *Ba.* 166–9, 748, 862–72, 1090–1, fr. 752.

CRESPHONTES

The title *Cresphontes* is given to Ennius six times, once by Macrobius, once by Gellius, twice by Verrius and twice by Nonius. Five of the fragments quoted illustrate verbs strange to classical Latin either in their form or in their usage. The sixth is alleged by Macrobius to come from a speech on which Virgil modelled that of the mother of Euryalus at *Aen.* 9.481–97. The author of the rhetorical treatise addressed to Herennius quotes a dialogue in trimeters between the wife of a Cresphontes and her father and an appeal by the Cresphontes (so one part of the tradition) of a play by Ennius for peace and reconciliation. Cicero gives no sign that he knew any Latin tragedy about a Cresphontes; at *Tusc.* 1.115 he translates himself some trimeters from Euripides' Κρεσφόντης (fr. 449) which he found in his source.[1]

---

[1] Probably Crantor. The trimeters are quoted frequently in Greek philosophical writing.

CRESPHONTES

In the stories connected with heroic Messenia two persons appear bearing the name Cresphontes, one the Heraclid who gained the kingdom by deceit in the famous lottery, the other his son whose recovery of the kingdom from the usurper Polyphontes provided the theme of Euripides' tragedy Κρεσφόντης.[1] This play was admired by Aristotle[2] and still had readers in the third century A.D.[3] The only clear reference to a tragic presentation of the elder Cresphontes seems to be at Ammianus Marcellinus 28.4.27.

Most students have interpreted the Latin remains as belonging to a version of Euripides' Κρεσφόντης.[4] Ribbeck[5] and L. Mueller[6] on the other hand reconstructed Ennius' play to deal with the elder Cresphontes.

Three fragments cause difficulty for the orthodox view. Two are textually insecure but the third seems to me to be quite unambiguous and fatal to this view.

Fragment LVIII was seen by Columna to refer to the lottery for Messenia, the richest part of Hercules' domain; cf. Sophocles, Ai. 1285–6, Euripides, fr. 1083 (Strabo 8.366), Plautus, Cas. 398–9, Apollodorus 2.8.4, Pausanias 4.3.5. The transmitted text, an inter se sortiunt urbem atque agros, suggests that the lottery took place during the very action of Ennius' play. Hartung[7] put the fragment in a separate play from the others. Other scholars have either emended an or referred the fragment to something else. The words transmitted are metrically defective and there may be something wrong with an.

It is difficult to see in what context the younger Cresphontes could make the appeal for peace and reconciliation quoted by the anonymous rhetorician at Her. 2.39 (fr. CLXII). Wecklein accordingly proposed that the hitherto received text Chresphontem Ennius induxit should be rejected in favour of either Polyphontem Ennius induxit or Thesprotum Ennius induxit. The latter is in fact the reading of the better class of manuscripts and the verses can be accommodated quite well in Ennius' Thyestes; see below, pp. 416 f.

---

[1] Apollodorus 2.8.5 and Pausanias 4.3.8 make his name Aepytus, Hyginus, Fab. 137 Telephontes. From Schol. Arist. Eth. Nic. 3.2.1111a12 and Epigr. Cyzic. A.P. 3.5 it is plain that Euripides gave him his father's name. See Robert, Die griech. Heldensage II ii, pp. 671 ff.

[2] Cf. Poet. 14.1454a5.

[3] See Pap. Oxy. 2458 (Part XXVII [London, 1962], pp. 73 ff.), Mette, Hermes XCII (1964), 391 ff. For the possibility that this comes from an actor's text see Turner, AC XXXII (1963), 120 ff.

[4] Columna, Q. Ennii Frag. p. 398, L. C. Valckenaer, Diatribe in Euripidis Dramatum Reliquias (Leiden, 1767), pp. 181 ff., Welcker, Die griech. Trag. pp. 828 ff., Hartung, Euripides Restitutus II, pp. 47 ff., Wilamowitz, Anal. Eur. p. 154, N. Wecklein, in Festschrift für L. Urlichs (Würzburg, 1880), 1 ff., Vahlen, Ind. lectt. Berlin 1888/9, 16 ff. (= Op. Ac. I 417 ff.).

[5] Quaest. scen. pp. 266 f., Die röm. Trag. pp. 186 ff.

[6] Enn. Rel. pp. 238 f.   [7] See Euripides Restitutus II, pp. 39 ff.

Fragment LIII consists of a dialogue between two persons who can only be Cypselus the king of the Arcadians and Merope his daughter, married at the moment of speaking to the elder Cresphontes.[1] Neither Columna nor Valckenaer tried to explain how this could be fitted into what they knew the action of Euripides' Κρεσφόντης to be. Hartung put it into his postulated second play. Welcker altered the transmitted reading *Chresphontem* to *Polyphontem* and proposed the following dramatic situation: on hearing about the price put on the head of his grandson (Hyginus, *Fab.* 137.2) Cypselus came to Messenia to remove his daughter from the house of Polyphontes; Merope in the meantime had recognised the younger Cresphontes and, in concert with him, pretended to be reconciled with Polyphontes; accordingly she had to resist her father if the plans for vengeance against Polyphontes were to succeed. Bergk[2] approved the alteration *Polyphontes* and offered a somewhat less incredible context: Cypselus had learnt of a rebellion brewing against Polyphontes and tried to persuade Merope to return home by revealing to her that Polyphontes had murdered her first husband Cresphontes, a fact of which, up until then, she had been ignorant. Wilamowitz[3] and Wecklein[4] avoided the need to provide a context by proposing the names *Ctesiphontem* and *Deiphontem* respectively as substitutes for *Cresphontem*. Wecklein's arguments persuaded Vahlen to remove the trimeters in question from his second edition of Ennius' remains.

Marx has seemed to many to dispose of the whole problem by treating the trimeters as the product of the rhetorical schools rather than the theatre. In his first edition of the anonymous treatise[5] he complained of their frigidity and the hiatus in *nam si improbum esse Cresphontem existimas*. In his second edition[6] he alleged significance in the fact that *existimare* occurs nowhere else in republican tragedy and is absent from the high genres of classical poetry. Marx's argument persuaded Ribbeck to expel the trimeters from his third edition of the remains of tragedy.

As to the alleged frigidity of the trimeters two opinions are possible; according to Columna: 'Enniana haec uerba nuda puraque sunt, ueterisque Romani sermonis candorem et elegantiam prae se ferunt.' Hiatus before the final diiambus is presented fairly often by the tradition of early second century iambic and trochaic verses, much less often by the tradition of those composed towards the time at which Marx's hypothetical rhetorician would have been operating. A considerable number of words absent from classical poetry, including the tragedies of Seneca, occur in the remains of republican

---

[1] Cf. Pausanias 8.5.6.

[2] *RhM* XXXV (1880), 244 ff.   [3] *Anal. Eur.* p. 154 n. 5.

[4] *Philologus* XXXIX (1880), 409, *Festschr. Urlichs*, 3 f. Wecklein appears to withdraw at *SB München* 1888, 117 and to return at *BPhW* XXXV (1915), 385.

[5] Leipzig, 1894, *Prolegomena*, p. 132.   [6] Leipzig, 1923, p. 58.

tragedy. Marx's case against the trimeters is obviously a flimsy one. On the other hand a good positive case can be made out in favour of their dramatic origin.

Along with the controversial trimeters there are quoted in the discussion of *uitiosae argumentationes* at 2.31–46 trimeters from the *Medea* of Ennius, trimeters from the *Trinummus* of Plautus, trochaic tetrameters from a tragedy by Pacuvius concerning Orestes, a tetrameter given by Ribbeck to tragedy (Trag. inc. 162) but possibly from comedy, two tetrameters from a tragedy by Ennius, three trimeters on a tragic theme (Trag. inc. 186–8), six trimeters spoken by an Ajax (Trag. inc. 49–54), and five trimeters given by Ribbeck to tragedy (Trag. inc. 177–81) but again possibly from comedy. An argument from Pacuvius' *Antiopa* is described. Among the *argumentationes* which Cicero refutes in his youthful rhetorical treatise *De inuentione* at 1.78–96 are five of the pieces of verse quoted in the anonymous treatise. The argument which the anonymous treatise attributes to Pacuvius' *Antiopa* is attributed to the Euripidean tragedy.[1] Hypothetical arguments quoted by the anonymous treatise without names (2.46) are referred by Cicero to Orestes and Ulysses (1.92). Cicero also quotes an argument mentioning the treachery of Eriphyle[2] which does not appear at all in the anonymous treatise. There can be no reasonable doubt that behind the two treatises, here as elsewhere, lies a common Latin source and behind this Latin source a Greek treatise which drew examples from the theatre as well as the assembly and the law court.[3] For direct quotation of drama the Latin source substituted quotations of Latin drama, the indirect quotations it merely translated. There is no evidence that our archetypal rhetorician made verse translations himself; the verses quoted at *Her.* 2.34 and 2.38 belong to a special category. Since Cicero does not quote or refer to the verses about Cresphontes[4] it is not certain whether they stood in the common source or were adduced by the author of the anonymous treatise from his own knowledge of the Latin theatre.[5] Marx's theory would demand that in the original Greek treatise there stood Greek verses saying the same things about Cresphontes as are said by the Latin trimeters in question. But while the remains of Greek rhetorical and philosophical writing quote with remarkable frequency the Κρεσφόντης

---

[1] *Item apud Pacuuium* at *Inu.* 1.94 is to be deleted as a harmonising gloss.

[2] 1.94. Valckenaer argued, *Diatribe*, p. 151, that we have here a direct quotation of tragedy (cf. Trag. inc. 143–4).

[3] Cf. Matthes, *Lustrum* III (1958), 81 ff.

[4] Cicero's language at 1.83 is like that of the anonymous treatise at 2.38 but his example is the one used by the anonymous treatise at 2.42 to illustrate a slightly different type of argument.

[5] The reference to Pacuvius at 2.43 must be his own; contrast Cicero 1.94.

of Euripides they contain nothing about any other tragic Cresphontes.[1] Evidence for free composition in verse on tragic themes in Greek rhetorical schools is scanty. It is difficult to believe that the practice went on in Latin schools of the Republican period. Common sense requires that the verses be treated as of the same character as the others providing examples of faulty argument at *Her.* 2.31–46; i.e. as coming ultimately from the Latin theatre, either from the writer's source or from his own knowledge.

If the verses belong to Ennius, attempts to reconstruct the Κρεσφόντης of Euripides with the fragments of Ennius' *Cresphontes* and *vice versa* must cease. There is no room for a discussion of the younger Cresphontes' virtues as a husband in the plot-structure of the Euripidean tragedy. Ribbeck's view that the Latin tragedy dealt with the overthrow of the elder Cresphontes must be reinstated.

LIII

Stephanus, Columna and Scriverius print all the poetic matter quoted, except the repeated *nam si improbum esse Cresphontem existimas cur me huic locabas nuptiis*, as the words of Ennius. Bothe excludes only the repeated *nam si improbum esse Cresphontem existimas*. Delrius[2] and L. Mueller exclude all the repeated matter and *duxi probum, erraui, post cognoui et fugio cognitum* as being the work of a rhetorician. The pre-Marx Ribbeck excludes the repeated matter and *nulla...incommodis*. The only course still untried is to exclude both replies to the argument of Cresphontes' wife. Something could be said in favour of every course. I have followed Delrius but think it possible that the rhetorician extracted *duxi probum, erraui, post cognoui et fugio cognitum* from a following speech and glued it to part of the speech of Cresphontes' wife already quoted so as to provide an illustration of a second method of answering the ἔλεγχος ἀναγκαῖον κατὰ δίλημμα. At 2.34 the trimeter *utinam ne era errans mea domo efferret pedem* is botched together from different parts of a tragic speech.

There are parallel situations in Menander's Ἐπιτρέποντες (510 ff.), in a fourth-century play whose character is disputed[3] and in Plautus' adaptation of Menander's Ἀδελφοὶ β', the *Stichus* (15 ff.). Behind the two Latin arguments lies the assumption that the woman's father had full legal power to

---

[1] It is significant that the 'non-dramatic' pieces of tragic verse in Cicero's philosophical writings are all translations of pieces frequently quoted in the remains of Greek philosophical writing.

[2] *Syntagma Tragoediae Latinae* (Antwerp, 1593) I, p. 164.

[3] Euripides fr. 953 = Menander I, p. 143 Körte = Anon. p. 180 Page (*G.L.P.*). See most recently W. Bühler, *Hermes* XCI (1963), 345 ff.

dissolve the marriage against her will.[1] The Greek arguments leave it quite unclear whether the father imagined he could use anything but persuasion or brute force. It is possible that the conditions of Roman society influenced the way Plautus and Ennius adapted their Attic originals. The Twelve Tables recognised a form of marriage *sine manu*[2] and such marriages could be legally dissolved by the woman's father until the time of Pius or Marcus.[3] Only one kind of marriage is known at Athens and it is doubtful whether the father could interfere against the expressed will of his daughter.[4]

For the type of argument employed by Cresphontes' wife cf. Euripides, *El.* 1015–17 τὸ πρᾶγμα δὲ | μαθόντας, ἢν μὲν ἀξίως μισεῖν ἔχῃς, | στυγεῖν δίκαιον· εἰ δὲ μή, τί δεῖ στυγεῖν;, *I.A.* 1034–5, *Hyps. ap.* Lydum, *De mens.* 4.7 (p. 48 Bond), Trag. Lat. inc. 178–80, Terence, *Hec.* 558–9.

For the content of the argument cf. Plautus, *Stich.* 130–1 *nam aut olim, nisi tibi placebant, non datas oportuit,* | *aut nunc non aequum est abduci pater illisce absentibus.*

125 iniuria abs te adficior indigna: cf. Terence, *Phorm.* 730 *uereor era ne ob meum suasum indigna iniuria adficiatur* (from a highly emotional speech). *Aliquem iniuria adficere* does not occur elsewhere in comedy. The legalism *alicui iniuriam facere* (cf. Lex XII tab. 8.4) is frequently used both properly and metaphorically (cf. Plautus, *Stich.* 12–16 *patrem tuom meumque adeo...* *uiris qui tantas absentibus nostris facit iniurias inmerito*).

pater: the simple vocative is regular in both comedy and tragedy; *mi pater* or *pater mi* would indicate a warmth evidently lacking here. See Köhm, *Altlat. Forsch.* pp. 179 ff.

126–7 si improbum esse Cresphontem existimas, | **cur me huic locabas nuptiis?:** 'If you really think Cresphontes is a bad man, tell me why you tried to make him my husband.' For the unusual arrangement of tenses in the conditional sentence cf. Plautus, *Asin.* 452 *sed si domi est,*

---

[1] The suspected verses *Stich.* 53–4, *uerum postremo in patris potestate est situm:* | *faciendum id nobis quod parentes imperant,* make the assumption quite explicitly. It is implicit in 15 f., 69, 128.

[2] Gaius 1.111.

[3] See H. F. Jolowicz, *Historical Introduction to the Study of Roman Law,* ed. 2 (Cambridge, 1952), pp. 242 ff., 561 f.

[4] The authorities differ. See J. H. Lipsius, *Das attische Recht und Rechtsverfahren* II ii (Leipzig, 1912), pp. 483 f., E. Levy, in *Gedächtnisschrift für E. Seckel* (Berlin, 1927), 154, R. Taubenschlag, *ZSavSt* XLVI, *Rom. Abt.* (1926), 74 ff., U. E. Paoli, *Aegyptus* XXXII (1952), 284. The passage of Demosthenes always quoted (41.3) says nothing about the woman's attitude.

Demaenetum uolebam, Terence, *Phorm.* 1023 *iam tum erat senex, senectus si uerecundos facit.*

Verse 126 as transmitted is metrically odd in two ways. There are few clear examples in Ennius' iambic and trochaic verses of the pure element of the metron being occupied by a long penultimate syllable and none of hiatus before the final diiambus. Both phenomena are rare in the tradition of early comedy but sufficient to deter all but the most extreme analogists among emenders; they are very much rarer in that of later comedy.[1] The only elegant emendation of the verse in question so far offered is Wilamowitz's *nam si inprobum esse Ctesiphontem existimas.* However Wilamowitz's motives were base and the rationale of the corruption is hard to explain. I leave the transmitted verse in the company of, on the one hand, 178 *necasset quo quis cruciatu* (Iunius: *necassat quos quis cruciatur* codd.) *perbiteret*, 280 *palam muttire plebeio piaculum est*, 388 *plebes in hoc regi antestat loco licet*, Pacuvius 278 *aetatem adiungas cruciatum reticentia*, Trag. inc. 17 *omnis aequalis uincebat quinquertio*, and, on the other, Pacuvius 5 *ita saeptuose dictio abs te datur*, 248 *pariter te esse erga illum uideo ut illum te* (*ted* Vossius) *erga scio*, Accius 301 *eloquere propere* (Iunius: *proprie* codd.) *ac pauorem hunc meum expectora.*

For *me huic locabas nuptiis* cf. Quintilian, *Decl.* 247, p. 10.14 *uxor est quae femina uiro nuptiis collocata in societatem uitae uenit.* Plautus, *Aul.* 192, 228, Terence, *Phorm.* 646 have *aliquam locare*; Plautus, *Trin.* 159 *collocare*; Terence, *Phorm.* 752 *nuptum locare*; Plautus, *Trin.* 735 *nuptum collocare*; Plautus, *Trin.* 782 *in matrimonium locare.* Ennius must be the one varying the regular legal phraseology.

128 inuitam inuitum: for the polyptoton cf. Aeschylus, *Hik.* 227–8 πῶς δ' ἂν γαμῶν ἄκουσαν ἄκοντος πάρα | ἁγνὸς γένοιτ' ἄν;, *Prom.* 19, 671, Euripides, *Hipp.* 319, Seneca, *Clem.* 2.1.2 *inuitus inuito cum... protulisset traderetque*, Suetonius, *Tit.* 7.2 *Berenicen statim ab urbe dimisit inuitus inuitam.*

linquere: the simple verb occurs six times in tragedy, *relinquere* only three. In comedy on the other hand *relinquere* is extremely common while *linquere* occurs only four times (in paratragic contexts: Plautus, *Asin.* 280, *Capt.* 282, *Cist.* 643, *Pseud.* 141).

---

[1] For the 'Dipody Law' see J. Draheim, *Hermes* xv (1880), 238 ff., W. Meyer, *Abh. Bayer. Ak.* xvii (1886), 36 ff., R. Klotz, *Grundzüge*, p. 315, F. W. Hall, *CQ* xv (1921), 99 ff. For the 'Locus Jacobsohnianus' see A. Luchs, in G. Studemund, *Studia in Priscos Scriptores Latinos* i (Berlin, 1873), 22 ff., R. Klotz, *Grundzüge*, pp. 132 ff., H. Jacobsohn, *Quaestiones Plautinae Metricae et Grammaticae* (Diss. Göttingen, 1904), pp. 2 ff., 26 ff., A. Klotz, *Hermes* ix (1925), 328 ff.

129 nata: vocative *gnata* occurs seven times in comedy as against *filia* four. There is nothing peculiarly tragic about Ennius' language here. Outside the vocative *gnata* does have a markedly lofty tone. It occurs 7 times in tragedy as against *filia* 4; in comedy 54 as against 183.

Mea gnata is the regular phrase. Simple *gnata* must indicate considerable lack of warmth (cf. Plautus, *Trin.* 1).

130 si probus est, collocaui: 'if as you say he is a good man, I will not alter the arrangement I made'. The tense of *collocaui* in contrast with that of *locabas* in *v.* 127 and the addition of the prefix indicate the completeness and fixity of the arrangement.

131 diuortio: the technical legal term (cf. Paulus, *Dig.* 50.16.191) for the dissolution of a marriage; it is used thus three times in comedy (Plautus, *Aul.* 233, *Mil.* 1167, *Stich.* 204).

incommodis: for the substantive plural cf. Terence, *Andr.* 627, *Haut.* 932, *Hec.* 165, 840, *Phorm.* 248 (Donatus remarks: *nimis comice non clades aut aerumnas posuit*), Accius, *Trag.* 350. Plautus has only the singular (*Amph.* 636, *Capt.* 146, *Merc.* 773, *Most.* 418).

LIV

Ribbeck made two suggestions about the context of this verse: first that it was spoken by Merope to her father after he had proposed the second marriage for her (cf. fr. LIII), the second that it was spoken to Polyphontes after the murder (cf. fr. LIX). The metre counts somewhat against the first suggestion. The verse could come from a prologue speech; the republican poets did not always use trimeters for these. If the play is about the younger Cresphontes a number of contexts are imaginable.

132 ducit me uxorem: doubtlessly legal phraseology; cf. Plautus, *Aul.* 170, *Cas.* 69, 107, 322 et al.

liberorum sibi quaesendum gratia: more legal phraseology; see above on *v.* 112.

Gratia modifies the legalistic tone; with the genitive, *mea* etc., *ea* etc., *gratia* seems to have had a loftier tone than *causa*; in tragedy the ratio of occurrence is 5:3, in comedy 50:142.

LV

Ribbeck took this verse as spoken by Merope to her father in the scene of the quarrel (cf. fr. LIII); Wecklein as spoken by the younger Cresphontes claiming the reward from Polyphontes for 'Cresphontes'' death (Hyginus, *Fab.* 137.3).

277

133 audi atque auditis: this kind of epanalepsis is comparatively uncommon in republican drama (cf. however Plautus, *Amph.* 278, *Aul.* 365–6, *Trin.* 127, *Truc.* 490, Terence, *Andr.* 298, *Eun.* 1057, Accius, *Trag.* 365 *sistis pelli, pulsum patimini*). It probably had a stylistic weight lacking in its Attic equivalent. The wealth of participles available to them allowed the Attic dramatists to employ it frequently (cf. Euripides, *Hik.* 743, *Hipp.* 313 et al.).

hostimentum: only here and Plautus, *Asin.* 172 (*par pari datum hostimentumst, opera pro pecunia*): *hostire* is equally rare, occurring only at Ennius, *Trag.* 149, Pacuvius, *Trag.* 346, Plautus, *Asin.* 377, Laevius, fr. 1; likewise *redhostire* (Naevius, *Praet.* 6, Accius, *Trag.* 92, *Didasc.* fr. 10). *Hostimentum* is unlikely to be a poetic coinage; Ploen finds only three formations in -*mentum* in tragedy as against 52 in comedy.

adiungito: to judge by Plautine usage the so-called future imperative form in -*to* had a highly formal tone even in the early second century; the material is collected by O. Riemann, *RPh* x (1886), 161 ff.

LVI

Ribbeck made two suggestions about the context of this fragment: first that it was spoken by Polyphontes in reply to someone advising him not to kill the elder Cresphontes; second that it was spoken by Cresphontes in reply to Merope warning him to be careful of his enemies. Welcker compared the verses of Euripides' Κρεσφόντης quoted at Schol. Eur. *Med.* 85: ἐκεῖνο γὰρ πέπονθ' ὅπερ πάντες βροτοί · | φιλῶν μάλιστ' ἐμαυτὸν οὐκ αἰσχύνομαι (fr. 452) and put it in a speech by Polyphontes defending his actions to Merope. The tense of *deprecer* excludes this interpretation. Vahlen made the speaker the younger Cresphontes replying to a plea by Merope to spare the life of Polyphontes.

The sentiment expressed must have been commonplace; cf. Seneca, *Thy.* 324–5 *male agis; recedis, anime; si parcis tuis | parces et illis*, Plautus, *Asin.* 177 *quae amanti parcet eadem sibi parcet parum.*

134 ego meae cum uitae parcam: the conjunction *cum* here seems to have a conditional force; cf. Plautus, *Capt.* 892 *dubium habebis etiam sancte quom ego iurem tibi*, Tibullus 2.3.5–6 *o ego cum aspicerem dominam quam fortiter illic | uersarem...solum.*

letum inimico deprecer: for the sake of concinnity Ennius avoids what must have been the normal construction, *deprecari ab*+abl.

For *mortem deprecari* cf. Cicero, *Verr.* 5.125, Caesar, *Gall.* 7.40.6, Sallust, *Iug.* 24.10, Ovid, *Fast.* 2.103, *Pont.* 1.2.57. For the poetic word *letum* see above on fr. xxxiv.

LVII

Hartung interpreted these words as coming from a messenger's speech describing the sacrifice at which the younger Cresphontes slew Polyphontes (cf. Hyginus, *Fab.* 137.6). Ribbeck accepted this interpretation and extended the plot of the tragedy accordingly. Vahlen (reading *o pietas, eam* [~ *ire*] *secum aduocant*. . .) took them as from a speech by Merope complaining of how she was not allowed to prepare the corpses of her husband and sons for burial (cf. fr. LIX). L. Mueller referred them to an account of Polyphontes and his fellow conspirators purifying themselves after the murder of the elder Cresphontes.

136 nitidant: only here and Accius, *Trag.* 602 in republican drama; from elsewhere in Latin the dictionaries quote only the agricultural writers Columella and Palladius; probably, therefore, a poetic neologism.

LVIII

For the context of this fragment see above, p. 271.

137 inter se sortiunt urbem atque agros: 'they draw lots to see who of themselves should have the state'. Probably the regular early second century usage; cf. Plautus, *Cas.* 395, 413. *Sortiri* meant 'to have lots drawn' (Plautus, *Cas.* 298, 342, *Merc.* 136*b*).

The phrase *urbem atque agros* would have recalled the official language: cf. Plautus, *Amph.* 226 *urbem agrum aras focos seque uti dederent*, Livy 1.38.2 et al.

LIX

The speaker must be Merope, the corpses mentioned those of the elder Cresphontes and two of her three children. The time of speaking may just as likely be straight after the murder as some years later.

Macrobius, or his source, ought to have provided more of the speech of Euryalus' mother: e.g. from *Aen.* 9.483: *nec te sub tanta pericula missum* | *adfari extremum miserae data copia matri?* | *heu terra ignota canibus data praeda Latinis* | *alitibusque iaces. nec te, tua funera, mater* | *produxi pressiue oculos aut uulnera laui,* | *ueste tegens tibi quam noctes festina diesque* | *urgebam et tela curas solabar anilis.* | *quo sequar? aut quae nunc artus auolsaque membra* | *et funus lacerum tellus habet?* It is not certain that this is modelled on the piece of Ennius' *Cresphontes* quoted. Laments at not being able to give the due rites to one's next of kin must have been common in republican tragedy; cf., in Attic, Sophocles, *Ant.* 21–30, *El.* 865–70, 1138–40, Euripides, *Hik.* 51–3. Certainly both Ennius and Virgil reverse the chronological order of events. But such

COMMENTARY

ὕστερον πρότερον is frequent in the *Aeneid*,[1] Attic tragedy, and the republican adaptations. It may even have been a particular feature of funeral descriptions; cf. Euripides, *Herakles* 1360–1 δὸς τούσδε τύμβῳ καὶ περίστειλον νεκροὺς | δακρύοισι τιμῶν.

The text transmitted is obviously unmetrical and its Latinity has been suspected. By changing the order *mihi corpora* to *corpora mihi* Bothe produced two iambic tetrameters. Scholars have been further worried by the very bold personification *miserae lacrimae*[2] and the departure from the common arrangement of words *lacrimis lauere*.[3] Hence Buecheler's *mihi licuit neque meae lauere lacrimae*, Usener's *mihi licuit nec miserai lauere lacrimis*, Ribbeck's *mihi licuit miserae, neque lauere lacrimae salsae*, O. Skutsch's *licuit neque miserae lauere lacrimae ⟨latice⟩ salsum sanguinem* (deleting *mihi* altogether).[4] In a genre which can produce the phrases *superstitiosis hariolationibus* and *curis suspirantibus* (see above on *v.* 33) one ought not to be worried by *miserae lacrimae*. The phrase *lauere lacrimae* is no bolder than *aures aucupant* (Ennius, *Trag.* 245) or *oculi uescuntur* (Accius, *Trag.* 189).

138 terram inicere: cf. Virgil, *Aen.* 6.365–6 *aut tu mihi terram | inice.* Ennius and Virgil import into the Greek heroic world the culminating act of the Roman funerary ritual, varying slightly the traditional phraseology; cf. Cicero, *Leg.* 2.57 *nec tamen eorum ante sepulchrum est, quam iusta facta et porcus caesus est. et quod nunc communiter in omnibus sepultis uenit usu, ut humati dicantur, id erat proprium tum in iis, quos humus iniecta contexerat, eumque morem ius pontificale confirmat; nam prius quam in os iniecta gleba est, locus ille, ubi crematum est corpus, nihil habet religionis; iniecta gleba †tum et illis† humatus est, et gleba uocatur, ac tum denique multa religiosa iura conplectitur,* Varro, *Ling.* 5.23, Paulus, p. 250.11 s.v. PRAECIDANEA.

cruenta conuestire corpora: the adjective *cruenta* could be corrupt; the blood was usually washed from corpses before they were dressed; cf. Homer, *Il.* 18.343 ff., Euripides, *Alk.* 158 ff., *Hik.* 765 ff.

---

[1] See Norden, *Aen. VI*², p. 379.

[2] *T.L.L.* VIII 1103.4 can offer no parallel; contrast Terence, *Hec.* 379 *lacrumans misera*, 385 *lacrumem miser*.

[3] Ennius, *Trag.* 276, Plautus, *Pseud.* 10, Afranius, *Com. tog.* 322, Accius, *Trag.* 420, Ovid, *Ars* 3.744, *Met.* 9.680. Accius, *Trag.* 578 makes a slight variation: *salsis cruorem guttis lacrimarum lauit.*

[4] The apparatus of Willis *ad* Macr. *Sat.* 6.2.21 is misleading. Skutsch refers me to such expressions as Euripides, *I.T.* 228 οἰκτρόν τ' ἐκβαλόντων δάκρυον, *Hik.* 96 et al. for the number and attribute of *lacruma* and points out the parallelism of the two infinitives *conuestire* and *lauere* and the two sets of triple alliteration arising from his emendation. See now *HSCPh* LXXI (1967), 135.

The compound verb *conuestire* occurs elsewhere in republican drama only at Trag. inc. 137. Comedy has the simple *uestire* nine times. Ennius formed the compound here for the sake of the triple alliteration. Other rare formations with *con-* in tragedy are *commiserescere* (Ennius 162, Pacuvius 391,Trag. inc. 246), *configere* (Accius 539), *conseruare* (Pacuvius 189), *consepire* (Ennius 252), *contegere* (Accius 540), *contremere* (Pacuvius 413), *conuisere* (Accius 598). Plautus seems to have produced them freely for comic and rhythmical purposes.[1]

139 miserae lauere lacrimae salsum sanguinem: the epithet *salsum*, from a subjective point of view, would fit *lacrimae* better than *sanguinem*.[2] Ennius and other republican tragedians preferred the effect of alliteration; cf. Accius, *Trag.* 322, Trag. inc. 77.

Lacrima was an old borrowing from Greek which drove the inherited word out of the ordinary language; the alliterative phrase *lacrimis lauere* looks like a creation of the dramatic poets; the only thing parallel in Attic tragedy which I can find is Euripides, *Herakles* 480–2 μεταβαλοῦσα δ᾽ ἡ τύχη | νύμφας μὲν ὑμῖν Κῆρας ἀντέδωκ᾽ ἔχειν, | ἐμοὶ δὲ δάκρυα λουτρὰ δυστήνοις φέρειν (Bothe: δύστηνος φρενῶν codd.).

Emotion rather than strict regard for chronology controls the order of events in Merope's discourse; cf. Plautus, *Men.* 509–10 *neque ego Erotio* | *dedi nec pallam surrupui*, Terence, *Haut.* 779 *illi neque do neque despondeo*. Comparatively speaking, tragedy describes events ὕστερον πρότερον quite often: e.g. Ennius 148 *id ego aecum ac iustum fecisse expedibo atque eloquar*, 249 *hoc ego tibi dico et coniectura auguro*, Pacuvius 91 *omnia animat format alit auget creat*, Trag. inc. 148 *uis quae summas frangit infirmatque opes*. The Latin poets could have been introducing artificialities from their Attic originals (cf. Euripides, *El.* 160 ff., *Hik.* 918 ff., *Ion* 154 f., *Or.* 814 f.) but the frequency of the phenomenon in comedy (add to the above quoted cases Plautus, *Cist.* 675, *Men.* 643, *Mil.* 773, *Pseud.* 133, 283, *Rud.* 996) suggests that ordinary Romans sometimes spoke in this way in their more excited moments.

ERECTHEVS

Gellius and Macrobius give the title *Erectheus* to Ennius. The pieces quoted could come ultimately from the dictionary of Verrius Flaccus. Festus quotes an *Erectheus* and the name of Ennius as the author may be restored in the defective manuscript. Nonius' one quotation comes from Gellius.[3]

---

[1] See Lorenz, *Plautus: Pseudolus* (Berlin, 1876), p. 38.
[2] Cf. Bentley, *Emendationes*, in J. Davies, *Cicero: Tusculanae Disputationes* (Cambridge, 1709), p. 8.
[3] See W. M. Lindsay, *Nonius Marcellus' Dictionary*, p. 69.

COMMENTARY

Euripides produced a tragedy Ἐρεχθεύς concerning the siege of Athens by Eumolpus and a Thracian army and the sacrifice of the eldest daughter of Erechtheus and Praxithea on the orders of the Delphic oracle.[1]

Cicero refers three times to the legend (*Sest.* 48, *Fin.* 5.62, *Tusc.* 1.116) without giving any sign that he knew a dramatic treatment of it.

Ribbeck assumed with Columna that Ennius adapted the Euripidean tragedy and assigned[2] a number of pieces of verse quoted with the name of Ennius to the *Erectheus*; that quoted by Varro at *Ling.* 5.14 (fr. CLXXXVI) to an apostrophe by Eumolpus to the land of Thrace; those quoted by Festus at p. 110.16 (fr. CCI) and p. 388.25 (fr. CCIV) to a patriotic speech by Cthonia, the princess who was to be sacrificed; that quoted by the Danieline Servius on *Aen.* 2.62 (fr. CCXXII) to a speech by Praxithea consenting to the sacrifice. Unnecessary violence has to be done to the transmitted text of frs. CLXXXVI and CCXXII to make them fit the plot of the Ἐρεχθεύς.[3] Frs. CCI and CCIV could belong to any of several plays.

LX

140 quos non miseret neminis: for the double negative cf. Plautus, *Mil.* 1411 *iura te non nociturum...nemini*, Lucilius 551 *proprium uero nil neminem habere*. A certain degree of emotion is indicated in the speaker.

Neminis occurs only here and at Plautus, *Capt.* 764–5 in republican drama. The desire for word play dictates Plautus' *neminis* | *miserere certum est, quia mei miseret neminem.*

LXI

The speaker is Praxithea. Columna compared Euripides, fr. 360.50–2 χρῆσθ᾽ ὦ πολῖται τοῖς ἐμοῖς λοχεύμασιν, | σῴζεσθε, νικᾶτ᾽· ἀντὶ γὰρ ψυχῆς μιᾶς | οὐκ ἔσθ᾽ ὅπως οὐ τήνδ᾽ ἐγὼ σώσω πόλιν. Ennius' language must have recalled the cant of contemporary politicians: cf. Cato, *Or.* fr. 164 Malcovati...*ne sub solo imperio nostro in seruitute nostra essent. libertatis suae causa in ea sententia fuisse arbitror*, Cicero, *Pis.* 15 *caedem illi ciuium, uos seruitutem expetistis. hic uos etiam crudeliores: huic enim populo ita fuerat ante uos consules libertas insita ut emori potius quam seruire praestaret*, *Phil.* 6.19 *aliae nationes seruitutem pati possunt, populi Romani est propria libertas.*

141 libertatem paro: *paro* rather than *pario* is guaranteed by the metre. The regular phrase in classical prose is *libertatem parere*; cf. Rhet. inc. *Her.* 4.66, Cicero, *Leg. agr.* 2.16, Livy 3.61.6 et al.

---

[1] See Lycurgus, *Leokr.* 98 ff., Apollodorus 3.15.4, Hyginus, *Fab.* 46, 238, Robert, *Die griech. Heldensage* II i, pp. 140 ff.

[2] *Quaest. scen.* p. 262, *Die röm. Trag.* p. 185.

[3] See *Introduction*, p. 62, below, p. 406.

EVMENIDES

LXII

These words probably come from a messenger's description of Eumolpus' besieging army.
There is an antithesis here between *arma* 'defensive' and *tela* 'offensive weapons'. *Arrigunt* gives a feeble effect and, in any case, the only reasonably near parallel seems to be Propertius 4.4.19–20 *uidit harenosis Tatium proludere campis | pictaque per flauas arma (frena* Palmer: *lora* Hartman) *leuare iubas.* There is much to be said for Bergk's *fulgoriunt*;[1] cf. Homer, *Il.* 22.133–4 σείων Πηλιάδα μελίην κατὰ δεξιὸν ὦμον | δεινήν· ἀμφὶ δὲ χαλκὸς ἐλάμπετο, Virgil, *Aen.* 7.525–7 *atraque late | horrescit strictis seges ensibus, aeraque fulgent | sole lacessita et lucem sub nubila iactant,* 11.601–2 *tum late ferreus hastis | horret ager campique armis sublimibus ardent.*

143 horrescunt tela: to the observer the lances appear to be shivering; cf. Ennius, *Ann.* 285 *densantur campis horrentia tela uirorum,* Virgil, *Aen.* 10.178 *mille rapit densos acie atque horrentibus hastis.* The aspect is slightly different at Homer, *Il.* 4.281–2 φάλαγγες...σάκεσίν τε καὶ ἔγχεσι πεφρικυῖαι, 13.339, Euripides, *Phoin.* 1105, Ennius, *Ann.* 393 *horrescit telis exercitus asper utrimque,* Horace, *Sat.* 2.1.13–14, Livy 44.41.6.

EVMENIDES

Nonius gives the title *Eumenides* four times to Ennius and sixty-six times to Varro. The pieces he quotes of Varro's *Eumenides* come from Lindsay's list 31 'Varro ii', a list apparently based on a volume containing eighteen of Varro's Menippean satires. The four pieces of Ennius' *Eumenides* illustrate unclassical verbs and verbal forms; their source is uncertain but it is possible that they all come from list 27 'Alph. Verb'. Ennius' work was clearly a tragedy which dealt with the trial of Orestes at Athens concerning the killing of his mother.
The Εὐμενίδες of Aeschylus was the only work of the three classical tragedians known at Alexandria to have presented this story[2] and there is thus a strong presumption that this was Ennius' model. Scaliger[3] interpreted Nonius' four quotations as versions of specific passages of Aeschylus' play.
It is possible that the title *Eumenides* does not come from the theatre but from a scholar who believed that Ennius' original was the Aeschylean

---

[1] *Philologus* xxxiii (1874), 290 (= *Kl. phil. Schr.* I 357).
[2] According to the extant hypothesis: παρ' οὐδετέρῳ κεῖται ἡ μυθοποιία.
[3] *Coniect. Varr. Ling.*, on 7.19.

283

tragedy.[1] The story of the transformation of Orestes' persecutors from
Ἐρινύες into Εὐμενίδες was of popular interest at Athens and of learned
interest elsewhere.[2] It does not seem a likely theme for the early second
century Roman stage. The final scene of the Athenian play has no relevance
to the preceding action and could have been omitted from a Latin version.[3]

Aeschylus opened his play with the scene set in Delphi and then shifted the
action to Athens. Such changes of scene took place rarely, if at all, in later
Attic drama[4] and it is worth pointing out that Ennius could have omitted
the Aeschylean opening or replaced it with another set in Athens, the scene
of the principal action.

Orestes was a popular figure on the Roman stage; he appeared quite
certainly in the *Electra* of Atilius, in the *Chryses*, *Dulorestes* and *Hermiona* of
Pacuvius, in the *Erigona* of Accius and in the *Orestes* of an unnamed author
(Donatus, *Gramm.* IV 375.25); possibly also in the *Hermiona* and *Aegisthus* of
Livius, the *Iphigenia* of Naevius, the *Agamemnonidae*, *Aegisthus* and *Clyte-
mestra* of Accius.

Cicero does not name the title *Eumenides* or any possible variant but in
referring to the trial of Orestes at *Mil.* 8 he seems to have the stage in mind.[5]
His references to the friendship of Orestes and Pylades at *Fin.* 1.65, 2.79,
5.63, and *Lael.* 24 concern a play by Pacuvius. Those to the madness of
Orestes at *Pis.* 47 and *Tusc.* 3.11 concern the stage but one cannot say more.
Three references to stage *Furiae* pursuing matricides with blazing torches
(*S. Rosc.* 67, *Pis.* 46, *Leg.* 1.40) have been thought to concern Ennius'
Alcmeo but since it is almost certain that the *Furiae* did not appear on stage
before the audience's eyes in that play (see above, p. 186) one should think
rather of the *Eumenides*.

At *De orat.* 1.199 Cicero refers half obliquely, half directly to a speech by
Apollo in a play by Ennius (fr. CLXVI). Ribbeck[6] set the words quoted in the
god's address to the Athenian jury, comparing Aeschylus, *Eum.* 576 ff. and
614 ff., but did not go so far as actually to print them alongside the quotations
of the *Eumenides* made by Nonius. Vahlen suggested that[7] they were spoken
by Apollo as he expelled the Furies from his oracular shrine, comparing
Aeschylus, *Eum.* 179 f., 185, 194 f. It seems to me equally possible that
Apollo spoke the prologue of Ennius' *Alcmeo* as we now know he did that of
Euripides' Ἀλκμέων ὁ διὰ Κορίνθου (fr. 73 a Snell), and that Cicero is quot-

---

[1] Cf. *Introduction*, p. 60 n. 3.   [2] Cf. Cicero, *Nat. deor.* 3.467.
[3] Cf. Terzaghi, *SIFC* N.S. VI (1928), 184 (= *Stud. Gr. et Lat.* 815).
[4] Cf. above on fr. 1.
[5] The references at *Inu.* 1.18 and 92 (cf. *Her.* 1.17, 25, and 26) may stem
from Greek rhetorical writing.
[6] *Quaest. scen.* p. 271. Cf. G. Hermann on Aesch. *Eum.* 608 (Leipzig, 1852).
[7] *E.P.R.*², p. 142.

ing this. There are no really striking correspondences between Cicero's quotation and anything in Aeschylus' Εὐμενίδες.

Discussing the temperate zones of the earth at *Tusc.* 1.68-9 Cicero describes that of the northern hemisphere as follows: *hic autem, ubi habitamus, non intermittit suo tempore 'caelum nitescere, arbores frondescere, | uites laetificae pampinis pubescere, | rami bacarum ubertate incuruescere, | segetes largiri fruges, florere omnia, | fontes scatere, herbis prata conuestirier'*. He is obviously quoting tragedy and Ribbeck imagined him quoting Ennius' version of the dialogue between Athena and the Erinyes at Aeschylus, *Eum.* 902-9: — τί οὖν μ' ἄνωγας τῇδ' ἐφυμνῆσαι χθονί; | — ὁποῖα νίκης μὴ κακῆς ἐπίσκοπα, | καὶ ταῦτα γῆθεν ἔκ τε ποντίας δρόσου | ἐξ οὐρανοῦ τε· κἀνέμων ἀήματα | εὐηλίως πνέοντ' ἐπιστείχειν χθόνα· | καρπόν τε γαίας καὶ βοτῶν ἐπίρρυτον | ἀστοῖσιν εὐθενοῦντα μὴ κάμνειν χρόνῳ, | καὶ τῶν βροτείων σπερμάτων σωτηρίαν. Hermann prefaced the five trimeters directly quoted by Cicero with *suo non intermittat tempore*.[1] Vahlen printed them as part of the Latin *Eumenides*. Even if the verbal parallelism were less superficial than it is this would be a rash proceeding. Furthermore, as I have argued above, there is no certainty that Ennius retained the final scene of Aeschylus' play.

At *Ling.* 7.19 Varro quotes a piece of Ennius now extremely corrupt but evidently about the *Areopagitae* (fr. CXCII). Scaliger compared Aeschylus, *Eum.* 690 and most editors have included it in the Latin *Eumenides*. It could come from any play set in Athens or referring to Athenian institutions.

In Paulus' epitome of Festus, p. 73.15, there is quoted a tragic address to Night without the author's name: *Erebo creata fuscis crinibus Nox te inuoco*. Ribbeck compared Aeschylus, *Eum.* 321 μᾶτερ ἅ μ' ἔτικτες, ὦ μᾶτερ Νύξ and assigned the fragment to Ennius' adaptation of the Furies' prayer. The address to Night is one of the commonest of tragic motifs (see above on fr. XXXIII) and I have therefore not accepted Ribbeck's assignation.

LXIII

Scaliger compared Aeschylus, *Eum.* 463-7: ἔκτεινα τὴν τεκοῦσαν, οὐκ ἀρνήσομαι, | ἀντικτόνοις ποιναῖσι φιλτάτου πατρός. | καὶ τῶνδε κοινῇ Λοξίας ἐπαίτιος, | ἄλγη προφωνῶν ἀντίκεντρα καρδίᾳ, | εἰ μή τι τῶνδ' ἔρξοιμι τοὺς ἐπαιτίους.

144 materno: 'matris': cf. Pacuvius, *Trag.* 144, Accius, *Trag.* 23; comedy has *maternus* only once and in the sense of 'maternal' (Terence, *Haut.* 637).

---

[1] On Aesch. *Eum.* 894.

sanguine exanclando: cf. Euripides, *Rhes.* 430–1 ἔνθ' αἱματηρὸς πέλανος ἐς γαῖαν Σκύθης | ἠντλεῖτο λόγχῃ Θρήξ τε συμμιγὴς φόνος, Cicero, *Sest.* 54 *me perculso ad meum sanguinem hauriendum . . . aduolauerunt*, Ovid, *Met.* 7.333, 13.331, Livy 7.24.5 et al. The full grim point of the Ennian Orestes' language is not revealed by these parallels; he thinks of the killing of Clytemnestra as the offering of her blood to the shade of Agamemnon: he will draw not the conventional draught of wine (cf. Aeschylus, *Pers.* 610 ff., Euripides, *I.T.* 159 ff., Paulus, *Fest.* p. 319.1 f. RESPARSVM VINVM *dixerunt quia uino sepulcrum spargebatur*) but one of blood. For *exanclare* as a ritual word see above on *v.* 103. The heroes of Attic tragedy frequently describe their deeds of bloodshed as if they were acts of sacrifice to divinities; cf., where Clytemnestra's death is concerned, Aeschylus, *Choe.* 904 ἕπου, πρὸς αὐτὸν τόνδε σὲ σφάξαι θέλω, Euripides, *El.* 1221–3 ἐγὼ μὲν ἐπιβαλὼν φάρη κόραις ἐμαῖς | φασγάνῳ κατηρξάμαν | ματέρος ἔσω δέρας μεθείς, *Or.* 562 ἐπὶ δ' ἔθυσα μητέρα, 842 σφάγιον ἔθετο ματέρα. Sometimes the audience is merely being presented with a horrific metaphor; sometimes there is a tone of blasphemy.[1] The Ennian Orestes is perhaps making an implicit defence of his deed. The Romans seem to have conceived of many kinds of legal and semi-legal killing in sacrificial terms.[2]

ulciscerem: cf. Pacuvius, *Trag.* 169, Accius, *Trag.* 293; to judge by comic usage the deponent form was normal in the common language of the second century; the only other examples of the active in recorded Latin seem to be Sallust, *Iug.* 31.8, Livy 5.49.3, and Valerius Flaccus 4.753.

LXIV

Scaliger compared Aeschylus, *Eum.* 741 νικᾷ δ' Ὀρέστης κἂν ἰσόψηφος κριθῇ, Ribbeck 752–3 ἀνὴρ ὅδ' ἐκπέφευγεν αἵματος δίκην· | ἴσον γάρ ἐστι τἀρίθμημα τῶν πάλων.

The seven Latin words must be spoken by Athena, president of the court, to the Furies, the prosecutors whose charge has failed. They imply that the decision is Athena's own and not the automatic result of the deadlock brought about by her equalising vote. In trials of the late republic equality of votes meant acquittal[3] and the president of the court had nothing to do except announce the jurors' decision but it is possible that in Ennius' day the

---

[1] See Fraenkel on Aesch. *Ag.* 1384 ff., 1432 f.

[2] Cf. Festus, p. 260.7 ff., Pliny, *Nat.* 18.12, Servius auct. *Aen.* 6.609, Suetonius, *Aug.* 15, Dionysius Hal. 2.10.3, 2.74.3, Plutarch, *Romul.* 22.3, Dio Cass. 43.24.4. But see Latte, *RE* Suppl. VII (1940), s.v. *Todesstrafe*, 1614 ff., for a different view of Roman conceptions.

[3] Cf. Cicero, *Cluent.* 74, *Fam.* 8.8.3, Plutarch, *Mar.* 5.5.

decision in some cases of homicide was purely that of a magistrate exercising jurisdiction and that Ennius gave his Athena the words *dico uicisse Orestem. uos ab hoc facessite* with contemporary Roman legal practice in mind.[1]

145 dico: cf. Terence, *Eun.* 961–2 *at ne hoc nesciatis, Pythias:* | *dico edico uobis nostrum esse illum erilem filium* (solemn, semi-legal context).

Orestem: a necessary correction; Greek terminations of proper names did not appear on the stage until the time of Accius.[2] The manuscripts of Plautus have the *en* termination much less frequently than that in *-em*; in no case is *-en* metrically necessary; in two (*Epid.* 612 [~ 197], *Truc.* 514) it is metrically impossible; at *Pseud.* 991, on the other hand (cf. Terence, *Hec.* 432, Accius, *Trag.* 657[1]), *-em* is metrically necessary. See Housman, *Journal of Philology* XXXI (1910), 236 ff., Leumann, *MusH* II (1945), 239 f. (= *Kl. Schr.* 110 f.).

ab hoc facessite: *facessere* occurs twice elsewhere in tragedy (Pacuvius 326, 343) and only four times in comedy (Plautus, *Men.* 249 [solemn warning to insolent slave], *Rud.* 1061, 1062 [semi-legal argument], Terence, *Phorm.* 635 [legal discussion]). The phrase may be an ancient formula of acquittal reflecting a state of affairs in which the prosecutor in person brought the defendant to court and exacted the penalty in the event of conviction.

LXV

Scaliger compared Aeschylus, *Eum.* 571–3 σιγᾶν ἀρήγει καὶ μαθεῖν θεσμοὺς ἐμούς | πόλιν τε πᾶσαν ἐς τὸν αἰανῆ χρόνον | καὶ τώδ᾽, ὅπως ἂν εὖ καταγνωσθῇ δίκη (Athena's address to the jury) and wrote Ennius' words as *tacere opino esse optumum, ut pro uiribus* | *sapere atque fabulari tute nouerint*. Bothe compared 276–9 ἐγὼ διδαχθεὶς ἐν κακοῖς ἐπίσταμαι | πολλοὺς καθαρμούς, καὶ λέγειν ὅπου δίκη | σιγᾶν θ᾽ ὁμοίως· ἐν δὲ τῷδε πράγματι | φωνεῖν ἐτάχθην πρὸς σοφοῦ διδασκάλου (Orestes' speech on arrival in Athens) and wrote *sapere esse opinor optimum pro uiribus: tacere ac fabulari tute noueris.* Ribbeck wrote *ita sapere opino esse optumum, ut pro uiribus* |

---

[1] Plautus sometimes refers to legal institutions that could have had no equivalent in his Attic original; cf. *Aul.* 416.

[2] Ennius has *aera* (acc.) and *crateras* in epic (*Ann.* 148, 511). It is difficult to give an account of *Salmacida* (voc.) at *Trag.* 347. Where comedy uses a proper name taken from the Greek first declension, the *a* of the nominative and vocative cases seems normally to be scanned as short; but the matter is disputed; cf. R. H. Martin, *CQ* N.S. v (1955), 206 ff., vi (1956), 197, O. Skutsch, *CQ* vi (1956), 90, vii (1957), 52.

tacere ac fabulari tute noueris, L. Mueller *ego sapere opino esse optumum pro uiribus:* | *tacere et fabulari tute noueris.* Vahlen kept what is transmitted and interpreted it rather tortuously as 'qua sum condicione tacere optumum esse censeo, et hoc si feceris, sapere pro uiribus (εἰς δύναμιν, ὅτι μάλιστα) et fabulari tute (ἀσφαλῶς) noueris: sed in hac causa iam mihi loquendum est, ut didici'. I think it better to assume that Ennius rewrote Orestes' speech according to his own ideas of what was rhetorically appropriate and to interpret the two trimeters transmitted as a general *sententia* rather than a statement about particulars: 'as a rule I think it the best policy to keep one's mouth shut and to show only such verbal cleverness as one's physical strength allows; but (*atque*) in some circumstances one may know how (*noueris*) to speak without risk'. Ennius was given to altering the tone and emphasis of the general statements he found in his originals (see below on frs. LXXXIV and CV) and to adding general statements quite foreign to his originals (see below on frs. CV and CVIII).[1]

146–7 tacere opino esse optumum et pro uiribus | sapere: cf. Sophocles, fr. 61.4 κόσμος ἡ σιγή τε καὶ τὰ παῦρ' ἔπη, Euripides, *Herakleidai* 476–7 γυναικὶ γὰρ σιγή τε καὶ τὸ σωφρονεῖν | κάλλιστον.

The active form *opino* occurs twice in tragedy, 12 times in comedy (not in Terence); the deponent only once in tragedy but extremely often in comedy.

147 atque: adversative; cf. Plautus, *Aul.* 287, Terence, *Andr.* 225 (and Donatus *ad loc.*), *T.L.L.* II 1077.15 ff.

fabulari...noueris: I can find no parallel for this construction in republican drama but cf. Propertius 2.25.38, 2.28.13, 3.23.5.

tute: cf. Accius, *Trag.* 590; *tuto* is regular in comedy.

LXVI

Scaliger compared Aeschylus, *Eum.* 463–9 ἔκτεινα τὴν τεκοῦσαν...καὶ τῶνδε κοινῇ Λοξίας ἐπαίτιος...σὺ δ' εἰ δικαίως εἴτε μὴ κρῖνον δίκην (Orestes speaking); Ribbeck 616–20 οὐπώποτ' εἶπον μαντικοῖσιν ἐν θρόνοις, | οὐκ ἀνδρός, οὐ γυναικός, οὐ πόλεως πέρι, | ὃ μὴ κελεῦσαι

---

[1] H. Fuchs, *Hermes* LXX (1935), 245, writes *tacere opino esse optimum, at pro uiribus* | *sapere atque fabulari tute noueris* and suggests that the trimeters belonged to a scene created independently by Ennius in which either Apollo briefs Orestes on how to behave in court or Orestes in soliloquy repeats advice given to him by Apollo. Such freedom in adaptation is not unexampled in what we know of republican drama but the scenes postulated by Fuchs are difficult to believe in.

EVMENIDES

Ζεὺς Ὀλυμπίων πατήρ. | τὸ μὲν δίκαιον τοῦθ᾽ ὅσον σθένει μαθεῖν, | βουλῇ πιφαύσκω δ᾽ ὕμμ᾽ ἐπισπέσθαι πατρός, 657 καὶ τοῦτο λέξω, καὶ μάθ᾽ ὡς ὀρθῶς ἐρῶ (Apollo speaking).

The verb *fecisse* makes it fairly plain that Orestes' deed and not Apollo's advice is in question.

The corrupt *accius* cries out to be altered to *ac ius* but this alteration leaves hiatus in two places in the trochaic tetrameter (each case tolerable in itself[1] but suspicious in company) and a very queer phrase *id ius facere* (for which *ius orare* is no parallel). Furthermore the normal order of the doublet seems to have been *ius atque aecum* (cf. Ennius, *Trag.* 155, Plautus, *Stich.* 423, Terence, *Haut.* 642, Cicero, *Brut.* 145, Tacitus, *Ann.* 14.18, Fronto, p. 81.15, Claudian 10.313).[2] On the other hand the adjectives usually arranged themselves *aequus ac iustus* (cf. Plautus, *Amph.* 16, Cicero, *Phil.* 2.72, *Fin.* 3.71, Seneca, *Epist.* 95.52; rhythm dictates the refractory instances at Cicero, *Fin.* 3.71 and Horace, *Sat.* 1.3.98). Accordingly I propose to write *id ego aecum ac iustum fecisse* with hiatus at the diaeresis of the tetrameter.

The substance of the Ennian verse, which is plain whatever the details of its restoration, departs a long way from the spirit of Aeschylus' Εὐμενίδες. The Aeschylean Orestes hesitates to claim even τὸ δίκαιον for his act (cf. *Choe.* 1027), the Aeschylean Apollo claims it for the will of Zeus. Ennius' personage pretends confidence about not only the justice but also the equity of his act. The notion of equity (τὸ ἐπιεικές) is absent from the Εὐμενίδες and quite rare elsewhere in Attic drama (cf. however Sophocles, *O.K.* 1125–7, fr. 703.2, Euripides, fr. 274, fr. 645.6, Aristophanes, *Neph.* 1437–8).

148 id ego aecum ac iustum fecisse: the subject of the accusative and infinitive is omitted quite frequently in republican drama; cf. Plautus, *Capt.* 256, Terence, *Haut.* 16–17, *Phorm.* 54 et al., A. Funck, *NJbb* CXXI (1880), 725–34. The context always precludes ambiguity.

expedibo atque eloquar: cf. Terence, *Phorm.* 197–8 — *cedo quid portas, obsecro. atque id, si potes, uerbo expedi.* | — *faciam.* — *eloquere.*

The form *expedibo* occurs three times elsewhere in tragedy (Pacuvius 66, 281, Accius 490), only once in comedy (Plautus, *Truc.* 138 [high-falutin dialogue]); *expediam* seems to have been the normal form (Plautus, *Amph.* 912, Terence, *Andr.* 617, *Phorm.* 238).

---

[1] For hiatus after the second arsis of the tetrameter see Jacobsohn, *Quaest. Plaut.* p. 4; for hiatus at the diaeresis see above on *v.* 17.

[2] Vahlen seems to have been dimly aware of this when he suggested *id ego ius atque aecum fecisse*; see *Ind. lectt. Berlin* 1888/9, 7 f. (= *Op. ac.* 1 406 f.).

HECTORIS LYTRA

Verrius is represented by the tradition as having given Ennius the title *Hectoris lyrae* (Festus, p. 334.16); Diomedes *Lustra* (*Gramm.* I 345.3, 387.30); Nonius *Hectoris* †lystra† (pp. 467.39, 472.23, 489.29, 490.6, 504.35, 511.10, 518.24), *Hectoris* †listra† (pp. 355.17, 407.24), *Hectoris lytra* (pp. 111.18, 399.8, 469.30) and *Lytra* (p. 222.27). The *Hectoris* †lystra† quotations all come pretty certainly from Lindsay's list 10 'Ennius', a list based on a volume or volumes containing this play and the *Telephus*. About the others there are varying degrees of uncertainty; the *Lytra* quotation may come from the work of Flavius Caper which seems to lie behind Nonius' third book.

Stephanus printed the sixteen quotations under two titles *Hectoris lytra* and *Lustra* but later editors have assumed the existence of only one play. The quotations can all be interpreted as from a tragedy set in the Myrmidon part of the Greek encampment before Troy and climaxed by Priam's ransom of Hector's body from Achilles. Welcker[1] made the tragedy begin with Priam's arrival at Achilles' tent and suggested that it was an adaptation of Sophocles' Φρύγες. Schöll[2] argued that it began even before Patroclus' departure to do battle with Hector and that Ennius combined the plots of Aeschylus' Μυρμιδόνες, Νηρεΐδες and Ἕκτορος λύτρα ἢ Φρύγες. Schöll's view has won an extraordinary number of adherents.[3]

There is nothing absolutely improbable, despite Aristotle, *Poet.* 5.1449 b 13, about a tragedy covering the events narrated in books XI–XXIV of the *Iliad*. Aeschylus' Ἀγαμέμνων and Εὐμενίδες, Sophocles' Τραχίνιαι, Euripides' Ἀνδρομάχη, Ἱκετίδες and Σθενέβοια have actions spread over long intervals of time. The notion that Ennius was responsible for combining the plots of three Attic tragedies is harder to swallow, there being no hard evidence that the republican poets ever worked as freely as this.

Only one of the sixteen quotations (fr. LXXIV) has to be taken as from a scene set in time before the arrival of Priam at Achilles' tent.

One might allow that Ennius himself added to the Aeschylean Ἕκτορος λύτρα a scene showing the arming of Achilles and his departure for battle but there remains the difficulty that Aeschylus employed a chorus of Phrygians, Ennius one of Myrmidon guards (fr. LXXV).

---

[1] *Die Aeschylische Trilogie*, p. 428, *Die griech. Trag.* p. 136.
[2] *Beitr.* pp. 472 ff.
[3] Bergk (*NJbb* LXXXIII [1861], 629 [= *Kl. phil. Schr.* I 299]), C. Bailey (*CR* XVIII [1904], 171) and Leo (*Gesch.* p. 193 n. 1) are the only scholars I can find expressing scepticism.

The title of the play obviously could not have been HECTORIS LYRAE. A second-century Roman would have smiled to see HECTORIS LVSTRA on a bill-board but many have thought this to be Ennius' title.[1] The subject-matter of the play would demand that *lustra* be interpreted as the equivalent of the Greek λύτρα. There is no evidence that the word was so used in the common language of the early second century; neither *luere* nor any of its compounds translated λύεσθαι; the Latin verb was *redimere* (Plautus, *Asin.* 106, 107, *Capt.* 337 et al.). Varro's etymology at *Ling.* 6.11, *lustrum nominatum tempus quinquennale a luendo, id est soluendo, quod quinto quoque anno uectigalia et ultro tributa per censores persoluebantur*, proves nothing about ordinary usage. HECTORIS LYTRA could not have been written thus by Ennius himself. Ribbeck accordingly made the title HECTORIS LVTRA. However what lies behind our muddled tradition may be simply a classical transliteration of "Εκτορος λύτρα.[2]

The title "Εκτορος λύτρα is recorded against the names of Dionysius and Timesitheus as well as Aeschylus. Hyginus, *Fab.* 106, which relates events from Agamemnon's seizure of Briseis to Achilles' surrender of Hector's body, is headed *Hectoris lytra*. The plot of an Attic tragedy often lies behind Hyginus' narrative but one can never be sure how much comes from the prologue and how much from the action.

Our ignorance of the precise extent of Ennius' plot makes it impossible to apportion a number of fragments relating to the siege of Troy between this play and the *Achilles*; see above, pp. 162 ff.

LXVII

This fragment appears to refer to the revenge taken (Scaliger's *hostiuit e manu*) or to be taken (Vahlen's *hostibitis manu*, Timpanaro's *hostibis eminus*) by Achilles for Patroclus' death.

For the phraseology of Scaliger's text and texts similarly constituted cf. Homer, *Il.* 20.462 τὸν μὲν δουρὶ βαλών, τὸν δὲ σχεδὸν ἄορι τύψας, Cicero, *Cato* 19 *neque eminus hastis aut comminus gladiis uteretur*, Ovid, *Met.* 3.119 *comminus ense ferit, iaculo cadit eminus ipse*.

149 machaera: only here in republican tragedy, frequent in comedy as a weapon of the mercenary soldier, twice in the *Annales* in obscure contexts (400, 597). The word is likely to have come from Greek through the common language rather than the scripts of Attic drama. Μάχαιρα occurs once in Attic tragedy (Euripides, *Hik.* 1206) and often in comedy but never indicates

---

[1] Most recently R. M. Ogilvie, *JRS* LI (1961), 35.
[2] See *Introduction*, pp. 59 f.

19-2

a military weapon.[1] Tragic soldiers wield the ξίφος or the φάσγανον, comic the σπάθη (Menander, *Perik.* 165, *Sam.* 314, 315, *Misoum.* B ↓ 5, C ↓ 25).

hasta: here and twice elsewhere in republican tragedy (Ennius 165, Trag. inc. 235), fairly common in comedy of the soldier's spear and the athlete's.

LXVIII

Schöll[2] regarded this fragment as having been spoken by Achilles before the departure of Patroclus for battle. It could as easily have reference to the decision to hand over Hector's body to Priam.

The words transmitted will not form any regular metrical pattern and the phrase *ut hoc consilium Achiuis auxili* (*auxilii* codd.) *fuat* is anomalous.[3] I have printed, without much confidence, Lindsay's arrangement of the text.[4] For the mingling of catalectic and acatalectic tetrameters cf. *vv.* 185–8, 219–21, 296–9.

150 at: makes the request more urgent; cf. Plautus, *Most.* 38–9 *at te Iuppiter | dique omnes perdant*, Livy 1.12.5 *at tu pater deum hominumque hinc saltem arce hostes* et al. Ἀλλά is similarly used in Greek; cf. Aeschylus, *Theb.* 116–19 ἀλλ' ὦ Ζεῦ πάτερ παντελές, | πάντως ἄρηξον δαΐων ἅλωσιν et al.

omnipotens: perhaps a poetic calque on παγκρατής. In the remains of archaic and classical Latin it appears to be restricted to poetry. Its early adoption by the Christians confirms that it was absent from the sacral language of the pagans. See Fraenkel on Aeschylus, *Ag.* 1648. For the form of the compound epithet see above on *v.* 45.

Omnipotens occurs unaccompanied elsewhere in Latin at Virgil, *Aen.* 4.220, 10.615.

151 ted: this and other *-d* forms were obsolescent in the early second century except in the language of religion and law; in the remains of Ennius'

---

[1] Cf. Shipp, *Glotta* XXXIV (1954), 149 f. The diminutive however seems to have been so used; cf. Menander, fr. 793 ἀσπίδιον ἐπριάμην τι καὶ μαχαίριον (~ Plautus, *Curc.* 574–5 *ita me machaera et clipeus…bene iuuent*, *Truc.* 506 *machaeram et clipeum poscebat sibi*).

[2] *Beitr.* p. 497.

[3] Contrast Plautus, *Amph.* 92, *Aul.* 715–16, *Curc.* 267, *Epid.* 676, *Poen.* 1137, 1277, Terence, *Haut.* 992–3. A. Reifferscheid, *Ind. lectt. Breslau* 1885/6, p. 7 (not seen by me), defends *auxili*.

[4] Cf. Timpanaro, *SIFC* XXI (1946), 79–80, O. Skutsch, *CQ* N.S. XIII (1963), 90 n. 2; *aliter* Strzelecki, *Eos* XLIII (1948/9), 159–61.

writings one case is transmitted (*Var.* 45 *med ego* [Manutius: *me et ego* codd.]), in comedy only a few; editors concur in restoring *med* and *ted* to avoid hiatus after the arsis of the first foot of iambic and trochaic verses. See Maurenbrecher, *Hiatus und Verschleifung*, pp. 107 ff.

exposco: only here and Plautus, *Persa* 495 (paratragic context) in republican drama; the simple form *poscere* is common in comedy.

fuat: this and compound forms do not occur in official inscriptions of the second century; they are relatively common in tragedy (4 instances as against 8 of *siem* etc., 19 of *sim* etc.) and uncommon in comedy (~22:196:684 in Plautus, 1 [*Hec.* 610]:85:254 in Terence, 2:1:8 in Naevius et al.); they tend in both genres to occur at the ends of iambic and trochaic verses and in formulaic expressions like *fors fuat*. See F. Thomas, *Recherches sur le subjonctif latin* (Paris, 1938), pp. 10 ff.

LXIX

We have here a periphrasis for *Acheruns* concerning the context of which it is useless to speculate.

For the periphrasis cf. Seneca, *Tro.* 178–80 *tum scissa uallis aperit immensos specus | et hiatus Erebi...iter...praebet*, 430–1 *Stygis profundae claustra et obscuri specus | laxantur*, *Thy.* 105–6 *gradere ad infernos specus | amnemque notum*.

152 inferum: probably the genitive plural of *inferi*, 'beings of the lower world' (cf. Plautus, *Aul.* 368, Pacuvius, *Trag.* 289, Accius, *Trag.* 57); not to be grouped with Ennius, *Trag.* 98, Accius, *Trag.* 479, Trag. inc. 75 (*infera*, 'lower world') or with Seneca, *Herc. O.* 15, 743 (*inferi*, 'lower world').

uastos: twice elsewhere in tragedy (along with *uastitas* once, *uastitudo* 4 times, *uastescere* once); only once in comedy (Plautus, *Bacch.* 1053).

LXX

Schöll referred this fragment to the fighting described in *Iliad* XI.[1] One might with equal plausibility refer it to any action involving Hector. It could come from a prologue relating events long past or from a messenger's speech describing a recent happening off stage, either the action in which Patroclus lost his life or that in which Hector lost his.

There is little talk of the strategical deployment of troops in the Iliad; the

---

[1] *Beitr.* p. 491. Cf. Homer, *Il.* 11.56–61.

early epic poets concentrate attention on the deeds of individual heroes.[1] In the battle-pieces of Attic tragedy,[2] on the other hand, the heroes are treated as στρατηγοί rather than πρόμαχοι. Ennius' two trimeters gave a Roman cast to what was an already established tragic motif.

153 Hector †ei summa† armatos educit foras: Mercerus' *ui summa* is universally accepted; the phrase occurs often in drama (Plautus, *Amph.* 210, *Cas.* 80, *Merc.* 45, Terence, *Ad.* 493); but one must ask why Hector should need to exercise *uis* either in arming or leading out his troops.

Ennius draws on the military language; cf. Plautus, *Amph.* 216–18 *Amphitruo castris ilico* | *producit omnem exercitum. contra Teloboae ex oppido* | *legiones educunt suas nimis pulchris armis praeditas*, Cato, *Orig.* 83 *tempus exercitus ex hoc loco educendi habebis* et al.

Foras frequently in republican drama accompanies verbs compounded with *ex-*; for *educere foras* cf. Plautus, *Cas.* 798 et al.

154 castrisque castra ultro iam ferre occupat: Vossius' alteration of *ferre* to *conferre* removes two anomalies. Hiatus after the thesis of the third foot is rarely transmitted in extant trimeters and scholars prepared to tolerate hiatus elsewhere deny it here.[3] Nevertheless Ennius 249, Pacuvius 293, 364, Accius 84, to say nothing of the comic examples,[4] are difficult to normalise. *Castra castris conferre* was a regular phrase of the military language; cf. Cicero, *Diu.* 2.114 *castra enim in Thessalia castris conlata audiebamus*, Caesar, *Ciu.* 3.79.3, Hirtius 8.9.2 et al.[5] But *castris castra ferre* is a possible poetic variation; for the replacement of the compound form of the verb with the simple in tragedy see above on *v.* 14.

---

[1] Cf., nevertheless, 15.281 ff., 16.171 ff. The general character of the Homeric narrative is well brought out by comparison of 16.394 ff. with Virgil's imitation at *Aen.* 10.238 ff., 285 ff.; Virgil makes Turnus a στρατηγός. See L. Wickert, *Philologus* LXXXV (1930), 455 ff.

[2] E.g. Euripides, *Hik.* 707 ff., *Herakleidai* 799 ff., *Phoin.* 1090 ff. Cf. Plautus, *Amph.* 216 ff.

[3] E.g. Lindsay, *E.L.V.* p. 231.

[4] These are collected by P. Friedländer, *RhM* LXII (1907), 73 ff., and A. Klotz, *Hermes* LX (1925), 332 ff.

[5] The polyptoton looks poetical (cf. Homer, *Il.* 13.131 ἀσπὶς ἄρ' ἀσπίδ' ἔρειδε, κόρυς κόρυν, ἀνέρα δ' ἀνήρ, Euripides, *Hik.* 666–7 ἱππεῦσι δ' ἱππῆς ἦσαν ἀνθωπλισμένοι | τετραόροισί τ' ἀντί' ἅρμαθ' ἅρμασιν, *Phoin.* 1095–6 ἐφέδρους δ' ἱππότας μὲν ἱππόταις | ἔταξε, *Herakleidai* 836–7 ποὺς ἐπαλλαχθεὶς ποδί, | ἀνὴρ δ' ἐπ' ἀνδρὶ στάς) but the employment of the phrase by Cicero and Caesar fixes it in the regular military language.

LXXI

This is almost certainly a fragment of a speech asking or advising Achilles to hand over Hector's corpse. From a similar speech in Aeschylus' Ἕκτορος λύτρα comes (fr. 266) καὶ τοὺς θανόντας εἰ θέλεις εὐεργετεῖν | εἴτ' οὖν κακουργεῖν, ἀμφιδεξίως ἔχει | τῷ μήτε χαίρειν μήτε λυπεῖσθαι φθιτούς. | ἡμῶν γε μέντοι Νέμεσις ἔσθ' ὑπερτέρα | καὶ τοῦ θανόντος ἡ Δίκη πράσσει κότον. The sentiment is more like that in a similar context of Euripides' Ἱκετίδες: 594–7 ἓν δεῖ μόνον μοι· τοὺς θεοὺς ἔχειν, ὅσοι | δίκην σέβονται· ταῦτα γὰρ ξυνόνθ' ὁμοῦ | νίκην δίδωσιν. ἀρετὴ δ' οὐδὲν λέγει | βροτοῖσιν, ἢν μὴ τὸν θεὸν χρῄзοντ' ἔχῃ. One may make the same point about the content of this fragment as about LXVI. Talk about equity was almost certainly absent from Ennius' original if this original was Aeschylus' Ἕκτορος λύτρα, quite probably absent if it was some other play; the personages of Euripides' Ἱκετίδες talk simply of νόμοι βροτῶν (378), ὁ Πανελλήνων νόμος (526, 671), νόμος παλαιὸς δαιμόνων (563) and δίκη.

Virtus here does not stand for virtue in general but rather for the particular virtue of the warrior; for the contrast between *uirtus* and justice, etc. cf. Trag. inc. 116–17 *eandem uirtutem istam ueniet tempus cum grauiter gemes* | *si neque leges neque mores cogunt*, Livy 1.26.12 *absolueruntque admiratione magis uirtutis quam iure causae*; justice, etc. are set alongside *uirtus* by Cicero at *Manil.* 36 *non enim bellandi uirtus solum in summo ac perfecto imperatore quaerenda est sed multae sunt artes eximiae huius administrae comitesque uirtutis. ac primum quanta innocentia debent esse imperatores, quanta deinde in omnibus rebus temperantia, quanta fide . . .* and by Augustus at *Mon. Ancyr.* 34 *clupeus aureus in curia Iulia positus quem mihi senatum populumque Romanum dare uirtutis clementiaeque iustitiae et pietatis caussa* (ἀρετὴν καὶ ἐπιείκειαν καὶ δικαιοσύνην καὶ εὐσέβειαν) *testatum est per eius clupei inscriptionem.*

156 ius atque aecum se a malis spernit procul: an odd phrase; *spernere* normally takes a simple object in republican drama. The genesis of the Ennian phrase can be seen in Plautus, *Mil.* 1232 *ille illas spernit, segregat ab se omnis extra te unam* and Plautus, *Capt.* 517 *spes opes auxiliaque a me segregant spernuntque se* (Dousa: *me* cod.).

LXXII

This fragment is grossly corrupt and no good purpose is served by attempts at restoration.[1] A little can be said about the subject-matter. There is no question of taming real horses on the field of battle or of curbing real horses with

---

[1] For the latest and by no means least intelligent attempt see Mariotti, *SIFC* XXXI (1959), 233–5: *duc et quadrupedum iugo* | *inuitam doma infrena et iunge, ualida quom tenacia* | *infrenari minis* ⟨*nequitur*⟩.

threats. Some person or persons has been acting obstreperously. The word *inuitam* suggests that it is a woman; one might parallel Aeschylus, *Ag.* 1066-7 χαλινὸν δ᾽ οὐκ ἐπίσταται φέρειν | πρὶν αἱματηρὸν ἐξαφρίζεσθαι μένος and 1071 εἴκουσ᾽ ἀνάγκη τῇδε καίνισον ζυγόν but hardly Lucilius 1041-2 *anne ego te uacuam* (Lachmann: *acuam* codd.) *atque animosam | Thessalam ut indomitam frenis subigam ante domemque* (cf. Anacreon 417.4 f. Page). However it is difficult to imagine who the woman could be in this play. *Quorum* suggests men; cf. Aeschylus, *Ag.* 1639-40 τὸν δὲ μὴ πειθάνορα | ζεύξω βαρείαις, Sophocles, *Ant.* 291-2 οὐδ᾽ ὑπὸ ζυγῷ | λόφον δικαίως εἶχον, ὡς στέργειν ἐμέ, *El.* 1460-3 ὡς εἴ τις αὐτῶν ἐλπίσιν κεναῖς πάρος | ἐξῆρετ᾽ ἀνδρὸς τοῦδε, νῦν ὁρῶν νεκρὸν | στόμια δέχηται τἀμά, μηδὲ πρὸς βίαν | ἐμοῦ κολαστοῦ προστυχὼν φύσῃ φρένας, Livy 39.25.13 *Philippum ut equum tenacem non parentem frenis asperioribus castigandum esse.* But again it is difficult to identify the men in question.

Infrenare occurs elsewhere in Latin only at Accius, *Trag.* 15, Cicero, *Pis.* 44, Virgil, *Aen.* 12.287, Livy 37.20.4, Pliny, *Nat.* 9.100. The simple *frenare* is absent from republican drama but quite common in classical prose and verse. For *in-* as a tragic prefix see above on *v.* 26.

Tenacia occurs only here in republican drama and may have been a tragic neologism. Cicero has *tenacitas* at *Nat. deor.* 2.122.

LXXIII

This fragment comes from an article put together from lists apparently compiled by Nonius himself from the original texts. *Constitit credo Scamander arbores uento uagant* is almost certainly what Nonius thought he saw in the text of the *Hectoris lytra*. Yet while *uento* could be taken ἀπὸ κοινοῦ with *constitit* (cf. Virgil, *Ecl.* 2.26 *cum placidum uentis staret mare*, *Georg.* 4.484 *Ixionii uento rota constitit orbis*) it makes no sense with *uagant*. Nonius must have misread a *uacant*.

Schöll referred the fragment to the fight between Achilles and the river-god narrated in *Iliad* XXI, Bergk to the fight between Achilles and Hector. Certain close parallels in Greek and Latin literature make it seem likely, however, that the fragment concerns some miraculous event or divine epiphany; the parallels are Euripides, *Ba.* 1084-5 σίγησε δ᾽ αἰθήρ, σῖγα δ᾽ ὕλιμος νάπη | φύλλ᾽ εἶχε, θηρῶν δ᾽ οὐκ ἂν ἤκουσας βοήν, Aristophanes, *Orn.* 777-8 πτῆξε δὲ φῦλά τε ποικίλα θηρῶν, | κύματά τ᾽ ἔσβεσε νήνεμος αἴθρη, *Thesm.* 43-4 ἐχέτω δὲ πνοὰς νήνεμος αἰθήρ, | κῦμα δὲ πόντου μὴ κελαδείτω, Limenius 7-9 (Powell 149) πᾶ[ς δὲ γ]άθησε πόλος οὐράνιος [ἀννέφελος ἀγλαός,] | [ν]ηνέμους δ᾽ ἔσχεν αἰθὴρ ἀε[λλῶν ταχυπετ]εῖς [δρόμ]ους, | λῆξε δὲ βαρυβρόμων Νη[ρέως ζαμενὲς ο[ἴδμα, Alcaeus of Messene, *A.P.* 7.412.5-6 ῥόον δ᾽ ἔστησεν...᾽Ασωπός (grief for death of Pylades), Virgil, *Aen.* 9.123-5 *obstipuere animis Rutuli, conterritus ipse* | *turbatis Messapus equis, cunctatur et amnis* | *rauca sonans reuocatque pedem Tiberinus ab alto,* 10.101–3 *eo dicente deum domus alta silescit* | *et tremefacta sono tellus, silet arduus aether,* | *tum Zephyri posuere, premit placida aequora pontus,* [Tibullus] 3.7.121–34.[1] The word *credo* suggests that nothing in the action of the play is referred to; rather that we have a hearsay report of earlier events (cf. Plautus, *Epid.* 34 *Mulciber credo arma fecit quae habuit Stratippocles*).[2]

LXXIV

The text of this fragment is corrupt and its specific interpretation obscure[3] but one can give it a fairly secure context: news of Patroclus' death has come and Achilles is without arms, powerless to avenge his beloved.[4]

160 cunctent: once elsewhere in tragedy (Accius 72) and only twice in comedy (Plautus, *Cas.* 792, *Epid.* 162); comparatively uncommon in Caesar and Cicero (who both use it as a deponent).

LXXV

This fragment must come from an address by Priam to the guards at Achilles' tent.

Ianus Palmerius[5] restored it as *per uos et nostrum imperium et fidem Myrmidonum, uigiles, commiserescite.* Bergk and Vahlen thought they could make sense of it with only one alteration: *per uos et uostrum imperium et fidem, Myrmidonum uigiles, conmiserescite.* However three grave difficulties can be made about the text they offer.

First, the words will not fit into any of the recognised verse patterns of republican drama.[6]

---

[1] One has to guess at the context of Ennius, *Var.* 9–12 *mundus caeli uastus constitit...constitere amnes perennes arbores uento uacant.*

[2] O. Skutsch (London seminar, 15 November 1955) proposes to replace *credo* with *cursu.* See now *HSCPh* LXXI (1967), 136 f.

[3] Ribbeck (cf. *Coroll.* p. xxiv, *Die röm. Trag.* p. 123) wrote in his final edition *ei ipsi cunctent...* and made the speaker some Achaean refusing Achilles' request for armour after the death of Patroclus. Vahlen (cf. *Ind. lectt. Berlin* 1888/9, 5 ff. [= *Op. ac.* I 403 ff.]) wrote *ut ipsi cunctent?* and made the speaker Achilles pointing out his lack of armour in reply to Iris' command to go into battle and recover Patroclus' body.

[4] The mood of *cupiant* makes it very difficult to accept Welcker's view (*Die griech. Trag.* p. 136) that the words are spoken by Achilles to Priam in an account of past events.

[5] *Spicilegium* (Frankfurt, 1580); repr. in Gruterus, *Lampas,* IV 787.

[6] For the trochaic pentameter alleged by Bergk see above on fr. XLIII.

Secondly, while the appeal *per uos* can be paralleled in Cicero's oratory (*Planc.* 103 *nolite iudices per uos per fortunas per liberos uestros inimicis meis... dare laetitiam*) and in the writings of the historians (Sallust, *Iug.* 14.25 *patres conscripti per uos per liberos atque parentis nostros per maiestatem populi Romani subuenite mihi misero*, *Hist.* 2.47.13, Livy 29.18.9, Curtius 9.2.28) and in classical poetry (Lygdamus 1.15) it has no parallel in republican drama. Here, in certain very solemn passages, *per* is disjoined from its object by the pronominal subject and/or object of the verb of supplication (see above on *v.* 3). The construction was already old-fashioned in tone in the early second century and Cicero's *nolite per uos* etc. seems to spring from a misunderstanding of its nature. One should not try to take *uos* as the object of an unexpressed verb of supplication. This was a Greek construction (cf. Euripides, *Andr.* 892–3 πρός σε τῶνδε γουνάτων, | οἴκτιρον ἡμᾶς) and seems to appear first in Latin at Rhet. inc. *Her.* 4.65 (*per te ea quae tibi dulcissima sunt in uita miserere nostri*), in what looks like a rhetorician's literal translation of a Greek story, and then sporadically in poetry (e.g. Lucan 10.370, Silius 1.658).

Thirdly, the idea that mere *uigiles* should possess a thing like *imperium* is absurd. The word *imperium* had a semi-religious tone lacking in Greek words for power and authority; it belonged properly to the official language and denoted the authority of the chief civil magistrates. Plautus uses it, perhaps in jest, of the authority of the head of the private Greek household[1] but there is no parallel anywhere for the use which Bergk and Vahlen foist on Ennius.[2]

I cannot see how to restore the fragment without extensive rewriting. That there stood in Ennius' text a variant of the appeal *per fidem* (Plautus, *Trin.* 153, Terence, *Andr.* 290, Sallust, *Iug.* 10.3 et al.) is fairly certain; for the coupling of *fides* and *imperium* cf. *Carm. deu. ap.* Macrob. *Sat.* 3.9.11 *ut me meamque fidem imperiumque legiones exercitumque nostrum qui in his rebus gerundis sunt bene saluos siritis esse.*[3] One should take *imperium et fidem Myrmidonum* together; according to some Roman politicians and political theorists *imperium* belonged in the last resort to the whole *populus Romanus* (cf. Cicero, *Phil.* 3.37 *cum senatus auctoritatem populique Romani libertatem*

---

[1] Cf. *Asin.* 87 *dote imperium uendidi.* It is possible that the juridical language already used it so; cf. Paulus, Fest. p. 55.9 *nuptiali iure imperio uiri subicitur nubens*, Ulpian, *Dig.* 50.17.4 *uelle non creditur qui obsequitur imperio patris uel domini.*

[2] O. Prinz, *T.L.L.* VII i 574.38 ff., puts the fragment at the end of his examples of *imperium, de certarum personarum potestate/apud exteros/de monarchis* but is obviously nonplussed.

[3] Ennius, *Ann.* 107 has *fides* and *regnum* together, Caesar, *Gall.* 2.3.2, 2.13.2, Cicero, *ad Q. fr.* 1.1.27, Curtius 8.4.21 *fides* and *potestas*, Livy 34.35.10, 37.45.3, 38.31.6 *fides* and *dicio.*

imperiumque defendat, Livy 4.5.1, Ulpian, *Dig.* 1.4.1) and the early tragedians were ready to transfer this collective *imperium* to the heroic world of Greece (cf. Accius 231 *Argiuom imperium*).

Ennius' Priam draws on the solemn formulae of the Roman *deditio in fidem* for his appeal. Something of the character of Euripides, *Med.* 709–11 ἀλλ' ἄντομαί σε τῆσδε πρὸς γενειάδος | γονάτων τε τῶν σῶν ἱκεσία τε γίγνομαι, | οἴκτιρον οἴκτιρόν με is likely to have stood in his original. Πρὸς τῶν θεῶν, πρὸς τοῦ γενείου, πρὸς τῶν γονάτων and πρὸς τῆς δεξιᾶς are the normal espressions in Attic tragedy; appeals to abstract qualities are rare (cf. Sophocles, *O.K.* 515 μὴ πρὸς ξενίας...). In Roman comedy the normal appeal is *per deos* or *per genium* or *per genua* or *per dexteram*; abstracts appear when the tone rises (cf. Plautus, *Asin.* 18 *ted obtestor per senectutem tuam*, *Capt.* 245–6 *per fortunam incertam et per mei te erga bonitatem patris,* | *perque conseruitium commune*).

162 commiserescite: a high tragic form; twice elsewhere in republican tragedy, only three times in all comedy (Plautus, *Rud.* 1090, Terence, *Hec.* 129, Turpilius, *Com.* 211); comedy has *miserescere* three times in very solemn contexts (Plautus, *Epid.* 526, *Trin.* 343, Terence, *Haut.* 1026); *misereri* is the regular form (37 times in comedy, 7 in tragedy).

LXXVI

The noisy arrival is a commonplace of tragedy (cf. Euripides, *I.A.* 317, *I.T.* 1307–8, *Rhes.* 11–16) as well as of comedy (cf. Plautus, *Bacch.* 583–6, 1120, *Curc.* 277, *Trin.* 1093). Schöll referred the fragment to the arrival of news of Hector' success in his attack on the Greek encampment. It could equally well concern that of news of Patroclus' death (so Ribbeck) or the arrival of Priam in quest of Hector's body.

163 quid hoc hic clamoris: cf. Plautus, *Aul.* 403 *sed quid hoc clamoris oritur hinc ex proximo ?*, *Trin.* 1093 *quid hoc hic clamoris audio ante aedis meas ?*, Caecilius, *Com.* 245 *quid hoc clamoris ?*

quid tumulti est: cf. Plautus, *Poen.* 207 *quid istuc tumulti est ?*, Turpilius, *Com.* 154 *quid hic tumulti ante fores ?*, Pomponius, *Atell.* 121 *quid hoc est tumulti ?*

nomen qui usurpat meum: contrast Plautus, *Bacch.* 1120 *quis sonitu ac tumultu tanto nominat me ?*, *Curc.* 304 *quis nominat me ?*, *Mil.* 901, *Most.* 784, *Rud.* 98, 678*b*, 868, Terence, *Phorm.* 739, 990, Trag. inc. 1 *quis enim est qui meum nomen nuncupat ?*, 97 *quis meum nominans nomen aede exciet ?*

Qui is transmitted quite often as an indefinite or interrogative substantive in both tragedy (Pacuvius 228, Accius 64, 343, 562, 625) and comedy.[1] Its enclitic position here is highly unusual.

For *usurpare*, 'nominare', cf. Cicero, *Off*. 2.40 *Laelius, is qui Sapiens usurpatur*. Plautus has the verb six times (*Bacch*. 149, *Cas*. 631, *Cist*. 505, *Persa* 736, *Trin*. 846, *Pseud*. 135), mostly as a high-falutin synonym of *uti*; elsewhere in republican drama it occurs only at Trag. inc. 127 and Accius, *Trag. praet*. 29.

LXXVII

Lindsay's analysis of the structure of Nonius' dictionary tends to confirm Columna's view that this fragment followed LXXVI directly. Nonius illustrated TVMVLTI and STREPITI with pieces taken successively from the list based on Ennius' *Hectoris lytra* and *Telephus*.[2]

LXXVIII

165 aes sonit: Nic. Faber's emendation is almost certain; cf. the corruption at Catullus 41.8. The phrase can hardly refer to the blast of trumpets (so *T.L.L.* I 1073.48). The clash of iron-tipped spears on brazen shields and helmets is meant; cf. Euripides, *Herakleidai* 832 πόσον τιν' αὐχεῖς πάταγον ἀσπίδων βρέμειν, Ennius, *Ann*. 363 *tum clipei resonunt et ferri stridit acumen*, Virgil, *Aen*. 9.666–7 *tum scuta cauaeque | dant sonitum flictu galeae*.[3]

franguntur hastae: cf. Euripides, *Phoin*. 1399–402 ἀπὸ δ' ἔθραυσ' ἄκρον δόρυ... μέσον δ' ἄκοντ' ἔθραυσεν, Ennius, *Ann*. 405 *semper abundantes hastas frangitque quatitque*, Hostius, *Carm*. fr. I *percutit atque hastam pilans prae pondere frangit*, Plautus, *Amph*. 232 *tela frangunt*.

terra sudat sanguine: a bizarre phrase imitated by Virgil (?) at *Aen*. 2.582 *Dardanium totiens sudarit sanguine litus*. Lucretius (5.1131–2, 6.1147–8) and Livy (22.1.8, 27.4.14) use *sanguine sudare* in somewhat more appropriate circumstances. Ennius has conflated two motifs of the traditional battle narrative, the sweat pouring from the bodies of the contestants (cf. Homer, *Il*. 16.109–11 αἰεὶ δ' ἀργαλέῳ ἔχετ' ἄσθματι, κὰδ δέ οἱ ἱδρὼς | πάντοθεν ἐκ μελέων πολὺς ἔρρεεν, οὐδέ πη εἶχεν | ἀμπνεῦσαι, Euripides, *Phoin*.

---

[1] See O. Seyffert, *BPhW* XIII (1893), 277 ff., Löfstedt, *Syntactica* II (Lund, 1933), pp. 79 ff.

[2] See Lindsay, *Nonius Marcellus' Dictionary*, p. 26, *RhM* LVII (1902), 202.

[3] Nevertheless, contrary to epic practice (the simile at *Il*. 18.219 is the significant exception), the battles of Attic tragedy are signalled by the trumpet; cf. Aeschylus, *Pers*. 395 (contemporary fighting), Sophocles, *Ai*. 289 ff., Euripides, *Herakleidai* 830, *Phoin*. 1102.

1388–9 πλείων δὲ τοῖς ὁρῶσιν ἐστάλασσ᾽ ἱδρώς | ἢ τοῖσι δρῶσι, διὰ φίλων ὀρρωδίαν, Ennius, *Ann.* 406 *totum sudor habet corpus*) and the blood pouring upon the ground (cf. Homer, *Il* 8.65 ῥέε δ᾽ αἵματι γαῖα, 10.484 ἐρυθαίνετο δ᾽ αἵματι γαῖα, Euripides, *Phoin.* 1152 ξηρὰν δ᾽ ἔδευον γαῖαν αἵματος ῥοαῖς). The alliterative pair *sanguis et sudor* is common in Latin writing (cf. Ennius, *Trag.* 347, Cicero, *Leg. agr.* 2.16, 2.69, Livy 2.48.2, 7.38.6 et al.).

LXXIX

The unexpressed subject of *cernunt* have good fortune as well as their weapons helping them. *Fortuna* never indicates impersonal chance (τύχη) in republican drama except at Pacuvius, *Trag.* 366 ff., where the speaker is discoursing on philosophical doctrines; when unqualified it is normally optimistic in tone. Its nearest equivalent in Attic drama would be θεός or δαίμων (contrast Aeschylus, fr. 395 φιλεῖ δὲ τῷ κάμνοντι συσπεύδειν θεός and Euripides, fr. 432.2 τῷ γὰρ πονοῦντι χὠ θεὸς συλλαμβάνει with Terence, *Phorm.* 203 *fortis fortuna adiuuat*).

166 saeuiter: the regular form in republican drama, 6 times in comedy, 3 times in tragedy; neither *saeuiter* nor *saeue* seems to occur in classical Latin.

fortuna ferro: for the asyndeton bimembre cf. the tragic examples listed above on *v.* 9 and the formulaic *forte fortuna* (Plautus, *Bacch.* 916, *Mil.* 287, Terence, *Eun.* 134, 568). Neither Columna's *fortuna ferri* nor Bergk's *ferro ac fortuna* is necessary but the latter emendation has the merit of directing attention to the fact that the longer word rarely precedes the shorter in these asyndeta.

For the combination of *fortuna* and *ferrum* cf. Virgil, *Aen.* 10.421–2 *da nunc Thybri pater ferro quod missile libro | fortunam*.

cernunt: Homeric κρίνονται (*Il.* 2.385, 18.209); a usage hard to explain;[1] to be found elsewhere only at Ennius, *Trag.* 232, *Ann.* 196, 555, Pacuvius, *Trag.* 24, Accius, *Trag.* 326, Lucretius 5.393, Virgil, *Aen.* 12.218, 709. The compound *decernere* is used with the same sense at Ennius, *Ann.* 133, frequently in Virgil and Livy, occasionally in Cicero and Caesar. Comedy has *decernere* 'decide' often and *cernere* with the same sense at Plautus, *Bacch.* 399, *Cas.* 516, *Trin.* 479. For *cernere* 'perceive' see above on *v.* 13. *Certare* seems to have been the regular word in the common language for 'fight for a decision' (Plautus, *Merc.* 345, *Mil.* 714, *Persa* 238, *Truc.* 948, 950, Terence, *Phorm.* 20, Pacuvius, *Trag.* 25).

---

[1] See Ernout, *BSL* XXIX (1929), 82 ff. (= *Philologica* I, pp. 83 ff.), Leumann, *Gnomon* XIII (1937), 31, *MusH* IV (1947), 133 (= *Kl. Schr.* 154).

301

LXXX

This fragment seems to describe an encounter between two warriors; while one is temporarily blinded, the other takes to his heels. The vision of Homer's warriors is frequently obscured on the field of battle by mists, etc. (cf. *Il.* 16.790 ff., 17.644 ff., 20.321 ff., 20.441 ff.) but there is no exact parallel in the *Iliad* for Ennius' Latin. I should guess that the final encounter between Achilles and Hector is being described; Homer's account is somewhat different (cf. *Il.* 22.136-7 Ἕκτορα δ' ὡς ἐνόησεν ἕλε τρόμος· οὐδ' ἄρ' ἔτ' ἔτλη | αὖθι μένειν, ὀπίσω δὲ πύλας λίπε, βῆ δὲ φοβηθείς) but so too is his account of several other events described or enacted in Ennius' tragedy.

The abrupt asyndeton and change of subject do not compel one to postulate a lacuna between *abstulit* and *derepente*. If there is something missing here it becomes doubly hard to understand why Nonius quoted *ecce...abstulit* in an article illustrating the adverb *derepente*.

167 ecce autem caligo oborta est; omnem prospectum abstulit: cf. Anon. *Bell. Afr.* 52 *nisi...puluis...uento flatus omnium prospectu offecisset*, Virgil, *Aen.* 8.253-4 *inuoluitque domum caligine caeca | prospectum eripiens oculis*, Livy 4.33.8, 10.32.6.

Ecce autem indicates either the speaker's surprise at an unexpected turn of the action (cf. Plautus, *Merc.* 748, 792), or as here, his feeling that the hearer will be surprised at what he is to narrate (cf. Virgil, *Aen.* 2.201-5 *Laocoon... taurum ingentem mactabat ad aras. | ecce autem gemini...angues | incumbunt pelago*).

Prospectus appears elsewhere in republican drama only at Plautus, *Mil.* 609.

168 contulit sese in pedes: cf. Plautus, *Bacch.* 374 *me continuo contuli protinam in pedes* (paratragic); *pedibus se dare* seems to have been the regular phrase (Naevius, *Com.* 35, Plautus, fr. 15); Plautus, *Capt.* 121 *si non est quod dem, mene uis dem ipse — in pedes* is humorously meant. L. Mueller was thus quite wrong to excise *contulit sese in pedes* from the Ennian fragment as being untragic.

LXXXI

Sublime iter (cf. *vv.* 190-1) indicates that the fragment refers to the horses of the sun-god (cf. Pindar, *Ol.* 7.71-2 ὁ γενέθλιος ἀκτίνων πατήρ, | πῦρ πνεόντων ἀρχὸς ἵππων, Euripides, *I.A.* 159 πῦρ τε τεθρίππων τῶν Ἀελίου, Virgil, *Georg.* 1.250 *nosque ubi primus equis Oriens afflauit anhelis, Aen.* 12.114-15 *cum primum alto se gurgite tollunt | solis equi, lucemque elatis naribus efflant*) rather than to those of any of the heroes (cf. Euripides, *Alk.* 493 πῦρ πνέουσι μυκτήρων ἄπο, Lucretius 5.29 *et Diomedis equi spirantes naribus ignem*, Virgil, *Aen.* 7.280-1 *geminosque iugalis | semine ab aetherio spirantis naribus ignem*). Omitting *ut* and comparing Ennius, *Var.* 11–12 *sol equis iter repressit ungulis uolantibus,* | *constitere amnes perennes, arbores uento uacant* Vahlen argued that the fragment belonged in the same context as LXXIII. This is an acute suggestion but I should prefer to leave *ut* and take the fragment as part of a simile.

169 quadrupedantes: an odd formation, restored at Accius, *Trag.* 603, securely transmitted at Plautus, *Capt.* 814 *qui aduehuntur quadrupedanti crucianti cantherio* (a tragically styled parody of a praetor's edict), Virgil, *Aen.* 8.595–6 *agmine facto* | *quadrupedante putrem sonitu quatit ungula campum,* 11.614–15 *perfractaque quadrupedantum* | *pectora pectoribus rumpunt*; perhaps concocted by Ennius himself for the sake of sound-play with *halitantes*. Tragedy has *quadrupes* commonly of animals (Naevius 25, Ennius 157, Pacuvius 2, Accius 315, 381), comedy only once (Terence, *Andr.* 865 [perhaps paratragic]). The formation *quadrupedans* is of the same type as *undans* (Ennius, *Trag.* 179), *uiridans* (Accius, *Trag.* 244), *unanimans* (Plautus, *Truc.* 435 [paratragic]), a type of formation rare in old Latin and confined to poetry in classical Latin.

halitantes: only here in Latin; *halare* itself is rare and confined to poetry.

LXXXII

Schöll took this fragment as spoken by Achilles to a worried Patroclus after Ulysses has come with bad news from the battle-field. It could as easily be spoken by Priam to a companion while on the way to Achilles' tent or by Achilles to Priam after the ransom has been arranged. The Attic tragedians made Ulysses the opponent of all just and merciful arrangements.[1]

170 nomus: probably the regular form in the common language; its absence from the rest of extant drama is accidental; *nouimus* does not appear either; the situations of drama leave little scope for the first person plural; *nosti, nossem* etc., *nosse* are common in Plautus and almost universal in Terence.

HECVBA

Aulus Gellius asserts at *Noctes Atticae* 11.4 that the *Hecuba* of Ennius was a version of Euripides' homonymous tragedy and quotes three verses of the Greek script along with the particular Latin rendering. At 2.23 he makes a

---

[1] Vahlen (*E.P.R.*[2], p. 145) appears to have taken the fragment as spoken by Menelaus to Ajax after the wounded Ulysses has shouted for help (Homer, *Il.* 11.463 ff.); such an interpretation would require a quite incredible change of scene.

similar but much more extended comparison between Menander's Πλόκιον and Caecilius' version. The extant scholia to Terence's comedies contain scraps of similar comparisons between Terence's Latin and the Greek of his originals. We may suppose that Gellius based his assertion about Ennius' *Hecuba* either on a detailed personal knowledge of the texts of this play and the Euripidean or on a didascalic notice of the type affixed to the extant texts of the six comedies of Terence and the *Stichus* of Plautus. It has a reliability quite lacking in apparently similar assertions by Varro and Cicero about particular Latin tragedies (see above, p. 236).

Nonius Marcellus gives Ennius the title *Hecuba* eleven times. The eight pieces quoted seem to come from grammatical sources rather than Nonius' own knowledge of the text. The wording of only two of them (frs. xc and xcπ) parallels Euripides' Greek[1] as closely as does that of Gellius' quotation (lxxxiv) but the others can be fitted into free versions of Euripidean speeches without upsetting at any point the framework of the Greek plot. This circumstance indicates clearly what others only suggest, namely that the republican poets rarely followed the exact wording of the Athenian classics they were hired to adapt. It is accordingly improper to use, as many have done, the text of Euripides' Ἑκάβη as an aid in restoring that of the Ennian fragments.

A trimeter, *ueter fatorum terminus sic iusserat*, is attributed by Priscian (*Gramm.* II 264.15) to a *Hecuba* of Accius. If *fata* be interpreted as 'oracles' the trimeter has no counterpart in Euripides' Ἑκάβη. If it be interpreted as 'fate' or 'destiny' there are a number of possible counterparts: cf., for example, *vv.* 43 ἡ πεπρωμένη, 584 θεῶν ἀνάγκαισιν. The imagery of the boundary stone is absent from Euripides' Ἑκάβη but can be found elsewhere in Attic tragedy (cf. Aeschylus, *Ag.* 1154–5 πόθεν ὅρους ἔχεις θεσπεσίας ὁδοῦ | κακορρήμονας, *Choe.* 927 πατρὸς γὰρ αἶσα τόνδε σουρίζει μόρον, Sophocles, *O.T.* 723 τοιαῦτα φῆμαι μαντικαὶ διώρισαν). Land division was a frequent source of metaphor in republican dramatic writing (cf. Plautus, *Poen.* 48–9) and it is possible that the author of *ueter fatorum terminus sic iusserat* drew upon it to express the rather un-Roman notion of a fixed immutable destiny.[2] Hermann[3] suggested that Priscian was in error in attributing the trimeter to Accius' *Hecuba* rather than to Ennius' *Hecuba*. Such errors are

---

[1] P. Victorius, *Variarum Lectionum libri XXV* (Florence, 1553), x 1, compared Euripides, *Hek.* 826 ff. and 497 ff.

[2] Cf. Lucretius, 1.75–7 *unde refert nobis uictor quid possit oriri,* | *quid nequeat, finita potestas denique cuique* | *quanam sit ratione atque alte terminus haerens* (Epicurean natural law), Virgil, *Aen.* 4.612–14 *si...necesse est* | *et sic fata Iouis poscunt, hic terminus haeret,* Horace, *Carm. saec.* 25–7 *uosque ueraces cecinisse Parcae* | *quod semel dictum est stabilisque rerum* | *terminus seruet.*

[3] On Eur. *Hek.* 578 (Leipzig, 1800).

common enough in the grammarians[1] and the singularity of the reference to Accius' *Hecuba* makes the existence of the play dubious. On the other hand the titles *Alcestis*, *Eriphyla* and *Persidae* are given by Priscian to Accius each on a single occasion and occur nowhere else in our sources; the existence of these it would be folly to doubt. Furthermore the usage of republican drama favours the interpretation 'oracle' for *terminus fatorum* rather than 'fate'.[2]

At *Ling.* 7.6 Varro illustrates the use of the word *templum* from the plays *Hecuba*, *Periboea* and *Andromacha*; copious quotations elsewhere give an *Andromacha* to Ennius and a *Periboea* to Pacuvius; but for the doubts about Priscian, *Gramm.* II 264.15 one would be tempted to assign Varro's first quotation to Accius, the third of the classical tragic trio. With some doubts I have followed editorial tradition and printed it alongside the pieces directly attributed to Ennius' *Hecuba* (fr. LXXXIII).

There is no unambiguous evidence that Cicero knew Ennius' *Hecuba*. On the other hand his works contain many quotations of Ennius' *Andromacha* and Pacuvius' *Iliona*, tragedies similar in many ways structurally to the *Hecuba*.[3] Accordingly quotations such as those at *Tusc.* 1.37[4] and *Orat.* 153[5] which recall structural elements of Euripides' Ἑκάβη (*vv.* 1–2, 837, 1040–4) need not be attributed to Ennius' adaptation.[6]

Where *sententiae* with parallels in Euripides' Ἑκάβη are concerned even greater scepticism is justified.[7] The remains of Euripides' tragic production are full of general statements about society, religion, politics, morality, etc.[8]

---

[1] Using a common source Priscian, *Gramm.* II 260.4 and Nonius, p. 223.2 attribute a fragment the one rightly to the *Niptra* of Pacuvius the other wrongly to a *Niptra* of Accius; cf. the clear errors at Nonius, pp. 75.8, 90.10, 116.8, 117.18, 170.12, 176.12, 209.25, 223.2, 382.12, 479.13, 515.12.

[2] Cf. Marx, *SB Leipzig* LXIII (1911), 62.

[3] On *Iliona* see Zieliński, *Tragodumenon Libri Tres* (Kraków, 1925), pp. 48, 124.

[4] See Columna, *Q. Ennii Frag.* p. 376.

[5] See Ribbeck, *Die röm. Trag.* p. 145, Havet, *RPh* XXVIII (1904), 219 ff.

[6] Scaliger, *Coniect. Varr. Ling.*, on 10.70, attributed to *Hecuba* the *canticum* quoted at *Tusc.* 3.44 on the grounds that it resembled Euripides, *Hek.* 158–60, overlooking that later, at 3.53, part of the *canticum* is quoted as coming from *Andromacha*.

[7] Two trimeters quoted by Cicero at *Tusc.* 2.13 were assigned by Columna to Ennius' *Hecuba* because of their similarity to Euripides, *Hek.* 592–5. In *RhM* XVI (1861), 443 ff., Mommsen published some Virgilian scholia (*Breu. exp. Georg.* 1.1, p. 199.3 Hagen) quoting the verses as from Accius' *Atreus* and thus confirming Muretus' restoration of Cicero's corrupt introductory words as *illud Accii* '*probae* (*illud acimprobe* RK: *acinprobe* GV).

[8] See C. W. Friedrich, *Die dramatische Funktion der euripideischen Gnomen* (Diss. Freiburg, 1955).

often repeated from one play to another. Vahlen printed the words *nimium boni est cui nihil est mali* attributed to Ennius at *Fin.* 2.41 (fr. CLXXIII) as a fragment of *Hecuba* on the grounds of its similarity to Euripides, *Hek.* 627–8 κεῖνος ὀλβιώτατος, | ὅτῳ κατ' ἦμαρ τυγχάνει μηδὲν κακόν.¹ The idea recurs at *Ba.* 910–11 τὸ δὲ κατ' ἦμαρ ὅτῳ βίοτος | εὐδαίμων μακαρίζω.² Vahlen also printed among the fragments of *Hecuba* the *amicus certus in re incerta cernitur* attributed to Ennius at *Lael.* 64 (fr. CLXXXV). The substance of this trimeter appears not only at *Hek.* 1226–7, ἐν τοῖς κακοῖς γὰρ ἀγαθοὶ σαφέστατοι | φίλοι,³ but also at *Or.* 454–5, ὄνομα γάρ, ἔργον δ' οὐκ ἔχουσιν οἱ φίλοι | οἱ μὴ 'πὶ ταῖσι συμφοραῖς ὄντες φίλοι.⁴ Ennius seems to have employed *sententiae* much more frequently than did his successors Pacuvius and Accius. He quite certainly altered the emphasis of some of those which he found in his originals (see below on LXXXIV) and added others totally absent (see below on CVIII); it is possible that he omitted some which did not appeal to him.⁵ In circumstances like this it seems pointless to try to localise *sententiae* in particular plays; too many possibilities are open.

LXXXIII

The personages of tragedy frequently address the open sky above the stage; cf. Aeschylus, *Prom.* 88 ὦ δῖος αἰθήρ, 1091–2 ὦ πάντων | αἰθὴρ κοινὸν φάος εἰλίσσων, Sophocles, *El.* 86, Euripides, *Ion* 1445, fr. 443. The heroine of Euripides' Ἑκάβη refers sarcastically to the practice at *vv.* 334–5 ὦ θύγατερ, οὑμοὶ μὲν λόγοι πρὸς αἰθέρα | φροῦδοι μάτην ῥιφέντες ἀμφὶ σοῦ φόνου.⁶ The only near parallel in the play with Ennius' iambic tetrameter is the anapaestic address to the lightning bolt of Zeus at *vv.* 68–70, ὦ στεροπὰ Διός, ὦ σκοτία νύξ, | τί ποτ' αἴρομαι ἔννυχος οὕτω | δείμασι φάσμασιν; But Ennius can be shown quite certainly in other places to have altered the metrical structure and the substance of his original no less drastically (see below on fr. LXXXIV).

---

¹ Muretus (*Variarum Lectionum libri VIII* [Venice, 1559], V 13) seems to have been the first to make this identification.

² Cf. also Euripides, *Herakles* 503 ff., *Hik.* 953 f., *Hipp.* 1111 ff., fr. 196, fr. 714.

³ Hartung (*Euripides Restitutus* I, p. 529) was the first to make this identification.

⁴ Cf. *Or.* 665–8.

⁵ Among the fragments of Menander's Ἀνδρία (43) and Ἑαυτὸν τιμωρούμενος (132) are *sententiae* which have no equivalents in Terence's adaptations. The substance of *Andria* 959–60 is said by Donatus to come from Menander's Εὐνοῦχος but it has no equivalent in the Latin version of this play.

⁶ Cf. Euripides, *Andr.* 91 ff., *I.T.* 42 f., *Med.* 57 f. Comedy parodies it; cf. Menander, *Sam.* 111, Plautus, *Trin.* 1070, Terence, *Ad.* 790.

171 **templa caelitum**: cf. (a) Accius, *Trag. praet.* 2, Varro, *Men.* 56, (b) Ennius, *Ann.* 541 *templum magnum Iouis altitonantis*, Lucretius 5.1188 *in caeloque deum sedes et templa locarunt*, (c) Ennius, *Ann.* 49 *caeli caerula templa*, Terence, *Eun.* 590 *templa caeli summa* ('sententia tragica'—Donatus), Lucretius 1.1014, 1105 et al., (d) Lucretius 5.1204–5 *magni caelestia mundi | templa super stellisque micantibus aethera fixum*, (f) Seneca, *Herc. f.* 3 *templa summi . . . aetheris*. The only comparable phrase in extant Attic tragedy seems to be Aeschylus, *Pers.* 365 τέμενος αἰθέρος.

The word *templum* probably came from the augural language (see above on *v.* 88).[1] It is difficult to say whether *caeles*, which occurs four times elsewhere in republican tragedy and only once (Plautus, *Rud.* 2) in comedy, was a sacral word or a poetic creation (~ οὐράνιος, οὐρανίων). It is absent from classical prose. Yet its second element is not common in poetic neologisms.

splendidis: elsewhere in tragedy at Accius 678; absent from comedy. This could be accident, for *splendere* occurs at Iuventius, *Com.* 6, Plautus, *Poen.* 314, *Rud.* 3 (*splendens stella*), *splendor* at Plautus, *Asin.* 426, *Aul.* 602, *Merc.* 880, *Mil.* 1. However the incidence of adjectives in -*idus* seems to be somewhat greater in tragedy than in comedy. Ploen counts 40 formations in comedy and 27 in tragedy, 10 of which do not occur in comedy.

LXXXIV

Ennius' opening *haec*, which has no counterpart in the Greek of *vv.* 293–4, τὸ δ' ἀξίωμα, κἂν κακῶς λέγῃ, τὸ σὸν | πείσει, must refer to the content of his version of *vv.* 288–92, ὡς ἀποκτείνειν φθόνος | γυναῖκας, ἃς τὸ πρῶτον οὐκ ἐκτείνατε | βωμῶν ἀποσπάσαντες, ἀλλ' ᾠκτίρατε. | νόμος δ' ἐν ὑμῖν τοῖς τ' ἐλευθέροις ἴσος | καὶ τοῖσι δούλοις αἵματος κεῖται πέρι. One may doubt whether he adapted the substance of *vv.* 291–2; this was an anachronistic reference to the protection which Athenian law gave to slaves against arbitrary acts on the part of their masters[2] and would have created sympathy for the speaker in the Athenian theatre; but in second-century Rome, where masters enjoyed unrestricted power over the lives of their slaves, it would have sounded merely paradoxical. At *Stich.* 446–8, *atque id ne nos miremini, homines seruolos | potare, amare atque ad cenam condicere: | licet haec Athenis nobis*, Plautus feels obliged to explain the behaviour of his Menandrian slaves.

---

[1] Ennius could be employing an architectural metaphor (see above on *v.* 3); for *templum*, 'roof-beam' cf. Lucretius 2.28, Paulus, Fest. p. 505.1 f., Vitruvius 4.2.

[2] Cf. Isocrates 18.52, Demosthenes 21.46–9, Ps. Xenophon, *Ath.* 1.10.

The substance of *vv.* 294–5 λόγος γὰρ ἔκ τ' ἀδοξούντων ἰὼν | κἀκ τῶν δοκούντων αὐτὸς οὐ ταὐτὸν σθένει was a commonplace both in the fifth century and later; cf. Euripides, *Andr.* 186–7 ἐγὼ δὲ ταρβῶ μὴ τὸ δουλεύειν μέ σοι | λόγων ἀπώσῃ πόλλ' ἔχουσαν ἔνδικα, fr. 327, Trag. Graec. inc. fr. 119, Cicero, *S. Rosc.* 2 *quia si qui istorum dixisset quos uidetis adesse, in quibus summa auctoritas est atque amplitudo, si uerbum de re publica fecisset, id quod in hac causa fieri necesse est, multo plura dixisse quam dixisset putaretur. ego autem si omnia quae dicenda sunt libere dixero nequaquam similiter oratio mea exire atque in uolgus emanare poterit.* For the purely general contrast between οἱ δοκοῦντες and οἱ ἀδοξοῦντες Ennius substitutes a particular one between *opulenti*, 'those with *opes*, with social power and influence', and *ignobiles*, 'those without a *nomen*, of obscure and humble family'. This contrast is not apt to the situation of Ulysses and the enslaved Hecuba. Ennius must have had in mind not the text of his original or even its plot but one of the themes of contemporary political debate. He would have known that critics chid Euripides for making his heroes and heroines speak like contemporary Athenian philosophers and politicians.[1] In making his Hecuba utter something quite incongruous with the dramatic situation he also had Euripides as a forerunner, if not in Ἑκάβη certainly in other plays.[2] His motive, like that of Euripides, would have been a straightforward desire for theatrical effect, something to which the Aristotelian canons of organic unity are not always relevant.

Euripides' spoken trimeters are replaced with musically accompanied trochaic tetrameters. These verses bring with them here, as elsewhere, an amount of figurated language absent from Euripides' trimeters (whose *breuitas* is noted by Gellius). Αὐτὸς οὐ ταὐτόν obviously inspires *aequa non aeque*, a type of polyptoton common in Attic tragedy but rare in Roman drama.[3] The phrase *facile... flexeris* is chosen for an alliterative effect quite rare in Attic tragedy but common in the republican adaptations.[4] Λόγος . . .

---

[1] Ennius may have read a commentary on the Ἑκάβη containing remarks like those in the extant scholia; cf. *ad* 254 ταῦτα εἰς τὴν κατ' αὐτὸν πολιτείαν λέγει. καὶ ἐστι τοιοῦτος ὁ Εὐριπίδης, περιάπτων τὰ καθ' ἑαυτὸν τοῖς ἥρωσι καὶ τοὺς χρόνους συγχέων, 898 οὐ καλῶς φησι ταῦτα ὁ Ἀγαμέμνων. ἔχρην γὰρ αὐτὸν ἅπαξ δόντα τὴν χάριν σιωπῆσαι καὶ μὴ ἐλέγξαι τὴν ἑαυτοῦ γνώμην· οὐ γὰρ ἀνάγκη τοιαύτῃ ὑπέκειτο βασιλεὺς ὤν.

[2] See Lucian, *Iou. trag.* 41.689, the scholiast on *Phoin.* 388, modern scholars on *Herakles* 1340–6.

[3] The only exact parallel I can find is Plautus, *Amph.* 355 *familiaris, accipiere faxo haud familiariter.*

[4] Cf. Naevius 13 *mea manu moriare,* 28 *lino linquant lumina,* Ennius 118 *spumant sanguine,* 165 *sudat sanguine,* 181 *modice morem gerit,* 184 *grauiter gemam* et al.

αὐτός is turned into the highly elaborate *eadem dicta eademque oratio*; the doubling of one word or phrase with another of much the same meaning, the anaphora, the balancing of one colon with another slightly longer are certainly to be found in some trimeter speeches of Attic tragedy and comedy but they are most at home in the long verses of the Latin adaptations (see above on *vv.* 9, 19). The units of sense of the Latin discourse are made to coincide with those of metre in the normal manner of republican drama.

173 nam cum opulenti locuntur: Porson's *nam opulenti cum locuntur* removes an instance of hiatus after a monosyllable in the thesis of a trochaic verse,[1] gives the general *opulenti* an emphasis corresponding with that of the particular *tu* placed in front of the conjunction *etsi* in *v.* 172 and produces an order of words common in republican drama but rarer later and therefore likely to be 'modernised'.[2] I am not sure however that these are grounds firm enough for altering the paradosis.

Opes usually stands for social power and standing rather than property (*diuitiae*) in the speeches of republican drama. *Opulentus* is sometimes difficult to distinguish from the much more commonly occurring *dives* (it is opposed to *pauper* at Plautus, *Aul.* 247, 461, 479, Caecilius, *Com.* 170 ff.) but at Plautus, *Curc.* 284–6, *nec usquam quisquamst tam opulentus, qui mi opsistat in uia | nec strategus nec tyrannus quisquam nec agoranomus | nec demarchus nec comarchus*, and *Rud.* 713, *de senatu Cyrenensi quemuis opulentum uirum*, it bears plainly the meaning 'socially powerful, influential'.[3]

ignobiles: the meaning here cannot be anything but 'socially obscure', as at Pacuvius, *Trag.* 221 and Terence, *Phorm.* 120. At Livius, *Com.* 3, Plautus, *Amph.* 440, *Pseud.* 592, 964 it is 'unknown to one individual or another'. *Nobilis* means 'known to one individual or another' at Plautus, *Poen.* 758, *Pseud.* 1112, *Rud.* 619, *Trin.* 828; 'socially eminent' at Plautus, *Cist.* 125 (suspected of lateness by some scholars), Terence, *Ad.* 15, 502, *Eun.* 204, 952,

---

[1] The only other tragic instance of this hiatus seems to be Accius 345. For a list of the instances transmitted by the codices of Plautus in which *cum* and *quom* stand unelided *in thesi* see Maurenbrecher, *Hiatus und Verschleifung*, pp. 35 ff.

[2] Cf. Plautus, *Amph.* 91–2 *histriones anno quom in proscaenio hic | Iouem inuocarunt, uenit*, 427–8 *legiones quom pugnabant maxume, | quid in tabernaclo fecisti ?, Cas.* 7–8 et al. However for the 'modern' type of order cf. Plautus, *Capt.* 77–9 *quasi mures semper edimus alienum cibum; | ubi res prolatae sunt, quom rus homines eunt, | simul prolatae res sunt nostris dentibus, Cas.* 417–18, *Curc.* 105–6 et al.

[3] Among the classical prose writers only the historians Sallust and Livy have *opulentus* at all commonly. On Livy's usage see Drexler, *RhM* CII (1959), 55–8.

Haut. 227, 609. Plautus uses *nobilitas* three times (*Capt.* 299, *Mil.* 1324, *Rud.* 933) of social eminence. The two sets of meanings must have been already coexistent before 184 B.C. By the first century *nobilis* was a fully technical term of the political vocabulary, denoting a member of one of those families whose names were known as a result of ancestral consulships and which enjoyed an almost complete monopoly of the principal magistracies. Ennius' first patron, Cato, had been forced to make his political way in a climate of opinion well described by *vv.* 173–4.

174 eadem dicta eademque oratio: the two phrases can be distinguished; *dicta* are the words and *oratio* the way they are uttered; cf. *v.* 258 *quam tibi ex ore orationem duriter dictis dedit.*

LXXXV

Tears drip in Attic tragedy rather less frequently than blood and sweat; but cf. Aeschylus, *Choe.* 185–6, *Prom.* 398–401, Euripides, *Herakles* 1354–6, *Ion* 876, as well as Euripides, *Hek.* 760 ὁρᾷς νεκρὸν τόνδ' οὗ καταστάζω δάκρυ; Mercerus thought that fr. LXXXV was a version of this latter passage, in which Hecuba draws Agamemnon's attention to the corpse of Polydorus, and restored it as *uide hunc meae in quem lacrumae guttatim cadunt.* Vossius restored it as *uide hanc meae in quam* etc. suggesting that the words are spoken by Hecuba to Ulysses as he grasps her daughter Polyxena. This suggestion involves less alteration to the paradosis and is none the worse for implying that Ennius altered slightly the form of the Euripidean Hecuba's appeal at *vv.* 277–81. Scaliger had let the words transmitted stand and set them in a version of Talthybius' account of the death of Polyxena (cf. *vv.* 519–20 νῦν τε γὰρ λέγων κακὰ | τέγξω τόδ' ὄμμα).

175 lacrumae guttatim cadunt: contrast the form of the expression at Propertius 4.1.144 *gutta quoque ex oculis...cadet.* The adverb *guttatim* occurs elsewhere in republican drama only at Plautus, *Merc.* 205 and not again until Apuleius.

LXXXVI

In moments of good fortune the personages of tragedy and comedy frequently, if not regularly, address thanks to the gods; cf. Sophocles, *Ant.* 330–1, *Tr.* 200–1, Euripides, *Herakleidai* 869, Menander, *Sam.* 269–70, Plautus, *Capt.* 768 ff., 922 ff., *Merc.* 842 ff., *Most.* 431 ff., *Persa* 251 ff., 753 ff., *Poen.* 1274 ff., *Rud.* 906 ff., *Stich.* 402 ff., *Trin.* 820 ff. Ennius' personage gives ironical thanks for ill fortune. The malignity of the gods is a constant theme of Euripides' Ἑκάβη—231–3 κἀγώ γ' ἄρ' οὐκ ἔθνησκον οὗ μ' ἐχρῆν θανεῖν, | οὐδ' ὤλεσέν με Ζεύς, τρέφει δ', ὅπως ὁρῶ | κακῶν κάκ' ἄλλα μεῖζον' ἢ τάλαιν' ἐγώ, 57–8 ἀντισηκώσας δέ σε | φθείρει θεῶν τις τῆς πάροιθ' εὐπραξίας, 199–201 οἶαν οἶαν αὖ σοι λώβαν | ἐχθίσταν ἀρρήταν τ' | ὦρσέν τις δαίμων, 721–2 ὦ τλῆμον ὡς σε πολυπονωτάτην βροτῶν | δαίμων ἔθηκεν ὅστις ἐστί σοι βαρύς, 958–60 φύρουσι δ' αὐτοὶ θεοὶ πάλιν τε καὶ πρόσω | ταραγμὸν ἐντιθέντες, ὡς ἀγνωσίᾳ | σέβωμεν αὐτούς—but there is nothing parallel with the Ennian irony in this play or elsewhere.[1] I suggest that the Latin words come from an outburst by Hecuba on hearing of the discovery of Polydorus' body.[2]

The words *Iuppiter* and *gratulor* (in the sense 'give thanks') belonged properly to the sacral language; the second was always used in auspicious circumstances. Of the Attic tragedians Aeschylus was particularly fond of employing sacral words and phrases in paradoxical contexts (cf. *Ag.* 645 πρέπει λέγειν παιᾶνα τόνδ' 'Ερινύων, 1144–5 στένουσ' ἀμφιθαλῆ κακοῖς | ἀηδὼν βίον, 1385–7 καὶ πεπτωκότι | τρίτην ἐπενδίδωμι, τοῦ κατὰ χθονός, | "Αιδου, νεκρῶν σωτῆρος, εὐκταίαν χάριν). Ennius indulges in similar paradox at *Trag.* 287: *qui illum di deaeque magno mactassint malo.*[3]

Fraenkel has argued[4] that Ennius' tetrameter parodies not just the Roman sacral language in general but the particular prayer offered to *Iuppiter Optimus Maximus* by the triumphing *imperator*.

176 Iuppiter tibi summe: the disjunction of the epithet by *tibi* moved to second place in the sentence[5] was unusual in Ennius' day and could be imitative of the style of sacral formulae.

Summus was a common epithet of *Iuppiter* in comedy (cf. Plautus, *Amph.* 933 et al.), along with *supremus* and *magnus*. It seems to be a poetic translation of ὕψιστος or ὕπατος rather than a borrowing from the sacral language. Cicero's public orations always refer to *Iuppiter Optimus Maximus*.

---

[1] Zeus is abused directly to his face at *Herakles* 339–47 … ἀρετῇ σε νικῶ θνητὸς ὢν θεὸν μέγαν· | … ἀμαθής τις εἶ θεός, ἢ δίκαιος οὐκ ἔφυς.

[2] Cf. Düntzer, *Zeitschr. f. d. Alt.* 1838, pp. 52 f., who alleges an oxymoron and compares Eur. *Hek.* 232 and 784. Columna's theory, accepted by Ribbeck and Vahlen, that the words form Hecuba's cry of triumph after the revenge taken upon Polymestor would require a *bene re gesta* in the text; cf. the context of Plautus, *Rud.* 1178–9 *quom istaec res male euenit tibi* | *Gripe gratulor.* A. Della Casa, *Dioniso* XXXVI (1962), 69 f., offers a good criticism of Columna's but no convincing interpretation of her own.

[3] Cf. also the way in which Lucretius expresses the Epicurean detestation of religion in language redolent of the traditional Roman cult at 1.82–3: *quod contra saepius illa* | *religio peperit scelerosa atque impia facta*; Propertius' use of the sacral *piare* at 1.1.20 and 3.19.18.

[4] *Pl. im Pl.* pp. 238 ff. (= *Elementi*, pp. 229 ff.), on Aeschylus, *Ag.* 1387.

[5] Cf. the disjunction of *per* and its object discussed above on *v.* 3.

tandem male re gesta: *tandem* is to be taken closely with *male*; 'really, positively'; cf. Plautus, *Curc. 7 tandem es odiosus mihi*.

The ablative absolute is not common in either republican comedy or tragedy and here the normal phrase would be a clause introduced by *quom*, *quod* or *quia*. There is some evidence that the absolute construction originated in the official language; the prayer of thanksgiving addressed by successful generals to Jupiter may have contained the phrase *re bene gesta*. Perhaps at one time *rem gerere* was proper to the official language but it is used so often in comedy of the doings of *priuati* (even the absolute phrase occurs eight times: Plautus, *Amph.* 655, *Persa* 754, *Stich.* 402, 411, 507, *Trin.* 592, 1182, Terence, *Ad.* 775) that we must suppose it to have been unremarkable in common parlance in the early second century.

gratulor: rare in the meaning 'gratias ago' (elsewhere in drama only at Caecilius, *Com.* 9, Terence, *Haut.* 879, Afranius, *Com. tog.* 21) and then only in addresses to gods.

LXXXVII

The general sense of this fragment is clear despite the corruption it has suffered; a person is addressed in whose state the written law provides no penalty for the murderer of a parent or guest. This was notoriously true of historical Athens, at least as far as parenticide was concerned;[1] the Roman Twelve Tables imposed various kinds of death penalty for various kinds of crime but seem to have left the punishment of homicide in general to private arrangement.[2] How the prosecution of L. Hostius, the first for patricide known to the Roman annalists, was mounted we do not know. At any rate the case must have been still fresh in the minds of Ennius' audience (see above on fr. xiv). The language and style of the fragment recall strongly the remains of republican *leges*.

There appear to be verbal links between the fragment and remarks made by the Euripidean Hecuba as she appeals to Agamemnon to punish Polymestor (*scriptis*... ~ 866 νόμων γραφαί; *quis parentem aut hospitem necasset* ~ 803–4 οἵτινες ξένους | κτείνουσιν ἢ θεῶν ἱερὰ τολμῶσιν φέρειν). Jacobus Nicolaus of Loo[3] accordingly made it belong to a version of *vv.* 798–805. Anachronistic talk of written law is common in Attic tragedy (cf. Aeschylus,

---

[1] On Solon's law see Cicero, *S. Rosc.* 70, Diogenes Laertius 1.59.

[2] See Latte, *TAPhA* LXVII (1936), 24 ff., *RE* Suppl. VII (1940), s.v. *Todesstrafe*, 1614, *ZSavSt* LXVII (1950), 51 ff., W. Kunkel, *Untersuchungen zur Entwicklung des römischen Kriminalverfahrens in vorsullanischer Zeit* (Munich, 1962), pp. 38 ff.

[3] *Miscellaneorum Epiphillidum Libri X*, VIII 7, apparently first published in J. Gruterus, *Lampas*, Tom. V, Suppl. (Frankfurt, 1606), p. 588. On Jacobus see W. Clausen, *CPh* LIX (1964), 96.

Hik. 707–9, Sophocles, *Ant.* 454–5, Euripides, *Hik.* 433–4, *Ion* 442–3) and Greek thought commonly associated offences against guests with those against parents (cf. Hesiod, *Erg.* 327–34, Aeschylus, *Eum.* 269–71, Aristophanes, *Batr.* 146–50). But it is difficult to associate the point of the fragment with that of 798–805 or indeed with anything in Hecuba's utterances at this stage. Vossius referred it to Hecuba's reply to Polymestor in the debate before Agamemnon. The absence here of any verbal counterpart to Ennius' Latin does not count against Vossius' theory but again it is difficult to see what point the Latin could have had. Osann[1] referred the fragment to Agamemnon's speech refusing to punish Hecuba and in particular to *vv.* 1247–8, but looked at as a whole it is no possible version of τάχ' οὖν παρ' ὑμῖν ῥᾴδιον ξενοκτονεῖν · | ἡμῖν δέ γ' αἰσχρὸν τοῖσιν Ἕλλησιν τόδε. Scholars may of course be mistaken in seeking a point related to the plot and arguments of the Euripidean play. Ennius may be making his actor speak of contemporary Rome or contemporary Athens. I must admit, however, that even so the point eludes me.

177–8 quis parentem aut hospitem | necasset: for relative *quis* cf. Lex XII tab. I 4 *proletario iam ciui quis uolet uindex esto*, II 2, Lex luci Lucer. *C.I.L.* I² 401.5, Lex Sil. *ap.* Fest. p. 288.34, Cato, *Agr.* 145.1, 148.2, Plautus, *Merc.* 991 *supplici sibi sumat quid uolt ipse ob hanc iniuriam*; it was clearly a legal archaism already in the early second century.

Necare, which occurs twice elsewhere in tragedy and nine times in comedy (not in Terence), probably also had an archaic tone, though much less pronounced than that of *quis*; comedy, reflecting the common language, preferred the compound *enicare* (28 times in Plautus, 5 in Terence; I include the metaphorical usage).

For the meaning 'murder' cf. Festus, p. 174.26, Rhet. inc. *Her.* 1.23.

The relative clause precedes the principal quite rarely in drama but does so regularly in republican legal texts.[2]

178 †quos quis† cruciatu perbiteret: if Junius' *quo quis cruciatu* be accepted we have either a very loose arrangement of relative and principal clauses, for which there is no parallel in particular but quite a few in general (cf. Plautus, *Aul.* 790–1 *qui homo culpam admisit in se, nullust tam parui preti | quin pudeat quin purget sese*, *Capt.* 941 *quod bene fecisti referetur gratia* et al.), or the use of *quis* as an indefinite after an interrogative/relative pronoun, for which the only exact parallel I can find is Ennius, *Sat.* 61–2 (*nam qui sese [si se* Usener] *frustrari quem frustra sentit, | qui frustratur is frustra est si non ille est frustra*).

---

[1] *Anal. crit.* 127 ff. [2] See W. Kroll, *Glotta* III (1912), 8 ff.

For *cruciatu perbiteret* cf. Plautus, *Pseud.* 776–8 *interminatust...si quis non hodie munus misisset sibi,* | *eum cras cruciatu maxumo perbitere, Rud.* 494–5, *Cas.* 300, *Epid.* 513, Cicero, *Nat. deor.* 3.81. The verb *baetere/bitere* seems to be evidenced from the Twelve Tables (Varro, *Men.* 553); it and its compounds occur sporadically in Plautine comedy as high-falutin variants of *ire,* etc. Tragedy appears to have affected the verb rather more frequently (*perbitere,* for example, occurs 3 times against *perire* 5; comedy has *perbitere* only twice but *perire* over 200 times) and for longer. The whole phrase *cruciatu perbitere* may come from the language of the law; the Romans regularly accompanied legal execution with torture (see above on fr. XIV).

LXXXVIII

This fragment might come from any of a number of contexts in Ennius' play; cf. Euripides, *Hek.* 26–7 κτανὼν ἐς οἶδμ' ἁλὸς | μεθῆχ', 28–9, 446, 634, 701, 781–2, 797, 938, 1259.

179 undantem salum: cf. Accius, *Trag.* 401 *undante in freto.*

The adjective *undans,* like other similar formations, seems to be restricted to poetry in classical Latin. It occurs in republican comedy only at Plautus, *Epid.* 436.

Salus masculine seems to occur only here in Latin. *Salum* neuter occurs sporadically in classical prose and verse. It must have been a borrowing from Greek first made in the nautical language; *mare* determined the gender perhaps from the beginning. Ennius may have been unsure of the gender or have varied it for poetic reasons with that of σάλος in mind.

LXXXIX

This fragment must have been uttered by Hecuba as Ulysses, unpersuaded by her arguments, left the stage with Polyxena. If the less well attested reading *heu me miserum* is correct the speaker was Polymestor as the Trojan women proceeded to slay his children. At neither point in the action has Euripides' Greek anything parallel.

Warriors normally washed in water after battle (cf. Homer, *Il.* 23.35 ff., *Od.* 22.478, Sophocles, *Ai.* 654–6, Virgil, *Aen.* 2.718–20). The Ennian Hecuba predicts a ghastly reversal of the normal practice. The murderers of Attic tragedy were ritually purified by animal blood (cf. Aeschylus, *Eum.* 283, 452, fr. 327, Euripides, *I.T.* 1223, *Sthen.* 17 ff.) but this practice seems to have been unknown at Rome and one cannot assume any allusion to it in Ennius' Latin.

180 lauere sanguen sanguine: for the idea of bathing in blood cf. Euripides, *Hek.* 1281 φόνια λουτρά, Furius *ap.* Gell. 18.11.4 *sanguine diluitur*

HECVBA

tellus, Virgil, *Georg.* 3.221 *lauit ater corpora sanguis*, *Aen.* 10.727–8 *lauit improba taeter* | *ora cruor*, 12.721–2 *sanguine largo* | *colla armosque lauant*, Propertius 4.10.37–8 *desecta Tolumni* | *ceruix Romanos sanguine lauit equos.* For the polyptoton cf. Sophocles, *O.T.* 100–1 φόνῳ φόνον πάλιν | λύοντας, Euripides, *El.* 857–8 αἷμα δ᾽ αἵματος | πικρὸς δανεισμὸς ἦλθε τῷ θανόντι νῦν, *Herakles* 40 ὡς φόνῳ σβέσῃ φόνον, *I.T.* 1223–4 ὡς φόνῳ φόνον | μυσαρὸν ἐκνίψω, Accius, *Trag.* 82–3 *cum patre paruos patrum hostifice* | *sanguine sanguen miscere* (Passeratius: *hiscere* codd.) *suo*, *Trag. praet.* 4 *lue patrium* (Buecheler: *ue patrum* codd.) *hostili fuso sanguen sanguine*, Lucretius 3.71 *caedem caede accumulantes.*

XC

This fragment clearly comes from a version of Euripides, *Hek.* 824–35 καὶ μήν — ἴσως μὲν τοῦ λόγου κενὸν τόδε, | Κύπριν προβάλλειν· ἀλλ᾽ ὅμως εἰρήσεται· | πρὸς σοῖσι πλευροῖς παῖς ἐμὴ κοιμίζεται | ἡ φοιβάς, ἣν καλοῦσι Κασάνδραν Φρύγες. | ποῦ τὰς φίλας δῆτ᾽ εὐφρόνας δείξεις, ἄναξ, | ἢ τῶν ἐν εὐνῇ φιλτάτων ἀσπασμάτων | χάριν τίν᾽ ἕξει παῖς ἐμή, κείνης δ᾽ ἐγώ; ...τὸν θανόντα τόνδ᾽ ὁρᾷς; | τοῦτον καλῶς δρῶν ὄντα κηδεστὴν σέθεν | δράσεις.

Absent from the Greek is the emphasis upon obedience to the will of the male during sexual intercourse (*morem gerit*) and upon restraint of the female's desires (*uerecunde et modice*). Even where marriage and concubinage in general are concerned Attic tragedy does not emphasise so strongly the virtue of female obedience; cf. the Euripidean Andromache's account of her relationship with Hector at *Tr.* 645–56, in particular 655–6 ἤδη δ᾽ ἀμὲ χρῆν νικᾶν πόσιν, | κείνῳ τε νίκην ὧν ἐχρῆν παριέναι, and Hecuba's advice to Andromache on how to treat her new master at *Tr.* 699–700: τίμα δὲ τὸν παρόντα δεσπότην σέθεν, | φίλον διδοῦσα δέλεαρ ἀνδρὶ σῶν τρόπων.

In the society depicted by comedy and its Roman adaptations obedience was the chief characteristic which distinguished the γυνὴ γαμετή/*matrona* from the ἑταίρα/*amica*; cf. Pap. Didot. 1.14–16 ἔστ᾽ ἀνδρὶ καὶ γυναικὶ κείμενος νόμος, | τῷ μὲν διὰ τέλους ἣν ἔχει στέργειν ἀεί, | τῇ δ᾽ ὅσ᾽ ἂν ἀρέσκῃ τἀνδρί, ταῦτ᾽ αὐτὴν ποεῖν, Plautus, *Men.* 787–9 *quotiens monstraui tibi uiro ut morem geras,* | *quid ille faciat ne id opserues, quo eat, quid rerum gerat* (father to married daughter), *Amph.* 839–42 *non ego illam mi dotem duco esse quae dos dicitur* | *sed pudicitiam et pudorem et sedatum cupidinem,* | *deum metum, parentum amorem et cognatum concordiam,* | *tibi morigera atque ut munifica sim bonis, prosim probis* (wife to accusing husband), Ovid, *Ars* 3.585–6 *hoc est uxores quod non patiatur amari* : | *conueniunt illas cum uoluere uiri.* There was always something a little paradoxical about female obedience outside legal wedlock; cf. Plautus, *Men.* 202, *Most.* 188 ff., Terence, *Andr.* 285 ff.

315

COMMENTARY

For restraint of female desire cf. Plautus, *Amph.* 840, Turpilius, *Com.* 37–9 *quae mulier uolet | sibi suum amicum* (Acidalius: *summam amicam* codd.) *esse indulgentem et diutinum, | modice atque parce eius seruiat cupidines*—Jason's denunciation of Medea's lust at Euripides, *Med.* 522 ff., Clytemnestra's boast about her σωφροσύνη at Euripides, *I.A.* 1159, and the story told by Plutarch at *Mor.* 140 c indicate that such restraint was not a peculiarly Roman marriage ideal.

The Euripidean Hecuba appeals to Agamemnon not only through the pleasure he has had of her daughter but also through the quasi-legal relationship which the association of Agamemnon and Cassandra has in her view established between the Greek king and herself (*vv.* 834–5 τοῦτον καλῶς δρῶν ὄντα κηδεστὴν σέθεν | δράσεις).[1] This would have been a difficult notion to put straight into Latin. Ennius seems to have substituted the notion that Cassandra's sexual behaviour was more like that of a legal spouse than that of an ordinary concubine. The notion assumed a climate of social ideas common to Rome and historical Athens. There is nothing specifically 'Roman' about the passage except its language.[2]

181 tibi in concubio...morem gerit: for *concumbere* of the female's part in sexual intercourse cf. Terence, *Hec.* 393. *Concubium* occurs elsewhere in republican drama only at Plautus, *Trin.* 886 (*concubium...noctis*). The phrase *morem gerere* and the adjective *morigerus*, to judge by Plautus, *Capt.* 966, *Cas.* 463, 897 and Terence, *Ad.* 214–15, seem to have served in the common language as sexual euphemisms.[3]

uerecunde et modice: cf. Cicero, *Tull.* 5 *uerecunde modiceque*, Livy 26.49.16 *uerecunde ac modeste*, Ammianus 16.7.3 *uerecunde et modice*.

XCI

Personages who have suffered misfortune frequently express the desire for suicide in both Attic and Roman drama; cf. Euripides, *Andr.* 841 ff., *Herakles* 1146 ff., 1247 ff., *Tr.* 1282 f., Plautus, *Asin.* 606 ff., *Cist.* 639 ff., *Mil.* 1240 ff., Terence, *Andr.* 606 (*non dixit 'gladium' aut 'laqueum' ne esset tragicum* —Donatus), *Phorm.* 552, Seneca, *Phoen.* 105 ff., *Herc. f.* 1221 ff. The Hecuba of Euripides' Ἑκάβη nowhere expresses this desire but frequently makes plain her distaste for life and asks others to kill her: *vv.* 167–8 οὐκέτι μοι βίος | ἀγαστὸς ἐν φάει, 386–7 ἡμᾶς δ' ἄγοντες πρὸς πυρὰν 'Αχιλλέως |

---

[1] Cf. Euripides, *Tr.* 308 ff.

[2] For a somewhat different view see G. W. Williams, *JRS* xLVIII (1958), 20.

[3] Cf. the use of *nubere* at Plautus, *Cist.* 43–4, *nuptiae* in the example of *translatio...obscenitatis uitandae causa* at Rhet. inc. *Her.* 4.45.

316

HECVBA

κεντεῖτε, μὴ φείδεσθ᾽, 391 ὑμεῖς δέ μ᾽ ἀλλὰ θυγατρὶ συμφονεύσατε, 396 πολλή γ᾽ ἀνάγκη θυγατρὶ συνθανεῖν ἐμέ, 505–6 ἆρα κἄμ᾽ ἐπισφάξαι τάφῳ | δοκοῦν ᾽Αχαιοῖς ἦλθες; ὡς φίλ᾽ ἂν λέγοις. The chorus of this play interpret the speech of the childless and blinded Polymestor at *vv.* 1096–106 as motivated by a suicidal urge. It is therefore anybody's guess where fragment xci would have stood in the action of Ennius' adaptation.

The text of the fragment is plainly corrupt. Vahlen printed the paradosis, perhaps having in mind such passages as Sophocles, *Phil.* 1004, *Tr.* 1089, Euripides, *Alk.* 837, *Herakles* 268–9, *Med.* 496–7, 1244, *Tr.* 1178, Neophron, fr. 2.12, Aristophanes, *Thesm.* 776. But the verb *date* rules out an apostrophe to the speaker's own hands and the absence of qualification an address to the hands of others. Scaliger's *anuis* runs up against the difficulty that *anus* in republican comedy (it is absent from tragedy) has a contemptuous tone when applied to women of the upper orders. It could be that two distinct quotations, *miserete manus date* and ...*date ferrum qui me anima priuem*, have been run together in Nonius' article as at pp. 467.32, 478.26 and elsewhere; *miserete manus date* might then belong to a version of Euripides, *Hek.* 59 ff. and ...*date ferrum qui me anima priuem* to some play other than *Hecuba*.

182 miserete: for the active form cf. Ennius, *Ann.* 171; the deponent form is regular in drama except for the impersonal *miseret*.

qui me anima priuem: cf. Sophocles, *Phil.* 1427 νοσφιεῖς βίου, Plautus, *Men.* 905 *anima priuabo uirum*, Lucretius 5.997 *donec eos uita priuarant uermina saeua*; contrast Plautus, *Trin.* 129 *dedisti...gladium qui se occideret*.

XCII

This fragment clearly belongs to a version of Euripides, *Hek.* 492–8 οὐχ ἥδ᾽ ἄνασσα τῶν πολυχρύσων Φρυγῶν, | οὐχ ἥδε Πριάμου τοῦ μέγ᾽ ὀλβίου δάμαρ; | καὶ νῦν πόλις μὲν πᾶσ᾽ ἀνέστηκεν δορί, | αὐτὴ δὲ δούλη γραῦς ἄπαις ἐπὶ χθονὶ | κεῖται, κόνει φύρουσα δύστηνον κάρα. | φεῦ φεῦ· γέρων μέν εἰμ᾽, ὅμως δέ μοι θανεῖν | εἴη πρὶν αἰσχρᾷ περιπεσεῖν τύχῃ τινί. The Talthybius of the Τρῳάδες refers explicitly to his own poverty (*v.* 415) but the matter of wealth and poverty is a constant theme of the ῾Εκάβη, discussed explicitly at *vv.* 317 ff., 492 f., 1218 ff., and it is not surprising that Ennius should make it explicit again in an otherwise fairly close version of *vv.* 497–8.

Ennius here for once keeps the spoken iambic verse of his original. Stylistically he moves away with the nominal phrase *mortem obpetam*, the repetition *senex...senex* and the alliteration of *grauiter gemam*.

183 mortem obpetam: a fairly common phrase in classical prose but absent from the rest of republican drama.

317

COMMENTARY

euenat: this form and *euenant* are restored with a fair degree of certainty five times in Plautine comedy (*Curc.* 39, *Epid.* 290, 321, *Mil.* 1010, *Trin.* 41),[1] each time at the end of a metrical unit and in a context of some solemnity; *eueniat* and *eueniant*, which occur 19 times in comedy, were clearly the normal forms in the common language.

184 senex: this type of pleonasm is hard to parallel in either Greek or Roman drama but cf. Ennius, *Trag.* 298–9 *neque sepulcrum...habeat, portum corporis,* | *ubi...corpus requiescat.*

grauiter gemam: cf. Trag. inc. 116, Virgil, *Georg.* 3.133, Ammianus 14.5.7.

IPHIGENIA

The title *Iphigenia* is given to Ennius by Verrius, the Virgilian scholiasts,[2] Aulus Gellius and Iulius Rufinianus; and to Naevius by Nonius Marcellus (p. 370.23). The piece which Nonius quotes as from Naevius' *Iphigenia* is corrupt to the point of almost complete obscurity[3] but since at least one piece of verse quoted with his name and no title comes from a play set on the Black Sea coast[4] we may suppose that he adapted Euripides' *I.T.* or another tragedy on the same theme.[5] The five pieces quoted as from Ennius' *Iphigenia* put this play without much doubt in Aulis.

Scaliger[6] considered that Ennius adapted the extant version of Euripides' *I.A.* and most scholars have accepted his opinion. Wilamowitz suggested[7] that *vv.* 590–7 of the extant *I.A.* is a remnant of a version of the play containing a chorus of soldiers and that Ennius adapted this version; M. Lenchantin De Gubernatis[8] had earlier suggested that Ennius' immediate model was a tragedy based on the Euripidean *I.A.* Certainly more than one acting

---

[1] Cf. *Pseud.* 1030 (*aduenat*), *Rud.* 626 (*peruenat*), *Trin.* 93 (*peruenant*).

[2] Schol. Veron. *Ecl.* 5.88 uses Verrius' lexicon either directly or indirectly. Servius auct. *Aen.* 1.52 probably draws on the same source; Festus (p. 510.19 ff., s.v. *uastus*) may have omitted the Ennius passage from his epitome.

[3] See the restorations attempted by Mariotti, *StudUrb* xxiv (1950), 176, *Il Bellum Poenicum e l'arte di Nevio* (Rome, 1955), p. 131, and O. Skutsch, *CR* N.S. 1 (1951), 146–7, viii (1958), 48.

[4] *Trag.* 62 (Cicero, *Orat.* 152).

[5] The 'Ιφιγένεια of Polyidus was set among the Taurians (Aristotle, *Poet.* 16.1455a6, 17.1455b10).

[6] *Coniect. Varr. Ling.*, on 7.73.

[7] *Hermes* LIV (1919), 51 ff. (= *Kleine Schriften* IV [Berlin, 1962], 289 ff.).

[8] *MAT*, LXIII (1913), 416.

318

version of the Euripidean *I.A.* must have existed in theatrical circles and since Lenchantin wrote there have turned up pieces of what looks like a post-Euripidean tragedy dealing with the sacrifice of Iphigenia.[1] However the five pieces attributed to Ennius' *Iphigenia* can be interpreted as coming from an adaptation of the Euripidean *I.A.* no more free than certain other republican adaptations whose originals are certainly known. The continuing popularity of the *I.A.* in Athens and other Greek cities[2] and Ennius' well-evidenced predilection for Euripides give Scaliger's opinion a certain advantage over the others. Bergk[3] tried to explain the divergences from the *I.A.* in terms of 'contaminatio' with Sophocles' Ἰφιγένεια, a play which certainly dealt with the sacrifice but was probably set in Argos rather than Aulis.[4]

A title *Iphigenia* seems to be referred to by the author of the rhetorical treatise addressed to Herennius (fr. XCIII) and by Cicero (fr. XCV a). Since in the one case the personages Agamemnon and Menelaus are named and in the other Achilles we may suppose that Ennius' tragedy rather than Naevius' is meant. Nonius appears to quote from Achilles' speech in an article of uncertain origin (fr. XCV d).[5]

No other republican play about events at Aulis is known but both Ennius and Accius wrote a *Telephus* dealing with a later episode in the saga. Behind Ennius' *Telephus* there stood quite probably Euripides' homonymous tragedy, a tragedy to which the *I.A.* bore a striking resemblance; in both plays there was a quarrel between Agamemnon and Menelaus and a speech by Achilles complaining of the delay in setting out for Troy; the baby Orestes was used in the *I.A.* by Iphigenia (on Clytemnestra's orders) to soften Agamemnon, in the Τήλεφος by Telephus (perhaps too on Clytemnestra's orders) to impel Agamemnon to protect him against the spy-hunting Greeks; various arguments and *sententiae* appeared in both plays.[6] A certain caution is therefore required in dealing with fragments not attri-

---

[1] Pap. Brit. Mus. 2560; Milne, *Cat.* p. 57 nr. 78; A. Körte, *APF* x (1932), 53.

[2] There are verbal allusions in Eubulus, fr. 67.10 (370), Philetaerus, fr. 4 (701), Menander, *Sam.* 329 (1602) and the Alexandrian Machon 21–4 Gow (22–3). Plautus refers to the story at *Epid.* 490–1, perhaps echoing his original. One of Euripides' two plays about Iphigenia was re-performed at the Great Dionysia of 342/1 (*I.G.* II² 2320). Euripides' name and scenes from the *I.A.* appear on a Megarian bowl (nr. 10 in U. Hausmann, *Hellenistische Reliefbecher aus attischen und böotischen Werkstätten* [Stuttgart, 1959]) of the late third century.

[3] *Ind. lectt. Marburg* 1844, XIV (= *Kl. phil. Schr.* I 229). In *Commentatio de Fragmentis Sophoclis* (Leipzig, 1833), p. 15, Bergk had proposed Sophocles' Ἰφιγένεια as Ennius' original.

[4] See Zieliński, *Tragodumenon Libri Tres*, p. 271.

[5] Verrius could be the source; cf. Paulus, p. 163.12.

[6] E.g. *Telephos* fr. 714 ∼ *I.A.* 17 ff., 446 ff.; fr. 719 ∼ *I.A.* 1255–75.

buted to any particular play but appearing to concern the events and the
arguments of the *I.A.*

Shortly after his specific quotation of Ennius' *Iphigenia* Iulius Rufinianus
quotes (fr. CI) without the name of either author or play three trochaic
tetrameters addressed by an Agamemnon to a Menelaus and referring to the
projected slaying of Agamemnon's daughter. Columna gave these to the
Iphigenia on the grounds of similarity between the Latin phrases and phrases
in *I.A.* 378–401. More decisive to my mind are the proximity of the specific
quotation of the *Iphigenia* and the lack of any other known republican
tragedy to which the tetrameters could belong.

Some anapaests quoted by Varro (fr. XCVI*a*, *b*) as spoken by an Agamemnon and attributed by Verrius (fr. XCVI*c*), apparently drawing on the same
source,[1] to Ennius were given by Scaliger to the *Iphigenia* on the grounds of
their similarity to *I.A.* 6–8. The similarity is not so very great but since it is
impossible to imagine an Agamemnon speaking thus at the beginning of the
Telephus or any other known Ennian tragedy we may accept Scaliger's
opinion.

A. F. Naeke[2] argued that in referring to Iphigenia in his catalogue of
patriots at *Tusc.* I.116 (fr. XCIV) Cicero had in mind the actual wording of a
passage of Ennius' *Iphigenia* based on *I.A.* 1475–6, ἄγετέ με τὰν Ἰλίου | καὶ
Φρυγῶν ἐλέπτολιν. Düntzer added the parallel *I.A.* 1484–6 ὡς ἐμοῖσιν,
εἰ χρεών, | αἵμασι θύμασι | θέσφατ' ἐξαλείψω. Here as elsewhere one may
be sceptical about attempts to extract the poet's phrases from Cicero's[3] but
Vahlen[4] goes much too far in asserting that no reference at all is made to a
poetic treatment of Iphigenia's death. It is perhaps true, but nevertheless
irrelevant, that Cicero's phrases show no trace of poetical rhythm. It is true,
but again irrelevant, that the parallels adduced from the *I.A.* are not verbally
close. It is not true that the metaphor in *sanguis hostium eliciatur sanguine suo* is
sufficiently mild to be Cicero's own making, that it is no bolder than, for
example, that in *oriens incendium belli Punici suo sanguine restinxissent.*
The words, as I shall argue later, recall the language of sacral practice and
it is well known how fond Ennius was of importing the Roman sacral
language and the ideas informing this language into his adaptations of Attic
tragedy.

---

[1] See J. Kretzschmer, *De A. Gelli fontibus* I (Diss. Greifswald, 1860), pp. 16,
41, 45, F. Mentz, *Comm. phil. Ien.* IV (1890), 51, R. Reitzenstein, *M. Terentius
Varro und Johannes Mauropus*, pp. 32–3, G. Goetz, *BPhW* XXI (1901), 1034, R.
Kriegshammer, *Comm. phil. Ien.* VII (1903), 80.

[2] *Ind. lectt. Bonn* 1822, III (= *Opusc.* I 86).

[3] See the attempts of Düntzer, *RhM* V (1837), 444, Bergk, *Ind. lectt. Marburg*
1844, XIII (= *Kl. phil. Schr.* I 256), Strzelecki, *Eos* XLIII (1948), 161.

[4] *Ind. lectt. Berlin* 1879/80, 14 (= *Op. ac.* I 101).

Study of the organisation of Cicero's argument gives positive grounds for thinking that he is not speaking with his own voice but alluding to the words of another writer. He is discussing the examples of patriotic self-sacrifice given by 'rhetores'. As a rule he brings forward the name of the hero or heroine (*repetunt ab Erectheo cuius filiae...Codrum* [*?*]...*Menoeceus non praetermittitur...Harmodius in ore et Aristogiton...Lacedaemonius Leonidas, Thebanus Epaminondas uiget*) and describes his or her deed with a preterite verb (*mortem expetiuerunt...se in medios inmisit hostes...largitus est patriae suum sanguinem*). Iphigenia's name, on the other hand, is not formally introduced like the other names and her deed is described in the present tense. Furthermore her death makes the number of mythical examples four, whereas one would expect three to balance the historical ones. I would suggest therefore that Cicero took the daughters of Erechtheus, Codrus and Menoeceus from his philosophical source and added Iphigenia as an afterthought with a speech from a Latin tragedy in mind. The present tense of *eliciatur* would suit such a speech but is quite out of place in Cicero's discourse. Ennius' *Iphigenia*, which Cicero knew well, was very probably the tragedy quoted.

Dobree[1] assigned the trochaic pieces of a stichomythic dispute between an Agamemnon and a Menelaus quoted by Cicero at *Tusc.* 4.77 to the *Iphigenia* on the grounds of their similarity to sentences in *I.A.* 317–33. Ribbeck and Vahlen both accept Dobree's idea. However the *Iphigenia* is not the only republican tragedy known that could have contained such a dispute. Hartung[2] gave the pieces to Ennius' *Telephus*.

In a letter to Atticus (13.47.1) Cicero alludes unmistakeably to a tragic speech addressed to an Agamemnon—*posteaquam abs te Agamemno non ut uenirem (nam id quoque fecissem nisi Torquatus esset) sed ut scriberem tetigit aures nuntius, extemplo instituta omisi; ea quae in manibus habebam abieci, quod iusseras edolaui.*[3] Cicero's identification of his addressee with the mythical Agamemnon means of itself very little[4] but the words *extemplo*[5] and *edolaui*[6] and the

---

[1] *Aduersaria* II (Cambridge, 1833), p. 373; cf. Düntzer, *RhM* v (1837), 444. Earlier scholars had mistakenly referred the pieces to a quarrel between Atreus and Thyestes.   [2] *Euripides Restitutus* I, p. 202.

[3] Cf. Varro *in epistula Iuli Caesaris* (Nonius, p. 263.3): *quem simul ac Romam uenisse mi adtigit auris nuntius extemplo* †*eas*† *in curriculum contuli propere pedes.*

[4] Cf. the passages of Plautus discussed by Fraenkel, *Pl. im Pl.* pp. 95 ff. (= *Elementi*, pp. 89 ff.), Cicero, *Att.* 1.18.3, *S. Rosc.* 98, Rhet. inc. *Her.* 4.46, Fortunatianus, *Ars rhet.* 3.7; cf. also the Athenian nicknames listed by Anaxandrides, fr. 34.

[5] Elsewhere in Cicero only at *Q. Rosc.* 8, absent from Caesar, common in drama.

[6] Elsewhere only at Varro, *Men.* 59 (quoting Ennius) and 332.

catalectic trochaic dimeter *tetigit aures nuntius*[1] are clearly of dramatic origin. *Iusseras* was not a natural word for Cicero to use in correspondence with Atticus. Ladewig[2] argued that Cicero had in mind Ennius' version of *I.A.* 607–34, the scene in which Clytemnestra arrived from Argos with Iphigenia in obedience to Agamemnon's first letter.[3] Other tragic contexts are imaginable.

Düntzer[4] compared the words *Thelis illi mater* attributed by Varro to Ennius at *Ling.* 7.87 with a passage of the first choral ode of the *I.A.*, 207–8 Ἀχιλῆα | τὸν ἁ Θέτις τέκε. Vahlen printed the three words among the fragments of the *Iphigenia*, comparing *I.A.* 701 and 708. The *Achilles*, the *Hectoris lytra* and the *Telephus* are equally likely to have contained such a reference to Achilles' parentage.

A. Grilli[5] argued that Cicero's words at *Tusc.* 2.33, *sin tectus Volcaniis armis, id est fortitudine, resiste*, refer to Ennius' version of *I.A.* 1072–3 ὅπλων Ἡφαιστοπόνων | κεκορυθμένος ἔνδυτα. Cicero may refer to a poetic account of the armour of Achilles but Ennius' *Iphigenia* is not the only possible source.

F. Skutsch[6] argued that Cicero's words at *Tusc.* 3.57, *nec siletur illud potentissimi regis anapaestum qui laudat senem et fortunatum esse dicit quod inglorius sit atque ignobilis ad supremum diem peruenturus*, refer not to Euripides, *I.A.* 16–18 but to Ennius' version. He seems to have convinced A. Klotz.[7] He was clearly right to think that Cicero had a Latin tragedian's verses in mind. Scholars now assume that in the case of direct verse quotations Cicero always draws on a Latin poet unless he names a Greek as the author[8] and the same assumption should be made in the case of indirect quotations. *Illud potentissimi regis anapaestum* refers to a Latin verse just as surely as does *qui hoc anapaesto citantur* at *Fin.* 2.18 where the run of the argument allows him to quote directly. However the Agamemnon of the *Iphigenia* was not the only *rex potentissimus* of republican tragedy and the sentiment in question not by any means an uncommon one.[9]

---

[1] Cf. Plautus, *Poen.* 1375–6 *quod uerbum auris meas | tetigit*, *Rud.* 233 *certo uox muliebris auris tetigit meas.*　　　　　[2] *Anal. scen.* p. 15.

[3] The most recent attempt at restoration is that of Strzelecki, in *Charisteria Thaddaeo Sinko...oblata* (Warsaw, 1951), 344. See the more sceptical approaches of F. Skutsch, *RhM* LXI (1906), 618 (= *Kl. Schr.* 308), and Dahlmann, *MusH* VII (1950), 216–18.

[4] *RhM* V (1837), 443.　　　　　[5] *Acme* X (1957), 75.

[6] *RhM* LXI (1906), 611 (= *Kl. Schr.* 302).

[7] *Scaenicorum Romanorum Fragmenta* I (Munich, 1953), p. 101.

[8] Cf. Przychocki, *Eos* XXXII (1929), 215 ff.

[9] Cf. Euripides, *Hipp.* 1028 ἢ τἄρ' ὀλοίμην ἀκλεὴς ἀνώνυμος, *Ion* 621 ff., Seneca, *Thy.* 393 ff. Cicero's philosophical source probably quoted Euripides, *I.A.* 16–18 (cf. Plutarch, *Mor.* 467 E–F, 471 C, 474 D).

At *Diu.* 2.56–7 the notion that the crowing of cocks has a supernatural divinatory significance (cf. *Diu.* 1.74) is refuted. Cicero takes from his source Democritus' explanation of the well-known fact that cocks crow before dawn and adds *qui quidem silentio noctis, ut ait Ennius, fauent faucibus russis cantu plausuque premunt alas* (see fr. CLXXIX). It is hard to say whether *silentio noctis* is meant to repeat or to complement *ante lucem*. In either case Ennius' anapaests must be interpreted to refer to the noise of the cocks. A reference to their silence would be quite absurd. The point is that cocks crow any old time and do not need divinity to prompt them. However that may be, the passages from the *I.A.* prologue compared by Ribbeck[1] and Vahlen,[2] 9–11 οὔκουν φθόγγος γ᾽ οὔτ᾽ ὀρνίθων | οὔτε θαλάσσης · σιγαὶ δ᾽ ἀνέμων | τόνδε κατ᾽ Εὔριπον ἔχουσιν, 156–7 λευκαίνει | τόδε φῶς ἤδη λάμπουσ᾽ ἠώς, refer to the particular situation by the Euripus. Ennius' anapaests, unless Cicero has altered them drastically, seem to have referred to the behaviour of cocks in general.[3]

In his letter consoling Heliodorus for the death of Nepotianus (*Epist.* 60.14.4) St Jerome appears to draw from Cicero's now lost *Consolatio*[4] an Ennian *sententia*—*plebes in hoc regi antestat: loco licet | lacrimare plebi, regi honeste non licet* (fr. CCXV)—similar to *I.A.* 446–9 ἡ δυσγένεια δ᾽ ὡς ἔχει τι χρήσι-μον. | καὶ γὰρ δακρῦσαι ῥᾳδίως αὐτοῖς ἔχει, | ἅπαντά τ᾽ εἰπεῖν. τῷ δὲ γενναίῳ φύσιν | ἄνολβα ταῦτα. On the grounds of this similarity Columna assigned the two trimeters to the *Iphigenia* and all editors have followed him. However such similarities can be treacherous where *sententiae* are concerned and no assignations should be based upon them. Homer's gods and heroes wept freely, likewise those of fifth-century Attic tragedy.[5] But the social etiquette of the Athenian aristocracy of the late fifth century condemned the public display of emotion.[6] So too that of the Roman republican aristocracy if we may judge from Pacuvius' alteration of Sophocles' Νίπτρα, Cicero's approval of this alteration,[7] and Cicero's own treatment

---

[1] *Quaest. scen.* p. 254, *Die röm. Trag.* p. 95.

[2] *Ind. lectt. Berlin* 1888/9, 10 (= *Op. ac.* 1 409).

[3] Columna, C. F. W. Mueller and F. Skutsch, *RhM* LXI (1906), 610 (= *Kl. Schr.* 301), include *silentio noctis* in the Ennian fragment. Zillinger, *Cicero und die altrömischen Dichter*, p. 115 n. 1, gives it to Cicero.

[4] See A. Luebeck, *Hieronymus quos nouerit scriptores et ex quibus hauserit* (Leipzig, 1872), pp. 105 f., 157, Kunst, *De S. Hieronymi studiis Ciceronianis*, p. 142.

[5] Cf. Sophocles, *Tr.* 1046–111, *Phil.* 785–820.

[6] See Plato's attack on the poets for allowing the heroes to moan and beat their breasts: *Politeia* 10.605 C.

[7] *Tusc.* 2.49.

of Sophocles' Τραχίνιαι.[1] One could imagine the sentiment of *plebes in hoc regi antestat: loco licet lacrimare plebi, regi honeste non licet*[2] in several of Ennius' tragedies.

XCIII

The words which the rhetorician quotes are plainly of tragic origin and make good sense but do not form a recognisable metrical unit.[3] It does not follow that because the memoriser is advised to think of actors preparing to perform a scene of Ennius' *Iphigenia* (see above, p. 319) the words necessarily come from this play.[4]

XCIV

For the rationale of Cicero's discourse see above, p. 321. *Sanguis* is to be understood with *hostium* from the previous sentence. Very probably the polyptoton *sanguis sanguine* (for which see above on *v.* 180) stood in the speech of Iphigenia which Cicero has in mind.

Sanguinem elicere was a common medical term (*T.L.L.* v ii.367.22 ff.) but the usage here is clearly metaphorical. The blood of the enemy will be made to flow like water from a fountain or rain from the sky (*T.L.L.* v ii.367.71 ff.). I suggest that Ennius parodied the language used in prayers to *Iuppiter elicius* at the *aquaelicium*.[5]

XCV

At *Rep.* 1.30 the tragic verses are directed in the first instance at C. Sulpicius Gallus, an aristocrat famous for his knowledge of astronomy, and in the second at those who would prefer to discuss a vision of two suns reported as a *prodigium* rather than the sedition threatening the welfare of the state. At *Diu.* 2.30 *physici* in general are the object of attack.

Donatus (Ter. *Ad.* 386) appears to have in mind the story of the natural philosopher Thales and the slave girl recounted by Plato (*Theait.* 174A) and many others (Hippolytus, *Phil.* 1.1, Diogenes Laertius 1.34, Aristides, *Or.*

---

[1] *Tusc.* 2.20–2: the hero's cries of pain at 1081–5 are omitted from an otherwise fairly close version.

[2] Cf. Ovid, *Fast.* 4.845–7 *haec ubi rex didicit lacrimas introrsus obortas | deuorat et clausum pectore uulnus habet. | flere palam non uult, exemplaque fortia seruat, Met.* 13.474–5 *at populus lacrimas quas illa* (i.e. Polyxena) *tenebat | non tenet.*

[3] The usual reading *iam domum itionem reges Atridae parant* produces a trimeter with the highly unusual division of syllables *At-ridae.* The transmitted reading makes equally good if not better sense (for the construction cf. Plautus, *Aul.* 201–2, *Stich.* 283) but produces a trochaic tetrameter lacking one trochee and afflicted with the same unusual division of syllables.

[4] Cf. Bergk, *Ind. lectt. Marburg* 1844, xiv f. (= *Kl. phil. Schr.* I 230 f.), C. Pascal, *RFIC* xxvi (1898), 30.

[5] See Aust, *RE* v ii (1905), 2366–7, s.v. *elicius*, Latte, *Röm. Rel.* pp. 78 f.

48.85, Tertullian, *Nat.* 2.4, Schol. Lucian, p. 147 Rabe) to illustrate the common man's distrust of philosophical speculation. The words *in Syrum* could be interpreted as referring to Thales; for the story of his Phoenician ancestry cf. Diogenes Laertius 1.22. Certainly Donatus had Thales in mind.[1] The words which Donatus puts in the slave girl's mouth obviously come in corrupted form from the tragic Achilles' speech. I suggest that some earlier commentary upon Terence's play contained not only the story of Thales and the slave girl but also a clearly designated quotation from the *Iphigenia*[2] and that in the course of time and successive epitomisations the two elements of the original note became conflated.

For Cicero's loose mode of introduction at *Rep.* 1.30, *ille de Iphigenia Achilles* 'the famous words of Achilles in the *Iphigenia*', cf. *De orat.* 3.217 *Atreus fere totus* 'almost everything said by Atreus', *Fam.* 7.6.2 *Medeam coepi agere* 'I have begun to act the role of Medea', *Att.* 12.45.3 *tu uero peruolga Hirtium* (~ 12.47.3 *Hirti librum...diuolga*), Horace, *Sat.* 2.3.11 *stipare Platona Menandro* et al.

The tragic verses have been much emended since the discovery of the palimpsest fragment of the *De republica*.[3] The emendations offered are extremely unconvincing and one may doubt whether the words and phrases transmitted are sufficiently anomalous to justify the search for replacements. Both tragedy and comedy mingle acatalectic and catalectic tetrameters in speeches of elevated tone; very often, as here, a catalectic verse concludes a series of acatalectic ones (cf. Plautus, *Aul.* 727–30). I should put a question mark after *obseruationis* and interpret the first verse as 'what right have *astrologi* to look for signs in the sky (and give men like us advice on how to conduct the affairs entrusted to us)?' Ennius' Latinity is admittedly peculiar. The normal phraseology would be *quid astrologis signa in caelo obseruatio est?* (cf. Plautus, *Amph.* 519 *quid tibi hanc curatio est rem, uerbero, aut muttitio?*, *Asin.* 920 *quid tibi hunc receptio ad te est meum uirum?*, *Aul.* 423 *quid tibi nos tactiost?* et al.).[4] The subjunctive verb indicates impatient expectation of the answer *nihil*; cf. Plautus, *Mil.* 615 *quis homo sit magis meus quam tu's?*, *Amph.* 576–7 *quid hoc sit | hominis?* The postponed *quid* and the locution *quid...obserua-*

---

[1] For Thales as the archetypal *sapiens* cf. Plautus, *Bacch.* 121 ff., *Capt.* 274 ff., *Rud.* 1001 ff.

[2] Cf. the way in which Cicero glosses the story of Anaxagoras' reception of the news of his son's death with a speech by a tragic Telamo, *Tusc.* 3.28, 3.58; his quotation of both Euripides and Ennius on the real nature of the supreme god at *Nat. deor.* 2.65.

[3] For an account of the emenders' attempts see K. Ziegler, *Hermes* LXXXV (1957), 495–501.

[4] See T. Bögel, *NJbb* Suppl. XXVIII (1903), 57 ff., Löfstedt, *Syntactica* I², p. 253, G. Pasquali, *RAI* VII iii (1941), 29 ff.

tionis perhaps also indicate impatience on the speaker's part. *Astrologorum* is the most difficult word to defend. In third and second century drama genitives accompanying verbal nouns in *-tus* are normally subjective while those accompanying verbal nouns in *-tio* (*-sio*) are objective.[1] Nevertheless the word cannot be emended and to take it with either *signa* or *nemo* is even harder to justify. One finds the pronominal adjective replacing the dative at Plautus, *Cas.* 261 *me sinas curare ancillas quae mea est curatio*, *Persa* 586 *tua mers est tua indicatio* et al. and subjective genitives of nouns all through official inscriptions of the late second century (e.g. *C.I.L.* I² 583 . III *de ea re eius petitio nominisque delatio esto*, VI *quaestio eius praetoris esto*).

At *I.A.* 919–74 the Euripidean Achilles denounces the Greek leaders one after the other, describing Calchas as an unreliable adviser: 956–8 τίς δὲ μάντις ἔστ' ἀνήρ, | ὃς ὀλίγ' ἀληθῆ, πολλὰ δὲ ψευδῆ λέγει | τυχών, ὅταν δὲ μὴ τύχῃ, διοίχεται. Calchas' mode of divination is not mentioned in the *I.A.* But elsewhere in early Greek epic and tragedy he is talked of as an οἰωνοπόλος, that is the equivalent of the Roman *augur*.[2] Earlier in the *I.A.* (520–1) Agamemnon and Menelaus, with Calchas in mind, denounce diviners as a class. Such general denunciations of diviners are common in Attic tragedy (e.g. Sophocles, *Ant.* 1055, Euripides, *Hel.* 744 ff., fr. 795).

The anti-intellectual sentiments of the Ennian Achilles are common in Attic tragedy (e.g. Sophocles, fr. 671 μισῶ μὲν ὅστις τἀφανῆ περισκοπεῖ, Euripides, *Hel.* 757 γνώμη δ' ἀρίστη μάντις ἥ τ' εὐβουλία, fr. 913 μετεωρολόγων . . . σκολιὰς ἀπάτας ὧν τολμηρὰ γλῶσσ' εἰκοβολεῖ περὶ τῶν ἀφανῶν, οὐδὲν γνώμης μετέχουσα, 973 μάντις δ' ἄριστος ὅστις εἰκάζει καλῶς). Whether or not astrological divination was known in fifth-century Athens[3] the tragedians certainly excluded it from the heroic world. The Aeschylean Prometheus does not reckon it among the types of divination he discovered for men.[4] He talks of the stars only as guides to the seasons.[5] There is remarkably little talk of the stars in either Ionian epic or Attic tragedy; they were of interest to farmers rather than to men of state. The only possible tragic reference to divination by the stars is in Euripides' account of Melanippe's learned mother Hippo: fr. 482 πρῶτα μὲν τὰ θεῖα προὐμαντεύσατο | χρησμοῖσι σαφέσιν ἀστέρων ἐπ' ἀντολαῖς.[6]

---

[1] See A. W. Blomquist, *De genitiui apud Plautum usu* (Diss. Helsingfors, 1892), pp. 111 ff., Marouzeau, *MSL* XVIII (1914), 146 ff.

[2] See Homer, *Il.* 1.68–72, 13.70, Euripides, *I.T.* 662, Propertius 4.1.109 ff.

[3] See W. Capelle, *Hermes* LX (1925), 373 ff.

[4] *Prom.* 484–99. Cf. Euripides, *Hik.* 211–13.

[5] *Prom.* 454–8. Cf. Sophocles, fr. 399.

[6] Wilamowitz, *SB Berlin* 1921, 74 n. 3 (= *Kl. Schr.* I 453 n. 2), declared that διοσημεῖα only are involved. A. Bouché-Leclercq, *L'astrologie grecque* (Paris, 1899), p. 37 n. 1, was less dogmatic.

Roman tragedy, on the other hand, both republican and imperial, is full of talk of astrologers, the planets and the zodiac: e.g. Pacuvius 407 *nam si quae euentura sunt prouideant aequiperent Ioui* (i.e. *astrologi*; see Gellius 14.1.34), Accius 331–2 *lucifera lampade Arietem exurat Iouis*, 678–80 *peruade polum splendida mundi sidera binis* (Popma: *bigis* cod.) *continuis sex apti signis* (Scaliger: *continui se cepit spoliis* cod.), Seneca, *Thy.* 836, 844–66, *Herc. f.* 944 ff., *Oed.* 40, 251. Roman epic treats the heroic world similarly: e.g. Virgil, *Aen.* 3.360, 10.176, Statius, *Theb.* 3.558.

It is possible to regard Ennius' verses as coming from an adaptation of *I.A.* 919–74. Elsewhere without any doubt (see below on fr. cviii) Ennius inserts *sententiae* absent from his originals or rewrites *sententiae* (see above on fr. lxxxiv) with the world of experience of himself and his audience in mind. To have ridiculed Calchas as an *augur* might have given offence to his aristocratic patrons[1] but the *astrologus*, like all private diviners, was generally despised.[2]

186 cum Capra aut Nepa aut exoritur nomen aliquod beluarum: for the series of alternatives cf. Plautus, *Aul.* 24 *aut turi aut uino aut aliqui semper supplicat*, *Capt.* 382 *pater exspectat aut me aut aliquem nuntium*, *Truc.* 53 *aut empta ancilla aut aliquod uasum argenteum*. For the periphrasis with *nomen* cf. Euripides, *I.T.* 662–4 τόν τ' ἐν οἰωνοῖς σοφὸν | Κάλχαντ' 'Αχιλλέως τ' ὄνομα, καὶ τὸν ἄθλιον | 'Αγαμέμνον', *C.I.L.* I² 581 (186 B.C.) *neue nominus Latini neue socium quisquam*, Cicero, *Fam.* 7.5.3 *huic ego neque tribunatum neque praefecturam neque ullius benefici certum nomen peto*; Vahlen, *Ind. lectt. Berlin* 1878, 8 ff. (= *Op. ac.* I 58 ff.), Löfstedt, *Eranos* x (1910), 22 ff., *Coniectanea* (Uppsala, 1950), pp. 42 ff.

Capra normally represents the constellation Αἴξ in later Latin poetry. However at *Anth. Lat.* 622.5 and 626.5 it represents Αἰγόκερως.[3] The astrological context does not demand necessarily a zodiacal constellation[4] but makes one likely.

Nepa represents Σκορπίος in later poetry but Verrius Flaccus[5] seems to have thought that Ennius could mean Καρκίνος.

187 caeli scrutantur plagas: Varro, *Men.* 233, Ovid, *Met.* 11.518, Seneca, *Oed.* 972 repeat the phrase *caeli plagas* as a mere periphrasis for

---

[1] Pacuvius comes close to attacking the state augurs at *Trag.* 83 ff.

[2] See Cato, *Agr.* 54 *augurem hariolum Chaldaeum nequem consuluisse uelit*, Appian, *Hisp.* 85, Plutarch, *Mor.* 201 B (on Scipio and μάντεις in the Roman camp at Numantia).

[3] For *Caper* = Αἰγόκερως cf. Manilius 2.179 and Housman's note.

[4] See on the constellation Αἴξ Manilius 5.128–39.

[5] Nonius, p. 145.12, Paulus, p. 163.12; see above, p. 319 n. 5.

caelum. Ennius' context (*exoritur*) suggests that he has the circle of the horizon in mind. Elsewhere in drama *plagae* denotes a (hemispherical, circular?) hunting net.[1] There may be the same link here as between Homer, *Il.* 5.487 ὡς ἀψῖσι λίνοι' ἁλόντε πανάγρου and Plato, *Phaidr.* 247 B ἄκραν ὑπὸ τὴν οὐράνιον ἀψῖδα πορεύονται. It is difficult however to understand within this area of metaphor Ennius, *Sat.* 65 *subulo quondam marinas propter astabat plagas* (circle of 'Ὠκεανός?).

<h2 style="text-align:center">XCVI</h2>

At *Ling.* 7.73–5 Varro quotes Ennius' anapaests as an illustration of how the poets represent *multa nox* and turns aside to discuss the Latin names of the constellation of the Great Bear. It is certain that the latter discussion comes from the work of another scholar and highly likely that this work is also the source of the anapaests.[2] If so, Varro's interpretation—*multam noctem ostendere uult*—may be determined by the general structure of his discussion of poetic accounts of time rather than by the dramatic context of Ennius' anapaests.

Scaliger accepted the manuscript division of speakers at Euripides, *I.A.* 6–8 and made a similar division of speakers in Ennius' anapaests after *uidetur*.[3] Hermann took over Scaliger's basic assumptions and put the division after *clipeo* to take account of *Ling.* 5.19. On any unprejudiced view the phrase *in altisono caeli clipeo* goes with *superat.* Vahlen[4] understood all the anapaests as uttered by the one speaker, Agamemnon, to himself. The word *uidetur* is hardly proper to a soliloquy. I therefore take *quid noctis uidetur* as a question addressed by Agamemnon to a second party and the other words of the quotation as information about the state of the sky designed to help the second party's reply. The relative positions of the stars do not of themselves fix the time of night.

The text of Varro's discussion as well as that of his quotation is corrupt and there is little hope of certain restoration. *Stellas* lacks a complement[5] and *sublime agens* presents a quite intolerable hiatus.[6]

---

[1] Plautus, *Mil.* 608, 1388, *Poen.* 648, *Trin.* 237b.   [2] See above, p. 320.

[3] Even quoting at first hand ancient writers were prone to make no reference to such divisions; cf. Cicero, *Diu.* 1.66 and above, p. 207.

[4] *Ind. lectt. Berlin* 1888/9, 14 (= *Op. ac.* 1 414).

[5] Vahlen (*Ind. lectt. Berlin* 1888/9, 14 [= *Op. ac.* 1 414], *Hermes* XLIII [1908], 514) seems to have taken *stellas* as one of the objects of *agens.* F. Skutsch (*RhM* LXI [1906], 605 [= *Kl. Schr.* 296]) took it as the object of *superat*, comparing Plautus, *Stich.* 365 *commodum radiosus sese sol superabat ex mari.* Neither explanation gives a very clear image. Ribbeck (*Coroll.* p. xxv) saw the difficulty.

[6] Leo, *Ausg. kl. Schr.* 1 196, pointed out that *agens* might be treated as having suffered iambic shortening. But this phenomenon is comparatively rare in tragedy even in iambo-trochaic verse (for anapaests cf. Accius 290).

Turnebus' *sublimis agens* and Vahlen's *sublime agitans* remove the hiatus. *Sublimum agens* would be a simpler change.[1] For the hiatus *sublimum agens* cf., in anapaestic verse, Plautus, *Bacch.* 1193 *mentem amabo*, *Curc.* 137 *plorā amabo*; in dactylic verse Ennius, *Ann.* 307 *aeuum agebant*,[2] 332 *militum octo*, *Var.* 3 *Scipiŏ inuicte*, Cicero, *Arat.* fr. 24 *etesiāe in uada ponti* (*Orat.* 152), Lucretius 6.716 *etesiāe esse*. Where hiatus in general is concerned the tradition of republican dramatic verses has it much more often after words ending in vowel + *m* than after words ending in *ĕ*.[3] However this may simply reflect the relative frequency of words ending in *m* and *e* in the lexicon.

Varro's remark *et plaustrum appellatum, a parte totum, ut multa* perhaps contains the clue to what is wrong with Ennius' *temo superat stellas*. I take *temo* literally as the yoke-pole formed by Alioth, Mizar and Benetnasch[4] and supply *plaustri* with *stellas*. Ennius would then be describing the relative positions of the seven stars when Mizar has reached its highest point in the sky.

In the anapaestic dialogue which opens the *I.A.* Euripides' Agamemnon either asks his aged servant or muses to himself about the appearance of the sky: 6–8 τίς ποτ' ἄρ' ἀστὴρ ὅδε πορθμεύει | σείριος ἐγγὺς τῆς ἑπταπόρου | Πλειάδος ἄσσων ἔτι μεσσήρης;[5] The mention of the Pleiades at the beginning of the campaigning season as still unset would have put the time somewhat before dawn. Sophocles describes Palamedes' discovery of how to divide the watches of the night by the stars at fr. 399.8 ff. and Euripides twice elsewhere (*Rhes.* 528 ff., *Phaeth.* fr. 773.19 ff.) uses the Pleiades to fix the time. The Bear is never so used in Attic tragedy. In classical Roman poetry, on the other hand, whatever the position of the observer, the position of the Bear seems regularly to fix the time of night and that of the Pleiades the season of the year. The parallelism of phrase ἄσσων ἔτι μεσσήρης ~ *sublimum agens etiam atque etiam noctis iter* confirms to some extent the external indications that the Greek and Latin anapaests are linked. Why Ennius changed the seven stars of the Pleiades for the seven of

---

[1] For the form see Nonius, p. 489.7. A number of adjectives swing in early Latin between -*us* -*a* -*um* and -*is* -*e* (*futtilus, pronus, sterilus* et al.).

[2] Cicero, *Brut.* 58; cf. Timpanaro, *SIFC* N.S. xxi (1946), 53.

[3] See Maurenbrecher, *Hiatus und Verschleifung*, pp. 16 ff.

[4] Cf. *Souda* 'Ρ 295 ῥυμός...καὶ τῆς Ἄρκτου οἱ κατὰ τὴν οὐρὰν γ' ἀστέρες ὑπὸ Ἡρακλείτου, Cicero, *Arat.* fr. 16 (*Nat. deor.* 2.109) *Arctophylax uulgo qui dicitur esse Bootes* | *quod QVASI TEMONE ADIVNCTAM prae se quatit Arctum* (~ Aratus 92–3 τόν ῥ' ἄνδρες ἐπικλείουσι Βοώτην | οὕνεχ' ἀμαξαίης ἐπαφώμενος εἴδεται Ἄρκτου), Ovid, *Met.* 10.446–7 *tempus erat quo cuncta silent interque triones* | *flexerat obliquo plaustrum temone Bootes*.

[5] For the interpretation of the Greek see Housman, *CR* xxviii (1914), 267.

the Bear it is hard to say.[1] Ancient critics were much divided on the precise
significance of Euripides' words.[2] Rome's different position on the globe
and the different times of the year at which her dramatic festivals were held
may have made astronomical observations comprehensible in Athens at the
time of the Great Dionysia seem ludicrous when literally translated. In any
case the Latin Agamemnon's question is a different one from the Greek.

188 quid noctis uidetur: 'how late do you think it is?'; cf. Plautus,
Amph. 153–4 *qui me alter est audacior homo ... qui hoc noctis solus ambulem?*, 164,
292, 310, *Curc.* 1. For the omission of personal pronouns in high dramatic
style see above on *v.* 17.

188–9 in altisono | caeli clipeo: it is not certain that Apuleius, *Socr.* 2
refers to this passage; for repetition of phrases in drama see above on
fr. xxxiv.

For images presenting the visible sky as a hemispherical container and
their absence from Attic tragedy see above on fr. xxxiii. The only classical
ancestors of Ennius' shield image are the descriptions of Achilles' shield and
its decoration by Homer (*Il.* 18.483–9) and Euripides (*El.* 464–9).

190–1 sublimum agens | etiam atque etiam noctis iter: 'making its
nightly way still high in the sky'. Comedy and classical prose employ
regularly the phrases *iter facere, conficere, perficere* (cf. Plautus, *Cas.* 968, *Merc.*
913, *Persa* 221); *iter agere*, etc. are absent. For Ennius' phrase cf. Ovid, *Ars*
2.84 *altius egit iter*, *T.L.L.* 1 1382.69 ff.

Etiam atque etiam normally means 'again and again' (cf. Plautus, *Aul.* 614,
Trin. 674) but for Ennius' usage cf. Gellius 2.30.3 *a uento quidem iamdudum
tranquilla sunt, sed mare est etiam atque etiam undabundum.*

XCVII

Verrius Flaccus commonly quoted republican poetry in metrical units and
the words which Festus transmits here will form an iambic trimeter if the
first syllable of *Acherontem* is treated as short. But Plautus has this name frequently enough for there to be no doubt about the prosody regular on the
early second century stage. We must suppose that Festus' quotation or the
tradition is defective and treat the words as an incomplete trochaic tetrameter.

---

[1] Cf. Virgil's imitation of *Od.* 5.270 ff. at *Aen.* 3.512 ff. and Macrobius'
discussion (*Sat.* 5.11.11).

[2] See Theon Smyrn. *De astr.* xvi, p. 202 Martin; there seems to have been
agreement about what is meant at *Rhes.* 527 ff. and general condemnation of
Euripides' ignorance.

IPHIGENIA

Columna thought that Ennius was adapting *I.A.* 1503 θανοῦσα δ' οὐκ ἀναίνομαι and later scholars have adduced other passages uttered by the Euripidean Iphigenia after her decision to go willingly to her death: 1375 κατθανεῖν μέν μοι δέδοκται, 1506–9 λαμπαδοῦχος ἁμέρα | Διός τε φέγγος, ἕτερον ἕτερον | αἰῶνα καὶ μοῖραν οἰκήσομεν. | χαῖρέ μοι, φίλον φάος. There are closer verbal parallels in other plays: e.g. Euripides, *Hek.* 414 ἄπειμι δὴ κάτω, *Hik.* 1022 Φερσεφονείας ἥξω θαλάμους, *Herakles* 1247 εἶμι γῆς ὕπο, *Tr.* 460 ἥξω δ' ἐς νεκρούς. From 1368 Iphigenia makes no mention of the underworld; at 1437 ff. she forbids any of the customary funeral rites and her wish is almost instantly approved; she is to be the possession of Olympian Artemis, not of Pluto. Before her change of heart Iphigenia expresses several times (1219, 1250–1, 1281–2) the traditional Greek horror of the underworld. *Acherontem obibo* etc. should therefore be treated as coming from an adaptation of some utterance by the Euripidean Iphigenia before *v.* 1368.[1]

192 Acherontem obibo: cf. Apuleius, *Met.* 4.20 *uitae metas ultimas obiret.* The phrases *mortem obire* and *diem (suum) obire* are frequent in comedy; *obire* does not occur in other contexts.

Etruria seems to have been the intermediary between 'Αχέρων, one of the rivers of the heroic underworld, and *Acheruns*, the underworld itself in the imagination of early second century Romans.[2]

Mortis thesauri: cf. the alleged epitaph of Naevius, *ap.* Gell. 1.24.2, *postquamst Orci traditus thesauro.* For the personification of *Mors* cf. Plautus, *Capt.* 692 *ob sutelas tuas te Morti misero, Cist.* 640 *recipe me ad te Mors amicum et beneuolum.* The third and second century dramatists usually speak of *Orcus.* Ennius' grandiose phraseology alludes obliquely to the name *Dis pater* given to the Greek Πλούτων when he was introduced to the Roman state cult in 249.[3] For similar obliquity cf. Sophocles, *O.T.* 29–30 μέλας δ' | 'Αίδης στεναγμοῖς καὶ γόοις πλουτίζεται; for the explicit etymology Ennius, *Var.* 78 *Pluto Latine est Dis pater, alii Orcum uocant,* Cicero, *Nat. deor.* 2.66.

The Greek borrowing *thesaurus* occurs frequently in comedy, usually in the singular; the plural is always accompanied by other signs of stylistic elevation (Plautus, *Aul.* 240, *Mil.* 1064, *Pseud.* 628, *Truc.* 245).

---

[1] M. L. Cunningham has interpreted the fragment as a question and compared *I.A.* 1219 τὰ δ' ὑπὸ γῆς μή μ' ἰδεῖν ἀναγκάσῃς; see O. Skutsch, *HSCPh* LXXI (1967), 142.

[2] See Pasquali, *Studi Etruschi* I (1927), 291 ff. (= *Pagine meno stravaganti di un filologo*, pp. 163 ff.). 'Αχέρων often indicates the underworld in Hellenistic poetry: cf. Asclepiades, *A.P.* 5.85.3 et al.

[3] See Latte, *Röm. Rel.* pp. 246 ff.

obiacent: not elsewhere in republican drama; tragedy has the simple *iacere* 4 times, comedy 16. Ennius chooses the unusual compound for the sake of word play with *obibo*; cf. his *expetunt* at *v.* 23 and *incinctae* at *v.* 26.

XCVIII

The speaker bids someone whom he esteems either to come towards him (cf. Plautus, *Mil.* 828 *procede huc*, Terence, *Eun.* 470 *procede tu huc*, Seneca, *Tro.* 705 *huc e latebris procede tuis*) or to move away (cf. Plautus, *Capt.* 954 *age tu illuc procede*); Ennius could be adapting either *I.A.* 1–2 ὦ πρέσβυ δόμων τῶνδε πάροιθεν | στεῖχε (Vahlen) or 139–40 ἀλλ᾽ ἴθ᾽ ἐρέσσων σὸν πόδα, γήρᾳ | μηδὲν ὑπείκων (Scaliger). The πιστότης of Agamemnon's servant is a constant theme of Euripides' play (*vv.* 45, 114, 304, 867).

193–4 gradum proferre pedum, | nitere, cessas: for the imperative in parenthesis cf. Aeschylus, *Theb.* 435 τοιῷδε φωτί, πέμπε, τίς ξυστήσεται;, *Choe.* 779 ἄγγελλ᾽ ἰοῦσα, πρᾶσσε, τἀπεσταλμένα, Ennius, *Ann.* 201 *dono, ducite, doque*, Plautus, *Merc.* 111–12 *ex summis opibus uiribusque usque experire, nitere,* | *erus ut minor opera tua seruetur*, Catullus 14.21–2 *uos hinc interea, ualete, abite* | *illuc unde malum pedem attulistis* et al. Some modern scholars put a stop after *nitere* and make the infinitive *proferre* its object—a construction absent from Caesar and Cicero but common enough in the historians and dactylic poets and therefore possible in archaic tragedy.

Plautus, *Men.* 754 has *gradum proferam* in bacchiacs. For the periphrasis *gradum…pedum* cf. Euripides, *Tr.* 333–4 ποδῶν | φέρουσα φιλτάταν βάσιν, Lucretius 5.914 *trans maria alta pedum nisus ut ponere posset.*[1] Verrius must have understood *gradum* as an internal object of *procede*.

194 o fide: the doctrine reported at Servius auct. *Aen.* 1.113, *quidam uelint fidum amicum, fidelem seruum dici*, appears to be refuted by this verse, *v.* 237, Ritschl's almost certain restoration of Plautus, *Most.* 785, and Livy 33.28.13. But it is clear from the comparative rarity of *fidus* in comedy (5 occurrences as against 24 of *fidelis*) and classical prose and from the contexts of occurrence that it conveyed much more emotion than *fidelis* and was more likely to appear in the dialogue of social equals. Applied to a person of servile status it perhaps indicated an out of the ordinary affection on the part of the speaker. Bergk's supplement *o fide ⟨senex⟩* is quite unnecessary; the absence of *fidus* as a substantive from our record of early Latin loses significance when one considers how rarely even the adjective occurs.

---

[1] No real parallel is provided by Pollio *ap.* Gell. 10.26.4 *transgressus a transgrediendo dicitur, idque ipsum ab ingressu et a pedum gradu appellatum.*

XCIX

The structure of the soldiers' argument is clear despite several corrupt words: a general statement about the employment of *otium* is followed by a reference to the particular dramatic situation. This structure has many parallels in republican drama: where stichic iambic trimeters are used at Plautus, *Poen.* 627 ff., *Pseud.* 767 ff.; where iambic tetrameters are used at Plautus, *Rud.* 290 ff.; where trochaic tetrameters are used at Pacuvius, *Trag.* 366 ff., Plautus, *Bacch.* 540 ff., *Poen.* 504 ff., Terence, *Ad.* 855 ff., *Eun.* 232 ff.; where different types of verse are mingled at Plautus, *Amph.* 633 ff., *Epid.* 166 ff., *Men.* 571 ff., Caecilius, *Com.* 142 ff. One cannot decide what metre Ennius gave his soldiers' words on *a priori* grounds. It is, however, significant that no such argumentative structure begins in the middle of a metrical unit.

Three kinds of measurement have been tried: one in stichic trochaic tetrameters,[1] one in corresponding lyric strophes,[2] and one in a mixture of trochaic lengths.[3] The third kind requires least alteration to the words transmitted.

The first thirteen words transmitted form a trochaic dimeter and a catalectic trochaic tetrameter without diaeresis but with caesura after the fourth arsis.[4] The extended word play, *otio...negoti...negotium...*, has few analogues in Attic drama (cf. however Philemon, fr. 23.3–4 ὁ λοιδορῶν γάρ, ἂν ὁ λοιδορούμενος | μὴ προσποιῆται, λοιδορεῖται λοιδορῶν) but seems to have been considered a stylistic ornament in early second century Rome (cf. Ennius, *Sat.* 59–62 *nam qui lepide postulat alterum frustrari | quem frustratur frustra eum dicit frustra esse. | nam qui sese frustrari quem frustra sentit, | qui frustratur is frustra est si non ille est frustra*, Plautus, *Amph.* 33–6, *Capt.* 255–6, *Pseud.* 704–5, Terence, *Andr.* 258–9). The interpretation of *negotium in negotio* has given difficulty. Vahlen offered the translation 'sehr viel Arbeit'. E. H. Warmington 'when he is awork at work'.[5] There is no parallel however for this particular kind of expression in republican drama although it is common in Attic (cf. Euripides, *I.T.* 197 φόνος ἐπὶ φόνῳ, ἄχεα ἄχεσιν et al.) and appears occasionally in classical Latin dactylic poetry (cf. Ovid, *Ars* 1.244 *et Venus in uinis ignis in igne fuit*). It would be better to translate the thirteen words as 'the man who has no job to do and does not know

---

[1] Cf., most recently, O. Skutsch, *RhM* XCVI (1953), 193 ff.

[2] First by Ribbeck, most recently by O. Crusius, *Die Responsion*, pp. 114 ff. (cf. Strzelecki, in *Tragica* I, 58).

[3] Cf. Vahlen, *Hermes* XV (1880), 262.

[4] For this type of tetrameter, which is comparatively rare, see W. Meyer, *Abh. Bayer. Ak.* XVII (1886), 75 ff.

[5] *Remains of Old Latin* I (London, 1935), p. 309.

how to employ the resulting leisure has more difficulty than when there is difficulty in a job on hand'. For the two meanings of *negotium* cf. Donatus, Ter. *Andr.* 2 *negotium modo pro molestia et cura, non labore.* For the switch of meaning in polyptoton cf. above on *v.* 105 (adjectives) and Plautus, *Bacch.* 323 *uerum uerum nescio, Capt.* 741 *post mortem in morte nihil est quod metuam mali, Epid.* 113 *in re dubia re iuuat, Mil.* 4 *praestringat oculorum aciem in acie hostibus, Pseud.* 90 *ante tenebras tenebras persequi,* Terence, *Haut.* 41 *mea causa causam hanc iustam esse animum inducite,* Accius, *Trag.* 109 *mala auxere in malis,* 422 *neque uita ulli propria in uita est.*

Three other treatments of the thirteen words are worth mentioning. Bothe wrote *otio qui nescit utier* as the end of a catalectic tetrameter. There is however a strong presumption that Ennius' discourse begins a metrical unit and Bothe's reading assumes a tetrameter without either diaeresis or caesura after the fourth arsis. Timpanaro suggested[1] that *otio qui nescit uti* should either be kept as the second half of a full tetrameter or changed to *qui uti nescit otio.* This has an order of words more modern in type than the one transmitted (cf. Plautus, *Poen.* 210 *negoti sibi qui uolet uim parare,* 627 *uiam qui nescit*) and it would be difficult to explain the corruption. Taking up a suggestion of A. M. Dale, O. Skutsch supplemented the thirteen words as follows: *otio qui nescit uti ⟨quom otio est, in otio⟩ | plus negoti habet quam, quom est negotium, in negotio.* This is free from metrical anomalies and the mode of expression attributed to Ennius perhaps no more twisted than that transmitted at *Sat.* 59–62.

The two word-groups, *cui quod agat institutum est in illis negotium* and *otioso initio animus,* are defective in sense and metre. Clearly one refers to the busy and the other to the idle and almost certainly the original rhythm was trochaic. No convincing restoration has been offered.[2]

Gellius introduces his quotation with the words *in eius tragoediae choro inscriptos esse hos uersus legimus.* Similar language is to be found at Varro, *Ling.* 6.94, *quare una origine inlici et inlicis, quod in choro Proserpinae est, et pellexit,* and *Gloss. Lat.* 1 128, *apud Romanos quoque Plautus comoediae choros exemplo Graecorum inseruit.* Varro could be referring to a tragedy *Proserpina*; the glossator's source must have had in mind the fishermen of the *Rudens* (290 ff.) or the *aduocati* of the *Poenulus* (504 ff.). Ennius' 'chorus' was composed of soldiers and of such there is no trace in the extant version of Euripides' *I.A.*[3] The Attic odes were sung and danced by women of Chalcis come out of mere curiosity to look at the army assembling at Aulis. Their content was to a quite unusual degree unconnected with the action of the

---

[1] *SIFC* N.S. xxi (1946), 76 f.

[2] O. Skutsch suggested *cui quod agat institutum in otio est negotium* and *otioso in otio ⟨aeger⟩ animus.*

[3] Verses 589 ff. have been, however, so interpreted. See above, p. 318.

I.A. There is no sign that Ennius adapted the text of any of them. Students o Roman tragedy seem all to have assumed that Ennius replaced them with utterances of the troop of soldiers. The only matter of dispute is the play from which Ennius extracted his soldier chorus.

There is no need to assume that Ennius made such radical alterations to the *I.A.* The soldiers, like the attendants of the Euripidean Hippolytus (designated χορός by our manuscripts),[1] may have appeared on the stage only once, accompanying Achilles to the tent of Agamemnon (*I.A.* 801–1035). In any case only the soldiers of Agamemnon could have been present throughout the action of the play and the utterance of the Ennian soldiers marks them plainly as Achilles' Myrmidons; the boredom and impatience of these were proverbial: cf. Homer, *Il.* 2.778–9 ...οἱ δ᾽ ἀρχὸν ἀρηΐφιλον ποθέοντες | φοίτων ἔνθα καὶ ἔνθα κατὰ στρατὸν οὐδὲ μάχοντο, Euripides, *I.A.* 812–18 γῆν γὰρ λιπὼν Φάρσαλον ἠδὲ Πήλεα | μένω 'πὶ λεπταῖς ταισίδ᾽ Εὐρίπου πνοαῖς, | Μυρμιδόνας ἴσχων· οἱ δ᾽ ἀεὶ προσκείμενοι | λέγουσ᾽· Ἀχιλλεῦ, τί μένομεν; πόσον χρόνον | ἔτ᾽ ἐκμετρῆσαι χρὴ πρὸς Ἰλίου στόλον; | δρᾶ γ᾽, εἴ τι δράσεις, ἢ ἄπαγ᾽ οἴκαδε στρατόν, | τὰ τῶν Ἀτρειδῶν μὴ μένων μελλήματα, *Telephos* in Pap. Berol. 9908 II 13–24 τί μέλλετ᾽; οὐ χρῆν ἥσυχον κεῖσθαι πόδα... αἰεί ποτ᾽ ἐστὲ νωχελεῖς καὶ μέλλετε | ῥήσεις θ᾽ ἕκαστος μυρίας καθήμενος | λέγει, τὸ δ᾽ ἔργον [οὐ]δαμοῦ πορεύεται. | κ[ἀγ]ὼ μὲν ὡς ὁρᾶ[τ]ε δρᾶν ἕτοιμος ὤν | ἥ[κ]ω, στρατός τε Μ[υρ]μιδῶν, καὶ πλεύσ[ομαι] | [τὰ τ]ῶν Ἀτρειδᾶ[ν οὐ μένων] μελλήματα, Accius, *Trag.* 611–12 *iam iam stupido Thessala somno | pectora languentque senentque.*

Terence admits himself to importing the persons of the parasite and the soldier into his adaptation of Menander's Εὐνοῦχος (19 ff.) and to adding a whole scene to the Ἀδελφοί (6 ff.). Donatus reports that he imported the persons of the freedman Sosia, the lover Charinus and the slave Byrria to the Ἀνδρία (*ad vv.* 14, 301; cf. Ter. *Andr.* 9 ff.) and that of the young man Antipho to the Εὐνοῦχος (*ad v.* 539). Terence never speaks of these alterations to the dramatic structure of Menander's plays as coming from his own creative imagination; he always claims the authority of a scene in another comedy. It therefore makes some sense to ask what tragic scene Ennius would have claimed as authority for the soldiers he imported into his adaptation of the *I.A.* Scholars in the past have asked a slightly different question but their answers could in principle be adapted to this new one.

Bergk[2] tied *otio qui nescit uti plus negoti habet quam cum est negotium in negotio* with a *sententia* quoted by Stobaeus (30.6) from Sophocles' Ἰφιγένεια —

---

[1] 61; cf. Aeschylus, *Eum.* 1032, Euripides, *Phaethon* fr. 781.14.

[2] *Ind. lectt. Marburg* 1844, XIV (= *Kl. phil. Schr.* I 229); cf. *De Frag. Sophoclis*, p. 15, Welcker, *Die griech. Trag.* p. 110.

τίκτει γὰρ οὐδὲν ἐσθλὸν εἰκαία σχολή (fr. 287), and deduced that Ennius replaced the odes of Euripides' play with versions of those of Sophocles' besides making other alterations.

The tie is not a close one. The Sophoclean *sententia* would be more likely uttered by a general than men of lower rank; it breathes the same spirit as Euripides, *I.A.* 1000–1 στρατὸς γὰρ ἀθρόος, ἀργὸς ὢν τῶν οἴκοθεν, | λέσχας πονηρὰς καὶ κακοστόμους φιλεῖ.[1] It concerns the man who has acquired leisure through some chance rather than from his own deliberate effort and the socially deleterious effect of such leisure. The Ennian *sententia* on the other hand concerns the man who does not know how to manage the leisure that comes to him and the personal effect of this ignorance. Even if the tie were a close one it would not show any structural link between Ennius' play and Sophocles'. Ennius at least once, perhaps twice (frs. cv, cviii), makes his Medea utter *sententiae* quite absent from his Euripidean original without apparently making any structural alteration to that original.

Where *sententiae* are concerned in Roman tragedy and comedy it may be a mistake always to look for a dramatic source. At least twice (frs. lxxxiv, cv) Ennius can be shown altering a *sententia* of his original in terms of his own experience of Roman life. Here he may be composing with the arguments of contemporary Greek philosophical schools[2] in mind rather than any dramatic context. Such detailed psychological analysis is scarcely appropriate in the mouths of soldiers. The mental effects described—*animus nescit quid uelit...incerte errat animus, praeter propter uitam uiuitur*—are those suffered by Democritus' ἀνοήμονες (fr. 202 τῶν ἀπεόντων ὀρέγονται, τὰ δὲ παρεόντα... ἀμαλδύνουσι), by the love-sick Phaedra (Euripides, *Hipp.* 181–5) and by those ignorant of the Epicurean science of living and dying (Lucretius 3.1057–67).

Leo[3] suggested that Ennius' soldiers were the chorus of Euripides' Τήλεφος. His only argument was that some anapaests quoted by Priscian (*Gramm.* 2.512.21) from Accius' *Telephus*—*iam iam stupido Thessala somno pectora languentque senentque*—prove Euripides to have employed a chorus of soldiers. They prove nothing of the sort, even if it were certain, as it is not, that

---

[1] O. Skutsch suggested that Sophocles' trimeter refers to the particular situation at Aulis and takes up a generalisation about leisure made in an earlier choral ode.

[2] On philosophical discussion of σχολή/*otium* see F. Boll, 'Vita contemplatiua', *SB Heidelberg, Phil.-hist. Kl.* Abh. viii, 1920 (= *Kl. Schr.* 303 ff.), W. Jaeger, 'Über Ursprung und Kreislauf des philosophischen Lebensideals', *SB Berlin, Phil.-hist. Kl.* 1928, 390 ff. (= *Scripta Min.* 1 347 ff.), J. L. Stocks, *CQ* xxx (1936), 177–87, Fraenkel, *Horace* (Oxford, 1957), pp. 212–13, J.-M. André, *Recherches sur l'otium romain* (Paris, 1962), pp. 27 ff.

[3] *De Trag. Rom.* p. 15 (= *Ausg. kl. Schr.* 1 204), *Gesch.* p. 192 n. 3.

Accius adapted Euripides. If soldiers did form the chorus of the Euripidean Τήλεφος they would have been Agamemnon's Argives, not Achilles' Myrmidons. One could imagine a sub-chorus of Myrmidons accompanying Achilles to Agamemnon's palace. However the fact that in the Berlin papyrus Achilles himself describes the Myrmidon discontent seems to rule out this possibility. We shall have to look outside the Τήλεφος for the origin of Ennius' soldiers but Leo's method of looking at the dramatic substance of the trochaic verses rather than their general argument remains the one to follow.

Mariotti[1] sees something of an 'andatura stilistica sommessa e conversativa' in the discourse of Ennius' soldiers, 'persone di categoria inferiore'. It is true that their manner of speaking does not possess the finished elegance of a Ciceronian oration or philosophical dialogue and that their vocabulary contains no element that we should think absent from the common language of the early second century. But one could say this of probably most of the sententious passages of republican tragedy and comedy. Peculiarly poetic vocabulary masses in the narrative and descriptive passages of the speeches of all social categories in tragedy. In the elaboration of phrasal patterns the discourse of Ennius' soldiers marks itself off even from the most ornate of the paratragic monodies of Plautine comedy; one notes the forward position of verbs and relative clause, the frequency of impersonal verbs, the asyndeta, the personification of *animus*, the extended word play with *otio...negoti... negotium...negotio*, the polyptota *negotium in negotio* and *cui* (*quoi*) *quod*, the ascending tricolon with anaphora *id agit id studet ibi mentem atque animum delectat suum*, the ascending doublet *mentem atque animum*, the etymological figure *uitam uiuitur*; all of these phenomena occur in comedy but nowhere in such mass as here.

198 ibi mentem atque animum delectat suum: for *ibi se delectat* or *ibi delectatur*. The doublet occurs in comedy only at Plautus, *Trin.* 454 *satin tu sanus mentis aut animi tui* and is rare in classical prose. Dactylic verse has it (Lucretius 1.74, 3.142, Horace, *Epist.* 1.14.8, Virgil, *Aen.* 6.11 et al.) perhaps partly on the analogy of Homer's κραδίην καὶ θυμὸν ἵκανεν (*Il.* 2.171), κατὰ φρένα καὶ κατὰ θυμόν (4.163), τοιόνδε νόον καὶ θυμόν (4.309).

199 †otioso initio† animus: Lipsius' *otioso in otio animus* can be taken in two ways: 'the mind in idle idleness' or 'the mind of a man idle at a time of idleness'; for the first cf. Cicero, *Planc.* 66 *cui fuerit ne otium quidem umquam otiosum* (Naevius, *Trag.* 35 *acrem acrimoniam*, Plautus, *Aul.* 215 *mala...malitia*,

---

[1] *Lezioni su Ennio*, p. 119. Cf. G. Luck, *Über einige Interjektionen der lateinischen Umgangssprache* (Heidelberg, 1964), p. 52.

COMMENTARY

Capt. 774 *amoenitate amoena, Cas.* 217 *nitoribus nitidis, Epid.* 120 *pretio pretioso,*
Mil. 959 *pulchram pulchritudinem, Poen.* 134 *gratas gratias, Pseud.* 882 *suaui*
suauitate, Lucretius 1.826 *sonitu... sonanti,* 3.993 *anxius angor*); for the second
cf. Cicero, *Cael.* 1 *quibus otiosis ne in communi quidem otio liceat esse* (Plautus,
Curc. 533 *iratus iracundia, Merc.* 191 *negotiosi eramus nos nostris negotiis,* 844
laetus laetitia).

animus nescit quid uelit: cf. Lucretius 3.772 *quidue foras sibi uult*
membris exire senectis, 1058 *quid sibi quisque uelit nescire,* Livy 41.20.4 *nescire*
quid sibi uellet quibusdam uideri. The omission of the pleonastic reflexive
pronoun perhaps raises the level of the style.

200 em neque domi nunc nos nec militiae sumus: *em* is rare outside
republican drama; it precedes statements at Plautus, *Asin.* 336 *em ergo is*
argentum huc remisit, Bacch. 274 *em accipitrina haec nunc erit.* Here it seems to
indicate an exasperated tone of voice. In a tragedy of the classical period it
would be an extreme colloquialism; one cannot be sure about its exact status
in early second century Latin.

Domi... militiae is official phraseology; cf. Terence, *Ad.* 495–6 *una semper*
militiae et domi | fuimus, Cicero, *Manil.* 48, *Mur.* 87, *Pis.* 1, *Lig.* 21 et al.

202 incerte errat animus: for *animi incerti eramus.* The Attic tragedians
commonly apply ἀλᾶσθαι, πλάζεσθαι, πλανᾶσθαι, φοιτᾶν to mental
behaviour. For the Latin phraseology cf. Ennius, *Trag.* 215–16 *era errans...*
animo aegro, ap. Cic. *Tusc.* 3.5 (fr. CLXXIV) *animus aeger semper errat,* Plautus,
Merc. 347 *tantus cum cura meost error animo,* Pacuvius, *Trag.* 302 *triplici pertime-*
factus maerore animi incerte errans uagat, Lucretius 3.463–4 *morbis in corporis*
auius errat | saepe animus, 3.1052 *animi incerto fluitans errore uagaris,* Cicero,
Carm. fr. 47.1 *ignaris homines in uita mentibus errant.*

praeter propter uitam uiuitur: the opposite of *recte uiuimus* (cf. Horace,
Epist. 2.2.213); the philosophical notion of living as an exact skill, like, for
example, carpentering, is implied.

Salmasius changed *uitam* to *uita.* A scribe could have mistaken *praeter*
propter for a preposition. On the other hand the accusative dependent on the
impersonal *uiuitur* has companions in republican drama which are difficult to
explain away: Plautus, *Cas.* 185 *pessumis me modis despicatur domi, Mil.* 24
epityra estur insanum bene, 254 *inducamus uera ut esse credat quae mentibitur,*
Pseud. 817 *teritur sinapis scelera,* 1261 *ubi mammia mammicula opprimitur.* The
rarity of the construction may simply reflect the rarity of the impersonal
passive in comedy (*uiuitur* occurs only at Plautus, *Persa* 17, *Trin.* 65, Terence,
Haut. 154).

338

IPHIGENIA

For the etymological figure cf. Plautus, *Epid.* 386–7 *cogitarent postea* | *uitam ut uixissent olim in adulescentia, Merc.* 473, Mil. 628, 726, *Persa* 346, 494, Turpilius, *Com.* 143, Cicero, *Verr.* 2.118 et al.

c

As often in rhetorical treatises[1] the illustration refers not only to the text of the dramatic speech but also to the mode of utterance; the words quoted scarcely of themselves illustrate ἀγανάκτησις. The Agamemnon of Euripides' *I.A.* is at his angriest in the scene of his quarrel with Menelaus. Accordingly scholars since Columna's day have wanted to put the Latin words in an adaptation of this scene, although there are no obvious verbal correspondences.

The words *Menelaus me obiurgat* would be spoken more naturally about Menelaus in his absence than to his face directly.[2] *Regimen* should be interpreted as 'my command of the Greek armada' rather than 'Menelaus' domineering behaviour' (cf. Trag. inc. 29 *proin demet abs te regimen Argos dum est potestas consili*). The Latin Agamemnon is describing the opposition that has arisen between his office and the welfare of his family. Accordingly I propose that Ennius' trochaic tetrameter be treated as coming from an adaptation of the scene preceding that of the confrontation of the two brothers. Some sort of stimulus can be seen in the iambics 84–6 κἀμὲ στρατηγεῖν †κᾶτα Μενέλεω χάριν † | εἵλοντο σύγγονόν γε. τἀξίωμα δὲ | ἄλλος τις ὤφελ' ἀντ' ἐμοῦ λαβεῖν τόδε. The anapaests 22–3 καὶ τὸ πρότιμον (Nauck: φιλότιμον codd.) | γλυκὺ μέν, λυπεῖ δὲ προσιστάμενον refer in general to the troubles that positions of worldly honour can bring.

My interpretation implies that the Latin Agamemnon put up a much stronger resistance to the proposed sacrifice than either the Euripidean Agamemnon claimed (97–8 οὖ δή μ' ἀδελφὸς πάντα προσφέρων λόγον | ἔπεισε τλῆναι δεινά) or the Euripidean Menelaus allowed (360 ἄσμενος θύσειν ὑπέστης παῖδα). Recognition of the force of circumstances rather than base ambition would have motivated his decision to acquiesce. The Euripidean Agamemnon was a most contemptible and unheroic figure. Ennius, if my interpretation is right, gave him a character more in harmony with the one which the Athenian philosophical schools and Roman aristocratic tradition thought appropriate to the statesman. Comparable are the alterations made by Pacuvius to the character of Sophocles' Ulysses (Cicero, *Tusc.* 2.48) and by Terence to Menander's Micio (Donatus, *Ad.* 938).[3]

---

[1] Cf. Charisius, p. 364.21 (Trag. inc. 123–4), 374.8 (Trag. inc. 120–2).
[2] They could be an angry aside; cf. Plautus, *Curc.* 572 f.
[3] For the 'Stoicising' of the heroes in epic poetry see Norden, *Aen. VI*², p. 154.

203 Menelaus me obiurgat; id meis rebus regimen restitat: Bentley's simple alteration produces a regular trochaic tetrameter. The fact that the intensive *restitare* is rare in archaic Latin compared with the positive and even rarer in classical Latin stands probably to the favour of *restitat* here; the same is true of many recorded intensives in *-itare*. For the predilection of tragedy for intensive forms see above on *v.* 68.

According to Festus, p. 348.15: REGIMEN *pro regimento usurpant poetae.* The extant texts do not seem to have *regimentum*; *regimen* occurs only here in republican drama, not at all in Caesar, Cicero and Sallust, five times in Livy. For the predilection of tragedy for nominal formations in *-men* see above on *v.* 13.

Restitat takes the place of expected *obstat, obest* (cf. Lucretius 1.110 *ratio nulla est restandi,* 2.450 *aeraque quae claustris restantia uociferantur*), perhaps for the sake of the triple alliteration at the end of the verse.

CI

In the Euripidean Agamemnon's attacks on his brother (*I.A.* 317–412) there is nothing as rhetorically figured as these three trochaic tetrameters; the nearest to them in form and substance are verses of Menelaus' speech of reconciliation: 481–4 καί σοι παραινῶ μήτ' ἀποκτείνειν τέκνον | μήτ' ἀνθελέσθαι τοὐμόν. οὐ γὰρ ἔνδικον | σὲ μὲν στενάζειν, τἀμὰ δ' ἡδέως ἔχειν, | θνῄσκειν τε τοὺς σούς, τοὺς δ' ἐμοὺς ὁρᾶν φάος.

204 ego proiector quod tu peccas: usually interpreted[1] as a syntactic graecism: i.e. ἐπιτιμῶμαι, 'mihi proicitur quod...'. Timpanaro[2] pointed out that *proicio/proiecto* is unexampled in the meaning normal to *obicio/obiecto* and offered the quite satisfactory interpretation 'io sono messo innanzi come capro espiatorio, sono esposto al biasimo pubblico a causa della tua colpa'. For the type of argument cf. Plautus, *Epid.* 139–40 *men piacularem oportet fieri ob stultitiam tuam,* | *ut meum tergum tuae stultitiae subdas succidaneum?* Ribbeck punctuated this and the next correctly as positive statements; the future indicative sometimes occurs in repudiating questions (e.g. Plautus, *Men.* 198 *ego saltabo?*), the present never, as far as I can see.

tu †delinquas† ego arguor: Stephanus' *delinquis* produces a metrical anomaly (see above on fr. xii) but quite good sense. O. Skutsch suggests[3]

---

[1] Cf. R. Frobenius, *Die Syntax des Ennius* (Diss. Tübingen, 1910), p. 81, Kroll, *Studien*, p. 249, Löfstedt, *Syntactica* ii, p. 412, J. B. Hofmann and A. Szantyr, *Lateinische Syntax und Stilistik* (Munich, 1965), p. 33.

[2] *Maia* iii (1950), 28. He would now, however, interpret (letter to O. Skutsch) 'I am being sacrificed in your interest' (cf. Catullus 64.81–2).

[3] London seminar, 29 November 1954; see now *HSCPh* lxxi (1967), 133 ff.

that *arguor* is a displaced gloss on *proiector* and replaces it with *luam* (cf. Horace, *Carm.* 3.6.1 *delicta maiorum immeritus lues*).

206 reconcilietur: only once in comedy (Plautus, *Capt.* 33; *reconciliassere* occurs at *Capt.* 168, 576) as against *conciliare* 14 times.

necetur: a word normally applied to criminal homicide (see above on *v.* 178) and the extermination of unwanted children, slaves, criminals and *prodigia* (see above on *v.* 18). The accepted notion that it refers at base to killing without bloodshed[1] appears to be contradicted by this passage and Pacuvius, *Trag.* 329. Both passages have a highly emotional tone and the speakers may be emphasising the word's brutal associations rather than its literal meaning.

CII

Ribbeck set these words in an adaptation of the lament uttered by the Euripidean Iphigenia after the rejection of her plea to Agamemnon (*vv.* 1279–335), comparing in particular her apostrophe to Helen (*vv.* 1333–5 ἰὼ ἰώ, | μεγάλα πάθεα, μεγάλα δ' ἄχεα | Δαναΐδαις τιθεῖσα Τυνδαρὶς κόρα). Vahlen set them in an adaptation of the dialogue between Agamemnon and Clytaemnestra about the proposed marriage (*vv.* 691–741), comparing in particular *vv.* 735–7 (— οὐ καλὸν ἐν ὄχλῳ σ' ἐξομιλεῖσθαι στρατοῦ. — καλὸν τεκοῦσαν τἀμά μ' ἐκδοῦναι τέκνα. — καὶ τάς γ' ἐν οἴκῳ μὴ μόνας εἶναι κόρας.

The attempt to find verbal parallels between Greek and Latin, here as so often elsewhere, falsifies interpretation of the Latin. In a play about the Trojan expedition one would naturally interpret the words *quae nunc abs te uiduae et uastae uirgines sunt* as part of a complaint uttered by a woman against the commander: because of his actions the young women of Greece have been left without suitors and the means of bearing children. The plight of the women of Greece during the siege of Troy is a constant theme of the speeches and odes of tragedy: cf. Euripides, *Hek.* 322–5, *Hel.* 1125, *Or.* 1134–6, *Tr.* 379–81. The Euripidean Clytaemnestra makes no such complaint in her attack upon Agamemnon (*vv.* 1146–208) but it would not be out of place in a free Latin version.

207 uiduae et uastae uirgines: the *uidua* and the *uirgo* are normally differentiated (e.g. Plautus, *Curc.* 37–8 *dum ted abstineas nupta uidua uirgine...*

---

[1] Cf. Festus, p. 158.17 NECI DATVS *proprie dicitur, qui sine uulnere interfectus est, ut ueneno aut fame,* 190.5 OCCISVM *a necato distingui quidam, quod alterum a caedendo atque ictu fieri dicunt, alterum sine ictu,* Priscian, *Gramm.* II 470.14 f., Wölfflin, *ALL* VII (1892), 278.

ama quidlubet) but cf. Seneca, *Ag.* 195 *uirgines uiduae*, Apuleius, *Met.* 4.32 *Psyche uirgo uidua domi residens*. For the tautology cf. Aeschylus, *Pers.* 288–9 ὡς πολλὰς Περσίδων | ἔκτισαν εὐνῖδας ἠδ᾽ ἀνάνδρους, Sophocles, *O.T.* 1502 χέρσους...κἀγάμους, Euripides, *Hipp.* 547 ἄνανδρον τὸ πρὶν καὶ ἄνυμφον, Cato, *Agr.* 141 (prayer to Mars) *uti tu morbos uisos inuisosque, uiduertatem uastitudinemque, calamitates intemperiasque prohibessis defendas auerruncesque*, Plautus, *Pseud.* 69–70 *harunc uoluptatum mi omnium atque ibidem tibi | distractio discidium uastities uenit*.

MEDEA EXVL; MEDEA

The title *Medea exul* is given to Ennius three times by Nonius (frs. CIX*c*, CXI*a* and *b*)[1] and once by a Virgilian commentator, the so-called Probus (fr. CX).[2] The Latin of the three pieces quoted is quite close to the Greek of three passages of Euripides' extant Μήδεια.[3] The other titles given to republican tragedians which consist of proper name and adjective may all be treated as transliterations or translations of the titles of the Attic originals.[4] Such titles were applied to Attic plays by grammarians wishing to distinguish two plays about the one hero or heroine by the one author. Among the seventy tragedies of Euripides known to the scholars of Alexandria there was one apart from the extant Μήδεια which dealt with the Colchian woman. But this is regularly quoted in our sources as Αἰγεύς. We should therefore suppose that *Medea exul* was a title applied by grammarians to an adaptation of Euripides' Μήδεια so as to distinguish this script from another by Ennius about Medea.[5]

---

[1] Pp. 39.2, 261.21, 292.20 probably depend on Lindsay's list 27 'Alph. Verb'.

[2] Probus' work exists only in humanist apographs of a lost medieval codex. Certain things in it could not possibly come from the mouth or pen of M. Valerius Probus Berytius. Whether or not the core of the work belongs to him is an insoluble problem; see Marx, *C. Lucilii carminum reliquiae*, vol. I (Leipzig, 1904), p. lxxii, J. Aistermann, *De M. Valerii Probi Berytii uita et scriptis* (Diss. Bonn, 1910), pp. 72 ff., Norden, *Ennius und Vergilius*, p. 10.

[3] Fr. CXI was compared with Euripides *vv.* 49–51 by Stephanus; fr. CIX with Euripides *vv.* 250–1 by Muretus (*Var. Lectt.* IV 7); fr. CX with Euripides *vv.* 1251–4 by Scaliger (*Coniect. Varr. Ling.*, on 7.9).

[4] See *Introduction*, p. 58.

[5] Hyginus, *Fab.* 25 gives the ὑπόθεσις of Euripides' Μήδεια under the title *Medea*; *Fab.* 26 an account of the birth of Medus to Aegeus and the exile of Medea from Athens for witchcraft under the title *Medea exul*; the latter could be but does not look like the ὑπόθεσις of a tragedy.

There is further and stronger evidence both that Ennius adapted the Μήδεια of Euripides and that he wrote another tragedy about Medea. This second tragedy was set in Athens. There is nothing either for or against the supposition that it adapted the Αἰγεύς of Euripides.

The title *Medea* is given to Ennius by Cicero (fr. CIII*d*), Varro (fr. CXXII*a*)[1] and Donatus (fr. CIII*m*) once each, by Priscian twice (frs. CIII*o*, CIII*p*)[2] and by Nonius five times (fr. CXII*b*, CXIII, CXIV, CXV, CXVI);[3] to Accius by Nonius sixteen times[4] and Priscian once;[5] to Pacuvius in error twice by Macrobius and once by a Virgilian scholiast.[6] Of the seven pieces quoted with Ennius' name one (fr. CIII) is said by Cicero (*Fin.* 1.4) to come from an adaptation of Euripides, and is used by Latin writers on logic and rhetoric to illustrate a fallacious type of argument (Rhet. inc. *Her.* 2.34, Cicero, *Inu.* 1.91, *Top.* 61, *Fat.* 34, Quintilian, *Inst.* 5.10.84, Iulius Victor, *Rhet.* 12) where Greek writers use the prologue of Euripides' Μήδεια (Clemens Alex. *Strom.* 8.9.27), and in fact follows fairly closely the Greek of Euripides

---

[1] The fact that the trimeter quoted by Varro at *Ling.* 7.9 does not form a sense unit and its mode of introduction (contrasting with the one discussed above on fr. XI) show that it comes from another grammarian's collection. In the seventh book Varro refers frequently to Aurelius Opilius, Servius Clodius and 'glossematum scriptores'. Reitzenstein, Dahlmann and Schröter have shown (see *Introduction*, p. 53 n. 5) how a mass of undigested glossographical material was jammed into the schematic framework of this book.

[2] The quotation at *Gramm.* II 320.15 occurs in an article of the sort which goes back at least to Flavius Caper and perhaps even as far as the source of Varro, *Ling.* 7.33. That at *Gramm.* III 423.35 probably comes from an earlier writer on metric (cf. 418.10). The view of Marx (*Ind. lectt. Greifswald* 1891, 10 ff.) and Jeep (*Philologus* LXVIII [1909], 12 and 16 n. 27) that Priscian drew it from Rhet. inc. *Her.* 2.34 is implausible. The quotations of Ennius, Accius and Turpilius in the treatise on Terence's metres are all lengthy and come from the beginnings of plays as do those of Plautus and Terence. Accius' plays like Terence's seem to have been chosen in alphabetical order. Most quite certainly could not have entered Priscian's treatise *via* a rhetorician and we should not treat the Ennius quotation as any different from its companions.

[3] The source in all cases is probably Lindsay's list 27 'Alph. Verb'.

[4] Pp. 12.6, 16.9, 16.13, 89.5, 90.5, 159.13, 179.25, 235.1 (?), 237.43, 307.21, 323.12, 362.5, 422.30, 467.37 and 504.10 from Lindsay's list 5 'Accius i'; p. 467.21 from list 27 'Alph. Verb'.

[5] *Gramm.* II 336.18.

[6] The error at *Sat.* 6.1.36 could come from Macrobius misreading his source (on which see *CQ* N.S. XIV [1964], 289 ff.). That at *Sat.* 3.8.7 is shared by Servius auct. *Aen.* 11.543 and must come from Donatus. Varro gives the correct title (drawing upon the ultimate common glossographical source) at *Ling.* 7.34.

vv. 1–8.[1] Petrus Victorius joined two together to form (fr. cxii) what are clearly the opening verses of a tragedy set outside the walls of heroic Athens.[2] The remaining four pieces have no close verbal parallels in the Greek of Euripides' Μήδεια but it could be argued that they have a place in an adaptation of this play no freer than that of the Ἑκάβη.[3]

Varro's quotation at *Ling.* 7.9 (fr. cxiia) is the plainest of the signs pointing to the existence of two plays by Ennius about Medea. Some have tried to push the words *asta atque Athenas...contempla* into adaptations of speeches and odes of the Euripidean Μήδεια: Plank[4] into the speech made by Medea after the departure of Aegeus, *vv.* 764–810; Ladewig[5] into the ode delivered by the chorus after Medea's revelation of her plans of vengeance, *vv.* 824–65; Pascal[6] and N. L. Drabkin[7] into the speech in which Aegeus promises Medea refuge in Athens, *vv.* 719–30. These four scholars all think that the speaker is talking of Medea's future domicile in Athens and conjuring up a picture of it in the present. This is the way in which prophets moved by the spirit of a god talk, e.g. the Cassandra of Ennius' *Alexander*. It is not appropriate to any personage of the freest adaptation of the Μήδεια imaginable.

Vahlen[8] argued that Cicero and Varro give no sign of knowing a second play by Ennius about Medea and that Nonius quotes pieces of the adaptation of the Μήδεια under the title *Medea* as well as under the title *Medea exul*. He explained away *asta atque Athenas...contempla* with the hypothesis that Ennius had combined in one monster tragedy the action of Euripides'

---

[1] This was first pointed out by A. Politianus, *Miscellaneorum Centuria Prima* (Florence, 1489), cap. 27.

[2] *Var. Lectt.* xiv 16. Cf. Scaliger, *Coniect. Varr. Ling.*, on 7.9. It is possible that a common glossographical source lies behind Varro, *Ling.* 7.9 and Nonius, p. 470.4 (= list 27 'Alph. Verb'): Varro excerpted the second trimeter without worrying about the sense while Nonius, who in excerpting actual texts liked to quote units of sense, excerpted the words *asta atque Athenas anticum opulentum oppidum contempla*. Victorius made Ennius' original a lost play by Euripides; P. Elmsley, *Euripidis Medea* (Oxford, 1818), p. 66 made it the Αἰγεύς.

[3] With fr. cxiii Stephanus compared Euripides, *vv.* 1069–70; with fr. cxiv Plank, *Q. Ennii Medea*, p. 96, compared *v.* 1258, Ribbeck *v.* 764, Vahlen *v.* 752; with fr. cxv Elmsley, *Euripidis Medea*, p. 151, compared *vv.* 431–2, Vahlen *vv.* 627–34; with fr. cxvi Columna compared *vv.* 131–3, Vahlen *vv.* 772–3, O. Skutsch, in *Nauicula Chiloniensis: studia philologa F. Jacoby...oblata* (Leiden, 1956), 112, *v.* 67.

[4] *Q. Ennii Medea*, pp. 97–8.   [5] *Anal. scen.* p. 16.

[6] *RFIC* xxvii (1899), 3.

[7] *The Medea Exul of Ennius* (New York, 1937), pp. 10 ff. (tentatively).

[8] *E.P.R.²*, pp. ccvii–ccviii, 162.

Μήδεια with that of his Αἰγεύς. Vahlen's view of things is now the orthodox one.[1] It will not stand up to a rigorous check.

There is admittedly no sign that Cicero knew of a *Medea* set in Athens. But many plays cited in Nonius' dictionary give no certain sign of their presence in Cicero's writings (e.g. Ennius' *Andromeda, Erectheus, Hectoris lytra, Hecuba, Nemea, Phoenix, Telephus*). Cicero's knowledge was that of the cultivated amateur, not the scholar.

Varro, although a piece of the Athenian *Medea* appears at *Ling.* 7.9, need not have known this play at first hand as he did the Corinthian *Medea*. His mode of quotation (see above, p. 343 n. 1) suggests that he took the piece from an earlier scholar's collection.

We can deduce little about the construction of Nonius' source, list 27 'Alph. Verb'. The introductory words *Ennius Medea* can be treated as an abbreviation of *Ennius Medea exule*, but equally well of something like *Ennius Medea Atheniensi*. Extant Greek anthologies, lexica and scholia, by dropping the distinguishing epithet, frequently leave us in doubt as to which of Euripides' Melanippe, Alcmeo and Phrixus scripts is being quoted.

The *Medea exul* which Vahlen visualises, in which a large and involved action reaches its climax in Corinth and is followed by another action set in another city at at least several years' remove, is not historically credible. No surviving contemporary adaptation of comedy exceeds by more than a few verses the length of fourteen hundred[2] and we can reason that second-century audiences did not allow more licence to tragedy. Even considerable pruning of the choral odes and the omission of a detachable scene like that involving Aegeus would not have reduced the length of the Corinthian section of Ennius' alleged tragedy much below a thousand verses. Aeschylus' Ἀγαμέμνων and Εὐμενίδες, Sophocles' Τραχίνιαι, Euripides' Ἀνδρομάχη, Ἱκετίδες and Σθενέβοια have actions spread over long intervals of time. Sophocles' Αἴας and Euripides' Ἑκάβη have actions which can scarcely be said to possess unity in the Aristotelian sense. But nothing we know resembles Vahlen's hypothetised monster; nor is there any good evidence that the Roman adapters of comedy and tragedy ever employed such a combinatory technique.

---

[1] It seems to have been accepted with varying degrees of enthusiasm by F. Skutsch (*RE* v [1905], 2594), Leo (*Gesch.* pp. 187 ff., 193 n. 1), Terzaghi (*SIFC* N.S. vi [1928], 191), Drabkin (*The Medea Exul*, pp. 10 ff.), Warmington, Klotz and Heurgon. C. Bailey (*CR* xviii [1904], 171) was sceptical.

[2] The *Pseudolus* has 1335 verses in our texts; the prologist remarks (*v.* 2) *Plautina longa fabula in scaenam uenit*, the slave Pseudolus (*v.* 388) *nolo bis iterari; sat sic longae fiunt fabulae*. The *Casina* has 1018 verses; the matron Cleustrata remarks (*v.* 1006) *hanc ex longa longiorem ne faciamus fabulam*.

One might try to salvage Vahlen's general theory by postulating only a small scene at the end of the *Medea exul* showing Medea's arrival in Athens. Our texts have what looks like a scene based on Sophocles' 'Αντιγόνη added at the end of Aeschylus' 'Επτὰ ἐπὶ Θήβας. Some of our texts have added to the end of Terence's *Andria* a scene in which Charinus and Philumena are betrothed.[1] Our texts of Plautus' *Captiui* and *Poenulus* show obvious traces of similar interference with Plautus' original versions. The prologue of Terence's *Adelphi* admits to the insertion of a scene into the action of Menander's comedy by the adapter. However the shift of scene from Corinth to Athens remains very difficult to accept (see above, p. 165).

The *Medea exul* was well known outside the ranks of lexicographers. We therefore expect to find among the unattributed quotations of tragedy made by Cicero, Varro and the rhetoricians quite a number belonging to it. The search for such quotations has not however always been sufficiently critical.

Cicero knew at least two other tragedies about Medea: Pacuvius' *Medus*,[2] which dealt with the reunion in Colchis between Medea and the son she bore to Aegeus, and Accius' *Medea*,[3] whose scene has been set by one scholar or another in practically every place mentioned in the stories about Medea.[4] Quotations of tragedy referring to Medea and accompanied by the name of Ennius should go to the *Medea exul*. Where Ennius is not mentioned too

---

[1] See O. Skutsch, *RhM* c (1957), 53 ff.

[2] *Off.* 1.114, *Nat. deor.* 3.48.

[3] *Nat. deor.* 2.89; one of the trimeters quoted by Cicero appears under *Accius Medea* at Nonius, p. 90.5; Priscian, *Gramm.* III 424.9 quotes six as by *Accius in Argonautis*. H. Keil (in app.) argued that Priscian drew on Cicero and that the title *Argonautae* was a mere error. However Priscian goes on to quote passages unknown elsewhere from Accius' *Persidae*, *Phoenissae* and *Telephus* in that order. All four seem to come from prologues and we should suppose that they came directly from texts to the source of Priscian's metrical treatise (see above, p. 343 n. 2). An even closer alphabetical arrangement appears in the titles if we suppose that the first play bore the title *Argonautae uel Medea* (cf. Aeschylus' Φρύγες ἤ "Εκτορος λύτρα, Accius' *Stasiastae uel Tropaeum* and *Aeneadae uel Decius*). Nonius would have used one, Priscian the other. Stephanus gave Accius two separate plays *Argonautae* and *Medea*, arguing (*Addenda*, p. 428) that Nonius was in error at p. 90.5. Ribbeck (cf. Manutius on Cic. *Fam.* 7.6, Bothe, *RhM* v [1837], 259) abolished not only the play but even the title *Argonautae*.

[4] In Colchis at the end of the heroine's wanderings by Welcker (*Die griech. Trag.* pp. 1214–16); in Athens by Mercerus (on Nonius, p. 237.43); in Corinth by Scaliger (*Coniect. Varr. Ling.*, on 7.9), in Scythia by Ribbeck (*In Tragicos Romanorum Poetas Coniectanea. Specimen I*, pp. 25 ff., comparing Apollonius Rhod. 4.315 ff. with the verses quoted by Cicero); in Colchis at the beginning by Manutius (on Cic. *Fam.* 7.6) and Ladewig (*Anal. scen.* p. 18).

many possibilities are open for a firm decision to be made. Similarity with the text of Euripides' Μήδεια is a quite treacherous guide. Study of Nonius' quotations of the *Hecuba* shows that Ennius departed radically from the wording of his original even more often than he adhered to it.

Turnebus[1] assigned the two trimeters quoted at *Tusc.* 3.63 (fr. CVI) to the *Medea exul.* Columna printed the Euripidean passage Turnebus had in mind: *Med.* 57–8. Succeeding editors have all followed Columna.

Politianus[2] compared the pieces quoted in *Fam.* 7.6 (fr. CVa) with Euripides, *Med.* 214 ff. Manutius[3] argued that there is no parallel for the tetrameter *qui ipse sibi sapiens prodesse non quit nequiquam sapit* in the extant Μήδεια but that it is rather like a Greek trimeter quoted by Cicero at *Fam.* 13.15.2 as by Euripides[4] and assigned it to the second Ennian *Medea* postulated by Victorius and Scaliger. Columna accepted Manutius' argument. Later editors have not. The substance of *qui ipse sibi sapiens prodesse non quit nequiquam sapit* is in fact no further removed from that of Euripides, *Med.* 294–301 than is the substance of the previous *sententia* from *vv.* 215–18. In any case, just as Athenian actors excised and transferred almost at will the general statements about religion, morality, society and politics they found in the scripts of classical tragedy and comedy,[5] so too did the Roman adapters of these scripts. Donatus, or his source, could not find the substance of Terence, *Andr.* 959–60 in Menander's 'Ανδρία but did in the Εὐνοῦχος. There is no trace, however, in Terence's adaptation of the latter play. The substance of Caecilius, *Com.* 143 is apparently absent from the speech of Menander's Πλόκιον which is being adapted. Ennius was much admired by early first century rhetoricians for the quality of his *sententiae*.[6] He seems to have used them much more frequently than did succeeding tragedians. They were an orator's device as much as clausula rhythm, antithesis, the figures of speech and thought and the rest and the handbooks of rhetoric gave precise instructions on their proper use.[7] It is likely that Ennius handled them with more art than my analogy with the behaviour of Athenian actors might suggest.

---

[1] *Aduersariorum tomus II* (Paris, 1565), XIX 5.   [2] *Miscell.* I 27.

[3] On Cic. *Fam.* 7.6; in volume VI of the edition published by Aldus (Venice, 1579). The 'Scholia' of 1540 do not discuss the matter.

[4] This had already been pointed out by Stephanus.

[5] Euripides, *Bakchai* 1028 is plainly inserted in our text from *Medeia* 54. *Andromache* 330–2, considered objectionable in its present context by Didymus and many later scholars, is ascribed by Stobaeus (104.14) to Menander. See C. W. Friedrich, *Die dramatische Funktion der euripideischen Gnomen*, p. 232.

[6] See Rhet. inc. *Her.* 4.7.

[7] Cf. Aristotle, *Rhet.* 2.21.1394a–1395b, Rhet. inc. *Her.* 4.24, Quintilian, *Inst.* 8.5.1–8.

Columna compared the tetrameter, *neque tuum umquam in gremium extollas liberorum ex te genus,* quoted by Cicero at *Orat.* 155 (fr. CLXX), with Euripides, *Med.* 803–4 οὔτ' ἐξ ἐμοῦ γὰρ παῖδας ὄψεταί ποτε | ζῶντας τὸ λοιπόν and editors included it in the *Medea exul* until they were persuaded by Elmsley and Bergk[1] to put it in the *Phoenix.* It is plainly a curse and, if placed in the *Medea exul,* would suit best an adaptation of Medea's taunts at Jason at the end of Euripides' play.

Four pieces of trochaic verse referring to Medea are quoted by Cicero at *Nat. deor.* 3.65–7 (fr. CVIII). The first three must come from the one speech by a tragic Medea. It would be difficult to make this speech concern any situation in Medea's life except that dealt with by Euripides' Μήδεια. The three pieces should therefore go into the *Medea exul.* With the third Columna compared Euripides, *Med.* 399–400[2] and Plank *vv.* 371–5.[3] With the first Osann compared *vv.* 365–9.[4] No parallel of any kind can be found for the second in the Euripidean text but since it forms a *sententia* this is not surprising. Ribbeck's placing of it among the *incerta incertorum* is quite unjustified. The fourth piece gives an account of Medea's flight from Colchis and the slaughter of her brother.[5] Neither the Euripidean Medea nor any of her friends alludes outright to this deed.[6] Jason throws it up at her after the slaying of his own children: 1334–5 κτανοῦσα γὰρ δὴ σὸν κάσιν παρέστιον | τὸ καλλίπρωρον εἰσέβης Ἀργοῦς σκάφος. This is the version of the story told by Sophocles (Schol. Apoll. Rhod. 4.228). The Latin tetrameters give a different one. However in order to put them in the *Medea exul* one need only make the assumption that Ennius gave one of Euripides' choral odes a new content. Greater changes than this to the Attic classics are well evidenced in the Roman adaptations.[7] Osann[8] and Bothe put them in the *Medea exul,* Ribbeck and Vahlen[9] excluded them. Vahlen's stated reason was the lack of correspondence in Euripides' Greek. A better reason would be the possibility of putting them in other plays known to Cicero. The problem is a difficult one and study of Cicero's mode of quotation does not help. Different poets' handlings of the one legend are sometimes indicated (*Tusc.* 3.62, 4.69), sometimes not (*Tusc.* 3.28, 39, 58).

---

[1] See below, p. 389.

[2] *Q. Ennii Frag.* p. 323. He did not include the three tetrameters in his actual collection.

[3] *Q. Ennii Medea,* pp. 100–2. [4] *Anal. crit.* pp. 117–18.

[5] Cf. Cicero, *Manil.* 22, Ovid, *Epist.* 6.129–30, *Trist.* 3.9.27–34.

[6] Medea herself comes nearest at *v.* 257; contrast the nurse at *v.* 32, the chorus at *vv.* 431 ff., Medea at *vv.* 476 ff.

[7] See above, pp. 333 ff.

[8] *Anal. crit.* p. 125.

[9] Cf. *Ind. lectt. Berlin* 1877, 1 ff. (= *Op. ac.* I 34).

The pieces quoted by Cicero at *De orat.* 3.217 (fr. CIV) and *Tusc.* 4.69 (fr. CVII) could hardly go anywhere except into an adaptation of the encounter between Medea and Jason, Euripides, *Med.* 446–626. With the first Stephanus compared *vv.* 502–4, with the second *vv.* 530–1.

In discussing the relations between his client and Ptolemaeus at *Rab. Post.* 28–9 Cicero quotes three royal utterances from tragedy: *ergo aderat uis, ut ait poeta noster, quae 'summas frangit infirmatque opes'…nemo nostrum ignorat etiam si experti non sumus consuetudinem regiam. regum autem sunt haec imperia 'animaduerte ac dicto pare et praeter rogitatum †sit pie†' et illae minae 'si te secundo lumine hic (hoc* codd.) *offendero moriere', quae non ut delectemur solum legere et spectare debemus, sed ut cauere etiam et fugere discamus.* Scaliger[1] assigned the second two to Ennius' *Medea exul*, comparing with the first Euripides, *Med.* 321 ἀλλ' ἔξιθ' ὡς τάχιστα, μὴ λόγους λέγε and with the second *vv.* 352–4 εἴ σ' ἡ 'πιοῦσα λαμπὰς ὄψεται θεοῦ | καὶ παῖδας ἐντὸς τῆσδε τερμόνων χθονός, | θανῇ. Whatever one may think of the first identification both pieces must be assigned to the one speech or series of speeches. Such a striking statement as *si te secundo…* might be recalled in any circumstances[2] but an unremarkable scrap like *animaduerte ac dicto…* would hardly be quoted except in conjunction with something remarkable from the same context. The behaviour of Ribbeck and Vahlen (in his second edition) in assigning one and not the other to the *Medea exul* is hopelessly unsystematic and makes a demonstrably false assumption about the fidelity of Roman dramatic adaptations to the wording of their originals. The Creon of the *Medea exul* is a possible speaker of the two pieces but so too are several other monarchs of republican tragedy. The first piece quoted by Cicero could, but need not, be given to the same speaker.[3]

There is nothing to be said either for or against Ladewig's assignation of the trimeter quoted by Cicero at *Deiot.* 25, *pereant amici dum inimici una intercidant*, to Ennius' adaptation of the speech made by Medea after the chorus's attempt to dissuade her from her plan for vengeance.[4]

K. O. Mueller identified the words *ut tibi Titanis Triuia dederit stirpem liberum*, quoted by Varro at *Ling.* 7.16 as by Ennius (fr. CXCI), with Euripides, *Med.* 714–15 οὕτως ἔρως σοὶ πρὸς θεῶν τελεσφόρος | γένοιτο παίδων. Vahlen found an equally if not more plausible context in the *Andromeda* (see above, p. 262).

Three anonymous pieces from extant rhetorical writing, *miseri sunt qui uxores ducunt—at tu duxisti alteram* from *Rhet. inc. Her.* 2.39, *quam magis*

---

[1] *Coniect. Varr. Ling.*, on 7.9.
[2] As it is by Cicero himself at *Att.* 7.26.1.
[3] Terzaghi (*BFC* XXXII [1925], 16) assigned it to the *Medea exul*.
[4] *Anal. scen.* p. 17.

aerumna urget tam magis ad male faciendum uiget from Quintilian, *Inst.* 9.3.15, *non commemoro quod* †latroni statui oppressi et dom ista uirorū et segetis armata ~ conis saeui sopiuit impetū non quod domauit uiros et segetis armatae† *manus* from Charisius, pp. 372.19 and 374.1, have been assigned to the *Medea exul.* Only the third with its fairly certain reference to the Colchian dragon need be seriously considered. Scriverius printed it among the fragments of the *Medea exul* with the wording of H. Putschius' text *non memoro, quod draconis sopiui impetum*; *non, quod uiros domaui et segetis armatae manus.* Plank complained of the lack of a verbal parallel in Euripides and Welcker[1] supplied *vv.* 476–82 ἔσωσά σ', ὡς ἴσασιν Ἑλλήνων ὅσοι | ταὐτὸν συνεισέβησαν Ἀργῷον σκάφος, | πεμφθέντα ταύρων πυρπνόων ἐπιστάτην | ζεύγλησι καὶ σπεροῦντα θανάσιμον γύην· | δράκοντά θ', ὃς πάγχρυσον ἀμπέχων δέρας | σπείραις ἔσῳζε πολυπλόκοις ἄυπνος ὤν, | κτείνασ' ἀνέσχον σοὶ φάος σωτήριον.[2] The uncertainty of the text makes further discussion profitless.[3]

CIII

(*a*) These nine trimeters are said by Cicero at *Nat. deor.* 3.75 to have been spoken by *illa anus*, 'that famous old woman', i.e. Medea's nurse. They must have been the opening verses of Ennius' *Medea exul* for at *Fin.* 1.5 Cicero refers to the whole play as *utinam ne in nemore*; ancient writers commonly referred to poems by means of their opening words.[4] The context of Priscian's quotation at *Gramm.* III 423.35 ff. suggests the same conclusion; the examples of comic trimeters in his treatise on Terence's metres all come from the prologues and opening scenes of plays; those of tragic trimeters look as if they come from similar places. Thus the theory once propounded by Fraenkel[5] according to which Ennius' tragedy opened with a dialogue between the paedagogus and the nurse with the paedagogus making the first utterance cannot be seriously entertained.

Behind Ennius' Latin lie the first eight trimeters of Euripides' Μήδεια:

εἴθ' ὤφελ' Ἀργοῦς μὴ διαπτάσθαι σκάφος
Κόλχων ἐς αἶαν κυανέας Συμπληγάδας,

---

[1] *Die griech. Trag.* p. 1378.

[2] The *sopiui* of the Latin tragedian makes his account closer to that of Apollonius Rhod. 4.123 ff.

[3] Cf., most recently, S. Boscherini, *SIFC* N.S. xxx (1958), 106–15. Boscherini's point that Accius would have written *dracontis* is unhelpful; classical rhetoricians and their scribes would have normalised to *draconis*.

[4] Cf. Theocritus 14.30, Propertius 2.24.2, Ovid, *Trist.* 2.261, 534, Persius 1.96, Martial 4.14.13–14, 14.185.2.

[5] *Hermes* LXVII (1932), 355 f.; not reprinted in *Kl. Beitr.*

μηδ' ἐν νάπαισι Πηλίου πεσεῖν ποτε
τμηθεῖσα πεύκη, μηδ' ἐρετμῶσαι χέρας
ἀνδρῶν ἀρίστων, οἳ τὸ πάγχρυσον δέρας
Πελίᾳ μετῆλθον. οὐ γὰρ ἂν δέσποιν' ἐμὴ
Μήδεια πύργους γῆς ἔπλευσ' Ἰωλκίας
ἔρωτι θυμὸν ἐκπλαγεῖσ' Ἰάσονος.

These were designed to suggest the atmosphere created by Jason's decision to marry Creon's daughter and by Medea's angry reaction as much as to narrate the background of the plot. The sudden mention of an earlier element in the traditional story at *v.* 3 and the anaphoric repetition μὴ...μηδ'...μηδ', much more unusual and striking in Attic trimeters than a similar phenomenon would be in Latin trimeters, indicate the nurse's nervous distraction. Euripides' verses were much admired in antiquity for their arrangement.[1]

As occasionally in his adaptation of the Ἑκάβη Ennius preserves the bones of Euripides' grammatical arrangement (see above on frs. LXXXIV and XCII): the series of negative wishes, the relative clause, the independent apodotic sentence. He removes some of the Euripidean flesh and adds some of his own. The dressing is typically Roman with little counterpart in Euripides' Greek.

The nurse's first wish with its rich geographical detail and the magnificent image of the Argo swooping like a bird through the Clashing Rocks is omitted, the second is filled out into two and the content of the third together with that of the relative clause is put into a relative clause and an adverbial explaining the etymology of the name Argo. Thus the events of the traditional story are referred to in chronological sequence. Whatever Ennius' motives were in securing this sequence they were pretty certainly in accord with the teaching of contemporary rhetoricians.[2] Euripides made the heroes themselves row the Argo; Ennius abandons this detail, perhaps thinking it inappropriate for men of the first social rank to perform such a menial task. Ennius may also have had contemporary naval expeditions in mind when he had his Argo built of fir-wood instead of the traditional pine. Ennius' etymology is his own but a commentary upon the Μήδεια, as well as his own individual love of etymologising, may have provoked him to include it; the mode of expression—*nunc nominatur nomine*—suggests the academic commentator with his mind on the present rather than a personage, albeit a minor one, of the heroic saga.

---

[1] Cf. *Med. hyp.* ἐπαινεῖται δὲ ἡ εἰσβολὴ διὰ τὸ παθητικῶς ἄγαν ἔχειν καὶ ἡ ἐπεξεργασία· μηδ' ἐν νάπαισι καὶ τὰ ἑξῆς· ὅπερ ἀγνοήσας Τιμαχίδας τῷ ὑστέρῳ φησὶ πρώτῳ κεχρῆσθαι, ὡς Ὅμηρος.
[2] Cf. Cicero, *Inu.* 1.29 *aperte autem narratio poterit esse si ut quidque primum gestum erit ita primum exponetur et rerum ac temporum ordo seruabitur ut ita narrentur ut gestae res erunt aut ut potuisse geri uidebuntur.*

Many of the words and forms used by Euripides in his eight trimeters were quite absent from everyday Attic. A few of Ennius' must have been rare in contemporary Roman speech but none could be labelled purely poetic. On the other hand, whereas Euripides played discreetly with only four sounds E, P, S, and T, Ennius plays extensively with A, B, C, E, R, S, and T. He adds the etymological figure *nominatur nomine*, more striking than the usual type because of its pleonasm, substitutes periphrases for nouns (*abiegna...trabes* ∼ πεύκη) and verbs (*inchoandi exordium cepisset*; *efferret pedem* ∼ ἔπλευσε) and loads his sentences with words conveying more weight than information (*securibus...ad terram...inchoandi...arietis...imperio regis...errans...saeuo*). The degree of rhetorical embellishment is not however so high as when Attic trimeters are turned into verses to be accompanied by the *tibiae* (cf. fr. LXXXIV).

208–9 utinam ne...securibus | caesa accidisset...ad terram: ∼ εἴθ' ὤφελ'...μηδ'...πεσεῖν ποτε | τμηθεῖσα.

It is possible that the readings of our codices reflect the rhetorician's own belief about the text. Cicero clearly believed the nurse to have said *caesae accidissent abiegnae* (see *Top.* 61 in his *trabibus*). However the statements of Varro at *Ling.* 7.33 and Priscian at *Gramm.* II 320.15 ff. must go back ultimately to a grammarian's examination of a text and, at least where Ennius is concerned, should be preferred to those of rhetoricians and literary amateurs relying on memory. The readings at Priscian, *Gramm.* III 423.35 ff. may be medieval corruptions.

Accidere, 'cadere', occurs frequently in tragedy (4 times elsewhere ∼ 5 *cadere*); it is relatively uncommon in comedy (7 times ∼ 29 *cadere*).

208 in nemore Pelio: ∼ ἐν νάπαισι Πηλίου.

Nemus, 'a grove of trees reverenced as belonging to a deity', was a word of the sacral language, absent from comedy (where *saltus* is common) and rare in classical prose.

The so-called 'poetic singular' is not common in the remains of republican tragedy but is in those of Ennius' *Annales* (85, 224, 277, 299, 439, 472, 484, 533).

The use of the adjective instead of the genitive of the noun raises the tone above the commonplace; cf. Livius, *Trag.* 35 *in Pelio...ocri* and above on *v.* 100.

209 abiegna...trabes: ∼ πεύκη.

For the periphrasis cf. Virgil, *Aen.* 2.112 *trabibus contextus acernis*, 6.181 *fraxineaeque trabes*.

Elsewhere the Argo is always said to have been made of pine wood (Herodotus 4.179, Euripides, *Andr.* 863, Apollonius 1.386, 525, Catullus

64.1 ff., Horace, *Epod.* 16.57 f., Propertius 3.22.11 ff., Ovid, *Am.* 2.11.2, *Met.* 1.94 f., Anon. *Culex* 137, Phaedrus 4.7.4 ff.). Mere caprice may have dictated Ennius' alteration[1] but his liking for sound play (better achieved with *abies* in this context than with *pinus*) and for rewriting the heroic myth in contemporary terms must be considered. A fir-wood Argo suggested to Ennius' audience a military expedition whereas a pine-wood one would have suggested commercial enterprise.[2]

210–11 neue inde nauis inchoandi exordium | cepisset: for *exordium cepisset* there are good early parallels: Plautus, *Poen.* 2 *inde mihi principium capiam*, Varro, *Rust.* 3.1.10 *initium capiam hinc*, Cicero, *Phil.* 5.35 *a Bruto... capiamus exordium*, *Fin.* 5.23, *Leg.* 1.8, 2.7 *a ceteris dis inmortalibus sunt nobis agendi capienda primordia*, *T.L.L.* III 324.1 ff.; for *exordium coepisset* the parallels are late and in authors ignorant of republican drama: Columella 3.6.4 *sol in eandem partem signiferi per eosdem numeros redit per quos cursus sui principium coeperat*, Tacitus, *Hist.* 2.79 *initium ferendi ad Vespasianum imperii Alexandriae coeptum*, Ammianus 26.6.19 *principia incaute coepta et temere*, *T.L.L.* III 1427.84 ff.

For the pleonastic gerund *inchoandi* cf. Plautus, *Mil.* 637 *ut apud te exemplum experiundi habeas*, *ne †titas† foras*, *Poen.* 34 *domum sermones fabulandi conferant*.

For *nauem incohare* cf. Livy 21.26.8. The word is rare in republican drama. According to Servius, *Aen.* 6.252: *est uerbum sacrorum*.

The metaphor from weaving may have been still alive in Ennius' *exordium*: cf. *Ann.* 477 *idem campus habet textrinum nauibus longis*.[3] The word occurs elsewhere in republican drama only at Trag. inc. 181.

211–12 quae nunc nominatur nomine | Argo: for the etymological figure cf. Sophocles, *Phil.* 605 ὄνομα δ᾽ ὠνομάζετο, Euripides, *Ion* 80–1, 800, Pacuvius, *Trag.* 239 *quis tu es mulier quae me insueto nuncupasti nomine?*, Trag. inc. 97, Plautus, *Asin.* 780, Terence, *Phorm.* 739. Ὀνομάζειν and *nominare* are normally unaccompanied. For etymological figure in general see above on *vv.* 6–7.

212–13 quia Argiui in ea delecti uiri | uecti petebant: ~ χέρας | ἀνδρῶν ἀρίστων οἳ... μετῆλθον.

This is the text that must have stood in the archetype of our manuscripts of the anonymous rhetorician's treatise and, with the exception of *delecti*, in

---

[1] At Euripides, *Hel.* 229 ff. the ship that took Paris to Sparta is made of pine, at *Hek.* 631 ff. of fir.

[2] See Theophrastus, *Hist. plant.* 5.7.1, Livy 28.45.18, *RE* 2 IV i (1932), 2216 ff., s.v. *Tanne*.

[3] Cf. also, in a different context, Plautus, *Pseud.* 399–400.

that of Cicero, *Tusc.* 1.45, where it is confirmed by the context of Cicero's discourse. Priscian, *Gramm.* III 424.5–6 offers the possible but much less good *qua uecti Argiui dilecti uiri petebant illam.* Imitations of Ennius' phraseology by Lucretius (1.86 *ductores Danaum delecti, prima uirorum*) and Virgil (*Ecl.* 4.34–5 *altera quae uehat Argo | delectos heroas*) put *delecti* beyond reasonable doubt.

The main verbal idea seems to be carried in the participle: 'because in her (N.B. the emphatic position of *in ea*) were carried the *Argiui* who went in search...'. The etymological explanation given by Ennius for the name Argo lies behind Cicero, *Arat.* 277 *Argolicam...nauem* (contrast Aratus 504) and Manilius 1.694 *Argiuumque ratem.* It is not to be found in Greek writings; the nearest is Hegesander's ὅτι ἐν Ἄργει τῇ πόλει κατεσκευάσθη.[1] It makes complete sense and does not contradict the traditional story only if *Argiui* is interpreted not as 'men of Peloponnesian Argos' but as '*Graeci* of the heroic age'. This was a regular usage of the republican stage; cf. Ennius, *Trag.* 330 *eloquere eloquere res Argiuum proelio ut se sustinet* (the Argives and others fighting before Troy), Plautus, *Amph.* 208 *abituros agro Argiuos* (the soldiers of the Theban king Amphitruo). Ennius himself probably concocted the etymology.[2] Plautus was given to introducing his own etymologies in comedy; cf. the Latinate explanation of Epidamnus at *Men.* 263.

It is hard to say whether with *delecti* Ennius is making explicit an element of the traditional story neglected by Euripides (cf. Apollonius 3.347–8 τῇ δ' ἐναγειράμενος Παναχαῖδος εἴ τι φέριστον | ἡρώων, Theocritus 13.17–18 ἀριστῆες...πασᾶν ἐκ πολίων προλελεγμένοι, Apollodorus 1.9.16) or merely heightening the tone of the nurse's speech with a technical term of the Roman military language (cf. *T.L.L.* vii.452.83 ff.).

213 pellem inauratam arietis: ∼ τὸ πάγχρυσον δέρας.
Comedy has *auratus* three times, *inauratus* not at all.

214 Colchis, imperio regis Peliae, per dolum: ∼ Πελία.
The preposition is omitted before *Colchis* as often in tragic style; see above on *v.* 43.

Imperio regis Peliae reminds modern scholars of Apollonius' βασιλῆος ἐφημοσύνη Πελίαο (1.3) but was probably designed to remind Ennius' audience of the style of official Roman military reports; cf. *C.I.L.* I² 626 (133 B.C., dedication to Hercules) *L. Mummi L. f. cos. duct. auspicio imperioque eius Achaia capt. Corinto deleto Romam redieit triumphans.* The *ductus* was Jason's and, in the view of the hostile nurse, there existed no valid *auspicium* at all.

---

[1] *Etym. mag.* s.v. Ἀργώ, Tzetzes, *Lycophr.* 883.
[2] Cf. B. Biliński, in *Tragica* i, 88 ff.

The designation of Pelias as *rex* both reflected the style of official reports,[1] in order to elevate the tone of the nurse's discourse, and grasped at contemporary Roman political prejudice, in order to excite sympathy for the plight of the nurse and her mistress.

Per dolum marked the behaviour of the Argonauts as reprehensible by both heroic (cf. Euripides, *I.A.* 1457 δόλῳ δ', ἀγεννῶς 'Ατρέως τ' οὐκ ἀξίως) and contemporary Roman standards (cf. Livy 1.53.4 *minime arte Romana, fraude ac dolo*, 42.47.5 ff.).

215 nam numquam...domo efferret pedem: ~ οὐ γὰρ ἂν... πύργους γῆς ἔπλευσ' 'Ιωλκίας.

Remote past apodoses, both dependent and independent, seem normally to have been expressed by the imperfect rather than the pluperfect subjunctive in the Latin of republican drama; see Thomas, *Recherches*, pp. 199 ff.

Numquam is often merely a strong *non* in republican drama; cf. Donatus, Ter. *Andr.* 384, 410.

Domo abire is the usual phrase in comedy (Plautus, *Amph.* 502–3, *Epid.* 46, *Merc.* 12, *Stich.* 29, *Trin.* 1010, Terence, *Eun.* 661). *Pedem efferre* appears in elevated contexts in Plautine comedy (*Bacch.* 423, *Capt.* 456–7, *Merc.* 831) as do similar periphrases with *pes*. The only thing parallel in Terentian comedy is *Andr.* 808 *nam pol si id scissem numquam huc tetulissem pedem*, a verse uttered under great emotional stress.

Medea's homelessness is referred to later in the Euripidean prologue (*vv.* 31 ff.) and often during the action of the play (*vv.* 328, 431, 441, 642, 798).

215–16 era errans mea... | Medea animo aegro: ~ δέσποιν' ἐμὴ | Μήδεια.

The Euripidean chorus refers to Medea's mental aberration at *vv.* 431–2: σὺ δ' ἐκ μὲν οἴκων πατρίων ἔπλευσας | μαινομένα κραδίᾳ.

Only the metrical pause separates Medea's name from the designation of her status in the Euripidean prologue. Ennius raises the tone by widening the gap; contrast Ennius, *Trag.* 291–2 *a socru* | *Oenomao*, Plautus, *Capt.* 26 *medicus Menarchus emit, Cist.* 171 *dat eam puellam meretrici Melaenidi* and compare Sophocles, *O.T.* 826–7, Euripides, *El.* 763–4, *Hipp.* 51–3, 581–2, *Tr.* 861–2, Plautus, *Bacch.* 589.

For the phraseology of *errans...animo aegro* cf. Ennius, *Trag. ap.* Cic. *Tusc.* 3.5 (see fr. CLXXIV) *animus aeger semper errat*, Plautus, *Merc.* 18–31 *nam amorem haec cuncta uitia sectari solent...aegritudo...sed amori accedunt etiam haec quae dixi minus...error....*

Era is the normal appellation in comedy; *domina* occurs only at Plautus, *Cist.* 773, *Stich.* 296, Terence, *Haut.* 298, 301, 628.

---

[1] Cf. *v.* 292 *Oenomao rege* and above on *v.* 34.

216 **amore saeuo saucia**: ~ ἔρωτι θυμὸν ἐκπλαγεῖσ᾽ Ἰάσονος.
For the wounding effect of love cf. Euripides, *Hipp*. 392 ἐπεί μ᾽
ἔρως ἔτρωσεν, Theocritus 11.15, 30.10, Callimachus, *A.P.* 12.134.1,
Plautus, *Cist*. 298, *Persa* 24, Lucretius 1.34, 4.1048, Virgil, *Aen*. 4.1,
Propertius 3.21.32, 3.24.18, Ovid, *Ars* 1.21-2, 166, 257, Seneca, *Ag*.
188-9.

῎Ερως, normally δεινός (Euripides, *Hipp*. 28 et al.), never receives an
epithet of the character of *saeuus* in Attic tragedy. Ennius' phrase appealed
to later Latin poets; cf. Virgil, *Ecl*. 8.47-8 *saeuus amor docuit natorum
sanguine matrem | commaculare manus*, *Aen*. 4.532 *saeuit amor*, Lygdamus
4.65-6 *saeuus amor docuit ualidos temptare labores, | saeuus amor docuit
uerbera saeua pati*, Seneca, *Med*. 849-51 *quonam cruenta maenas | praeceps
amore saeuo | rapitur?*

CIV

There are grounds for thinking that Cicero's quotation is as defective as those
of Terence, *Eun*. 46-9 at *Nat. deor*. 3.72, *Eun*. 114-15 at *Att*. 7.3.10, and
Andr. 117-28 at *De orat*. 2.327, which would cause some difficulty in the
absence of a direct tradition of Terence's comedies.

Ennius' apparent trimeters must come from an adaptation of the Euripidean Medea's verbal assault on Jason, *vv*. 465-519. One would expect
Ennius to have turned such a highly emotional utterance into musically
accompanied verse, especially as he did so with Jason's reply (see fr. CVII).
Both Attic tragedy and Roman comedy on occasion insert a series of trimeters into musically accompanied scenes but always for good cause:
Aeschylus, *Pers*. 176-214 (narration of dream); Euripides, *I.A.* 402 to end of
scene (sharp drop in emotional tone); Plautus, *Amph*. 1006 to end of scene,
Cist. 747 to end of scene, *Curc*. 635 to end of scene (sharp drop in emotional
tone); *Rud*. 1338 to end of scene (recitation of oath); *Bacch*. 997 to end of
scene, *Persa* 501-12, 520-7, *Pseud*. 998 to end of scene (reading of letter);
Stich. 762-8 (piper takes time off for a drink); Terence, *Andr*. 215-24, *Eun*.
323-51, *Haut*. 265-311 (narration). In Accius' *Brutus* Tarquin recounts his
dream in trimeters (*Trag. Praet*. 17-28) while the *coniectores* interpret it in
trochaic tetrameters (29-38). Ennius' Andromache seems to have described
Hector's death in trimeters and expressed her own emotions in musically
accompanied verses (*Trag*. 78-94). There is no reason why Ennius' Medea
should descend to trimeters for rhetorical questions like *quo nunc me uortam?
quod iter incipiam ingredi?* In any case such tautological phrasal doublets
normally occur in musically accompanied verses rather than trimeters (see
above on *v*. 19).

One could treat the trimeters as 'lyric', like those at Plautus, *Bacch*.
669, *Epid*. 24, 46-7, 177, *Stich*. 300 et al. The unusual arrangement of

words at the beginning of the verse ∪−, ∪−−[1] might be excused by a musical setting.

After her rhetorical question νῦν ποῖ τράπωμαι; the Euripidean Medea poses a dilemma: πότερα πρὸς πατρὸς δόμους, | οὓς σοὶ προδοῦσα καὶ πάτραν ἀφικόμην; | ἢ πρὸς ταλαίνας Πελιάδας; καλῶς γ' ἂν οὖν | δέξαιντό μ' οἴκοις ὧν πατέρα κατέκτανον (502–5). The fact that Ennius' *domum paternamne? anne ad Peliae filias?* does not follow the Euripidean dilemma closely would not of itself be significant. But such dilemmata seem regularly, in both Greek writing[2] and Latin,[3] to be formed like Euripides, *Med.* 502–5. Furthermore the famous dilemma of Caius Gracchus, *quo me miser conferam? quo uortam? in Capitoliumne? at fratris sanguine madet. an domum? matremne ut miseram lamentantem uideam et abiectam?* (Cicero, *De orat.* 3.214; cf. Cicero, *Mur.* 88, Ps. Sall. *Inu.* 1), must have been uttered with Ennius' Medea in mind. Norden[4] thought that the absence of the customary answers to each question of the dilemma in the Ennian fragment showed that Gracchus' inspiration lay elsewhere. Things are the other way about. The presence of the answers in the Gracchan fragment may show that Cicero misquoted Ennius.

217 quod iter incipiam ingredi: the pleonastic *ingredi* is added to make the phrase longer than the preceding one (see above on *v.* 19). Plautus has *iter incipere* three times (*Cas.* 164, 817, *Merc.* 913), *iter inceptare* once (*Truc.* 130), *iter capere* once (*Bacch.* 325). For *ingredi incipere* cf. Cicero, *Catil.* 3.6, Phaedrus 5.7.17.

218 domum paternamne: contrast Plautus, *Rud.* 116 *ad alienam domum*, *Stich.* 506 *in patriam domum*. But even if the text of the trimeter were above suspicion there would be no need to understand an *ad* ἀπὸ κοινοῦ (on the analogy of Plautus, *Asin.* 163, *Pseud.* 124 et al.). Tragic style frequently dispenses with prepositions (see above, *v.* 43). *Domus paterna*, 'home of my father', occurs only here in republican drama; *domus patria* was the regular phrase (Plautus, *Merc.* 831, *Stich.* 506, Ennius, *Trag.* 84); for *paternus* as a synonym of *patrius* cf. Plautus, *Stich.* 88 (paratragic), Pacuvius, *Trag.* 144, 328.

---

[1] For an attempt to emend out of existence this and other tragic examples of the arrangement see Havet, *RPh* XIV (1890), 33 f.

[2] Cf. Sophocles, *Ai.* 457 ff., Euripides, *Hik.* 1094 ff., *Herakles* 1281 ff., *I.T.* 96 ff., Diodorus 13.31.1.

[3] Cf. Terence, *Phorm.* 185–6, Catullus 64.177 ff., Sallust, *Iug.* 14.17, Virgil, *Aen.* 4.534 ff., Seneca, *Med.* 451 ff.

[4] *Die antike Kunstprosa* I, edition of 1915, *Nachträge*, pp. 13 ff.

CV

Cicero advises his friend Trebatius to take the same attitude towards being an expatriate as did Medea in Ennius' tragedy. He quotes three trochaic verses verbatim, the first two being revealed by their rhythm and vocabulary (*gessere, patria procul, aetatem agerent*), the third by its mode of quotation as well. It has long been realised that in his account of the context Cicero interweaves Ennius' words and phrases with his own.[1] Quite foreign to the style of his correspondence are the phrases *quae Corinthum arcem altam habebant*,[2] and *matronae opulentae optumates*.[3] The superlative form of the verbal participle *gypsatissimis* would have indicated considerable violence of feeling even on the stage.[4] It is quite out of keeping with Cicero's urbane admonitions to Trebatius. The alliterative phrase *uitio...uerterent* also stands out. It is common in drama[5] but absent elsewhere in Cicero's letters and formal writing.[6]

Sixteenth and seventeenth century scholars gave to Ennius a form of words like *matronae opulentae optumates quae Corinthum arcem altam habetis* corresponding with Euripides' Κορίνθιαι γυναῖκες; Bentley[7] the trochaic tetrameter *quae Corinthum arcem altam habetis matronae opulentae optimates*. It would be in Ennius' manner to expand a simple vocative with adjectives and a relative clause, especially when turning trimeters into musically accompanied verses (see above on *v.* 34). A post-classical Attic tragedy has Medea addressing the women of Corinth with a similar relative clause: [φίλαι γ]υναῖκες αἳ Κορίνθιον πέδον | [οἰκεῖ]τε χώρας τῆσδε πατρῴοις νόμοις.[8] However the order of words in Bentley's text with the relative

---

[1] Cf. *Sest.* 121, *De orat.* 1.199, *Diu.* 1.132, *Tusc.* 1.69.

[2] Cicero does not have *urbem, oppidum* etc. *habere* elsewhere; however such phrases are common in the historians (see *T.L.L.* VI iii.2401.29 ff.).

[3] *Opulentus* does not occur elsewhere in Cicero's own letters and is rare in his formal writings. The asyndeton bimembre has no real parallel among those collected by C. A. Lehmann, *Quaestiones Tullianae* (Prague and Leipzig, 1886), pp. 24 ff., and H. Sjögren, *Eranos* XVI (1916), 32 ff. The formulaic *certa clara* at *Att.* 16.13 A.2 is the nearest. There are plenty in drama; see above on *v.* 9.

[4] Cf. Plautus, *Asin.* 282–3 *maxumas opimitates gaudio ecfertissimas | suis eris ille una mecum pariet, gnatoque et patri, Aul.* 723 *perditissimus ego sum omnium in terra*, 824–5 *egon te emittam manu | scelerum cumulatissime?, Capt.* 775, *Cas.* 694, *Curc.* 16, *Men.* 698.

[5] Cf. Plautus, *Amph.* 1142 et al. (not in Terence).

[6] *Vitio dare* occurs at *Off.* 1.71, 1.112, 2.58.

[7] *Emendationes Cic. Tusc.* p. 26.

[8] Pap. Brit. Mus. 186 (Milne, *Catal.* 77): cf. Euripides, *Hipp.* 373–4 Τροζήνιαι γυναῖκες, αἳ τόδ' ἔσχατον | οἰκεῖτε χώρας Πελοπίας προνώπιον.

clause preceding the vocative *matronae* has no exact parallel that I can find in republican drama.[1] The older texts on the other hand leave it difficult to explain why Cicero adopted such an unusual order of words in his own sentence. If a guess has to be made at Ennius' exact words I would suggest *uos Corinthum arcem altam habetis matronae opulentae optumates.* There is no equivalent of these words in Euripides' play but the adaptation of the ῾Εκάβη provides many parallels for the freedom I am allowing Ennius.

Petrus Victorius[2] took *illa manibus gypsatissimis* to be Ennius' description of a Medea who acquired her white complexion by means of cosmetics. Jacobus Nicolaus[3] argued that the phrase was Cicero's own description of the male actor playing the role of Medea and drew attention to Isidore, *Etym.* 10.119, *nomen autem hypocritae tractum est ab specie eorum qui in spectaculis contecta facie incedunt distinguentes uultum caeruleo minioque colore et ceteris pigmentis, habentes simulacra oris lintea gipsata et uario colore distincta, nonnumquam et colla et manus creta perungentes ut ad personae colorem peruenirent et populum dum in ludis agerent fallerent; modo in specie uiri modo in feminae. . . .* The passage of Isidore is now neglected[4] but Jacobus Nicolaus' explanation of Cicero's discourse seems to be universally accepted.[5]

Jacobus' explanation multiplies hypotheses unnecessarily. Cicero does not mention the stage, except in a notional way with *quoniam Medeam coepi agere* much later in his letter. *Illa manibus gypsatissimis* must reflect Medea's description of herself or her report of someone else's description. There was a contrast between *uos matronae opulentae optumates* and *ego peregrina manibus gypsatissimis.* The normal whitening cosmetics were, in Attic drama, ψιμύθιον (Aristophanes, *Ekkles.* 878, Eubulus, fr. 98 et al.) and, in Roman, *cerussa* (Plautus, *Most.* 258) and *creta* (Plautus, *Truc.* 289–94). The only mention of γύψος/*gypsum* used for this purpose is at Rufinus, *A.P.* 5.19, as far as I can see (contrast *A.P.* 11.374 and 408). It may have been used in elaborate preparations for very dark complexions or persons wishing to disparage the use of

---

[1] Cf., however, Plautus, *Amph.* 1066 *exsurgite . . . qui terrore meo occidistis prae metu.*

[2] *Var. Lectt.* XX 13. Cf. Turnebus, *Aduersariorum libri XII* (Paris, 1564), XII 18 (comparing Valerius Flaccus 2.150 and Rufinus, *A.P.* 5.19).

[3] *Misc. Epiph.* II 8 (in Gruterus, *Lampas,* V Suppl., 309 ff.).

[4] Cf. for example Blümner, *RE* VII ii (1912), 2100.19 ff., s.v. *Gypsum,* Warnecke, *RE* VIII ii (1913), 2118.40 ff., s.v. *Histrio,* Bieber, *RE* XIV ii (1930), 2082.53 ff., s.v. *Maske.*

[5] T. B. L. Webster and O. Skutsch, in *Nauicula Chiloniensis,* 110 n. 1, vary this explanation slightly: '. . . oder könnte etwa Cicero *Eur.* 30 πάλλευκον δέρην ungenau als πάλλευκον χέρα in Erinnerung gehabt und diese schneeweisse Hand scherzhaft, da es sich um Schauspieler handelte, als *gypsatissima* bezeichnet haben ? '

creta may have deliberately misdescribed it as *gypsum*, a substance normally used for decorating walls and ceilings.[1]

The substance of *ne sibi uitio illae uerterent quod abesset a patria* certainly appeared in Ennius' play, the expression *uitio uertere* probably. Attempts at complete restoration could not hope to be universally convincing. O. Skutsch[2] makes the plausible suggestion *ne mihi uitio uos uortatis exul a patria quod absum.*

In Euripides' Μήδεια the heroine's first entry is preceded by a lyric dialogue between the nurse and the chorus of Corinthian citizen women. The latter express friendship and sympathy for Medea, distaste for what they consider to be Jason's wrongdoing. Neither here nor elsewhere in the play do they criticise anything in Medea except her violent reaction to Jason's behaviour. When Medea enters she is afraid lest the Corinthian women regard her as an arrogant person (*vv.* 214–21)[3] and a foreigner hard to get on with (*vv.* 222–4).[4] She is depressed by the thought of how defenceless her foreignness makes her (*vv.* 252–8; cf. *vv.* 591, 801–2). Euripides makes considerable play with the fact that his heroine is not a Greek, giving her most of the characteristics associated in fifth-century Athens with foreign women, proneness to excessive lamentation, servility before men in authority, inability to understand broken promises, knowledge of magic and witchcraft.[5] He repeats over and over again the theme of her absence from home (*vv.* 32–5, 166, 255–6, 328, 431–8, 502–3, 642–51, 798–9) but allows only Jason to make it a matter of reproach (*vv.* 1329–32). Medea and the Corinthian women treat each other as being of equal dignity.[6]

Behind Ennius' contrast of the Corinthian *matronae opulentae optumates* and the barbarian Medea *manibus gypsatissimis* must lie Euripides, *Med.* 252–8:

> ἀλλ' οὐ γὰρ αὐτὸς πρὸς σὲ κἄμ' ἥκει λόγος·
> σοὶ μὲν πόλις θ' ἥδ' ἐστὶ καὶ πατρὸς δόμοι
> βίου τ' ὄνησις καὶ φίλων συνουσία,
> ἐγὼ δ' ἔρημος ἄπολις οὖσ' ὑβρίζομαι
> πρὸς ἀνδρός, ἐκ γῆς βαρβάρου λελῃσμένη,
> οὐ μητέρ', οὐκ ἀδελφόν, οὐχὶ συγγενῆ
> μεθορμίσασθαι τῆσδ' ἔχουσα συμφορᾶς.

---

[1] See Blümner, *RE* vii ii (1912), 2094 f. Pliny (*Nat.* 35.199) speaks of *creta* being used to mark the feet of slaves in the market; Tibullus (2.3.60) and Ovid (*Am.* 1.8.64), both writing emotively rather than descriptively, use the verb *gypsare* in this connection.   [2] In *Nauicula Chiloniensis*, 109.

[3] For the Athenian dislike of σεμνότης see Euripides, *Hipp.* 91 ff., *Alk.* 799 ff.

[4] For the Athenian attitude to foreigners see Aeschylus, *Hik.* 200 ff., Euripides, *Hik.* 891 ff.

[5] Cf. D. L. Page, *Euripides: Medea* (Oxford, 1938), pp. xviii ff.

[6] Note Medea's form of address Κορίνθιαι γυναῖκες at *v.* 214; φίλαι at *vv.* 227, 377, 765, 1116, 1236.

Significantly Ennius uses the word *matronae* rather than *mulieres*. The Corinthian women are bound to their mates by *iustum matrimonium* and hence protected by all the majesty of the city-state's law and custom. Medea, by implication, is only a *concubina*. Her powdered limbs make even plainer her foreignness and friendlessness. A fair complexion was much prized in Rome and Greek-speaking communities[1] and seems to have been a common indicator of class.[2] Considering the attitude to cosmetic aids in Greece,[3] an attitude reflected plainly in Plautus' adaptations of Attic comedy,[4] it is unlikely that any women except foreign-born harlots used them in early second century Rome.

The formal structure of Ennius' *sententia*

$$\overset{A^1}{\qquad} \qquad \overset{A^2}{\qquad}$$

A ⌊*multi suam rem bene gessere at publicam patria procul;*

B ⌊*multi qui domi aetatem agerent propterea sunt improbati*

imitates that of Euripides *Med.* 214–17

A ⌊οἶδα γὰρ πολλοὺς βροτῶν

$$\overset{A^1}{\qquad}$$
σεμνοὺς γεγῶτας τοὺς μὲν ὀμμάτων ἄπο,

$$\overset{A^2}{\qquad}$$
B τοὺς δ' ἐν θυραίοις. ⌊οἱ δ' ἀφ' ἡσύχου ποδὸς

δύσκλειαν ἐκτήσαντο καὶ ῥᾳθυμίαν

However not only are Euripides' trimeters replaced with musically accompanied trochaic verses and the triple alliteration of *publicam patria procul* and the anaphora of *multi...multi*[5] but a different accusation is replied to, one of

---

[1] Cf. Catullus 13.4, Propertius 2.13.53, Chariton 2.2.2; for defence of a dark one cf. Theocritus 10.26–9, Asclepiades, *A.P.* 5.210, Philodemus, *A.P.* 5.121, Virgil, *Ecl.* 2.15–18, 10.38–9.

[2] Cf. Cicero, *Pis.* fr. 8, Propertius 1.4.13, Horace, *Epist.* 1.18.3–4, Lucian, *Parasit.* 41.   [3] Cf. Xenophon, *Oik.* 10, Lucian, *Dial. deor.* 20.10.

[4] *Most.* 258 ff., *Truc.* 289 ff.

[5] Anaphora of adjectives, nouns and verbs is very uncommon in the trimeters of Attic tragedy and comedy. It is quite common in the trimeters of Roman comedy and very common in the long musically accompanied verses (see Haffter, *Untersuchungen*, p. 84).

COMMENTARY

peregrinatio rather than σεμνότης. *Grauitas* is probably the nearest Latin equivalent of σεμνότης and that of course was no vice at Rome. Absenting himself from the family circle left a Roman open to serious rebuke.[1] The Ennian *sententia* drew on the experience of Roman magistrates, whose *prouinciae* had begun in recent times to be commonly assigned abroad, and on the language with which they boasted of political and military success.[2]

The second *sententia* quoted by Cicero probably comes from Ennius' adaptation of Medea's address to Creon, Euripides, *Med.* 292–315. It would have replaced the *sententia* on σοφία at *vv.* 294–301:

χρὴ δ' οὔποθ' ὅστις ἀρτίφρων πέφυκ' ἀνὴρ
παῖδας περισσῶς ἐκδιδάσκεσθαι σοφούς·
χωρὶς γὰρ ἄλλης ἧς ἔχουσιν ἀργίας
φθόνον πρὸς ἀστῶν ἀλφάνουσι δυσμενῆ.
σκαιοῖσι μὲν γὰρ καινὰ προσφέρων σοφὰ
δόξεις ἀχρεῖος κοὐ σοφὸς πεφυκέναι·
τῶν δ' αὖ δοκούντων εἰδέναι τι ποικίλον
κρείσσων νομισθεὶς ἐν πόλει λυπρὸς φανῇ.

These verses were full of meaning for the Athenians of the fifth century but had little for the Romans of the early second, among whom traditional wisdom had not yet been seriously challenged. Ennius' replacement was a commonplace of vulgar talk among both Greek and Latin speakers.[3]

---

[1] Cf. Naevius, *Com.* 92–3 *primum ad uirtutem ut redeatis* (Fabricius: *reductis* cod.) *abeatis ab ignauia* | *domi* (Ribbeck: *domos* cod.) *patres patriam ut colatis potius quam peregri probra* (Ribbeck: *probro* cod.), Cicero, *Planc.* 29 *ut uiuat cum suis, primum cum parente — nam meo iudicio pietas fundamentum est omnium uirtutum — quem ueretur ut deum, Cael.* 18 *reprehendistis a patre quod semigrarit. quod quidem in hac aetate minime reprehendendum est. qui cum et ex publica causa iam esset mihi quidem molestam sibi tamen gloriosam uictoriam consecutus et per aetatem magistratus petere posset, non modo permittente patre sed etiam suadente ab eo semigrauit.*

[2] Cf. Cicero, *Cat.* 3.15 *quae supplicatio si cum ceteris supplicationibus conferatur, hoc interest quod ceterae bene gesta, haec una conseruata re publica constituta est, Pis.* 97 *sin autem aliquid speraueras, si cogitaras id quod imperatoris nomen, quod laureati fasces, quod illa tropaea plena dedecoris et risus te commentatum esse declarant, quis te miserior, quis te damnatior, qui neque scribere ad senatum a te bene rem publicam esse gestam neque praesens dicere ausus es?* Plautus parodies the phraseology at *Amph.* 195–6 *me a portu praemisit domum ut haec nuntiem uxori suae* | *ut gesserit rem publicam ductu imperio auspicio suo,* 523–4 *operam hanc surrupui tibi,* | *ex me primo ut prima scires rem ut gessissem publicam.*

[3] Cf. Aeschylus, *Prom.* 473–5 κακὸς δ' ἰατρὸς ὥς τις ἐς νόσον | πεσὼν ἀθυμεῖς καὶ σεαυτὸν οὐκ ἔχεις | εὑρεῖν ὁποίοις φαρμάκοις ἰάσιμος, Euripides, fr. 61 μισῶ σοφὸν ⟨ὄντ'⟩ ἐν λόγοισιν, ἐς δ' ὄνησιν οὐ σοφόν, fr. 905 μισῶ σοφιστὴν ὅστις οὐχ αὑτῷ σοφός (= 'Menander', *Monost.* 457 Jäkel), Plato, *Hipp. meiz.* 283 B τὸν σοφὸν αὐτὸν αὑτῷ μάλιστα δεῖ σοφὸν εἶναι, Isocrates, *Ad Nicoclem* 52 ὁ

362

MEDEA EXVL; MEDEA

219 patria procul: the preposition is absent only here in republican drama; contrast Plautus, *Capt.* 551 *proin tu ab istoc procul recedas* et al.

220 qui domi aetatem agerent propterea sunt improbati: Wesenberg wrote *quod*; Vahlen suggested tentatively *quia*, thinking no doubt of palaeography and Plautus, *Capt.* 174–5 *quia mihist natalis dies | propterea a te uocari ad te ad cenam uolo*, *Mil.* 1257 *quia me amat propterea Venus fecit eam ut diuinaret.* But relative and principal clauses tend to be loosely arranged in old Latin, particularly where the relative precedes (see above on *vv.* 177–8, below on *v.* 228).

221 nequiquam: avoided by Caesar and Cicero, preferred to *frustra* by the classical poets but, according to Wölfflin (*ALL* II [1885], 9) 'in der archaischen Literatur...keinen bestimmten Charakter trägt'. The situation is in fact far from clear. Tragedy has *nequiquam* twice, *frustra* not at all. Terence has *nequiquam* only once (*Haut.* 344), *frustra* 11 times. Plautus has *nequiquam* 24 times and *frustra* 24 (including the locution *frustra esse* 14): both words occur preponderantly in musically accompanied verse, *frustra* more so than *nequiquam*. It therefore looks as if in Ennius' day *nequiquam* belonged fully to the common language but very soon after dropped out, to be employed henceforth only by poets and poeticising historians.

CVI

These two trimeters must come from Ennius' adaptation of the conversation between the paedagogus and the nurse, Euripides, *Med.* 49–95. They reflect the wording of *vv.* 56–8:

ἐγὼ γὰρ ἐς τοῦτ' ἐκβέβηκ' ἀλγηδόνος,
ὥσθ' ἵμερός μ' ὑπῆλθε γῇ τε κοὐρανῷ
λέξαι μολούσῃ δεῦρο δεσποίνης τύχας.

Ennius adds only the word play *miseram...miserias.*

222 cupido cepit...me: republican drama has *cupido* quite rarely (not elsewhere in tragedy, 5 times in comedy) compared with *lubido.* For Ennius' locution cf. Terence, *Hec.* 88–9 *edepol te desiderium Athenarum arbitror | Philotium cepisse saepe.*

μηδὲν ὧν αὐτῷ χρήσιμος οὐδ' ἂν ἄλλον φρόνιμον ποιήσειεν, N.T. Mark, *Euang.* 15.31 ἄλλους ἔσωσεν, ἑαυτὸν οὐ δύναται σῶσαι, Plautus, *Truc.* 495–6 *sine uirtute argutum ciuem mihi habeam pro praefica, | quae alios collaudat, eapse sese uero non potest*, Pacuvius, *Trag.* 348 *odi ego homines ignaua opera et philosopha sententia*, Phaedrus 1.9.1–2 *sibi non cauere et aliis consilium dare | stultum esse*, Ovid, *Ars* 1.84 *quique aliis cauit non cauet ipse sibi.*

363

proloqui: compare Virgil, *Aen.* 2.10–11, 6.133–4 and contrast Livy 1.6.3 *Romulum...cupido cepit...urbis condendae*, 32.5.3, 33.38.11, 38.16.4, 40.21.1. Grammarians[1] dispute about the extent to which the Ennian type of expression is a conscious graecism where it occurs in Augustan poetry. In the passage under discussion Ennius is unlikely to have retained the Greek syntax if it was grossly inconsistent with contemporary Latin usage. One finds in fact a state of apparent anarchy in comedy where the infinitive and the gerund are concerned. Plautus has *occasio est* with the infinitive 3 times, with the gerund 4; *tempus est* with the infinitive 3 times, with the gerund 6.

223 Medeai miserias: Turnebus' emendation restores the iambic rhythm. The manuscripts of Cicero's writings frequently modernise archaic forms in quotations of dramatic verse: e.g. *De orat.* 2.193 *extinxisti*, *Off.* 3.98 *percepisset*, *Tusc.* 3.26 *socero*, 3.28 *sciebam*. The manuscripts of Plautus' comedies either corrupt the genitive in *-ai* where it occurs or modernise it to *-ae*.[2]

The genitive in *-ae* appears to have been normal in tragedy. Epic had *-ai* (Ennius, *Ann.* 16, 33 *bis*, 119, 191, *203, *343, *489) and *-as* (see Priscian, *Gramm.* II 198.8 ff.) quite frequently as well as *-ae*. Plautine comedy had *-ai* occasionally in formulaic and stylised passages.[3]

CVII

In her denunciation of Jason (*vv.* 465–519) the Euripidean Medea speaks of their relationship as one of φιλία (*vv.* 470, 499) and implies that she had thought him an ἀγαθὸς ἀνήρ (*vv.* 465, 488, 498, 518, 586, 618). She mentions in passing the χάρις (*v.* 508) she had shown him. Jason accepts the definition of their relationship (*vv.* 549, 622) but argues that it was not so much the socially honourable feeling of χάρις that motivated her actions as sexual lust (*vv.* 527–31 Κύπριν νομίζω τῆς ἐμῆς ναυκληρίας | σώτειραν εἶναι θεῶν τε κἀνθρώπων μόνην. | σοὶ δ' ἔστι μὲν νοῦς λεπτός — ἀλλ' ἐπίφθονος | λόγος διελθεῖν, ὡς Ἔρως σ' ἠνάγκασε | τόξοις ἀφύκτοις τοὐμὸν ἐκσῷσαι δέμας, 555, 568–75). Medea interprets Jason's actions similarly (*vv.* 623–4). Neither party makes anything of Medea's juridical status[4] and the chorus refers to Medea as Jason's ἄλοχος (*v.* 578).

---

[1] Cf. Hofmann–Szantyr, *Lat. Synt. u. Stil.* p. 351.
[2] See Leo, *Pl. Forsch.*², pp. 342 ff.
[3] See Leumann, *MusH* II (1945), 253 n. 37, IV (1947), 121 (= *Kl. Schr.* 125 n. 2, 143).
[4] But cf. *vv.* 591–2 οὐ τοῦτό σ' εἶχεν, ἀλλὰ βάρβαρον λέχος | πρὸς γῆρας οὐκ εὔδοξον ἐξέβαινέ σοι.

Ennius' trochaic tetrameter with its antithesis and rhyming metra[1] reflects the stylistic traditions of the Roman stage and the ethical notions of Roman society as much as it does Euripides' trimeters and their substance. For the fifth-century Athenian χάρις was the attitude of a man volunteering to do something to which he was not bound.[2] This for the Roman was *benignitas* or *beneuolentia* rather than *honos*. Cicero distinguishes the two attitudes at *Off.* 2.21: *quaecumque igitur homines homini tribuunt ad eum augendum atque honestandum, aut beneuolentiae gratia faciunt, cum aliqua de causa quempiam diligunt, aut honoris, si cuius uirtutem suspiciunt quemque dignum fortuna quam amplissima putant, aut cui fidem habent et bene rebus suis consulere arbitrantur, aut cuius opes metuunt, aut contra, a quibus aliquid exspectant, ut cum reges popularesue homines largitiones aliquas proponunt, aut postremo pretio ac mercede ducuntur.* Plautus and Terence normally use the word *honor* in this subjective sense where persons of comparable social status are concerned, e.g. citizen man and wife: Plautus, *Stich.* 48–9 *nolo ego soror me credi esse inmemorem uiri | neque ille eos honores mihi quos habuit perdidit*, Terence, *Haut.* 687 *quam ego scio esse honore quouis dignam*. A tone of irony or high-falutin banter is to be detected in contexts like that of Plautus, *Mil.* 1074 ff., *Truc.* 589 ff. The formulae *honoris causa* and *honoris gratia*[3] should not be identified completely with the Attic χάριν τινός, εἰς χάριν, χάριτος ἔνεκα.[4] I suggest therefore that Ennius made his Medea speak of the *honor* she paid Jason in adaptation not of Euripides, *Med.* 508 σοὶ χάριν φέρουσα but of the whole tone of *vv.* 465–519. Ennius' language assimilated Medea's status to that of *uxor* (γυνὴ γαμετή), whereas in legal reality she would have been only a *concubina*.[5]

224 amoris magis quam honoris ... gratia: cf. Cicero, *Pis.* 65 *conuiuium publicum non dignitatis causa inibit ... sed plane animi sui causa*, Seneca, *Contr.* 1.6.9 (Latro) *puellam non misericordia motam sed libidine et ideo non esse beneficium.*

CVIII

Behind Ennius' tetrameters lie Euripides, *Med.* 364–75:

> κακῶς πέπρακται πανταχῇ· τίς ἀντερεῖ;
> ἀλλ' οὔτι ταύτῃ ταῦτα, μὴ δοκεῖτέ πω.
> ἔτ' εἴσ' ἀγῶνες τοῖς νεωστὶ νυμφίοις
> καὶ τοῖσι κηδεύσασιν οὐ σμικροὶ πόνοι.
> δοκεῖς γὰρ ἄν με τόνδε θωπεῦσαί ποτε,

---

[1] See above on *v.* 8. [2] See Fraenkel on Aeschylus, *Ag.* 182 f.
[3] Plautus, *Amph.* 486, 867, *Asin.* 191, *Aul.* 25, *Mil.* 620, *Poen.* 638, *Stich.* 338, Terence, *Phorm.* 928.
[4] As is done by F. Mehmel, *Philologus* XC (1935), 505 f.
[5] Cf. Hecuba's description of Cassandra at Ennius, *Trag.* 181.

εἰ μή τι κερδαίνουσαν ἢ τεχνωμένην;
οὐδ' ἂν προσεῖπον οὐδ' ἂν ἡψάμην χεροῖν.
ὁ δ' ἐς τοσοῦτον μωρίας ἀφίκετο,
ὥστ' ἐξὸν αὐτῷ τἄμ' ἑλεῖν βουλεύματα
γῆς ἐκβαλόντι, τήνδ' ἀφῆκεν ἡμέραν
μεῖναί μ', ἐν ᾗ τρεῖς τῶν ἐμῶν ἐχθρῶν νεκροὺς
θήσω, πατέρα τε καὶ κόρην πόσιν τ' ἐμόν.

and 399–400:

πικροὺς δ' ἐγώ σφιν καὶ λυγροὺς θήσω γάμους,
πικρὸν δὲ κῆδος καὶ φυγὰς ἐμὰς χθονός.

Ennius imports the *sententia* — *qui uolt quod uolt ita dat se res ut operam dabit*, the metaphors *mente trauersa* and *repagula quibus...recludam*, and the elaborately arranged pair of antitheses *mihi maerores illi luctum, exitium illi exilium mihi*.

Cicero breaks off his quotation of the tetrameters at one point, expecting his readers to fill in the gap for themselves.[1] Vahlen restored the beginning of the third tetrameter with the almost certain *ni ob rem*[2] and placed the query mark immediately afterwards. However heavy pauses are rare after the first trochee in Ennius' tetrameters and in those of the other third and second century playwrights. Ennius' mode of expression is usually much fuller. I suggest therefore that with *parumne ratiocinari uidetur et sibi ipsa nefariam pestem machinari?* Cicero twists the content, if not the wording, of the remainder of the tetrameter into his own argument about the potential evil of reason.[3] In any case Cicero shows no tendency to break quotations at pauses of sense where he does not break them at pauses of metre.

Language like *qui est uersus omnium seminator malorum* usually appears when Cicero quotes full metrical units (*Fam.* 13.15.2, *Diu.* 1.17, 2.12, 2.25, *Nat. deor.* 3.79, *Rep.* 5.1, *Off.* 3.82, *Tusc.* 1.106, 2.26, 4.63, *Fin.* 2.105, *Cato* 16) or the beginning of one (*Att.* 2.19.3, *Cato* 1). But *qui uolt quod uolt ita dat se res ut operam dabit* is a trochee short either at the beginning or internally. Three fifteenth-century codices supply an *esse* after the first *uolt* but this destroys the figure of speech. A *semper* before *se* does less damage to Ennius' rhetoric and its loss in the tradition is more easily explained.[4]

225 nequaquam istuc istac ibit: ~ οὔτι ταύτῃ ταῦτα. *Sic abire* seems to have been the normal phrase (cf. Terence, *Andr.* 175, Catullus 14.16, Cicero, *Att.* 14.1.1, *Fin.* 5.7, Seneca, *Herc.f.* 27).

---

[1] Cf. frs. xv*b*, xvii*a*, xxvii*a*.
[2] *Ind lectt. Berlin* 1877, 1 ff. (= *Op. ac.* 1 34 ff.).
[3] Cf. the manner of quotation at *Sest.* 121.
[4] O. Skutsch, in *Nauicula Chiloniensis*, 110 ff., inserts the transmitted six and a half trochees directly after *ni ob rem*.

magna inest certatio: 'there is plenty of fighting ahead'. Verbal nouns in *-tio* are usually accompanied by *est*; for the use of *in-* to form poetic compounds see above on *v.* 26.

226–7 nam ut ego illi supplicarem tanta blandiloquentia | ni ob rem: ~ δοκεῖς γὰρ ἄν με τόνδε θωπεῦσαί ποτε, | εἰ μή τι κερδαίνουσαν ἢ τεχνωμένην; Ribbeck's *illi* is enforced not by Euripides' τόνδε but by the *ille* of *v.* 229 and the *illi*...*illi*...*illi* of *vv.* 230–1. *Vt* frequently introduces questions about impossible or incredible acts and situations in the dialogue of Latin drama; cf. Plautus, *Bacch.* 197–8 *egon ut quod ab illoc attigisset nuntius | non impetratum id aduenienti ei redderem?*, 375, *Mil.* 962, *Rud.* 1063, 1244, *Truc.* 441, Terence, *Andr.* 618, *Phorm.* 304. The normal mode of introducing such questions was plainly with *egone ut* but Ennius perhaps wished to emphasise *illi* rather than *ego*.

Blandiloquentia does not occur elsewhere in archaic or classical Latin. Plautus, *Trin.* 239 has *blandiloquentulus* and Laberius, *Mim.* 106 *blandiloquens*. *-loquentia* type nouns are rare: Plautus has at *Rud.* 905 *uaniloquentia*, *Trin.* 222 *stultiloquentia*, Novius, *Atell.* 38 *tolutiloquentia*, Trag. inc. 110 *superbiloquentia*, Cicero, *Orat.* 191 and *Fam.* 13.15.2 *magniloquentia*, *Brut.* 58 *suauiloquentia*.[1] They must have been created originally by the adapters of tragedy.

For *ni ob rem* cf. Terence, *Phorm.* 525–6 *non pudet | uanitatis? —minime dum ob rem*, Sallust, *Iug.* 31.5 *id frustra an ob rem faciam in uostra manu situm est Quirites.*

228 qui uolt quod uolt ita dat semper se res ut operam dabit: cf. Caecilius, *Com.* 290–1 *fac uelis: | perficies.*

The figuration of *qui uolt quod uolt* is common in Greek[2] and Latin[3] dramatic writing. For the sentiment cf. Cicero, *Att.* 14.1.2 *de quo quidem ille ad quem deuerti Caesarem solitum dicere:* 'magni refert hic quid uelit sed quicquid uolt ualde uolt'.

For *ita dat se res* cf. Terence, *Hec.* 380 *omnibus nobis ut res dant sese ita magni atque humiles sumus*, Cicero, *Att.* 3.23.5 *ut se initia dederint.*

Dat has a future reference; cf. Ennius, *Ann.* 100 *nam mi calido das sanguine poenas.*

For the lack of close syntactic connection between relative and principal clause cf. Ennius, *Trag.* 256 *ea libertas est qui pectus purum et firmum gestitat*, Plautus, *Asin.* 323 *em ista uirtus est quando usust qui malum fert*, Terence, *Hec.*

---

[1] Cf. Seneca *ap.* Gell. 12.2.7.
[2] Cf. Aeschylus, *Ag.* 67, 1287, *Choe.* 780, *Eum.* 679, Sophocles, *O.T.* 1376 *O.K.* 273, 336, *Tr.* 1234, Euripides, *El.* 85, 289, *Med.* 1011, *Or.* 79, *Tr.* 630.
[3] Cf. Plautus, *Epid.* 554 *memini id quod memini*, *Most.* 1100 *quod agas id agas*, *Trin.* 242 *qui amat quod amat* (cf. *Merc.* 744), *Poen.* 874 *qui homo eum norit norit.*

608 *istuc est sapere qui ubiquomque opus sit animum possit flectere*, Com. inc. 76 *onus est honos qui sustinet rem publicam*, Cicero, *Leg.* 2.19 *qui secus faxit deus ipse uindex erit*.

229 ille trauersa mente: ~ ὁ δ' ἐς τοσοῦτον μωρίας ἀφίκετο. For Ennius' metaphor cf. Cato *ap.* Gell. 6.3.14 *secundae res laetitia transuorsum trudere solent a recte consulendo atque intellegendo*, Seneca, *Epist.* 8.4 *coepit transuersos agere felicitas*.

229–30 mi hodie tradidit repagula | quibus ego iram omnem recludam: ~ τήνδ' ἀφῆκεν ἡμέραν | μεῖναί μ', ἐν ᾗ.... The Euripidean Medea refers to her anger later in the speech: *Med.* 395–8 οὐ γὰρ...χαίρων τις αὐτῶν τοὐμὸν ἀλγυνεῖ κέαρ. It is a major theme of the play (*vv.* 91, 93 f., 99, 172 f., 176 f., 260 f., 271, 395 ff., 446 f., 520, 589 f., 615, 870, 878 f., 898, 909).

Repagula are regularly the bars placed across the leaves of a door on the inside (Cicero, *Verr.* 4.94, *Diu.* 1.74, Apuleius, *Met.* 1.14.1, Paulus, Fest. p. 351.3 f. *repagula sunt quae patefaciendi gratia ita figuntur ut e contrario oppangantur. haec et repages dicuntur*). It is difficult to interpret closely Ennius' metaphor. The same area provides Plautus' quite intelligible metaphor at *Truc.* 603 *meamque iram ex pectore iam promam*.

230–1 atque illi perniciem dabo, | mihi maerores, illi luctum, exitium illi, exilium mihi: ~ τρεῖς τῶν ἐμῶν ἐχθρῶν νεκροὺς θήσω, πατέρα τε καὶ κόρην πόσιν τ' ἐμόν...πικροὺς δ' ἐγώ σφιν.... The surface meaning of the Greek is belied by the action of the play. Only the king's daughter will be destroyed. Jason will not die; his children will. If Cicero reports Ennius' Latin correctly, Ennius substituted vagueness and confusion for dramatic irony. *Maerores* must allude to the plan to kill Jason's children but this has nothing to do with the grief she is going to impose on Creon. One might assume a lacuna[1] in Cicero's quotation after *dabo* and take the next verse as referring to the vengeance to be wreaked on Jason much more explicitly than do Euripides' verses. The Greek play does not refer to the killing of Jason's children until *v.* 792.

The nouns *pernicies* and *permities* are confused in Cicero's manuscripts as they often are in those of Plautus. I see no way of sorting out the confusion.

The phrase *perniciem dare* must have been based on *malum dare*, a phrase which refers regularly in comedy to the punishment of slaves. Cf. Seneca's *letum dare* (*Med.* 17–18).

Maeror normally occurs in the singular in both tragedy (5 times) and

---

[1] Cf. the passage discussed above, pp. 356 f..

comedy (14 times). The plural occurs elsewhere at Plautus, *Capt.* 840, 841, *Epid.* 105.

Luctus occurs 9 times in tragedy and only twice (Plautus, *Vid.* fr. 2, Terence, *Hec.* 210) in comedy. This perhaps reflects a difference of subject-matter rather than one of style.

CIX

Behind Ennius' trochaic verse[1] lie the trimeters, Euripides, *Med.* 248–51:

λέγουσι δ' ἡμᾶς ὡς ἀκίνδυνον βίον
ζῶμεν κατ' οἴκους, οἱ δὲ μάρνανται δορί·
κακῶς φρονοῦντες· ὡς τρὶς ἂν παρ' ἀσπίδα
στῆναι θέλοιμ' ἂν μᾶλλον ἢ τεκεῖν ἅπαξ.

232 sub armis: in the first century certainly and in the second probably *in armis* and *armis* were the regular expressions of the common language (see *T.L.L.* II 597.26 ff.); only the poets and the historians (Anon. *Bell. Afr.* 42.2, Livy 9.37.4, 28.15.4) used *sub armis*.

uitam cernere: a most peculiar phrase, paralleled only at Ennius, *Ann.* 195–6 *non cauponantes bellum sed belligerantes,* | *ferro non auro uitam cernamus utrique.* The verbs *certare, decertare, cernere* and *decernere,* when used in the present manner (see above on *v.* 166), are regularly accompanied by *de* and the ablative; cf. Cicero, *Quinct.* 43, *Phil.* 11.21, *Att.* 10.9.2, Virgil, *Aen.* 12.765 et al.

CX

These words come from Ennius' adaptation of the first strophe of the dochmiac prayer uttered by the Euripidean chorus as Medea leaves the stage to kill her children: *vv.* 1251–60:

ἰὼ Γᾶ τε καὶ παμφαὴς
ἀκτὶς Ἀελίου, κατίδετ' ἴδετε τὰν
ὀλομέναν γυναῖκα, πρὶν φοινίαν
τέκνοις προσβαλεῖν χέρ' αὐτοκτόνον·
†σᾶς γὰρ ἀπὸ χρυσέας γονᾶς
ἔβλαστεν, θεοῦ δ' αἷμά τι πίτνειν†
φόβος ὑπ' ἀνέρων.
ἀλλά νιν, ὦ φάος διογενές, κάτειρ-
γε κατάπαυσον, ἔξελ' οἴκων τάλαι-
ναν φονίαν τ' Ἐρινὺν ὑπαλάστορον.

Since the time of Vossius scholars have usually wanted to arrange Ennius' words in catalectic trochaic tetrameters.[2] At least two alterations to the

---

[1] O. Skutsch, however, emends to produce trimeters: *nam ter sub armis malim uitam cernere* | *quam semel modo parire.* See *HSCPh* LXXI (1967), 137.

[2] Osann, *Anal. crit.* p. 123, produced 3½ cretic tetrameters.

paradosis, in places where sense and Latinity appear quite sound, are needed to produce the required tetrameters. Furthermore it seems unlikely that a stage adaptation which turned the relatively calm trimeters 364–409 into stichic tetrameters should use the same form of verse as a replacement of the excited dochmiacs 1251–70.

Ennius' words can be divided into three rhetorical units. The units of verse in republican drama, particularly in the early period, tend markedly to coincide with units of rhetoric. Any attempt to analyse the rhythm of Ennius' words must take account of this tendency.

The first unit, *Iuppiter tuque adeo summe Sol qui res omnis inspicis*,[1] can be treated as a cretic trimeter followed by a catalectic trochaic dimeter. In proposing this scansion Strzelecki[2] compared Plautus, *Epid.* 330 *is nummum nullum habes nec sodali tuo in te copiast*, which appears in a dialogue of paratragic character along with other types of cretic verse, trochaic verses and iambic.

The second unit, *quique tuo lumine mare terram caelum contines*, is metrically obscure but sound in sense.[3] Strzelecki scanned the words transmitted as two catalectic trochaic dimeters.

The first part of the third unit, *inspice hoc facinus priusquam fit*,[4] forms a possible trochaic dimeter.[5] The second part is corrupt. Bothe's *prohibessis scelus* satisfies the sense of the whole passage, the stylistic level[6] and palaeography. The metre however remains obscure.

In adapting the Euripidean ode Ennius preserved the salient features of its

---

[1] Vahlen's *spicis* (*RhM* XIV [1859], 566 [= *Ges. phil. Schr.* 1 406]) destroys a common type of sentence arrangement in which a verb of the preceding relative clause is taken up in the principal (see above on *v.* 8). Where co-ordinate clauses are concerned simple verbs frequently pick up their compound forms (see above on fr. IX); less frequently compound picks up simple (e.g. in such pleonastic doublets as Plautus, *Amph.* 551 *sequor subsequor*, *Poen.* 221 *poliri expoliri*, 223 *lauando eluendo*, Caecilius, *Com.* 212 *ploro atque inploro*, Terence, *Eun.* 962 *dico edico*, Ennius, *Trag.* 337 *neque pati neque perpeti*).

[2] *Eos* XLII fasc. 2 (1947), 98 n. 52, in *Tragica* I, 55.

[3] Vahlen's *quique tuo cum lumine* spoils the sense; likewise Leo's *qui igneo tuo lumine* (*De Trag. Rom.* p. 14 [= *Ausg. kl. Schr.* 1 203]).

[4] The indicative *fit* is unexceptional in early Latin; cf. Plautus, *Capt.* 831–2, *Curc.* 210, *Truc.* 115, Terence, *Phorm.* 1037.

[5] *Priusquam* is much more often an anapaest than a bacchius in republican drama; see Lindsay, *E.L.V.* p. 212.

[6] The form occurs only in apotropaic prayers of great solemnity: Plautus, *Aul.* 611, *Pseud.* 13–14, Cato, *Agr.* 141.2, Cicero, *Leg.* 3.6, 3.9, Contrast Terence, *Andr.* 568 *quod di prohibeant*, *Haut.* 1038, *Hec.* 207, *Ad.* 275. The only other -*ss*- form of a second conjugation verb in republican drama seems to be at Plautus, *Asin.* 603 (*licessit*).

grammatical framework, the address to the Sun, the imperative verb of seeing, the adverbial reference to the crime to come and the imperative verb of preventing. However, while Euripides made the Corinthian women give expression to traditional religious ideas still valid for at least some members of his fifth-century Athenian audience, Ennius put in their mouths an amalgam of traditional Roman religious thought and Hellenistic philosophical speculation.[1] For the special poetic vocabulary of Greek choral lyric Ennius substituted the words and formulae of the Roman sacral language.

A major theme of the Athenian tragedy was the punishment of Jason for perjury through the destruction of his children. Hence the constant complaints by the heroine and her friends centering on Jason's breaking of his oath rather than his act of taking a new consort (vv. 21–2, 161–3, 168–70, 208–9, 439, 492, 1391–2) and the elaborate description of the binding of Aegeus (vv. 734–55). At the culminating point of the drama, as Medea enters the palace to carry out a just act of vengeance, the Corinthian women beseech Earth and Sun to prevent her. These are the deities by which not long ago on the very stage Medea made Aegeus swear and by which, we are given implicitly to understand, on the fatal day in Colchis Jason himself swore. They are asked to remove an Ἐρινύς from the house. This Ἐρινύς is not Medea herself but a real demon,[2] one of those who in the world of epic and tragic poetry[3] (probably too in that of Euripides' audience) were supposed to punish perjury among other misdemeanours. She is urging Medea on to destroy Jason's children in punishment for Jason's crime rather than waiting to punish Medea for the act she has not yet committed. This act, a crime as well as an act of justice, will be dealt with by another Ἐρινύς.[4]

Sophisticated Greeks of the second century, even in Athens, would have found the ideas underlying the words of Euripides' chorus hard to fathom and there were no precise parallels in Roman religious belief. It is not surprising that Ennius did not try to reproduce them. In any case it is possible

---

[1] Scholarly discussion has concerned itself solely with the replacement of Earth by Iuppiter. According to Ribbeck (Die röm. Trag. p. 157) 'der Name Iuppiter war populärer als die uralte Mutter Erde...'. G. Herzog-Hauser (Comment. Vindob. 1 [1935], 48) added some psycho-analytical sophistication, suggesting that Ennius' preference for the father-god Iuppiter over the mother-god Earth reflects the patriarchal structure of Roman society. R. Goossens (Latomus v [1946], 288–91) approached the same narrow question from another angle, suggesting that in Ennius' text of the Greek play stood the word δᾶ (= γᾶ) and that this was misunderstood by Ennius, who learnt the West Doric dialect of Greek in Tarentum, where Δᾶ would have been the equivalent of Ζεῦ.   [2] So one of the scholiasts; contra Page on v. 1260.

[3] Cf. Homer Il. 19.258–65.

[4] Cf. Jason's curse, vv. 1389–90 ἀλλά σ' Ἐρινὺς ὀλέσειε τέκνων | φονία τε Δίκη.

that he had abandoned Euripides' subtly sympathetic view of Medea and presented her simply as a foreign-born *concubina* opposing her master's arrangements of his own affairs (see above on frs. CV, CVII, below on *v.* 237). His chorus appears to be requesting *Iuppiter prodigialis* (cf. Plautus, *Amph.* 739) and the Αἰθήρ in which this deity dwells and whose nature he shares to make some sign by which the Corinthians might be warned of Medea's evil intentions and thus enabled to prevent *scelus* affecting their community. In his epic poem on his own consulship Cicero writes of *Iuppiter* much more explicitly in terms of philosophical theory (*Carm.* fr. 3.1–5 [*Diu.* 1.17])

—*principio aetherio flammatus Iuppiter igni* | *uertitur et totum conlustrat lumine mundum* | *menteque diuina caelum terrasque petessit,* | *quae penitus sensus hominum uitasque retentat* | *aetheris aeterni saepta atque inclusa cauernis*—before describing the *prodigia* sent to warn Rome of the troubles in store for her.

The substance of *inspice hoc facinus priusquam fit* (∼ κατίδετ' ἴδετε τὰν | ὀλομέναν γυναῖκα, πρὶν φοινίαν | τέκνοις προσβαλεῖν χέρ' αὐτο-κτόνον) looks on the surface to be absurd. But as early as the time of the composer of *Od.* 20.351 ff.[1] gods and human seers were wont to see future events as if they were happening in the present before their very eyes. Many philosophers regarded all events, past present and future, as linked together and capable of being known by an intelligent divine cosmic principle; in their view human seers foresaw the future in so far as their minds were connected with a principle which observed the eternal process unaffected by temporal divisions. Some philosophers identified this principle with the lower atmosphere and their theory lies behind Philemon's prologising Ἀήρ: fr. 91 ὃν οὐδὲ εἷς λέληθεν οὐδὲ ἓν ποιῶν | οὐδ' αὖ ποιήσων οὐδὲ πεποιηκὼς πάλαι, | οὔτε θεὸς οὔτ' ἄνθρωπος, οὗτός εἰμ' ἐγώ, | Ἀήρ, ὃν ἄν τις ὀνομάσειε καὶ Δία. Other philosophers, perhaps Heraclitus and Empedocles and certainly the Stoics, made the fiery upper atmosphere the source of prophetic knowledge:[2] *inspice hoc facinus priusquam fit* would be a natural prayer to address to the Αἰθήρ of Stoic theology.

Probus took the relative clause *quique tuo lumine mare terram caelum contines* as co-ordinate with *qui res omnis inspicis* and thus qualifying *Sol*.[3] The verb *contines* will hardly apply to the normal activity of the sun[4] and for this

---

[1] See above on *vv.* 43–4.

[2] Cf. Ps. Hippocrates, *De carnibus* 2 δοκέει δέ μοι ὃ καλέομεν θερμὸν ἀθάνατόν τε εἶναι καὶ νοέειν πάντα καὶ ὁρῆν καὶ ἀκούειν καὶ εἰδέναι πάντα ἐόντα τε καὶ ἐσόμενα. τοῦτο οὖν τὸ πλεῖστον, ὅτε ἐταράχθη ἅπαντα, ἐξεχώρησεν εἰς τὴν ἀνωτάτω περιφορήν, καὶ αὐτό μοι δοκέει αἰθέρα τοῖς παλαιοῖς εἰρῆσθαι.

[3] Cf. Plautus, *Amph.* 677–8, *Capt.* 271, *Men.* 549, 1133–4, *Mil.* 1229, *Poen.* 1189, *Rud.* 28–9, 128–9, Terence, *Andr.* 481, *Haut.* 444–5.

[4] Vahlen adduces Ennius, *Ann.* 542–3 *qui fulmine claro* | *omnia per sonitus arcet, terram mare caelum.* But the antecedent here was plainly *Iuppiter* or *aether*.

reason Janus Rutgersius[1] conjectured *contuis*. On the other hand the clause as transmitted makes an excellent description of the αἰθήρ, the outer element of the Empedoclean four.[2] I therefore suggest that *quique tuo lumine mare terram caelum contines* is co-ordinate with *Iuppiter* and *Sol*[3] and refers to the divinised αἰθήρ in an allusive manner common in ancient prayers; cf. Homer, *Il.* 3.276–9 Ζεῦ πάτερ... Ἥλιος... καὶ ποταμοὶ καὶ γαῖα καὶ οἳ ὑπένερθε καμόντας | ἀνθρώπους τίνυσθον (contrast 19.258), Aristophanes, *Thesm.* 315–19 Ζεῦ μεγαλώνυμε χρυσολύρα τε | Δῆλον ὃς ἔχεις ἱεράν. | καὶ σὺ παγκρατὲς κόρα γλαυ|κῶπι χρυσόλογχε πόλιν οἰ|κοῦσα, περιμά-χητον, Virgil, *Georg.* 1.12–15 *tuque o... Neptune et cultor nemorum cui pinguia Ceae | ter centum niuei tondent dumeta iuuenci*, Seneca, *Med.* 1–4 *tuque genialis tori | Lucina custos, quaeque domituram freta | Tiphyn nouam frenare docuisti ratem, | et tu profundi saeue dominator maris.*

Probus' interpretation might be saved by supposing that Ennius identified in a very bold way Ἥλιος and Αἰθήρ. Varro remarks (*Rust.* 1.4.1) that *eius* (i.e. *agriculturae*) *principia sunt eadem quae mundi esse Ennius scribit, aqua terra anima et sol*. These are plainly the Empedoclean four.[4] Stoic theological

---

[1] *Variarum lectionum libri sex* (Leiden, 1618), VI 1.

[2] Cf. Empedocles, fr. 38 γαῖά τε καὶ πόντος πολυκύμων ἠδ' ὑγρὸς ἀὴρ | Τίταν ἠδ' αἰθὴρ σφίγγων περὶ κύκλον ἅπαντα, Achilles, *Eisag.* 5, p. 36.19 Maass Ζήνων γοῦν ὁ Κιτιεὺς... οὐρανός ἐστιν αἰθέρος τὸ ἔσχατον... τοῦτο δὲ καὶ πάντα περιέχει πλὴν αὐτοῦ, Cicero, *Nat. deor.* 2.58 *mundi qui omnia complexu suo coercet et continet*, 101 *restat ultimus et a domiciliis nostris altissimus omnia cingens et coercens caeli complexus, qui idem aether uocatur, extrema ora et determinatio mundi, in quo cum admirabilitate maxima igneae formae cursus ordinatos definiunt... e quibus sol*, 117 *quem complexa summa pars caeli quae aetheria dicitur*. Euripides gives no sign of acquaintance with the theory of four elements but he frequently talks of the atmosphere as a whole embracing the earth: *Ba.* 292–3 μέρος τι τοῦ χθόν' ἐγκυκλουμένου| αἰθέρος, fr. 919 κορυφὴ δὲ θεῶν ὁ περὶξ χθόν' ἔχων | †φαεννὸς† αἰθήρ, fr. 941 ὁρᾷς τὸν ὑψοῦ τόνδ' ἄπειρον αἰθέρα| καὶ γῆν πέριξ ἔχονθ' ὑγραῖς ἐν ἀγκάλαις; |τοῦτον νόμιζε Ζῆνα, τόνδ' ἡγοῦ θεόν. Cf. Aristophanes, *Neph.* 264 ἀὴρ ὃς ἔχεις τὴν γῆν μετέωρον, Pacuvius, *Trag.* 86–7 *hoc uide circum supraque quod complexu continet* | *terram*, Lucretius 5.318–19 *tuere hoc circum supraque quod omnem | continet amplexu terram.*

[3] Cf. Plautus, *Curc.* 473 *ibidem erunt scorta exoleta quique stipulari solent, Stich.* 4–5, Terence, *Hec.* 478. At Plautus, *Bacch.* 1087, *Curc.* 480 et al. there is one grammatical antecedent but two notional ones.

[4] In a fragment of the *Annales*—521–2 *corpore Tartarino prognata paluda uirago, | cui par imber et ignis spiritus et grauis terra*—an Italian underworld demon appears to be identified with the Νεῖκος of Empedocles; see Norden, *Ennius und Vergilius*, pp. 10 ff., E. Bignone, *RFIC* N.S. VII (1929), 10 ff. (= *Studi sul pensiero antico*, pp. 327 ff.), H. Fränkel, *Hermes* LXX (1935), 62 ff.; *contra*, W.-H. Friedrich, *Philologus* XCIII (1948), 291 ff.

treatises, while keeping Ἥλιος and Αἰθήρ distinct, nevertheless disputed as to which should be identified with the Ζεύς of traditional cult.[1]

234 Iuppiter tuque adeo summe Sol: for *tuque* introducing a further addressee cf. *Carm. deu. ap.* Macr. *Sat.* 3.9.11 *Tellus mater teque Iuppiter obtestor,* Virgil, *Aen.* 8.71–2 *nymphae...tuque o Thybri,* Livy 1.32.10 *audi Iuppiter et tu Iane Quirine,* Seneca, *Phaedr.* 959–60 *o magna parens Natura deum | tuque igniferi rector Olympi.* The same ἀπὸ κοινοῦ arrangement is common in Greek dramatic prayers; cf. Aeschylus, *Theb.* 109–48, 151–65, Euripides, *Kykl.* 350–4, 599–605, *Hel.* 1093–8, Aristophanes, *Thesm.* 315–26.

For *adeo* in invocations cf. Turpilius, *Com.* 118–19 *te Apollo sancte... uosque adeo uenti,* Virgil, *Georg.* 1.5–25 *uos o clarissima mundi | lumina...tuque adeo...Caesar.*

For the epithet of *Sol* cf. Cicero, *Rep.* 6.9.

qui res omnis inspicis: for relative clauses in invocations of deity see above on *v.* 4. For the content of this clause cf. Homer, *Il.* 3.277 Ἠέλιός θ' ὃς πάντ' ἐφορᾷς καὶ πάντ' ἐπακούεις, Aeschylus, *Choe.* 985–6 ὁ πάντ' ἐποπτεύων τάδε | Ἥλιος, *Prom.* 91 τὸν πανόπτην κύκλον ἡλίου καλῶ, fr. 192.5 ὁ πανόπτας Ἥλιος, Sophocles, *O.K.* 869 ὁ πάντα λεύσσων Ἥλιος.

235 mare terram caelum: such tricola were probably common in the formulae of the sacral language; cf. *Carm. aug. ap.* Varr. *Ling.* 7.8 *conregione conspicione cortumione, Carm. euoc. ap.* Macr. *Sat.* 3.9.7–8 *eique populo ciuitati metum formidinem obliuionem iniciatis, Carm. deu. ap.* Macr. *Sat.* 3.9.10 *illam urbem Carthaginem exercitumque...fuga formidine terrore compleatis,* Livy 8.25.10 *quod bonum faustum felix Palaeopolitanis populoque Romano esset, tradere se ait moenia statuisse.* For this particular tricolon cf. Ennius, *Ann.* 542–3 *qui fulmine claro | omnia per sonitus arcet, terram mare caelum,* Plautus, *Amph.* 1055 *uidentur omnia mare terra caelum consequi, Trin.* 1070 *mare terra caelum di uostram fidem,* Terence, *Ad.* 790 *o caelum o terra o maria Neptuni,* Afranius, *Com. tog.* 9 *mare caelum terram ruere ac tremere diceres,* Cicero, *Fin.* 5.9 *ut nulla pars caelo mari terra, ut poetice loquar, praetermissa sit* (contrast *S. Rosc.* 131 *cuius nutu et arbitrio caelum terra mariaque reguntur), Tusc.* 5.105 *et in hoc ipso mundo caelum terras maria cognoscimus, Ac.* 2.105 *oculis quibus iste uester caelum terram mare intuebitur.*

236 inspice hoc facinus priusquam fit: for the singular verb following a plurality of divine invocations cf. Aeschylus, *Prom.* 1091–3 ὦ μητρὸς ἐμῆς σέβας, ὦ πάντων | αἰθὴρ κοινὸν φάος εἱλίσσων, | ἐσορᾷς μ' ὡς ἔκδικα

---

[1] Cf. Cicero, *Ac.* 2.126.

πάσχω; Sophocles, *El.* 86–9 ὦ φάϊο ἁγνὸν | καὶ γῆς ἰσόμοιρ' ἀήρ, ὥς...ἦσθου, Aristophanes, *Thesm.* 315–19 Ζεῦ μεγαλώνυμε χρυσολύρα τε...καὶ σὺ...ἐλθὲ δεῦρο.

The etymological figure *facinus facere* occurs once elsewhere in tragedy (Trag. inc. 64), is extremely common in Plautus (*Aul.* 220, *Bacch.* 641, 682, 925 et al.) but rare in Terence (only at *Eun.* 644; in trochaic tetrameters). Cf. Sophocles, *O.T.* 1374 ἔργα...εἰργασμένα, Euripides, *Hik.* 1072 ἔργον ἐξειργάσω.

prohibessis scelus: the word *scelus* here denotes the state of religious unhealthiness which will arise from the act rather than the act itself; cf. Livy 22.10.5 *si quis clepsit ne populo scelus esto neue cui cleptum erit.*

CXI

Ribbeck and Vahlen printed Mercerus' restoration of the second of Ennius' two trimeters—*quid sic te extra aedis exanimata eliminas?* F. Skutsch argued in favour of Stephanus' and Columna's restoration—*quid sic extra aedis exanimata eliminas?*[1] Lindsay's analysis of the composition of Nonius' lexicon permits a more systematic restoration.

Nonius' lexicon has two articles on *eliminare*, one in the first book at p. 38.29–p. 39.7 illustrating the lemma *extra limen eicere* and one in the fourth book at p. 292.20–33 illustrating two lemmata, *exire* and *excludere.* Four quotations of drama appear in both articles. The source of the first article, both lemma and illustrative quotations, is Lindsay's list 27 'Alph. Verb' (possibly list 26 'Gloss iii'). One should not expect to find disharmony between lemma and quotations here. The second article appears in a book whose lemmata are dictated by Nonius' own arrangement of the material, one designed to show that individual words have a multiplicity of meanings. Nonius twists the material provided by his sources, often in an extremely unintelligent manner, to fit his new lemmata. At p. 292.20 ff. he makes the quotations of Ennius' *Medea exul* and Accius' *Meleager*, which at p. 38.29 ff. illustrated the lemma *extra limen eicere*, illustrate the quite different lemma *exire* along with a quotation of Accius' *Phoenissae.* The latter quotation comes from list 5 'Accius i', the former from list 27.[2]

When composing p. 292.20–33 Nonius must have imagined he could read something like *antiqua erilis fida custos corporis quid sic extra aedis exanimata*

---

[1] *Glotta* III (1912), 387 (= *Kl. Schr.* 487).

[2] Lindsay seems to me quite wrong in assigning the quotation of Accius' *Meleager* to list 27 at p. 39.5 and to list 8 'Accius ii' at p. 292.25, especially as similar corruptions appear at both places. No significance need be seen in the position of the quotation of Ennius' *Medea exul* at the head of the p. 292.20 ff. article.

375

eliminat in list 27 and took the verb *eliminat* as intransitive and the noun *custos* as its subject. But the lemma in list 27 was something like ELIMINARE, *extra limen eicere* and could not have been effectively illustrated by such a sentence; in any case the descriptive phraseology attaching to *custos* requires a noun in the vocative rather than the nominative case. I therefore propose *quid sic te extra aedis exanimatam eliminat* as the second trimeter quoted by the compiler of list 27, already corrupt in Nonius' copy, transferred along with the lemma of list 27 at p. 38.29 and placed under a different and inappropriate lemma at p. 292.20.[1]

Ennius' two trimeters have been regarded since the sixteenth century as an adaptation of the address of the Euripidean paedagogus to the nurse, *vv.* 49–51:

παλαιὸν οἴκων κτῆμα δεσποίνης ἐμῆς,
τί πρὸς πύλαισι τήνδ' ἄγουσ' ἐρημίαν
ἔστηκας, αὐτὴ θρεομένη σαυτῇ κακά;

P. Maas[2] objected that the word *exanimata* has no counterpart in the Greek and would more aptly apply to the nurse's reaction to the catastrophe of 1271–8. There is considerable weight in Maas's second point. Euripides pictures the nurse as sympathetic with Medea (*vv.* 54–6, 78–9) and afraid of where her anger might lead (*vv.* 37, 90 ff. et al.) but not distraught. Nevertheless Ennius' adaptations of the nurse's utterances employ language of greater emotional colouring than the Greek (215–16 *errans...animo aegro amore saeuo saucia*, 222–3 *miseram...miserias*) and the same exaggerating tendency may be in play here.

The present tense normally indicates that the personage referred to enters the stage at the moment of speaking (e.g. Plautus, *Most.* 419 *sed quid tu egredere Sphaerio?*), the perfect that he or she has been there for some time (e.g. Plautus, *Amph.* 1078–9 *sed quid tu foras | egressa es?*). Accordingly Fraenkel argued[3] that the Ennian paedagogus was already on stage when the nurse entered. For reasons which I have given above (p. 350) this could not have been the case. But the link between the Latin trimeters and Euripides, *Med.* 49–51 need not be abandoned. *Eliminas/-t* can be treated as a resultative present along with Plautus, *Amph.* 368 *immo equidem tunicis consutis huc aduenio, non dolis*, *Mil.* 1299 *a matre illius uenio*, *Most.* 440 *triennio post Aegypto aduenio domum*, Turpilius, *Com.* 52–3 *me curae somno segregant | forasque noctis excitant silentio.*[4]

---

[1] If the transmitted text of the quotation of Accius' *Phoenissae, egredere exi ecfer te elimina urbe*, is correct this quotation does illustrate correctly the lemma *exire*.
[2] *Hermes* LXVII (1932), 243 f.   [3] *Hermes* LXVII (1932), 355–6.
[4] See G. Monaco, *SIFC* N.S. XXIV (1950), 249–53. Nevertheless it must be admitted that *eliminare*, an emphatically perfective verb, could not have been used thus in the common language.

237 antiqua: ~ παλαιόν; a solemn and honorific word when applied to persons (Plautus, *Bacch.* 261, Curc. 591, Terence, *Phorm.* 67, Aprissius *ap.* Varr. *Ling.* 6.68), but not markedly poetical like the Greek παλαιός.

erilis fida custos corporis: ~ οἴκων κτῆμα δεσποίνης ἐμῆς. The nurse came into Jason's possession along with Medea. Ennius' use of the word *custos* rather than *ancilla* is perhaps meant to emphasise that Medea has not the status of a *matrona*, that Jason regards her as a *concubina* who needs watching. Elsewhere in republican drama *custos* is used of the attendants of unmarried young men[1] and women[2] of free status, of *concubinae*[3] and *meretrices* of servile status,[4] never of *matronae*.

Fidus was a word of great solemnity, not normally applied to slaves; see above on *v.* 194. For its substance cf. Euripides, *Med.* 821 ἐς πάντα γὰρ δὴ σοὶ τὰ πιστὰ χρώμεθα.

For the periphrasis *erilis corporis* (= *erae*) cf. the Attic tragedians' use of δέμας (e.g. Aeschylus, *Eum.* 84 κτανεῖν...μητρῷον δέμας, Euripides, *I.A.* 417, *Med.* 388, 531 et al.), Ennius, *Trag.* 241 *optima corpora*, Naevius, *Trag.* 21-2 *uos qui regalis corporis custodias | agitatis*, Accius, *Trag.* 547 *pinnigero non armigero in corpore*, Ennius, *Ann.* 93-4 *cedunt de caelo ter quattuor corpora sancta | auium*, 521 *corpore Tartarino prognata paluda uirago*, Lucretius 1.770-1 *terrae ...corpus*, 2.232 *corpus aquae*, 2.472 *Neptuni corpus*, Virgil, *Aen.* 5.318 *ante omnia corpora*, 6.21-2 *septena quotannis | corpora natorum*, 11.690-1 *Orsilochum et Buten duo maxima Teucrum | corpora*, Ovid, *Met.* 3.58 *fidissima corpora*. For the stylistic level of the adjective, see above on *v.* 100; for that of *erilis* see Löfstedt, *Syntactica* I², pp. 116 ff.

238 quid...te...eliminat: ~ τί...ἕστηκας. *Quid* only once elsewhere in republican drama so far as I can see governs a transitive verb (Terence, *Eun.* 162). Questions are normally introduced by *quid* adverbial or *quid est quod.* But the high tragic style much affects abstract nouns and incorporalia as the subjects of transitive verbs; see above on *v.* 17.

The noun *limen* had much more solemn associations for the Roman mind[5] than did οὐδός et sim. for fifth-century Athenians. It occurs in comedy only in very formal contexts (Plautus, *Cist.* 650, *Merc.* 830, *Mil.* 596, *Most.* 1064,

---

[1] Plautus, *Asin.* 655, *Capt.* 708, *Merc.* 92, Terence, *Phorm.* 287.

[2] Plautus, *Truc.* 812.

[3] Plautus, *Mil.* 146, 153, 271, 298, 305, 467, 550.

[4] Plautus, *Curc.* 76, 91, *Truc.* 103.

[5] See K. Meister, 'Die Hausschwelle in Sprache und Religion der Römer', *SB Heidelberg, Phil.-hist. Kl. Abh.* III (1924/5). On the verse of the Arval hymn *satur fu fere Mars limen sali sta berber* see Norden, *Aus altrömischen Priesterbüchern* (Lund, 1939), pp. 146 ff.

Terence, *Hec.* 378), in tragedy once in an elaborate periphrasis (Accius 531 *ab limine caeli*).[1] The verb *eliminare* occurs three times elsewhere in republican tragedy; according to Quintilian, *Inst.* 8.3.31, *inter Pomponium ac Senecam ...esse tractatum an 'gradus eliminat' in tragoedia dici oportuisset.* Elsewhere in extant literature it occurs only at Pomponius, *Atell.* 33, Varro, *Men.* 459 and Horace, *Epist.* 1.5.25. It was clearly a creation of the tragedians.

sic: ~ τήνδ᾽ ἄγουσ᾽ ἐρημίαν.

extra aedis: ~ πρὸς πύλαισι. Plautus has *ex aedibus* and *extra portam* regularly. Terence's *interdico ne extulisse extra aedis puerum usquam uelis (Hec.* 563) apes the style of public edicts. Pomponius' *eliminabo extra aedis coniugem (Atell.* 33) is plainly paratragic.

exanimatam: ~ αὐτὴ θρεομένη σαυτῇ κακά.

CXII

This fragment comes from a play set in Athens; see above, p. 344.

Elmsley[2] compared Ennius' two trimeters with the opening of Sophocles' Ἠλέκτρα, a play set on the citadel of heroic Argos before the palace of the king: 1–10 ὦ τοῦ στρατηγήσαντος ἐν Τροίᾳ ποτὲ | Ἀγαμέμνονος παῖ, νῦν ἐκεῖν᾽ ἔξεστί σοι | παρόντι λεύσσειν, ὧν πρόθυμος ἦσθ᾽ ἀεί. | τὸ γὰρ παλαιὸν Ἄργος οὑπόθεις τόδε, | τῆς οἰστροπλῆγος ἄλσος | Ἰνάχου κόρης· | αὕτη δ᾽, Ὀρέστα, τοῦ λυκοκτόνου θεοῦ | ἀγορὰ Λύκειος· οὑξ ἀριστερᾶς δ᾽ ὅδε | Ἥρας ὁ κλεινὸς ναός· οἳ δ᾽ ἱκάνομεν, | φάσκειν Μυκήνας τὰς πολυχρύσους ὁρᾶν, | πολύφθορόν τε δῶμα Πελοπιδῶν τόδε. With this comparison in mind Wilamowitz[3] set Ennius' play before the palace of Aegeus in the Κῆποι south of the citadel. One would expect the king's palace to be on the citadel. In any case the imperative *adsta* suggests that the person addressed is walking across the stage in front of the audience and the phrase *opulentum oppidum* that he or she has the entrance to the citadel facing at the end of the road. Whether we interpret the two trimeters in terms of the topography of fifth-century Athens[4] or according to

---

[1] Meister finds in Attic drama only Aeschylus, *Choe.* 571 ἀμείψω βαλὸν ἑρκείων πυλῶν.   [2] *Euripidis Medea*, p. 66.

[3] 'Burg und Stadt von Kekrops bis Perikles', *Philologische Untersuchungen* I (Berlin, 1880), p. 128 n. 48.

[4] The site of the Ἐλευσίνιον τὸ ὑπὸ τῇ ἀκροπόλει (Clem. Alex. *Protr.* 3.45; cf. *I.G.* II² 1078.14–15, 41) is now established with certainty on the north-west slope of the Ἀκρόπολις, that is on the left of the Panathenaic Way as one proceeds from the Dipylon gate; see T. L. Shear, *Hesperia* VIII (1939), 207–12, IX (1940), 268, E. Vanderpool, *Hesperia* XVIII (1949), 134–6, H. A. Thompson, *Hesperia* XXIX (1960), 334–8.

the normal conventions of the Roman stage[1] we must imagine the action of Ennius' play as taking place before the precinct of the underworld deities, Demeter, Kore and Plouton. A better parallel is provided by the opening of Sophocles' Οἰδίπους ὁ ἐπὶ Κολωνῷ, a play also set outside the citadel of Athens and in front of a precinct of chthonic deities: 14–16 πάτερ ταλαίπωρ' Οἰδίπους, πύργοι μὲν οἳ | πόλιν στέγουσιν, ὡς ἀπ' ὀμμάτων, πρόσω· | χῶρος δ' ὅδ' ἱρός.

239 Athenas anticum opulentum oppidum: the words *oppidum* and *urbs* were differentiated in early second century Latin as ἀκρόπολις and ἄστυ. Plautus normally uses *oppidum* in contexts of real or metaphorical siege and occasionally where the city as a whole is concerned (*Men.* 73, *Mil.* 88, *Poen.* 175, 560, 994, 1403). Terence, however, twice (*Andr.* 342, *Ad.* 715) uses it clearly of the residential quarters and public places, in contexts where Plautus uses *urbs* (*Epid.* 195, 197, 719, *Merc.* 175, 805, *Stich.* 113).

With the alliterative phrase *opulentum oppidum* Ennius is perhaps playing with an etymology (cf. Varro, *Ling.* 5.141 *oppidum ab opi dictum quod munitur opis causa ubi sint*) as well as with sound. Livy, who in other contexts is as shy of *opulentus* as are Caesar and Cicero, employs the phrase repeatedly (1.2.3, 2.63.6 et al.) along with *urbs opulenta*.

The epithet *antiquus* would reflect the feelings that fifth-century Athenians had about their city; cf. Euripides, *Med.* 824 Ἐρεχθεῖδαι τὸ παλαιὸν ὄλβιοι.

240 templum Cereris: Ennius probably refers here to the τέμενος rather than the ναός. *Templum* is never used unambiguously of the god's *aedes* in republican drama.

For *templum Cereris* ~ Ἐλευσίνιον cf. Plautus' *Cereris uigiliae* (*Aul.* 36, 795 ~ October festival of Eleusinian deities).

CXIII

Of the five pieces quoted by Nonius as from Ennius' *Medea* this has the closest verbal and thematic parallel in Euripides' Μήδεια, Medea's farewell to her children at 1069–73: δότ', ὦ τέκνα, | δότ' ἀσπάσασθαι μητρὶ δεξιὰν χέρα. | ὦ φιλτάτη χείρ, φίλτατον δέ μοι στόμα | καὶ σχῆμα καὶ πρόσωπον εὐγενὲς τέκνων, | εὐδαιμονοῖτον. There are similar passages in other plays (e.g. Euripides, *Hek.* 409–10, *Tr.* 757–63, fr. 362.32–3) but it

---

[1] Travellers from abroad seem regularly to have entered from the audience's left; see Plautus, *Amph.* 333, *Men.* 555, *Rud.* 156, Terence, *Andr.* 734. The Attic convention may have been different; see *Introduction*, p. 20.

is difficult to imagine one, especially one addressed to a plurality, in a play about Medea set in Athens.

Nevertheless there are difficulties in the traditional identification. *Saluete* alone is normally a term of greeting and the closest parallels with the Ennian fragment in Roman drama are Plautus, *Curc.* 305–7 *o mea opportunitas | Curculio exoptate salue...saluom gaudeo | te aduenire. cedo tuam mi dexteram, Epid.* 548–59 *salua sies...salue...cedo manum. —accipe, Poen.* 1259–61 *hic pater est uoster, date manus. —salue insperate nobis | pater; te complecti nos sine. cupite atque exspectate | pater salue* (cf. Euripides, *I.T.* 902–3, *Ion* 517–19, Seneca, *Thy.* 508–9). In farewells *salue* seems always to be accompanied by *uale* (Plautus, *Asin.* 592–3, *Capt.* 744, *Cist.* 116, *Curc.* 522, 588, *Merc.* 830). If the Ennian fragment does come from a greeting and does belong to the Athenian *Medea* it is still difficult to give it a plausible context. The metre is hard to establish and the words transmitted by the codices of Nonius' lexicon may be corrupt.

241 optima corpora: for this periphrasis see above on *v.* 237.

242 cette: 3 times elsewhere in tragedy against *date* once; only once in comedy (Plautus, fr. 160) against *date* 46 times. There was more life in *cedo* (128 times in comedy against *da* 70).

CXIV

The descriptive relative clause makes it likely that we have here an address to *Sol* rather than a piece of narrative. For the relative clause in invocations of deity see above on *v.* 4; for the use of the third person verb in invocations cf. Homer, *Il.* 17.248–50 ὦ φίλοι...οἵ...πίνουσιν καὶ σημαίνουσι, Ennius, *Ann.* 620 *uosque Lares tectum nostrum qui funditus curant*, Trag. inc. 35 *Danai qui parent Atridis quam primum arma sumite*.

Ἥλιος is invoked thrice in Euripides' Μήδεια and often elsewhere in tragedy. He was the grandfather of Medea (Euripides, *Med.* 404 ff., 954 ff.) and thus particularly likely to be invoked in any play about this heroine.

243 candentem in caelo sublimat facem: for Ἥλιος/*Sol* strongly personified as a man with a torch cf. Theodectes, fr. 10.1–2 ὦ καλλιφεγγῆ λαμπάδ᾽ εἱλίσσων φλογὸς | Ἥλιε, Lucretius 5.401–2 *Solque cadenti | obuius aeternam suscepit lampada mundi*, 976 *dum rosea face Sol inferret lumina caelo*, Seneca, *Herc. f.* 37–8 *Sol...* | *binos propinqua tinguit Aethiopus face.* The conventional image of fifth-century Attic tragedy was that of a man driving a four-horse chariot (Sophocles, *Ai.* 845–6 et al.) but cf. Euripides, *I.A.* 1505–7 ἰὼ ἰώ. | λαμπαδοῦχος ἀμέρα | Διός τε φέγγος....

Candere occurs twice elsewhere in republican tragedy, is absent from comedy and classical prose.

For the tragic character of *sublimis* see above on *v.* 3. *Sublimare* occurs only here and at Cato, *Orig.* 2.63 in literature before the time of Apuleius.

CXV

The theme of Medea's lustfulness runs all through Euripides' Μήδεια but the only possible parallels for this fragment as a whole are the nurse's words at *vv.* 6–8 οὐ γὰρ ἂν δέσποιν' ἐμή | Μήδεια πύργους γῆς ἔπλευσ' Ἰωλκίας | ἔρωτι θυμὸν ἐκπλαγεῖσ' Ἰάσονος turned by Ennius as *nam numquam era errans mea domo efferret pedem* | *Medea animo aegro amore saeuo saucia,*[1] and the chorus' words at *vv.* 431–2 σὺ δ' ἐκ μὲν οἴκων πατρίων ἔπλευσας | μαινομένᾳ κραδίᾳ. There would be nothing against placing the fragment in a free version of the choral ode *vv.* 627–62 or the long speech made by Jason after the discovery of his murdered children (*vv.* 1323–50), but a play about Medea set in Athens could contain it equally well; Aegeus had to banish her from this city after an attempt on the life of Theseus.[2]

244 †mede† cordis cupido corde: there is some evidence that Euphorion employed a form Μήδη (fr. 14.3 Powell) but one ought not impose on republican drama either the termination *-e* or variation in the form of a proper name[3] towards an obscure Alexandrinism. The obvious connection between Euphorion's ἦλ (fr. 153 *a*) and the *gau* and *cael* of Ennius' epic poetry (*Ann.* 574, 575) has no relevance here.

Cordis...corde should probably be allowed to stand; cf. *Carm. Sal. ap.* Varr. *Ling.* 7.27 *diuom deo*, Plautus, *Curc.* 388 *ubi reliquiarum reliquias conderem*, *Stich.* 126 *edepol uos lepide temptaui uostrumque ingenium ingeni*, *Trin.* 309 *dum uiuit uictor uictorum cluet*, *Truc.* 24–5 *Venus* | *quam penes amantum summa summarum redit*, Seneca, *Med.* 233 *nam ducem taceo ducum*, *Thy.* 912 *regumque regem*.

For *cupido corde* cf. Ennius, *Trag. ap.* Cic. *Tusc.* 3.5 *animus aeger...cupere numquam desinit* (see fr. CLXXIV), Plautus, *Bacch.* 1015 *ego animo cupido...fui*, *Mil.* 1215 *moderare animo; ne sis cupidus*, Terence, *Haut.* 208 *animus ubi semel se cupiditate deuinxit mala*, 367 *ut illius animum cupidum inopia incenderet*, *Phorm.* 821–2 *eiusmodi in animo parare cupiditates* | *quas...mederi possis*. Comedy doubles *animus* with *cor* (Plautus, *Pseud.* 1321) or replaces it with the physical organ (Plautus, *Epid.* 146, Caecilius, *Com.* 79) in high-falutin contexts.

---

[1] Plank thought that Nonius had misquoted Ennius' prologue.
[2] Hyginus, *Fab.* 26.1.
[3] Ennius has *Medea* at *v.* 216, *Medeai* at 223. Cf. Plautus, *Pseud.* 869.

CXVI

If this were a comic fragment one would most naturally interpret it as spoken by an eavesdropper standing on stage. In a tragedy it is likely to have been spoken by the chorus hearing something off stage or by a character who has just entered the stage and speaks of what he has heard from off[1] (resultative present; see above on fr. CXI) or by a character reporting a past act of eavesdropping (historic present). As far as *aucupant* is concerned Columna's identification of the fragment with Euripides, *Med.* 131–2 and O. Skutsch's with *Med.* 67–9 are possible. But *fructus* is damning to them both. Nothing overheard in the Μήδεια profits the hearer or anyone else.

245 fructus uerborum: for this type of periphrasis see above on *v.* 21.

aures aucupant: the metaphor is from fowling. This and related metaphors are common in early comedy (e.g. Plautus, *Mil.* 598–9, 607–8, 955, 990, *Most.* 473, *Stich.* 102, Caecilius, *Com.* 62–4). They are absent from Terence and from the copious remains of fourth and third century Attic comedy. It is likely that they originated in Roman tragedy (cf. Pacuvius 185 *sermonem hic nostrum ex occulto clepit*, Accius 292) as an extension of such locutions as Homer, *Il.* 1.201 καί μιν φωνήσας ἔπεα πτερόεντα προσ-ηύδα, Aeschylus, *Hik.* 657–8 ἐκ στομάτων ποτά|σθω φιλότιμος εὐχά, *Prom.* 115 τίς ἀχώ... προσέπτα μ' ἀφεγγής, 555 τὸ διαμφίδιον δέ μοι μέλος προσέπτα, Accius, *Trag.* 449 *simul ac nota uox ad auris accidit*, Virgil, *Aen.* 11.380–1 *uerbis | quae tuto tibi magna uolant.*[2]

MELANIPPA

The title *Melanippa* is given to Ennius three times by Nonius using Lindsay's list 27 'Alph. Verb' and once each by Gellius, Macrobius and Priscian; to Accius once by Varro (*Ling.* 7.65) and once by Nonius using list 28 'Alph. Adverb' (p. 154.15). *Melanippus* is given to Accius eight times by Nonius using list 5 'Accius i' (pp. 15.23, 85.4, 219.1, 233.22, 234.23, 485.31, 500.14, 521.8) and once using list 28 'Alph. Adverb' (p. 349.2), three times by Verrius (Festus and Paulus, pp. 180.28, 320.27, 340.25; cf. p. 256.15), and once by Cicero (*Tusc.* 3.20); to Ennius once by Nonius after a series of entries from list 5 (p. 469.7). The attributions at Varro, *Ling.* 7.65

---

[1] Cf. Sophocles, *O.T.* 634 ff., Euripides, *Herakleidai* 474 ff.
[2] Cf. Plautus' parodies: *Amph.* 325–6 *uox mi ad auris aduolauit* (*Merc.* 864, *Rud.* 332) *—ne ego homo infelix fui, | qui non alas interuelli! uolucrem uocem gestito.*

and Nonius, pp. 154.15 and 469.7 are clearly erroneous.¹ The *Melanippa* referred to by Cicero at *Off.* 1.114 is probably the Ennian tragedy quoted by the grammarians, although Cicero gives no other sign of knowing this play.

Two tragedies about Melanippe, the daughter of Aeolus, were composed by Euripides. One, Μελανίππη ἡ σοφή,² dealt with how, when the twins the heroine had borne to the god Poseidon and secretly exposed were discovered being suckled by a cow, Aeolus, on the advice of his father Hellen, decided to have them burnt as prodigies. Melanippe, having received the task of dressing them in funeral robes, delivered a speech criticising Hellen and explaining the apparent prodigies in naturalistic terms. Euripides' other tragedy, Μελανίππη ἡ δεσμῶτις, dealt with an episode in the later life of the twins.³

The first fruitful attempt to interpret the fragments cited under the title *Melanippa* was made by Bergk,⁴ who assigned frs. CXIX, CXX and CXXI to a version of Euripides' Μελανίππη ἡ σοφή and CXXII and CXXIII to one of the Μελανίππη ἡ δεσμῶτις. Scholars since have usually tried to interpret all six fragments as coming from a version of the Μελανίππη ἡ σοφή.

CXVIII

The prose hypothesis of Euripides' Μελανίππη ἡ σοφή describes the heroine as κάλλει διαφέρουσαν. The Ennian passage referred to by Gellius must have been uttered by someone with Melanippe's illegitimate offspring in mind.

For the substance of the Ennian passage cf. Euripides, fr. 928 οὐ γὰρ ἀσφαλὲς (Grotius: ἀφελές *codd.*) | περαιτέρω τὸ κάλλος ἢ μέσον λαβεῖν.⁵ Ovid, *Fast.* 2.161 *foedera seruasset si non formosa fuisset, Am.* 3.4.41–2 *quo tibi formosam si non nisi casta placebat?* | *non possunt ullis ista coire modis,* 3.14.1 *non ego ne pecces cum sis formosa recuso, Epist.* 16.290 *lis est cum forma magna*

---

¹ Delrius appears to have thought that Accius' tragedy was a *Melanippa*. Welcker, *Die Griech. Trag.* pp. 854 ff., and Hartung, *Euripides Restitutus* II, pp. 375 ff., pressed the fragments into a version of Euripides' Μελανίππη ἡ δεσμῶτις. Scaliger, *Coniect. Varr. Ling.*, on 7.65, said all that is necessary.

² For the prose hypothesis see the rhetorical work published by H. Rabe, *RhM* LXIII (1908), 145 f., and Pap. Oxy. 2455, fr. 2, col. 1.

³ See Hyginus, *Fab.* 186, Pap. Berol. 5514, 9772, Wilamowitz, *SB Berlin* 1921, 63 ff. (= *Kl. Schr.* I 440 ff.), Pickard-Cambridge, in *New Chapters in the History of Greek Literature* III (Oxford, 1933), 117 ff.

⁴ *RhM* III (1835), 71–3.

⁵ Compared by Hartung, *Euripides Restitutus* I, p. 116, and assigned to Μελανίππη ἡ σοφή.

383

pudicitiae, Petronius 94.1 *raram fecit mixturam cum sapientia forma*, Juvenal 10.297–8 *rarast adeo concordia formae | atque pudicitiae*.

It is idle to attempt to restore Ennius' actual verse. His descriptive ablative *stata forma* is hard to interpret closely (∼ Plautus, *Merc.* 13 *forma eximia mulierem, Mil.* 782 *forma lepida mulierem* et al.); perhaps *forma* has been given something of its etymological sense (cf. *C.I.L.* I² 592.2.2 *pecunia...signata forma p[ublica] P[opuli] R[omani]*) and the phrase is to be interpreted as 'of the legally fixed stamp or mould, not departing from the norm, neither strikingly beautiful nor strikingly ugly'.

CXIX

The words transmitted will scan as a hypermetric trimeter[1] or a versus reizianus.[2] Acidalius' removal of the second -*que* produces a regular trimeter.

On Nonius' interpretation the subject of *sospitent superstitentque* could be either the twins Aeolus and Boeotus or the gods. The redundancy is typical of the language of tragedy (see above on *v.* 9) and prayer; cf. Sophocles, *O.T.* 1349–51 ὄλοιθ' ὅστις ἦν ὃς... ἀπό τε φόνου | ἔρρυτο κἀνέσωσέ με, Plautus, *Asin.* 16–17 *sicut tuom uis unicum gnatum tuae | superesse uitae sospitem et superstitem*, Cato, *Agr.* 141.3 *pastores pecuaque salua seruassis duisque bonam salutem ualetudinemque mihi domo familiaeque nostrae*, Lucilius 739 *sospitat salute inpertit plurima et plenissima*. However the only other time the verb *superstitare* occurs (Plautus, *Persa* 331 *ut mihi supersit suppetat superstitat*) it is intransitive. If Ennius' use is parallel we have a ὕστερον πρότερον of the type discussed above on *v.* 139 and the verse must come from a prayer by a member of the king's family to allow the twins to survive.

246 sospitent: the adjective *sospes* occurs twice in republican tragedy and five times in comedy (against *saluus* 180 times); it doubtless belonged to the sacral language. The denominative *sospitare* occurs twice in tragedy and twice in comedy (Plautus, *Asin.* 683, *Aul.* 546); it may have been a tragic neologism.

CXX

With one alteration the words transmitted will scan as a cretic tetrameter. Something other than iambo-trochaic verse is suggested by the word order. *Ausculta mihi* seems to have been regular (Plautus, *Aul.* 237, *Most.* 586, 634, *Persa* 574, *Poen.* 311; but cf. Plautus, *Cas.* 204 [anapaestic], *Stich.* 602,

---

[1] So Vahlen, *Ind. lectt.* Berlin 1878, 6 (= *Op. ac.* I 56), comparing *Trag. inc.* 191–2.

[2] So Strzelecki, *Eos* XLII (1947), 26–9, comparing Naevius, *Trag.* 13 *numquam hodie effugies quin manu mea moriare* (see Lindsay, *E.L.V.* p. 279 n. 2).

MELANIPPA

Cicero, *S. Rosc.* 104 [*auscultare* does not occur elsewhere in Cicero]). The imperative *iube* normally preceded the infinitive (but cf. Plautus, *Capt.* 668, *Men.* 517, *Merc.* 777, *Rud.* 1095, *Truc.* 585 [cretic]). Nevertheless the substance is of a dramatic importance hard to parallel in the certainly established cretics of republican drama. Bothe's *cremitari* is the neatest further correction; the absence of the intensive form from recorded Latin and the apparent lack of any intensive force do not count greatly against it; for tragic use of the intensive see above on *vv.* 68, 203.

The speaker would be Hellen; cf. the prose hypothesis of Euripides' tragedy: τὰ βρέφη τινὲς τῶν βουκόλων φυλαττόμενα μὲν ὑπὸ τοῦ ταύρου, θηλαζόμενα δὲ ὑπὸ μιᾶς τῶν βοῶν ἰδόντες ὡς βουγενῆ τέρατα τῷ βασιλεῖ προσήνεγκαν· ὁ δὲ τῇ τοῦ πατρὸς Ἕλληνος γνώμῃ πεισθεὶς ὁλοκαυτοῦν τὰ βρέφη κρίνας....

247 nate: the use of *gnatus* has no stylistic significance here; vocative *fili* does not occur in republican drama. *Mi gnate* and *gnate mi* are the normal forms of address. The absence of the pronoun indicates a certain peremptoriness on the speaker's part (cf. Plautus, *Trin.* 362, Terence, *Haut.* 843, 1065).

cremari: not elsewhere in republican drama; probably from the sacral language; Cicero and Caesar use it of burning corpses and executing criminals (*Gall.* 1.4).

CXXI

Hellen is speaking of the twins. Ennius makes him use the technical language of a Roman augur; cf. the behaviour of Virgil at *Aen.* 3.58–60: *delectos populi ad proceres primumque parentem | monstra deum refero, et quae sit sententia posco. | omnibus idem animus, scelerata excedere terra.*

248 monstrum: 'sign of divine displeasure'; a word of the sacral language; cf. Plautus, *Most.* 505 *quae hic monstra fiunt anno uix possum eloqui,* Terence, *Phorm.* 705–8 *quot res postilla monstra euenerunt mihi | intro iit in aedis ater alienus canis; | anguis per inpluuium decidit de tegulis; | gallina cecinit,* Festus, p. 122.8 *ut Aelius Stilo interpretatur a monendo dictum est, uelut monestrum. item Sinnius Capito quod monstret futurum et moneat uoluntatem deorum,* Paulus, p. 147.10 *monstra dicuntur naturae modum egredientia, ut serpens cum pedibus, auis cum quattuor alis, homo duobus capitibus, iecur cum distabuit in coquendo.*

siet: the full forms *siem* etc. were still employed in official inscriptions during the second century but had little life in the common language. The republican poets used them in comedy as an ornament of style but much less frequently than in tragedy; F. Thomas, *Recherches*, p. 10, counts 284 examples in extant comedy as against 967 of *sim* etc. and 8 in tragedy as against 19.

25   385

249 hoc ego tibi dico et coniectura auguro: the second statement, chronologically prior to the first, is given even greater emphasis by the hiatus in caesura.[1]

For *coniectura augurare* cf. Pacuvius, *Trag.* 78, Cicero, *De orat.* 1.95, *Att.* 2.9.1. Ennius' Hellen, however, proposes not to make a prediction but rather to give advice on what the gods desire; his statement comes as a result of reasoning (*coniectura*) not of second sight (*hariolatio, uaticinatio*).

CXXII

The words transmitted will scan as a dactylic hexameter. They should be treated as such rather than divided between incomplete anapaestic dimeters. There is a strong tendency noticeable in Macrobius, *Sat.* 6.4–5 for the quotations of pre-Virgilian poetry to form metrical units.[2] Hexameters are found commonly enough in Attic tragedy (Aeschylus, *Ag.* 104, 111, 119, 123, 129, 137, 155–7, *Xantr.* Pap. Ox. 2164, fr. 1.16 ff., Sophocles, *Phil.* 839–42, *Tr.* 1010–14, Euripides, *Andr.* 103 ff., 117 ff., *Hel.* 164–5, *Tr.* 595–602) and in imperial Roman (Seneca, *Med.* 110–15, *Oed.* 233–8).

Bergk[3] referred the words to the restoration of Melanippe's sight after her imprisonment; Hartung[4] to a discussion of natural philosophy by the chorus; Ribbeck[5] to a version of the Euripidean Melanippe's famous speech on this subject (cf. fr. 484.4 τίκτουσι πάντα κἀνέδωκαν εἰς φάος). Many, including Wilamowitz,[6] have accepted Ribbeck's idea without explaining either the presence of the dactyls or how a sentence introduced by *sic* would fit into a narrative of the creation of things. Welcker[7] took the words to be part of a simile while Ribbeck allowed that it might come from a version of fr. 486 δικαιοσύνας τὸ χρύσεον πρόσωπον | οὔθ᾽ ἕσπερος οὔθ᾽ ἑῷος οὕτω | θαυμαστός (Meineke's arrangement). The dactyls suggest to me an utterance by the seer Hellen (cf. *vv.* 43–6) and the talk of light the epiphany

---

[1] For this type of hiatus, frequently disallowed by students of republican drama, see above on *v.* 154. Ribbeck scanned *tibi* as an iambus and W. Ax, *De Hiatu qui in Fragmentis Priscae Poesis Romanae inuenitur* (Diss. Göttingen, 1917), p. 29, proposed *hoc tibi ego dico et coniectura id auguro.* On iambic *tibi*, extremely rare in this part of the iambic trimeter, see P. W. Harsh, *Iambic Words and Regard for Accent in Plautus* (Stanford University, 1949), pp. 110 ff., O. Skutsch, *Mnemosyne* 4.XIII (1960), 231 f.

[2] See *CQ* N.S. xv (1965), 129 ff.   [3] *RhM* III (1835), 73.

[4] *Euripides Restitutus* I, p. 121.

[5] *Quaest. scen.* p. 265, *Die röm. Trag.* p. 179.

[6] *SB Berlin* 1921, 74 n. (= *Kl. Schr.* I 453 n.).

[7] *Die griech. Trag.* p. 850.

of a god, probably Poseidon.[1] Poseidon must have appeared at the end of the play to rescue Melanippe and the children he had sired.

250 lumine... tremulo: cf. Apollonius Rhod. 3.756 ἠελίου... πάλλεται αἴγλη, Lucretius 4.404–5 *iamque rubrum tremulis iubar ignibus erigere alte | cum coeptat natura*, 5.697 *sub terris ideo tremulum iubar haesitat ignis*, Virgil, *Aen*. 7.9 *splendet tremulo sub lumine pontus*, 8.22–3 *sicut aquae tremulum labris ubi lumen ahenis | sole repercussum*, Ovid, *Epist*. 18.59 *luna fere tremulum praebebat lumen eunti*.

caerula: adjectives terminating in -*ulus* etc. are rare in republican tragedy, as are similarly terminating diminutive and instrumental nouns. The employment of two in the one sentence perhaps sought some special effect.

CXXIII

Most scholars refer this fragment in some way to the imprisonment of Melanippe.[2] It is difficult, however, to imagine an imprisonment in an adaptation of Euripides' Μελανίππη ἡ σοφή. I can find no satisfactory interpretation of the three words transmitted.

NEMEA

The title *Nemea* is given to Ennius by Nonius and Priscian. Nonius' source appears to be Lindsay's list 1 'Gloss. i', Priscian's the work of Flavius Caper, going back through Probus to Pliny and perhaps beyond. One of the two pieces quoted must have been spoken by a woman whose liberty of movement had been restricted; the other is quite enigmatic.

Columna thought that Ennius' play dealt with the story of the death of Opheltes while under the care of the enslaved Hypsipyle and with the institution of the Nemean games in his memory, a story which has since proved to be the theme of Euripides' Ὑψιπύλη. Columna's view has often been maintained, most recently by Przychocki.[3] Ennius' play perhaps referred to the

---

[1] Cf. Homer, *Il*. 4.75 ff., *Hymn*. 2.189, 3.440–4 ... σέλας δ' εἰς οὐρανὸν ἷκεν ... πᾶσαν δὲ Κρίσην κάτεχεν σέλας, Euripides, *Ba*. 1082–3 πρὸς οὐρανὸν | καὶ γαῖαν ἐστήριξε φῶς σεμνοῦ πυρός, *Ion* 1549–50, Lucretius 1.2–9, Virgil, *Aen*. 1.402, 2.589–90, 2.615–16, 3.151–2, 4.358–9, Ovid, *Fast*. 1.94.

[2] Welcker, however, referred it to a discussion of miracles by the philosophical heroine.

[3] *WSt* xxxi (1909), 300–5.

institution of the Nemean games in the aetiological manner of Attic tragedy but it is scarcely credible that the title should have done so. One would naturally expect the title to be the name of the daughter of Asopus, in honour of whose son Archemoros, according to another story, the Nemean games were instituted. The only Attic tragedian credited with a Νεμέα is Aeschylus.[1] Whether or not Ennius adapted this play, no fragments of which survive, must remain an open question.[2]

CXXIV

252 teneor consaepta: cf. Euripides, *Herakles* 83 φυλακαὶ γὰρ ἡμῶν κρείσσονες κατ' ἐξόδους, *Or.* 444 κύκλῳ γὰρ εἰλισσόμεθα παγχάλκοις ὅπλοις, 760 φυλασσόμεσθα φρουρίοισι πανταχῇ, *Hyps.* fr. 20/21.12 φυλάσσεται γῆ φρουρίοισιν ἐν κύκλῳ.

Consaepire does not occur elsewhere in republican drama; the simple verb occurs 5 times in tragedy and 3 times in comedy. Paulus, Fest. p. 54.22 CONSIPTVM *apud Ennium pro conseptum inuenitur* probably has nothing to do with the piece cited by Nonius; Vahlen draws attention to the article at p. 56.13 CONSIPTVM *clauis praefixum.*

undique uenor: for *undique circumuenior* (cf. Caesar, *Gall.* 3.26 *hostes undique circumuenti* et al.), if Nonius is to be believed. *Venor* for *uenior* seems to be quite unparalleled. Nonius, however, may merely be using a word with some affinity of sound to gloss the passive use of *uenari* 'hunt' (cf. Priscian, *Gramm.* II 387.12).

CXXV

Przychocki referred the words transmitted to the oracle which bade Adrastos marry his daughters to a lion and a boar.[3] This cannot be so. *Pecu, pecus* etc. normally refer to domesticated animals or animals capable of being domesticated (cf. Lucretius 1.14, Varro, *Rust.* 2.1.12); there is a tone of irony in Ovid, *Ib.* 455 *inque pecus subito Magnae uertare parentis,* as in Livius, *Trag.* 5 *lasciuum Nerei simum pecus. Marito* would suggest that the animal already has a consort.

---

[1] See Mette, *Der verlorene Aischylos* (Berlin, 1963), pp. 38 f.
[2] Cf. F. Skutsch, *RE* v (1905), 2594, Leo, *Gesch.* p. 190.
[3] Euripides, *Hik.* 138 ff., *Phoin.* 409 f., *Hyps.* fr. 8/9.13 ff., Apollodorus 3.6.1.3.1.

PHOENIX

The title *Phoenix* is given to Ennius by Aulus Gellius, Helenius Acro and Nonius Marcellus.[1] The eight pieces quoted are each open to a variety of interpretations. Cicero mentions on one occasion (*De orat.* 3.57) a *Phoenix apud Homerum* and on another (*Mur.* 60) quotes a piece of tragic verse which might have been spoken by Achilles' old tutor Phoenix in a play about the events of *Iliad* IX (see above, p. 164).

Among the known Greek tragedians, Sophocles, Euripides, Ion, Astydamas and a certain ?]nedoros[2] are credited with a Φοῖνιξ. Euripides' play was set before the palace of Phoenix's father Amyntor in Boeotian Eleon and dealt with the false accusations made against Phoenix by Amyntor's concubine Phthia and Amyntor's violent treatment of his son.[3] Columna asserted that none of the fragments preserved prevents us from identifying the Ennian and Euripidean plays, and Valckenaer[4] remarked on the lofty moral tone of the two sets of fragments.[5] Fr. CXXX looks like the utterance of Phoenix, and the sort of Phoenix we know Euripides to have portrayed.[6]

At *Orat.* 155 Cicero quotes, apparently from a grammatical source,[7] a dramatic tetrameter by Ennius (fr. CLXX): *neque tuum umquam in gremium extollas liberorum ex te genus*. Columna gave this to the *Medea exul* but Elmsley[8] spotted a similarity with Amyntor's curse as reported at Homer, *Il.* 9.453–6 (πατὴρ δ' ἐμὸς...πολλὰ κατηρᾶτο...μή ποτε γούνασιν οἷσιν ἐφέσσεσθαι φίλον υἱὸν | ἐξ ἐμέθεν γεγαῶτα) and gave it to the *Phoenix*. The assignation is plausible but far from certain. Vahlen's alteration of the transmitted text to *neque tu meum umquam* etc. cannot be accepted even if Elmsley's assignation is. Two unjustified assumptions are made, first that Euripides followed Homer exactly, second that Ennius followed Euripides exactly.[9]

---

[1] Nonius' immediate sources seem to have been Lindsay's list 27 'Alph. Verb' and list 28 'Alph. Adverb'; at p. 518.6 list 1 'Gloss i' is a possible source. Gellius and Acro may depend on Verrius Flaccus.

[2] *I.G.* II² 2363.18.   [3] Cf. *Souda* A 1842.

[4] *Diatribe*, pp. 262 ff.

[5] This is not completely without significance; one would certainly expect this tone in the quotations of a Stobaeus but not necessarily in those of a Nonius Marcellus.

[6] Cf. Schol. A. Hom. *Il.* 9.453 καὶ Εὐριπίδης δὲ ἀναμάρτητον εἰσάγει τὸν ἥρωα ἐν τῷ Φοίνικι.   [7] See above, p. 348.

[8] *Euripidis Medea*, p. 201. Ribbeck and Vahlen wrongly credit Bergk (*RhM* III [1835], 73) with the idea.

[9] *In gremium extollere* may be a variant of the Roman formula discussed above on *vv.* 59–60.

Two dramatic pieces quoted by Charisius, one to illustrate epanalepsis—
pater inquam hospites me lumine orbauit pater,[1] the other apoclisis—*egone illam:
pudor est eloqui: quam comperi,*[2] could be interpreted as coming from a version
of Euripides' Φοῖνιξ.[3]

CXXVI

Since Gellius is discussing *obnoxius* 'dependent' we might expect to find this
word and this sense exemplified in the verses of Ennius which he quotes. But
ancient lexicographers frequently included etymologically related words
under one lemma.[4]

Ennius' first two verses make a statement about *uirtus*, conventionally the
successful exercise of a man's physical powers in warfare, statecraft and pro-
creation,[5] his second two about *libertas*, conventionally the state of being a
free man and not a slave.[6] In both cases conventional notions are being corrected or reinterpreted but textual corruptions obscure the dramatist's point.

The phrase *uirtute... animatum* has no exact parallel; cf., however, Plautus,
Trin. 650 *cape sis uirtutem animo.* The preservation of *animatum* would also
provide some link between the first *sententia* and the second (*pectus purum et
firmum ∼ uera uirtute... animatum... fortiter*). *Vera uirtus* may have meant not
'true, genuine *uirtus*' but rather '*uirtus* accompanied by a sense of fair-
dealing' (cf. Virgil, *Aen.* 12.694–5 *me uerius unum | pro uobis foedus luere et
decernere ferro* and Servius *ad loc.*). The alliterative phrase was a cliché of
Roman public moralising (cf. Plautus, *Cas.* 88, *Cist.* 198, Cicero, *Pis.* 57,
Livy 4.31.5, 24.14.6, Horace, *Carm.* 3.5.29, *Epist.* 1.1.17, 1.18.8).

The sentence *ea libertas est qui pectus purum et firmum gestitat* can stand; for
similar structures see above on *v.* 228.

Res obnoxiosae must be an attempt to represent the abstract idea of dependence in a context where words like *seruitus* and *clientela* would sound too
paradoxical. For this manner of dealing with the abstract cf. Ennius, *Trag.*
318 *res... turbidas,* Plautus, *Merc.* 134 *malae res, Trin.* 344 *in rebus aduorsis.* The
point seems to be that men whose minds are unfree, i.e. men with a bad
conscience, keep out of public sight.

---

[1] P. 370.9; cf. Diomedes, *Gramm.* I 445.29, Sacerdos, *Gramm.* VI 458.11.
[2] P. 374.6.
[3] So Ribbeck, *Quaest. scen.* p. 264, *Die röm. Trag.* pp. 195 f., *T.R.F.*[3], p. 61.
Mariotti, *SIFC* N.S. XXIV (1949), 87 f., replaced *hospites* with *hospes* in the first
piece, assuming a change of scene from Amyntor's palace to that of Peleus in
Phthia.
[4] Cf. Festus, p. 334.8 REDHOSTIRE, Nonius, p. 255.1 CREPARE.
[5] See above on fr. LXXI.
[6] So always in republican drama except at Plautus, *Bacch.* 168, 'free speech',
and *Mil.* 702, 'bachelorhood'.

The substance of the four Latin verses would have been something like that of Euripides, *Hipp.* 421–30: ἀλλ' ἐλεύθεροι | παρρησίᾳ θάλλοντες οἰκοῖεν πόλιν | κλεινῶν 'Αθηνῶν, μητρὸς οὕνεκ' εὐκλεεῖς. | δουλοῖ γὰρ ἄνδρα, κἂν θρασύσπλαγχνός τις ᾖ, | ὅταν ξυνειδῇ μητρὸς ἢ πατρὸς κακά. | μόνον δὲ τοῦτό φασ' ἀμιλλᾶσθαι βίῳ, | γνώμην δικαίαν κἀγαθήν, ὅτῳ παρῇ. | κακοὺς δὲ θνητῶν ἐξέφην' . . . χρόνος.

255 aduersarios: more general than *hostis* or *inimicos*; six times elsewhere in republican drama; comedy has 99 formations in *-arius* according to Ploen's reckoning, tragedy only this one.

256 pectus purum et firmum gestitat: the normal phrase was *animum gerere* (cf. Terence, *Hec.* 311 *qui eos gubernat animus eum infirmum gerunt*); *pectus* was a fairly common high-falutin substitute for *animus* in both tragedy and comedy; *gestitare* replaces *gerere* only here and seven times in Plautus.

For *pectus purum* cf. Euripides, *Med.* 659–61 ἀχάριστος ὄλοιθ', ὅτῳ πάρεστιν | μὴ φίλους τιμᾶν καθαρᾶν ἀνοί|ξαντα κλῇδα φρενῶν, Lucilius 296 *quod gracila est, pernix, quod pectore puro,* | *quod puero similis*, Horace, *Sat.* 1.6.64, *Epist.* 1.2.67–8, Lucretius 5.18, Anon. *Culex* 68.

257 obnoxiosae: '*obnoxiae,* dependent'; cf. Plautus, *Epid.* 695, *Trin.* 1038. With *obnoxiosus* I count 13 formations in *-osus* in tragedy (*aerumnosus, aestuosus, bellicosus, dusmosus, globosus, malitiosus, otiosus, religiosus, scruposus, saeptuosus, uillosus, unose*). They are common in Plautine comedy, rare in Terentian.

nocte in obscura: an order of words highly unusual in republican drama, fairly common in Ennius' epic (*Ann.* 187, 378, 380); see Marouzeau, *REL* xxv (1947), 321.

CXXVII

Somebody, perhaps the chorus leader, comments on Amyntor's denunciation of Phoenix.

258 ex ore orationem: for the word play cf. Plautus, *Merc.* 176 *tu quidem ex ore orationem mi eripis*, Cicero, *Phil.* 5.20 *in me absentem orationem ex ore impurissimo euomuit.*

duriter: not elsewhere in tragedy, four times in comedy (always at the end of a metrical unit); *dure* occurs nowhere in republican drama and is rare in classical prose and verse, which appear to prefer *durius*.

duriter dictis dedit: triple alliteration of D is significantly rare in tragedy; it occurs only here, Ennius, *Trag.* 303 *delectat ductat Delphicus*, Trag. inc. 184–5 *dispari dominare domino*. M and T begin about the same number of words in the tragic lexicon and produce 12 and 8 triple alliterations respectively. On triple alliteration in general see above on *v.* 4.

<h2 style="text-align:center">CXXVIII</h2>

Text and context are obscure. Mariotti[1] commends Ribbeck's *stultust qui cupita cupiens cupienter cupit*,[2] comparing with *cupita cupere v.* 228 *qui uolt quod uolt.*

For the sentiment cf. Plautus, *Pseud.* 683–4 *stulti hau scimus frustra ut simus, quom quod cupienter dari | petimus nobis, quasi quid in rem sit possimus noscere*, Lucilius 806 *cupiditas ex homine cupido et stulto numquam tollitur.*

259 cupiens cupienter cupit: cf. Plautus, *Cas.* 267 *quid istuc tam cupide cupis?*; for the figure in general see above on *v.* 63; for the triple polyptoton cf. Aeschylus, *Pers.* 1041 δόσιν κακὰν κακῶν κακοῖς, Sophocles, *Ai.* 866 πόνος πόνῳ πόνον φέρει, Euripides, *Ba.* 905–6 ἑτέρᾳ δ' ἕτερος ἕτερον | ὄλβῳ καὶ δυνάμει παρῆλθεν, Euripides, *Kykl.* 120 ἀκούει δ' οὐδὲν οὐδεὶς οὐδενός, Plautus, *Amph.* 34 *iuste ab iustis iustus sum orator datus*, *Capt.* 774 *ita hic me amoenitate amoena amoenus onerauit dies*, *Cas.* 826 *mala malae male monstrat*, *Poen.* 1216 *bonus bonis bene feceris.*

Cupienter occurs here, Accius, *Trag.* 543 and Plautus, *Pseud.* 683 in republican drama; *cupide* occurs six times in comedy, not at all in tragedy.

<h2 style="text-align:center">CXXIX</h2>

Wilamowitz and Snell (*WSt* LXIX [1956], 90) accept Haupt's *tum tu isti crede te* etc. (*Hermes* II [1867], 216 [= *Op.* III 375]) and compare the trimeters quoted by Stobaeus 2.15.25 and 3.13.14 and very plausibly assigned to the Φοῖνιξ by O. Hense (*ad* Stob. 3.13.14, p. 456): καὶ τῷδε δηλώσαιμ' ἄν, εἰ βούλοιο σύ, | τἀληθές, ὡς ἔγωγε καὐτὸς ἄχθομαι, | ὅστις λέγειν μὲν εὐπρεπῶς ἐπίσταται, | τὰ δ' ἔργα χείρω τῶν λόγων παρέσχετο.

260 exerce linguam: cf. Ovid, *Met.* 6.374–5 *turpes | litibus exercent linguas*, Tacitus, *Dial.* 31 *linguam modo et uocem exercerent.*

argutarier: Plautus has *argutus* 'talkative in an idle, useless way' a number of times, *argutari* twice (*Amph.* 349 *pergin argutarier?*, fr. 81 *superaboque omnis argutando praeficas*).

---

[1] In private conversation, 8 February 1966.

[2] *T.R.F.*[1], p. 43; withdrawn in favour of *stultus est qui non cupienda cupiens*..., *T.R.F.*[3], p. 59.

CXXX

Phoenix replies to advice suggesting that he resist his father with actions as well as words.

261 plus miser: *miserior* is normal in drama; for this form of the comparative cf. Plautus, *Cas.* 676–7 *tibi infesta solist | plus quam cuiquam.*

scelestum: not elsewhere in tragedy, frequent in comedy of the behaviour of slaves.

The manuscript *scelestim* would in itself be acceptable; Vossius drew attention to the variation *diserte/disertim, caute/cautim, arcte/arctim, exquisite/exquisitim.*

faxim: this form was probably still alive in the common language, unlike other *-s-* and *-ss-* subjunctive/optative forms. Plautus has *faxim* 10 times against *fecerim* 5; Terence has them twice each. See Thomas, *Recherches*, pp. 53 ff.

quod dicam fore: Vahlen pointed out that this was a periphrasis of the type discussed below on *v.* 300. It can be objected that *dicam* is normally so used in direct and indirect questions, not in relative clauses.

CXXXI

Someone, perhaps Phoenix, speaks of Amyntor's angry reaction to Phthia's accusations.

262 saeuiter...ferre: cf. Afranius, *Com. tog.* 301.

ferre falsam futtilum: triple alliteration of F is significantly rare in tragedy; it occurs only here and at Naevius 45 *flammis fieri flora*; the letter begins about the same number of words in the tragic lexicon as D, M and T (see above on *v.* 238).

For *futtilis/-us* of persons cf. Terence, *Andr.* 609 *seruon fortunas meas me commisisse futtili*, Afranius, *Com. tog.* 35, Cicero, *Fin.* 3.38, *Diu.* 1.36, Virgil, *Aen.* 11.339, Phaedrus 4.18.33.

CXXXII

Phoenix must be speaking of his failure to stand up to Amyntor.

Feratis is an absolutely necessary correction (cf. Plautus, *Asin.* 323 *em ista uirtus est...qui malum fert fortiter*) but leaves the trochaic tetrameter with an oddly divided third foot (see above on fr. XII).

COMMENTARY

CXXXIII

It is difficult to fit this tetrameter into a dramatic treatment of the story of Phoenix. No one has been convinced by Hartung's suggestion[1] that a messenger describes Phoenix receiving back his sight on top of Mount Pelion.

264 ibi tum: cf. Terence, *Andr.* 131, 634, Cicero, *Quinct.* 16, *Verr.* 2.3.139, *Caecin.* 27.

TELAMO

The title *Telamo* is given to Ennius six times by Nonius,[2] once by Verrius and once by Diomedes. Two of the seven pieces quoted (frs. cxxxv, cxxxix) clearly fix the action of the play in Salamis at the time of Teucer's return from Troy. Aeschylus' Σαλαμίνιαι, Sophocles' Τεῦκρος and Pacuvius' *Teucer* also dealt with the confrontation between Teucer and his father but there is no Τελαμών among those titles which are recorded against the names of Attic tragedians.

At *Nat. deor.* 3.79, *Diu.* 1.132 and *Diu.* 2.104 Cicero quotes a tragic speech setting out the Epicurean view of gods and diviners; he names Ennius twice in connection therewith and the hero Telamo once. With the exception of Delrius all editors since Columna have printed the speech with the grammatical fragments of the *Telamo*.

At *Tusc.* 3.28, 3.39 and 3.58 Cicero quotes from two tragic speeches clearly labelled as uttered by a Telamo. At 3.44 he quotes a third speech which we can deduce to have come from a tragedy by Ennius (fr. clxxv; see above on fr. xxvii *h*). Columna printed the remains of the three speeches under the title *Telamo* and argued that the action of the play began with the exile of Telamo himself from his original home in Aegina.

Scholars have continued to assign the speech quoted at *Tusc.* 3.28 and 58—*ego cum genui tum morituros sciui et ei rei sustuli,* | *praeterea ad Troiam cum misi ob defendendam Graeciam,* | *scibam me in mortiferum bellum, non in epulas mittere*—to the *Telamo* although it is difficult to see why it could not equally well go into Pacuvius' *Teucer*.

The speech quoted at 44—*pol mihi fortuna magis nunc defit quam genus.* |

---

[1] *Euripides Restitutus* 1, pp. 75–6.
[2] Nonius' source at p. 172.19 seems to be Lindsay's list 1 'Gloss. i'. At the other five places there is considerable uncertainty; list 27 'Alph. Verb' could be the source.

namque regnum suppetebat mi ut scias quanto e loco, | *quantis opibus, quibus de rebus lapsa fortuna accidat*—has been given to the principal personage of several Ennian tragedies, to Hecuba by Bothe,[1] to Telephus by Düntzer,[2] and to Thyestes by Ribbeck.[3] A careful look at Cicero's argument from 39 to 44 enables one to exclude both Telamo and Thyestes as possible speakers; Cicero is adapting a criticism of Epicurus' doctrine on pain and suffering and adorns his adaptation with quotations from and references to Roman tragedy; at 39 he names Thyestes, Aeetes (with a backward glance at his actual quotations of speeches by them at 26) and Telamo, at 43 Telamo again; at 44 *qui ita dicat,* whoever he is, and Andromache provide further examples of tragic suffering.

The speech quoted at 39—*hicine est ille Telamo modo quem gloria ad caelum extulit,* | *quem aspectabant, cuius ob os Grai ora obuertebant sua?* | *simul animus cum re concidit*—obviously cannot go in the same play either with the speech quoted at 28 and 58 or with the grammatical fragments. Hermann's attempt[4] to interpret it as spoken by Teucer recalling the banishment of his own father from Aegina many years previously is quite unconvincing. Welcker[5] suggested that Cicero quotes a play about Telamon's banishment from Aegina unrecorded by the grammarians. Ribbeck,[6] having reconstructed Accius' *Eurysaces* so as to make Aegina the scene of action and Telamon, expelled from Salamis in old age by revolutionaries, one of the personages, included the quotation therein. Since there is nothing in the mythographical tradition about Telamo losing his Salaminian kingdom in old age Welcker's view is much to be preferred.

Acceptance of the view that Cicero knew three plays about Telamo would raise a doubt as to the propriety of placing the verses quoted at *Nat. deor.* 3.79, *Diu.* 1.132 and *Diu.* 2.104 together with those quoted by the grammarians. Nevertheless Cicero's verses look as if they were spoken by a man exercising authority, not an exile bowed by misery. With some hesitation I have printed them under the title *Telamo* (fr. CXXXIV).

---

[1] Despite Cicero's *eum.*

[2] *Zeitschr. f. d. Alt.* 1838, 53; cf. Ladewig, *Anal. scen.* p. 25.

[3] *Quaest. scen.* p. 268; cf. *Die röm. Trag.* p. 201.

[4] *De Aeschyli Tragoediis Fata Aiacis et Teucri Complexis,* p. 17 (= *Opusc.* VII 381).

[5] *Die griech. Trag.* pp. 1379–80; cf. Robert, *Die griech. Heldensage* III 2 i, p. 1044.

[6] *Coniect.* pp. 31 ff., *Quaest. scen.* pp. 328 f., *Die röm. Trag.* pp. 419 ff.

CXXXIV

(a) G. Hermann's view[1] that Telamo is speaking after receiving news of Ajax's death seems to have prevailed among later scholars. But the principal point of Telamo's speech was surely the unreliability of diviners' advice. No diviner is known to have foretold Ajax's return home, and the utterances of Calchas reported at Sophocles, *Ai.* 746 ff. were justified by events. We must have in fact a situation like that of Homer, *Od.* 2.178 ff., Sophocles, *Ant.* 1033 ff., *O.T.* 380 ff., Euripides, *I.A.* 955 ff. But what advice Telamo had been given I cannot guess.

The general prosperity of the wicked and the misery of the righteous are common themes in the speeches of the unfortunate in ancient drama: cf. Euripides, fr. 286. 1–12 φησίν τις εἶναι δῆτ' ἐν οὐρανῷ θεούς; | οὐκ εἰσίν, οὐκ εἶσ', εἴ τις ἀνθρώπων θέλει | μὴ τῷ παλαιῷ μῶρος ὢν χρῆσθαι λόγῳ. | σκέψασθε δ' αὐτοί, μὴ ἐπὶ τοῖς ἐμοῖς λόγοις | γνώμην ἔχοντες. φήμ' ἐγὼ τυραννίδα | κτείνειν τε πλείστους κτημάτων τ' ἀποστερεῖν | ὅρκους τε παραβαίνοντας ἐκπορθεῖν πόλεις · | καὶ ταῦτα δρῶντες μᾶλλόν εἰσ' εὐδαίμονες | τῶν εὐσεβούντων ἡσυχῇ καθ' ἡμέραν. | πόλεις τε μικρὰς οἶδα τιμώσας θεούς, | αἳ μειζόνων κλύουσι δυσσεβεστέρων | λόγχης ἀριθμῷ πλείονος κρατούμεναι, Trag. Graec. inc. fr. 465 τολμῶ κατειπεῖν, μήποτ' οὐκ εἰσὶν θεοί · | κακοὶ γὰρ εὐτυχοῦντες ἐκπλήσσουσί με. The gods themselves and some mortals take a different view: cf. Euripides, *El.* 1350–3 τοῖς μὲν μυσαροῖς οὐκ ἐπαρήγομεν, | οἷσιν δ' ὅσιον καὶ τὸ δίκαιον | φίλον ἐν βιότῳ, τούτους χαλεπῶν | ἐκλύοντες μόχθων σῴζομεν, *Ion* 1619–22, Plautus, *Capt.* 313–15 *est profecto deus qui quae nos gerimus auditque et uidet... bene merenti bene profuerit, male merenti par erit, Rud.* 9–21.

265 nam si curent: the present subjunctive normally expresses the unreal present in the Latin of republican drama.

bene bonis sit, male malis: cf. Plautus, *Bacch.*660 *bonus sit bonis malus sit malis.*

quod nunc abest: 'which is at present not the case'; *T.L.L.* I 210.18 ff. offers no exact parallel.

(b) The substance of Cicero's argument is complete at the word *harioli*. The four trochaic tetrameters *aut inertes... reddant cetera* are merely decorative; indeed they repeat some of the substance of the foregoing discourse (*inertes ~ non... scientia aut arte*; *insani ~ superstitiosi*; *quibus egestas imperat ~*

---

[1] *De Aeschyli Tragoediis Fata Aiacis et Teucri Complexis*, pp. 15 f. (= *Opusc.* VII 378 f.).

inpudentes).[1] Stephanus and Columna began the tragic quotation at *non habeo denique nauci*[2] but most recent editors follow Bothe and begin where the transmitted text falls into trochaic rhythm, i.e. at *sed*. Many scholars nevertheless seem to believe that Cicero's sentence conveys the substance if not the exact wording of the first part of the tragic speech.[3]

A parallel distinction between true prophecy and quackery is made at Euripides, *El.* 399–400: Λοξίου γὰρ ἔμπεδοι | χρησμοί, βροτῶν δὲ μαντικὴν χαίρειν ἐῶ.[4] But if the tragic hero had made anything like Cicero's point it is difficult to understand why most of his speech should be paraphrased. *Aut insani aut inertes* covers all classes of diviners, those like the Pythia who prophesy in ecstasy and those like Calchas and Teiresias who employ natural signs. Telamo clearly denounced all classes. Cicero's use of *superstitiosus* and *hariolus* as straight-out terms of insult conforms with the aristocratic usage of his time. But in the Latin of the second century the two words had very precise meanings. *Superstitiosus* meant 'clairvoyant'.[5] It could not have been used at that time as a near synonym of *inpudens*. The *hariolus* was a diviner who used different methods from the *haruspex*. Plautus (*Amph.* 1132, *Mil.* 693, *Poen.* 791) and Terence (*Phorm.* 708–9) couple them in lists of diviners. *Hariolus* (~ *hariolari*) is nowhere recorded in second-century Latin with its later sense 'talker of nonsense'.[6] *Vates* seems to be recorded only three times before the first century (Ennius, *Ann.* 214 *uersibus quos olim Fauni uatesque canebant*, 380 *satin uates uerant aetate in agunda?*, Plautus, *Mil.* 911 *bonus uates poteras esse; nam quae sunt futura dicis*) but not even in first-century usage is it ever unambiguously a term of insult.[7] Second-century aristocrats might well have denounced *superstitio*, *uates* and *harioli*, especially as clairvoyancy was not one of the methods employed by the state diviners,[8] likewise the professional *sortilegi*, *augures*, *haruspices*, *astrologi*, *coniectores* and *interpretes somniorum* whom less privileged people consulted. However, we should not expect a tragic hero using their language to blur the distinction they made between one diviner and another.

---

[1] Cf. *Diu.* 1.42 (fr. XVIII).

[2] This phrase occurs nowhere else in Cicero but occasionally in drama; to the examples quoted by Festus, p. 166.11 ff. add Plautus, *Bacch.* 1102.

[3] Cf. M. S. Salem, *JRS* XXVIII (1938), 56–9.

[4] Cf. *Phoin.* 954–9.

[5] See above on *v.* 35.

[6] See Latte, *Röm. Rel.* p. 268.

[7] See Dahlmann, *Philologus* XCVII (1948), 337 ff., F. Bickel, *RhM* XCIV (1951), 257 ff.

[8] The Sibylline oracles of course depended historically on clairvoyancy but their contemporary keepers did no more than consult the books in which they were recorded.

Vahlen was right to give *sed* to Cicero rather than the tragedian but should have gone further. We might grant that Ennius could have composed the phrase *superstitiosi uates inpudentesque harioli* without the particular colour that the context of Cicero's discourse gives it but the rude and undigested pile of adjectives and adjectival clauses in *superstitiosi uates inpudentesque harioli...* *monstrant uiam* looks like the work of a hasty quoter rather than that of a competent dramatist.[1]

What particular diviner Ennius' Telamo had in mind it is impossible to say. It looks as if Telamon had been given some advice on what course of action to take (or not to take) and, after rejecting it, had launched into a general denunciation of divination and diviners. The class of diviners mentioned—those who *diuitias pollicentur*—do not appear in the remains of Attic tragedy; there is some point in Vossius' remark 'sed mihi ut et amicissimo Scriuerio omnes hi uersus socci potius quam cothurni esse uidentur'. We have perhaps yet another instance of Ennius turning aside from the drama he is adapting and commenting upon contemporary affairs (see above on fr. LXXXIV).

266 inertes: 'without *ars*, i.e. skill acquired by training'; cf. Varro, *Men.* 359 *artem...expromis inertem*, Horace, *Epist.* 2.2.126–8 *praetulerim scriptor delirus inersque uideri...quam sapere.*

quibus egestas imperat: cf. Plautus, *Asin.* 671 *quiduis egestas imperat.*

For the bad moral effects of poverty cf. Euripides, *El.* 375–6 ἀλλ᾽ ἔχει νόσον | πενία, διδάσκει δ᾽ ἄνδρα τῇ χρείᾳ κακόν, Terence, *Andr.* 275 *coactum egestate ingenium inmutarier.* The word *egestas* has a bad odour in the public orations of Cicero (cf. *Prou. cons.* 43, *Phil.* 2.50, 2.62 et al.); for him and his aristocratic audiences it denoted one of the prime causes of political radicalism.

267 qui sibi semitam non sapiunt alteri monstrant uiam: cf. *v.* 221 *qui ipse sibi sapiens prodesse non quit nequiquam sapit* and my notes thereon.

Semita denotes a side-track, *uia* the highway; cf. Plautus, *Cas.* 675 *sciens de uia in semitam degredere.*

Semitam...sapiunt is an odd phrase; its nearest parallel is Plautus, *Pseud.* 496 *recte ego meam rem sapio.* Desire for concinnity with *monstrant uiam* may have been Ennius' motive. On the other hand one could understand a *monstrare* with *sapiunt*; cf. Plautus, *Asin.* 248 *nam si mutuas non potero certumst sumam faenore*, 354–5 *si erum uis Demaenetum,* | *quem ego noui, adduce*, Capt.

---

[1] Cicero likes the collocation of *harioli* and *uates* (cf. *Diu.* 1.4, 2.9, *Nat. deor* 1.55).

238 *pol ego si te audeam meum patrem nominem*, 303 *memini quom dicto haud audebat; facto nunc laedat licet, Pseud.* 120 *si neminem alium potero tuom tangam patrem.*

Monstrare was perhaps still redolent of its origin in the sacral language (~ *monstrum*); it occurs twice elsewhere in tragedy, 21 times in Plautus but only once in the rest of comedy (Terence, *Ad.* 570); it is absent from Caesar and rare in Cicero. *Ostendere* on the other hand seems to be common in all genres in all authors both during the second century B.C. and later.

268 quibus diuitias pollicentur, ab iis drachumam ipsi petunt: the venality of diviners was a commonplace of Ionian epic[1] and Attic tragedy.[2] The Roman aristocracy always drew a firm distinction between the priests, who advised the senate and magistrates on the will of the gods and who were recruited from wealthy families of Latium and Etruria, and itinerant foreign professionals.[3] It is not therefore very surprising that the adapters of Attic tragedy should here and elsewhere[4] allow the advisers of the Greek heroes to be identified with money-grubbing quacks.

Plautus, *Merc.* 777, *Pseud.* 85 ff., 808 make it clear that for second-century Roman audiences the *drachuma* was a coin of very little value. Coined metal was a source of imagery for the Attic tragedians (cf. Euripides, *El.* 558–9, *Med.* 516–19) but the names of particular coins do not seem to occur in the remains.

For the sneer at the lowness of the diviner's charges cf. Aeschylus, *Ag.* 1273–4 καλουμένη δὲ φοιτὰς ὡς ἀγύρτρια | πτωχὸς τάλαινα λιμοθνὴς ἠνεσχόμην (Cassandra speaking), Juvenal 6.546–7 *aere minuto* | *qualiacumque uoles Iudaei somnia uendunt.*

269 sibi deducant drachumam: 'let them deduct their drachma fee'; cf. Cato, *Agr.* 144.3 *id uiri boni arbitratu deducetur...si non praebuerit quanti conductum erit aut locatum erit, deducetur; tanto minus debebitur.*

reddant cetera: 'and hand over the remainder according to the bargain'; cf. Plautus, *Bacch.* 329–30 *id signumst cum Theotimo, qui eum illi adferet,* | *ei aurum ut reddat.*

---

[1] Cf. Homer, *Od.* 2.178 ff.

[2] Cf. Sophocles, *Ant.* 1033 ff., *O.T.* 380 ff., Euripides, *Ba.* 255 ff.

[3] Cf. Plautus, *Mil.* 692–4 (a passage of specifically Roman colouring), Rhet. inc. *Her.* 4.62, Cicero, *Diu.* 1.88–92, Propertius 4.1.81–2, Livy 25.1.8, Gellius 14.1.2.

[4] Accius, *Trag.* 169–70 *nil credo auguribus qui auris uerbis diuitant* | *alienas, suas ut auro locupletent domos*, Ennius, *Trag.* 343 *qui sui quaestus causa fictas suscitant sententias* (Stephanus' attribution [p. 129] of this verse to the *Telamo* is not even plausible).

(c) The two propositions 'the gods do not exist' and 'the gods do not interfere in human affairs' are different from the propositions 'the gods are not powerful (whatever they may have been in the past)' and 'the gods do not exercise their power justly'. They remove one of the foundation stones of the heroic story. Not surprisingly the first appears only thrice in the remains of Attic tragedy[1] and the second not at all. Plato refers to the second at *Nom.* 10.885 B and it was commonly associated in later times with the name of Epicurus.[2] It appears at Menander, *Epitr.* 726–8 οἴει τοσαύτην τοὺς θεοὺς ἄγειν σχολήν, | ὥστε τὸ κακὸν καὶ τἀγαθὸν καθ᾽ ἡμέραν | νέμειν ἑκάστῳ; and Plautus may have taken *Merc.* 4–7 *Nocti aut Dii | aut Soli aut Lunae...quos pol ego credo humanas querimonias | non tanti facere quid uelint, quid non uelint* from Philemon's Ἔμπορος. It is possible that the original of the *Telamo* was composed sometime in the fourth century or later and contained the Epicurean sentiments in question, equally possible that Ennius, with his fondness for philosophical speculation, introduced them himself.

270–1 deum genus... caelitum... humanum genus: for the first periphrasis cf. Euripides, *Hek.* 490 δοκοῦντας δαιμόνων εἶναι γένος, Virgil, *Aen.* 4.12 *credo equidem, nec uana fides, genus esse deorum*; for the second Euripides, fr. 898.13 βρότειον...γένος, Plautus, *Poen.* 1187 *Iuppiter qui genus colis alisque hominum*; for both Lucretius 5.1156 *diuom genus humanumque*. Plautus parodies the way of speaking with his *genus lenonium* (*Curc.* 499, *Persa* 582).

270 dixi et dicam: cf. Bacchylides 1.159 φαμὶ καὶ φάσω, Plautus, *Mil.* 1058 *dixi hoc tibi dudum et nunc dico*, Terence, *Hec.* 722 *iamdudum dixi idemque nunc dico*. The figure appears occasionally in Attic drama[3] and with considerable frequency in Roman.[4] The dramatists were probably aping the magistrates' manner of speech; cf. the examples collected from early public inscriptions by O. Altenburg, *NJbb.* Suppl. xxiv (1898), 494 f.

---

[1] Euripides, *Hek.* 488–91, fr. 286, Trag. Graec. inc. 465.
[2] Cf. Cicero, *Nat. deor.* 1.43–5.
[3] Cf. Euripides, *Tr.* 468 πάσχω τε καὶ πέπονθα κἄτι πείσομαι, 499 οἵων ἔτυχον ὧν τε τεύξομαι.
[4] Without searching systematically I find Pacuvius, *Trag.* 297, Accius, *Trag.* 227–8, Plautus, *Aul.* 216, *Bacch.* 1087, *Capt.* 392, 933–4, *Cist.* 12, 43, *Curc.* 168, *Men.* 118, 991, *Merc.* 539, *Mil.* 1058, *Persa* 777, 847, *Trin.* 56, 106, 619, Terence, *Eun.* 1009, *Hec.* 722, 739.

CXXXV

Telamo addresses Teucer whom he suspects of having murdered or partici-
pated in the murder of Ajax with a view to usurping the kingship.

272 scibas: the normal form in republican drama.

natum ingenuum Aiacem: cf. Plautus, *Rud.* 738 *haec est nata Athenis
ingenuis parentibus.* The jurists use *ingenuum nasci* as a technical term.

Ajax was born of Eriboea, daughter of Alcathous who received Telamo
when he fled to Salamis from Aegina (Pindar, *Isth.* 6.45, Bacchylides
13.102, Sophocles, *Ai.* 569); Teucer on the other hand was the bastard son of
Hesione whom Heracles had given Telamo as part of the spoil of Troy
(Sophocles, *Ai.* 1299 ff.).

cui tu obsidionem paras: language proper to the description of attacks
on walled cities; parodied at Plautus, *Asin.* 280, *Mil.* 219, 222, *Most.* 1048,
Rud. 838; for more elaborate parody of the tragedians' hyperbolic use of
military language cf. Plautus, *Bacch.* 232, 709 ff., 925 ff., 1094, *Epid.* 158 ff.,
Pseud. 585 ff., 761 ff.; for similar hyperbole in Attic tragedy cf. Euripides,
Or. 762 ὡσπερεὶ πόλις πρὸς ἐχθρῶν σῶμα πυργηρούμεθα.

CXXXVI

Bergk's restoration of the name Aeacus[1] seems certain; cf. Pindar, *Pyth.*
8.98–100 Αἴγινα φίλα μᾶτερ, ἐλευθέρῳ στόλῳ | πόλιν τάνδε κόμιζε Δὶ
καὶ κρέοντι σὺν Αἰακῷ | Πηλεῖ τε κἀγαθῷ Τελαμῶνι σύν τ' Ἀχιλλεῖ,
Apollonius Rhod. 3.363–4 Τελαμὼν δ' ὅγε κυδίστοιο | Αἰακοῦ ἐκγε-
γαώς· Ζεὺς δ' Αἰακὸν αὐτὸς ἔτικτεν, Ovid. *Met.* 13.22–8.

Nonius' remark 'uel clareat' is peculiar; after *clara est* one would expect
'clara sit'. In any case the verb *clarare* on the few occasions it occurs in recorded literature is, as one would expect, transitive. *Clarere* leads a shadowy
existence in poetry and is regularly intransitive. The fragment cannot therefore be taken as the beginning of an asseveration of the type *ita me di ament
ut....*[2] It may come from a statement made by Teucer on arrival in Salamis
expressing pride in his ancestry and joy at having survived the voyage from
the Troad; i.e. at a point in the drama before Telamo's anger breaks out.

---

[1] *RhM* III (1835), 73 (FACI ~ (A)EACI). TOVIS for IOVIS was another mistake
in capital script.

[2] The formula is very occasionally varied with *ita me di amabunt* etc. but such
phrases do not justify Vahlen's *nam ita mihi...esse est atque hoc lumen candidum
claret mihi ⟨ut ego mortis huius insons sum⟩* (*SB Berlin* 1888, 32–40 [= *Ges. phil.
Schr.* II 263–71]).

274 hoc lumen candidum claret: cf. Plautus, *Aul.* 748 *luci claro deripi-amus, Amph.* 547 *inlucescat luce clara et candida,* Com. pall. inc. 70 *prior ire luci claro non queo.* The verb *clarere* seems to be a tragic neologism.

With *hoc* the speaker would have pointed to the sky; cf. Ennius, *Trag.* 301 *aspice hoc sublime candens,* 342 *hoc quod lucet,* Pacuvius, *Trag.* 86–7 *hoc uide circum supraque quod complexu continet* | *terram,* Plautus, *Amph.* 543 *lucescit hoc iam.*

CXXXVII

Lipsius[1] thought that this was a statement that could be made only by an Orestes. It could be made by a monarch asked by suppliants for protection against potential enemies of his city (cf. Aeschylus' Ἱκετίδες, Euripides' Ἡρακλεῖδαι). None of the dilemmas suggested for Ennius' tragedy (e.g. whether or not Telamo should banish Teucer, whether or not Teucer should lead a rebellion against Telamo) seems sharp enough.

275 deum... pietas: 'the gods whom I revere'; Ennius seeks parallelism of phrase with *ciuium pudor.*

sentit: 'sententiam dicit, censet'; cf. Catullus 64.21 *tum Thetidi pater ipse iugandum Pelea sensit,* Cicero, *Orat.* 195 *ego autem sentio omnes in oratione esse quasi permixtos et confusos pedes,* Fam. 11.21.2 *cum ego sensissem de iis qui exercitus haberent sententiam ferri oportere,* Virgil, *Aen.* 10.622–3 *si...meque hoc ita ponere sentis.*

porcet pudor: cf. Pacuvius, *Trag.* 67 *mi gnate ut uerear eloqui porcet pudor.* The verb *porcere* occurs three times in republican tragedy but is absent from comedy.

CXXXVIII

Tecmessa, Ajax's mother Eriboea and Teucer's mother Hesione have all been suggested as the person to whom the speaker refers. Eriboea seems to me the most likely. Pacuvius, *Trag.* 422–3 *flexanima tamquam lymphata aut Bacchi sacris* | *commota in tumulis Teucrum commemorans suum* must refer to Hesione; two opinions are possible about 313–14 *quae desiderio alumnum paenitudine* | *squales scabresque inculta uastitudine* (from *Teucer*).

276 strata terrae: 'stretched on the ground'. There seems to be no comparable dative in the rest of republican drama.[2] Accius has at *Trag. praet.* 25 *prostratum terra. Terrae* may have been written as an artificial variant of *humi* (cf. Cicero, *De orat.* 3.22, Virgil, *Aen.* 9.754, 10.697 et al.).

---

[1] *Epistolicarum Quaestionum Libri V* (Antwerp, 1577), IV 19.
[2] See P. Lejay, *MSL* XII (1903), 85 ff.

squalam: not transmitted elsewhere in Latin; restored at Plautus, *Men.* 838 and *Truc.* 934; *squalidus* occurs three times in comedy, three in tragedy. Leumann's interpretation[1] of the phrase as 'squal- et sord-idam', 'ein sprachliches Kunststück', is hard to take but there seem to be no parallels for the formation.

CXXXIX

Teucer complains that Telamo suspects him as well as the Atreids of being implicated in the death of Ajax. It is impossible to get a reference to the charge once levelled against Telamo of killing his half-brother Phocas into the words transmitted.

277 eandem me in suspicionem: monosyllabic prepositions apart from *cum* do not normally follow personal pronouns; the only other two recorded instances, Plautus, *Mil.* 1265 *nescio tu me ex hoc audieris an non*, Cicero, *Tusc.* 2.15 *hunc post*, are suspect.[2]

partiuit: the deponent form does not occur in republican drama.

CXL

Telamo agrees to hear Teucer's defence.

278 more antiquo: cf. Plautus, *Rud.* 624–5 *qui Veneri Veneriaeque anti-stitae | more antiquo in custodelam suom commiserunt caput*, Varro, *Men.* 303 *antiquo more silicernium confecimus*, Lucretius 2.610–11 *hanc uariae gentes antiquo more sacrorum | Idaeam uocitant matrem*, Livy 7.2.11 *iuuentus histrionibus fabellarum actu relicto ipsa inter se more antiquo ridicula intexta uersibus iactitare coepit*.

audibo: only here in tragedy; at Plautus, *Capt.* 619, *Poen.* 310, Ennius, *Com.* 4, Caecilius, *Com.* 24, 113 in comedy; *audiam* etc. seem to have been the regular forms (twice in tragedy, 9 times in Plautus, 5 in Terence).

atque auris tibi contra utendas dabo: repeats the substance of the preceding *audibo*; for the pleonasm cf. Aeschylus, *Choe.* 4–5 τύμβου δ' ἐπ' ὄχθῳ τῷδε κηρύσσω πατρὶ | κλύειν, ἀκοῦσαι, Euripides, *Phoin.* 919 οὐκ ἔκλυον, οὐκ ἤκουσα. *Contra* is to be taken ἀπὸ κοινοῦ with *audibo* in the sense of 'ἐν μέρει,[3] in turn, having had my say'; cf. Terence, *Ad.* 50.

---

[1] *Lat. Gramm.* I, p. 225 n. 1.
[2] See Marouzeau, *REL* xxv (1947), 312.
[3] Cf. Euripides, *Kykl.* 253 ἄκουσον ἐν μέρει.

26-2

Vahlen's attempt to interpret the phrase as 'I shall answer you'[1] clashes with the common usage of the phrases *alicui aliquid utendum dare/rogare*.[2] The phrase *aures dare* was probably a colloquialism;[3] likewise *auribus uti*.[4] The two together doubtlessly had a pompous tone; cf. Plautus, *Bacch.* 995 *aurium operam tibi dico*, Mil. 954 *auris meas profecto dedo in dicionem tuam*.

CXLI

279 abnuebunt: probably an artificial form modelled on *prohibebunt*; in the rest of republican drama *abnuere* and *adnuere* behave according to the pattern of the third conjugation.

TELEPHVS

The title *Telephus* is given to Ennius six times by Nonius[5] and once by Verrius, to Accius fourteen times by Nonius (pp. 13.17, 136.18, 155.9, 174.14, 226.3, 227.29, 307.31, 347.14, 352.8, 426.22, 485.9, 488.3, 488.10, 503.28),[6] twice by Priscian (*Gramm.* II 512.4, III 424.24) and once by Macrobius (*Sat.* 6.1.57).

Telephus, the son of Auge and Hercules, was king of the Mysians when Agamemnon brought his first expedition against Troy to Asia Minor. He led the Mysians to victory over the Greeks but suffered himself a wound which would not heal. After an oracle had informed him that ὁ τρώσας καὶ ἰάσεται, he went to Greece and eventually reached Argos where Agamemnon was preparing his second expedition. He agreed to guide the expedition to the site of Troy and Achilles healed his wound by touching it with the spear that caused it. Both[7] Latin tragedies seem to have been set in Argos.

---

[1] Cf. *SB Berlin* 1888, 34 (= *Ges. phil. Schr.* II 265).

[2] See O. Seyffert, *BPhW* XXIV (1904), 1325.

[3] Cf. Plautus, *Trin.* 11, Cicero, *Att.* 1.5.4, 2.14.2, *Arch.* 26, Persius 4.50.

[4] Cf. Plautus, *Mil.* 799, and, where other people's ears are concerned, Cicero, *Fam.* 7.33.2 *nam et Cassius tuus et Dolabella noster uel potius uterque noster studiis iisdem tenentur et meis aequissimis utuntur auribus*, Pliny, *Epist.* 7.30.3 *qui auribus meis post longum tempus suo iure abutuntur*, Symmachus, *Epist.* 1.3.3 *si nobis utendas aures datis, dicam, quid diebus superioribus egerim*.

[5] The origin of the quotations at p. 537.24 ff. is obscure. The rest come from Lindsay's list 10 'Ennius'.

[6] The quotation at p. 155.9 comes from list 27 'Alph. Adverb', the rest from list 5 'Accius i'.

[7] For the legends attaching to Telephus' name see Robert, *Die griech. Heldensage* III 2 i, pp. 1138 ff.

Aeschylus, Sophocles, Euripides, Agathon, Cleophon, Iophon and Moschion have the title Τήλεφος recorded against their names. Junius and P. Leopardus[1] emended the fragment quoted by Nonius at p. 537.27 (fr. CXLIII) on the assumption that Ennius adapted Euripides' tragedy. Euripides was famous for having brought the Mysian king to Argos dressed in a beggar's rags.

J. Geel[2] interpreted the other fragments on the same assumption. The quite considerable amount of Euripides' tragedy which has come to light during the present century contains nothing destructive of this assumption.

Düntzer[3] assigned the Ennian verses quoted by Cicero at *Tusc.* 3.44 (fr. CLXXV; see above on fr. XXVII h)—*pol mihi fortuna magis nunc defit quam genus.* | *namque regnum suppetebat mi ut scias quanto e loco,* | *quantis opibus, quibus de rebus lapsa fortuna accidat*—to a speech by Telephus without suggesting a context. The Euripidean Telephus seems to have left his kingdom of his own free will and to have assumed the disguise of a beggar.[4] However the Latin words could have been uttered by a Telephus suspected as a result of his regal mannerisms of not being a real beggar and trying to prevent his particular identity being discovered; cf. Accius, *Trag.* 619–20 *nam si a me regnum Fortuna atque opes* | *eripere quiuit at uirtutem nec quiit* (Ribbeck: *nequit* codd.).

Hartung[5] assigned the piece of dialogue between Agamemnon and Menelaus quoted by Cicero at *Tusc.* 4.77—*quis homo te exsuperauit umquam gentium inpudentia?*::*quis autem malitia te?*—to Ennius' *Telephus* on the grounds that there was a quarrel between the two brothers in Euripides' play.[6]

To the alleged quarrel in Ennius' *Telephus* Ribbeck[7] assigned verses quoted by Seneca at *Epist.* 80.8, *quod nisi quieris Menelae hac dextra occides,* and an anonymous metrician at *Gramm.* VI 613.9, *proin demet* (Lachmann: *proinde et* cod.) *abs te regimen Argos dum est potestas consili* (Lachmann: *consulendi* cod.).

It is possible that when his identity was revealed the Ennian Telephus

---

[1] *Emendationum et Miscellaneorum Libri Viginti. Tomus Prior* (Antwerp 1568), VIII 24.

[2] *De Telepho Euripidis Commentatio.* I have seen the copy sent by Geel to G. Hermann and now in the Cambridge University Library. The date of publication is usually given as 1830.

[3] *Zeitschr. f. d. Alt.* 1838, 53. Cf. Ladewig, *Anal. scen.* p. 25.

[4] Cf. Aristophanes, *Ach.* 440–1, which a scholiast alleges to be ἐκ Τηλέφου Εὐριπίδου (fr. 698). Horace, *Ars* 96–7 seems to refer to a tragedy which represented Telephus as banished from his kingdom.

[5] *Euripides Restitutus* I, p. 202.

[6] Cf. Schol. Arist. *Neph.* 891 (fr. 722), Stobaeus 3.39.9 (fr. 723).

[7] *Quaest. scen.* p. 264, *Die röm. Trag.* p. 109.

COMMENTARY

seized the baby Orestes and took refuge at an altar.[1] Ribbeck assigned to such a scene the verses quoted by Cicero at *De orat.* 3.102 *nam sapiens uirtuti honorem praemium haud praedam petit.* | *sed quid uideo? ferro saeptus possidet sedis sacras.*

Any play about Telephus set in Argos would have to end with Telephus being appointed to guide the Greek army to Troy. Ribbeck assigned to a speech by Telephus at this point two iambic pieces quoted as from Ennius by Cicero at *Off.* 1.51: *homo qui erranti comiter monstrat uiam,* | *quasi lumen de suo lumine accendat facit;* | *nihilo minus ipsi lucet cum illi accenderit* (fr. CLXV), and by Varro at *Ling.* 7.89: *si uoles aduortere animum comiter monstrabitur* (fr. CXCVI).

The scholia make it plain that Dicaeopolis' denunciation of the warlike policies of the Athenian government at Aristophanes, *Ach.* 496–556 parodies an attack by the Euripidean Telephus on Agamemnon and Menelaus. Timpanaro has suggested[2] that the words quoted as from Ennius by the Danieline Servius on *Aen.* 2.62—*ut uos nostri liberi* | *defendant, pro uostra uita morti occumbant obuiam* (fr. CCXXII)—come from an adaptation of this speech.

None of the assignations I have described is without probability but it must be remembered that many tragic heroes could have claimed to have lost their kingdom, that a quarrel between Agamemnon and Menelaus took place in Ennius' *Iphigenia*, that the justice of the war against Troy was questioned in this play and that in the *Alexander* a suppliant at an altar was threatened with death. Furthermore there is a lack of hard evidence that Cicero knew Ennius' *Telephus* and a constant possibility that Seneca and the metricians quote imperial rather than republican tragedy. I have therefore printed under the title *Telephus* only the pieces quoted with this title by Verrius and Nonius.

CXLII

Geel interpreted this verse as spoken by Telephus, while still unrecognised, to the Greek princes; he compared the verses of Euripides, μή μοι φθονήσητ', ἄνδρες Ἑλλήνων ἄκροι, | εἰ πτωχὸς ὢν τέτληκ' ἐν ἐσθλοῖσιν λέγειν (703), parodied by Aristophanes at *Ach.* 496–8 μή μοι φθονήσητ', ἄνδρες οἱ θεώμενοι, | εἰ πτωχὸς ὢν ἔπειτ' ἐν Ἀθηναίοις λέγειν | μέλλω περὶ τῆς πόλεως.[3] E. W. Handley makes[4] the speaker someone trying to silence Telephus. This is much more plausible. The reply of Aristophanes' chorus to Dicaeopolis—557–8 ἄληθες ὠπίτριπτε καὶ μιαρώτατε; | ταυτὶ σὺ

---

[1] Cf. Aristophanes' parody of the Euripidean scene at *Ach.* 326 ff., *Thesm.* 689 ff.
[2] *SIFC* N.S. XXII (1947), 73–6.
[3] For parallel sentiments cf. Euripides, *Ion* 670 ff.
[4] *BICSL* Suppl. V (1957), p. 34.

406

τολμᾷς πτωχὸς ὢν ἡμᾶς λέγειν;—may reflect the Greek that Ennius was adapting. *Muttire* and *piaculum* are both strongly abusive words, unlikely to be used by a person, even one apparently destitute, of his own behaviour.

280 muttire: 'speak out of place, at the wrong time, in the wrong company'; normally applied to the behaviour of slaves in comedy.

plebeio: elsewhere in republican drama only at Plautus, *Poen.* 515; *plebs* is likewise rare (Ennius, *Trag.* 388, Plautus, *Pseud.* 748, Caecilius, *Com.* 185); *populus* and *popularis* on the other hand are fairly common. *Plebs* was probably already in the early second century confined to certain set phrases of the constitutional lawyers.

piaculum est: cf. Plautus, *Truc.* 220–3 *nos diuitem istum meminimus atque iste pauperes nos:* | *uorterunt sese memoriae; stultus sit qui id miretur.* | *si eget, necessest nos pati: amauit, aequom ei factum est.* | *piaculumst miserere nos hominum rei male gerentum.* Elsewhere the associations of the word *piaculum* are unquestionably sacral; cf. Varro, *Ling.* 6.29 *dies fasti per quos praetoribus omnia uerba sine piaculo licet fari*, Gellius 10.15.10 (from Fabius Pictor) *si quis ad uerberandum ducatur, si ad pedem eius supplex procubuerit, eo die uerberari piaculum est.* The dramatists may simply be using a sacral word that had become one of general abuse in the common language (cf. μιαρός, *scelestus*) but it is possible that they are consciously giving a Roman cast to their personages' sentiments. The notion that the inherited class structure, distribution of political power and constitutional forms were divinely sanctioned was firmly rooted in the thought of the republican aristocracy. The annalists (cf. Livy 4.1–6, 6.39–41) represented both sides in the struggle of the orders as taking seriously the question of divine approval for projected social and political change. A similar ideology appears in Ionian epic (cf. *Il.* 2.196–7 θυμὸς δὲ μέγας ἐστὶ διοτρεφέων βασιλήων, | τιμὴ δ' ἐκ Διός ἐστι, φιλεῖ δέ ἑ μητίετα Ζεύς, 204–6 εἷς κοίρανος ἔστω, | εἷς βασιλεύς, ᾧ ἔδωκε Κρόνου πάϊς ἀγκυλομήτεω | σκῆπτρόν τ' ἠδὲ θέμιστας ἵνα σφίσι βουλεύῃσι) but it is noteworthy that neither Homer's Odysseus (*Il.* 2.246–64) nor his quiescent lower orders (2.272–7) bring religious arguments against the behaviour of Thersites. Attic tragedy on the whole represents the power of princes as resting on popular consent rather than divine grant. Sophocles' Agamemnon denies the right of the bastard Teucer to be heard (*Ai.* 1226–63) but defends his own authority in naturalistic terms. The fragments suggest that the princes of Euripides' Τήλεφος spoke similarly.[1]

---

[1] Cf., however, Aeschylus, *Eum.* 625 ff., Euripides, *Or.* 1167 ff.

CXLIII

The beggar's rags in which Euripides dressed the Mysian king caused an immediate sensation and were probably a necessary part of all later dramatic presentations of the story; cf. Aristophanes, *Ach.* 432 ff. and the scholia, Diogenes, *Epist.* 34.2 Τήλεφόν τε τὸν Ἡρακλέους ἡνίκα εἰς Ἄργος παρεγένετο, πολὺ χείρονι σχήματι τοῦ ἡμετέρου ἐμφανισθῆναι πτώχ' ἀμφίβληστρα (Burges: ἀμφίβλητα codd.) σώματος λαβόντα ῥάκη ἀλκτήρια τύχης (~ Euripides, fr. 697), Accius, *Trag.* 613–16 *quem ego ubi aspexi, uirum memorabilem | intui uiderer, ni uestitus taeter uastitudo | maestitudo praedicarent hominem esse*, 617 *nam etsi opertus squalitate est luctuque horrificabili* (Vossius: *horrificali* codd.).

The source from which Nonius drew these two quotations is obscure and Lindsay put a question mark against his suggestion[1] that they are made in the order in which they occur in the text of the play. Strzelecki[2] has repeated Lindsay's suggestion much more dogmatically. However even where his own excerptions are concerned (e.g. in the case of Lucilius) Nonius sometimes seems to quote in reverse order. 'Lindsay's law' can be a treacherous guide to the student of republican poetry. The trimeter *regnum reliqui septus mendici stola* could come from a speech of Telephus revealing himself to one of the Greek personages of the play (so Vahlen and Strzelecki) but Geel's assignation of it to the prologue seems much more likely.

281 squalida saeptus stola: cf. Sophocles, *O.K.* 1597 ἔλυσε δυσπινεῖς στολάς (of Oedipus), Euripides, *Rhes.* 503 πτωχικὴν ἔχων στολήν, 712 ῥακοδύτῳ στολᾷ πυκασθείς (of Odysseus). The word *stola* is used thrice elsewhere in republican tragedy apparently like the Attic στολή but does not occur in comedy. In the mid first century it denoted the particular dress of the aristocratic *matrona*.[3]

Saepire is properly used of fences, walls etc. (cf. Plautus, *Curc.* 36, Ennius, *Trag.* 88); for Ennius' hyperbole cf. Plautus, *Cas.* 921–2 *saepit ueste id qui estis ⟨mulieres⟩* (add. Loman). | *ubi illum saltum uideo opsaeptum, rogo ut altero sinat ire.*

CXLIV

The phrase *haec enodari* was taken by Geel to refer to Menelaus' desire to continue the war and by Welcker[4] to Telephus' defence of the Mysian resistance. Wecklein[5] interpreted it much more plausibly as Telephus'

---

[1] *RhM* LVII (1902), 202.   [2] *Eos* XLII, fasc. I (1947), 30–5.

[3] Cf. Horace, *Sat.* 1.2.69–71 *numquid ego a te | magno prognatum deposco consule cunnum | uelatumque stola mea cum conferbuit ira*, 99 *ad talos stola demissa et circumdata palla.*

[4] *Die griech. Trag.* p. 488.   [5] *SB München* 1878, vol. 2, 221.

explanation of the oracle ὁ τρώσας καὶ ἰάσεται and put the fragment in a speech by Achilles rejecting the pleas of the Achaean leaders to help his enemy Telephus and recalling the number of Greeks killed by Telephus' Mysians during the earlier expedition.

283 leto dati: a phrase from the sacral language,[1] taken up by Pacuvius (*Trag.* 148), Lucretius (5.1007), Virgil (*Aen.* 5.806, 11.172, 12.328), Ovid (*Met.* 1.670 et al.) and others; varied by Plautus with *morti dare* (*Asin.* 608, *Merc.* 472; cf. Horace, *Sat.* 2.3.197) and *ad mortem dare* (*Amph.* 809), by Accius with *leto offerre* (*Trag.* 117) and *leto mittere* (491; cf. Plautus, *Capt.* 692 *te morti misero*).

284 sunt: not normally separated from its complement by a heavy metrical pause. Vahlen compared Plautus, *Capt.* 884–5 *quid tu per barbaricas urbis iuras? —quia enim item asperae | sunt ut tuom uictum autumabas esse*, Terence, *Ad.* 330–2 *me miseram. quid iam credas aut quoi credas? nostrumne Aeschinum, | nostram uitam omnium, in quo nostrae spes opesque omnes sitae | erant? qui sine hac. . . .* An excited tone of voice is perceptible in both the comic passages.

enodari: three times elsewhere in tragedy, once in comedy (Turpilius 14).

CXLV

Geel, Schöll,[2] Welcker and Jahn[3] reconstructed a scene of Euripides' Τήλεφος in which the hero appealed to Clytemnestra for help and was advised to seize the baby Orestes and fly to the altar at the moment of discovery.[4] Wecklein however showed[5] that none of the evidence adduced demands the presence of Clytemnestra at any point in the action and argued that the seizure of Orestes (parodied by Aristophanes at *Ach.* 326 ff. and *Thesm.* 689 ff.) was Telephus' own sudden stratagem.

This leaves the word *illam* in the Ennian fragment, which Geel took to refer to Clytemnestra, a little difficult to handle on the supposition that Ennius was adapting Euripides' tragedy. However the collocation *aduorsum illam mihi* at

---

[1] Cf. Varro, *Ling.* 7.42 *in funeribus indictiuis quo dicitur 'ollus leto datus est'*, Festus, p. 304.1 ff.

[2] *Beitr.* pp. 134 ff.

[3] *Telephos und Troilos. Ein Brief an Herrn F. G. Welcker in Bonn* (Kiel, 1841), pp. 16 ff.

[4] Cf. the story of Themistocles and the wife of Admetus (Thucydides 1.136 f.).

[5] *SB München* 1878, vol. 2, 201 ff.; cf. Wilamowitz, *Griechische Dichterfragmente* II (Berlin, 1907), pp. 69 ff., Robert, *Die griech. Heldensage* III 2 i, p. 1157 n. 8.

the beginning of an iambic trimeter is odd[1] if not impossible[2] and *mihi* seems quite otiose. Textual corruption may therefore bar all possibility of understanding the Latin fragment, to say nothing of using it to reconstruct the original Greek tragedy.

285 profiteri: once elsewhere in tragedy (Trag. inc. 52) where the quantity of the first syllable is indeterminate; three times in comedy where the syllable is twice short (Plautus, *Capt.* 480, Terence, *Eun.* 3) and once long (Plautus, *Men.* 643).

286 aduorsum: 'in the presence of'; cf. Plautus, *Bacch.* 698 *immo si audias quae dicta dixit me aduorsum tibi* et al.

CXLVI

Geel took Ennius' trimeter to be a version of the Euripidean verse quoted by the scholiast on Aristophanes, *Ach.* 8—κακῶς ὀλοίατ' (Dobree: ὄλοιτ' ἄν codd.) · ἄξιον γὰρ Ἑλλάδι (720)—and made Telephus the object of a curse uttered by Achilles. A view of this kind is much more plausible than that of Welcker, according to which the disguised Telephus is uttering a curse upon himself. The verse of Euripides quoted by the scholiast on Aristophanes, *Ach.* 446—καλῶς ἔχοιμι, Τηλέφῳ δ' ἀγὼ φρονῶ (fr. 707)—is more oblique than the Ennian.[3] In any case, to the ancient mind curses were dangerous things likely to rebound on the head of the deliverer even when directed elsewhere. Ennius' Telephus would have had to be an extraordinarily enlightened character to make so light of the power of evil words as to speak them against himself.

287 qui illum di deaeque: the regular order of words in curses and blessings introduced by a particle; cf. P. Langen, *RhM* XII (1857), 428 f.

Qui ablative is restricted in republican drama almost entirely to curse formulae; even these are much more frequently introduced by *ut* or have no particle at all.

Di deaeque was a traditional Roman way of referring to deity (see the examples collected at *T.L.L.* v i 909.14 ff.); the Attic dramatists used a similar formula very occasionally (cf. Aeschylus, *Theb.* 88 ἰὼ ἰὼ θεοὶ θεαί τε, 93–4, Menander, *Sam.* 184–5 τοῖς θεοῖς . . . καὶ ταῖς θεαῖς).

---

[1] See above on *vv.* 126–7.

[2] Cf. Plautus, *Epid.* 179 *neque sexta aerumna acerbior Herculi quam illa mihi obiectast* (iambic tetrameter) and F. Skutsch, *Plaut. u. Rom.* p. 136 n. 1.

[3] At *Ach.* 509 ff. Dicaeopolis curses the Lacedaemonians and at *Thesm.* 466 ff. Mnesilochus says he hates Euripides. A speech by Euripides' devious hero lies behind both the comic speeches.

magno mactassint malo: cf. Afranius, *Com. tog.* 264 *di te mactassint malo,* Pomponius, *Atell.* 137 *at te di omnes cum consilio calue mactassint malo*; the normal dramatic curse however employs the verb *perdere.* Ennius' phrase is yet another example of the use of auspicious words in inauspicious circumstances.[1] Behind *mactare* seem to lie such phrases as *macte hac illace dape polucenda esto* (Cato, *Agr.* 132.1) and *macte esto uirtute* (Pacuvius, *Trag.* 146), which appeal for an augment of strength.[2] The phrase *deum aliquo mactare* (cf. Cicero, *Vat.* 14 *cum puerorum extis deos manis mactare soleas*) probably preceded in use the regular classical *aliquid deo mactare.* It is possible that the oxymoron was a coinage of popular slang rather than of tragedy, for Plautus uses *infortunio mactare* and similar phrases too often for one to be comfortable in labelling them paratragic.

CXLVII

The Aldine editor changed *incendere* to *incendier* while Mercerus declared *incendere* to be used intransitively. *T.L.L.* VII i 870.22 produces only one dubious example of this use: Ps. Hieronymus, *in Ioh.* p. 580D *maxime incendente zelo Iudaeorum.* Vahlen suggested that the subject of *incendere* was expressed in the following verse.

Geel interpreted the fragment as spoken by the chorus after the quarrel between Agamemnon and Menelaus. But *ciuitatem...Argiuum* must refer to the whole Argive state, not just its leaders. Vahlen interpreted it as spoken by one of the Greek princes after the disguised Telephus' defence of the Mysian resistance and compared Aristophanes' parody of Euripides: *Ach.* 576–7 ὦ Λάμαχ', οὐ γὰρ οὗτος ἄνθρωπος πάλαι | ἅπασαν ἡμῶν τὴν πόλιν κακορροθεῖ; (~ Euripides, fr. 712). But *incendere* in metaphorical usage was no equivalent of κακορροθεῖν; it denoted the stirring up of passion (cf. Plautus, *Asin.* 420 *qui semper me ira incendit, Pseud.* 201 *nimis sermone huius ira incendor,* Terence, *Phorm.* 185–6 *quod eius remedium inueniam iracundiae?* | *loquarne? incendam*). Telephus' speech was meant to allay passion.

288 ciuitatem...Argiuum: 'ciues Argiui'; cf. Cicero, *Font.* 14 *quid coloni Narbonenses?...quid Massiliensium ciuitas?* For the type of periphrasis cf. Euripides, *Or.* 612 ἔκκλητον Ἀργείων ὄχλον, 846 Ἀργεῖον... λεών.

---

[1] See above on fr. LXXXVI.
[2] See H. J. Rose and O. Skutsch, *CQ* XXXII (1938), 220 ff., XXXVI (1942), 15 ff.

COMMENTARY

CXLVIII

Geel took this verse to refer to the journey of the Greeks to Troy. Scarcely a happy idea. Welcker interpreted it as spoken to the Greeks by Calchas about Telephus' journey to Argos at the behest of Apollo. A view of this type is likely to prove correct. Handley[1] compared the aeolic verses uttered by Euripides' chorus after the decision of Agamemnon and Menelaus to accept Telephus as guide on a second journey to Troy (Pap. Berol. 9908, col. II 7–10 σὲ γὰρ Τε[γ]εᾶτις ἡμῖν | Ἑλλάς, οὐ[χ]ὶ Μυσία, τίκτει | ναύταν σύν τινι δὴ θεῶν | καὶ πεμπτῆρ' ἁλίων ἐρετμῶν) but the operative phrase of these verses, σύν τινι . . . θεῶν, seems to have a much wider reference than Ennius' *deum . . . de consilio*.

289 itiner . . . conatum: cf. Pacuvius, *Trag.* 44–5 *dolet pigetque magis magisque me conatum hoc nequiquam itiner*, Virgil, *Aen.* 10.685 *ter conatus utramque uiam*.

The form *itiner* occurs 6 times in tragedy against *iter* twice; comedy on the other hand has *iter* 15 times, *itiner* only 3 (Plautus, *Merc.* 913, 929, Turpilius, *Com.* 207).

THYESTES

The title *Thyestes* is given to Ennius by Cicero, Verrius and Nonius; to Pacuvius by the unreliable Fulgentius[2] and to Gracchus by Priscian (*Gramm.* II 269.8). Cicero once (*Orat.* 184) names the title alone. I have followed all editors since Columna in giving the verse here quoted to Ennius' *Thyestes* (fr. CLI). It seems to me possible that the words attributed to Pacuvius' *Thyestes* by Fulgentius, *non illic luteis aurora bigis* (uulgo: *biiugis* codd.) are the work of neither Pacuvius nor the grammarian but come from Ennius' tragedy.

The stories told about the feud between the two sons of Pelops, Atreus and Thyestes, over the kingship of Mycenae were many and various.[3] Most students have accepted Welcker's view[4] that Ennius' tragedy was set in

[1] *BICSL* Suppl. V (1957), 38.
[2] *Serm. ant.* 57 *Pacuuius in tragoedia Thyestis* (uulgo: *Tietis* [*ti&Zis* R: *Tiethis* D: *tegetis* BE] codd.). On the character of Fulgentius' quotations of republican poetry see Wessner, *Comment. phil. Ienenses* VI 2 (1899), 135 ff., F. Skutsch, *RE* VII i (1910), 219, Timpanaro, *SIFC* N.S. XXII (1947), 199 ff.
[3] See Robert, *Die griech. Heldensage* I, pp. 285 ff., 293 ff., A. Lesky, *WSt* XLIII (1922/3), 172 ff. (= *Gesammelte Schriften* [Bern, 1966], 519 ff.).
[4] *Zeitschr. f. d. Alt.* 1838, 229 ff. (= *Die griech. Trag.* pp. 678 ff.).

Mycenae and showed how Atreus punished Thyestes for an act of adultery with his wife Aerope by first banishing him, then recalling him and offering him at a feast the limbs of his murdered children to eat.

I propose to argue that these events took place before the action of the *Thyestes* and that Ennius' tragedy was set at the court of Thesprotus in Epirus. Thyestes cursed his brother and inquired of Apollo how he might be avenged. Apollo replied that a son sired on his own daughter would be the avenger. In the meantime drought struck Mycenae and Apollo told the inquiring Atreus that it would only end when Thyestes returned. Thyestes came to Epirus where his daughter Pelopia was being cared for by king Thesprotus, saw Pelopia unprotected and raped her (doubtlessly in ignorance of her true identity).[1] Atreus arrived in Epirus just afterwards, was struck by Pelopia's beauty and took her in marriage from Thesprotus, believing her to be Thesprotus' daughter. The rape of Pelopia and her marriage with Atreus in my view formed the action of the *Thyestes*.

Ladewig[2] seems to have included not only these events but also certain that took place at Mycenae many years later in his reconstruction of the *Thyestes*. Pelopia exposed in the mountains by Mycenae the child she conceived as a result of Thyestes' assault. This child was found being reared by herdsmen and accepted by Atreus as his own with the name of Aegisthus. In young manhood Aegisthus discovered who his real father was and fulfilled Apollo's prophecy by killing Atreus.

Of the pieces quoted by Nonius as from Ennius' *Thyestes* four (frs. CLIV, CLV, CLVI, CLIX) have a content relevant to the discussion of the theme of the tragedy.

Ribbeck,[3] who accepted Welcker's view of the plot, interpreted fr. CLIV, *eheu mea fortuna ut omnia in me conglomeras mala*, and fr. CLIX, *quam mihi maxime hic hodie contigerit malum*, as spoken by Thyestes after he discovered what he had eaten at the feast. In the language of both fragments (see below, pp. 424, 426) there is an element of oxymoron implying that the speaker's woes are not unmixed. I would therefore suggest that Thyestes' discovery that he had lain with his daughter was the cause of his remarks; confidence that Apollo's oracle will be fulfilled tempers horror at the thought of incest.

Welcker interpreted fr. CLV, *set me Apollo ipse delectat ductat Delphicus*, as referring to an oracle delivered during Thyestes' first period of exile (after his intrigue with Aerope) and advising him to return to Mycenae. This

---

[1] Two versions of the story of Thyestes' incest are conflated at Hyginus, *Fab.* 87–8. Robert (*Die griech. Heldensage* I, p. 299) rightly treated the reference to Sicyon at 88.3 as an error.

[2] *Anal. scen.* p. 38.

[3] *Die röm. Trag.* p. 203. The fragments are not mentioned at *Quaest. scen.* pp. 267 f.

oracle is not recorded anywhere in the mythographical tradition. There are two versions of the story of his return; according to one he returned secretly in quest of vengeance;[1] according to the other he came back openly on Atreus' invitation.[2] I should interpret fragment CLV as either from a speech by Thyestes about the oracle concerning his daughter[3] or from a speech by Atreus about the oracle telling him to recall Thyestes from his second spell of exile.[4]

Ribbeck interpreted fr. CLVI, *sin flaccebunt* (Gulielmius: *inflaccebunt* codd.) *condiciones repudiato et reddito*, as spoken by Thyestes to supporters of a plot to overthrow Atreus. Ladewig, who believed that Thyestes' recognition of the grown Aegisthus was Ennius' central theme, argued that the words of the fragment are taken most naturally as those of a father betrothing his daughter and that the only possible marriage offered by the later history of the Pelopids is that which Atreus contracted with Pelopia in the belief that she was Thesprotus' daughter.[5] He nevertheless failed to realise that his acute observation necessarily set Ennius' tragedy outside Mycenae and at a time some years before the discovery of Aegisthus' identity.

Thyestes was a personage of at least two other republican tragedies, the *Atreus* and the *Pelopidae* of Accius. The *Atreus* quite certainly dealt with the feast while the meagre remains of the *Pelopidae* can be very plausibly interpreted[6] as dealing with the recognition of Aegisthus. If Thyestes had any role in Accius' *Chrysippus* it could only have been a minor one.

Cicero nowhere names the title *Atreus*[7] but frequently quotes from the Accian tragedy that bore it.[8] Where utterances by Atreus are concerned, those at *Off.* 3.102 and *Tusc.* 4.55 (cf. *De orat.* 3.217) are quoted along with Accius' name; those at *Sest.* 102 (cf. *Planc.* 59), *Phil.* 1.34 and *Off.* 1.97 are associated with the age of Sulla by Seneca at *Dial.* 3.20.4; those at *Nat. deor.* 3.68, which certainly come from a play about the feast, were given to the *Atreus* by Columna[9] and have been left there by scholars ever since; that at

---

[1] Accius, *Trag.* 198 ff.; cf. Aeschylus, *Ag.* 1583 ff.
[2] Hyginus, *Fab.* 88.1, Seneca, *Thy.* 288 ff.
[3] Hyginus, *Fab.* 87, Apollodorus, *Epit.* 2.14, Schol. Stat. *Theb.* 1.694, Servius, Verg. *Aen.* 11.262; cf. Sophocles, fr. 226, Seneca, *Ag.* 28–36, 48–9, 294.
[4] Hyginus, *Fab.* 88.5.   [5] Hyginus, *Fab.* 88.6.
[6] Cf. Welcker, *Die griech. Trag.* p. 370, Ribbeck, *Quaest. scen.* p. 335, *Die röm. Trag.* 457 ff., Robert, *Die griech. Heldensage* I, p. 298.
[7] At *De orat.* 3.217 the phrase *Atreus fere totus* refers to the speeches made by a personage Atreus; see above on fr. XCV.
[8] A Virgilian scholium (*Breu. Exp. Georg.* 1.1) ties the quotation at *Tusc* 2.13 to the *Atreus*.
[9] *Q. Ennii Frag.* p. 419.

THYESTES

Tusc. 5.52 was given by Welcker to the *Atreus*[1] and restored to the *incerta* by Ribbeck; the trimeter quoted at *Pis.* 82 is said by Asconius to have been spoken to Atreus by Thyestes in a play by Accius.

A verse which is quoted four times in *Nat. deor.* (2.4, 2.65, 3.10, 3.40), twice with Ennius' name, is quoted by Festus as from the *Thyestes* (fr. CLIII). Its context is obscure.

Columna gave the curse of Thyestes quoted at *Pis.* 43 and *Tusc.* 1.106 (at the latter place with Ennius' name) to the tragedy *Thyestes* (fr. CL). In Welcker's view the verses were uttered by Thyestes as he prepared to leave Mycenae.[2] The verb *habeat* suggests to me that Thyestes is speaking about Atreus to a third party.[3] Drowning was thought by the ancients to be a particularly terrible form of death[4] and may have been wished on Atreus as the worst fate Thyestes, gorged with his own children's flesh, could think of at that moment. However, the verses would have had much more dramatic force if at the time of speaking the sea separated Thyestes from Mycenae and Atreus was known to be coming in search of him. One might compare the prayer of Aeschylus' Danaids that Zeus should wreck the ships of their Egyptian pursuers (*Hik.* 29–39).

The lyric dialogue between Thyestes and a number of 'hospites' which Cicero quotes at *De Orat.* 3.164 and *Tusc.* 3.26 was also given by Columna to the *Thyestes* (fr. CXLIX). Welcker interpreted this dialogue as having taken place between a chorus of Cretan women, the attendants of Atreus' wife Aerope, and Thyestes when the latter emerged from the dining hall. Ribbeck, Mueller, Vahlen and Robert held to Welcker's view, although, in the meantime,[5] one of its main supports, Valckenaer's identification of Euripides' Κρῆσσαι with the Θυέστης, had collapsed. If one believes that both the *Thyestes* and the *Atreus* dealt with the feast and accepts Welcker's interpretation of the dialogue there is no reason for assigning the verses to one play rather than the other. On the other hand my reconstruction of the plot of the *Thyestes* and a more careful interpretation of the wording of the verses permits a rational decision.

Warmington, whatever one might think of his reconstruction of the whole play,[6] was right to set the scene of the dialogue at the court of Thesprotus. Thyestes has been standing on the stage for some time and

---

[1] *Zeitschr. f. d. Alt.* 1838, 221 ff., *Die griech. Trag.* 357 ff.
[2] Cf. Aeschylus, *Ag.* 1600–1 μόρον δ᾽ ἄφερτον Πελοπίδαις ἐπεύχεται, | λάκτισμα δείπνου ξυνδίκως τιθεὶς ἀρᾷ, Horace, *Epod.* 5.86 ff.
[3] Cicero writes *penderes* at *Pis.* 43 to suit his own discourse.
[4] See Synesius, *Epist.* 4, Immisch, *RhM* LXXX (1931), 98 ff. See below on fr. CL. [5] See below, p. 418.
[6] *Remains of Old Latin* I, pp. 346 ff.; Warmington proposed two scenes, one at the court of Atreus in Mycenae, the second at that of Thesprotus in Epirus.

addresses his command to the chorus of 'hospites' as they enter. The scene would be roughly parallel with that opening the Ἡρακλεῖδαι of Euripides, where a chorus of citizens enter to find the foreigner Iolaos standing by the altar of a temple and are addressed as ξένοι (78, 84, 93).[1] If Bentley was right in assigning the trochaic verses *Tantalo prognatus Pelope natus qui quondam a socru* (Bentley: *socero* codd.) | *Oenomao rege Hippodameam raptis nanctus nuptiis* to the same play as the bacchiacs, they must come from the same context; i.e. they are spoken by Thyestes either in a prologue speech or, more likely, in a reply to a question from the 'hospites'. Welcker's interpretation[2] has the absurd result of putting this background information at the end of the play at a time when the chorus would know quite well who Thyestes was.

Welcker interpreted the words quoted by Cicero at *Orat.* 184 as from a *Thyestes* (fr. CLI)—*quemnam te esse dicam qui tarda in senectute*—as a question addressed by Atreus to a servant come to reveal Thyestes' plans for revolution. They look to me like the question whose answer is quoted at *Tusc.* 3.26 (fr. CXLIX *b*).

An account by a tragic Thyestes of the proceedings of the feast is quoted by Cicero at *De orat.* 3.217 and *Tusc.* 4.77: *ipsus hortatur me frater ut meos malis miser | mandarem natos*. Scriverius gave these words to the Thyestes of Accius' *Atreus*, along with the words of Atreus quoted in addition at *Tusc.* 4.77: *maior mihi moles maius miscendumst malum, | qui illius acerbum cor contundam et comprimam*. The latter clearly belong to a play whose principal theme was the feast. The former however need not come from the same play. Indeed they look as if they come from an account of the feast given by Thyestes some time afterward. The immediate reaction of a father so treated would have been one of disgust rather than anger. The possibility should be weighed that the words *ipsus hortatur me frater ut meos malis miser mandarem natos* belong to Ennius' *Thyestes*.

To illustrate a type of fallacious argument the anonymous rhetorician quotes as from a tragedy by Ennius two tetrameters—*eho tu di quibus (studiis* M) *est potestas (est potest at* M) *motus (motum* M) *superum atque inferum,* | *pacem (pacem enim* M) *inter sese (se* E) *conciliant, conferunt concordiam* (Rhet. inc. *Her.* 2.39 = fr. CLXII) and names the speaker. Editors of the rhetorician's treatise (including Marx) make the speaker Cresphontes and most collectors of the tragic fragments put the verses in Ennius' homonymous play (see

---

[1] For *hospites* in an address by a foreigner to citizens cf. Plautus, *Poen.* 678.

[2] Hartung (*Euripides Restitutus* I, p. 176) gave the trochaic verses to the *Atreus* and interpreted them as spoken by Thyestes on arrival at Mycenae near the beginning of Accius' play. Ribbeck (*Quaest. scen.* p. 268, *Die röm. Trag.* p. 201) separated them from the bacchiacs and put them at the beginning of the *Thyestes*.

above, p. 271). In 1888 Vahlen[1] pointed out that the manuscript tradition (*thesprotum* M: *threspontem* [*thespontem* d] E) was best interpreted so as to make Thesprotus the speaker and assigned the verses to the *Thyestes*, without, however, abandoning Welcker's view that the feast was the principal theme of this play. Warmington accepted Vahlen's assignation of fr. CLXII and interpreted it as spoken by Thesprotus to Atreus when the latter came to Epirus in search of Thyestes. Nevertheless, in view of the conflict in the manuscript tradition, I have left fr. CLXII among the *incerta*.

In the rhetorical section of his work Charisius quotes two pieces of tragic verse addressed to Thesprotus: at p. 364.21 ff. illustrating the trope 'sarcasmos'—*rite Thesprotum pudet* (Grotius: *pudeat* cod.) *Atrei* (Buecheler: *rei* cod.) *quod ipse a Tantalo ducat genus*; at p. 374.8 ff. illustrating the figure of thought 'transmutatio personarum'—*Thesprote si quis sanguine exortam tuo | prolem inter †arass† sacram immolet, | quid meritus hic sit dubium an cuiquam fuat* (Fabricius: *fiat* cod.)? The distinction between figures of speech and figures of thought makes its first appearance in extant literature in the anonymous treatise addressed to Herennius. The source of this treatise must have contained examples of dramatic poetry to illustrate fully the two kinds of figure but true to his principles[3] the anonymous rhetorician quotes only illustrations of vicious figures. At least two of his illustrations turn up again and again in work not directly dependent on his[4] and it is possible that his source was also the ultimate source of most of the quotations of republican drama in the later discussion of rhetorical figures, including those at Charisius pp. 364.21 ff. and 374.8 ff.

Welcker assigned Charisius' two quotations to Accius' *Pelopidae*,[5] offering no interpretation of the first and taking the second to be addressed to Thesprotus in his absence. Ladewig[6] seems to have accepted Welcker's interpretation of the second and gave both to the *Thyestes*. Ribbeck[7] argued that the two quotations must come from speeches delivered at the court of Thesprotus in a play whose theme was the marriage of Atreus and Pelopia. Believing that the *Thyestes* and the *Pelopidae* were set in Mycenae he had no title to attach to his postulated play. If my reconstruction of Ennius' *Thyestes* is correct and if Charisius and the anonymous rhetorician draw on a common source there is a good chance that the *Thyestes* was the play quoted.

---

[1] *Ind. lectt. Berlin* 1888/9, 17 (= *Op. ac.* I 417). Cf. Wecklein, *Festschr. Urlichs*, 1 ff.
[2] 4.18.
[3] 4.18 *nam hic nihil prohibet in uitiis alienis exemplis uti*.
[4] 2.34 (Ennius, *Trag.* 208–16), 4.18 (Ennius, *Ann.* 103, 109).
[5] *Die griech. Trag.* p. 370. See above, p. 414.
[6] *Anal. scen.* p. 40.
[7] *Quaest. scen.* p. 335, *Die röm. Trag.* pp. 628 f.

COMMENTARY

A number of Ennius' tragic verses quoted by Cicero without the name of the play or the speaker (*Tusc.* 3.44 [fr. CLXXV], *Off.* 1.26 [fr. CLXIX*b*], 2.23 [fr. CLXXXII], 3.104 [fr. CLXXXIV], *Rep.* 1.49 [CLXIX*a*]) have been more or less tentatively given to the *Thyestes*.[1] The quotation at *Tusc.* 3.44 can be proved not to come from here.[2] Contexts for the others can be imagined in several of Ennius' plays.

Many Greek tragedians have the title Θυέστης recorded against their names: Sophocles,[3] Euripides, Apollodorus of Tarsus, Carcinus, Chaeremon, Cleophon, Diogenes of Sinope and Agathon. Valckenaer[4] suggested that in Euripides' case Θυέστης was an alternative title of Κρῆσσαι, that Ennius adapted this script, that fr. CLIII, *aspice hoc sublime candens quem uocant omnes Iouem*, was part of Ennius' version of the three Euripidean trimeters ὁρᾷς τὸν ὑψοῦ τόνδ' ἄπειρον αἰθέρα | καὶ γῆν πέριξ ἔχονθ' ὑγραῖς ἐν ἀγκάλαις; | τοῦτον νόμιζε Ζῆνα, τόνδ' ἡγοῦ θεόν (fr. 941) and that the trimeters therefore belonged to the Κρῆσσαι/Θυέστης.

Ribbeck[5] dismissed the idea of a direct link between Euripides, fr. 941 and Ennius, fr. CLIII on the grounds that Cicero would not have made his own version for *Nat. deor.* 2.65 if this were the case. But Cicero's philosophical source may have introduced the Greek trimeters merely with the name of Euripides; in that case Cicero would have been quite ignorant of their specific origin. Nevertheless the similarity between Euripides and Ennius is not as great as Valckenaer thought and the doctrine is such as might have been mentioned in many Euripidean tragedies.

An inscription found in the Piraeus (*I.G.* II² 2363; cf. *C.I.G.* III 6047). revealed that Κρῆσσαι and Θυέστης denoted separate scripts[6]

Most of the citations of Θυέστης occur in anthologies of moral apophthegms and give no information about the plot of Euripides' tragedy. A scholium on Aristophanes, *Ach.* 433 enables one to deduce that Thyestes appeared on stage at one point dressed in rags. Two fragments of Aristophanes' Προαγών (461, 462) have been thought to parody a description given somewhere in Θυέστης of the cannibal feast.[7] Even if this were the

---

[1] See Ribbeck, *Quaest. scen.* p. 267. Vahlen printed them all under the title *Thyestes* in his first edition but only those quoted at *Tusc.* 3.44 in his second.
[2] See above, p. 395.
[3] The distinctive symbols, ᾱ, β̄ and γ̄ (Pap. Mus. Brit. 2110) and the epithet Σικυώνιος appear in various citations.
[4] *Diatribe*, pp. 12, 47.
[5] *Quaest. scen.* p. 267.
[6] See Wilamowitz, *Anal. Eur.* p. 153 (cf. *Obseruationes Criticae in Comoediam Graecam Selectae* [Diss. Berlin, 1870], p. 12).
[7] See Bergk, *Aristophanis Fragmenta* (Berlin, 1840), pp. 248 ff., Wilamowitz, *Anal. Eur.* p. 153 n. 4.

418

case one should not conclude that Euripides' tragedy was set in Mycenae and included the feast within its action. It remains a possible model of the Ennian *Thyestes*.

CXLIX

(*a*) For the context of this fragment see above, p. 415.

Bentley[1] altered the *abnutas* of Cicero's manuscripts to *renutas* in order to procure a complete bacchiac tetrameter; Vahlen in his first edition altered *adiri* to *adirier* for the same purpose. However such 'contracted' tetrameters commonly occur in the company of full tetrameters; cf. Plautus, *Bacch.* 1127, 1128, *Cas.* 658, 662, 675, 685, 691, 694, 695, 702, 703, *Cist.* 35, *Men.* 763, 763 *a*, 771, *Most.* 125, 783, Terence, *Andr.* 483; Pacuvius, *Trag.* 202 and 340 can be scanned similarly.[2]

290 quidnam est... quod: a common variant of adverbial *quid* (*quidnam*); cf. Plautus, *Cas.* 630, *Curc.* 166, *Epid.* 560, 570, *Men.* 677, *Most.* 69 (*quid est quid* CD), *Pseud.* 9, *Truc.* 238, 295, Terence, *Haut.* 613, *Eun.* 558, 559, *Ad.* 305.

te adiri abnutas: cf. Euripides, *Herakles* 1218 τί μοι προσείων χεῖρα σημαίνεις φόνον;

The intensive form *abnutare* occurs only here and at Plautus, *Capt.* 611 in republican drama; perhaps with some difference of meaning from *abnuere* (Plautus, *Capt.* 481, *Merc.* 50, *Truc.* 6); 'why do you keep nodding...?'

(*b*) Scriverius had suspected the existence of poetic rhythm in *qualis enim tibi ille uidetur Tantalo prognatus Pelope natus qui quondam a socero Oenomao rege Hippodameam raptis nanctus nuptiis Iouis iste quidem pronepos*, and Bentley procured trochaic verse from *Tantalo* down to *pronepos* by altering *socero* to *socru*. The phrase *Iouis iste quidem pronepos*, however, looks like Cicero's own interjection. In a tragic quotation one would expect the sequence Iuppiter–Tantalus–Pelops (cf. *Trag. inc.* 101–3) or Pelops–Tantalus–Iuppiter (cf. Ennius, *Trag.* 273).

To procure three regular bacchiac tetrameters Bentley inserted *meo* before *tanta uis sceleris in corpore haeret*. Several scholars since have tried to achieve the same purpose with different additions, none nearly so plausible. The words in question form a unit of verse (cretic dimeter + trochaic metron) occasionally found in Plautine comedy (e.g. *Amph.* 245, *Rud.* 667).[3] Bacchiacs and cretics sometimes occur in the same monologue or dialogue but it is diffi-

---

[1] *Emendationes Cic. Tusc.* pp. 45 ff.   [2] Cf. Strzelecki, in *Tragica* I, 64.

[3] A. Spengel detected several Plautine examples in his *De Versuum Creticorum Vsu Plautino* (Diss. Berlin, 1861), pp. 43 f. but later recanted (*Reformvorschl.* pp. 105 ff.). See also Ribbeck, *Coroll.* p. xxxiii, Leo, *Die plaut. Cant.* p. 17, Strzelecki, in *Tragica* I, 65.

cult to find switches from one verse form to the other accompanied by such little apparent change of verbal tone as there is here; Plautus, *Men.* 579 ff. and *Pseud.* 1126 ff. are as near to the form which Cicero's manuscripts give Ennius' canticum as I can find.

291 Tantalo prognatus: 'the grandson of Tantalus'; cf. Plautus, *Cas.* 398–9 *utinam tua quidem ⟨ista⟩ (add.* Guyet) *sicut Herculei praedicant | quondam prognatis, in sortiendo sors deliquerit.* The word *prognatus* occurs in the epitaph of Scipio Barbatus (*C.I.L.* I² 7), comparatively often in early epic and tragedy, 14 times in Plautus (only once however in trimeters [*Capt.* 170]), not at all in the rest of comedy.¹ It is normally a high-falutin variant of *natus*.

socru: cf. Nonius, p. 223.21 *socrus et masculino genere ueteres dici posse uoluerunt*, Priscian, *Gramm.* II 233.7. The normal forms in republican drama are *socer* (*socerus*), *soceri* etc.

292 raptis nanctus nuptiis: cf. Livy 30.14.2 *raptae prope inter arma nuptiae.*
There is no need to restore *nanctu'st*; for this type of nominal phrase in republican drama see above on *v.* 78.

293 nolite hospites ad me adire: this mode of expressing the negative imperative is very rare in republican drama compared with others; I count only 21 instances in Plautus and eight in Terence. The tone can be gathered from the edictal formula *nequis fecisse uelit.*²

ilico istic: compare and contrast Plautus, *Bacch.* 1140 *ilico ambae manete*, *Merc.* 912 *atque istic sta ilico*, *Most.* 1064 *ilico intra limen isti astate*, *Rud.* 836 *illic astate ilico*, Caecilius, *Com.* 118 *manete ilico*, Terence, *Ad.* 156 *ilico hic consiste*, *Phorm.* 195 *sta ilico*. A gesture by the actor (cf. *v.* 290 *abnutas*) would have taken the place of the verb.

294 contagio mea: 'contact with me'; cf. Plautus, *Amph.* 30–1 *atque ego quoque etiam, qui Iouis sum filius, | contagione mei patris metuo malum.* In Attic tragedy the sight,³ voice⁴ and physical proximity⁵ of the polluted

---

¹ See Fraenkel, *Horace*, p. 82 n. 4.
² Cf. D. Daube, *Forms of Roman Legislation* (Oxford, 1956), pp. 37 ff.
³ Sophocles, *O.T.* 1424–8, *O.K.* 1483–4, Euripides, *El.* 1195–7, *Herakles* 1155–6, 1231, *Or.* 512–15.
⁴ Aeschylus, *Eum.* 448, Euripides, *El.* 1292–4, *Herakles* 1218–19, *Or.* 428, 481.
⁵ Aeschylus, *Theb.* 597 ff., Euripides, *Herakles* 1233, *Hipp.* 946–7, *I.T.* 1159 ff., 1226 ff., *Or.* 512–15.

person was generally thought to be dangerous. For the pollution of touch cf. Seneca, *Thy.* 104.

umbraue obsit: for the idea that the shadow has personality and power cf. Pliny, *Nat.* 28.69 *magi uetant eius causa contra solem lunamque nudari aut umbram cuiusquam ab ipso respergi,* N.T. *Act. ap.* 5.15 ὥστε καὶ εἰς τὰς πλατείας ἐκφέρειν τοὺς ἀσθενεῖς...ἵνα ἐρχομένου Πέτρου κἂν ἡ σκιὰ ἐπισκιάσῃ τινὶ αὐτῶν.

CL

For the context of this fragment see above, p. 415.

Bentley was the first to recognise its metrical character, i.e. two trochaic tetrameters followed by catalectic tetrameters. Garatoni took the words *naufragio expulsus uspiam*[1] as the end of a catalectic tetrameter. Such tetrameters, lacking in diaeresis after the second metron but with caesura after the fourth arsis, are transmitted in the remains of republican drama a number of times.[2] However, although *uspiam* occurs only once elsewhere in the orations (*Flacc.* 29), the phrase should be taken as Cicero's own gloss on the poetic matter he intended to quote verbatim.[3]

The contents of Thyestes' curse, shipwreck, no grave or rest for the dead man, are commonplace in Greek poetry[4] and Roman.[5] It would, however, have sounded more horrible to Roman ears than to Greek; the Romans allowed even criminals burial.[6]

296–7 ipse summis saxis fixus asperis, euisceratus, | latere pendens: cf. Euripides, *Tr.* 448–50 κἀμέ τοι νεκρὸν φάραγγες γυμνάδ' ἐκβεβλημένην | ὕδατι χειμάρρῳ ῥέουσαι, νυμφίου πέλας τάφου, | θηρσὶ δώσουσιν δάσασθαι, Virgil, *Aen.* 8.668–9 *et te Catilina minaci | pendentem scopulo.*

One might have expected *saxis affixus;* cf. Plautus, *Persa* 295 *te cruci ipsum adfigent propediem alii,* fr. 48.

Euiscerare occurs only once elsewhere in republican drama (Pacuvius, *Trag.* 4); for similar formations see above on *v.* 93.

For *latere pendens* cf. Plautus, *Cas.* 390 *pedibus pendeas.*

297 tabo sanie et sanguine atro: for the syntax *a, b et c* cf. Plautus, *Amph.* 1011, *Asin.* 571, *Merc.* 548, 678–9 et al.

---

[1] Before *naufragio* cod. V has the scholium 'uersus Ennii'.
[2] See above on fr. XCIX.
[3] For this mode of quotation see above on fr. XVIII.
[4] Cf. Archilochus, fr. 79a Diehl³, Sophocles, *Ai.* 1177.
[5] Cf. Catullus 108, Horace, *Epod.* 5.86 ff., 10.21 ff., Virgil, *Aen.* 4.620, Propertius 4.5.3, Ovid, *Ib.* 165 f.   [6] See *Dig.* 48.24.

For *tabum* and *sanies* of the recently dead cf. Virgil, *Aen.* 8.487, Valerius Flaccus 4.749.

For *sanguis ater* of the dead cf. Virgil, *Georg.* 3.221, *Aen.* 3.28, 33, 622, Livy 38.21.9 et al.

298 neque sepulcrum quo recipiat habeat: for *recipere* intransitive (perhaps from the nautical language) cf. Plautus, *Bacch.* 294 *rursum in portum recipimus.*

portum corporis: the idea of Hades as the λιμήν to which the soul passes after the voyage of life is common in Greek poetry.[1] The classical Roman writers frequently took it up.[2] Ennius' Thyestes expresses much more primitive sentiments. Whether they come from fifth-century Athens or early second century Rome is hard to say.

299 remissa humana uita: the phrase *uitam reddere* might have been expected; cf. the alternation *leto dare/mittere* (above on *v.* 283).

corpus requiescat malis: cf. Virgil, *Ecl.* 10.33 *molliter ossa quiescant, Aen.* 6.328, 6.371, Tibullus 2.4.49–50, 2.6.30, Ovid, *Am.* 3.9.67–8. The Greek poets frequently used εὕδειν of the dead; cf. Homer, *Il.* 14.482, Sophocles, *O.K.* 621 et al.

Requiescat picks up *recipiat* and *remissa*; the compound is quite rare in republican drama (Plautus, *Capt.* 505, *Epid.* 205, *Truc.* 209, Terence, *Eun.* 405) compared with the simple form.

CLI

For the context of this fragment see above, p. 416.

The context of Cicero's discourse demands *illa in Thyeste* rather than *ille in Thyeste*. The latter reading cannot be defended on the analogy of those phrases discussed above on fr. xcv.

Bothe made Cicero's quotation into a regular bacchiac tetrameter by substituting the archaic form *senecta* for *senectute*. But Cicero's whole argument is that the tragedian's words would sound prosy without the accompanying pipe music. In the mid first century *senecta* was a highly poetic word; it occurs only here in Cicero's writings, not at all in Caesar's, only six times in

---

[1] Cf. Sophocles, *Ant.* 1284, Euripides, *Herakles* 770, *Ba.* 1361–2, Trag. inc. fr. 369, Leonidas, *A.P.* 7.264.2, 7.452.2, 7.472*b*.1.

[2] Cf. Cicero, *Tusc.* 1.118, 5.117, Virgil, *Aen.* 7.598–9, Seneca, *Ag.* 591–2.

Livy's and then for special effect.[1] Bacchiacs are not always arranged in tetrameters κατὰ στίχον: cf. Plautus, *Men.* 571 ff., *Rud.* 185 ff., Varro, *Men.* 405.

300 quemnam te esse dicam qui: a pompous variant of *quis tu es qui* (cf. Plautus, *Epid.* 637, fr. 44). The comedians quite often insert *dicam* + accusative and infinitive in direct and indirect questions of a solemn or mock-solemn character; cf. Plautus, *Cas.* 616 *qua ego hunc amorem mi esse aui dicam datum?, Curc.* 1 *quo ted hoc noctis dicam proficisci foras?, Merc.* 516 *quid nomen tibi dicam esse?, Most.* 1042 *quod id esse dicam uerbum nauci nescio, Pseud.* 744 *sed quid nomen esse dicam ego isti seruo?, Trin.* 2 *sed finem fore quem dicam nescio, Truc.* 70–1 *quos quidem quam ad rem dicam in argentariis | referre habere nisi pro tabulis nescio,* 689 *quam esse dicam hanc beluam?,* Terence, *Phorm.* 659–60 *utrum stultitia facere ego hunc an malitia | dicam...incertus sum.* The manner of speech may have originated in tragedy; cf. Euripides, *Rhes.* 38–9 τί σε φῶ | νέον ἀγγέλλειν;, fr. 1 ποίαν σε φῶμεν γαῖαν ἐκλελοιπότα | πόλει ξενοῦσθαι τῇδε;

tarda in senectute: cf. Plautus, *Poen.* 508–9 *fugitaui senes: scibam aetati tardiores,* Horace, *Sat.* 2.2.87–8 *seu | dura ualetudo inciderit seu tarda senectus,* Virgil, *Aen.* 9.610–11 *nec tarda senectus | debilitat uiris animi mutatque uigorem,* Tibullus 2.2.19–20 *dum tarda senectus | inducat rugas inficiatque comas.*

CLIII

The context of this fragment is obscure.

In his second edition of Ennius' remains Vahlen withdrew his adherence to the view that Ennius had written *aspice hoc sublimen candens...*[2] but argued that Festus' lemma was SVBLIMEN. The existence of this word is highly dubious and Virgil, *Georg.* 1.242 does not exemplify it. The reading SVBLIMEN of some of Paulus' manuscripts can be explained as arising from the etymology which Paulus reports. The Festus manuscript's SVBLIMEM could come from a quotation in Verrius' lexicon omitted in Festus' epitome without change of lemma.

For the identification of the chief element and the chief god cf. Euripides, *Tr.* 884–6 ὦ γῆς ὄχημα κἀπὶ γῆς ἔχων ἕδραν, | ὅστις ποτ' εἶ σύ, δυστόπαστος εἰδέναι, | Ζεύς, εἴτ' ἀνάγκη φύσεος εἴτε νοῦς βροτῶν, fr. 877 ἀλλ' αἰθὴρ τίκτει σε, κόρα, | Ζεὺς ὃς ἀνθρώποις ὀνομάζεται, fr. 941 ὁρᾷς

---

[1] See R. M. Ogilvie on 2.40.5 (Oxford, 1965).
[2] Cf. Scaliger, *Notae ad Varronis Libros de Re Rustica* (Paris, 1573), p. 235, Ritschl, *RhM* VII (1850), 556 ff. (= *Op.* II 462 ff.); for the contrary view see W. Heraeus, *Philologus* LV (1896), 197 ff., Haffter, *Glotta* XXIII (1935), 251 ff.

τὸν ὑψοῦ τόνδ' ἄπειρον αἰθέρα | καὶ γῆν πέριξ ἔχονθ' ὑγραῖς ἐν ἀγκάλαις; | τοῦτον νόμιζε Ζῆνα, τόνδ' ἡγοῦ θεόν, Philemon, fr. 91.4 ἀὴρ ὃν ἄν τις ὀνομάσειε καὶ Δία, Ennius, *Trag.* 356–7 *istic est is Iuppiter quem dico, quem Graeci uocant* | *aerem.* For other pantheistic re-interpretations of divine names cf. Euripides, *Ba.* 275–6, *Phoin.* 685–6, fr. 781.11–13, fr. 944.

It is noteworthy that at fr. 941 Euripides makes the chief element the fluid lower atmosphere.[1] The Stoic philosophers nevertheless interpreted these verses as representing the doctrine they took from Empedocles, according to which the outer fiery element of the universe was identifiable with Ζεύς. The source of Probus, Verg. *Ecl.* 6.31 corrupted part of Euripides' Greek into τὸν περιέχοντα ὑγρὰν ἀγκάλαις τὸν νόμιζε Ζῆνα while Cicero at *Nat. deor.* 2.65, adapting a Stoic source, turned ὑγραῖς ἐν ἀγκάλαις into the vague *tenero circumiectu.* It is therefore not out of the question that Ennius had fr. 941 or another Euripidean passage of similar character before him when he wrote *aspice hoc sublime candens quem uocant omnes Iouem.* For a fairly clear case of the importation of philosophical ideas foreign to the drama being adapted see above on fr. cx.

301 hoc sublime candens: for the adjective and present participle in asyndeton cf. Virgil, *Georg.* 2.377 *grauis incumbens, Aen.* 3.70 *lenis crepitans,* 8.559 *inexpletus lacrimans.*

quem uocant omnes Iouem: for the gender of the relative cf. Lucretius 4.132 *in hoc caelo qui dicitur aer.*

For *uocare* in the sense of *nominare* cf. Ennius, *Trag.* 64 *quapropter Parim pastores nunc Alexandrum uocant.* Cicero may have believed that Ennius wrote *inuocant;* the context of his own argument gave support to such a belief.

CLIV

For the context of this fragment see above, p. 413.

The strongest rebuke to *fortuna* in the rest of republican drama seems to be Terence, *Hec.* 406 *o fortuna ut numquam perpetuo's data.* There is a certain oxymoron in Ennius' expression that could hardly have stood in his original. Whereas τύχη usually denoted a purely neutral chance and θεός and δαίμων powers that were as likely to be hostile as beneficent, the *fortuna* of the republican dramatists was a benevolently positive power.[2]

302 conglomeras: only here and at Pacuvius, *Trag.* 20a in republican drama; the simple verb *glomerare* does not occur at all; in classical Latin it is rather more frequent than the compound.

---

[1] Cf. fr. 839.   [2] See above on fr. lxxix.

CLV

For the context of this fragment see above, pp. 413 ff.

Bergk[1] was the first to see that the transmitted words could be scanned as a cretic dimeter followed by a catalectic trochaic dimeter; cf. Aeschylus, *Choe.* 585–6, 594–5, *Eum.* 491–2, 500–1, 956–7, 976–7, *Pers.* 126–7, 133–4, Plautus, *Amph.* 223, 233, *Cas.* 628, *Rud.* 677.[2]

303 delectat ductat Delphicus: where two nearly synonymous words stand together in asyndeton the shorter normally precedes the longer but cf. Plautus, *Bacch.* 934 *misere male*, *Merc.* 681 *disperii perii*, *Mil.* 1204 *donaui dedi*, Terence, *Andr.* 248 *contemptus spretus*, 855 *confidens catus*, *Haut.* 404 *disperii perii*, *Eun.* 377 *abduc duc*, Pacuvius, *Trag.* 263 *retinete tenete*; in general see Lindholm, *Stilistische Studien*, pp. 80 ff.

CLVI

For the context of this fragment see above, p. 414.

304 sin flaccebunt condiciones repudiato: the metaphorical use of *flaccere* is odd but cf. Cicero, *Ad Q. fr.* 2.15.4 *Messalla flaccet*, 'Messalla's candidature is not standing up straight, support for it is weak'. Ennius may have been employing a current colloquialism; cf. Terence's use of *stare* in connection with plays that gained public support (*Phorm.* 10, *Hec.* 15).

For *condicionem repudiare* cf. Plautus, *Trin.* 454–5, Rhet. inc. *Her.* 4.34, Cicero, *Quinct.* 46, *Phil.* 13.37 et al.

CLVII

The context of this fragment is obscure.

305 sonitus auris meas pedum pulsu increpat: contrast Plautus, *Curc.* 203 *sonitum et crepitum claustrorum audiu*, *Aul.* 811, *Cist.* 543, *Curc.* 229, *Mil.* 1393, *Rud.* 661, *Trin.* 1093; compare Homer, *Il.* 10.535 ἵππων μ' ὠκυπόδων ἀμφὶ κτύπος οὔατα βάλλει, Sophocles, *Ant.* 1187–8 καί με φθόγγος οἰκείου κακοῦ | βάλλει δι' ὤτων, Accius, *Trag.* 479–80 *sonitus . . . peruasit auris*, Plautus, *Amph.* 333 *hinc enim mihi dextra uox auris ut uidetur uerberat*, Virgil, *Aen.* 8.582–3 *grauior neu nuntius auris | uolneret*, 12.618–19 *impulit auris | confusae sonus urbis*, Seneca, *Med.* 116 *aures pepulit hymenaeus meas*. For the alliterative *pedum pulsu* cf. Virgil, *Aen.* 12.334–5 *gemit ultima pulsu | Thraca pedum*, 445 *pulsuque pedum tremit excita tellus*, Livy 27.37.14

---

[1] *Philologus* XXXIII (1874), 274 (= *Kl. phil. Schr.* I 342).
[2] W. Christ (*Metrik der Griechen und Römer*[2], Leipzig, 1879, pp. 407 ff.) seems to have been the first to set out the Plautine examples of this unit of verse.

sonum uocis pulsu pedum modulantes. For *pede (pedibus) pellere (pulsare)* cf. Ennius, *Ann.* 1 *Musae quae pedibus magnum pulsatis Olympum,* Lucretius 5.1402, Catullus 61.14, Horace, *Carm.* 1.4.13, 1.37.1–2, 3.18.15–16, Ovid, *Ars* 1.112, Seneca, *Oed.* 433 et al.

CLVIII

The context of this fragment is obscure.

306 impetrem facile ab animo ut cernat: cf. Livy 43.23.8 *temptare eum destitit cum appareret quantum in eo praesidii esset nec tamen impetrare ab animo posset ut impensam in rem maximi ad omnia momenti faceret;* Ennius' phrase was perhaps an elevated variant of *impetrem facile a me ut cernam* (cf. Caelius *ap.* Cic. *Fam.* 8.12.1, Petronius 52.5).

CLIX

For the context of this fragment see above, p. 413.

Vahlen[1] was the first to perceive that the words transmitted form a cretic dimeter followed by a catalectic dimeter; cf. *v.* 303.

There is in the phrase *contigerit malum* an oxymoron parallel with that in *v.* 302. Unlike Greek τυγχάνειν Latin *contingere* is normally used of fortunate events; cf. Caper, *Gramm.* VII 98.8 *accidere aliquid aduersi dicito, contingere aliquid pulchri,* a statement which applies quite well to the usage of republican drama.

307 hic hodie: cf. Plautus, *Cist.* 16, *Most.* 1129, *Persa* 710, *Rud.* 1417, Terence, *Haut.* 162, 176, *Eun.* 230, 800.

CLX

The context of this fragment is obscure.

The iambic word *parat* standing in the fifth foot of the iambic trimeter offends against the laws established by Bentley and Luchs[2] regarding word division in the final metron of this type of verse and similar ones. Only four other tragic verses (Ennius 388, Accius 442, 618, Trag. inc. 21) offend in the same way. Nevertheless there seems to be nothing against *parat* from the point of view of usage; cf. Cicero, *Verr.* 1.67 *id agi atque id parari ut...,* *Fam.* 2.5.2 *ea para meditare cogita quae esse in eo ciui ac uiro debent,* Accius, *Trag.* 634 *atque id ego semper sic mecum agito et comparo.*

308 putat: 'reputat'; cf. Caecilius, *Com.* 41 *non haec putas? non haec in corde uersantur tibi?,* Virgil, *Aen.* 6.332 *multa putans sortemque animo miseratus iniquam,* 8.522 *multaque dura suo tristi cum corde putabant.*

---

[1] *Ind. lectt. Berlin* 1888/9, 9 n. (= *Op. ac.* 1 408 n.).
[2] In G. Studemund, *Studia in priscos scriptores Latinos* 1, 8 ff.

ADDENDA

p. 5   On performances in foreign languages at Roman *ludi* see Mariotti, *Belfagor* xx (1965), 37.

p. 53 n. 5   On Cicero's methods of quoting republican poetry see also E. Malcovati, *Cicerone e la poesia* (Pavia, 1943 [*Ann. d. fac. di Lett. e Filos. d. Univ. di Cagliari*, xiii]), pp. 89 ff.

p. 167   Phrases such as *uersus Ennianus* and *hemistichium Ennii* in the Virgilian scholia refer to Virgil; the Ciceronian scholiast's *Ennianum hemistichium*, however, can only refer to Ennius (Mariotti).

p. 169   Treating *deum* as a monosyllable would produce a normal diaeresis (Mariotti).

p. 176   *Male uolentes famam tollunt, bene uolentes gloriam* could be Achilles' reply to an ambassador's *summam tu tibi pro mala uita famam extolles et pro bona paratam gloriam* (Mariotti).

p. 192   Vahlen linked the words *uitae cruciatum* in his 'index sermonis'.

p. 193   F. H. Sandbach, however, reminds me of ἀποτυμπανισμός.

p. 213   *Neque...inuitam* could be defended as a colloquial lapse by a speaker intending to say *neque...non inuitam* and being distracted by the positive attribute *dementem*. For such lapses in accumulations of negatives see Mariotti in *Lanx satura N. Terzaghi oblata* (Univ. of Genoa, 1963), 263.

p. 227   Menander, *Sam.* 140, 159, 196 are not strictly relevant: Chrysis alleges, and Demeas believes, the child to be her own. Plutarch, *Mor.* 489 F is hard to explain away (Sandbach).

p. 246   However for molossic words at head of cretic tetrameter see Plautus, *Most.* 109 et al. (Mariotti).

p. 294   Mercier must have intended *ui* as an ablative of quality; cf. Ennius, *Ann.* 303–4 *Cornelius suauiloquenti | ore Cethegus*, Accius 636 *Tereus indomito more atque animo barbaro* (Mariotti).

p. 362   For the undesirability of those who *uolucri semper spe et cogitatione rapiuntur a domo longius* see Cicero, *Rep.* 2.7.

p. 372   For Probus' interpretation cf. Rutilius Namatianus 1.57 *qui continet omnia Phoebus*.

p. 388   *Marito* could be interpreted as 'ita ut eius maritus sit' (Mariotti).

p. 405 n. 4   The common version of the two myths to which Horace refers could be restored by taking *pauper et exul* with *Telephus et Peleus* as a form of 'double zeugma' (Brink).

p. 423   Cf. Lucretius 1.414–15 *ne tarda prius per membra senectus | serpat*.

BIBLIOGRAPHY

I list (*a*) those collections of the fragments of Ennius' tragedies which have furthered in some measure the establishment and understanding of the text and (*b*) those editions of the sources which I have used in making my own collection. Work pertaining to particular tragedies or fragments is not listed here but cited where it has relevance. Serial titles are abbreviated according to the system of *L'Année philologique*.

(*a*)

STEPHANVS, R. & H. *Fragmenta poetarum ueterum Latinorum quorum opera non extant...undique a Rob. Stephano summa diligentia olim congesta, nunc autem ab Henrico Stephano eius filio digesta...* (Geneva [?], 1564), pp. 108–28.

COLVMNA, H. Q. *Ennii poetae uetustissimi quae supersunt fragmenta ab Hieronymo Columna conquisita disposita et explicata ad Ioannem filium* (Naples, 1590), pp. 305–475.

DELRIVS, M. A. *Martini Antonii Delrii ex societate Iesu syntagma tragoediae Latinae* (Antwerp, 1593), pp. 96–107, 163–7.

SCRIVERIVS, P. *Petri Scriuerii collectanea ueterum tragicorum...fragmenta et circa ipsa notae breues. quibus accedunt singulari libello castigationes et notae uberiores Gerardi Ioannis Vossii* (Leiden, 1620), pp. 8–38, 13–60.

BOTHE, F. H. *Poetae scenici Latinorum: recensuit Fridericus Henricus Bothe: vol. v: fragmenta* (Leipzig, 1834), pp. 23–78.

RIBBECK, O.[1] *Scenicae Romanorum poesis fragmenta: recensuit Otto Ribbeck: vol. i: tragicorum Latinorum reliquiae* (Leipzig, 1852), pp. 13–62, 248–78.

VAHLEN, J.[1] *Ennianae poesis reliquiae: recensuit Ioannes Vahlen* (Leipzig, 1854), pp. 91–150.

RIBBECK, O.[2] *Scaenicae Romanorum poesis fragmenta: secundis curis recensuit Otto Ribbeck: vol. i: tragicorum fragmenta* (Leipzig, 1871), pp. xvi–xxxviii, 15–75.

MVELLER, L. Q. *Enni carminum reliquiae...emendauit et adnotauit Lucianus Mueller* (St Petersburg, 1884), pp. 91–135, 212–44.

RIBBECK, O.[3] *Scaenicae Romanorum poesis fragmenta: tertiis curis recognouit Otto Ribbeck: vol. i: tragicorum fragmenta* (Leipzig, 1897), pp. 17–85.

VAHLEN, J.[2] *Ennianae poesis reliquiae: iteratis curis recensuit Ioannes Vahlen* (Leipzig, 1903), pp. cc–ccxi, 118–203.

428

WARMINGTON, E. H.¹ *Remains of Old Latin: newly edited and translated by E. H. Warmington*: vol. I: *Ennius and Caecilius* (London, 1935), pp. 217–383.

KLOTZ, A., SEEL, O., VOIT, L. *Scaenicorum Romanorum fragmenta*: vol. I: *tragicorum fragmenta: adiuuantibus Ottone Seel et Ludouico Voit edidit Alfredus Klotz* (Munich, 1953), pp. 44–111.

WARMINGTON, E. H.² *Remains of Old Latin: newly edited and translated by E. H. Warmington*: vol. I: *Ennius and Caecilius*: revised edition (London, 1956), pp. 217–383.

(b)

[Acro]
    in carmina Horatii commentarius, ed. O. Keller (Leipzig, 1902).

Apuleius
    pro se de magia liber (apologia), ed. R. Helm (Leipzig, 1905).
    metamorphoseon libri, ed. R. Helm (Leipzig, 1907).
    de mundo liber, ed. P. Thomas (Leipzig, 1908).
    de deo Socratis liber, ed. P. Thomas (Leipzig, 1908).

Aurelius
    'ad Frontonem epistulae', ed. M. P. J. van den Hout (in *M. Cornelii Frontonis epistulae* [Leiden, 1954]).

Catullus
    carminum liber, ed. R. A. B. Mynors (Oxford, 1958).

Charisius
    artis grammaticae libri, ed. C. Barwick (Leipzig, 1925).

Cicero
    Academicorum priorum liber secundus, ed. O. Plasberg (Leipzig, 1908).
    ad Atticum epistularum libri, I–VIII ed. W. S. Watt (Oxford, 1965); IX–XVI ed. D. R. Shackleton Bailey (Oxford, 1961).
    pro L. Cornelio Balbo oratio, ed. A. Klotz (Leipzig, 1916).
    de claris oratoribus liber qui Brutus inscribitur, ed. H. Malcovati (Leipzig, 1965).
    pro M. Caelio oratio, ed. A. Klotz (Leipzig, 1915).
    de diuinatione libri, ed. O. Plasberg, W. Ax (Leipzig, 1938).
    ad familiares epistularum libri, ed. H. Sjögren (Leipzig, 1923–25).
    de fato liber, ed. O. Plasberg, W. Ax (Leipzig, 1938).
    de finibus bonorum et malorum libri, ed. T. Schiche (Leipzig, 1915).
    rhetorici libri (de inuentione), ed. E. Ströbel (Leipzig, 1915).
    de amicitia liber qui Laelius inscribitur, ed. K. Simbeck (Leipzig, 1917).
    de natura deorum libri, ed. O. Plasberg (Leipzig, 1911).
    de officiis libri, ed. C. Atzert (Leipzig, 1923).
    de optimo genere oratorum liber, ed. A. S. Wilkins (Oxford, 1903).
    oratoris liber, ed. P. Reis (Leipzig, 1932).

BIBLIOGRAPHY

Cicero (*cont.*)
  de oratore libri, ed. A. S. Wilkins (Oxford, 1902).
  in L. Calpurnium Pisonem oratio, ed. R. G. M. Nisbet (Oxford, 1961).
  de republica libri, ed. K. Ziegler³ (Leipzig, 1955).
  pro Sex. Roscio Amerino oratio, ed. A. Klotz (Leipzig, 1922).
  pro P. Sestio oratio, ed. A. Klotz (Leipzig, 1915).
  topicorum liber, ed. A. S. Wilkins (Oxford, 1903).
  Tusculanarum disputationum libri, ed. M. Pohlenz (Leipzig, 1918).
  in C. Verrem actionis secundae libri, ed. A. Klotz (Leipzig, 1923).
  'scholia Gronouiana', ed. T. Stangl (in *Ciceronis orationum scholiastae*
    [Vienna, 1912], pp. 279–351).
Diomedes
  'artis grammaticae libri', ed. H. Keil (in *Grammatici Latini*, vol. 1
    [Leipzig, 1857], pp. 297–530).
Donatus
  'artis grammaticae liber', ed. H. Keil (in *Grammatici Latini*, vol. IV
    [Leipzig, 1864], pp. 367–402).
  in comoedias Terentii commentarius, ed. P. Wessner (Leipzig, 1902–5).
Festus
  de uerborum significatu libri, ed. A. Thewrewk de Ponor, W. M.
    Lindsay (Leipzig, 1913).
Gellius
  noctium Atticarum libri, ed. M. Hertz, C. Hosius (Leipzig, 1903).
Hieronymus
  epistulae, ed. I. Hilberg (Vienna, 1910–18).
Horatius
  epodon liber, ed. F. Klingner (Leipzig, 1939).
Isidorus
  de differentiis uerborum libri, ed. F. Arévalo (Rome, 1802).
Iulius Rufinianus
  'de figuris sententiarum et elocutionis liber', ed. C. Halm (in *Rhetores
    Latini minores* [Leipzig, 1863], pp. 38–47).
Iulius Victor
  'artis rhetoricae liber', ed. C. Halm (in *Rhetores Latini minores* [Leipzig,
    1863], pp. 371–448).
Lucretius
  de rerum natura libri, ed. H. Diels (Berlin, 1923).
Macrobius
  conuiuiorum primi diei Saturnaliorum libri, ed. J. Willis (Leipzig, 1963).
Nonius
  de compendiosa doctrina libri, ed. J. H. Onions, W. M. Lindsay (Leipzig,
    1903). I quote according to Mercier's pagination.

Orosius
  historiarum aduersum paganos libri, ed. C. Zangemeister (Leipzig, 1889).
Ouidius
  artis amatoriae libri, ed. E. J. Kenney (Oxford, 1961).
  heroidum epistulae, ed. A. Palmer (Oxford, 1898).
Paulus
  excerpta ex libris Pompei Festi
Phaedrus
  fabularum libri, ed. J. P. Postgate (Oxford, 1920).
Plautus
  comoedia quae Bacchides inscribitur, ed. F. Ritschl, G. Goetz (Leipzig, 1886).
  comoedia quae Poenulus inscribitur, ed. F. Ritschl, G. Goetz, G. Loewe (Leipzig, 1884).
Poeta incertus
  Aetnae liber, ed. F. R. D. Goodyear (Cambridge, 1965).
Pompeius
  'commentum artis Donati', ed. H. Keil (in *Grammatici Latini*, vol. v [Leipzig, 1868], pp. 95–312).
Priscianus
  'institutionum grammaticarum libri', ed. M. Hertz (in *Grammatici Latini*, voll. II–III i [Leipzig, 1855–9]).
  'de metris fabularum Terentii liber', ed. H. Keil (in *Grammatici Latini* vol. III ii [Leipzig, 1860], pp. 418–29).
[Probus]
  'in libros Vergilii commentarius', ed. H. Hagen (in *Appendix Seruiana* [Leipzig, 1902], pp. 323–87).
Quintilianus
  institutionis oratoriae libri, ed. L. Radermacher (Leipzig, 1907–35).
Rhetor incertus
  de ratione dicendi ad C. Herennium libri, ed. F. Marx (Leipzig, 1923).
Rutilius Lupus
  'de figuris elocutionis libri', ed. C. Halm (in *Rhetores Latini minores* [Leipzig, 1863], pp. 3–21).
Sallustius
  de bello Iugurthino liber, ed. A. W. Ahlberg, A. Kurfess[2] (Leipzig, 1954).
Seneca
  controuersiarum libri, ed. H. J. Mueller (Vienna, 1887).
Seneca
  liber qui Diui Claudii ἀποθέωσις *per saturam inscribitur* (*Apocolocyntosis*), ed. C. F. Russo[3] (Florence, 1961).

431

BIBLIOGRAPHY

Seruius

in libros vergilii commentarius et scholia quibus commentarius auctus est.
I–V *Aeneidos*, ed. E. K. Rand et al. (Lancaster–Oxford, 1946–65);
VI–XII *Aeneidos*, ed. G. Thilo (Leipzig, 1884); I–IV *georgicorum*, ed.
G. Thilo (Leipzig, 1887).

Terentius

comoedia quae Adelphi inscribitur, ed. R. Kauer, W. M. Lindsay,
O. Skutsch (Oxford, 1958).

comoedia quae Eunuchus inscribitur, ed. R. Kauer, W. M. Lindsay,
O. Skutsch (Oxford, 1958).

Tacitus

annalium libri, ed. C. Halm, G. Andresen, E. Koestermann (Leipzig,
1936).

Varro

de lingua Latina libri, ed. G. Goetz, F. Schoell (Leipzig, 1910).

Vergilius

Aeneidos libri, ed. R. Sabbadini (Rome, 1930).

eclogarum liber, ed. R. Sabbadini (Rome, 1930).

georgicorum libri, ed. R. Sabbadini (Rome, 1930).

'scholia Veronensia', ed. H. Hagen (in *Appendix Seruiana* [Leipzig,
1902], pp. 393–450).

CONCORDANCE I

This edition	Ribbeck³	Vahlen²
i	13–15	1–3
1	9	15
2	16	16
3–4	2–3	10–11
5	7–8	4
6–7	4–5	13–14
8	1	6
9	6	5
10–12	10–12	7–9
13	336–7	19
14	18	20
15	17	17
16–20	20–4	22–6
21	32	34
22–30	25–31	27–33
31	19	21
32–46	39–53	54–68
47–9	54–6	69–71
50–61	Inc. inc. 5–16	35–46
62–3	34–5	47–8
64	38	53
65	62	78
66	36	50
67	33	51
68	37	49
69–71	57–9	72–5
72–3	60–1	76–7
74–7	Accius 357–60	—
78–9	91–2	100–1
80	89	85
81–94	75–88	86–99
95	340–1	376
96–7	95–6	112–13
98	70–1	107–8
99	65	105
100	93	82
101	94	111
102	68	103
103	90	102
104–5	63–4	80–1

CONCORDANCE I

This edition	Ribbeck[3]	Vahlen[2]
106–7	72–3	83–4
108	69	106
109–10	66–7	104
111	74	79
112	97	120
113	100	115
114	102–3	117
115	101	114
116	104	116
117–18	105–6	118–19
119	98–9	122
120–4	107–11	123–7
125–31	[114–19]	—
132	120	129
133	113	133
134	121	134
135–6	124–5	130
137	112	128
138–9	126–7	131–2
140	130	139
141–2	128–9	137–8
143	131	140
144	134	147
145	136	149
146–7	132–3	145–6
148	135	148
149	149	178
150–1	141–2	177
152	155	193
153–4	139–40	158–9
155–6	160–1	188–9
157–8	156–7	190–2
159	151	185
160	148	179
161–2	158–9	186
163	143	156
164	144	157
165	150	181
166	145	180
167–8	146–7	182–3
169	152–4	184
170	137–8	160
171	163	196
172–4	165–7	199–201
175	172	206

CONCORDANCE I

This edition	Ribbeck³	Vahlen²
176	176	209
177–8	173–4	211–12
179	162	195
180	164	202
181	175	207
182	168–9	197–8
183–4	170–1	203–4
xciv	Iphigenia fr. x	—
185–7	199–201	242–4
188–91	177–80	215–18
192	202	245
193–4	181–2	213–14
195–202	183–90	234–41
203	193	224
204–6	194–6	225–7
207	203	233
208–16	205–13	246–54
217–18	231–2	276–7
219–20	220–1	260–1
221	240	273
222–3	216–17	257–8
224	233	278
225–7	226–7	266–8
228	Inc. inc. 161	269
229–31	228–30	270–2
232–3	222–3	262–3
234–6	237–9	284–6
237–8	214–15	255–6
239–40	243–4	287–8
241–2	235–6	282–3
243	234	280
244	241	279
245	218	281
cxviii	Melanippa fr. vi	294
246	249–50	295
247	246–8	291
248–9	245–6	289–90
250	251	292
251	252	293
252	254	297
253	255	296
254–7	257–60	300–3
258	265	306
259	256	298
260	262–4	304–5

28-2

CONCORDANCE I

This edition	Ribbeck³	Vahlen²
261	261	308
262	266	307
263	267	309
264	268	310
265	271	318
266–9	273–6	320–3
270–1	269–70	316–17
272	278	324
273–4	279–80	325–6
275	282	328
276	283	311
277	281	327
278	277	315
279	284	329
280	286	331
281	287	330
282	285	339
283–4	289–90	334–5
285–6	293–4	337–8
287	288	333
288	291	332
289	292	336
290	306	352
291–2	Inc. inc. 108–9	357–8
293–5	303–5	349–51
296–9	309–12	362–5
300	298	348
301	302	345
302	307	353
303	295	361
304	301	344
305	296	341
306	299–300	346–7
307	308	360
308	297	340
clxi	372	380
309–10	122–3	342–3
311	400	422
312	313	173
313–15	366–8	398–400
316–18	351–3	142–4
clxvii	398–9	412–13
319	374	381
320	381–2	404–5
321	363	299

436

CONCORDANCE I

This edition	Ribbeck³	Vahlen²
322–33	314–25	161–72
334	332	176
335	354	205
336–7	360–1	392–3
338–40	369–71	354–6
341	378	395
342	375	401
343	364	394
344–5	356–7	219–21
346	——	429
347	338	18
348	379	402
349	389	409
350	380	403
351	388	210
352–3	347–8	388–9
354	396	411
355	——	*Varia* 48
356–60	——	*Varia* 54–8
361	335	187
362	355	420
363	362	121
364	349	150
365–6	——	*Annales* 9
367	385	396
368	392	232
369	365	397
370	333–4	417–18
371	402	419
372	393	421
373	390	408
374	387	407
375	——	423
376	330	175
377	386	406
378	——	428
379	342	430
380	328–9	416
381	339	52
382	407	378
383	408	379
384	404	415
385	373	383
386	345–6	386–7
387	331	382

CONCORDANCE I

This edition	Ribbeck³	Vahlen²
388–9	197–8	228–9
390	394	425
391	Com. 5	424
392–3	358–9	390–1
394	343–4	384–5
395	395	426
396	391	410
397–8	383–4	135–6
399	406	174
400	397	427
ccxxv	Hecuba fr. xi	194
401	403	414
402	405	Inc. 3

CONCORDANCE II

Ribbeck³	This edition	Ribbeck³	This edition
1	8	63–4	104–5
2–3	3–4	65	99
4–5	6–7	66–7	109–10
6	9	68	102
7–8	5	69	108
9	1	70–1	98
10–12	10–12	72–3	106–7
13–15	i	74	111
16	2	75–88	81–94
17	15	89	80
18	14	90	103
19	31	91–2	78–9
20–4	16–20	93	100
25–31	22–30	94	101
32	21	95–6	96–7
33	67	97	112
34–5	62–3	98–9	119
36	66	100	113
37	68	101	115
38	64	102–3	114
39–53	32–46	104	116
54–6	47–9	105–6	117–18
57–9	69–71	107–11	120–4
60–1	72–3	112	137
62	65	113	133

CONCORDANCE II

Ribbeck³	This edition	Ribbeck³	This edition
[114–17]	125–8	193	203
[118–19]	liii	194–6	204–6
120	132	197–8	388–9
121	134	199–201	185–7
122–3	309–10	202	192
124–5	135–6	*Iphigenia* fr. x	xciv
126–7	138–9	203	207
128–9	141–2	205–13	208–16
130	140	214–15	237–8
131	143	216–17	222–3
132–3	146–7	218	245
134	144	219	cv*a*
135	148	220–1	219–20
136	145	222–3	232–3
137–8	170	224–5	see p. 349
139–40	153–4	226–7	225–7
141–2	150–1	228–30	229–31
143	163	231–2	217–18
144	164	233	224
145	166	234	243
146–7	167–8	235–6	241–2
148	160	237–9	234–6
149	149	240	221
150	165	241–2	244
151	159	243–4	239–40
152–4	169	245	248–9
155	152	246–8	247
156–7	157–8	249–50	246
158–9	161–2	251	250
160–1	155–6	252	251
162	179	*Melanippa* fr. vi	cxviii
163	171	254	252
164	180	255	253
165–7	172–4	256	259
168–9	182	257–60	254–7
170–1	183–4	261	261
172	175	262–4	260
173–4	177–8	265	258
175	181	266	262
176	176	267	263
Hecuba fr. xi	ccxxv	268	264
177–80	188–91	269–70	270–1
181–2	193–4	271	265
183–90	195–202	272	cxxxiv*b*
191–2	see p. 321	273–6	266–9

CONCORDANCE II

Ribbeck[3]	This edition	Ribbeck[3]	This edition
277	278	349	364
278	272	350	clxvi
279–80	273–4	351–3	316–18
281	277	354	335
282	275	355	362
283	276	356–7	344–5
284	279	358–9	392–3
285	282	360–1	336–7
286	280	362	363
287	281	363	321
288	287	364	343
289–90	283–4	365	369
291	288	366–8	313–15
292	289	369–71	338–40
293–4	285–6	372	clxia
295	303	373	385
296	305	374	319
297	308	375	342
298	300	378	341
299–300	306	379	348
301	304	380	350
302	301	381–2	320
303–5	293–5	383–4	397–8
306	290	385	367
307	302	386	377
308	307	387	374
309–12	296–9	388	351
313	312	389	349
314–25	322–33	390	373
326–7	see p. 164	391	396
328–9	380	392	368
330	376	393	372
331	387	394	390
332	334	395	395
333–4	370	396	354
335	361	397	400
336–7	13	398–9	clxvii
338	347	400	311
339	381	402	371
340	95	403	384
342	379	405	402
343–4	394	406	399
345–6	386	407	382
347–8	352–3	408	383

CONCORDANCE III

Vahlen[2]	This edition	Vahlen[2]	This edition
1–3	i	107–8	98
4	5	109–10	see pp. 255–6
5	9	111	101
6	8	112–13	96–7
7–9	10–12	114	115
10–11	3–4	115	113
12	see p. 164	116	116
13–14	6–7	117	114
15	1	118–19	117–18
16	2	120	112
17	15	121	363
18	347	122	119
19	13	123–7	120–4
20	14	128	137
21	31	129	132
22–6	16–20	130	135–6
27–33	22–30	131–2	138–9
34	21	133	133
35–46	50–61	134	134
47–8	62–3	135–6	397–8
49	68	137–8	141–2
50	66	139	140
51	67	140	143
52	381	141	clxvi
53	64	142–4	316–18
54–68	32–46	145–6	146–7
69–71	47–9	147	144
72–5	69–71	148	148
76–7	72–3	149	145
78	65	150	364
79	111	151–5	see p. 285
80–1	104–5	156–7	163–4
82	100	158–9	153–4
83–4	106–7	160	170
85–99	80–94	161–72	322–33
100–1	78–9	173	312
102	103	174	399
103	102	175	376
104	109–10	176	334
105	99	177	150–1
106	108	178	149

Vahlen[2]	*This edition*	*Vahlen*[2]	*This edition*
179	160	266–72	225–31
180	166	273	221
181	165	274–5	*see p. 350*
182–3	167–8	276–7	217–18
184	169	278	224
185	159	279	244
186	161–2	280	243
187	361	281	245
188–9	155–6	282–3	241–2
190–2	157–8	284–6	234–6
193	152	287–8	239–40
194	ccxxv	289–90	248–9
195	179	291	247
196	171	292	250
197–8	182	293	251
199–201	172–4	294	cxviii
202	180	295	246
203–4	183–4	296	253
205	335	297	252
206	175	298	259
207	181	299	321
208	*see p. 305*	300–3	254–7
209	176	304–5	260
210	351	306	258
211–12	177–8	307	262
213–14	193–4	308	261
215–18	188–91	309	263
219–21	344–5	310	264
222–3	*see p. 321*	311	276
224	203	312–14	*see p. 394*
225–7	204–6	315	278
228–9	388–9	316–17	270–1
230–1	*see pp. 321–2*	318	265
232	368	319	cxxxiv *b*
233	207	320–3	266–9
234–41	195–202	324	272
242–4	185–7	325–6	273–4
245	192	327	277
246–54	208–16	328	275
255–6	237–8	329	279
257–8	222–3	330	281
259	cv *a*	331	280
260–1	219–20	332	288
262–3	232–3	333	287
264–5	*see p. 349*	334–5	283–4

CONCORDANCE III

ENNIUS' TRAGIC VOCABULARY

I refer with Arabic numerals to verses actually quoted as Ennian, with Roman numerals to passages from which Ennian words have been or could be extracted. My lists attempt to be inclusive rather than critical. Square brackets mark corruption, italic numerals conjecture, asterisks conjecture which I reject but consider to be specially interesting. I use the following abbreviations:

a.	accusative	n.	neuter
ab.	ablative	nom.	nominative
adj.	adjective	p.	plural
adv.	adverb	part.	participle
conj.	conjunction	perf.	perfect
d.	dative	pres.	present
f.	feminine	prp.	preposition
g.	genitive	s.	singular
imp.	imperative	sub.	substantive
ind.	indicative	subj.	subjunctive
indef.	indefinite	vb.	verb
interr.	interrogative	voc.	vocative
m.	masculine		

ADIVVO adiuuerit, 74
ADSTO asta, 239; astitit, 2; adstante, 89; adstantem, [89]
ADSVM adest, 41, 41; adsunt, 23; ades (ind.), *70
ADVENIO aduenit, [45]; adueniens, 322; adueniet, 45, 49
ADVENTO aduentant, 68
ADVERSARIVS aduersarios, 255
ADVERSVM 255, 286 (aduorsum)
ADVERTO aduortite, i; aduortere, 369
ADVOCO aduocant, 136
AEACVS Aeaci, 273
AEDIS aedis (p.a.), 238
AEGER aeger, 336; aegra (f.s.nom.), [216]; aegro (m.s.ab.), 216
AEGRE aegerrume, 78
AEQVALIS aequalis (p.a.), 37
AEQVE 174
AEQVVS aequa (f.s.nom.), 174; aequum (n.s.nom.), 170; aecum (n.s.a.), 148; (n.s.nom.) 156
AER aer, 358; aerem, 357
AERVMNA aerumna (ab.), 141; aerumnis (ab.), 103
AES aes, 165; aere, 2
AESCVLAPIVS Aesculapi, 326 (Aesculapii)
AETAS aetatem, 220
AEVVM aeui, 401
AGER ager, 394; agros, 137
AGO agit, 198; agat, 197, 271, 308; agens, 190; agerent, 220
AIAX Aiax, [14]; Aiacem, 272
ALA alas, 345
ALACRIS alacris (m.s.nom.), 124
ALEXANDER Alexandrum, 64
ALIQVI aliquod (nom.), 186; (a.), xi c
ALIQVIS aliquis (m.s.nom.), 48; aliquid, [391]
ALIQVOT 346
ALIVS alii (m.p.nom.), 68, [85]; aliae (f.p.nom.), [257]; alia (n.p.a.), 117
ALMVS alma (f.s.voc.), 350

ALTER alter, [18]; alteri (m.s.d.), 267, 328
ALTERNVS alterna (f.s.ab.), 123
ALTISONVS altisono (m.s.ab.), 88, 188
ALTVS altum (n.s.a.), 264; altam, cva; alto (n.s.ab.), 111, 264; alti (m.p.nom.), *85; alta (n.p.voc.), 98
AMBO ambo (m.nom.), 170
AMICVS amicus, 351; amici (p.voc.), 263
AMOR amoris, 224; amore, 216
AN [102], 137, 374, [391]; see ANNE
ANDROMACHA Andromachae (d.), 99
ANGVIS angui (ab.), *26; angue, 384
ANIMA anima (ab.), [17], 182
ANIMO animatum, [254]
ANIMVS animus, 62, 199, 202, 336; animum (a.), i, 198, 369; animo (ab.), 74, 216, 306
ANNE 218
ANNVS annos, 42, 104
ANTE (adv.), 33; (prp.), 187
ANTESTO antestat, 388 (antistat)
ANTIQVVS antiqua (f.s.voc.), 237; anticum (n.s.a.), 239; antiquo (m.s.ab.), 278
APOLLO Apollo, 28, 36, 59, 303; Apollinem, 56
APPELLO appellat, 66; appellare, [218]
APPLICO applicem, 83
APTVS apta (f.s.voc.), 350
ARA aram, 94; arae (p.nom.), 84
ARBITROR arbitror, 349
ARBOR arbores (p.nom.), 159 (arboris)
ARCVS arcum, 29
ARDEO ardentem, 50; ardente, clxvii; ardentibus (ab.), 27, 32
ARDVVS ardua (n.p.a.), 73, [379]
AREOPAGITES Areopagitae (p.nom.), 364
ARGIVVS Argiui (m.p.nom.), 212; Argiuum (m.p.g.), 288, 330

446

ARGO Argo, 212
ARGVOR arguor, 204
ARGVTOR argutarier, 260
ARIES arietis (s.g.), 213
ARMA arma (a.), 143, 160; armis (ab.), 232
ARMO armatos, 153; armatis (ab.), 72
ARRIGO arrigunt, [143]
ARX arcem, cva; arce, 83
ASPECTVS aspectu, 21
ASPER aspera (n.p.a.), 379; asperis (n.p.d.), 296
ASPICIO aspice, 240, 301
ASTROLOGVS astrologorum, 185
AT 150; see ATQVE
ATER atro (m.ab.), 297
ATHENAE Athenas, 239
ATQVE, i, 6, 16, 20, 41, 62, 86, 113, 133, 137, 147, 148, 149, 156, 173, [174], 191, 198, 223, 230, 239, 260, 273, 274, 278, 309, 358, 360, 382
AVCVPO aucupant, 245
AVDIENTIA audientiam, i
AVDIO audis, [133]; audiunt, 284; audire, i; audi, 133; audibo, 278; auditis (part.n.p.d.), 133
AVEO auent, 62
AVFERO abstulit, 167
AVGIFICO augificat, 102
AVGVRO auguro, 249
AVIDE 63
AVRIS aures (p.nom.), 62, 245; auris (p.a.), 278, 305
AVRO auratum (m.s.a.), 29
AVRVM auro (ab.), 91
AVSCVLTO ausculta, 247
AVT *33, 71, [77], 81, 82, 109, 109, 177, 186, 186, 266, 266, 266, [309], 373
AVTEM 167
AVVS aui (s.g.), *273
AVXILIVM auxilium (a.), 24, 322; auxili, [151 auxilii]; auxilio (d.), 151; (ab.), 82

BACCHICVS Bacchico (m.ab.), 124
BACCHVS Bacchus, 120
BALO balantibus (f. ab.), 54
BARBARICVS barbarica (f.s.ab.), 89
BELLVM bellum (a.), 105; bello (ab.), 284
BELVA beluas, 360; beluarum, 186
BENE 12, 219, 265; see MELIVS
BENEFACTVM benefacta (a.), 349
BENEFICIVM beneficia (a.), [349]
BIGAE bigis (ab.), 97
BLANDILOQVENTIA blandiloquentia (ab.), 226
BLANDVS blandi (m.p.nom.), 108
BONVS bonum (n.s.nom.), i; boni (n.s.g.), 335; bona (f.s.ab.), 11; (n.p.a.), clxvii; bonis (m.p.d.), 265; (n.p.d.), 294; see MELIOR, OPTIMVS
BROMIVS Bromius, 120
BRVGES (nom.), 334 (Phryges)
BRVGIVS Brugio (n.ab.), *312

CADO cadunt, 175, 385; cadens, [301]; cecidit, 370; cecidissent, [209]
CAEDES caede, [23], [23]
CAEDO caesa (f.s.nom.), 209; caesae (f.p.nom.), [209]
CAELES caelitum, 171, 270
CAELO caelatis (part.n.p.ab.), 90
CAELVM caelum (a.), 235; caeli, 96, [171], 187, 189, clxia, 319, 366, 387; caelo (d.), 223; (ab.), 13, 67, 185, 243, [366]
CAEMENTA caementae (p.nom.), 385
CAERVLEVS caeruleo (m.ab.), *26; (n.ab.), 365; caeruleae (f.p.nom.), 26
CAERVLVS caerula (n.p.nom.), 250
CALIGO caligo, 167
CANDEO candent, 250; candens, 301; candentem, 243
CANDIDVS candidum (n.s.nom.), 274
CANIS canis (s.g.), 384
CANTVS cantus, [345]; cantu (ab.), 345

447

CAPIO cepit, 222; cepisset, 211
CAPRA Capra (nom.), 186
CAPVT caput, [114]; capiti, 77
CARDO cardine, 88
CASTRA castra (a.), 154; castris (d.), 154; (ab.), 164
CAVEO caueo, [281]
CAVSA causa (nom.), [365]; (ab.), 112, 343
CAVVS caua (f.s.nom.), 365; (n.p. nom.), 250; (n.p.a.), 96
CEDO cedo, [281]
CERES Ceres (nom.), clxxxviii; Cereris, 240
CERNO cerno, 13; cernunt, 166; cernitur, 351; cernat, 306; cernere, 232
CERTATIO certatio, 225, *248
CERTE clxxib
CERTVS certus, 351; certo (ab.), 74, [248]; certos, 317
CESSO cessas, 194; cessat, 376
CETERVS cetera (n.p.a.), 269
CETTE 242
CIBARIVM cibaria (a.), clxxxviii
CIEO ciet, 36; cita (f.s.nom.), 43
CIRCVM 114
CIRCVMSTO circumstant, 27
CIRCVMVENIO circumuentus, 16
CISSEVS Cissei, ccxxv
CITVS see CIEO
CIVIS ciues (voc.), 42; (a.), 8; ciuis (p.a.), 341 (ciues); ciuium, 275
CIVITAS ciuitatem, 288
CLAMOR clamoris, 163
CLAREO claret, 274
CLASSIS classis (s.nom.), 43
CLIPEVS clipeus, 370; clipeo (ab.), 107, 189
COEPI coepisset, [211]
COETVS coetus (s.nom.), 123
COGITO cogitat, 308; cogitet, [308]
COGNOSCO cognoui, liii; cognitum (n.s.a.), liii
COGO cogis, 128
COLCHVS Colchis (ab.), 214, *244

COLLOCO collocaui, 130
COMES comiti, [313]
COMITER 313, 369
COMMINVS 149
COMMISCEO commixta (n.p.voc.), 171
COMMISERESCO conmiserescite, 162
COMMVNITER [313]
COMPLEO complebit, *46; compleuit, 46
COMPOS compotes (m.p.a.), 317
CONATVS conatu, *110
CONCEDO concedit, 5
CONCIDO concide, 372
CONCILIO conciliant, 310
CONCIPIO concepta, [252]
CONCORDIA concordiam, 310
CONCVBIVM concubio (ab.), 181
CONCVTIO concutit, clxia
CONDICIO condiciones (nom.), 304
CONFERO conferunt, 310; conferre, *154; contulit, 168
CONFICIO conficis, 97
CONFIDENTIA confidentia (ab.), 19
CONGLOMERO conglomeras, 302
CONIECTVRA coniecturam, 55; coniectura (ab.), 249
CONOR conare (ind.), 7; conatur, [110]; conatum (n.s.a.), 289
CONSAEPIO consaepta (f.s.nom.), 252 (consepta)
CONSENTIO consentit, 21
CONSILIVM consilium (nom.), 151; (a.), clxvi, 382; consili, 317; consilio (ab.), 289; consiliis (ab.), *5
CONSISTO consistere, 324; constitit, 159
CONTAGIO contagio, 294
CONTEMPLO contempla, 240
CONTEMPLOR contemplatur, 115
CONTINEO contines, 235
CONTINGO contigerit, 307
CONTRA 278
CONVENIO conueniat, 311
CONVERTO conuertere, [138]

EXITIVM exitium (a.), 61, 231, 328; (p.g.), 44
EXITVS exitum, [231], [328]
EXORDIVM exordium (a.), 210
EXORIOR exoritur, 186
EXPECTORO expectorat, 17
EXPEDIO expedibo, 148
EXPELLO expulsus, cl*a*
EXPETO expetit, 348; expetunt, 23, clxvi
EXPOSCO exposco, 151
EXSACRIFICO exsacrificabat, 54
EXSECROR exsecrabor, 342
EXSEQVOR exequar, 81
EXSPECTO exspectantes (m.nom.), 63
EXSVRGO exsurge, i
EXTEMPLO 362
EXTOLLO extolles, 10; extollas, 321
EXTRA (prp.), 39, 238

FABVLOR fabulari, 147
FACESSO facessit, [145]; facessite, *145*
FACILE 172, 306; facilius, clxvii
FACINVS facinus (a.), 236
FACIO facit, 314; facimus, [236], [372]; fac, i; facito, *372*; facere, 275; faciet, [273]; fecisse, 148; faxim, 261; factum (n.s.nom.), i, 31, 263; facto (n.ab.), 51; factas, [343]; factum (n.p.g.), 37; factis (n.p.d.), 331; *see* BENEFACTVM, MALEFACTVM
FALSVS falsam, 262
FAMA famam, 10, 12
FAMILIA familiae (g.), 112
FANVM fanum (a.), 352; fana (nom.), 85
FAVEO fauent, 344
FAVX faucibus (ab.), 344
FAX fax, 41; facem, 30, 50, 243
FEMINA feminae (p.nom.), cxviii
FERE cxviii
FERO feratis, *263*; fer, 24; ferte, 42; ferre, 154, 262
FERRVM ferrum (nom.), 109; (a.), 182; ferro (ab.), 166, 312, 399

FERVS fera (f.s.nom.), 45; feram, [116]
FESTINO festinant, 395
FESTIVVS festiuum, *395*
FIDES fides, 320; Fides (voc.), 350; fidem, xv*b*, 162
FIDVS fide, 194; fida (f.voc.), 237
FIGO fixus, 296
FILIA filia (nom.), 206, ccxxv; filias, 218; filiis (d.), 119
FILIVS filium, 362
FINGO fictas, 343
FIO fit, [102], 236, 358
FIRMVS firmum (n.s.a.), 256; firmo (n.s.ab.), 19
FLACCEO flaccebunt, 304
FLAGITIVM flagiti, 341 (flagitii)
FLAMMA flamma (nom.), 22; flammam, 169, clxvii; flamma (ab.), 85
FLAMMIFER flammiferam, 25
FLECTO flexeris, 172
FLVCTVS fluctus (s.nom.), 116, 117; (p.nom.), 1
FOEDO foedati (m.p.nom.), 399
FONS fontem, *136*
FOR fandis (n.p.ab.), 36; fatis (n.p.ab.), 36
FORAS 153
FORMA forma (ab.), cxviii
FORNIX fornices, 319
FORTIS fortem, [136]
FORTITER 255, 263
FORTVNA fortuna (nom.), 333, 338, 340; (voc.), 302; (ab.), 166
FRANGO franguntur, 165; fractae (f.p.nom.), 84
FREMITVS fremitu, 394
FRETVS fretum (a.), 387
FRETVS freta (f.s.nom.), 82
FRIGVS frigus (nom.), 358
FRVCTVS fructus, [116]; (p.a.), 245
FRVX fruges (a.), clxxxviii
FVGA fugae (g.), *82*; fuga, (ab.), [82]
FVGIO fugio, liii; fugiat, [20]
FVRIA Furiarum, 49
FVTTILE 263
FVTTILVS futtilum (n.s.nom.), 262

GEMITVS gemitum, 110
GEMO gemam, 184
GENA genam, 400; genae (d.), 400
GENS gentis (p.a.), 355
GENVS genus (nom.), 271, 338; (a.), 270, 321
GERMANVS germane, 69
GERO gerit, 181, clxxxviii; gerentes, 105; gesserunt, 15; gessere, 219; gesta (f.s.ab.), 176
GESTITO gestitat, 256
GLORIA gloriam, 11, 12
GNATA nata (voc.), 129
GNATVS nate (voc.), 247; natum (a.), 100
GRADVS gradum, 6, 193
GRAECVS Graeci (p.nom.), 356
GRATIA gratia (nom.), [274]; (ab.), 132, 224
GRATVLOR gratulor, 176
GRAVIDVS grauidus, 72; grauida (f.s.nom.), 50
GRAVITER 184
GREMIVM gremium (a.), 321
GVTTATIM 175
GYPSO gypsatissimis (f.p.ab.), cv a

HABEO habet, 196, 381; habetis, cv a; habeat, 298
HAEREO haeret, 295
HALITO halitantes, 169
HARIOLATIO hariolationibus (ab.), 35
HARIOLVS harioli (p.nom.), cxxxiv b
HASTA hasta (voc. ?), 149; hastae (p.nom.), 165
HAVD haut, 77; haud, 95, 376
HECTOR Hector (nom.), 153, 376; (voc.), 69, 80; Hectorem, 79; Hectoris, 100, 333
HECVBA Hecuba (nom.), 51, ccxxv
HEHAE 370
HELENA Helena (nom.), 205
HEV 180, 371
HIC hic, 5, clxxxib; haec (f.s.nom.), 22; hoc (n.s.nom.), 39, 151, 163, 200, 274; hunc, *175; hanc, 25,

*175; hoc (n.s.a.), 236, 249, 285, 289, 301, 342; huic (m.), 127; hoc (m.s.ab.), 145, 388; haec (n.p.a.), 92, 172, 284, [359]; his (m.p.d.), 120, 120; (m.p.ab.), [268], 269
HIC (adv.), 163, [248], 307
HINC [175], 201
HIPPODAMEA Hippodameam, 292
HODIE 229, 307
HOMO homo, 313, 375; hominem, 66, clxxxib
HONESTE 389
HONOR honoris, 224
HORRESCO horrescunt, 143
HOSPES hospitem, 177; hospites (voc.), 293
HOSTIA hostiis (ab.), 54
HOSTILIS hostili (f.s.ab.), 323
HOSTIMENTVM hostimentum (a.), 133
HOSTIO see fr. lxvii; hostibis, *149; hostiuit, *149
HOSTIS hostes (a.), 8; hostium, xciv
HVC 201
HVMANVS humanum (n.s.nom.), 271; humana (f.s.ab.), 299
HVMVS humum, 354

IACEO iacent, 84, 399
IACIO iacit, 30
IACTO iactari, 100
IAM 31, 43, 62, 154, [208]; see ETIAM
IBI 58, 198, 264, 308, 312
IDEM eadem (f.s.nom.), 174; idem (n.s.nom.), 200; eandem, 277; eadem (f.s.ab.), [212]; (n.p.nom.), 174
IGNIS igni (ab.), 26
IGNOBILIS ignobiles (m.p.nom.), 173
IGNOTVS ignotus, 123
ILICO 293
ILLE ille, 229 (ill'), 380; illa (f.s.nom.), 33; illum, 103, 287; illam, [213], [286]; illi (m.s.d.), 226, 230, 231, 231, 315, 368, [391]; illo, [197]; illos, 40, 40; illis (f.p.d.), 121, [197], [226]; see POSTILLA

ILLIC illic, 375; illaec (f.s.nom.), 386
ILLINC [201], 201
ILLVC 201, 201, [201], [375]
IMBER imber, 4, 357; imbre, 358; imbrium, 394
IMMOLOR immolandam, xciv
IMPERATOR imperator, i
IMPERIVM imperium (a.), 162; imperio (ab.), 214
IMPERO imperat, 266
IMPETRO impetrem, 306
IMPLORO imploro, xvb
IMPRIMO inprimit, 400
IMPROBO improbati (m.p.nom.), 220
IMPROBVS inprobus, 130; inprobum (m.s.a.), 126
IMPVDENS inpudentes (m.p.nom.), cxxxivb
IN (+a.), xxviiie, 168, *175, 264, 277, 302, 321; (+ab.), 13, [23], [23], 51, 107, 120, 164, 181, 184, 185, 188, 196, [197], *199, 208, 212, 243, 257, 284, 295, 300, clxvii, 342, 351, 365, 374, 388
INAVRO inauratam, 213
INCEDO incedunt, 26; incede, [23], [23]
INCENDIVM incendio (ab.), 41
INCENDO incendere, 288; incendier, *288
INCERTE 202
INCERTVS incerta (f.s.ab.), 6, 351; incerti (m.p.nom.), clxvi; incertis (m.p.ab.), 317
INCINGO incinctae (f.p.nom.), 26
INCIPIO incipiam (subj.), 217
INCLINO inclinatam, 333
INCLVTVS inclutum (n.s.a.), 352; inclitum (n.s.a.), 48
INCOHO inchoanda, [210]; inchoandum, [210]; inchoandi (n.s.g.), 210; inchoandae, [210]; inchoandas, [210]
INCOLVMIS incolumi (ab.), cxviii
INCOMMODVM incommodis (ab.), 131

INCREPO increpat, 305
INDE [4], 210, 367
INDO indidit, 99, 99
INDIGNVS indigna (f.s.ab.), 125, 129
INDVCO inducta, [396]
INDVO induta (f.s.nom.), 396
INDVSTRIA industria (ab.), 105
INEO inibat, 124
INERS inertes (m.p.nom.), 266
INFERVS infera (n.p.voc.), 98; inferum (n.p.g.), 152, 309
INFLAMMO inflammari, 92
INFRENO infrena, 158; infrenari, 158
INGENIVM ingenium, [272]; ingenio (ab.), 19
INGENS ingentes, 319
INGENVVS ingenuum (m.s.a.), 272
INGREDIOR ingredi, 217
INGVRGITO ingurgitandum (n.s. nom.), xxviiie
INICIO inicere, 138
INIMICVS inimico (m.s.d.), 134
INITIVM initio, [199]
INIVRIA iniuria (ab.), 125, 129
INNITOR innixus, 29
INNOCENS innocens, 119, 205
INNOXIVS innoxium, [255]
INOPIA inopia (ab.), 16
INORATVS inorata (f.s.ab.), 6
INQVAM inquam, [175]
INSANVS insani (m.p.nom.), 266
INSPICIO inspicis, 234; inspice, 236
INSTITVO institutum (n.s.nom.), 197
INSTRVO instructam, 91
INSVLTO insultas, [124]; insultans, 124
INSVM inest, 225
INTEGER integros, 401
INTELLEGO intellegit, 66
INTENDO intendit, 28
INTER 9, 48, 137, 310, 341
INTEREA *9
INTEREO interii, 180
INTRODVCO introducta (f.s.nom.), 106

ENNIUS' TRAGIC VOCABULARY

INTVS [48]
INVENTOR inuentor, 121
INVESTIO inuestita, 113
INVITVS inuitum (m.s.a.), 128; inuitam, 36, 128, [157]; inuitis
(m.p.ab.), 367
INVOCO inuocant, [301]
IOVIS Iouem, 301; Iouis (g.), 94, 273,
cxlixb, 350; see IVPPITER
IPSE ipse, 52, [160], 221, 296, 303,
370, *371; ipsum, 285; ipsi (m.s.d.),
315; (m.p.nom.), *160, 268
IRA iram, 230
IRATVS irati (m.p.nom.), 108
IS is, [120], 356, 381; ea (f.s.nom.),
256, [274]; id (nom.), 203; eum,
61, [103], [239], 329 (eum), 390;
eam, xxviiie, 136 (? see EO); id
(a.), 148, 198, 198, *263, 371; eius,
[155]; ei, [99], [153]; ea (f.s.ab.),
[141], 212; eae, cxviii; eos, 271,
392 (eos); iis (m.p.ab.), 268; see
INTEREA, POSTEA, PROPTEREA
ISTAC 225
ISTE iste, cxlixb; isti (m.s.d.), [260];
ista (n.p.nom.), 359
ISTIC istic, 356; istuc, 225
ISTIC (adv.), 293
ITA 1, *9, 70, 228, 273
ITER iter (a.), 169, 191, 217
ITINER itiner (a.), 289
IVBAR iubar (a.), 13
IVBEO iubet, i, [201]; iube, 247
IVDICIVM iudicium (a.), 48; iudicio
(ab.), 49
IVDICO iudicauit, 48
IVGVM iugo, [157]
IVNGO iunge, 158
IVPPITER Iuppiter (nom.), 356 (Iu-
piter), 359 (Iupiter); (voc.), 176
(Iupiter), 234, 361 (Iupiter); see
IOVIS
IVRO iurandum (voc.), 350
IVS ius (nom.), 155, 156; (voc.), 350;
(a.), *5, [148]
IVSTVS iustum (n.s.a.), 148

IVVENIS iuuenem, [123]; iuuenum,
123
IVVO iuuat, 360

LABO labat, 385
LABOR labuntur, 385; lapsa (f.s.nom.),
340
LABOR laboris, 332
LACEDAEMONIVS Lacedaemonia (f.s.
nom.), 49
LACERO lacerato (n.s.ab.), 70
LACRIMA lacrimae (p.nom.), 139,
175 (lacrumae); lacrimis (ab.), 276
LACRIMO lacrimare, 389; lacrimari,
[389]
LACTO lactari, [100]
LAETVS laeto, [283]
LAEVVS laeuam, 240; laeua (ab.), 30
LAPIDEVS lapideo (n.s.ab.), 140
LAPIS lapis, 109
LAQVEATVS laqueatis (n.p.ab.), 90
(lacuatis)
LASCIVIO lasciuis, *66
LASCIVVS lasciui, [66]
LATEO latent, 257; latuit, 42
LATVS latere, 297
LAVO lauere (pres. inf.), 180, 276;
lauerent, 106; lauere (perf.ind.), 139
LETVM letum (a.), 134; leti, xxxiv;
leto (d.), 283
LIBENTER lubenter, 284
LIBER Liberi, 352
LIBERI liberi, 283, 397; liberorum,
132, 321, 326; liberum, 112, 363
LIBERO libero, [131]; liberabo, 131
LIBERTAS libertas, 256; libertatem,
141; libertate, [141]
LIBET lubet, 201
LICET licet, [342], 388, 389; licuit,
139
LINGVA linguam, 260; lingua, [260]
LINQVO linquere, 128
LITVS litora (p.a.), 46
LOCO locant, 106; locabas, 127;
locaui, [130], 353; locauit, *353;
locata (n.p.a.), 349

454

LOCVS loco (ab.), 339, 388; loca (p.voc.), xxxiv
LONGINQVE 104
LOQVOR locuntur, 173
LVCEO lucet, 315, 342; luceat, [315]
LVCTVS luctum, 231
LVDVS ludis (ab.), 62
LVGVBRIS lugubri (f.ab.), 386
LVMEN lumen (nom.), 274; (a.), 13, 314; lumine, 235, 250, 314
LVNA luna (ab.), 29
LVX lux (voc.), 69
LYAEVS Lyaeus, 121

MACHAERA machaera (voc.?), 149
MACHINOR see fr. cviii
MACTO mactassint, 287
MAEROR maerores (a.). 231
MAGIS 224, 325, 338
MAGNVS magna (f.s.nom.), 225; magno (n.s.ab.), 43, 287; magni (m.p.nom.), 1; magna (n.p.voc.), 171; maximo (m.s.ab.), 72
MALE 12, 176, 265
MALEFACTVM malefacta (a.), 349; malefactis (ab.), 205
MALO malim, 232; malui, 393; maluit, [393]
MALVS malum (n.s.nom.), 307; malam, 323; mali (n.s.g.), 335; mala (f.s.ab.), 10; malo (n.s.ab.), 287; mali (m.p.nom.), 155; mala (n.p.a.), 302; malis (m.p.d.), 265; (m.p.ab.), 156; (n.p.ab.), 299
MANDO mandatam, 323
MANVS manus (nom.), 46; manu, [149], 323; manus, [182]; (p.a.), 242, 322; manibus (ab.), cva
MARE mare (a.), 235, 264; mari (ab.), 43; maria, [43]; (nom.), 118
MARITVS marito (d.), 253
MARO Maro, 353
MATER mater (nom.), 50, 368; (voc.), 34, 38; matrem, 112
MATERNVS materno (m.ab.), 144
MATRONA matronae (p.voc.), cva

MAXIME 307
MEDE Mede (nom.), [244]
MEDEA Medea (nom.), 216, *244, Medeai, 223 (Medeae)
MEDICVS medici, [282]
MELIOR melior (voc.), 34; melius (nom.), 155
MELIVS (adv.), 378
MEMBRVM membra (a.), 118
MENDICVS mendici (g.), 282
MENELAVS Menelaus, 203
MENS mentem, 198; mentis, 52; mente, 229
METVO metuunt, 348
METVS metus, 374; metu, 20, 52
MEVS mea (f.s.nom.), 206, [206], 215, 294; (f.s.voc.), 38, 149 (?), 302, 371; meam, [142]; meum (n.s.a.), 163; mei (m.s.g.), 37; meae (f.s.g.), 380; meae (f.s.d.), 134; meo (m.s.ab.), xciv, *295; mea (f.s.ab.), 141 (mea͞), 142 (mea͞), 184 (mea͞), 316; meae (f.p.nom.), [175], [175]; meas, 242, 305; mea (n.p.a.), i; meum (n.p.g.), 37; meis (f.p.d.), 203
MILITIA militiae (loc.), 200
MINA minis (ab.), 158
MINITOR minitatur, [18]
MINOR minatur, 18
MINVS (adv.), 315
MISER miser, 70, 261; miserum, [180]; miseram, 180, 222; miserae (f.p.nom.), 139
MISEREO miseret, 38, 140; miserete, 182
MISERIA miseriam, [142]; miseria (ab.), 142; miserias, 223
MITTO missa (f.s.nom.), 35; misso (m.s.ab.), 14
MODESTIA modestia (nom.), 33
MODICE 181
MODO 233, 289
MODVS modo (ab.), 124; modis (ab.), 16

MONSTRO monstrat, 313; monstrant, 267, [313]; monstrabitur, 369
MONSTRVM monstrum (s.nom.), 248
MORBVS morbo (ab.), 16
MORIOR moriar, [183], 374
MORO *see fr. ccxvii*
MORS mors, 325; mortem, 183; Mortis, 192; morti, 398
MORTALIS mortales (nom.), 9; mortalis (p.a.), 360
MOS morem, 181; more, 278
MOTVS motum, [309]; motus (g.), 309
MVCRO mucronem, 402
MVLIER mulier (nom.), 49; (voc.), 34; mulierem, 373, 373; mulierum, 34
MVLTO 34
MVLTVS multi (m.p.nom.), 68, 140, 219, 220; multos, 42, 104; multa (n.p.a.), [232]; multis (m.ab.), 16
MVRVS muro (ab.), 100
MVSSO *see frs. xxxvii, cxcix*; musset, *372
MVTTIO muttire, 280
MYRMIDONES Myrmidonum, 162

NAM [5], 72, 95, 106, 108, 126, 155, 173, 197, 215, 226, 232, 265, 273; *see* QVIANAM, QVISNAM, VTINAM
NAMQVE *36, *173, 326, 339
NANCISCOR nanciscuntur, 156; nanctus, 292 (nactus)
NASCOR nascuntur, [156]; natus, 60, 291; natum (a.), 272; *see* GNATA, GNATVS
NAVCVM nauci, 375
NAVFRAGIVM naufragio (ab.), cl a
NAVIS nauis (s.nom.), 210; naũes (p.a.), 111, [210]; nauibus (ab.), 46
-NE 13, 40 (men), [102], 218; *see* ANNE
NE 208, cv a, 244, 294, 318; *see* NEMO, NEQVAQVAM, NEQVIQVAM, NEVE, NEVTIQVAM

NEC 77, 84, *200*, 320
NECESSE [95], 346
NECO necetur, *206*; necato (imp.), *362*; necasset, *178*
NEGO neget, 311; negetur, [206]; negato, [362]
NEGOTIVM negotium (nom.), 196, 197; negoti, 196 (negotii); negotio (ab.), 196, [197]
NEMO nemo, 19, 187, 378; neminis, 140
NEMVS nemore, 208
NEPA Nepa (nom.), 186
NEQVAQVAM 225
NEQVE [36], 108, 108, 138, 138, 139, 200, [278], 298, 321, 324, 337, 337, [339]
NEQVIQVAM 221 (nequicquam)
NEREVS Nerei, 119
NESCIO nescit, 195, 199
NEVE 210
NEVTIQVAM 21
NEX necem, 18
NI 227
NIHIL nihil, 335, [375]; nihili, *375*; nihilo, 315
NIMIVM nimium, 335
NIOBE Niobem, [227]; Niobe, [227]
NISI 144
NITIDO nitidant, 136
NITOR nitere (imp.), 194
NOLO nolite, 293
NOMEN nomen (nom.), 186; (a.), 99, 163; nomine, 211; nomina (a.), 68
NOMINO nominatur, 211
NON 66, xxviii e, 140, 174, [187], 221, 267, 271, 284, 312, 327, 331, 346, 375, 389
NOSCO nomus, 170; noueris, 147
NOSTER nostram, 333; nostrum (n.s.a.), *161*, 246; nostri (m.p. nom.), 397
NOX noctis, 188, 191, clxxix; nocte, 257
NVBES nubes (p. nom.), 357

456

NVBILVS nubila (n.p.voc.), xxxiv
NVDO nudare, 341
NVGATOR nugator, 375
NVLLVS nulla (f.s.nom.), [248], 320, 374; nullum, [248]; nulla (f.s.ab.), 129
NVMERVS numerus, [102]; numeros, *102
NVMQVAM 177, 215, 337
NVNC 6, 64, [72], 81, 141, 200, 207, 211, 217, 222, 265, 338, [346]
NVNTIVS nuntium, 63
NVPTIAE nuptiis (d.), 127; (ab.), 292

O 69, 87, 87, 87, [135], 171, 194, 322, 350, 352
OB 227; see OBVIAM
OBDVCO obducere, 376
OBEO obibo, 192
OBIACEO obiacent, 192
OBICIO obiecta (f.s.nom.), 119
OBIVRGO obiurgat, 203
OBNOXIOSVS obnoxiosae (f.p.nom.), 257 (obnoxiose)
OBNOXIVS obnoxio, [257]
OBORIOR oborta (f.s.nom.), 167
OBRVO obrutus, 372
OBSCVRO obscurat, 68
OBSCVRVS obscura (f.s.ab.), 257
OBSECRO obsecro, 290; obsecrans, 56
OBSEQVOR obsequi, 40
OBSERVATIO obseruationis, 185
OBSIDIO obsidionem, 272, 376
OBSTO obstare, 40
OBSVM obsit, 294; obesse, 40
OBVARO obuarant, 5
OBVIAM 398
OBVOLVO obuoluta (f.s.nom.), 41
OCCVMBO occumbant, 398
OCCVPO occupat, 154
OCVLVS oculorum, 21; oculis (ab.), 32
ODI odit, 348; oderunt, 348
OENOMAVS Oenomao (ab.), 292
OFFERO offerre, 77
OMNINO 95

OMNIPOTENS omnipotens (m.s.voc.), 150
OMNIS omnem (m.), 167, 387; (f.), 17, 230; omnes (m.nom.), 301, 382; omnis (f.p.a.), 234, 355, 360; omnia (a.), 92, 302, 346, 382
OPERA operam, 228
OPINO opino, 146
OPINOR opinor, 271
OPORTET oportet, 285, 329
OPPETO oppeto, 323; obpetam, 183 (oppetam)
OPPIDVM oppidum (a.), 239
OPPLEO opplent, 326; oppletus, 394
OPPRIMO opprimi, clxvii
OPS opem, 42; opis, 80; ope, 89, 316; opibus (ab.), 80, 340
OPTIMATES optumates (voc.), cva; optumatum, 34
OPTIMVS optuma, [34]; optumum (n.s.a.), 146; optumam, 39; optumi (m.s.g.), 38; optima (n.p.voc.), 241; optumarum, *34
OPVLENTVS opulentum (n.s.a.), 239; opulenti (m.p.nom.), 173; opulentae (f.p.voc.), cva
ORACVLVM oraclo (ab.), 58
ORATIO oratio, 174; orationem, 258
ORBVS orba (f.s.nom.), 83
ORCVS Orci, 98
ORDO ordo, 5
ORESTES Orestem, 145 (Oresten)
ORIOR oritur, 4, 22, 387
OS ore, 120, 258, clxvii
OSTREVM ostreis (ab.), 113
OTIOSVS otioso, [199]
OTIVM otio (ab.), 195, *199

PACTVM pacto (ab.), 324
PALAM 280
PALLIDVS pallida (n.p.voc.), xxxiv
PAR parem (f.), 329
PARCO parcam (subj.), 134; pepercit, [77]; pepercerit, 77
PARENS parentem, 177, 377
PARIES parietes (nom.), 85

457

PARIO parere, 50, 233; peperisti, *39*; peperit, 355
PARIS Parim, 64
PARITER 122, 173
PARITO paritat, **308*
PARO paro, 141; paras, 272; parat, 308, 328; paratum (n.s.a.), **329*; paratam, 11, 329
PARTICIPO participet, 329
PARTIO partiuit, 277
PARTVS partu, 73
PASTOR pastores (nom.), 64
PATEFACIO patefecerunt, 334
PATER pater (nom.), 51, 120, 277; (voc.), 87, 125; patrem, 144; patris (s.g.), 37, 273
PATERNVS paternam, 218
PATIOR pati, 337; passa (f.s.nom.), 78
PATRIA patria (voc.), 87; (ab.), cv *a*, 219
PATRICOLES Patricoles (voc.), 322
PATRIVS patriae (f.s.g.), 84
PAVCVS paucis (n.p.ab.), 95
PAVLO 33
PAVOR pauor, 17
PAVPERIES pauperie, 184
PAVPERTAS paupertas, 68
PAX pacem, 55, 310; pacis, 380
PECCO peccas, 204
PECTVS pectus (a.), 256
PECVS pecudi, 253
PEDVM *see fr. xcviii*
PELIA Peliae (g.), 214, 218
PELIVS Pelio (n.s.ab.), 208
PELLIS pellem, 213
PELOPS Pelope, 291
PENDEO pendens, 297
PER 3, **161*, 214
PERBITO perbiteret, 178
PERCELLO perculsus, 53
PERDO perdat, 73
PERDVELLIS perduellibus (ab.), 367
PEREO pereat, 205; periisse, 348 (perisse)
PERGAMVM Pergamo (d.), 61; Pergama (a.), 73

PERGO pergunt, 180
PERICVLVM periculum (nom.), [280]
PERNICIES perniciem, 230 (permitiem?)
PERPETIOR perpeti, 337
PERTINAX pertinaci (f.s.ab.), 383
PERVERSE 172
PERVICACIA peruicaciam, [383]; peruicacia (ab.), 383
PERVINCO peruince, 383
PERVOLO peruolat, 387
PES pedem, 215, 244; pedes (a.), 114, 168, 187; pedum, 193, 305
PESTIS pestem, 24, 61, cviii, 323, 329
PETO peto, 323; petunt, 268; petam (subj.), 81; petens, 55; petebant, 213
PHILOSOPHIA philosophia (ab.), xxviii *e*
PHILOSOPHOR philosophari, [95]; philosophandum (n.s.nom.), 95
PHRYGIVS Phrygio (n.ab.), 312
PIACVLVM piaculum (nom.), 280
PIE [135]
PIETAS pietas, 275
PIGET piget, 38
PINNA pinnis (ab.), 350
PINSIO pinsibant, 354
PLACEO placet, 95
PLAGA plagas, 187
PLAVSTRVM plaustri, *190*
PLAVSVS plausu (ab.), 345
PLEBEIVS plebeio (m.d.), 280
PLEBES plebes, 388 (plebs); plebi, 389
PLVS plus (a.), 196, 261
POL 338
POLLICEOR pollicentur, 268
POPVLVS populo (d.), i; populi (p.nom.), clxvi
PORCEO porcet, 275
PORTICVS porticus (p.a.), 326
PORTVS portum, 298
POSSVM potes, 8; potest, [309], 325, 327, 331, 337; possis, 260
POST (adv.), liii, 358
POSTEA 357

POSTILLA 60
POSTVLO postulat, 55
POTESTAS potestas, 309
POTIOR potiri, 380
POTIS potis (m.nom.), 324, 380
POTIVS 373
PRAECO praeco (voc.), i
PRAESIDIVM praesidi, 81 (praesidii)
PRAETER (adv.), 202
PREMO premunt, 345
PRIAMVS Priamus, 52; Priami, 87;
Priamo (d.), 39, 59, 93
PRIMVS primus, 59
PRINCIPIVM principium (nom.), 341
PRIVO priuem, 182
PRIVSQVAM 183, 236, 323
PRO (interjection), 361; (prp.), 10,
11, 146, 205, 398
PROAVVS proaui (s.g.), 273
PROBVS probus, 127, 130; probum
(m.s.a.), liii
PROCEDO procede, 193
PROCVL 156, 219
PROELIO proeliant, 9
PROELIVM proelio (ab.), 330
PROFERO proferre, 193; prolato
(n.ab.), 2
PROFITEOR prōfiteri, 285
PROFLVO profluens, 324
PROGENIES progeniem, 39
PROGNATVS prognatus, 291
PROHIBEO prohibe, [236]; prohi-
bessis, 236
PROIECTO proiector, 204
PROLOQVOR proloqui, 222, 285
PRONEPOS pronepos, cxlixb
PROPTER (adv.), 202; (prp.), 119,
[359]; see PROPTEREA, QVAPROPTER
PROPTEREA 220
PRORSVS 116
PROSPECTVS prospectum, 167
PROSVM prodesse, 40, 221
PVBLICVS publicam, 74, 219
PVDET pudet, 37
PVDICITIA pudicitia (ab.), cxviii
PVDOR pudor, 275

PVELLA puella (voc.), 371
PVER puerum, 59, 106; pueros, 247
PVGNO pugnant, 9
PVLSVS pulsu, 305
PVLVIS puluis, 387
PVRVS purus, 65; purum (n.s.a.), 256
PVTO putat, 308
PVTVS putus, 65

QVA [360]
QVADRIIVGVS quadriiugo (m.ab.),
79
QVADRINGENTI quadringentos, 114
QVADRVPEDANS quadrupedantes, 169
QVADRVPES quadrupedum, [157]
QVAERO quaesendum (m.p.g.), 112,
132
QVAESTVS quaestus (g.), 343
QVAM [113], 196, 224, 233, 307,
clxvii, 338, 373, 378, 392, 392; see
NVMQVAM, PRIVSQVAM, QVISQVAM
QVANTVS quantum (n.s.nom.), 331;
quanto (m.s.ab.), 339; quantis
(f.p.ab.), 103, 340
QVAPROPTER 64
QVASI 109, 314
-QVE i, *36, 43, [70], 106, 154, 174,
234, 235, 242, 246, 246, 255,
cxxxivb, 287, 289, 317, 345, 360,
400; see NAMQVE, QVISQVE, VNDI-
QVE
QVEO quit, 221
QVI qui (relative), 59, 73, 74, 99,
[141], ^177, 195, 221, 228, 234, 235,
243, 256, [259], 291, 300, clxia,
313, 328, *342, 357, 376; quae
(f.s.nom.), 25, 96, 181, 211, 386;
quod (nom.), 187, 263, 265, 342,
342, [391]; quem, *175, 301, 348,
348, 356, 356; quam, *175; quod
(a.), 78, 184, 197, 228, 261; cui
(m.), [141], 197, 272, 335, [342];
(f.), 84; qua, [212]; quo (n.), 49,
51; qui (n.s.ab.), 182; (m.p.nom.),
15, 160, 220, 267, 343; quae
(f.p.nom.), 207, cva, cxviii; quos,

459

QVI (*cont.*)
140, [178], 316; quae (n.p.a.), 19, 149, 359; quorum (m.), 68, 158, 283; quibus (m.d.), 5, 142, 266, 268, 309; (n.ab.), 230
qui (interr.), 163; quam, 258, [364]; quod (a.), 217 quo (m.ab.), *178; (n.ab.), 81; quibus (f.ab.), 340
qui (= utinam), 287
QVIA 212
QVIDEM cxlix*b*, clxxi*b*, 371
QVIESCO quiescere, 170
QVIN 20, 248, [300], 367
QVIS quis (interr.m.), 312; (f.), 386; quid (nom.), 163, 163, 164, 185, 188, 238; (a.), 32, 66, 70, 81, [102], 199, 271, [290], 308, 364, 373; qui (m.p.nom.), 71.
quis (indef.), 177, [178]; qui (n.s.ab.), 325
QVISNAM quidnam (nom.), 290; quemnam, 300
QVISQVAM quisquam, 311; quicquam (a.), 108 (quiquam), 311; quemquam, [311]
QVISQVE quisque, 311, 348; quemque, 311; quaeque (n.p.a.), 365
QVISQVIS quicquid (nom.), 342
QVO 6, 57, 83, 83, 217, 298
QVOD 204, cv*a*, 290, clxxxviii
QVONDAM 291

RABIO rabere, *32
RAPIO rapit, 44, 111; rapere, 32; raptis (f.p.ab.), 292
RAPTO raptarier, 79
RARENTER 110
RECEPTO receptat, 366
RECIPIO recipiat, 298
RECIPROCO reciprocat, 116
RECLVDO recludam, 230
RECONCILIO reconcilietur, 206
RECTE 99
REDDO reddant, 269; reddito (imp.), 304

REDEO redeat, 205
REDVCO reduci, 392
REFERO reterte, [42]
REFVGIO refugiat, 20
REGIFICE 91
REGIMEN regimen (nom.), 203
REGIVS regio, [388]
REGNVM regnum (nom.), 339; (a.), 246, 282; regni, 320
REGREDIO regredere, 7
RELINQVO relinquere, [128]; relinqui, 392; reliqui, 282
REMITTO remissa (f.s.ab.), 299
REPAGVLVM repagula (p.a.), 229
REPERIO repperisti, [39]
REPVDIO repudiato (imp.), 304
REQVIESCO requiescat, 299
RES res, 228, 330; rem, 15, 74, 219, 227; re, 6, 76, 176, 351; res (p. nom.), 257; (p.a.), 234, 318; rerum, clxvi; rebus (d.), 203; (ab.), 340
RESPECTO respectantibus (ab.), 71
RESTINGVO restinguite, 42
RESTITO restitat, 203
RESTO restat, [203]
RESVMO resumit, 355
REX rex, 52; regis, 214; regi, 388, 389; rege, 292; reges (nom.), clxvi
RISCVS riscus, [116]
RVRSVS 116
RVSSVS russis (f.ab.), 344

SACER sacrae (f.s.g.), 121
SACRIFICO sacrificabat, [54]
SAEPE 155
SAEPIO saeptus, 281, 282 (septus); saeptum (n.s.voc.), 88
SAEVITER 166, 262
SAEVVS saeuo (m.s.ab.), 4, 216; saeua (f.s.ab.), 396
SALMACIDES Salmacida (voc.), 347
SALSVS salsum (m.s.a.), 139; salsa (n.p.nom.), 118
SALTVS saltu, 72
SALVEO saluete, 98, 241
SALVS salum, 179

SANCTVS sancta (f.s.nom.), 320

SANGVEN sanguen (nom.), 20; (a.),180

SANGVIS sanguis, [20], xciv, 324; sanguinem, [94], 139, [180]; sanguine, 14, [20], 41, 94, 118, 144, 165, 180, xciv, 297, 347

SANIES sanie, 297

SAPIENTIA sapientiam, 17; sapientia (ab.), 325

SAPIO sapit, 221; sapiunt, 267; sapere, 147; sapiens (f.), 33; (m.), 221; sapienti (m.ab.), clxvii (sapiente)

SAVCIVS saucia (f.s.nom.), 216; saucii (m.p.nom.), 326

SAXVM saxum (a.), 251; saxo (ab.), 113; saxa (nom.), 385; (a.), 297, 379; saxis (d.), 296

SCABREO see fr. xlvib; scabrent, *113

SCAMANDER Scamander, 159

SCELESTIM [261]

SCELESTVS scelestum (n.s.a.), 261

SCELVS scelus (a.), 236; sceleris, 277, 295

SCINDO sciciderit, 251

SCIO scit, 378; scias, 339; scire, 329; scibas, 272

SCRIBO scripstis, 177 (scripsistis)

SCRVPEVS scrupeo (n.s.ab.), 113

SCRVTOR scrutantur, 187

SE se (a.), 50, 56, 137, 156, 228, [257], [310], 330; sese, 9, 57, 114, *137, 168, 310; sibi, 132, 221, 267, 269, clxvi, 329; se (ab.), 136, 308

SECO sectae, [209]

SECVM see CVM

SECVRIS securibus (ab.), 208

SED sed, 21, 32, 109, 254, cxxxivb, 271, 288, 305, 346, [391]; set, 177, 303

SEDITIO seditio, [102]

SEMEL 233

SEMITA semitam, 267

SEMPER 228, 270, 336

SENECTA senecta (ab.), *300

SENECTVS senectute, 300

SENEX senex, 183, 184; (voc.), 361

SENTENTIA sententias, 343

SENTIO sentit, 275

SEPVLCRVM sepulcrum (a.), 298

SERVITVS seruitutem, 142

SERVO serua, 8; seruetis, i; seruauisti, 224 (seruasti)

SI 126, 130, 261, 265, 325, 369; see ETSI, QVASI

SIC 71, 238, 250

SIGNITENENS signitenentibus (f.ab.), 97

SIGNVM signa (a.), 185

SILENTIVM silentio (ab.), clxxix

SILEO silete, i

SIN 127, 130, 304

SINCERE 108

SINE 347

SOCIETAS societas, 320

SOCER socero, [291]

SOCRVS socru, 291

SOL sol, 243; Sol (voc.), 234

SOMNIVM somnio (ab.), 52; somnia (p.nom.), 346; somnium (p.g.), 57

SOMNVS somnis (ab.), 51

SONITVS sonitus (s.nom.), 305; sonitu, 4, clxxia

SONO sonit, 165; sonunt, 108

SORDIDVS sordidam, 276

SORS sortes (nom.), 57

SORTIO sortiunt, 137

SOSPES sospitem, 377

SOSPITO sospitent, 246

SPARGO spargens, 297

SPECTO spectat, 187

SPECVS specus (p.a.), 152

SPERNO spernit, 156

SPES spe, [371]

SPIRITVS spiritu, 4

SPLENDIDVS splendidis (f.ab.), 171

SPOLIVM spolia, 347

SPVMO spumant, 118

SQVALIDVS squalidam, [276]; squalida (f.ab.), 281

SQVALVS squalam, 276

SQVAMA squamae (p.nom.), *113

STATIM 15
STATVO statuerit, 75
STATVS stata (f.s.ab.), cxviii
STELLA stellas, 190; stellis (ab.), 171
STERNO strata (f.s.nom.), 276
STIRPS stirpem, 363
STO stant, 84, 85; stare, *255; steterit, 75
STOLA stola (ab.), 281, 282, 386, 396
STOLIDVS stolide (voc.), 66
STREPITVS strepiti (g.), 164; strepitu, [4]
STVDEO studet, 198
STVDIVM studiis, [309]
STVLTVS stultus, [259]
SVB 232
SVBEX subices (a.), 3
SVBLIMIS sublimis (m.s.nom.), *190; sublime (n.s.a.), 169, [190], 301
SVBLIMO sublimat, 243
SVBLIMVS sublimum (n.s.a.), 190; sublimas, 3
SVCCENSEO succenset, 371
SVCCINGO succincta (f.s.nom.), 386
SVDO sudat, 165
SVDOR sudore, 347
SVM sum, 83, 183, [261]; es, *70; est, 19, 95, 127, 130, 130, 155, 163, 164, 170, 187, 196, 200, [248], 256, [259], 262, [274], 280, 290, 309, 320, 324, clxxi b, 335, 335, 341, 342, 342, 346, 356, 357, 374, 375, 386; sumus, 200; sunt, 140, 207, cxviii, 359; omitted 346; sim, 82, 261; sit, 185, [236], [238], 265; siet, 248; esse, [i], 61, 126, 146, *228, [236], 270, 300, [309]; erat, 120; fuat, 151; fore, 261; fueratis, [263]; fuisse, *148
    sum (auxiliary verb), 16, 35, 119; omitted 78; est, 31, 32, 51, 106, 167, 197, 201, 263, *292, 312, 386; omitted 292; sunt, 220, 284; foret, 59; fuĩt, 396
SVMMVS summe, 176, 234; summam, 10; summum (n.s.a.), 105;

summa (f.s.ab.), 105, [153]; (n.p. a.), clxxi a; summarum, [clxvi]; summis (n.d.), 296; (f.ab.), 80
SVMO sumpserint, 367; sumptus, 53
SVPERO superat, 189; superauit, 72
SVPERSTITIOSVS superstitiosi (m.p. nom.), cxxxiv b; superstitiosis (f.p. ab.), 35
SVPERSTITO superstitent, 246
SVPERVS superum (n.p.g.), 309
SVPPETO suppetit, 331; suppetebat, 339
SVPPLICO supplicarem, 226
SVSCITO suscitant, 343
SVSPICIO suspicionem, 262, 277
SVSPIRO suspirantibus (f.p.ab.), 53
SVSTINEO sustinet, 330
SVVS suum (m.s.a.), 198; suãm, 219; suĩ (m.s.g.), 343; suo (m.s.ab.), 73; (n.s.ab.), 314 (suõ); suos, [102]; suarum, clxvi

TABEO tabet, *102
TABES tabes, [102]
TABVM tabo (ab.), 297
TACEO tacete, i; tacere, 146
TAEDA taedis (ab.), 27
TAENIA taeniis (ab.), 67
TALIS talem (m.), 128
TAM 5, 19, 380
TAMETSI [172]
TANDEM 176
TANTALVS Tantalo (ab.), 291
TANTVS tanta (f.s.nom.), 295; tantum (n.s.a.), 331; tanta (f.s.ab.), 19, 226; tantae (f.p.nom.), 57
TARDVS tarda (f.s.ab.), 300
TECTVM tectis (ab.), 90
TELAMO Telamonis, 273
TELVM tela (nom.), 143
TEMERE 318
TEMO temo, 189
TEMPERO temperaret, 60
TEMPLVM templum (voc.), 88; (a.), 240; templa (voc.), 98, 171; (a.), clxxi a; see EXTEMPLO
TEMPTO temptaret, [60]

TENACIA tenacia (nom.), 158
TENEBRAE tenebris (ab.), xxxiv
TENEO teneor, 252; teneat, clxvii
TEPIDVS tepido (m.s.ab.), 14
TER 232
TERRA terra (nom.), 165, 250; (voc.), 352; terram, 138, 209, 235; terrae (d.), 223, 276; terra (ab.), 114, [276]; terris (ab.), 355
TERRIBILIS terribilem (m.), 18
TESCVM tesca (a.), 379
TEXO texitur, 44
THELIS Thelis, 368 (Thetis)
THESAVRVS thesauri (p.nom.), 192
THRAECVS Thraeca (f.s.voc.), 352 (Treca)
TIMIDVS timido (m.s.d.), 20
TITANIS Titanis, 363
TOLLO tollunt, 12; tollere, 60
TOPPER 378
TORREO tosti (m.p.nom.), 85
TRABES trabes (s.nom.), 209
TRABS trabem, [110]; trabes (p. nom.), [209]
TRACTO tractent, 318; tractauere, 71
TRADO tradidit, 229
TRAHO trahens, *110
TRAVERSVS trauersa (f.s.ab.), 229
TREMVLVS tremulo (m.s.ab.), 250
TRES tris (a.), 48
TRIVIA Triuia (nom.), 363
TROIA Troiae (g.), 69; (d.), 61
TROIANVS Troiano (m.s.ab.), 100
TV tu, 10, 172, 204, 204, 224, 234, [260], 272, [321]; (voc.), 309; te, 71, 89, 119, 129, *130, 131, [151], 238, *260, 285, 290, 300, 361; ted, 151; tui, 38; tibi, 10, 176, 181, 249, 258, 278, 359, 363 (tĭbĭ), 371; te (ab.), 125, 207, 321; uos (nom.), 263; (voc.), 145, cva; (a.), i, [161], 322, 397
TVEOR tucor, 361
TVLLIVS tullii (p.nom.), 14
TVM 17, [34], 55, 122, [171], [224], [260], 264

TVMVLTVS tumulti (g.), 163
TVOR tuor, 379
TVRBIDVS turbidas, 318
TVRPO turpari, 94
TVTE 147
TVVS tua (f.s.nom.), 206; tuum (n.s. a.), 321; tuae (f.s.g.), 80, 112; tuo (n.s.ab.), 70, 235

VACO uacant, 159; uacare, [255]
VAGO uagant, [159]
VALEO ualet, 174
VALIDVS ualida (f.s.nom.), 158
VANVS uanum (n.s.a.), 382
VASTVS uastae (f.p.nom.), 207; uastos, 152
VATES uates (p.nom.), cxxxivb
VBI 33, [58], 106, 192, 299, 333, 352
-VE 81, 294; see NEVE
VEHO uecti (m.p.nom.), 213
VELIVOLANS ueliuolantibus (f.p.ab.), 45
VELIVOLVS ueliuolas, 111
VENIO uentum (n.s.nom.), 201
VENO uenor, 252
VENTVS uentus, 357, 358; uento (ab.), 159; uentis, [358]
VERBVM uerba (a.), *253; uerborum 245
VERE uerius, 373
VERECVNDE 181
VEREOR uereor, 37
VERO [37]
VERSO uersat, 402
VERTO uertite, cva; uortam, 217; uertant, 57
VERVM 283
VERVS uera (f.s.ab.), 254; (n.p.nom.), 346
VESTER uostrum (n.s.a.), [161]; uestra (f.s.ab.), 325; uostra (f.s.ab), 398; uestri (m.p.nom.), [397]; uestras, 242, 322
VESTIO uestitus, [281]
VESTIS uestem, 276
VIA uiam, [77], 267, 313; see OBVIAM

463   30-2

VICIS uice, 123
VICTORIA uictoria (f.s.ab.), 166, 381
VIDEO uideo, 288; uident, [187];
  uidetur, 188; uide, [175]; uidete,
  47; uidere, 78; uidi, 78, 89, 92; uisa
  (f.s.nom.), 32, 51
VIDVVS uiduae (f.p.nom.), 207
VIGIL uigiles (voc.), 162
VILLOSVS uillosi (m.s.g.), 384
VINCO uicisse, 145; uictis (m.p.ab.),
  *367
VINDICTA uindictam, *367
VIR uirum (s.a.), 254; uiri (s.g.), 38;
  (p.nom.), 212
VIRGINALIS uirginali, [33]
VIRGO uirgo, 205; (voc.), xvb;
  uirgines (nom.), 207; (a.), 37
VIRTVS uirtutem, 155; uirtute, 155,
  254
VIS uis, 295; uim, 25; ui, 93, *153,
  334; uiribus (ab.), 146
VISCERATIM 118
VITA uita (nom.), *202; uitam, 77, 93,
  202, 232; uitae (d.), 18, 134; uita
  (ab.), 10, [232], 299, 398
VITALIS uitalem, [306]
VITIS uitis (s.g.), 121
VITIVM uitio (d.), cva
VITO uitari, [93]
VITVLOR uitulans, 381
VIVO uiuitur, 202; uiuam, 374;
  uiuere, 254
VIVVS uiua, [253]; uiuam, 253
VLCISCO ulciscerem, 144

VLIXES Vlixem, 170
VLLVS ullo (n.s.ab.), 324
VLTRO 154
VMBRA umbra (nom.), 294
VMIDVS umidas, 4
VMQVAM 244, 321
VNDE 4, 22, 115, clxvi
VNDIQVE 252
VNDO undantem (m.), 179
VNVS una (f.s.nom.), 49
VOCO uocant, 64, 301, 356; uocare,
  [255]
VOLO uolant, 14; uolans, 67
VOLO uolt, 228, 228; uelit, 199;
  uolentes, 12, 12; uoles, 369
VOLVPTAS uoluptatem, 382
VOX uoce, 58; uocibus (ab.), 372
VRBS urbem, 137; urbe, 83; urbes
  (a.), 360
VRVO uruat, 114
VSPIAM cla
VSVRPO usurpat, 163
VT i, 56, [77], 106, 151, [160], 169,
  xciv, 226, [228], 228, 246, 260,
  263, 302, 306, [309], [315], 318,
  329, 330, 339, 363, 397
VTI [208]
VTINAM 183, 208, [215], 244
VTIQVAM see NEVTIQVAM
VTOR uti, 195; utendos, [278];
  utendas, 278
VVLNERO uulneratus, 312
VVLNVS uulnere, 115
VXOR uxor, 206; uxorem, 132

ENNIUS' METRES

159	tetr. troch. cat.	246	uersus Reizianus
160–161	(?)	247	tetr. cret.
162	tetr. troch. cat.	248–249	trim. iamb. (248 ?; 249
163–164	tetr. iamb. (163 quid hŏc		dico ǀ et)
	hic; 164 quid incastris?)	250	hexameter dactylicus
165–168	tetr. troch. cat. (168 ?)	251	trim. iamb. (?)
169	(?)	252	dim. anap.
170	tetr. troch. cat. (?)	253	(?)
171	tetr. iamb.	254–258	tetr. troch. cat. (254–
172–174	tetr. troch. cat. (173		255, 257 ?; 258
	cum ǀ opulenti)		tibi ex ore)
175	trim. iamb. (?)	259–260	(?)
176	tetr. troch. cat.	261–278	tetr. troch. cat. (274 ?)
177–179	trim. iamb. (179 ?)	279	(?)
180–181	tetr. troch. cat. (181 tĭbi	280	trim. iamb.
	in concubio)	281	tetr. troch. cat. (?)
182	(?)	282	trim. iamb.
183–184	trim. iamb.	283–284	tetr. troch. cat. (283 ?)
185–186	tetr. troch.	285–288	trim. iamb. (286 ?)
187	tetr. troch. cat. (quŏd	289	tetr. troch. cat.
	est)	290	tetrameter bacchiacus
188–190	dim. anap. (190 sub-		contractus
	limum ǀ agens)	291–292	tetr. troch. cat.
191	paroem(iacus)	293–294	tetrametri bacchiaci
192	tetr. troch. cat. (?)	295	dim(eter) cret(icus)+
193	dim. anap.		monometer trochaicus
194	paroem.	296–297	tetr. troch.
195	dim(eter) troch(aicus)	298–299	tetr. troch. cat.
196–207	tetr. troch. cat. (197,	300	tetrameter bacchiacus
	199, 204, 207 ?)		hypermetricus
208–218	trim. iamb.	301–302	tetr. troch. cat.
219	tetr. troch. cat.	303	dim. cret.+dim. troch.
220	tetr. troch.	304	tetr. troch. cat.
221	tetr. troch. cat.	305	trim. iamb.
222–223	trim. iamb.	306	(?)
224–233	tetr. troch. cat. (226	307	dim. cret.+dim. troch.
	nam ǀ ut; 227, 232–	308	trim. iamb.
	233 ?)	309–312	tetr. troch. cat. (311–
234–236	(?)		312 ?)
237–240	trim. iamb.	313–319	trim. iamb. (316, 319 ?)
241–242	(?)	320	(?)
243	trim. iamb.	321	tetr. troch. cat.
244	(?)	322–332	tetr. iamb. (323 mălam;
245	trim. iamb. (?)		327 pŏtěst ?; 328 ?; 331
			pŏtěst; 332 ?)

333	tetr. troch. (?)	369	tetr. troch. cat.
334	trim. iamb. (?)	370	(?)
335	(?)	371–372	trim. iamb. (?)
336	dim. troch.	373	tetr. troch. cat.
337–343	tetr. troch. cat. (337	374	trim. iamb. (?)
	ᴗ ᴗ	375	(?)
	potest; 338, 342 ?)	376	trim. iamb.
344–345	dim. anap. (344 ?)	377–380	(?)
346	(?)	381	trim. iamb.
347	trim. iamb.	382	tetr. troch. cat.
348	tetr. troch. cat.	383–385	trim. iamb. (384 ?)
349	trim. iamb.	386	(?)
350	tetr. troch. cat.	387	tetr. troch. cat.
351–354	trim. iamb. (353–354 ?)	388–390	trim. iamb. (390 ?)
355–360	tetr. troch. cat. (359–	391	(?)
	360 ?)	392–393	tetr. troch. cat. (393 ?)
361–362	trim. iamb. (361 ?)	394	(?)
363	tetr. troch. cat.	395–396	trim. iamb. (?)
364	trim. iamb. (?)	397–398	tetr. troch. cat. (397 ?)
365	dim. anap.	399	trim. iamb. (?)
366	paroem.	400	(?)
367	trim. iamb.	401–402	trim. iamb. (?)
368	(?)		

MATTERS DISCUSSED IN
INTRODUCTION AND COMMENTARY

'Lindsay's law', 300, 408
Livius Andronicus, date of first play,
3 n. 4; *Achilles*, 161f.; *Ajax*, 177;
Andromeda, 262; *Odyssea*, 46 n. 4,
180; *Teucer* (?), 47 n. 5
Livy on history of theatre, 3, 13
'locus Jacobsohnianus', 276
'Luchs' law', 184, 426
ludi, 3, 12

Macrobius' quotations, 261, 279,
343 n. 6, 386
Magna Graecia, drama in, 16f.
Menander, posthumous popularity
of, 10
messenger speeches, 163, 165, 229f.,
265, 283, 293
metaphor, 170, 180 n. 1, 182, 190,
210f., 212, 215, 216, 220, 223, 225,
232, 233, 242, 259, 260, 283, 296,
304, 307, 324, 328, 330, 338, 353,
368, 382, 425
metre and dramatic content, 31, 34ff.,
40f., 163, 190, 209, 243, 253 n. 4,
333, 356f., 370, 385, 386, 419f.
metre and verbal style, 40f., 175,
176 n. 3, 195, 197, 308f., 317, 352,
356, 361f.
metrical division and syntax, 176,
182, 228, 309, 333, 355, 366, 370,
409
metrical terminology, 32 n. 3
military language, 173, 270, 294, 338,
354, 401
morphology, abnormal, 211, 214,
226, 232, 243, 263, 264, 289, 293,
318, 364, 370 n. 6, 385, 403, 412,
420
music, 29ff., 46f., 253f.

Naevius, *Acontizomenus*, 60 n. 3;
Iphigenia, 318
neologism, 265, 279, 296, 307, 378,
402, 404
nominative for vocative, 247f.
non-Attic Greek drama, 7f.

Nonius Marcellus, quotations by, 56,
180f., 296, 300, 317, 345, 375f.,
389 n. 5, 408; misunderstandings
by, 172, 296
non-Latin vocabulary, *see* Italic vocabulary, Greek vocabulary
nouns, terminating with -*en*, 197;
-*entia*/-*antia*, 196, 367; -*ex*, 169;
-*men*, 182, 340; -*mentum*, 278; -*or*,
195; -*tio*, 212; -*tor*, 268; -*tus*, 199;
-*ura*, 225

oaths, 169
official language, 166, 173, 175, 184,
226, 241, 246, 249, 255, 268, 270,
279, 298, 312, 338, 354f., 400,
420
orchestra, 18
Orcus, 255, 331
order of words, 172, 228, 233, 289,
296, 300, 309, 332, 334, 357, 358f.,
374, 384f., 391, 403, 410; *see also*
disjunction
orthography, 52, 184 n. 2, 220, 234,
258, 260, 291
Ovid, *Medea*, 48
oxymoron, 259, 411, 424, 426

Pacuvius, *Armorum iudicium*, 47, 178,
254; *Iliona*, 305; *Medus*, 346
παράφρασις, 25
parechesis, *see* assonance
parody, by comedians of tragic language, 39, 172, 175, 220, 242, 255,
276, 378, 401; by tragedians of
sacral language, 286, 311, 324, 411
participle, perfect with present force,
183
Paulus, *see* Verrius
periphrasis, 199, 200, 228, 231, 250,
255, 293, 327, 332, 352, 355, 377,
393, 400, 411, 423
personification, 195, 210f., 224, 280,
331, 380
philosophy, 168f., 174 n. 3, 191, 252,
255, 336, 372ff., 400, 424

INDEX TO INTRODUCTION AND COMMENTARY